FACING THE MUSIC

FACING THE MUSIC

Irish Poetry
in the
Twentieth Century

EAMON GRENNAN

CREIGHTON UNIVERSITY PRESS
Omaha, Nebraska
Association of Jesuit University Presses

Library of Congress Cataloging in Publication Data

Grennan, Eamon.
    Facing the music : Irish poetry in the twentieth century / Eamon Grennan.
        p.   cm.
    ISBN 1-881871-28-2 (cloth). -- ISBN 1-881871-29-0 (paper)
    1. English poetry--Irish authors--History and criticism. 2. English poetry--20th century--History and criticism. 3. Irish poetry--20th century--History and criticism. 4. Ireland--Intellectual life--20th century. I. Title.
PR8771.G74   1998
821'.91099417--dc21   98-30500
                                                                                          CIP

EDITORIAL
Creighton University Press
2500 California Plaza
Omaha, Nebraska 68178

MARKETING & DISTRIBUTION
Fordham University Press
University Box L
Bronx, New York 10458

Printed in the United States of America

For George O'Brien

and

To the Memory and Generous Spirit

of

Gus Martin (1935-1995)

Irish poets, learn your trade
Sing whatever is well-made,
Scorn the sort now growing up
All out of shape from toe to top.

W.B. Yeats

Irish poets, open your eyes,
Even Cabra can surprise;
Try the dog tracks now and then—
Shelbourne Park and crooked men.

Patrick Kavanagh

--Mr. Brodsky, what is the poet's political responsibility?
--To the language.

At a poetry reading

Contents

Acknowledgements

Grateful acknowledgment is made to the editors of the following books or magazines, in which many of these essays first appeared, under their original titles.

"Language and Politics: A Note on Some Metaphors in Spenser*'s A View of the Present State of Ireland.*" *Spenser Studies*, III (1982).

"The Poet Joyce." in *The Artist and the Labyrinth, Essays on Joyce*, ed. Augustine Martin (Ryan Publishing, 1990).

"The Poetry of John Hewitt." *Éire-Ireland*, 12 (1977).

"Careless Father: Yeats and his Juniors." *Éire-Ireland*, 14 (1979).

"In a Topographical Frame: Ireland in the Poetry of Louis MacNiece." *Studies*, (Autumn 1981), 145-61.

"Pastoral Design in the Poetry of Patrick Kavanagh." *Renascence*, 34 (1981).

"Affectionate Truth: Critical Intelligence in the Poetry of Padraic Fallon." *Irish University Review* (Autumn 1982).

"To the Point of Speech: The Poetry of Derek Mahon." In *Contemporary Irish Writing*, edited by James Brophy and Ray Porter (Boston: Twayne, 1982).

"Mastery and Beyond: Speech and Silence in Yeat's *The Tower.*" *Etudes Irlandaises* (Lille), 7 (1982).

"Riddling Free: Richard Murphy's The Price of Stone." *Poetry Ireland Review*, 15 (1985-86).

"'Naming These Things': A Piecemeal Meditation on Kavanagh's Poetry." In *Patrick Kavanagh: Man and Poet*, edited by Peter Kavanagh. National Poetry Foundation: University of Maine at Orono (1986).

"Random Pursuit: Mining One and A Technical Supplement." In *Tracks*, Thomas Kinsella Issue, 7 (1987).

"Two Part Invention: Reading into Durcan and Muldoon." In *New Irish Writing*, ed. by James D. Brophy and Eamon Grennan (Twayne, 1988).

"'Of so, and so, and so': Re-Reading Some Details in Montague." *Irish University Review* (Spring 1989).

"Opening the field: The Poetry of Michael Longley." *Poetry Ireland Review* 33 (1991).

"Gathering Poets" is an amalgam drawn from pieces in the following magazines: (1) *The Honest Ulsterman* (Winter 1986); (2) *Verse* (1986); (3) *The Colby Quarterly* (December 1992).

"John McGahern: Vision & Revisionism." *The Colby Quarterly* (March 1995)

"The American Connection: An Influence on Modern and Contemporary Irish Poetry." In *Poetry in Contemporary Irish Literature*, ed. Michael Kenneally (Colin Smythe, 1995).

"Wrestling with Hartnett. *Southern Review* (Summer 1995).

"A Mazing." *Poetry Ireland Review* (Summer 1995).

"Real Things." *Poetry Ireland Review* (Summer 1995).

"Works & Days: The Poetry of Paul Muldoon." *The Recorder* (Spring 1996).

"Passwords." *The Harvard Review* (Spring 1996).

"Prime Durcan: A Collage," *in The Kilfenora Teaboy: A Study of Paul Durcan*, ed. Colm Tóibín (Dublin: New Island Books, 1996).

"Little Room: Bloom and the Politics of Space." *The Recorder* (Fall 1997).

Grateful acknowledgment is also made to the various Directors of the Yeats International Summer School, where the Yeats essays in Part One were delivered; to the directors of the James Joyce Summer School, where the Joyce essays were delivered; to the Wolfe Institute of Brooklyn College, where "Little Room: Bloom and the Politics of Space" was first delivered; and to the Directors of the Kerry International Summer School, where "Public Positions, Private Parts" was first delivered.

An abridged version of "The American Connection" was given as a Thomas Davis Lecture on RTE radio, and appeared in *Irish Poetry Since Kavanagh,* ed. Theo Dorgan (Dublin: Four Courts Press, 1996).

Acknowledgements also to the *The Irish Times, Rostrum,* and *The Crab Orchard Review*, where "A Decade for A.C.," "Kavanagonistes," and "In the Kitchen with Yeats" first appeared.

My gratitude to Vassar College for sabbatical leaves during which some of these essays were written.

I wish to thank the National Endowment for the Humanities for a grant which supported the writing of some of these essays.

And thanks to Rachel.

Preface

The following essays, lectures, and reviews represent most of what I have written over the past twenty years as a reader of Irish literature, most specifically of modern and contemporary Irish poetry. The pieces—mostly readings of the work of individual poets—were not designed as a unit, nor should they necessarily add up to one. What they represent are the responses of one reader faced by various items (a book, a poem, an author's *oeuvre*, a theme, a topic, an idea) drawn from a particular literary field. How these responses took the particular shape they have taken, however, may bear a little explanation.

In 1977-78, not too long after finishing graduate studies and starting work as a full-time teacher, my field of academic interest gradually shifted from the English Renaissance to the Irish Revival, from thinking about issues inherent in the linguistic and theatrical codes of Renaissance literature to issues concerning Yeats, the Irish poets who came after him, and the stage on which recent Irish literary history had happened. One of the first pieces I wrote around that time was the essay I call "Careless Father," on Yeats's actual relationship with and effect on some of the Irish poets who immediately followed him. At that time, I hoped such an essay might be the prelude to a book I planned to call *The Domesticated Muse*. Such a book would have focused on the ways in which Yeats's immediate successors managed to deal with that difficult, often inhibiting influence and, by doing so, how they managed to provide a new beginning for Irish poetry in English.[1] As it turned out, I had neither the scholarly patience nor industry for this particular project. I believe, however, that the essays gathered here are in some sense the natural children of that first stirring, their lineaments for the most part bearing some likeness to whatever related concepts or originating ideas I had around that time.

Since, on its own, the above would not adequately explain the precise nature of my own critical involvement, the particular tilt of my perceptions and so on,[2] I would have to say that this swerve of direction was accompanied by a (to me) more important shift of emphasis and attention, towards the practise of poetry itself. And while I would not want to argue the case too eagerly, I might at least suggest that whatever principles inform these essays could be connected somehow with my own practises as a poet, although the specific nature of the connections might better be judged by others. Even general information of this kind, however—focused on the simultaneous drift in my critical as well as creative commitment towards the environment of modern and contemporary Irish poetry—may help explain why some of these essays enter their subjects at the particular angle they do, why it is that certain issues more than others seem to command my attention, and where a possibly recurrent argument might in fact be coming from.

Looking at them as a collection, I can see that what may be common to all these pieces is a respect for the craft of close reading. A history of my own habits of reading would include the following: In secondary school, in a boarding school run by Cistercian monks, my enthusiasm for what I read—Shakespeare, Wordsworth, Longfellow, Lamb, Milton, Yeats, Dickens, *Dubliners*—was first awakened by Gus Martin, then a very young teacher (and graduate student). In the way he communicated his own relish for the language of a speech from *Julius Caesar*, the humorous edges of an essay by Lamb, or the rolling cadences of "Tintern Abbey," Gus fostered whatever latent literary appetites I had as an adolescent. As a college student at University College, Dublin in the early Sixties, then, it was the meticulous verbal probes I heard Denis Donoghue making into the recesses of a speech by Shakespeare—his unfolding of implication in Ophelia's tearful tribute to Hamlet, for example, or in Edgar's creation of the non-existent Dover cliff in *King Lear*—that, as memorable acts of critical reading, held my attention, triggered my enthusiasm, and awakened me to nuance, subtlety, and possibility within a line, a stanza, a speech alerted me to the use of language as artistic instrument and agent.[3] As far as "theory" went, it was mostly implicit or explicit versions of New Criticism that excited us in those days at UCD. "Empson, Richards, Ransom, Brooks" was all our cry. We relished the activity of "text," the tang of language as actor, agent, even *agent provocateur*. As the readings I've done in this collection will show, I have remained more or less committed to the habits of critical response fostered by these early influences.

When I went to graduate school in the later Sixties, my love for what Edmund Spenser called "the brightness of brave and glorious words" was still probably the only reason I could offer for my continuing engagement with books, poems, plays, language, a reason given heartening endorsement and legitimacy by the inspired teaching of two close protegés of Reuben Brower——Anne Ferry and the late David Kalstone—whose performances on a passage by Milton or Shakespeare, by Dryden or Sidney or Wyatt were unfailing models of critical excellence and sources of intellectual inspiration. Though not a teaching member of Harvard's legendary "Hum. 6" (a freshman "introduction to reading" established by Brower), I took its influence indirectly, and shaped what I was trying to do as a reader according to its tenets of verbal scrupulosity and what seemed to me its basically decent, serious, yet at the same time exhilarating and liberating respect for the palpable body of the text, its organic and mechanical operations, its shifting, subtle, prismatic, but decisively present *thereness*, the way it rewarded in what seemed almost endless ways the simple but strenuous act of honest attention.

Finally—still at graduate school and writing a dissertation on Shakespeare's History Plays—I learned a few crucial things from the example of Sigurd Burckhardt's book, *Shakespearean Meanings*. In this innovative (unhappily posthumous) volume of criticism, Burckhardt's sceptical but intellectually passionate engagement with the implied possibilities of meaning inherent in an apparently unremarkable detail of a play's language or action brought text and biographical possibilities into alignment in complex, subtle, and sophisticated ways, making palpable and persuasive (for me, anyway) the Keatsian dictum that "Shakespeare led a life of Allegory; his works are the comments on it." I think that in these essays and lectures I am drawn in my own way to some of the implications of this statement, old-fashioned though this must seem in light of the critical orthodoxies and bracing theoretical practises of the last twenty years or so. For, in thinking about a text, I seem to be alert usually to the presence in its details of "the author"—a tone of voice, a pressure of syntax, a habit of diction, a beat—and my attempt to discover something that would be useful in clarifying the nature and function of such things has always informed my habits as a critic.[4]

What this amounts to, I guess, is a tendency to treat the text as an independent but not free-floating entity, rooted in the "presence" of an author and, by implication, the author's context. Such a tendency—if thought about long enough—might itself be a sign of my belonging to probably the first generation in modern Ireland to begin to feel itself independent of the determinative factors—political, cultural, religious—that shaped our elders' view of the world. Coming of intellectual age in the Sixties was to experience oneself as belonging to a context, even an intellectual community ("students") in which many of the cultural enclosures taken for granted up to then were being opened, dismantled, or at least questioned closely, in the ways we were also learning to question texts. Cultural constructs were texts, I suppose, and could be argued about with a kind of liberal, passionate impartiality. Given my own apolitical upbringing as a middle-class suburban Dubliner, I found it easy to lend myself to a mode of reading that took the text in its verbal presence as the primary critical fact. Another item of my upbringing was a resistance to absolutism. I don't know where this came from. Sceptical of exclusive opinions, I was inclined to an absolute belief in the provisional nature of any "truth." It became my sense of things that the Ireland to which I belonged was in fact not a homogenous single thing, but (as Louis MacNeice says of the world) "incorrigibly plural," full of incidentals that created a whole that would not be easily defined or limited. Some such unconscious primary "information" must have prepared the ground for me to become the kind of reader I became, and has led me to see the "scene" of Irish literature, especially poetry, as I see it in these readings, which are my own reiterated acts of attention.

Contemporary critical writing is often, it seems to me, taking to the barricades. It displays a great deal of agenda-making, position-taking, and a considerable amount of exploitation of the "primary" works as ammunition in theoretical and polemical debates—debates often associated with the current academic orthodoxies of gender studies and studies of post-colonial culture. Such debates are conducted with great energy and intelligence in the field of Irish studies and, more specifically, Irish literature.[5] A by-product of these forces, however, is that in such debates "Ireland" can become (as it does in the more explicitly political field) the site of opposing needs, itself a text meaning now one thing, now another, depending on the angle of vision of its "readers." Such discussions have much to offer, and they open up familiar literary texts to innovative and illuminating inquiry. But I feel they can do so, at times, at the expense of the practical, substantive presence of the actual literary text itself in its body of language. And it is this presence that I want to make palpable, through whatever critical means seem apt to me at the time of writing. By dwelling in the realm of what I might call "advanced description," I want to make visible, audible, and if possible understandable, just what kind of thing the text in question is, and what kind of things are going on in it. As a critic, that is, I don't want to tell my readers what to think about these poems or about the work of these authors. What I want is to be as clear as possible in my account of what I think and feel about them, what I think they are like. Description, in this business, seems superior to prescription (not to mention that other critical tendency, proscription). If I have a ruling purpose at all, I'd say a large part of it is to lead readers back to whatever poems (or stories or authors) I'm talking about, so they can experience or re-experience for themselves the particular life-in-words they find there. And by concentrating mostly on individual writers (rather than explicitly on cultural or political issues), I want to allow the poets' solo voices to be heard. My aim, therefore, is to be as catholic a reader as possible, as well as more than a touch protestant in what I hope is my loyalty to the word.

The first section of this volume contains four lectures I presented at the Yeats International Summer School in Sligo, on three separate single volumes of Yeats. What these add up to, I hope, is a partial take on some of the most compelling issues in that monumental and exemplary career. In what has to look like an anomalous Part Two, then, I include essays on other areas of Irish literature (with the piece on Spenser's *Present View* an anomaly within the anomaly). I have included these because the issues raised here, what I choose to focus on, are intrinsically connected in my mind to issues raised in the essays on poets and poetry contained in the next section. Some of what I have to say—about Joyce, McGahern, Spenser's use of metaphors—are, that is, "compass readings" by which my own subsequent readings of poets and poetry take their bearings. (Of course this was not an intention of such pieces: it is, rather, the meaning and design I extrapolate from them after the fact. The point is, that precisely in this unconscious manner they reveal to me some of my own persistent preoccupations, and represent ways of dealing with these that stand a little outside the field which is my main subject.) Part Three contains essays on individual poets, from Yeats to McGuckian. Part Four, finally, contains a number of pieces which consider modern and contemporary Irish poetry as a whole or in broader national or international contexts. One is assembled from a review and a couple of introductions to the subject. In it I include both a personal view of what I see as indispensable elements of the "picture" of Twentieth Century Irish poetry, as well as some brief incidental acknowledgement of poets to whom I have not devoted separate commentaries. Another considers how American poetry has in the last hundred years helped shape the nature of Irish poetry. Yet another attempts to suggest one of the ways in which Irish poetry, in both Irish and English, has exercised a political and cultural function. The concluding very short piece contains a brief personal reflection on the awarding of the Nobel Prize to Seamus Heaney.

Part Three is the largest section. The Yeats piece that inaugurates it establishes a connection to Part One, while suggesting a necessary condition for the three generations of poets that follow. Each is a discrete piece, and they are not as a group intended to follow any line of argument, merely that of chronology. What I hope they will compose between them is a sort of collage of modern and contemporary Irish poetry, claiming neither comprehensive coverage nor historical fullness,[6] but nonetheless giving the reader some sense of the vitality and variety of Irish poetry over the past three poetic generations. (Because of their separation in time, and because of their various circumstances of composition, some repetition was bound to creep into the essays. While it might have been desirable to eliminate it, I decided to let it stand, in order to preserve the integrity of each piece.)

Aside from their immediate purposes of explication, clarification, thematic exposition, and so on, these discussions will serve incidentally, I hope, to demonstrate how wide of the mark are certain unnecessarily limiting assumptions about the nature of modern and contemporary Irish poetry. "Ideological critique" of the "politics of identity," for example, can be a very narrow lens through which to look at the subtle nature and shifting implications of a poet's work, and can risk reducing it to a set of arbitrary gestures within a predetermined frame of meaning. And, beyond this (to take another example), it should not be possible on the evidence of the works I discuss—stretching from Yeats's 1899 volume, *The Wind Among the Reeds*, to a 1994 collection by Medbh McGuckian—to draw any firm and final conclusion about the nature of those critical straw men, "the Irish poem," or "the Irish political poem," terms that have become current in some recent critical discourse. Used as blunt (because hopelessly generalised) critical instruments, such terms—no matter how just the cause in which they are enlisted—lead only to reductive polemical cartoons of Irish literary history.

For what strikes me most forcefully when I consider the poets and the poems that occupy the following pages is the sheer plenitude and variety of the offerings. Whether one thinks of language, theme, or attitude; of subject matter, frame of reference, or texture of allusion, one has to admit that among the few things common to these poets and their works is the simple fact that they belong by birth or blood to the shared island of Ireland (a descriptive term that, in my use of it, wants to be innocent of any coded political implication). And in their variety, in the way they cross boundaries of language, religion, gender, in how they move beyond boundaries set up by cultural, social, and political backgrounds, they are—better than anything else I know—a living embodiment of what (in its various political, cultural, and social constituencies) the island of Ireland in the Twentieth Century has been, and has come to be, in all its complexity, vitality, and contradiction, in the sheer ordinary weight of the ways in which it knows itself and belongs to the world.

As far as the essays themselves are concerned, I'd be loath to try fitting them into a single description—thematic, theoretical, or any other kind. I might simply say that among the things that seems to occupy repeatedly my attention in these pages is the way a poet's work is often, it seems, a deliberate attempt to "keep pace" with the poet's life. And, in the larger picture, these essays between them might suggest that Irish poetry as a whole over the past century has been marked by a stubborn commitment to this same impulse: to keep pace with the life of the whole island. Something else I revert to more than once is the sense that what goes on in the poetry through the century represents the achievement of a sort of "full independence" for Irish poetry in English. The poets I have dealt with, that is, seem to have completed (in what, from the perspective of 1898, would seem unimaginably complicated ways) the work begun by the Irish Literary Revival—whether they intended to or not. Yet another recurrent motif in these essays consists of a celebrated quotation from Yeats. The poet, said Yeats in 1937, "never speaks directly as to someone at the breakfast table, there is always a phantasmagoria." And, he adds, "even when the poet seems most himself . . . he is never the bundle of accident and incoherence that sits down to breakfast; he has been reborn as an idea, something intended, complete." Simpleminded as I may have to sound, I would argue that Irish poetry since Yeats has—among many other things—been a journey back to that (real and metaphorical) breakfast table. And, to join these various strands, I would add that this latter journey is one of the major means by which poetic independence is achieved, and by which the poetry itself keeps pace not only with the life of each individual poet, but—taken collectively—with the life of the island.

I suppose it should go without saying that to be Irish is less important than to be human. In the poetry and other work which I deal with in the following pages, however, it is often the curious, complicated relationship between being "Irish" and being "human" that charges the writer's imagination. I wonder if the young poets and writers already knocking on the door, already crowding into the hall called Irish Literature (a recent publication, for example—a volume by contemporary Irish poets of poems prompted in some way by the poems of the great Italian Romantic, Leopardi, who was born in 1798—contains ninety contributors), will be attached in the same way to such an issue. Or will the end of the century see a shift by these men and women away from such a need to others more immediately pressing, the nature of which may even be adumbrated in some of the work dealt with in the following pages?

Stephen Dedalus wanted to wake from the nightmare of history. In their various ways and various work (in common with those who have—in the Irelands that have evolved on the island over the past hundred years, right up to today—have given themselves in their own way to the process of drawing the possible out of the hopeless), these poets and writers have been helping us towards just such an awakening. In the pages that follow, I hope the reader may come to understand a little better how this has been lived through, and how it has been registered on the pulse and in the body of our common language.

Vassar College
Poughkeepsie
10 April 1998

NOTES

[1] A comprehensive monograph remains to be written on the actual recorded responses of later poets to Yeats. To look at the specific poems and other writings by Clarke, Kavanagh, Fallon (all three of whom wrote quite a lot, both in prose and verse, on their indomitable predecessor), by MacNeice (who wrote one of the earliest critical books on Yeats), and by Kinsella, Montague, Heaney, and Boland, would be a way of charting the evolution of contemporary Irish poetry along a single set of coordinates.

[2] Studies of Irish literature since the Seventies, after all, and more decisively since the Eighties, are marked by various theoretical tendencies, from Marxist criticism to those that emphasise issues of gender and post-colonial conditions, modes to which my own critical habits and practise obviously do not belong.

[3] In addition, the lectures of Roger McHugh—a founding father of the study of "Anglo-Irish" literature—reminded me of writers closer to home, of the names that went into the making of the Irish Literary Revival.

[4] I should add that my reading (and teaching) of the works of Shakespeare was in itself—and continues to be—probably the single most important literary instruction I have had in my life as a reader. The aspect of this instruction I would especially want to single out here is my sense of how, in play after play, the act of reading itself, literally or metaphorically understood, lodges in the very grain of ethical action and interrogation, whether in comedy or history or tragedy. Think, for example, of the cause of Malvolio's misfortune, of Portia and Shylock, of how any of the kings is an "unreliable" text; think of Hamlet trying to teach his mother to be a better reader, of how poorly Lear sees and hears the word and the world, of the wicked misreading Leontes performs of his wife, and the kind of redemptive possibility in reading as an act of faith with which he has to

end, happily, their story. Think of Prospero and Caliban, reader and reluctant text, and all the versions *The Tempest* provides of that (textual) isle that is "full of noises" which are at the same time "sounds, and sweet airs, that give delight and hurt not." In all such examples, and they could be multiplied many times, Shakespeare seems to be nudging us towards a refinement of our own natures as readers, coaxing us into ever more subtle and inclusive acts of "readerly" discrimination.

I should further add that, in addition to my preparatory life as a student proper, I've also been tutored by my own experience as a teacher of literature (for the past twenty-five years in the English department of Vassar College) trying to steer undergraduate readers into some sort of primary acquaintance with the language and formal strategies of poems and plays and stories. From the energy and, so often, the surprise of such "primary acquaintance" on their part I have learned again the pleasure of the particular and the satisfaction of seeing again—in teacher as well as in students—how an honest, patient engagement with the language of any literary text can lead to some amplified understanding of the world and, not to be forgotten, of the self.

[5]Probably the most prominent Irish critics of Irish literature among my own contemporaries are Seamus Deane, Declan Kiberd, Edna Longley, David Lloyd, and W. J. McCormack, in each of whose responses to Irish literature one may find close attention to the text married to a leading idea, some extra-textual commitment or agenda (historical, political, cultural). That the marriage in question—however fruitful—has not always been a union of equals is what gives the particular texture, tone and effect to the books, articles, lectures and essays produced by each of these critics. The same would have to be said of Eavan Boland's variously inflected feminist interventions in the critical debates that have marked the Irish literary scene over the past couple of decades. As a commentator on poets and poetry from the North of Ireland, Terence Brown has done significant work. Seamus Heaney's critical commentaries on Irish poets, especially on Yeats and Kavanagh, stand in a category of their own, I'd say, revealing important things not only about these poets, but also about poetry in general, and his own poetry in particular. (In addition to these Irish commentators, I'd especially like to note—among a number of worthwhile American responses to the subject—Dillon Johnston's illuminating and informative *Irish Poetry After Joyce* and Robert Garratt's *Modern Irish Poetry: Tradition and Continuity from Yeats to Heaney*.)

[6] In the contemporary field, for example, the absence of an extended essay on Seamus Heaney, as well as the absence of a piece devoted explicitly to the work of Eavan Boland or to the poems of Ciaran Carson would make any claim to "coverage" an empty one.

1

READING YEATS

Yeats's Monodrama of Desire:
Listening to *The Wind Among the Reeds*

In 1937, the poet Austin Clarke met Yeats to discuss his projected biography of the great man. Clarke had been asked by the director of his publishing firm "whether the love affair between Maud Gonne and Yeats had been Platonic or not, as this would give interest to the book and help sell it." Clarke, somewhat rashly, had decided to ask Yeats. So, at a lull in their conversation in the Saville Club in London, he popped the question:

> Carefully wrapping up my question in as many vague words as was possible, I said: "Mr. Yeats, I would like to discuss with you *The Wind Among the Reeds*, a book which I have always liked immensely. It would help me very much in writing my study to have a general idea of your inclination in those love-poems. Would it be too much to ask if there is any basis in actual fact for them?"
>
> Yeats caught my implication at once. His manner changed and looking down at me like an eminent Victorian, he exclaimed: "Sir, are you trying to pry into my personal life?" Then, seeing my startled expression, he must have felt he had gone too far, for in a trice he had become confidential and, smiling pleasantly, continued with a vague wave of the hand, "Of course, if you wish to suggest something in your biography you may do so, provided that you do not write anything that would give offence to any persons living."

Clarke's final, and hardly unexpected, comment on the whole affair is "I never wrote the book." (This story is told in Clarke's autobiographical volume, *Twice Round the Black Church*.)

Now, thanks in large part to Yeats's own candour (his wife used to call him William Tell), the biographical findings of the past fifty years have erased the need for any such discretion. Any ordinarily informed reader *of The Wind Among the Reeds* will know, in general terms at least, the "basis in actual fact" for many of the poems. Will know, that is, how Yeats's unquenchable erotic obsession with Maud Gonne underlies such poems as "The Lover Tells of the Rose in His Heart," "The Fish," or "He Hears the Cry of the Sedge." Will know too that the poet's brief sexual liaison with Olivia Shakespeare in 1895 and 1896 is the ground and occasion for "The Travail of Passion," "The Lover Mourns for the Loss of Love," and "He Bids His Beloved Be at Peace." And will know, in ranging beyond the explicitly erotic poems, that "The Everlasting Voices" or "The Valley of the Black Pig" grow directly, as a number of recent critics have shown, out of Yeats's other master passion of the Nineties—the occult, tangibly incarnate in the rites and ceremonies of the Order of the Golden Dawn.

All well and good so far, then, and indeed such facts might have satisfied Clarke's publisher, eager to sell the "life" of the poet. But how far, in fact, does such practical knowledge carry us, in our attempts to understand what the poems in *The Wind Among the Reeds* are like, what they are about? In truth, I don't believe it takes us very far. And while Yeats's own motives in distancing the finished poems from their factual roots may have been due in part to what Clarke characterises as Victorian propriety, even prudishness, they may also owe something to Yeats's confident knowledge of the kind of poems he had written, poems in which the external facts were of less moment than the particular state or states they had induced in their subject, the poet himself. The meaning of these poems, that is, lies in this internal life, not in their external circumstances. And while to one degree or another this is true of all those many later poems which rise out of Yeats's relationship with "history," public and private, I believe it was the making of *The Wind Among the Reeds* that first revealed to him this special, necessary truth. In the last analysis, it is through a proper understanding of these inner meanings that we discover biographical truths as deep or deeper than any that could come to us in the idiom of circumstance and historical accident. Judged in this way, *The Wind Among the Reeds* provides the first major example of Yeats's critical distinction between the poet as a mere "bundle of accident and incoherence that sits down to breakfast" and that reborn "idea," his true identity, that "something intended, complete."[1] And if we attend closely enough to the poems, indeed, we may even get behind Yeats's own projected intentions and completeness, to discover a truth that is all the more true for being unintended, incomplete.

The most pressing question in my own mind when I first encountered these poems was "What is *The Wind Among the Reeds* about?" Are we to be left in the state of critical exhaustion of one of my students who complained that "the reader gets a bit tired slogging through constant references to the heart, heavy hair, wind, love, and pale brows." Is there no more to it than Richard Ellmann claims, when he refers to "the quicksands of the poetry of *The Wind Among the Reeds*, a poetry where one sinks down and down without finding a bottom," in a style that is "suitably escapist."[2] No more than Joyce's accusation that such poetry was "onanistic"? (Although Joyce also said that "In aim and *form The Wind Among the Reeds* is poetry of the highest order.")[3] No more than Yeats's own account of it as spoiled by sentimentality, "dreamy" and "purposefully vague," as a recent critic has said?[4] Or should we be content with John Unterecker's view that the book charts the rise and fall of an essentially unhappy love affair?

For me such views were more than adequately countered by Allen Grossman's exhaustive and probably definitive study of the book. His 1969 volume, *Poetic Knowledge in the Early Yeats: A Study of The Wind Among the Reeds* answered my question, "What is the book about?" in rich and illuminating ways, making a coherent map of its circumstantial and biographical environment. I offer what follows as a small addition to Grossman's work, putting into sharper, because isolated, focus one of the issues that concerns him, namely, the issue of desire. In answering my own question for myself, I kept returning to this issue of desire, how it operates in *The Wind Among the Reeds*, how the book itself may be said to be about desire, and what exactly this rather bald statement means—for the book as a whole, for the individual poems, and for the relationship between this volume and the rest of Yeats's verse.

I

Published in 1899, the book contains poems written between 1892 and 1898, between Yeats's twenty-seventh and thirty-third year. First, it can do no harm to take a closer look at the title. What sort of emotional and imaginative vibrations did the phrases have for the poet? To begin with, they are pre-literary vibrations. Before it hardened into image or symbol, the wind among the reeds was a fact of the poet's life, rooted in childhood. He spoke in 1894 of "recollections which are our standards and our beacons," and placed at the head of his own "a certain night scene long ago, when I heard the wind blowing in a bed of reeds by the borders of a little lake."[5] The potency of this remembered fact lies in its being pure fact: it holds no meaning but its own self, its own unadorned being. In its radical self-reference and self-containment it is a perfect solipsism, a kind of (memorial) haiku.

Aside from its climactic service as the first true title for a volume of his verse (see the "Preface" to *Collected Poems*, 1895), Yeats made a number of revealing literary uses of this image. Its earliest recorded occurrence is in the poem "Ephemera," written in 1884. The lady responds to her lover (in lines deleted after their first publication in 1889):

> 'The innumerable reeds
> I know the word they cry, "Eternity!"
> And sing from shore to shore, and every year
> They pine away and yellow and wear out,
> And ah, they know not, as they pine and cease,
> Not they are the eternal—'tis the cry.'
> (Variorum, 81)

Picturesque and conventional, what we have here is a predictable post-Romantic contrast between temporal and eternal. Essentially static, the image simply illustrates a resonant cliché, and belongs to those Pre-Raphaelite tapestry effects of some of Yeats's verse before *The Wind Among the Reeds*. Later examples of the image, however, deepen its possibilities, impelling us towards the field of reference peculiar to this volume.

In one of the essays in *The Celtic Twilight* ("A Visionary," 1893), the narrator speaks of the poems of a young acquaintance:

> They, with their wild music as of winds blowing in the reeds,
> seemed to me the very inmost voice of Celtic sadness, and of
> Celtic longing for infinite things the world has never seen.
>   [Signet Classic (1962), 37]

Uttering Celtic melancholy and Celtic desire, this wind is the authentic voice of an indigenous poetry. When "Celtic" is later glossed as "a striving after something never to be completely expressed in word or deed . . . to express a something that lies beyond the range of expression" (39) it points us towards the territory of impossible desire and to the kind of poetry likely to inhabit such territory. In another essay in *The Celtic Twilight* ("The Golden Age," 104), a reference to the faeries who "lamented over our fallen world in the lamentation of the wind-tossed reeds" turns the image into an elegiac voice of loss, with an Edenic undertow. Caught between desire and loss, then, the dual image of the wind among the reeds represents an untenable present poised between an irrevocable past and an impossible future. Its identity lies in its registration of these two absences, and in registering them it is a species of poetry, specifically "Celtic" poetry.

A further explicit linking of this image with poetry occurs in Yeats's preface to the *Book of Irish Verse* he edited in 1895. The Irish peasant of the eighteenth century, he says, made "fine ballads by abandoning himself to the joy or sorrows of the moment, as the reeds abandon themselves to the wind which sighs through them." Emblem of a poetry of literal inspiration, this reveals not only Yeats's re-fashioning of the Romantic notion of the Aeolian lyre as symbol of the poet, but also his passionate devotion of energy at this time to the occult. The implicit sexual tremor of this vocabulary is also hard to miss, and adds another layer of meaning to the image. Sexual implications also vibrate through a related image in *The Speckled Bird*, the autobiographical novel Yeats began in 1896 and abandoned in 1903, companion work to *The Wind Among the Reeds*. After he falls disastrously in love, the sound of the wind was for the hero "Eden sighing with a love like that of a woman over a fallen world." Finally, in "The Crucifixion of the Outcast" from *The Secret Rose* (1897), "the wind among the salley gardens" is an image of a man's soul—always vulnerable to desire, incapable of rest.[6]

We can see from all this that for Yeats, as well as some epiphanal childhood wonder (a hard fact at the very foundations of feeling), the image signified also a suggestive conjunction of sexual, occult, and poetic meanings, the common denominator of which is a condition of reaching after or harking back, a risky, painful but self-hypnotising residence in an untenable present. The comprehensive name for this complex condition is desire, and the book as a whole gives a body to this name, this condition, as its primary subject matter. Yeats himself, in one of the rather baroque notes which propped up the first edition of *The Wind*

Among the Reeds, lends his support to this point. In reference to "The Lover Asks Forgiveness because of his Many Moods" he says

> I use the wind as a symbol of vague desires and hopes, not merely because the Sidhe are in the wind, or because the wind bloweth where it listeth, but because wind and spirit and vague desire have been associated everywhere.

Casually gathered together here are the strands that link the wind to the occult, to arbitrary (poetic) visitation, and to (presumably sexual) desire.

Given this rich mixture of associations, then, it's no wonder that sometime in 1893 Yeats wrote in the manuscript album, in which many of the poems for this collection were drafted, an obviously excited marginal note. Beside the first draft of "The Host of the Air" he scribbled "Name for a book of verse 'The Wind Among the Reeds!'"[7] The exclamation point suggests either the exaltation with which he greeted the gift, which he saw would unify his next collection, or it may have been intended as part of the title itself, turning the phrase into a gesture of passionate recognition. (Remember "The Second Coming!") In either case, it is clear that the phrase and the image it conveyed were for Yeats an objective correlative for the dominant mood, feeling, and even purpose of the collection he was projecting as a whole. And although it was five years before the volume was ready for the press, during which time his life and his style underwent important changes, the titular phrase still fashioned a symbolic arch, containing and giving a decisive family resemblance to almost all the poems in the book.

II

So, by this rather circuitous route, we come upon the substance of the book itself. Instructed by the title, with its sexual, occult and poetic reverberations, I'd argue that we should see *The Wind Among the Reeds* as an "anatomy" of desire. In the first place, any simple description of subject matter would demonstrate that most of the poems in this collection deal with two major species of desire. One of these draws the speaker away from the ordinary world of space and time; the second condemns him to suffer one particular manifestation of this world: sexual frustration. Poems that seek a fairly simple form of escape from the world of human accident—a major impulse in poetry earlier than this volume—are "The Hosting of the Sidhe," "Into the Twilight," "The Lover tells of the Rose in his Heart," "The Moods," and, by implication, "The Unappeasable Host." A more savage drive towards apocalypse—the ending of the world rather than an escape from it, the desire to terminate desire—characterises poems like "He Mourns the Change that has come upon Him and his Beloved, and Longs for the End of the World," "He Remembers Forgotten Beauty," "The Valley of the Black Pig," and "The Secret Rose." The vagaries of sexual desire usually form some part of the experience of the poems I have just named (the imagery of "The Valley of the Black Pig," for example, is unmistakably phallic, whatever the political ramifications of this folk tradition).

It is the explicitly sexual form of desire, however, that compels the poet's attention in almost all the other poems of the collection, poems such as "The Fish," "He Reproves the Curlew," "The Song of Wandering Aengus," "The Travail of Passion," or "He Hears the Cry of the Sedge." Indeed it might be plausibly argued that sexual desire is the form of desire underlying all the other forms of desire in the book. Sexual desire, that is, is the formal source. Forms that seem overtly to belong to another kind, more transcendental in nature, are in reality but strategic displacements of this fundamental form. I've mentioned the phallic possibilities in the imagery of "The Valley of the Black Pig" with its "unknown spears," its ritual bowing before a terrible Eros, "Master of the still stars and of the flaming door" (images which are elsewhere in Yeats explicitly sexual). There's also the distinct sexual content of Niamh's invitation in "The Hosting of the Sidhe," with its provocative description of the faery host:

> Our cheeks are pale, our hair is unbound,
> Our breasts are heaving, our eyes are agleam,
> Our arms are waving, our lips are apart.

The erotic content of poems like "He Remembers Forgotten Beauty," "He Mourns the Change that has Come Upon Him," or "The Secret Rose" is visible in image (white deer with no horns, hound with one red ear) or in direct statement ("When my arms wrap you round I press / My heart upon the loveliness / That has long faded from the world").

To establish, with this scattering of evidence, the book's preoccupation with desire and its fundamentally sexual orientation, however, is little more than a prologue to genuine understanding. More important than this is some awareness of how the poems themselves work, how they embody in their own terms the very experience of desire which is their subject, so that they are no longer simply "about" the poet's unhappy sexual experience but compose its proper poetic body. How does Yeats manage, that is, to create in language the real presence of desire. By looking closely at a few poems in detail and then by observing some general features of the book as a whole, we may find some answers.

III

I begin by looking at one of the volume's earliest poems (dated—in the Variorum—Sligo, November 1892), "The Lover Tells of the Rose in His Heart":

> All things uncomely and broken, all things worn out and old,
> The cry of a child by the roadway, the creak of a lumbering cart.
> The heavy steps of the ploughman, splashing the wintry mould,
> Are wronging your image that blossoms a rose in the deeps of my heart.

The wrong of unshapely things is a wrong too great to be told;
I hunger to build them anew and sit on a green knoll apart
With the earth and the sky and the water, re-made, like a casket of gold
For my dreams of your image that blossoms a rose in the deeps of my heart.

Simply rendered, these stanzas record the profound antithesis between the ordinary world and the poet's perfect image of his love, as well as his desire to remedy this distressing state of affairs. Beyond such an unadorned summary of its matter, however, the poem's manner harbours interesting revelations. For it performs rather than describes the nature of desire itself, giving that condition a poetic/linguistic body. One of the first things to notice as one reads or listens to the poem is its intrinsic repetitiveness. The largest architectural blocks of the stanzas, for example, exactly repeat one another in metre, rhyme scheme, and actual rhyme sounds. Indeed there are only two such sounds, with the last line of each stanza actually repeating the crowning rhyme-word, "heart." The smaller units of the phrase also deliberately repeat one another (all things . . . all things; the cry of . . . the creak of . . . the wrong of; and the climactic repetition of "Your image that blossoms a rose in the deeps of my heart.") Even the smallest semantic units of all, the words, are repetitive: all those 'and's, for instance, as well as those generalising definite and indefinite articles, and that 'wronging,' 'wrong,' 'wrong.' Such repetitions enact an emotional condition that's hypnotic and confined; they reveal the speaker's state as a perpetual circling on itself, a state perfectly imaged in the "casket of gold," which is at once a symbol for the poem itself and for the enclosure of that desire which is its true subject.

The kind of containment suggested here is also communicated by the poem's verbs. Most are present participles, one is passive infinitive, two are active infinitive, and one ('re-made') a past participle with a future perfect meaning. These suggest a cycle of recurrence or impossibility in the present, and a future branded by fantasy. (The future perfect, indeed, must be desire's aptest tense.) The two strongest forms of the verb, plain statements of present fact, appear as "your image that blossoms" and "I hunger." By such means the two central figures of the poem, lover and beloved, are frozen into postures of irreconcilable opposition, the beloved simply present and therefore endlessly provocative and the lover endlessly yearning towards the impossible future.

Technically dry as they may sound when subjected to such exaggerated scrutiny as I've just given them, it is out of such particulars that the poet composes an adequate equivalent in his poetic medium—language—for his human emotion—desire. As I've said, he doesn't so much describe desire, he gives it a body in the language. This in turn has the paradoxical result of both controlling desire and at the same time ensuring that it maintains its control over him, neither dissipating it nor satisfying it. Just such a paradox, I suspect, lies at the heart of all poetry of sexual desire, most notably and emphatically since Petrarch's *Canzoniere*, to which tradition it seems proper to assign *The Wind Among the Reeds*. (It might even be said that this book is an honorary member of the great European tradition of the love-sonnet sequence, although none of its poems is formally a sonnet.)

Something it does share with this essentially male tradition, however, is its very sharp sense of distance from the woman. She is an "image" that becomes a "rose" in the lover's heart in the first stanza, and in the second she has receded even further, becoming the dream of an image. The actual woman is impossibly remote, a virtually unseen, unspeaking presence. Desire itself is absence: her presence is an absence, an absence given tangible life in the sense of distance created by these words. Desire inhabits the empty space between lover and beloved, it is that space. The poem itself, making that absence present to us in its own terms, becomes the body of desire. It is only by maintaining this distance— expressed in the circular, static nature of the poem—that desire itself may continue to live in its own "casket of gold" (prefiguration, maybe, of a later golden bird, icon of another but related species of desire). In fact the animating paradox is that were this distance to be eliminated and desire satisfied by possession, then the love of which it is the signature would itself become one of the uncomely and broken things of the ordinary world. Desire then, which must seek at once its own destruction and its own survival, is a living paradox, in the anguished equilibrium of which the subject, the lover, must persist. Such factors, composing the phenomenology of desire, are responsible for that striking repetitiveness which is a major formal determinant of "The Lover Tells of the Rose in his Heart."

This trope of repetition is hard to miss in "He Reproves the Curlew:"

> O curlew, cry no more in the air,
> Or only to the water in the West;
> Because your crying brings to my mind
> Passion-dimmed eyes and long heavy hair
> That was shaken out over my breast:
> There is enough evil in the crying of wind.

Here it is noticeable especially in the poem's phonetic elements, in those alliterative and assonantal patterns that shape the lines for our ears (curlew/cry; water/West; heavy hair; o/no/more/only; cry/crying/my mind/eyes/crying/wind). Within such strict auditory limits, the poem seems to mime the monotonous cry of the bird, itself a symbolic displacement of the monotonous condition of desire itself, a perpetual moan (all those open vowels) of sexual longing. The repetition of those prepositional phrases ("in the air," "to the water," "in the west," "over my breast," "in the crying") also suggests a certain fixity, an articulate paralysis of the erogenous zones. Once again, that is, desire is not so much being described, as enacted in the poet's own medium of language. Given his emotional state, this is the only authentic power he's got.

A number of things, however, distinguish this poem (written in 1896) from the obviously earlier "The Lover Tells of the Rose in His Heart" (1892); although desire is still its subject, there's a very different feel to its literary surfaces. It is at once more direct and more mysterious, its knowledge of desire more practical and, as a result, more sensual. The directness shows in the language. As an address, it is far more immediate than the earlier poem. Here, speaker and creature spoken to inhabit the same plane of being, a condition prohibited by the more reverential gestures of the earlier poem. The mystery, then, lies in the provenance of this voice, suddenly addressing us out of nowhere. Practical identification eludes us here: we must content ourselves simply with the presence of the voice and its strange utterance, its allusions to explicitly sexual events in a context that remains hidden from us. Whereas the relationship in "The Lover Tells of the Rose in his Heart" seemed pre-sexual in its knowledge, the practical sensuality of "He Reproves the Curlew" is undeniable, however pre-Raphaelite and emblematic those "passion-dimmed eyes" and that "long heavy hair" may seem. Through such elements, the poem gives a body in language to sexually experienced desire, inevitably an unnerving compound of directness, mystery (the known and what must always remain unknown), and sensual memory.

Where the earlier poems hungered for a possible future, however, this one grieves over a past impossible to hold onto. The result for the speaker, however, is the same in both cases: he is trapped in a present and before a presence which he can only experience as absence, an absence he embodies in speech. As the site, the sentient locale of an absence, he sums up the state of desire in himself. That's what this voice is. The crying of the curlew is a surrogate presence for that absence, an objectifying of his own condition in an inevitably limited attempt to assuage it. His negative invocation ("cry no more") seeks to exorcise that painful presence, seeks some power over what the cry stands for. The spell itself, however, only succeeds in making concrete, in perpetuating, the memory it seeks to erase. The paradox of desire is alive and well. It may also be experienced in the opening invocation itself. For isn't the summoning gesture a sign of powerlessness disguised (by hope) as power, a symbolic recognition of the separateness of the Other, on which hinge the anguish of desire must turn. By filling the void between speaker and Other, the invocation acknowledges the reality of the space between them at the same time as it appears to be dealing with this reality, redressing it in some way. Such an operation is a metaphor for the poem of desire itself, in which the very act of dealing with its dilemma is, more deeply, a recognition of its hopelessness. The surprising number of invocations which appear in *The Wind Among the Reeds* is due on the one hand to the book's occult environment and on the other to its embodiment of the state of desire itself. (The occult, it might also be added, is at once a species of desire given concrete form and a means of mastering it. In that case the magus replaces the poet and the lover.) Because of such a high proportion of invocations (a fact which must also be responsible for one of the book's most prominent tonalities), *The Wind Among the Reeds* might be described as being in the "invocative mood," the principle mood, along with the optative, in any genuine grammar of desire.

To return to "He Reproves the Curlew": In external form this six-line poem is quite different from the two quatrains of "The Lover Tells of the Rose in his Heart." While the experience of those earlier quatrains is one of decisive closure, the rhymes here (abcabc) are effectively countered by the way the sense moves in uneven blocks of 2-, 3-, and 1-line units. Such openness enacts the infinite hollowness that is desire as it contemplates a past irrevocably lost. Such interminable openness is beautifully confirmed, I believe, in the brusque stoicism of the last line. "There is enough evil in the crying of wind" brings us up short against the infinite, eternal fact of desire itself, symbolised, as we know already from the book's title, by the wind.

Finally, a brief word or two on some other relevant elements in this short lyric. Again the image of the woman is both passive and remote. Subjected to passion and imprisoned in the past tense, she exists only metonymously for the speaker as eyes and hair, features which offer a location for the lover's own desire but convey no sense of an inward reality. Desire, in this light, is distinctly solipsistic. Even the woman's hair is hardly given its own life, being something "That was shaken out over my breast." It is also worth noting, because true of many other poems in the collection, that the speaker-lover himself is passive under the influence of desire, put upon by natural phenomena and the memories they evoke. It is his victimage that grants him identity. (The graphic picture created by the image of the woman's hair falling over the man's breast also suggests a literal, physical inferiority.) The speaker's only positive strength sounds in the last line, coming, significantly enough, from his straightforward acknowledgment of the incurable nature of desire. (As the most specific acknowledgment of this kind in the book, it was important enough for Yeats to think it worth repeating: the cry of the sedge, in the poem of that name, tells him that until the world ends "Your breast will not lie by the breast / Of your beloved in sleep." And in "He Thinks of his Past Greatness," the poem that concluded the collection in its first edition, the one sure truth the speaker-lover is left with is "that his head/ May not lie on the breast nor his lips on the hair / Of the woman that he loves until he dies." Such a recognition touches the very quick of desire and is the book's center of gravity.) To go back to the last line, "There is enough evil in the crying of the wind": The plain language and colloquial rhythm break up for a moment the ritual sounds and postures which characterise the other lines and act as stylistic metaphors for the helpless state in which the speaker finds himself. The line, too, both defeats expectation and completes the poem, suspending us in a curious way that must mime the speaker's distressed poise between sexual expectation and completion, the state of desire that lives in memory. The abruptness of the line also serves to remind us how much a monologue the poem is, how, in common with so many of the poems of the volume, it has no hope of any response. The drama of desire is a mono-drama, a one-man show.

The third and last poem I want to deal with in this way, to show how it gives appropriate body to the book's subject, is "The Song of Wandering Aengus," one of the most popular and highly regarded of the pieces in the volume. The reason for such prominence, I'd argue, is because it embodies with wonderful objectivity and clarity the phenomenon of desire itself. It is Yeats's most finished attempt to cope with this difficult, demanding presence in his life, this presence that was a perpetual absence. The poem is an allegory for this condition, a myth in miniature that compresses into its three eight-line stanzas, into their style as well as into their substance, the whole experience of desire—its obsessive, enchanting, irremediable nature. It discovers no way around or out of the lover's dilemma. But there is such fullness of strength in its execution that it at least allows the poet to achieve a kind of resolving distance from the lover, a perspective that enables him to acknowledge completely the harsh incurable truth of the condition and at the same time to stand aside from it in the integrity and independence of the work of art itself. Part of this artistic stepping aside is indicated by the title. The poem, after all, is a song sung by a character (its original title was even more distancing, releasing the poet from a sense of responsibility for the content; it was called "Mad Song"). It is a song, with all the distance and control this form implies.

It's simple enough as far as its content is concerned: in the terms I've been using here, the poem represents the epiphany that arouses, gives birth to desire, and the interminable quest that is its consequence. The phallic imagery of the first stanza is hard to ignore.

> I went out to the hazel wood,
> Because a fire was in my head,
> And cut and peeled a hazel wand,
> And hooked a berry to a thread;
> And when white moths were on the wing,
> And moth-like stars were flickering out,
> I dropped the berry in a stream
> And caught a little silver trout.

Fire in the head, hazel wand, berry, and "little silver trout" are all suggestive of a coming to sexual consciousness, the condition preparatory to desire itself. From this sexually alerted solitude the poem moves in its second stanza to a realised object for this desire, a "thou" for the "I" of the first stanza.

> When I had laid it on the floor
> I went to blow the fire aflame,
> But something rustled on the floor,
> And some one called me by my name:
> It had become a glimmering girl
> With apple blossoms in her hair
> Who called me by my name and ran
> And faded through the brightening air.

This other, then, gives practical sexual identity (or if, as is possible, this is also a version of the muse, practical poetic identity?) to the speaker by calling his name, becoming a glimmering girl with his name like a spell in her mouth. That brightening air gathers its own sexual connotations from Yeats's *Memoirs*, where he tells of a dream in which "growing brightness" had a palpably sexual meaning.[8] While the girl is objectively there, then, the fact that the only utterance she makes is of his name suggests the powerful identification between her and his desire. The epiphanal event, that is, identifies him in terms of his own desire. (At the same time some objectivity is enhanced by the fact that the image of apple blossom, as we know from the autobiography, evokes Maud Gonne.) The third and final stanza summarises the consequences of this erotic identification.

> Though I am old with wandering
> Through hollow lands and hilly lands,
> I will find out where she has gone,
> And kiss her lips and take her hands;
> And walk among long dappled grass,
> And pluck till time and times are done
> The silver apples of the moon
> The golden apples of the sun.

Solitary again and in endless pursuit, hopeful and barren at the same time, the speaker postpones to an impossible future the fruition of his desire, the plucking of those obviously male and female magic apples (which, as a reference to "apples of the sun and moon" in *Baile and Ailinn* of 1903 shows, belong to a future beyond death). The poem is about arousal, hope, and unfulfillment—a diagram of desire that contains, as part of its diagnostic nature, the obligatory death wish.

So, what does the poem's style tell us about this experience? How does it embody it? The first thing I'm struck by is its ritualistic nature. Everything is deliberate, hieratic, in slow motion, suggestive of the hypnotic reflexes of the experience itself. Grammar and syntax are responsible for this. The syntax is simply cumulative, with phrases (each unfailingly with one line) added paratactically to each other until the whole experience has been precisely charted. The most strategic instrument in this respect is the conjunction: the word 'and' occurs 14 times, linking each act and object in a chain of remorselessly simple eventuality, stretching from remote past to impossibly distant future through a present that is known only as a painful absence from both, a ceaseless "wandering / Through hollow lands and hilly lands." The grammar enhances this effect, being straightforward and secretive. Cause and effect are clearly determined (I went . . . because; / I dropped . . . and caught; / When I had laid . . . I went; / though I am old . . . I will find out). From such grammatical and syntactical elements the poem derives its deliberate unchanging rhythm and the sense this creates of an eternally recurrent playing-out of this scenario of erotic somnambulism. Grammar, syntax, and rhythm (as well as other obvious elements of repetition) also display the essentially uncentred nature of desire, as it circles around itself and its own necessary emptiness and stretches irrevocably forward in time, its object always ahead of it, never attained. Lost in its own exclusive world, it is solipsism instead of relationship; aspiration rather than confrontation; monodrama, not drama proper.

Yeats evades the defeating consequences of such solipsism by making it the fully aware subject of this poem, as it is of almost all the poems in *The Wind Among the Reeds*, giving the condition itself an enduring literary body. It is the act itself of making the book that in a sense frees the poet from his dead-end subjection to desire, the cul-de-sac of being merely, as the speaker is here, its servant. It is the act of book-making that releases him to be what he became in later books, the fierce, randy, tragic antagonist to desire. The objectifying action he performs in "The Song of Wandering Aengus" is an important step towards such freedom. This poem, along with some others in the book, allows him to see himself as the subject of desire, and in that honest perception of his own bondage lies the seed of his liberation from it. But, as with Keats, the world of difficulty and circumstance must be the forge for Yeats's soul-making. *The Wind Among the Reeds* represents his authentic response to that world, is a genuine vessel for that element in his spiritual biography.

I'll end with a few general observations. The first of these concerns the relationship of the reader to the book. The second examines how desire is woven into the very texture of the book as book. Firstly, how might my response as a reader mime or act out (or, in a sense, complete) the experience of these poems as I have described them? As an approximate model for this relationship, consider "The Moods."

> Time drops in decay,
> Like a candle burnt out,
> And the mountains and woods
> Have their day, have their day;
> What one in the rout
> Of the fire-born moods
> Has fallen away?

Having read this poem, I find my initial response takes the form of questions. Who speaks the poem? Where does this voice come from? What does "moods" actually refer to? All this is hardly surprising, since the whole poem, or at least the second part of its single compound sentence, is a question. My response, in other words, extends the internal experience of the poem. As a reader, I have no satisfactory answers to these questions. I must simply accept them, learn to live with them and with myself, as it were, in the interrogative mood. The odd thing is that the manner of the poem is decidedly assertive: it has an authority which insists upon acceptance. Assailed by claims and questions which address me arbitrarily out of the air, taking over my consciousness, I am stricken as the subject of desire himself is stricken. My act of reading, that is, becomes an aspiration towards some knowledge, some possession, some experience which never comes to pass. Poise or paralysis, it may be hard to say which, but the experience is most intensely itself when it has no resolution, no outlet, no objective satisfaction. What I understand is that I don't understand. That is the nature of the poem's experience for me, of far more importance than some objective meaning that might be illuminated by learned commentary. This remains true even if Yeats's own view of what he meant is precise and concrete, although in fact, given the occult nature of the subject matter, this can hardly have been the case. So I know this poem as unquestionable fact (first four lines) followed by non-factual question (last three lines). I know it as a contrapuntal coexistence of the tangible (candle, mountains, woods; the colloquial phrase, "Have their day") and the intangible (the mystery attending the moods themselves; the poetic word "rout"). Fact and question; indicative and interrogative; certainty and uncertainty; tangible and intangible: such binary combinations are of the nature of desire itself, with its problematic participation in two realms, that of self and that of some objective and/or imagined other. As a reader of these poems, then, I must while the poem endures occupy this ambiguous territory, thereby duplicating in my own response the state of the poet's subject.

Finally, the book as a whole: how exactly is *The Wind Among the Reeds* Yeats's book of desire? Well, some of what I have said or implied has shown that the heart of desire is uncertainty. It could also be postulated that its soul, or some other vital member, is evasive indirection, a need at once to speak out of and to conceal its own source. The poems embody such an ambivalent need. This is seen with instructive clarity in the draft of a poem written around the same time as some of those in *The Wind Among the Reeds*. Significantly enough, he never published the poem, leaving it in an incomplete state. It is addressed directly, we must assume, to Maud Gonne: "You only know it is / Of you I sing when I tell / of the swan on the water / or the eagle in the heavens / or the faun in the wood."[9] Here Yeats is reflecting on the literary manners of the book itself: showing his hand, as it were, he reveals them to be in a simple way the manners of symbolism. Such manners, we see, are deliberately evasive, granting a body to that which cannot be actually named. But that, of course, is the nature of desire itself, which can only survive as desire by realising itself as what it is not, as, in literary terms, symbols. To consummate it would be to quench it; to name it would be to void it of all meaning. By uttering it by indirection and evasively, on the other hand, the poet grants it a continually living body. By being symbolist in spirit and execution (perhaps Yeats's only purely symbolist text) the book embodies an aesthetics of desire. And an aesthetics of desire is, it might be argued, only another way of describing a symbolist aesthetics. Within the boundaries of such an aesthetic commitment, Yeats could not include a poem like the following (the second section of what I have just quoted) in *The Wind Among the Reeds*. For it names too much and too practically, and so destroys the purity of the category of desire itself, within which he wanted these poems to exist:

> O my beloved. How happy
> I was that day when you
> came here from the
> railway, and set your hair
> aright in my looking glass
> and then sat with me at
> my table, and lay resting
> in my big chair. I am
> like the children o my
> beloved and I play at
> marriage—I play
> with images of the life
> you will not give to me o
> my cruel one.[10]

The way this poem, even in its raw state, intends to work is by describing ("subject for a lyric") desire rather than enacting it. The fact that such a poem, in even a final state, does not appear in *The Wind Among the Reeds* tells us much about the nature of Yeats's book of desire.

Other factors relating to the book as a whole further strengthen my argument. Take the titles, for example. Those in the *Collected Poems* are almost all changed from those that appeared in the first edition. Those that appeared in the first edition, in their turn, were not the same as the titles used when the poems were first published individually. The fact is that with no more than one exception ("The Everlasting Voices"), the poems were retitled one or more times before realising their final form in the *Collected Poems*. This is all the more significant in that between *The Wind Among the Reeds* and the *Collected Poems* the individual poems themselves saw remarkably few textual revisions. While the fact itself is of interest for all the poems, it is especially revealing as far as my present discussion is concerned in the following cases: The poem originally entitled "The Rose in my Heart" becomes "Aedh tells of the Rose in His Heart" which in turn became what you see in your text, "The Lover Tells of the Rose in his Heart." "Aedh to Dectora" was the first title of what later became "Aedh Laments the loss of his Love," which ultimately became "The Lover Mourns for the Loss of His Love." The poem we know in its final version as the expansive "He Mourns for the Change that has Come upon Him and his Beloved and Longs for the End of the World" began originally as the much more explicit "The Desire of Man and Woman," which was then softened to the more "dramatic" "Mongan Laments the Change that has come upon him and his Beloved." The poem which in its original incarnation was called "O'Sullivan the Red to Mary Lavell" became "Aedh Tells of Perfect Beauty" and is finally simplified to "He Tells of Perfect Beauty." The common tendency of such

changes, is towards depersonalisation, towards the representative nature of the
speaker and away from his individual (personal or dramatic) nature. So the
process is one of decisive distancing. First there's a shift to a more or less
dramatic mask. This is not very successful since, no matter what Yeats calls
them, all the voices have a suspicious likeness to one another and were, as Yeats
himself said rather defensively in a note, to be understood "more as principles of
the mind than as actual personages." (Given the actual content of the poems,
mind, in this case, is another example of strategic distancing.) From the
dramatic mask, then, he moves on to the more generalised persona of "the
lover."

Such title changes extend by analogy some of the discoveries we've already
made. First of all, they underline that uncertainty of identity which we've seen
attends desire. And, like the canceled poem I quoted above, they especially
show Yeats's concern that the completed symbolic action of the poem itself
would be quite distinct from what he called "the bundle of accident and
incoherence that sat down to breakfast." (Breakfast must have been the most
fearfully actual time of day for Yeats, the moment when the self was least
composed.) In alchemical terms, never too far from the poet's mind, I imagine,
the alteration of titles represents the purging of the accidental dross of
experience, leaving in the poem its pure essential gold. In *The Wind Among the
Reeds*, the presentation of the state of desire itself is this purified symbolic
action—individually of the poem and cumulatively of the book as a whole—
adding up to a one-act monodrama of desire.

A final general feature of the book as a whole that has some bearing on this
issue of desire is the elaborate set of notes with which, as I've said before, Yeats
propped up the first edition of *The Wind Among the Reeds*. In fact, this edition
has sixty-two pages of poems and forty-four pages of notes—a proportion far in
excess of anything in earlier or later volumes (all the notes in the definitive
Collected Poems run to no more than fifteen pages). Yeats himself was uneasy
with such a disproportionate bulk and eliminated the greater part of them in later
editions, explaining that they contained "all the little learning I had, and more
wilful phantasy than I now think admirable."

A curious, idiosyncratic mixture of folklore, comparative mythology, and
what Yeats called "the magical tradition," the notes, at least on the surface, are
explanatory of some of the more esoteric personages, allusions, and symbols in
the poems. Explanatory as their overt aim may be, however, I am not in fact
convinced they truly represent a sincere wish that the poems be more exactly
understood. Indeed, by drawing our attention very deliberately to the subject
matter of the poems, Yeats succeeds in displacing our queries about their
subject. Sexual desire is scarcely mentioned in these notes. One of the few
explicit references to it concerns the opening images of "He Laments the
Change," where white deer and red hound are, as the notes explain—after
tracing their sources in myth and folklore—"Plain images of the desire of man
'which is for the woman,' and 'the desire of the woman which is for the desire
of the man.'" (Such a statement, of course, is an interesting revelation of Yeats's

notion of desire, a notion that fits with what I have been saying: for in this description, desire is a living paradox, the man seeking its consummation, the woman its perpetuity.) Aside from this reference, however, which is itself oddly sanitised by unexplained quotation marks, the notes for the most part steer us away from sexual meanings. The author's explanation of "The Cap and the Bells," for example, avoids its implicitly phallic nature by concentrating on what he makes the more innocuous fact: that it was written directly out of a dream. Then, by saying it has always "meant a great deal to me" he seems to reveal something, but by adding "it has not always meant quite the same thing" he forestalls our own search for meaning, dissuading us even farther from this by saying that his own search for meaning and explanation ended up "confused and meaningless." It's impossible, therefore, to say what the poem really "means." What the note insists is that the poem must always remain in the idiom of desire, the image without the meaning. The note to "The Song of Wandering Aengus" is also rather evasive, first offering examples from myth and folklore that might be analogous to the happenings in the poem, and then distancing us even farther from any personal sexual relevance by insisting that "The poem was suggested to me by a Greek folksong." In their active refusal to name what stirs at the heart of so many of these poems, therefore, the notes constitute an important part of the constellation of desire that encompasses the individual poems and the book as a whole. The notes, that is, are often composed of contradictory forces—the will to reveal and the will to conceal, the will to be known and at the same time to remain unknown. The notes show how deliberately and (since he was using the idiom of clarification for purposes of concealment) how paradoxically Yeats fostered this twin ambition, letting the book as a whole personify desire, the state itself. As icon, you might say, the book reiterates its subject, desire, paralyzed between concealment and revelation. And it might even be possible to argue for some related implication regarding the book's cover, designed by Yeats's friend, the symbolist artist Althea Gyles. On front and back it has a stylised picture of curved and woven reeds, which it might not be too fanciful or sexist (at least in the context of the 1890s) to call "female," rising out of a stylised image of water and one of fire, and these are divided, even pierced, by the distinctly phallic blade of sedge on the book's spine.

IV

To sum up: *The Wind Among the Reeds* enacts one of the principle elements in Yeats's own state of being in the 1890s, a time of deep sexual distress, of inexorable but essentially unsatisfied desire. As a kind of oblique but distinct autobiographical statement, it creates one component in a style that will allow him to negotiate between his art and his life in an extraordinarily rich, complex, and lasting way. It also constitutes the first chapter in the autobiography of his spiritual or "poetic" identity, later chapters of which will be entitled *Responsibilities, The Wild Swans at Coole, The Tower*, and so on. This earliest layer of his identity is composed of pure desire and is a sort of ground, seed-bed, or forcing-house for his imagination. The books he wrote after *The Wind Among the Reeds*, those later chapters in this symbolic autobiography, perform an anatomy of the self-in-the-world, that begins in this anonymous lover's erotic paralysis of desire and ends in the erotic fury of the wild old wicked man of the later poems. One of the central discoveries of this great book of the self is that life itself is desire, that death finishes us off unappeased, not knowing the truth but embodying it. *The Wind Among the Reeds* presents this truth, embodies it, with a dreadful, diagrammatic simplicity. In fact I believe these poems set up Yeats's way of being in the world as a poet—which "being-in-the-world" is the subject of the *Collected Poems.* In the way it purely embodies the state of desire itself, that is, *The Wind Among the Reeds* is the true beginning of Yeats's spiritual autobiography. What precedes it (even *The Wanderings of Oisin*) is prologue, and what follows confronts, with a style constantly expanding and toughening, the desperate logic of the discoveries he is opened to and to which he gives voice in these early poems. The issue amounts to no more than yet another illustration of the extraordinary (willed and unwilled) coherence, unity, and integrity of the life and work.

I realise, of course, that to point to the presence of desire in Yeats's work, any of Yeats's work, early or late, is hardly going to win the prize for critical originality. What I hope to have shown in a more or less persuasive way, however, is what the word "desire" may mean in literary terms, and that *The Wind Among the Reeds* is, even if we take *The Wanderings of Oisin* into account, the volume in which Yeats puts down imaginative taproots which are the source of an enormous amount of his poetic productivity for the rest of his life. And this, I might observe in passing, is one of the many areas where the contrast between Yeats and Joyce is a striking one. Most of us are familiar with Stephen Daedalus's deliberate antithesis between himself and the "Michael Robartes" of the first edition of *The Wind Among the Reeds* (who "remembers forgotten beauty"). Even beyond this, it is clear that for Joyce, desire, as distinct from something we might call love, became essentially a comic condition. Think of Bloom's erotic attachments (detachments might be a better word) with the invisible Martha Clifford and the all too visible Gerty McDowell. But for Yeats, on the other hand, desire in all its incarnations was probably the single most important fact that determined his tragic sense of life. There is that aphorism of 1905, for example, in which he crystallises a metaphysics of desire: "life, apart from ecstasy, is perpetual preparation for what never happens." Desire, in other words, rarely interrupted by some gift or grace of fulfillment, is the natural condition. The same thought, but revised towards an honest relativism and with the elimination of ecstasy, turns up in the *Autobiography*: "All life weighed in the scales of my own life seems to me a preparation for what never happens." It's hard to imagine a more succinct definition of the state of desire tragically apprehended. For this is something Yeats knows in his bones, and which he first set down in *The Wind Among the Reeds*, in a way too complex to be understood in terms of the biographical issues with which I began this talk.

"Would it be too much to ask if there is any basis in actual fact for them?" asked Austin Clarke of the poems in *The Wind Among the Reeds*. Too much and not enough, I'd say. For the "actual fact" is that with all its strategic evasions of breakfast-table truths the book, as a monodrama of desire, is a perfect self-portrait of the artist as a young lover. And however Yeats may have felt about the shortcomings of the book and its style when he had grown into his later, tougher, more astringent self, *The Wind Among the Reeds* establishes a decisive, necessary point of departure for our understanding of his poetic identity, as this is revealed, fully embodied, by the *Collected Poems*.

1983

NOTES

[1] See "A General Introduction for My Work," 1937.

[2] Richard Ellmann, *Yeats, The Man and the Masks* (New York: Macmillan, 1948) 159, 147.

[3] *James Joyce, the Critical Heritage*, ed. Robert H. Deming (London: Routledge & Kegan Paul , 1970) 114.

[4] Douglas Archibald, *Yeats* (Syracuse: Syracuse University Press, 1983) 95.

[5] W.B. Yeats, *Uncollected Prose*, ed. John P. Frayne vol. I (New York: Macmillan, 1970) 324.

[6] In this paragraph, I am especially indebted to the findings of Allen Grossman. See *Poetic Knowledge*, 55-61.

[7] Curtis Bradford, *Yeats at Work* (Carbondale: Southern Illinois University Press, 1965) 29.

[8] W.B. Yeats, *Memoirs*, ed. Denis Donoghue (New York: Macmillan, 1973) 127.

[9] In Jon Stallworthy, *Between the Lines* (Oxford: Clarendon Press, 1963) 2.

[10] *Ibid.*

"A Living Thing":
Responding to Responsibilities

If verse, even great verse is to be alive it must be occupied with the whole of life.
Synge, letter to WBY, 1908

If verse is to remain a living thing it must be occupied, when it likes, with the whole of a poet's life and experience.
WBY, "amendment" of letter

Re-reading *Responsibilities* recently, I was curious about the widely accepted opinion that this was the first major collection in Yeats's career. Why do we see it, I wondered, as such a cardinal occasion, as that pivotal moment when Yeats achieves or happens into his maturity as a poet? What follows here is a mulling over some of the things that held my attention as I pursued an answer to this question.

My first stop was the title itself. *Crossways; The Rose; The Wind Among the Reeds; In the Seven Woods; The Green Helmet; Responsibilities*: in the procession of Yeatsian titles up to 1914, this last is clearly the odd one out. Neither mystical nor heraldic nor evocative of the natural world, the abstract and soberly suited *Responsibilities* seems a deliberate swerve away from a world in which any self-respecting Romantic lyricist would feel at home, towards one antagonistic to Romantic inspiration, the conventional antithesis of Romance itself. In its cool refusal of mood and mystery—exchanging their wavering illuminations for a harder, more realistic light—the title is a convincing token of some decisive change in the poet's way of being in the world. Through it he alerts expectation, preparing his readers for poems that will embody a revised, a re-made self. The title is the first sign we have of the particular quality that, in my opinion, makes Yeats the great poet he is. For it reveals his ability (and willingness) to perform those great sweeping swerves of self and style that transform his life as a poet into an enterprise in perpetual self-renewal.

Between the title and the text stand two unusual epigraphs. Since an epigraph can be a poet's way of lining up a book's sights, even, perhaps, of cocking its trigger, and since Yeats was not in the habit of using them (only *Crossways* and *The Rose*, among his other volumes, have one apiece), this brace of miniature signposts seemed to merit more than the casual glance I'd usually given them.

"In dreams begins responsibility." The first thing this does is temper the surprising title. In place of a definitive break with the past it implies a certain continuity between past and present selves. For 'dreams' are emblematic of the Romantic self embodied by the earlier poems, those volumes the poet himself referred to as "the books of my numberless dreams."[1] In fact, the word 'dream' in one form or another appears no less than nine times in the first poem of *Crossways*, and makes twenty-eight appearances in *The Wind Among the Reeds*. In terms of relative frequency it appears less in *Responsibilities* than in any earlier volume. By making dreams the source of responsibility, however, the epigraph shows that change can acknowledge rather than deny the past. And so the poet's revision of self is rooted in an *evolutionary* energy that knits apparently opposing forces into a fresh, complex harmony.

In Yeats's lexicon, the word 'dream' is also close to the notion of 'ideal.' For this reason, the epigraph may also be taken to mean that the moral realism of responsibility can derive from the idealism of dream, and/or in the disillusion in which idealism often ends (as Yeats's own national and amorous ideals ended). Responsibility, then, is an active, positive reaction to the idealist's disenchantment, a counterforce to despair and moral inertia. The potentially barren solipsism of the dream can be the seedbed of that altruism we name responsibility, the originating site of what Keats calls "soul-making." An end can be a beginning; the world can be an open-ended drama of evolution and continuity, a going-on. In its compound gesture of recognition and resolve, then, this epigraph may distill into a phrase of near-proverbial stability the poet's emotional and moral condition in the poems that follow.

In its Eastern inscrutability, the possible meanings of the second epigraph surrender themselves less readily to the reader. "How I am fallen from myself, for a long time now / I have not seen the Prince of Chang in my dreams." First of all, I suppose, like the title and the first epigraph, these lines are an acknowledgement of change. Fallen from a former dreaming self, the speaker experiences the world in a new way, as centered in radical absence. This simple acknowledgement may register a new, accepting self, able to reach beyond the oneiric into the actual. The fall may also be understood as from a state of innocent unity into one of historical experience and separation. And since a sexually-charged meaning is not impossible (perhaps the speaker is a woman) the lines may make allegorical reference to Yeats's relationship with Maud Gonne. As such, they could be an admission of loss and a confession of detachment. Physically consummated in 1908, that remarkable affair was restored quickly to the conditions of a "spiritual marriage" entered into in 1898.[2] Perplexed and unhappy, Yeats had, in the years that followed, other sexual liaisons ("I was never more deeply in love," he said in 1909, "but my desires must go elsewhere if I would escape their poison").[3] Between 1914 and 1916, however, when he chose to add the epigraphs to the second edition of *Responsibilities*, he was aware that his dreamlife was not inhabited as formerly by the woman he loved.[4] While many poems from *The Wild Swans at Coole* (1919), which were written in 1914 or 1915, deal passionately with that condition of loss ("O who could have foretold / That the heart grows old"), this epigraph simply recognizes it. In doing so, however, it suggests an evolutionary movement parallel to that in the first epigraph. This one, however, is more private and emotionally charged: their dreams, after all, were the privileged zone in which most of Yeats's and Maud Gonne's amorous and sexual activity seems to have, however metaphorically, taken place.[5] Here, then, we're in the realm of private emotion, whereas in the first epigraph we're in the realm of public 'truth.' And in the private realm, it should be added, one part of responsibility is to admit to unpalatable facts, to utter unwelcome truths. Between them, so, the epigraphs provide a twin signpost to the *experience* of responsibility in different aspects of a single life. And this experience, in turn, acknowledges within that life the felt presence of change, change that grows out of the past even as it separates from it.

Once beyond the title and epigraphs, one of my strongest interests in the book itself is the way the poems are assembled into groups to compose the larger design of the volume as a whole. Such patterns are worth considering. Although to look at elements of the book's architecture, (rather than at its furniture), is bound to lead to somewhat speculative and impressionistic readings, such an approach may serve as a summary introduction to a more detailed engagement with the poems themselves.

The first nine poems constitute a distinct pattern, one of broadening, perhaps concentric, spheres of responsibility. First (in "Introductory Rhymes") Yeats recognizes a responsibility to his lineage, his family, his "old fathers." Idiosyncratic as his position may be ("I have no child, I have nothing but a book"), he claims through confessional supplication (the repeated 'pardon' is the single main verb in one remarkably marshaled sentence of twenty-eight lines) he claims his place in the biological, and notably male, line. Next, in "The Grey Rock," his (equally male) poetic lineage is his subject. He records and judiciously praises his dead "tavern-comrades," those "poets with whom I learned my trade," offering the poem-within-the-poem as a gift of unfashionable narrative in token of his sense of responsible belonging.

The next sphere of responsibility (I am not moving in strict *sequence* here: the individual poems in a sub-group don't necessarily follow each other) is inscribed by two poems: "To a Friend Whose Work Has Come to Nothing," and "On Those That Hated 'The Playboy of the Western World,' 1907." In accents of pride, encouragement, and anger the poet speaks out of the responsibility of active friendship, against the enemies of Synge and Lady Gregory. In this way he expands the private commitment into the public world: the private man speaks in a deliberately public way. In the next sub-group of poems—"To a Wealthy Man," "September 1913," and "To a Shade"—he intensifies this engagement with the public world, speaking out as a citizen, accepting his place within the sphere of civic responsibility. In the lists of local controversy and local politics he seeks—by satire, ideal exemplars, and the pose of ironic detachment—to educate his fellow citizens on the proper responsibilities of citizenship, as found in places like Athens and Urbino, the city-states of Greece and the Italian Renaissance. Since citizenship is the primary sphere of political reality, these are poems of original *political* action.

A subtext in each of these smaller sets of poems is Yeats's own membership in a particular, exclusive group—familial, personal, social, or aesthetic. Each poem posits a "we" (positive) and a "they" (negative). This exclusive stance is softened by two poems which broaden the sphere of responsibility. "When Helen Lived" admits to a frailty and vulgarity in common with the rest of an unenlightened humanity. And, in "Paudeen," the sphere is even farther expanded into a responsible moment of visionary democracy. In this there is a recognition like that which Yeats saw (and had once separated himself from) in AE ("To the religious genius all souls are of equal value: the queen is not more than an apple woman"),[6] a recognition that "on the lonely height where all are in God's eye, / There cannot be, confusion of our sound forgot, / A single soul that lacks a sweet crystalline cry."

What I experience in this first large group of poems, then, is a pattern formed by the poet's journey through an amplifying series of spheres of acknowledged responsibility, from that of blood to that of soul, from biology and genealogy through poetry, politics, and history, to divinity. And in this pattern I find a kind of diagram of autobiographical essence, drawn up in the idioms of relationship, of personal (private and public) responsibility.

The next pattern-making group contains "The Three Beggars," "The Three Hermits," "Beggar to Beggar Cried," "Running to Paradise," and "The Hour Before Dawn." Different as they may seem from the previous group, they remain nonetheless rooted in the same fundamental issues, and manage to expand even farther the notions of autobiography and responsibility. In their marked change of style, however—brisk colloquial manner, dramatic masks, absence of that authorial self that was such an informing presence in the earlier group— they probe experience with different means and towards altered, if related ends.

Beside the "exorbitant dreams of beggary"—all of them located in a world of conventional responsibilities (marriage, trade, social status)—which incite "The Three Beggars" to futile quarrels, the wise passiveness of the crane might seem to be the poem's point. Certainly the bird's climactic utterance—"Maybe I shall take a trout / If but I do not seem to care"—could adumbrate a higher form of personal responsibility (as well as a fresh attitude to the anxieties of desire). In "The Three Hermits" I find a comparable redefinition of responsibility. Responsibly, if lugubriously, two of the hermits argue over the duties of prayer and the finer points of incarnation doctrine. The third, who neither says prayers nor cracks fleas (images of the religious and the secular life?), seems to bear the poet's seal of approval, for he, "Giddy with his hundredth year, / Sang unnoticed like a bird." Described by Yeats as "my first poem which is comedy or tragicomedy,"[7] "The Three Hermits" may offer, from the oblique angles of "comedy or tragicomedy," another view of responsibility. An implicit critique of his fellows' behavior, the happy, and passively anarchic quietism of the unnoticed singer may lay claim to a higher form of responsibility, for and to the self—beyond desire, acquisitiveness, action, even prayer.

After this, the vigorous, mocking quatrains of "Beggar to Beggar Cried" stand the habits of normal responsibility on their head. The Beggar's ironically conventional ambitions sound like nothing but moral truancy and arrant egotism, for he intends to "get a comfortable wife and house / To rid me of the devil in my shoes, / . . . And the worse devil that is between my thighs. / . . . And then I'll grow respected at my ease." Written, it is thought, in reaction to "sensible" advice given to Yeats to marry his mistress, Mabel Dickinson, whom he had, it was mistakenly believed, made pregnant, encourages my sense of it as a critique of conventional notions of responsibility.[8] Read thus, it insists that responsibility to an anarchic and therefore irresponsible ("frenzy-struck") version of the self is a more generous and encompassing notion than those more conventional forms endorsed, for example, in the poems of the previous group.

"Running to Paradise" ventures into the same zone of anarchy and unconventional blessedness as other poems in the second group. With his own socially anarchic vision of the ordinary world and of paradise ("And there the king *is* as the beggar"), and in the stark contrast between himself and his respectable, socially active brother, this beggarman turns conventional notions of respectability and responsibility topsy-turvy ("The poet," Yeats wrote in 1909, "is a good citizen turned inside out").[9] In the Beggar's joyous embrace of freedom and solitude, and in the rapt engagement of the wonderfully lightfooted stanzas themselves, there lies farther confirmation of an ecstatic commitment to self. Once again, apparent irresponsibility must be seen, I believe, as (in Yeats's view) a higher form of responsibility.

This group ends in "The Hour Before Dawn," whose drunken sleeper embodies an articulate renunciation of all responsibility: nothing in the *world* is of any value, "For all life longs for the Last Day / . . . And there be nothing but God left." Like Keats pursuing the nightingale, however, Yeats draws back from this edge where even the self must be extinguished. He gives to the opposing beggarman—a "cursing rogue with a merry face" and less a saint than a beggar out of Synge—a responsible defence of life itself, without any of those attached values which create normal responsibilities. Life itself has to suffice. Finally, in this strange debate between a species of despair and a beggarly Everyman (with shades of Dante and Spenser and *Measure for Measure*—texts much taken up with notions of responsibility—hovering around Hell Mouth in Cruachan), the beggar arbitrarily resolves the issue with his fists. In this rough, speechless embodiment, however, Yeats may be offering us the most ample and containing circle of responsibility in the book. For here, in full, articulate knowledge of the worst about life (the debate could look back to Synge and forward to Beckett), is a desperate commitment to life itself, and to the self—unpropped by any external values—in the ordinary world ("I'd have a merry life enough / If a good Easter wind were blowing"). And as the poem ends in the natural landscape, where "The clouds were brightening with the dawn," it is hard for me not to imagine the shadow of Wordsworth's leech-gatherer, in all his resolution and independence, falling over it. Out of the darkest hour has come this illuminating affirmation of secular responsibility, answering and, I suppose, complementing, the (also dawning) *religious* vision of "Paudeen," with its sense of divine organization in the world of souls. Similarly, this second group of poems counterpoints and extends those notions of responsibility presented in the previous group, as well as widening the net of autobiography to include the felt pressure and presence of Yeats's own anarchic individualism, free of all ties except his passionate attachment to life itself. And from this revised perspective it is possible to see the title, *Responsibilities*, as no longer simply signifying a plural concrete noun, but in addition signifying an interrogative meditation on the very *nature* of responsibility itself. Such an understanding of the title would give even greater unity to the volume as a whole.

"The Hour Before Dawn" falls roughly at the center of the book. By putting off the beggar's mask and returning to a recognizable self, Yeats seems to imply that the meditation on responsibilities, having reached its most capacious point, can return to the world of the actual. The actual, in this case, is the poet's relationship with women.

It is striking how absent women are from the poems of the first two groups. With the exception of Aoife and an extended, bitter reference to Maud Gonne in "The Grey Rock," women receive only incidental (and usually unflattering) mention in these poems. Women occupy the center of the next group, however, in poems that offer this fundamental relationship up for scrutiny in the hard light of the notion of responsibility.

The "Song From a Play" evokes, in the world of women, a primal male failure of responsibility—abandonment of the mother and child. Since the girl here is "the mad singing daughter of a harlot," and since in "Presences," a poem written in 1915, Yeats probably refers to Mabel Dickinson as a "harlot," and since Maud and Iseult Gonne are referred to in the same poem as queen and child, it is possible that this song (from *The Player Queen*) is woven out of Yeats's inmost experience. Perhaps as answers to this covert admission of some responsibility in that sexual zone, the three enigmatic short poems that follow ("The Realists," "The Witch," "The Peacock") are statements of self-affirming constancy—to himself, to a singular object of desire, and to his own art—in a world of conventional "riches," temptation, and change. Endangered and vulnerable, stubborn and proud, preoccupied with some unspoken sense of responsibility that has a distinctly sexual edge to it—it is the speaker of these three poems who takes up in the poems that follow the issue of responsibility in the sphere of sexual love.

Enigmatic at first, some light may enter "The Mountain Tomb" if it is opened to potential biographical connections. In 1908, not long after the physical consummation of the affair with Maud Gonne, Yeats—having been pushed back from the physical to the "spiritual marriage of 1898"—is meditating on the connection between "initiation in the coffin of Father Rosy Cross . . . and mystic marriage."[10] This meditation leads him to a spiritual sense of "a great union" with Maud Gonne. The poem in question, then, written in her house in Calvados four years later, may contain an admission that the old conjuring methods no longer work ("In vain, in vain"). As a confession of failure—a sort of confession of sexo-spiritual impotence—it echoes the second epigraph, where the Prince of Chang comes no longer into the speaker's dreams. Such a change in his sexual life, the hardest experience for the poet-lover to find an adequate language for, is what the other poems in this group responsibly encounter.

In its splendid sense of the actual, "To a Child Dancing" is a responsible antidote to dreaming. Yeats insists on the differences between himself and Iseult Gonne, on the fact that, because of their ages, they speak different tongues. His references to "love lost as soon as won," and to the girl's mother as having been "broken in the end" take a certain kind of realistic courage, free of dreaming desire. So in finding the adequate language, Yeats deepens the private operation of responsibility as well as enlarging the autobiographical capacity of his verse.

In "A Memory of Youth" and in "Fallen Majesty" the intimate life of love is seen as in itself a responsibility. Here his duty is two-fold: to place his love for Maud Gonne in the stream of time, and to speak honestly, casting aside the props of dreaming desire. This lover sees clearly and admits candidly that "even the best of love must die." And yet he can surround this truth with an even larger one—that Love itself can endure, as it did between them. In "Fallen Majesty," the responsibility is to "record what's gone." His hand "records what's gone." Ignoring the presumably unintended pun (in a very early letter he spelt her name "Miss Gone"), it's possible to say that such a task, such a conscious responsibility, is a new element in this central relationship of his life. So the framing idiom of responsibility can also contain this inner, most vulnerable area of his experience. This conscious sense of responsibility—to record the past and give due praise—is also what animates "Friends": "Now *must I* these three praise." Having praised Lady Gregory and Olivia Shakespeare, he goes beyond praise of Maud Gonne ("How could I praise that one?") to evaluation, a responsible recognition of the damage she wrought and the benefits she brought ("I count my good and bad"). The responsible love poem is also a poem of critical self-knowledge.

In "The Cold Heaven" and "That the Night Come," this love is also located within a context of evaluative awareness, whether he is summing up the nature of Maud Gonne's soul, or whether he's accepting, in a context of moral dread, responsibility for "love crossed long ago," taking "all the blame out of all sense and reason." Yeats removed these three poems ("Friends," "The Cold Heaven," "That the Night Come") from *The Green Helmet* and deliberately placed them in *Responsibilities* because, I'd say, they are different from the other love poems in the earlier volume. They belong to the complicated, evaluative idiom of responsibility, whereas—while recognizing the corrosive abrasions of time—the other love poems in *The Green Helmet* maintain an idiom of desire, regret, reconciliation, or the simple consciousness of loss. The love poems he placed in *Responsibilities*, however, as well as underscoring his conscious craft as book maker, fill out the scope of the volume by enacting the presence of responsibility in the intimate area of personal sexual love.

The final group of poems—"An Appointment," "The Magi," "The Dolls," "A Coat"—offers a series of emblematic summaries of political, mystical, sexual, and aesthetic topics already touched on by other poems in the book. As a political poem, "An Appointment" (1907) adopts a stance of passive, contemplative responsibility towards a political, public event. As a small *meditation* on the nature of instinctive energy and bureaucratic energy it serves to show by difference the nature of responsible *action* in the other political poems. "The

Dolls" and "The Magi" are complementary poems that compose, in their reactions to two versions of nativity, a spectrum that runs from the brute frenzy of life to the remote stillness of art. In both, the notion of responsibility is present: the Magi are bound to an endless quest, whereas the man and woman in "The Dolls" resist responsibility for the accidental birth of "A noisy and filthy thing." The two poems between them answer the responsibility to compose a whole picture: between them they accept the responsibility, embody it, indeed, of multiple being. "A Coat," too, in a more personal tone of voice, is another responsible summary, speaking back to "The Grey Rock." But where that poem had proclaimed membership of a group, this one proclaims a sturdy, bitter independence, the poet showing a responsibility to himself as a poet ("There's more enterprise / In walking naked").

The Epilogue brings the book full circle. In terms of responsibility it is a conclusive gesture. For where the prologue of "Introductory Rhymes" was a plea for pardon, an apology for the self, the epilogue is an extraordinarily affirmative, magniloquent presentation and declaration of self—a self fully conscious of living and dead friends, a self with "a sterner conscience," a self responsibly secure in its own state of public and private consciousness. And to this guaranteed sense of self there comes the largest sense of responsibility possible. For after all the hatred and bitterness, the being besieged in the world, he can "forgive even that wrong of wrongs" (an "outrageous article" by George Moore attacking Yeats's attitude to the middle classes).[11] In a context of such self-affirming magnanimity and textured consciousness, the circle of responsibility that is forgiveness is the largest circle possible. And in this gesture, to contain the largest moral responsibility possible, he has achieved a palpable fullness of speech (the poem is one massive, embracing rhetorical sentence, subtle in rhyme, magniloquent in diction, majestic even in its crude image). Such a fullness of speech is the largest *poetic* responsibility possible. As the book closes, these moral and expressive conditions represent a complete anatomy of the notion first offered to our attention by the title, *Responsibilities*.

Before one is trapped by such speculative and general considerations, however, it is usually the style of single poems that startles one to attention—features of voice, rhythm, syntax or image that are, in effect, the poem's body. In fact, it was the style of *Responsibilities* that first captured critical attention. Leavis called it "spare, hard and sinewy and in tone sardonic;" Pound praised its "quality of hard light," its manifestly "new note," how it is "gaunter, seeking greater hardness of outline;" and Eliot commended Yeats's "power of speaking as a particular man to men . . . this freedom of speech . . . is a triumph."[12] A few examples are enough to see, in some detail, what the critics mean. Here is the first stanza of "September 1913":

> What need you, being come to sense,
> But fumble in the greasy till
> And add the halfpence to the pence
> And prayer to shivering prayer, until

> You have dried the marrow from the bone?
> Romantic Ireland's dead and gone,
> It's with O'Leary in the grave.

Here, as never before in Yeats, is the abrasive voice of a man thoroughly engaged in action. The first political poem he wrote, for example (for Parnell's death, in 1891), is full of bardic gestures ("Ye on the broad high mountains of old Eri," that sort of thing), while his next poetic excursion into practical politics—"An Appointment," written in 1907 and included in *Responsibilities*— though vastly more sophisticated in speaking voice and the suppleness of syntax—is still a mannered, essentially meditative performance. In "September 1913," however (the specific title plunges us into time, history, immediacy), all is action. The question grabs at that "you," enforcing attention like a headline. (The poem, in fact, first appeared in *The Irish Times*.) The adjectives "greasy" and "shivering" skewer their nouns unmercifully, while the adjective "Romantic," in this context, shines with its own bleak splendor—so out of place, so dead and gone. The colloquial diction and turns of speech leave the Davisite rhetoric of 1891 and the slow courtly gestures of 1907 far behind. The syntax is at once headlong and poised, the enjambed lines forcing us always forward, that "until" a miracle of almost indecent suspense. The laconic, sardonic voice can manage the sharpest particularity and the most expansive generalization: after all the lethal brawling it can reach the plangent strain of the last two lines, the almost swaggering magniloquence of "O'Leary" as heroic talisman. Hard, various, stuffed with personality, this verse is a "speaking out," the style itself an exact embodiment of the responsibility the speaker feels in the facts. Here is a verse that manages to be public and private at the same time, dealing with public issues without loss of private passion and energy.

Similar qualities may be found, in a different register, in the new "folk" style of the beggar poems. The older ballad manner sounded like this:

> When I play on my fiddle in Dooney,
> Folk dance like a wave of the sea;
> My cousin is priest in Kilvarnet,
> My brother in Mocharabuiee.

Here is a stanza from "Running to Paradise":

> My brother Mourteen is worn out
> With skelping his big brawling lout,
> And I am running to paradise;
> A poor life, do what he can,
> And though he keep a dog and a gun,
> A serving-maid and a serving-man:
> *And there the king is but as the beggar.*

This language is rough, crude, densely colloquial. Speech, not musical song, is responsible for the rhythmic velocity. While the lines are end-stopped, each has a rhythmically surprising life of its own, while the fluent, continuous syntax never lets you lose sight or sound of a sentence building. The dancing anapaests of "The Fiddler of Dooney" take over the ear, whatever the sense, while the beggar's lines resist any such allurements (through their lively rhythmic and metrical variety). In image and diction, as well as in rhythm, a line like "With skelping his big brawling lout," double meaning and all, would wreck the dancing surfaces of the earlier ballad.

Finally, here is a snatch of a *love poem* from *Responsibilities*:

> Although crowds gathered once if she but showed her face
> And even old men's eyes grew dim, this hand alone,
> Like some last courtier at a gypsy camping-place
> Babbling of fallen majesty, records what's gone.

In such a passage, Yeats's speech manners are so much more concrete and matter of fact than they were, for example, in the perfumed gestures of *The Wind Among the Reeds* (e.g. "Fasten your hair with a golden pin / And bind up every wandering tress; / I bade my heart build these poor rhymes"). While rhythm here is audible iambic, the rhythm picked up in the later piece has only a faint iambic shadow across it: sense rather than metre makes up those rhythmic units. Apart from the more surprising imagery of the later poem, one could also notice how that rich and complicated music puts us in palpable touch with time (the poem's subject, after all), as poems in the timeless erogenous zones of *The Wind Among the Reeds* never intend to. For the tenses of "Fallen Majesty" move about in a bewildering, exhilarating way, registering time on one's nerve-ends in a way a Romantic image like "Time's bitter flood" (from *Reeds*) never could. Such stylistic toughness guarantees a fine sense of emotional truth rising out of the lines, out of this complicated sweetness. And this truth leads to a sense of actual presence—of poet and woman—presences the lyrical manners of *The Wind Among the Reeds* are always dissolving into the diffused atmospherics of mood.

Encountering this style (prepared for by the work in *The Green Helmet*), I was curious about the influences that might have enriched the mixture. A few possibilities suggested themselves. During 1908 and 1909, while he was incubating this new manner, Yeats felt very strongly the force of Synge (who died in 1909). Synge's urge to unite "asceticism, stoicism, and ecstasy," for example, may have affected the layered, various texture of many poems in *Responsibilities*.[13] Yeats admired the "astringent joy and hardness" in Synge, and as he was editing Synge's poems he must surely have given alert attention to the point Synge makes in his preface about "the rough poems that give weight to the more ecstatic."[14] And Synge's most striking formulation, "that before verse can be human again it must learn to be brutal," surely did not fall on deaf ears.[15]

I suspect, too, that the work of Donne, which Yeats was reading "constant-ly" in late 1912 when he got the Grierson edition, was another significant influ-ence on the new style.[16] He is impressed by Donne's combinations of subtlety and passion, "his pedantry and his obscenity," and later he will speak with ad-miration of his "natural momentum in the syntax."[17] Such qualities surely nour-ish the style of *Responsibilities*, as did the new connection with Ezra Pound. In January 1913, in fact, Yeats tells Lady Gregory how good a critic of his work Pound is, who "helps me get back to the definite and the concrete away from modern abstraction."[18] And Pound's views on syntax were certainly in tune with Yeats's own, since in 1913 Pound was mildly rebuking William Carlos Wil-liams because "your syntax still strays occasionally from the simple order of natural speech."[19]

Adding a profoundly important personal weight to such external influences was, I believe, Yeats's own *Journal*—begun in late 1908 and kept extensively to 1910 and sporadically from 1911 to 1914 and beyond. Aside from the fact that many observations or meditations on culture, class, religion, nationalism, emo-tional life, and poetry that are crucial to the poems of *The Green Helmet* and *Responsibilities* appear here, the habits of style he was deliberately subjecting himself to in the *Journal* ("Every note must first come as a casual thought, then it will be my life")[20] encourage a new ease and spontaneity of expression, quali-ties which bring to the verse some of the virtues of good prose. Quite a number of prose notes lead directly to poems (e.g. pp. 229, 225, 141), and in fact many of the poems of *The Green Helmet* are actually drafted in the *Journal*. Kept during a climactic emotional period in his life (because of the affair with Maud Gonne, the death of Synge, the changing political scene), the *Journal* must be seen as an important stylistic contribution to the new manners of *Responsibili-ties*.

Almost all the *Journal's* entries are written in immediate reaction to public and private events that impinge directly upon Yeats's own life. More than any other, I'd argue, it is this fact that shapes the style of *Responsibilities*. Conven-iently enough, the precise nature of that style may be discovered by looking again at the book's title. For the style is, of course, a style of *response*, it is style *as* response. In response, indeed, begins *Responsibilities*.

Preparatory gestures in this responsive mode are a number of *The Green Helmet* poems drafted in the *Journal*. "Reconciliation" and "King and No King," for example, are marvelous demonstrations of living speech, of a voice speaking directly *back* to an immediate, present listener. The energizing fact of response is also, I'd say, part of the poet's turn to epigram, a habit also revealed by the Journal. Most of these epigrams (perhaps Ben Jonson was an external influence here) are immediate reflexes to events or persons (see 182, 221, 230, 234-5, 244), in an essentially *momentary* language that hasn't time to be grace-ful, gestured, mannered. The epigram is a miniature model of response: it com-pels a language of immediate performance, a language that is, well, epigram-matic. And in Yeats's hands, too, this responsive mode is a distinctly social form—preparing his entrance into the hurly-burly of history and politics in *Re-sponsibilities*.

Any even cursory look at these poems will show the degree to which they are poems *of response*. In the largest sense, indeed, the style of the book may be seen as a response to Synge, to Donne, to Pound (whose 1912 volume, interestingly enough, full of fragments of intense lyric dramas, is called *Ripostes*—Responses). In the particular sense too, response is an integral part of the style of the individual poems. So often these are a speaking back at, or to: many of the titles reveal this, and it is audible in those first lines that imply—as Donne's poems so often do—an immediate listener or listeners. The poems, that is, give the impression of having their life in larger *dramatic* occasions.

Aside from being an informing principle, response is also built into many of the poems' own interior or exterior occasions. "Beggar to Beggar Cried," for example, is likely an oblique response to attempts made on Yeats's own sense of personal freedom, "A Coat" is a direct response to his imitators, and the Epilogue responds to the "outrageous article" written by Moore. In addition, the beggar poems themselves are bristling with interior arguments and debates. The world of all these poems is a world of dramatic action (even in vision there is an image of response, as in "Paudeen" when "a curlew cried . . . a curlew answered"), a world in which the lyric poet must re-make himself in order as a poet, to survive. It is this sense of pressure, of living in a risky, shared world (that *response entails* and that *entails response*), that is for me, in terms of substance and in terms of style, one of the most marked and satisfying characteristics of these poems. It is, to turn the word a little, the responsible and responsive style of *Responsibilities* that gives the book its particular charge.

After all this tugging and pulling at the text, my final curiosity seems simpleminded. What, I find myself wondering, is the true subject of *Responsibilities*? What is it *about*? The answer I am drawn to is itself simple enough, but I'll offer it as a kind of conclusion. Put simply, the subject of *Responsibilities* is the poet's power to find a language adequate to the *fullness* of his own experience, to the multiple reality that is his own life, its layered texture, its existential scepticism, its variety. None of the previous books had done that, although *The Green Helmet* is a first, probably unconscious, move in that direction. *Responsibilities*, however, is conscious of the enterprise and, in its arrangement and its contents, carries its own deliberate intentional force.

Outside the book itself, it's possible to discover some involuntary probes towards what I am calling its subject. In February 1909 in the *Journal*, for example, Yeats fears the loss of his "lyric faculty," as a result of the "heterogeneous labours of these last few years." But he adds then, in a note of significant resolve, "Whatever happens I must go on that there may be a man behind the lines already written. I should have avoided the thing—but being in it!" In this statement of germinal responsibility to himself as a poet, he reveals his ambition that his verse should have the solidity, the body, of the life lived. What this amounts to is a declaration of athletic surrender to the accidental nature of life. Like Hamlet on what Yeats calls "the storm-beaten threshold of sanctity," he does not like the conditions, but with that last exclamatory sentence he, on his own more secular storm-beaten threshold, says, with Hamlet, "Let be."

Again, in March 1909, he says, "perhaps I must do all these things that I may set myself into a life of action, so as to express not the traditional poet but that forgotten thing, the normal active man."[21] While it is hard to think of Yeats as "the normal active man," he is making a point worth attending to. By drawing a distinction between poetry that expresses "the traditional poet" and that which expresses "the normal active man," he adumbrates a poetry that has as its expressive ambition the fullness of a man's life rather than a segregated part of it, which part is probably what's expressed in the books through *In the Seven Woods*. In 1909, then, Yeats is percolating thoughts, attitudes, and moral directions which result immediately in the poems of *The Green Helmet* and, after that, in the more matured and developed plan and poetry of *Responsibilities*. The *Journal* is an attempt to understand himself in his fullness, and this is reflected in the collage-like nature of its composition, the space of a few pages (182-85) containing discussions of the artist and society, the national identity and the literary movement, an epigram on George Moore, a childhood memory, comments on Abbey actors, dreams, a haunted house, psychical research, and more.

Beyond the *Journal*, the continuous dialogue with his father might have also stimulated Yeats's drive for fullness. In a letter written in 1913, J. B. Yeats pointed out "that art embodies not this or that feeling, but the whole totality—sensations, feeling, intuitions, everything—and that when everything in us is expressed there is peace and what is called beauty—this totality is personality.[22] He then adds that "portraiture in art or poetry [is] the effort to keep the pain alive and intensify it, since out of the heart of the pain comes the solace." The son's response to the father puts the matter at its most complete. He says (in a letter of August 1913), "Of recent years instead of 'vision,' meaning by vision the intense realization of a state of ecstatic emotion symbolized in a definite imagined region, I have tried for more self portraiture. I have tried to make my work so convincing with a speech so natural and dramatic that the hearer would feel the presence of a man thinking and feeling."[23] Self portraiture, that is, is the thrust at fullness, the felt "presence of a man thinking and feeling." It may be said that the cumulative effect of the many and various self-portraits provided by the poems of *Responsibilities*, this multiplicity of voices, composes a textured fullness of being as it finds its proper embodiment in language. Beginning by, in a sense, apologizing for his personality, and setting himself (as a "normal active man" might) in the line of his ancestors (identifying himself, that is, as a descendant), he moves through self portraits as poet, citizen, friend, member of social group and class, impassioned visionary, passionate anarchist, lover of life, singer, lover of women, avuncular adviser, moral being, aesthetic critic, solitary poet, to end with a ferocious affirmation of absolute identity both as a poet ("A Coat") and as man ("Epilogue"), a self full enough for forgiveness. So an assured fullness of life—sealed by this proud capacity for forgiveness (no longer a descendant but an articulate full self)—closes a book of "self portraiture" that inaugurates the great second half of Yeats's career as a poet.

Obviously there are omissions that prevent *Responsibilities* being a complete portrait. On the negative side there are Yeats's shadowy sectarian attacks (in private) on Catholic education and the Catholic response to what *he* saw as "cultural" ideals. Such criticisms (observable in the *Journal*) take a bitterly partial view, seeing the consequences but not, in a sufficiently sympathetic way, the causes of the Catholic condition he's diagnosing. On the positive side, there is the necessary exclusion of the Mabel Beardsley poems, "On a Dying Lady," which would have shown his generous and enlightened capacity for admiration and praise, his articulate and simple admiration for the dying woman's understated gallantry, witty courage, and human dignity in the face of the real enemy.

On positive and negative sides, then, there are omissions, and the self-portrait is not complete. In spite of this, however, it seems right to talk about fullness as the book's subject, and leave the circle open. And this *fullness finding adequate expression* is a useful reminder of how *partial* some revisionist critical re-evaluations of Yeats really are, how unlikely they are to respond to the whole picture. (The first true revisionist of Yeats, of course, was Yeats himself.) As *Responsibilities* shows, there is a multiplicity about the poet and the poetry that in itself, in a way usually overlooked by current revisionists, could be a moral and a political model of possibility. But that is another story. Enough to say here that the self-portraiture of *Responsibilities*—that Portrait of the Artist as a Man in Middle Age—embodies a fullness of self that shows, in a phrase of Ben Jonson's about Shakespeare that Yeats was fond of, a man and a poet "so rammed with life he can but grow in life with being."[24]

To end, I return to my *own* epigraphs: in 1908 Synge wrote, "If verse, even great verse is to be alive it must be occupied with the whole of life."[25] Yeats, who certainly agreed with the sentiment, could not resist "improving" its expression when he quotes it in his 1909 preface to Synge's poems, changing it, I'd say, to mirror his own ambitions a little more exactly. "If verse is to remain a living thing," he writes, "it must be occupied, when it likes, with the whole of a poet's life and experience." Not "the whole of life," but "the whole of a poet's life and experience." *Responsibilities*, I'd argue, is Yeats's first major attempt to compose a book that responds to that implicit exhortation. And the fullness of self, of the poet's life and experience, that that book embodies, as well as the renewals in it we create by our attention, certainly make of it, without question, "a living thing."

1989

NOTES

[1] In "A Poet to His Beloved," from *The Wind Among the Reeds.*

[2] See Nancy Cardozo, *Lucky Eyes and a High Heart: The Biography of Maud Gonne* (New York, 1978), 263; *William Butler Yeats: Memoirs*, ed. Denis Donoghue (New York: Macmillan, 1972) 132; A. Norman Jeffares, *W.B. Yeats, A New Biography* (New York: Farrar, Straus, & Giroux, 1988) 160-61.

[3] Cardozo, 263. See Jeffares 162-63.

[4] The Macmillian edition of 1916 has the epigraphs, which are not in the Cuala edition of 1914.

[5] See Jeffares, 163-66.

[6] Memoirs, 168.

[7] *The Letters of W.B. Yeats*, ed. Allan Wade (London: Rupert Hart-Davis, 1954) 577.

[8] Jeffares, 195.

[9] *Memoirs*, 140-41.

[10] Cardozo, 117.

[11] *Memoirs*, 269.

[12] *W.B. Yeats, the Critical Heritage*, ed. A. Norman Jeffares (London: Routledge & Kegan Paul, 1977) 310; *Poetry* (April/May 1914) 66; Joseph Hone, *W.B. Yeats* (New York: Macmillan, 1943) 294.

[13] *Memoirs*, 202.

[14] J.M. Synge, Preface to the Poems, in *Collected Works* (New York, 1983), xxii.

[15] Ibid.

[16] *Letters*, 570.

[17] *Letters*, 570, 710.

[18] Jeffares, *W. B. Yeats: Man and Poet* (New Haven: Yale University Press, 1949) 167.

[19] Ezra Pound, *Letters of E.P.*, ed. D.D. Paige (New York: Harcourt, Brace, 1950) 28.

[20] *Memoirs*, 139.

[21] *Memoirs*, 181.

[22] J.B. Yeats, *Passages From the Letters of John Butler Yeats* (selected by Ezra Pound, Cuala Press, 1917), 161.

[23] Wade, *Letters*, 583.

[24] *Memoirs*, 165.

[25] Synge, Preface to the Poems, *Collected Works*, vol. 1, xv.

Mastery and Beyond:
Speech and Silence in *The Tower*

> *You must write poetry as if you were shouting to*
> *a man at the other side of the street and were*
> *afraid he wouldn't hear you.*
>   Yeats to Frank O'Connor

> *I do not listen enough.*
>   Yeats to himself

The kinds of speech that may be heard in *The Tower* compose the identity of the poet, mastering and surrendering to experience. By the spectrum they extend between anonymity and acknowledged self, between absence and presence, they constitute his mode of being in and to the world. Because of the completeness with which the poems of *The Tower* cover this speech-spectrum, the volume provides the best and most accessible model of Yeats's latest poetic identity (what he distinguished from his "character")[1]—his being in, reacting to, and being acted upon by the world. "Identity," that is, as the ideogram of his experience. Speech in *The Tower* may be said to fall into two main kinds. The first of these has a number of specific modes, related in the way each one impresses itself upon the world, opposing it or shaping it to the desire of the speaker by sheer force or a strategy of exclusion. The other kind of speech is itself shaped by experience, speech disposing itself as a kind of listening, not the mastering of experience but what I would call the admission of being.

I

Yeats discovered early that in the actual world speech was power. "I must learn to speak," he told himself in the late eighties; "A man must know how to speak in Ireland just as a man in old times had to carry a sword."[2] By a natural extension, speech was also a desirable force in the world Yeats wanted to create in his verse. It was speech that granted vigour and authenticity to poetry. He assumed that "all the old writers . . . wrote to be spoken or sung, and in a later age to be read aloud."[3] By 1913 he could say that he had been trying for some years "to make [his] work so convincing with a speech so natural and dramatic that the hearer would feel the presence of a man thinking and feeling."[4] Speech, that is, is the genuine registration of identity, the poet's most efficacious "I am." Speech is the palpable, persuasive element in Yeats's verse, its informing power: his persistent aim is "to make the language of poetry coincide with that of passionate, normal speech."[5] The "normality" of such speech must be qualified, however, by Yeats's contentious notion of speech as oratorical performance, his conviction that the poet "never speaks directly as to someone at the breakfast table."[6] Always, or almost always, speech remains the deliberative instrument and act of power, the poet's way of shaping the world around his own meanings.

The poems in *The Tower* comprise a spectrum of speech acts which embody Yeats's poetic identity as he enters the final phase of his life and work. Across much of this spectrum, speech operates as power, identity is the will imposing itself upon the world. The first of these acts of power presents speech as a possessing activity. Here the speaker is rendered anonymous by the force of some external utterance. This exotic speech phenomenon belongs to such poems as "Wisdom," "Fragments," and "Two Songs from a Play." Most importantly, it is to be heard in "Leda and the Swan."[7] I would call this speech "oracular," remembering especially what Cleomenes in *The Winter's Tale* says of the oracle at Delphi: "the burst / And the ear-deaf'ning voice o'th' oracle / . . . so surprised my sense, / That I was nothing." As Yeats manages it, the provenance of such speech seems mysterious; it registers a potent, enigmatic impersonality: "Where got I that truth? / Out of a medium's mouth, / Out of nothing it came."[8] It is a speech made strange because its allusive ground lies beyond our common experience, its voice remote, hieratic, and decisive.[9]

The voice that utters "Leda and the Swan" seems to come "out of nothing," a speech carrying the impact of some fearsome physical intrusion. In its suddenness and physicality it enacts the event it describes, speaking its speaker and overwhelming the reader as the transformed deity possesses "the staggering girl." The speech of the first quatrain swells with anonymous description: "A sudden blow . . . her thighs caressed . . . her nape caught . . . her helpless breast." Speech assaults the reader with violent facts: speech is the thing itself. The unanswering voice of the second quatrain seems equally anonymous, the speech of a generic human terror trapped inside unanswerable questions ("How can those fingers? . . . How can body?") which, by their simply hanging in the air, sustain the mysterious nature of the whole thing. This oracular quality is especially evident in the sestet, its first segment that extraordinary exposition of mytho-historical destiny stirring in the engendering act, the conclusion a question ("Did she put on his knowledge with his power?") that abandons the reader to a condition of perplexed anxiety. Finishing the poem, my most vivid sensation is of having been spoken *to*, as the poet has been spoken *through*. Mystery, rapture, unanswerable question become the defining shape of the experience, and in this haunted anonymity of expression pure oracular speech exercises total supremacy over the world. We are possessed by the enigma of the final question, as the poet himself is "caught up" in a speech that is his and not his, word as absolute shaper of world. Such an extremity of speech establishes a limit in the proper anatomy of the poet's identity. Lying farthest off from that self which sustains its existence in the ordinary world, it is still an authentic element in his identity, a condition of the visionary self registering as a kind of speech.

The second sort of mastering speech I wish to consider is closer to what I'm calling the "ordinary self." A decisive distance, however, still persists between what this speech enacts and that ordinary self, a distance created this time by a dramatic fiction. Where oracular speech pre-empts, as it were, the poet's voice, dramatic speech takes over the voice of a fictional other—"Browning talking aloud through Caliban," as Eliot puts it.[10] This speech, too, shapes the world to the poet's design. It is a means of granting, by strategic exclusions, a certain acceptable shape to the experience of the "actual" self.

In *The Tower*, the outstanding use of this dramatizing voice is in "A Man Young and Old," originally entitled "Songs from the Young Countryman" and "Songs of an Old Countryman."[11] The explicitly performative nature of the poems in this sequence—acting out a single (predominantly sexual) element in the poet's experience as if it were the whole life—underscores their existence as speech and their function as a deliberate, almost allegorical shaping of his experience. The dramatic sequence, therefore, is an emblem of speech as power, the invented character "speaking" the experience into the writer's chosen meanings, with a rhythmic emphasis and musical excitement that validates the description of the poems as "songs."

The strong colloquial lyricism and rhythmic buoyancy of these poems establish a counterforce to the pressure of an experience in which the speaker is the mostly passive victim. Such speech communicates a meaning which in substance is defeat but in style is a kind of victory. Speech in this dramatic fiction is a strategy for survival, survival being understood as the ability to speak the experience into satisfactory shapes. With its decisive grammatical units, its verbal confidence, and its uncompromising metrical beat, the following stanza reveals such qualities:

> She smiled and that transfigured me
> And left me but a lout,
> Maundering here, and maundering there,
> Emptier of thought
> Than the heavenly circuit of the stars
> When the moon sails out.

One way this speech exercises its power is through its detachment from any recognizable historical context. Where oracular speech is supra-historical, dramatic speech is extra-historical, its speaker locatable in a landscape of symbolic phenomena—moon and stars, stones, a broken tree—and in the grip of theatrical passions which are a distillation and a distancing of actual experience in the life of the writer—Yeats's sexual experiences with Maud Gonne and Olivia Shakespeare.

The power of the poet's speech to shape experience (as if this were the "subtext" of the poems themselves) may be felt especially in the way the tough plainness of these verses contrasts with the wandering melancholy sweetness of those poems in *The Wind Among the Reeds* which we can assume were written

out of the same, or a comparable, body of actual experience. In the earlier volume, poetry itself seems to be the speaker (in spite of titles which, in early versions, "gave" the poems to fictive speakers), creating a lyricism independent of
character, whereas the speech of these later poems is intense, personal, and idiosyncratic. Speech here is an implicit expression of mastery over the experience,
even if the speaker is still its victim. In *The Wind Among the Reeds* the same
experience dictates a speech as apparently passive as the protagonist, both of
them only the site where the languorous, unalterable emotions make their presence felt. The intensity and idiosyncratic energy of "A Man Young and Old," on
the other hand, particularly startles us, the speech of the "old man" forecasting
the more frenzied utterances of Crazy Jane and Mad Tom, as that of the "young
man" revises the mannered hieratics of *The Wind Among the Reeds*. In all the
poems of the sequence it is the liberated simplicity of speech that creates the
main effect, composing an identity within the power of the speaker, an unarguable presence inside this limited but passionate world.

Both the above modes of mastering speech represent comparatively simple exercises of power. And while each of them makes a critical contribution to an
understanding of Yeats's poetic identity, each also stands at a decisive distance
from that bundle of accident and incoherence which, according to Yeats, sat
down at the breakfast table. At the center of gravity of *The Tower*, however,
stand three poems which represent the poet's attempt to create a speech capable
of accommodating more of his actual experience than ever before. These are
"Nineteen Hundred and Nineteen," "Meditations in Time of Civil War," and
"The Tower." As oracular and dramatic speech were respectively supra- and
extra-historical, the various speech of these great meditations is, as the titles
would begin to suggest, fundamentally historical in the public and private sense.
The most obvious feature of these poems is the extraordinary shaping activity of
their speech. They not only bring this power to a new level of complexity in
Yeats's work, however, but they go beyond the notion of speech as mastery to
an embodied understanding of speech as the actual surrender of such mastery.
The speech of "Nineteen Hundred and Nineteen" exhibits a power deriving in
part from the speaker's sense that his speech is a communal possession, the repository of values antithetical to the forces fast overwhelming the world. The
poet speaks as one who is in the service of a certain (cultural) group to which he
owes this speech-as-power, having elsewhere referred to the crowning endowment of this group as "Gradual Time's last gift, a written speech / Wrought of
high laughter, loveliness and ease."[12] Implicitly the poem is a monument to a
certain kind of speech and its civilized ability to shape, even under dreadful
pressure, the world to its willed meanings, as the following stanza from Part I
shows:

> We too had many pretty toys when young:
> A law indifferent to blame or praise,
> To bribe or threat; habits that made old wrong
> Melt down, as it were wax in the sun's rays;

Public opinion ripening for so long
We thought it would outlive all future days.
O what fine thought we had because we thought
That the worst rogues and rascals had died out.

Such speech possesses a kind of casual magniloquence, an aristocratic ease of expression that can modulate from gorgeous metaphor to gruff colloquialism. Here is a speech thronged with gesture, the private man upon the public stage, striding from rhetorical question ("What matter that no cannon had been turned / Into a ploughshare?") to an imagery of grand assertiveness ("Now days are dragon-ridden, the nightmare / Rides upon sleep") or bitter intensity ("Who are but weasels fighting in a hole"). This speech is a limber image in itself of the mind in motion: "He who can read the signs . . . Has but one comfort left . . . But is there any comfort to be found?" Such speech is itself a metaphor for those civilized values being destroyed in what Yeats called in an earlier title to the poem "the present state of the world." What we hear is a voice stamping its own communal and personal identity on the world. The voice stages the identity and is its proper site. The speech, through all sections of the poem, confronts the dissolution of the world with its own *controlled* violence ("A civilization is a struggle to keep self-control," remarked Yeats elsewhere).[13]

Having proceeded through meditative gravity and colloquial deflation (Section III), epigrammatic shapeliness (IV), and vaunting parody (V), the poem ends in the most public speech of all, that of the oracle. In Section VI, that is, the poet permits himself to be spoken into truth: a series of images that embody statement-without-explanation brings the absolute counterforce of speech directly to bear upon the unleashed mindless violence of the world. So the public speech of the whole poem—a speech the poet claims as his own by virtue of his belonging to a certain value-community, a speech that is the last repository of those values savaged by a turbulent world—culminates naturally in the oracular speech of Section VI. Explanatory truths here emanate from mystery ("Herodias' daughters have returned again"), the poet surrendering his own voice to the voice of mystery itself, which grants a shape, however enigmatic, to the chaos he perceives in the world.

The speech of "Meditations in Time of Civil War" and "The Tower" has something of the assured magniloquence of "Nineteen Hundred and Nineteen." That public plangency is a necessary element in Yeats's articulate defense against a growingly unacceptable world. But in these two poems, which enter and render up more private areas of his life, he achieves a greater variety and freedom than ever before. For the speaker of both these poems, however, the reassurances of communal identity are no longer available. He is a private, withdrawn figure for whom speech is a last resort and place of refuge, such speech being a kind of emblem of the tower itself where the poems were written, a place of "solitude and silence" on the one hand, but also "a permanent symbol of my work, plainly visible to the passerby."[14]

Speech as the exercise of power is clearly exemplified in many parts of these two poems. In "Meditations in Time of Civil War," for example, the content of "Ancestral Houses" is doubt about the value of those things which in "Nineteen Hundred and Nineteen" opposed the decay of the world. The poem's rhetoric, however, with its magnificent antiphonal dynamics of assertion and interrogation, rings with triumphant certitude. So the incredible brimming plenitude of the first stanza is answered by the complex, muscular scepticism of the second:

> Mere dreams, mere dreams! Yet Homer had not sung
> Had he not found it certain beyond dreams
> That out of life's own self-delight had sprung
> That abounding glittering jet; though now it seems
> As if some marvellous empty sea-shell flung
> Out of the obscure dark of the rich streams,
> And not a fountain, were the symbol which
> Shadows the inherited glory of the rich.

In the same poem the poet speaks "My House" and "My Table" into emblematic significance. The simple yet suggestive act of naming the phenomena that comprise his dwelling (bridge, tower, rose bush, elm tree, water-hen, cows, winding stair) is the adequate analogue for the fact that he has "founded here," so these stern particulars of place may become his children's "Befitting emblems of adversity." Speech is itself the act of claiming and of proclamation, organizing a world of things into a constellation of meanings. We are asked to experience his speech itself as the act of granting meaning to the world. The orderly, discreet speech of "My Table" (metaphor for the ideal interconnection of art and life nostalgically endorsed by the poem) is the individual's private act of resistance to the chaos of civil war, his means of turning enforced retreat into creative freedom, of moralizing "My days out of their aimlessness."

The sense, shared by all the parts of this poem, of intimate self as powerful speaker is especially in evidence in "My Descendants." Here Yeats proudly proclaims his independence of ties even of blood, his commitment to self-begotten values that link him not with an anonymous group, as in "Nineteen Hundred and Nineteen," but with two equally private individuals (Lady Gregory and his wife). The expansive public speech of the poem guarantees its private commitment. As it powerfully moulds the world to the desired shape, its power may be felt as the stress of syntax compelling the world to adopt the speaker's magnificently egotistical and generous design:

> The Primum Mobile that fashioned us
> Has made the very owls in circles move;
> And I, that count myself most prosperous,
> Seeing that love and friendship are enough,
> For an old neighbour's friendship chose the house
> And decked and altered it for a girl's love,
> And know whatever flourish and decline
> These stones remain their monument and mine.

"Meditations in Time of Civil War" counters public violence with a private, embattled truth. In "The Tower," speech is the instrument of personal resistance to the general indignities of old age. The shaping power of this speech is especially magisterial in Parts II and III. In II, the massive blocks of meaning that make up the stanzas find their power in a style of oratorical conversation. Brilliant talk, it moves effortlessly between casual, grand, lyrical, and enigmatic, moulding life to the sinewy shapes of direct speech salted by idiosyncrasies of phrasing, syntax, and what John Holloway calls "emphatic terseness."[15]

In Part III the poet makes his will, a gesture that might be seen as symbolic of the intrinsic action of so many of these poems. Here speech is trimmed to the imperative urgencies of one who has made the very causes of perplexity and regret (old age, mortality) the source of a powerfully renewed energy. The verbs ("I choose," "I declare," "I mock," "I have prepared") force his will upon the world, compelling attention. Allusions to history, nature, and culture magnanimously expand upon the theme of his own pride and faith in man's creative potency. Speech opposes its present reality to those abstract philosophic schemes that would counsel quietude and despair, for "Death and life were not / Till man made up the whole." The vivid kinetic energy of such speech rebuts "this absurdity . . . decrepit age" which has been tied to the poet "As to a dog's tail" at the beginning of the poem. Here, as elsewhere, poetic speech is an act of power, a shouting across the street in order to be heard.[16] Such speech would appear to be, on the strength of the poems we have looked at so far, the poet's main mode of existence, his chief way of being in the world.

II

But this speech, with its aggressive imperatives, its magisterial shaping of the world to its will, its "equestrian authority,"[17] is not the whole of Yeats's poetic identity in *The Tower*. For in some of the poems of this collection quite a different kind of speech becomes audible. Instead of masterfully imposing an ego upon the world, this speech wonderfully accommodates the world of external reality, enacting less a habit of masterful talk than a condition of listening. Two of the poems in "Meditations in Time of Civil War" and part of the final section of "The Tower" exemplify my meaning here. All three portray the speaker as a listener, in the deepest sense, to the final meanings of experience, engaged not in some decisive shaping of the world, but in what amounts to a tougher discipline, the admission of being.

Both "The Road at My Door" and "The Stare's Nest at My Window" shift the focus of "Meditations in Time of Civil War" from the self to something outside the self. The self is neither subjective nor possessive but, as it were, prepositional: door and window are means of exit or entrance, ways of letting the world in or the poet out. Situated at a threshold between different zones, insisting on a sort of liminality of being, each of these poems portrays the involuntary self, the man caught in circumstance rather than the man forcing his will upon it.

The casual speech of "The Road at My Door" exactly expresses this condition. In the nature of simple communication, it is neither imposition nor interpretation; it is recognition, not revelation, the self listening to, not instructing, the world:

> An affable Irregular,
> A heavily-built Falstaffian man,
> Comes cracking jokes of civil war
> As though to die by gunshot were
> The finest play under the sun.

Such heroic impulses as the poetic voice might rise to are challenged before they happen by Falstaffian deflations. The poet permits himself into this picture, but engaged only in casual conversation. Neutralised between the two sides of the Civil War, feeling peculiarly marginalized and irrelevant, he is brought to a condition which must simply admit being—the weather, the war: "and I complain / Of foul weather, hail and rain, / A pear-tree broken by the storm." In the last stanza the poet, in speech that never raises its voice, permits his own vulnerability to be seen if not explained:

> I count these feathered balls of soot
> The moor-hen guides upon the stream,
> To silence the envy in my thought;
> And turn towards my chamber, caught
> In the cold snows of a dream.

Engaged in an act of enumeration, not interpretation, the poet's speech is as devoid of assertive mastery as is such an action. Speech here is his record of silence, "caught" (we register the surrender of power in the nature and placement of the passive verb) in "a dream." The unspoken meaning confronting us at the end of this poem (how to explain the "envy") provokes us to sympathize with Yeats in a way few of the poems allow us to do. Such speech, brooding in its unique maternal way upon silence, makes his actual self manifest to himself and to us in a way most of the poems do not.

"The Stare's Nest at My Window" continues and extends the mode of the previous poem. First, the simple acknowledgement of facts (bees, birds, loosening wall) leads to a sort of prayer. As speech, such prayer is the opposite of a shaping power in being the implicit admission of helplessness, a condition that might even be said to reach beyond silence:

> The bees build in the crevices
> Of loosening masonry, and there
> The mother bird brings grubs and flies.
> My wall is loosening; honey-bees
> Come build in the empty house of the stare.

Such images transcend any suggestion of masculine heroics, creating a context of maternal nurturing power in a context of violence and decay. The life that goes on is a natural process independent of history, a gift of grace to the speaker. The efficacy of such speech lives in the silence that follows the invocation. The rest of the poem, in a speech that is, though it uses the plural "we," intensely private and in no way assertive, realizes this condition more completely. For what Yeats admits to is a state of passive anxiety: he simply acknowledges helplessness in the face of violent experience:

> We are closed in, and the key is turned
> On our uncertainty; somewhere
> A man is killed or a house burned,
> Yet no clear fact to be discerned.

Underscored by the hesitations of rhythm and syntax, the quietness in the accumulation of -r sounds, his condition might be described as a perpetual listening for news: for, as he put it elsewhere, "one never knew what was happening on the other side of the hill or of the line of trees."[18]

The speech of this poem makes no attempt to shape the world. Rather, it owns up to it: "We had fed the heart on fantasies, / The heart's grown brutal at the fare." From this acknowledgement of things as they are the poem moves by a natural progression to a prayer that out of this savage state some nurturing sweetness may be born. It is vulnerability that speaks here, seeking no palliative in the mastering articulate exercise of the will: "The maternal is apprehended, intimated, and warmly cherished."[19]

An image of maternal nurturing also seals the last part of "The Tower." In the masterful act of making his will, the poet claims he has established his peace with the grand phenomena of culture and love, "All those things whereof / Man makes a superhuman / Mirror-resembling dream." At this point in the poem, however, perhaps at the realization of what is implied in "dream," the speech takes a sudden, surprising turn into a new mode. With no apparent preparation, the natural environment intrudes upon the poet's meditation:

> As at the loophole there
> The daws chatter and scream,
> And drop twigs layer upon layer.
> When they have mounted up,
> The mother bird will rest
> On their hollow top,
> And so warm her wild nest.[20]

The speaker sees his heroic, mastering activity as a nest-building, a noisy masculine action with the silence of maternal nurturing as its end. The particularity of the description and its use provides in speech the proper antidote to the anxiety and suppressed outrage against "Decrepit age" with which the poem begins. Charged by the marvelously fertile image of the nesting bird (turning the masculine image of the earlier lines, as overtly phallic as the tower itself, into the language of female sexual allusion, the nest a procreant cradle), the poem passes beyond the emotions of desire, fear, and aggressive pride into a speech that can relinquish the actual world as a dream, thereby achieving a concrete peace in which speech is no longer even necessary. "Wreck of body," "death of friends," are radically qualified by this sudden, involuntary revelation and

> Seem but the clouds of the sky
> When the horizon fades,
> Or a bird's sleepy cry
> Among the deepening shades.

When the masterful ego surrenders its will to dominate its world, all the brutal phenomena of mortal life appear in an almost oriental light, not of negation but of total admission: speech itself draws the speaker into a condition of perfect listening, a mystical being-at-one with the natural world. What has been transcended is the need to shape reality by the exercise of speech as power. Such a speaking into silence is, appropriately, the point at which the poet swaps will-making for soul-making ("Now shall I make my soul," he says at the start of this last section). This making, like Keats's (whose famous phrase he consciously or unconsciously echoes), is in the nature of active surrender, the hero about to cross that "storm-beaten threshold" where identity is achieved in its own disappearance.

III

Two of the greatest poems in this volume represent in an emblematic way that spectrum of speech which the whole collection embodies. "Sailing to Byzantium" is a crowning example of speech as an act of power. In its tense, compact, wonderfully confident rendering of a world lost to the sensual forces of generation and decay, it is a masterful counter-force to these antagonistic forces themselves. Speech is the instrument of the poet's voluntary withdrawal from this natural (and historical) world. In the first stanza such speech is dramatic and meditative: the poet speaks in his own person and through the mask of a "character" (perhaps that "poet of the Middle Ages" who was a *persona* in an early draft)[21]—acting out in fact the imagined voyage. By means of the dynamic energies of this powerful speech ("That is no country for old men"), involuntary subjection to the mortal world becomes a voluntary, proud withdrawal from it. An act vibrating with self-assertion, it commits the speaker to a kind of Coriolanus pose, and seems intended to set the tone for the book as a whole.[22] The expository force of the opening scarcely needs commentary: we hear this magisterial voice passing from the plenitude of a hypnotically named natural world of "dying generations" to the decisive grammar and cadences of "And therefore have I sailed the seas and come / To the holy city of Byzantium."

The variety of fluent speech is one of the more striking aspects of the poem. The confessional can be buoyant with excited vigor ("An aged man is but a paltry thing, / A tattered coat upon a stick, unless / Soul clap its hands and sing") and despair itself can translate its fall into a rising imperative: "Consume my heart away . . . and gather me / Into the artifice of eternity."

By the end of the poem, even a kind of oracular speech can be made to seem almost intimate. Everything stresses the activity of the voluntary will: the poet, become a golden bird, achieves a condition of oracular speech that is, as it were, second nature to him, singing "out of nature" and beyond his "bodily form" "To lords and ladies of Byzantium / Of what is past, or passing, or to come." Supremely shaped, the act of power that is speech twists the intractable matter of the world into those formal designs which answer the speaker's desire, just as the final image controls the world of mortal flux and inevitable decay. From first utterance to last this poem is all potency of expression, speech embodying an identity that first composes itself and then the world.

"Among School Children" enacts the other area of Yeats's poetic identity as this is revealed in the kinds of speech overheard in *The Tower*. The difference between this poem and "Sailing to Byzantium" is apparent in their respective openings. While the start of the latter poem is aggressive in its definition, its decisive unarguability a sort of shouting across the street to ensure being heard, the beginning of "Among School Children" is remarkably quiet. In this it corresponds to the speaker's own engagement not only in the historical world as a "sixty-year-old smiling public man," but in conversation (speaking and listening) with another: "I walk through the long schoolroom questioning; / A kind old nun in a white hood replies." Carrying out the logic of this opening, the poem proceeds easily in the accents of one who is being acted upon by experience, letting the meditative stream take what flows involuntarily into it.

Where "Sailing to Byzantium" has in form, and reaches towards in fact, a kind of architectural stasis, "Among School Children" is all kinesis, an active, open-eyed surrender to process. Here the poet is the willing object of experience as much as its subject, stared upon by the children's wondering eyes. The verbs suggest this condition of, as it were, listening to experience: "I dream," "I look upon," "I wonder," an image "floats into the mind." In such a condition he can employ a speech that can even cope in an ironic or comical way with serious matter (Stanza VI, on the philosophers) and yet rise to the involuntarily mystical accents of the conclusion. Fluid, unhurried, biographical reminiscence mounts unobtrusively to the wonder of the last stanza and the mysterious hanging-upon-the-air of those final questions.

Speech here is at once potent in its masterful energy, its confidence of definition, and is yet a great, generous admission of being: speech finding its ultimate power in its allowance of the world to be. This condition is embodied in the profound *agreeing* silence that must follow these questions, a condition of peace (since the last line can be heard as a rhetorical question that is *also* a declarative statement indicating the speaker's acceptance of the state of unknowing) that contrasts with the state of anxiety to which the concluding oracular question of "Leda and the Swan" abandon the reader:

> O chestnut-tree, great-rooted blossomer,
> Are you the leaf, the blossom, or the bole?
> O body swayed to music, O brightening glance,
> How can we know the dancer from the dance?

The triumphant use of tree and dancer here suggests a peculiar sexual wholeness of experience, which may itself be seen as a rich (and not necessarily intended) metaphor for the wholeness of speech which the poem embodies. Each image contains in itself the fullness of sexual identity—the phallic tree a female blossomer, the dancer either female or male. Admission of being becomes here an exalted celebratory gesture, a world achieved and accommodated by the speaker's own clear-sighted surrender to it. Such gestures find their exact expression in a speech that is an impeccable equilibrium of assertion and interrogation, definition and a being-defined.

The distance covered by Yeats's speech in *The Tower* stretches between the remote oracular heights of "Leda and the Swan" and the richly intimate depths of a statement like that I have just quoted, or that represented, in a different tone, by "The Stare's Nest at My Window." With all its intermediate stages (and variety is what gives such power and vitality to the book), this spectrum can suggest the nature and range of Yeats's poetic identity—from the magniloquent self forcing magnificent egotistical shapes upon the world, to the meditative self admitting the being of the world. As an aggregation of speech modes, the book projects a multiple identity that can only be incidentally "mythologized," a fact which animates the agonized dialectic of myth and mortality informing (here and elsewhere) so many of the poems. As mastering act of power, speech is the mythologizing instrument; as a mode of listening, speech becomes the admission of being. In its major forms, then, speech is the legitimate arbiter of this persistent dialectic: it is speech that makes manifest the site and end of this dialectic as the palpable present self.

One of the great achievements of the speech spectrum I have tried to describe is its persistent ability to communicate in a definitively public way while revealing the truly private self. And while this self may not be "the bundle of accident and incoherence that sits down to breakfast,"[23] it is nonetheless the involuntary heart of an identity willed into and upon the world. The presence of such elastic energies of speech in *The Tower* is surely an important factor among those which would prompt us (as Yeats himself was prompted)[24] to claim for this volume the pre-eminence many presume it holds among his poetic works. In no other single volume is speech so various and so accomplished and, in consequence, is the projected poetic identity so fully realised. Yeats himself said, "I have but one art, that of speech."[25]

Such fullness is not only the result of Yeats's shouting to the man at the other side of the street, but of his quietening beyond such mastery into a speech that is also a part of listening, a mysterious condition which extends the borders of speech until it becomes a silence made articulate. In this silence, after all the shouting (and in a way that forecasts the illumination of one of the triumphs of his later verse, "A Long-legged Fly"), Yeats's deepest identity knows itself.

1982

NOTES

[1] "Poetic identity" is the phrase I use to suggest that identity emerging from the poems themselves. Yeats separated this from what he called "my character," referring to his poems as "my true self." *Explorations* (New York: Collier books, 1962) 308.

[2] W. B. Yeats, *Memoirs*, transcribed and edited by Denis Donoghue (New York: Macmillan, 1972) 21.

[3] *Samhain* (rpt. in one vol. London, 1970) 1906, 14, 9.

[4] *The Letters of W. B. Yeats*, ed. Allan Wade (London: Rupert Hart-Davis, 1954) 583.

[5] *W. B. Yeats, Essays and Introductions* (London: Macmillan, 1961) 521.

[6] *Ibid*, 509. On the whole question of the unique, idiosyncratic nature of Yeats's poetic speech, see John Holloway's fine essay "Style and World in *The Tower*" in *An Honoured Guest: New Essays on W. B. Yeats*, ed. Denis Donoghue and J. R. Mulryne (London: Edward Arnold, 1965) 88-105, esp. 90.

[7] Apart from its parodic intent, the original title, "Annunciation," stresses the poem's existence as speech.

[8] My text for the poems throughout is *The Collected Poems of W. B. Yeats* (London: Macmillan, 1950, rpt. 1969).

[9] It is a speech connected with Yeats's occult interests. "Leda" appears as prologue to "Dove or Swan?" in *A Vision*.

[10] T. S. Eliot, *On Poetry and Poets* (New York: Farrar, Straus, and Cudahy, 1957) 103.

[11] *The Variorum Edition of the Poems of W. B. Yeats*, ed. Peter Allt and Russell K. Alspach (New York: Macmillan, 1977) 451-58.

[12] "Upon a House Shaken by the Land Agitation," *Collected Poems*, 106.

[13] *A Vision*, 268.

[14] *Letters*, 686; *W. B. Yeats and T. Sturge Moore, their Correspondence*, 1901-1937 (New York: Oxford University Press, 1953) 109.

[15] Holloway, 91.

[16] See Frank O'Connor, *A Short History of Irish Literature* (New York: G.P. Putnam's Sons, 1967) 178. The relevant passage forms the first epigraph to my essay.

[17] Seamus Heaney, *Preoccupations* (London and Boston: Faber and Faber, 1980) 73. The adjective is Denis Donoghue's.

[18] A. Norman Jeffares, *A Commentary on the Collected Poems of W.B. Yeats* (Stanford: Stanford University Press, 1968) 272.

[19] Heaney, 112.

[20] A curiosity of this poem is the small grammatical difficulty that appears at this point. Yeats seems to want to claim (by his use of the conjunctive "As") a continuity with what has gone before or (if "As" is adverbial) with what follows. But the broken grammar betrays him, forcing an uncharacteristic ambiguity and revealing a point of pivotal importance in the poem.

[21] Jon Stallworthy, *Between the Lines: Yeats's Poetry in the Making* (Oxford: Clarendon Press, 1963) 96.

[22] For Yeats's interest in *Coriolanus*, see *The Autobiography of William Butler Yeats* (New York: Collier Books, 1974) 42. Many of the poems have as their symbolic action the translation of a condition of subjection into a mastering of circumstance.

[23] *Essays and Introductions*, 509.

[24] He described it as "the best book I have written." *Letters*, 742.

[25] "Literature and the Living Voice,"*Samhain* (1906) 12.

Embattlements, Embodiments:
Pursuing Truth in *The Tower*

"A Man can embody truth, but he cannot know it." After a lifetime's pursuit of some satisfactory notion of "truth," this was the formulation Yeats stumbled on a few weeks before his death, when he tried to "put all into a phrase."[1] And a suggestive phrase it is, implying that genuine understanding derives only from wholeness of experience and not from the partial operations of the intellect. In "The Gift of Harun al-Rashid," speaking allegorically of his wife's part in the occult business of *A Vision,* he says the same thing in a slightly different way: "All, all those gyres and cubes and midnight things / Are but a new expression of her body." "The Gift of Harun al-Rashid" appeared in the first edition of *The Tower,* the volume which, to my mind, embodies in the most satisfying way the truth of the claim that "Man can embody truth, but he cannot know it." In its dazzling range of emotional registers, in the supple mastery of its language, in its rhythmic animation of so many areas of the poet's experience of himself and his world, *The Tower* embodies more fully than ever before or after the complex difficult truth of Yeats's own life. It is his most complete self-portrait and, according to himself, "the best book I have written."

Of course there's a price to be paid, at least by the critic, for such adequacy and abundance. In my own case, when I was invited to give this talk, the price could be summed up as first perplexity, then dismay. Which of the many allurements of the text should I try to develop into one critical thesis or another? Where, on all this wonderfully undulant ground, should I try to set up a theme, solidify an insight, steady an opinion? Given the flashily masculine iconography of the tower itself, should I make a fuss over the many references to motherhood which appear throughout the collection? Or, given Yeats's own brand of cultural nationalism, should I seek out reasons for the way he seems to set himself, by means of almost subliminal allusion, at the end of a major lineage in English poetry: Chaucer, Shakespeare, Milton, Wordsworth, Keats, Yeats? Or what about casting a critical cold eye or two on the book's bleak sexual prospect, since arguably no more than a couple of references in it allude to contented sexual love? Or would it be useful to explore the fact that the book's main or most interesting grammatical mood seems to be the interrogative? Or, on another level of style, should I dwell on one of the greatest pleasures of Yeats's mature verse, his athletic control of syntax, the way he uses it to make sense by making music?

These are only a handful of the possibilities that flashed before me as, "I sought a theme and sought for it in vain, / I sought it daily for six weeks or so." In the end, being "but a broken man," I decided not to try to force the book into the procrustean bed of some single topic or theme, but to follow a more Protean course, bending to what took my fancy. The result is a series of small medita-

tions on some of the items and issues that held my attention during this reading
of the poems.

First, a few small points about the collection:

(i) Coming to *The Tower*, after reading in sequence through the earlier volumes, one may notice right away a small but quite striking difference between it
and its predecessors: an unusual number of its poems bear dates. Before *The
Tower*, Yeats rarely dated the published versions of his individual poems. Lyrics, monologues, dialogues—all seemed to stand and deliver themselves in a
performative world of timeless gestures, a world in which a dateline would
seem odd and out of place. *Crossways*, *The Rose*, and *The Wind Among the
Reeds*, for example, are all innocent of dates, their various protagonists—even if
a melancholy apprehension of time was their subject matter—somehow standing apart from the lowest common denominators of time—the actual day,
month, year. Indeed dating may have seemed to Yeats uneasily close to the
loathed culture of the newspapers, and such exceptions as there are to the rule
are for the most part provoked by public controversies, such as those over the
Lane pictures or Synge's *Playboy*. Before *The Tower* only nine poems (in the
individual collections as printed in *Collected Poems* of 1933) carry explicit
dates.

Then, in *The Tower* volume itself, dates are attached to no less than seven
poems. Their titles suggest a broad range of subject matter, well beyond public
controversy: "Sailing to Byzantium," "The Tower," "Meditations in Time of
Civil War," "Nineteen Hundred and Nineteen," "Youth and Age," "Leda and
the Swan," "All Souls' Night": Gathered under these titles are poems about the
private world of the soul and the public world of the state; poems about the end
of a cultural era or the death of an individual; poems with local or mythological
inhabitants; poems containing theories of history and theories of the after-life.
So why do they all bear dates? The question is unanswerable, of course; but
speculation is possible, and my own thought is that Yeats uses these small,
scarcely observable notations perhaps unconsciously to call attention to something that stirs at the heart of the whole collection: his obsession with time at its
most palpable, in the actual quotidian corrosiveness of age and aging. The dates,
that is, are emblematic: they are the proper seal upon one of the common symbolic actions of these poems—to embody the unpalatable, unavoidable truth of
time.

(ii) So much for the small anomaly of dates. Another minor point of interest concerns the shape of *The Tower* as an organized collection, the whole of
which might be greater than the sum of its parts. From almost the outset of his
career Yeats was a composer of books as well as a maker of poems. In his case,
as in that of many poets, what might be called an aesthetics of sequence and
design prompts the final exercise of the will in eliciting as complete a meaning

as possible from material which, in itself (as individual poems), exists for the most part outside the scope and regulation of the will.

To be quite simple-minded about this: in its first edition, *The Tower* is a collection of twenty-one poems. Its three naturally cardinal points are its beginning and end, and the poem that occupies the middle position. "Sailing to Byzantium" and "All Souls' Night" open and bring to a close the collection. It is hard not to see them as deliberately symbolic extremities. In a collection preoccupied with time, each concerns itself with a world after death. The first is the volume's passionate prologue, a triumphant vantage point of possibility—outside nature and above time—from which to view the tragic time-bound action of the poems that follow. Setting the poet's soul up in its own solitude, it proceeds to surround it with its ideal audience—the lords and ladies of Byzantium. "All Souls' Night," then, may be seen as the appropriately much quieter epilogue to the volume. Resignation and urbanity replace rejection and ecstasy. Instead of a timeless Byzantium, here is Oxford, midnight, November 2nd, 1920. Instead of an audience of imagined lords and ladies, here the poet invites three old friends to listen not to golden birdsong but to mummy truths. In place of bright daylight he offers a spooky darkness. In one, the poet speaks as artist, in the other as philosopher of the occult. In consequence, the poems offer different but complementary ways of coming to terms with the over-riding concern of the whole book—the way of art and the way of a certain philosophy in dealing with the human toll of time.

In the first edition, the poem standing midway between these two extremities is "Leda and the Swan," and it isn't difficult to see its placement as serving a comparably symbolic function. For here is another spectacular connection between the human world of time and a world beyond its borders. In "Sailing to Byzantium" the poet wishes himself from one of these worlds to the other. In "All Souls' Night" he attempts in a much more urbane way to call that other world into his presence. "Leda and the Swan," then, is a marvelously emblematic conjunction of the two worlds, dramatizing the god's brutal descent into sexual union with the human girl, and the consequent stirring of the divine through the tangible, martial and erotic, stuff of history. A terrible beauty is conceived. It's proper, too, that at the centre of a book much engaged by the turbulence of human action should stand a poem dramatizing a pivotal moment of violent annunciation, the cataclysmic beginning of a new age. Placed as it is, it embodies in a single incandescent image a truth about history which Yeats tests in his own experience in many of the other poems.

There may be an approximate sense too, in which the whole book turns on this pivotal poem. For the first ten poems show the poet in relationship mainly with the world of history and a world of occult forces. "Leda and the Swan," then, as I've said, dramatizes a violent confrontation between history, the occult, and sexuality. This clash leads to the poems in the second half of the book, which are mainly, though not exclusively, dominated by the poet's preoccupa-

tion with his own sexual experience and, in the narrative "Harun al-Rashid,"
between that sexual experience and occult forces.

This evidence suggests, I hope, that not only does *The Tower* as a collection
have a conscious design (you could say that a sense of architectural determination is built into the title), but that its shape gives *poetic body* to a claim Yeats
made in 1927, when he declared himself "of the opinion that only two topics
can be of the least interest to the serious and studious mind—sex and the dead."
(iii) Yet another feature of *The Tower* that catches my attention is Yeats's recurring use of a particular figure. So often does a balance of opposites appear in the
very grain of the work, so frequently does the poet establish a tenuous poise
between elements contradictory in nature but of necessity coexistent, that the
figure itself becomes a kind of hieroglyph embodying the truth of his experience. By giving adequate body to a truth that cannot otherwise be known, it
lives out the logic of his claim that unknowable "ultimate reality" can only be
expressed "by a series of contradictions."[2] Of course the presence in his work of
such a figure is nothing new. Developing out of a doctrine of Blakean antithesis,
it informs his theories of history, of politics, of psychology, and finds its major
philosophical expression in *A Vision*, and its most intimately personal expression in his *Autobiography*. What seems fresh to me about his use of this figure
in *The Tower* is just how unschematic it is: it seems a natural way of *feeling*
now, not a deliberate way of *shaping* the chaos of experience.

A couple of moments in "The Bounty of Sweden," written during *The Tower*
period, show how intrinsic this figure was to Yeats's felt sense of life. He's
meditating on the Nobel medal he has just received: "It shows a young man
listening to a Muse, who stands young and beautiful with a great lyre in her
hand, and I think as I examine it, 'I was good-looking once, like that young
man, but my unpracticed muse was full of infirmity, my Muse old as it were;
and now I am old and rheumatic, and nothing to look at, but my Muse is
young.'" Contradiction, he insists, lies in the very texture of life itself. Then, at
the end of the autobiography, an image otherwise enigmatic may be seen to
serve as a seal on this central intuition. He meets in Stockholm, when snow has
fallen and there's central heating everywhere, a young American poet, whose
paradoxical words conclude Yeats's own biographical excursions: "'I was in the
South of France,'" he says, "'and I could not get a room warm enough to work
in, and if I cannot get a warm room here, I will go to Lapland.'"[3] Endless pursuit, endless desire, and endless contradiction: it is the poet's picture of the
world, embodying truth but not knowing it.

A few more trivial examples reveal this figure in the probably unconscious
grain of Yeats's life. In the summer of 1922, for instance, he says he is "reading
Ulysses and Trollope's Barchester novels alternately.[4] Pure balance in contradiction, as is apparent in the simple act of naming his tower "Thoor Ballylee"
because, as he says, "I think the harsh sound of 'Thoor' amends the softness of
the rest." The structure itself, with its Norman keep and small farmhouse at-

tached together, is a solid icon of similar meaning, of which he says, "My idea is to keep the contrast between the medieval castle and the peasant's cottage."[5] Opposites, as he says, amend one another to produce a satisfactory embodiment of the truth. During the violent political upheavals in Ireland his health and his literary style send him a similar message: "I write better from all the uncertainty," he says in 1922, "just as I am better in body for having left Oxford for this stormbeaten place."[6]

Oxymoron is the most distilled linguistic form of this figure—the attempt to reveal truth in the short-circuiting flash of verbal contradiction. Although Yeats used this rarely—perhaps it smacked too suspiciously of "wit"—it does appear on a couple of notable occasions to illuminate its surroundings. The most famous example before *The Tower* is the "terrible beauty" of "Easter 1916," focusing unforgettably the distraught doubleness of his response to that event—to celebrate and interrogate, to grieve and cast doubt. In "A Prayer for My Daughter" the figure is also central to the poem's meanings, where it appears as "the murderous innocence of the sea," and signifies something of the morally neutral violence of historical movement, and suggests something of the ambiguity in the poet's own "excited reverie" as he contemplates this phenomenon.

Those few oxymorons that crop up in *The Tower* perform a similarly focusing operation. Hanrahan's "horrible splendor of desire" in the title poem, for example, is a phrase that resonates at the heart of the second section, summarizing its experience of human sexual desire as man's distinction and debasement. Then there are those "monstrous familiar images" of apocalypse confronting the poet in the last section of "Meditations in Time of Civil War," their contradictory doubleness expressive of their intensity and his appalled rapture. The same climactic urgency and centrality mark the most famous example in the book—"those dying generations" that compel the poet's voyage to Byzantium. The phrase fuses life and death into a single trap-like figure, the intolerably contradictory equilibrium of which drives the poet towards its only antidote, the singular unchanging "artifice of eternity." The figure of speech reveals at a stroke the reasons for his impassioned leave-taking.

Beyond such serious verbal play, many examples of this figure are to be found in the substantive areas of the book. Two short poems could serve as exemplary models. "The Wheel" shows human life to be a cyclic progression of unsatisfied states:

> Through winter time we call on spring,
> And through the spring on summer call,
> And when abounding hedges ring
> Declare that winter's best of all.

What is this but an image of life as an ontological oxymoron? Being itself, in time, is condemned to a condition of contradictory poise; our living is but the perpetual vibration of antithesis. "Youth and Age" narrows the focus to Yeats's own life, but keeps the same figure:

> Much did I rage when young,
> Being by the world oppressed,
> But now with flattering tongue,
> It speeds the parting guest.

He discovers on the pulse of his own experience that contradiction is the fundamental scheme of things, not in grandiose conceptions of history or natural cycles but in the more mundane matter of personal ambition. The neatness of rhyme and rhythm here, the tightness of the quatrain's formal pattern, suggest something of the sense of entrapment such an understanding of experience must generate. High and low, as both these poems show, life is the same noose of contradictions, of which this recurrent figure is the proper body.

These brief poems, like the last stanza in "Two Songs from a Play" (which in a radically compressed way—"Love's pleasure drives his love away, / The painter's brush consumes his dreams"—sums up a truth central to the whole collection) provide a simple model for the phenomenon in question, and utter a truth embodied in many places by the larger, greater poems of *The Tower*.

Think of the speaker of the title poem, for example, who is himself a living contradiction, at once derided by "decrepit age," yet his imagination "more / Excited, passionate, fantastical than ever." Or, in "Ancestral Houses" (section I of "Meditations in Time of Civil War"), think of those bitter men who "rear in stone" sweetness and greatness (the clash of concrete and abstract an image of the contradiction he sees alive in the heart of civilization itself). Then there's the historical paradox that civility itself destroys greatness; the artistic contradiction that "only an aching heart / Conceives a changeless work of art;" the sociopolitical surprises, as it were, of the soldier "cracking jokes of civil war" (not to mention the oxymoron of "civil war"). And, there is also (in "Leda and the Swan") the mythological opposition of violence and tenderness, the god and the frightened girl. Elsewhere the poet's own imagination is figured under the double nature of a black centaur, while the vigorous, unleashed lyrics of "A Man Young and Old" add up to a musical meditation on the sexual distress of old age, its passionate mixing of memory and desire, diminution of act, intensification of will.

Finally (though this brief summary in no way exhausts the subject), there's the existential doubleness of the poet himself in "Among Schoolchildren," the sixty-year-old smiling public man coexisting with the dreamer, the railer against old age, the visionary. The startling power of this poem, in fact, comes from the way he acknowledges in his person the tragic paradoxes of being, then ends with a desperate, exhilarating attempt to rise out of contradiction—but by embracing it, not by fleeing from it. The conclusion of this poem, indeed, might be an answer to "Sailing to Byzantium," the poem, as a whole, being about staying at home and managing. As a result it earns the right to ascend out of contradiction into a fruitful doubleness that sees life not as dying generations, but as those living operations of the elemental chestnut tree, great-rooted blossomer, and of that whirling male/female dancer (something embodied, not known) inextricable from the dance. Here oxymoron, antithesis, contradiction are themselves the embodiment of genuine unity. Here Yeats finds a language adequate to his need, a language to give body to a celebratory as well as a tragic truth—the truth that contradiction itself, if fully lived and lived through is unity of being. He gives this truth its fullness by expressing it as a double question: the completeness of affirmation shines through these last interrogatives:

> O chestnut tree, great-rooted blossomer,
> Are you the leaf, the blossom, or the bole?
> O body swayed to music, O brightening glance,
> How can we know the dancer from the dance?

To such questions, what answers? Presumably, in the spirit of the poem, an exclamatory "Yes!" to the first, and to the second an equally exclamatory "No!" (The no/know pun could also be important.) Here contradicting doubleness is successfully expressed, embodied, and the man who so expresses it in an entirely honest way is, for a moment, free of it, his speech giving body to some larger, unknowable truth.

II

So much, then, for some of the minor points that interested me in my current reading of *The Tower*. In what follows I'll deal with two issues that seemed to call for more expansive treatment.

The first of these concerns a point of style. Roughly speaking, the poems in *The Tower* may be divided into three main poetic idioms or kinds of poetic speech. I call these dramatic speech, Delphic speech, and the speech of the self. Between them they compose a portrait of poetic identity which to me is the most rounded and complete self-portrait Yeats managed in any of the single volumes.

Here's how Yeats himself describes the first of these poetic idioms, that of dramatic speech:

> Every now and then, when something has stirred my imagination, I begin talking to myself. I speak in my own person and dramatise myself, very much as I have seen a mad old woman do upon the Dublin quays, and sometimes detect myself speaking and moving as if I were still young, or walking perhaps like an old man with fumbling steps. . . .

When I begin to write I have no object but to find for them some natural speech, rhythm and syntax, and to set it out in some pattern, so
seeming old that it may seem all men's speech.[7]

(An incidental point to notice here is how this speech begins in the mimic action
of the whole body: bodily imitation gives it dramatic coherence as speech.) The
poem "Owen Aherne and His Dancers" provides a simple example of that manner. In its dramatic invention and fictive speech, the poet manages to deal with
some painful episodes in his love for Maud Gonne's daughter, Iseult:

> A strange thing surely that my Heart, when love had come unsought
> Upon the Norman upland or in that poplar shade
> Should find no burden but itself and yet should be worn out.
> It could not bear that burden and therefore it went mad.

Probably the first thing that strikes any reader is the determined cadence of
these lines. This seems mainly the result of simple diction and an emphatic caesura that divides each line into seven- or eight-syllable and six-syllable units on
a fairly audible iambic base. Logical syntax underlines this division, each half-
line unit containing a minor clause of the main sentence (of time, of place).
While it may sound colloquial, it actually has the tight musical structure of lyrical song, and you could imagine it having a tune. Such musical balances ma-
noeuver the experience into manageable shapes, keep it, in a sense, at a safe
distance.

On top of this musical design, various compressions enhance the effect of
dramatic speech. The verb "to be" is suppressed in the first line, and the balance
of clauses becomes hypnotic; at the same time its deliberateness is drawn out by
such elements as that "and therefore": passion is being turned into grave play.
That "surely," too, in its particular usage, gives an impression of rural Irish
speech, but with an echo of Synge's stage, not out of Yeats's life. The manner is
dramatically natural, a sophisticated miming of a sort of emotional simplicity—"a pattern so seeming old that it may seem all men's speech." Its tunable
rhythms lift the experience out of normal time and space into the timeless world
of song, drama, character, symbol. This unhappy lover is a more complicated,
linguistically more supple and subtle, yet lineal descendant of that amorous
protagonist half in love with desire and half in love with death who cries his
songs out above the wind among the reeds. He is the ancestor of those more
accomplished examples of his kind—"A Man Young and Old" (originally
"Songs of an Old and Young Countryman") in *The Tower*, and, later, "A
Woman Young and Old" and Crazy Jane.

I call the second poetic idiom "Delphic speech." Unlike "dramatic speech,"
which presents the poet's own experience through a mask, this idiom is designed to utter what is not his own private experience at all. Instead, it articu-

lates an experience for which he is simply the mouthpiece. In "Fragments" he seems to describe just such a style: "Where got I that truth? / Out of nothing it came." This enigmatic utterance forms, in *The Tower*, a fitting prologue to "Leda and the Swan," probably the most satisfying example of that mode of poetic speech that we have, as can be heard in its opening lines:

> Above the staggering girl, her thighs caressed
> By the dark webs, her nape caught on his bill,
> He holds her helpless breast upon his breast.
>
> How can those terrified vague fingers push
> The fastened glory from her loosening thighs?
> And how can body, laid in that white rush,
> But feel the strange heart beating where it lies?

Probably one of the first things you realize here is that the poem is anonymous; it has no recognizable speaker as "Owen Aherne" has. And yet the speech has an extraordinary emotional immediacy. We are not audience to a dramatic monologue, but communicants in mystery. Someone is being strangely spoken through, the speech adapting constantly to new phrase units, the caesura shifting its position from line to line. The effect is of intense muscular action within a limited frame (it is, after all, a sonnet) : a bodily action. Enjambment heightens the effect of heady forward, unpredictable yet contained action. As readers we become as helpless as the girl—ravished, maybe, by the poem. (In "Owen Aherne," even where sense was carried over, the lines themselves called constantly for end-stopping, creating its particular musical effect.) Syntax is not the regular organization of action here as it was in "Owen Aherne" either, but a limber enforcement of surprise. At every phrase it redirects our mesmerised attention, at every startling transition. Then, without explanation, the rape generates a whole theory of history. That half of the poem consists of questions enhances its weird impersonality, forcing us—especially by means of that last question, uneasily suspended—to be possessed by the experience in a disturbing, unresolved way.

Yeats says somewhere that the poet is a woman to his work: one fanciful reading of this poem may see in it one of the relationships he had with his Muse. It could also be emblematical of a relationship between his work—taken as speech—and his audience. His own account of the composition of "Leda" suggests something of the mode I've been describing. Asked by AE for a poem for *The Irish Statesman*, Yeats began a poem of metaphysical speculation on political change "preceded by some violent annunciation." "My fancy," he goes on, "began to play with Leda and the swan for metaphor and I began this poem: but as I wrote, bird and lady took such possession of the scene that all politics went out of it." Literally, the poem is the result of an act of possession.

In "Owen Aherne" the poet possesses his experience and turns it to dramatic character and speech; in "Leda and the Swan" he is, as he says, possessed by the experience and its impersonal Delphic speech. The third sort of speech, the third poetic idiom I mentioned, is in every sense the speech of self-possession. Richer than either of the others, it contains elements of both, and is in my opinion the mode that gives *The Tower* its special distinction and power among his single volumes.

Beyond the dramatic tune-making of "Owen Aherne," and beyond the anonymous utterance of "Leda and the Swan," this speech has a voice for every twist and turn of the psyche, every vibration of the spirit, every flicker of the body's nervous life. More than any other poetic mode it embodies the truth of an experience Yeats cannot finally know because he cannot get outside it. Here, lyrical meditation replaces dramatic lyric and the lyric of possessed utterance. Its major examples are "Nineteen Hundred and Nineteen," (first called "Thoughts on the Present State of the World"), "Meditations in Time of Civil War," "The Tower" (which might be called "Meditations on Growing Old"), and "Among School Children," (which could be subtitled "Reveries Over Childhood, Youth, and Old Age"). A few fairly random examples should suffice.

Here's the opening stanza of "Meditations in Time of Civil War" (225):

> Surely among a rich man's flowering lawns,
> Amid the rustle of his planted hills,
> Life overflows without ambitious pains;
> And rains down life until the basin spills,
> And mounts more dizzy high the more it rains
> As though to choose whatever shape it wills
> And never stoop to a mechanical
> Or servile shape, at others' beck and call.

The first thing to notice, I suppose, is how this passage fills the mouth, fills the ear. Such civil grandiloquence is a sort of elevated oratory of the mind, human speech at the full stretch of its own possibility. The muscular welding of syntax, shaping more and more clauses into a final (for the stanza) amplified meaning, creates in the poet's lines an effect of abundance that serves as a metaphor in style for the fertility and spontaneity of the rich man's lawns and fountain. Such resonant urbanity perfectly embodies the life it invokes, celebrates, laments the loss of. (You might contrast the use of "surely" here with its use in "Owen Aherne"—"A strange thing surely." The different use of the same word shows, in a way, the difference between these two styles of poetic speech.)

The speech of the great meditations is not confined to this one style. A difference is clearly audible between it and the anguished crabbed passion in the opening lines of "The Tower":

> What shall I do with this absurdity—
> O heart, O troubled heart—this caricature,
> Decrepit age that has been tied to me
> As to a dog's tail?

Instead of oratorical magniloquence, here is a hurried, almost colloquial crying out, the stress of pressured speech dismantling all metrical sweetness—iambic pentameter only a ghostly presence. No tuneful lyric address, no excited oracular poise; plain human bafflement is all that finds its voice here, as the quality of the question itself shows. The collision between the passionate prosiness of the main sentence ("What shall I do with this absurdity, decrepit age?") and the slightly archaic poeticality of the ejaculation—"O heart, O troubled heart"— demonstrates the expansive pliancy of speech this meditative mind has access to.

The speech of meditation has other manners in which to register the fullness of self, compose the literary body of the self. The masterful public speech and passionate speech of the last two examples can give way to the relaxed, almost uninflected ordinariness of "The Road at my Door" in "Meditations":

> A brown Lieutenant and his men,
> Half dressed in national uniform,
> Stand at my door, and I complain
> Of the foul weather, hail and rain,
> A pear-tree broken by the storm.

As appropriate to the relationship he implies here, the stanza's formality of meter and rhyme is almost inaudible within what sounds like the perfectly common forms of speech. The poet is no longer a grand or passionate speaker, but a banal conversationalist at his own front door. This style of speech embodies an intimacy unusual in Yeats. But the speech of self does not stop even here. For in later segments of the same poem it can extend to the helpless sweet cadences of prayer ("O honey-bees, / Come build in the empty house of the stare"), or rise to the rapt impersonal excitement of "Frenzies bewilder, reveries perturb the mind; / Monstrous familiar images swim to the mind's eye."

To match its range of speech registers, this poetic idiom of the self has a wonderful thematic fluency, extraordinary powers of transition. The three separate sections of "The Tower" poem itself show this. The first section is passionately present, anchored in his aching body. The second inhabits memory— "Images and memories"—and follows the thread of a thought towards—"O towards I have forgotten what—enough!" Instinct with casual mastery, it moves cavalierly from one area of thought to another. The third section begins with astounding suddenness, pulling itself out of the dead end of section II with the

almost businesslike determination of "It is time that I wrote my will," and shifting metre, rhythm, line length, rhyme pattern with almost nonchalant ease. This
rich subjective mobility is never more animated than in "Among School Children," where the entrancing flow of the whole poem is created by transitions
which capture exactly and without strain the momentum of a mind moving
among its own intellectual and emotional contents and inhabitants. Reading
these meditations, you feel the poet can go anywhere and say almost anything,
that he has found a style to embody to perfection the variety and the velocity of
this old man's eagle mind.

As far as I know, Yeats has no objective description of this style, this mode
of meditation, this speech of self. In the later parts of his *Autobiography*, however, passages can be found that illustrate the nature of the imaginative action
which he dramatises in these poems. I have condensed one of them, his account
of receiving the Nobel Prize:

> During our first long wait all kinds of pictures had passed before me in
> reverie and now my imagination renews its excitement. I had thought
> how we Irish had served famous men and famous families, and had
> been . . . good lovers of women . . . I had thought how, before the emi-
> gration of our poor began, our gentlemen had gone all over Europe, of-
> fering their swords at every court. . . . Then my memory had gone back
> twenty years. . . . I remembered a cry of Bembo's. . . . I had repeated to
> myself what I could remember of Ben Jonson's address to the court of
> his time. . . . And now I begin to imagine some equivalent gathering to
> that about me. . . . Then suddenly my thought runs off to that old
> Gaelic poem made by the nuns of Iona.[8]

And so on and so on, to thoughts of "hereditary honour," nature and family,
Japan and the individualistic age, "the use of the mask in acting . . . the omission
from painting of the cast shadow . . ." No wonder he says, in a pause to draw
breath, "But my thoughts have carried me far away." Such a reverie suggests (in
a less intense form) something of the procedures of those poems which contain
what I've called the speech of self. The various nature of this speech, I want to
say, best embodies the truth of the poet's inner life, offers us the most complete
self-portrait of his poetic identity. It is a self-portrait, however, which is not
truly finished.

III

I began with a few small points of possible interest: about Yeats as not just a
maker of poems but as a shaper of books, about the pervasive element of time in
The Tower, about the figure of balanced contradiction as an embodiment of

life's difficult fullness and truth. I will end with a somewhat more elaborate treatment of these issues as they appear in the first four poems of the collection. These four poems form a coherent group. What particularly interested me was that they seemed to have one sort of coherence as a group when read in the order of art—as Yeats arranged them for book publication—and another kind of coherence when read according to the order of time—the chronological order of their composition, exactly the reverse of the order of art. The four poems are "Sailing to Byzantium" (1927), "The Tower" (1926), "Meditations in Time of Civil War" (1923), and "Nineteen Hundred and Nineteen" (dated 1919, but much of it written in 1921).

First, the order of art. The four poems compose a kind of drama in four acts. "Sailing to Byzantium" is a powerful opening act, celebrating the desperate gesture of the will—"And therefore I have sailed the seas and come. . . . Once out of nature I shall never take . . . " It gives bright body to the poet's dream of escape from the entrapments of time, "those dying generations." Like King Lear's dream of sanctuary in a prison cell, the poet's golden bird of art will take upon itself the mystery of things. Elevated out of the whirligyres of time and natural process, all time itself becomes its natural subject, matter for song. As if he were God's spy (laureate to a drowsy emperor), his singing will be memorial, existential, prophetic—of what is past, and passing, and to come.

Such a dream state cannot, however, last. In this drama, after all, it is only the first act. In *King Lear*, the old man's dream of such Yeatsian pastimes as telling old tales, hearing court news, and laughing at gilded butterflies, is shattered by the tragic conjunction of ambitious evil and arbitrary chance (rooted in specific temporality). And after his great speech of blessedly pastoral retreat, the next words we hear out of the king, as he bears onstage his dead daughter, are "Howl, howl, howl, howl . . . ," perfect counterpoint, in style as well as subject matter, to the musical cadences and lyric images of his earlier utterance. In moving from "Sailing to Byzantium" to "The Tower" Yeats makes a similarly brilliant, theatrical transition: the musical and substantive resolution of the first poem—"Of what is past, or passing, or to come"—is abruptly broken on the first hard words of the second ("What shall I do with this absurdity— / O heart, O troubled heart") and we are jolted from the image of the calmly omniscient singing bird surrounded by an ideal audience to the cacophonous image of a dog with tin cans tied to its tail. Jagged cadences and rough vocabulary tumble us off the golden bough into the shambles of actuality. In place of the gold mosaic of a wall, here is a storm-beaten stone tower in an environment not of sages, singing masters, and holy fire, but of ruins, ancient trees, memories, the ache of individual personality. Time and space prove intractable, and though that may be "no country for old men," this old man has to live there.

And yet this poem is a journey too. From the clamorous outrage of its opening scene, it travels through the labyrinth of memory and desire in Section II, through the determined resolutions of pride in the first part of Section III, to the simple meditative hush of its soul-making conclusion. At the end, the poet rests in the warm quietude of the natural world. There, reconciled to the body, he finds a sort of redemption for the sexual and imaginative self he had despaired of at the start. All the indignities of being human and being old now "Seem but the clouds of the sky / When the horizon fades; / Or a bird's sleepy cry / Among the deepening shades."

But as in *King Lear*, where every seeming resolution opens into another crisis, the muted reconciliations of "The Tower" poem is followed by "Meditations" upon the upheavals of the self in a context of civil war. In this act of the drama, too, the sphere of crisis has been enlarged. The subject of the first act, "Sailing to Byzantium," is the artist's soul in the purity of its own isolation and self-delight. It is, I suppose, a poem of perfect egotism. The second act, "The Tower," is a poem of imperfect egotism, being a heroic attempt to reconcile the artist's soul to his human body, the self acknowledged both as a member of "The people of Burke and Grattan" and as a cultural being who has "prepared my peace / With learned Italian things / And the proud stones of Greece." That accomplished, the subject of the third act—"Meditations in Time of Civil War"—is the poet in his immediate social and political environment, an environment which dismantles the compound self of "The Tower" in yet another crisis of confidence for this embattled individual.

The transition from one poem to another is, once again, startling and dramatically effective. The faint echo of the first line of "The Tower" ("Among the deepening shades") in the first line of "Ancestral Houses" ("Surely among a rich man's flowering lawns") only heightens the contrast, as the poet moves from natural solitude to civil society, from the environment of the soul to that of culture and social class. From soul-making solitude we're carried into a world where the poet is a conscious participant, seen in the shift of pronoun from first-person singular to first-person plural—our greatness, our violence, our ancestors, our bitterness.

Choosing to reside in a world of inherent decay and destructive violence, the poet is preoccupied with all kinds of belonging and continuity, with forging a place for himself in this precarious environment. "My House," "My Table," and "My Descendants" try to compose a self out of the palpable sign of those cultural values—literary, artistic, familial—which have been called drastically into question by civil war. Yet the inexorable logic of the situation forces the poet, in "The Road at My Door," to recognise his own isolation, at one with neither of the sides in the civil war, a social and cultural and temperamental outsider, grasping in the end at the minute evidence of natural continuity in the image of the mother moorhen and her chicks.

The almost domestic intimacy of the self-portrait he composes through "Meditations" is never more intense nor more touching than in the section I've just discussed and the one that follows it—"The Stare's Nest at my Window." The poet's own felt limits and vulnerability are also the subjects of the latter poem, as he desperately affirms, in the context of desolation, of "loosening masonry," the continuity of a natural sweetness that may redeem, but barely, the heart brutalized by fantasies. And here again, for all his feeling of being an outsider, he insists on some group identity—"More substance in our enmities / Than in our love." And the group this time, I'd say, as well as being his own family confined to Thoor Ballylee, is the whole fractured community of Ireland: "We are closed in, and the key is turned / On our uncertainty." This section of the poem concludes in the tenuous resolution of prayer: "O honey-bees, come build."

This resolution, however, is broken by the visionary climax of the last section, with its remarkable title, which in turn restores him to the predicament of the self in a context, again, of actual and symbolic "broken stone." "I climb to the tower-top and lean upon broken stone" is the emblematic sketch of the self with which he begins the poem. From this point he advances through three visionary moments (of violent participation, of artistic self-delight and detachment, of "the coming emptiness"—all of them temptations that could, that would, annihilate the self) to the image of the self in isolation. But this is an emphatically accepted isolation that regretfully but without flinching acknowledges the surrounding community as it leaves it:

> I turn away and shut the door, and on the stair
> Wonder how many times I could have proved my worth
> In something that all others understand or share.

In this isolation, finally, he makes a self by affirming, in an echo of Wordsworth that sounds almost parodic, the only continuity left him, that of his own imaginative self, that between "the ageing man" and "the growing boy."

Seen in this way, "Meditations" suggests that even in the turbulence of civil war the business of soul-making can continue. For the whole poem ends on a note of precarious, sadly resigned self-confidence: such egotism as there is here seems considerably more bruised by the world than those versions of it dominating "Sailing to Byzantium" and "The Tower." The ending does offer, nonetheless, a kind of resolution, no matter how provisional it may sound.

By opening on yet another contrapuntal note, the last poem of the group— "Nineteen Hundred and Nineteen"—adheres to the dramatic pattern I've already described. The solitary, self-sufficient individual of the end of "Meditations" is heard here grieving over the fact that "Many ingenious lovely things are gone / That seemed sheer miracle to the multitude." A line of cultural continuity back to the Greeks is broken in the present, and the poet is spokesman for the sense of loss ("We too had many pretty toys when young"). This surprisingly representative status is matched by a still more ample environment of actuality in which the self must struggle for identity. (The four poems widen from a golden bough in Byzantium, to a tower in County Galway, to all Ireland at civil war, to

"Thoughts on the Present State of the World," the first title of "Nineteen Hundred and Nineteen.") The Yeats of this poem is European idealist, the articulate and disenchanted member of a distinct culture group who "Learns that we were crack-pated when we dreamed." (The fierce, self-lacerating confessionalism of this must have been one of the features of *The Tower* that commended it so highly to the next generation of poets.) The self, which we have seen becoming more and more embattled through the tragic drama of these four poems, seems to vanish into the general meditation of this concluding act. So, in Section II, history is seen as a dance and "All men are dancers and their tread / Goes to the barbarous clangour of a gong." While the intimate soul-making of the earlier poems in the sequence becomes in Section II a distinct philosophy of the soul, the solitary philosophic self implied by the whole poem is becoming the generalised "A man in his own secret meditation." The outmoded culture group was general, even abstract, in ideals ("We . . . / Talked of honour and of / truth") and general, finally, in their habitual reactions, mocking all that was great, wise, and good "for we / Traffic in mockery." The final vanishing away of the self for which this prepares us is accomplished in the last section with its impersonal apocalypse—"Violence upon the roads: violence of horses." The general collapse of all the civilized values the poet and his group have stood for culminates in the sinister misalliance between "That insolent fiend Robert Artisson" and "the love-lorn Lady Kyteler." In the disappearance of the self there is no resolution, merely the horrified recognition of a new and terrible age. A little as *King Lear* does, this drama ends with the ultimately tragic acknowledgement: the world is in bits, this is the promised end, and the image of that horror, so "Fall and cease." From "Sailing to Byzantium," then, to these last lines of 1919, Yeats charts a tragic journey: from the artist's dream of the escape of his individual soul from time and place, to the loss of the individual in the impersonal violence of history.

This, or something like it, could be the tragic pattern composed by these four poems, when read according to what I've called the order of art. Between them, too, they offer a spectrum of self-hood, a self-portrait, richer and more revealing than any Yeats had composed before this. The full span of being available to the individual soul is seen here in a tragic light. These poems embody at least some of the truth of Yeats's own experience of himself, an oscillating movement from crisis to resolution and back to crisis, with no exit in the end from the inevitable and inexorable horror of historical violence. The poems dramatise, that is, the descent of the soul into larger and larger labyrinths of actuality.

When we read the poems in the order of time, however, in the order of chronological composition, the significance of the pattern they make is a little different. The order of art offers a tragic movement that begins at the bright centre of the self and moves in widening circles to those spheres of action where the self must live and find, if it can, fullness of being, however tragic the realisation of the nature of that being may be. The more involuntary order of time, on the other hand, begins in the wide world and in a general scheme of things. It begins, that is, in "Nineteen Hundred and Nineteen," dramatising how the tyrannies of circumstance compel the poet to abandon—in the mixed tones of urbanity, irony, and bitterness—the values of his chosen culture group. The drama of these four poems, that is, begins with a kind of elegy for a world the poet had hoped for, a world of idealistic dreams "to mend / Whatever mischief seemed / To afflict mankind." But the collapse of this world throws him into "ghostly solitude." Things have truly, as in "The Second Coming" (composed in 1919), fallen apart, and the individual learns upon his nerves that he will have to compose a life for himself outside (or without) the protection of the group. It might even be possible to say that "Nineteen Hundred and Nineteen" dramatises the plight of the individual who must continue to live in the world of "The Second Coming."

There's a logical movement from here to "Meditations in Time of Civil War," which may be read as an attempt, after the collapse of the value world of "1919," and in the uncertain and turbulent world of civil war, to forge a personal system of values. In "Ancestral Houses" collapse and decay are seen as inherent in the nature of civilisation itself, not external to it; from this seminal recognition the poet moves to fashion a self and a small space for it ("My House," "My Table," "My Descendants") inside the violent world of history. Having managed to compose such an enclave, he discovers such a protective space is itself an enclosure—"We are closed in, and the key is turned / On our uncertainty." Like "Nineteen Hundred and Nineteen," "Meditations" may be read as an elegy, an elegy this time for the self in the world, in the cultural and political community. His dwelling-place is the residence of "a lonely mind" and the most telling elements of self portraiture in the whole poem are contained in the poet's repeated gesture of turning away. In "The Road at My Door," he says "I turn towards my chamber," retreating from the world outside, of which he cannot be a part. In the last poem of the sequence he is definitively cut off from "something that all others understand or share," and consequently "I turn away and shut the door."

Chronologically, the next poem in the series is "The Tower," the very title of which suggests that this voyage of retreat continues still. This symbolic and real edifice stands as a blunt affirmation of the self, beyond the issues of time, history, culture, political upheaval. Europe and Ireland have narrowed to this emblematic dwelling-place. Refuge and fortress, it is, as Yeats called it, "a setting for my old age" and "a permanent symbol of my work plainly visible to the passerby." The self-sufficiency (albeit isolated) that he recognises and embraces at the end of "Meditations," however, with its consolation of "the half-read wisdom of daemonic images," collapses in the far more painful recognition of absurd old age. Even the reduced, drastically circumscribed self has a further crisis to face, and in consequence we have in this poem what amounts to another remarkable elegy. This one is essentially the self's farewell to the body, not by resorting to abstraction and philosophy, but by means of the more difficult affirmation of spirit: soul-making while the body breaks. The result is that at the end of "The Tower" he can—having suffered through and spoken out of his own actual condition—accept the state that time and nature have forced upon him. Having reviewed and summarised his experience, having made his will and begun to make his soul, the poet's last gesture here is a lovely valediction to his own bodily self. So "the wreck of body / Slow decay of blood / Testy delirium or dull decrepitude" become natural processes of which he is a part—clouds of the evening sky, the sleepy cry of the bird. He can bid the body such a farewell by learning how to live with it, as Prospero's redemption of his own humanity is crowned by his gruff embrace of Caliban—"This thing of darkness I acknowledge mine"—or as Keats warmly reconciles himself to Autumn and its "gathering swallows" that "twitter in the sky," readying themselves for their migratory voyage. With this moment of elegiac poise, the journey of internal exile Yeats began in "Nineteen Hundred and Nineteen" has reached its limit.

But emotionally satisfying as this may be to us as readers, the poet cannot rest even in such a moment of brilliant but precarious equilibrium. For the body itself still remains, and there can be no final resolution until it itself has been cast off. No surprise, then, that the dominant image of what is chronologically the last poem of the group is that of a voyage, nor that in early drafts of the poem some lines read "For many loves I have taken off my clothes . . . but now I will take off my body." From the fixity of "The Tower" to the pervasive fluency of "Sailing to Byzantium," the distance is palpable. The soul he made in "The Tower" cannot endure in a world of natural processes that is "no country for old men." So the soul must journey out of the body itself, turning elegy into celebration, a celebration of imagination and "unageing intellect." (Conventional elegies usually end—think of "Lycidas"—with just such celebratory resurrections.) It travels "out of nature" into its only proper resting place, "the artifice of eternity." Here is its last exile where, as pure artifact (a "lovely ingenious thing" that completes the circle from the first stanza of "Nineteen Hundred and Nineteen") it can turn the matter of the first three poems of this sequence into song—"Of what is past, or passing, or to come." This almost pastoral, tragicomic resolution is fashioned out of constant farewell, out of acts of exile that take the soul into smaller and smaller spaces, the smallest of which blossoms contradictorily into an immensity of imagination. For what the soul sails into in this wish world is an ecstatic freedom of imagination, a world of cultural values purely of the poet's own imagining.

Read according to the order of time, then, this group of poems enacts a *Commedia*-like journey out of time—from the infernal shambles of history in Europe in "Nineteen Hundred and Nineteen" to the supra-historical, paradisal songs of Byzantium. But such a destination, of course, just sets us up for the return journey—from art's Byzantium to the apocalypse of historical horror that concludes "Nineteen Hundred and Nineteen." For the soul must be shuttling perpetually between these two extremities, and the truth of the self, the completion of the self-portrait, results from holding both journeys in the mind at once, like a physical enactment of Yeats's favorite figure for human life—the interlocking gyres he describes in *A Vision*. In their balance of contradictions, the essentially unknowable truth of the poet's experience is brilliantly embodied. And, to complete the picture I've been sketching with an apt contradiction, the "truth"—given the destination you reach when you read in either direction (artifice of eternity on the one hand; historical apocalypse on the other)—is embodied by being disembodied. And that, perhaps, surely, is the truth. Or at least a version of it, the version the poet himself put into final words a decade later and some three weeks before his death, in that short, very moving letter which I quoted from in the beginning of this essay. It is only fair to give the poet the last word (or almost): "I know for certain," he says, "that my time will not be long":

> I have put away everything that can be put away that I may speak what I have to speak, and I find 'expression' is a part of 'study.' In two or three weeks . . . I will begin to write my most fundamental thoughts and the arrangement of thought which I think will complete my studies. I am happy, and I think full of an energy, of an energy I had despaired of. It seems to me that I have found what I despaired of. When I try to put all into a phrase I say 'Man can embody truth but he cannot know it.' I must embody it in the completion of my life. The abstract is not life and everywhere draws out its contradictions. You can refute Hegel but not the Saint or the Song of Sixpence.

Whatever about Hegel and the Song of Sixpence, the one thing that seems clear after perusing this 1928 collection is that—read as the richly orchestrated embodiment of the life-embattled self—*The Tower* remains the volume in which this final "truth" achieves, beyond contradiction, its inaugural, prophetic, and most enduring expression.

1985

NOTES

[1] Allan Wade, *Letters of W.B. Yeats* (London, 1954), 922 (January 4, 1939).

[2] Richard Ellmann, *Yeats, The Man and the Masks* (New York, 1948), 235.

[3] *The Autobiography of W.B. Yeats* (1916; New York, 1965), 377.

[4] Allan Wade, *Letters of W.B. Yeats* (London, 1954), 681.

[5] *Letters*, 625.

[6] *Letters*, 680.

[7] *Autobiography*, 359. While my points about speech intersect with what was said in the previous essay, I have included them here for what they might add, by way of detail and difference, to that discussion.

[8]*Autobiography*, 368.

2

SOME COMPASS READINGS

The Poet Joyce

I am not a poet.
Joyce to Padraic Colum

My generic title offers a variety of possible topics. It might be possible to argue, for example, that poetry was for Joyce a central imaginative zone in which he revealed with the least number of disguises and overlays of 'genius' the most intimate recesses of his own consciousness. The poems, as it were, emerge from a seminal area of self and identity. "Can you not see the simplicity which is at the back of all my disguises?" he asks Nora in 1904, and telling her (in 1909) how "my true love for you" is identical with "the love of my poems."[1] Such a topic would take into account the youthful love poems of *Chamber Music* (published in 1907), written, as he said, as "a protest against myself," against the outer actions of his dissipated life and as a log book for the "journey of the soul."[2] Such a topic might confirm Ezra Pound's observation (made in 1920) "that the real man is the author of *Chamber Music*, the sensitive. The rest is the genius; the registration of realities on the temperament, the delicate temperament of the early poems."[3] Pursuit of such a topic might also see how, in his only other volume of poems (*Pomes Penyeach*, published in 1927), the "real man . . . the sensitive" resorted to what his brother called "a few incidental songs of a very personal nature" to utter his raw distress over the passing of youth, the onset of age, the vanishing possibility of passion (he is all of 40 plus years at the time), and to give expression to a melancholy but tender sense of himself as son and father, a familial self beyond the critical isolation of the self as artist. Such a topic might argue, in other words, that in verse Joyce probed— without the protective carapace of irony, humour, multiple perspectives, linguistic invention—his own most deeply rooted, unmediated, and in a sense inarticulate identity.

I could also have chosen to deal in a more specifically stylistic way with the poems, asking along the way why the greatest and most revolutionary prose stylist of the century was so timid in verse; asking what in the nature of poetry (as he conceived of it) and in his own nature made him in verse the decidedly minor figure he is. What kept Joyce, in biographical, circumstantial, and aesthetic terms, so conservative and conventional as a poet (even if the metrical and rhythmic freedom of a couple of poems in *Chamber Music* might seem remarkable enough, while the manner of one or two of the pieces in *Pomes Penyeach* could suggest a liberation of consciousness into verse that might, just might, anticipate something in the later manner of Thomas Kinsella)?[4] Such an investigation of style might reveal some of Joyce's underlying assumptions about the relationship between language, imaginative expression, and actuality.

There was also the possibility of tracing the curiously recurring presence of *Chamber Music* through the biography. It appears in at least one of his clandestine and more or less unconsummated affairs. But its most interesting appearance is in 1909 as an element in the graphically sexual letters exchanged by Joyce and Nora. It is just at this time that Nora "discovers" the book, giving the poems a fresh lease of life for Joyce himself.[5] In this new context he can clearly see how the poems relate to his love for Nora (although not written for her), for they hold "the desire of my youth and you, darling, were the fulfillment of that desire."[6] Through these letters, mixing the idealised lyricism of the poems with the graphic coarseness of active lust, Joyce discovered in rudimentary form a mode of expression that would, when developed, approximate, as he believed a literary style could and should, the complex fullness of reality. In his need to express his loving and lustful fervour for Nora he stumbles on a style that will animate in language the brimmingly various (and rootedly sexual) consciousness of Leopold and Molly Bloom. This rediscovery and validation of the poems leads to a new creative fluency, the rudimentary preparations for which can be seen in the remarkable transitions observable in the letters from the lyricism of "My beautiful wild flower of the hedges! My dark-blue, rain-drenched flower!" to the pornographic urgency of "Fuck me in your dressing gown (I hope you have that nice one) with nothing on under it, opening it suddenly and showing me your belly and thighs and back and pulling me on top of you on the kitchen table," to the mundane details of "O, I am hungry now. The day I arrive get Eva to make one of the threepenny puddings and make some kind of vanilla sauce without wine. I would like roast beef, rice-soup, capuzzi garbi, mashed potatoes, pudding and black coffee. No, no I would like stracotto di maccheroni, a mixed salad . . . ," and so forth.[7] By setting the poems in this startling epistolary context (he frequently quotes from them, and he is making during this time a fancy manuscript of the whole collection on parchment and covered in vellum as a gift for Nora, a book that was to be her particular treasure and which "missal-like volume . . . lay throned . . . on a reading desk, ecclesiastical in style" in their flat in Trieste),[8] by setting them in such a context, Joyce found a way to accommodate in language the whole self, an imaginative accommodation that would lead to the expansive wholeness and harmonies of *Ulysses* and even of *Finnegans Wake*.

These, then, were among the possibilities. With a mixture of modesty and desperation, however, I finally narrowed my focus to *Chamber Music* alone. (*Pomes Penyeach*, after all, in spite of some interesting features, is more a ploy than a book proper, a ploy to prove that Joyce, under fire for the lunacies of *Work in Progress*, could still be "grammatically sane" if and when he wanted to be).[9] So my subject here is the verse in *Chamber Music*, what (or at least some of what) those poems can tell us about the writer Joyce.

To begin, a sample, so we know the kind of thing we are talking about:

> My love is in a light attire

Among the apple trees,
Where the gay winds do most desire
To run in companies.

There, where the gay winds stay to woo
The young leaves as they pass,
My love goes slowly, bending to
Her shadow on the grass;

And where the sky's a pale blue cup
Over the laughing land,
My love goes lightly, holding up
Her dress with dainty hand.

(VII)

Of all Joyce's works *Chamber Music*—complete by or in 1904 and published in 1907—was the only one to get an almost unanimously positive critical reception. "It is a slim book and on the frontispiece is an open pianner," is Joyce's own laconic description, but the collection was widely praised in Ireland and England. Arthur Symons, who had been instrumental in their publication, was not alone in being "reminded of Elizabethan, more often of Jacobean lyrics" (as well as, no doubt, of his own symbolist poems and those of his friends of the Nineties: "No one who has not tried," he said, "can realize how difficult it is to do such tiny evanescent things").[10] In Ireland, Tom Kettle praised "these delicate verses which have, each of them, the bright beauty of a crystal." Other reviewers were happy to inform their readers that "Mr. Joyce flows in a clear delicious stream that ripples" or that "the casual reader will see nothing in his verses to object to, nothing incapable of an innocent explanation" in the "old-fashioned sweetness and flavour" of the collection. They had much of music and quaintness," in spite of some "bold liberties taken with rhyme and rhythm"; they were "sweet, reposeful and sublime"; they formed "a very promising little volume"; and were a "welcome contribution to contemporary poetry."

One discordant, dissenting voice was raised in this chorus of approval and praise: "I don't like the book," said young James Augustine Joyce himself when he saw it. "Nearly all the poems seemed to me poor and trivial: some phrases and lines pleased me and no more."[11] Posterity has not been as hard on this "capful of light odes" as their own author was.[12] Nor, however, has posterity echoed the fulsome tributes of those early critics, being more inclined to offer a measured appreciation of the distinctly minor work of a major writer, his status unquestionably due to his work in prose. In spite of a certain liking for the poems, most readers now would be likely to find themselves in agreement with Richard Ellmann's judgement of "the rather anemic style Joyce reserved for his verse."[13] or with another critic who describes the poems as "a limited selection from Joyce's life and a simplification of it for the convenience of tenors."[14] For this reason, the few critics who have written about the poems at length have resorted to various tactics of validation. William York Tindall's definitive edition, for example, resorts to a marvelously inventive over-reading in psycho-allegorical terms (stressing scatology rather than eschatology), and is in spite of its mischievous excesses the anatomy lesson to which we're all indebted.[15] Chester Anderson's tactic is a scrupulously exacting stylistic analysis and evaluative summary. And Robert Boyle's excellent essay on "The Woman Hidden in James Joyce's *Chamber Music*" revises the published order of the poems (back to Joyce's original order) with fascinating results.[16] Like these critics, I have taken an approach that is, I suppose, a species of validation, thereby hoping to cast a little more light on the meaning of this small plot of ground in the Joycean landscape.

One of the curious facts connected with *Chamber Music* concerns a dedication. On the copy of the poem XXI which Joyce gave to Constantine Curran in 1904 he had written "Dedication. To Nora." Since poem XXI, the last line of which is "His love is his companion," was the opening poem of the sequence as Joyce himself arranged it (the "Yale" Ms), Tindall presumes that "in dedicating this poem to Nora he was dedicating the whole suite."[17] Whatever the truth of this last point, and it has to remain in doubt, (along with the possibility of other poems being about Nora), the fact of the matter is that the published volume contains no dedication, neither particular nor general. The actual reason for this is not known. As I read the poems over, however, I wondered if it might not be connected with the sense the book as a whole was giving me, of being in itself a sort of dedication of the poet himself to certain crucial elements in his art. At any rate, it was this sense of *Chamber Music* as the young Joyce's own act of self-dedication as a literary artist that caught and held my attention, and this is what I want to share in what follows. It is possible, I feel, that it was his own awareness of something like this that prompted him, not long after publication, and when he had become a somewhat more tolerant reader of his own book, to refer to "the expression of myself which I now see I began in *Chamber Music*."[18]

There are three forms of self-dedication I want to address. The first of these is to craft, the craft of language. Thirty years and more before Yeats's celebrated injunction, here is an Irish poet who has certainly learned his trade and, with a youthfully dandified air, flaunts it. In fact, in 1903, Yeats's first praise of the cocky young poet was couched in precisely such terms: "Your technique in verse is very much better than the technique of any young Dublin man I have met during my time."[19] Yeats's judgement (its geographical qualification may be a touch mischievous) was echoed by the critics and reviewers, who stressed Joyce's mastery over the technique of poetry, "the poems' integrity of form," their "accomplished execution."[20] Even a casual ear will pick up the elegance with which the following quatrains are managed:

> Strings in the earth and air
>   Make music sweet;
> Strings by the river where
>   The willows meet.

> There's music along the river
> > For Love wanders there,
> Pale flowers on his mantle
> > Dark leaves on his hair.
>
> All softly playing,
> > With head to the music bent,
> And fingers straying
> > Upon an instrument.
> > > (I)

Here craft coaxes language towards the condition of music. Its chief strategy is repetition, dominating sound, rhythm, structure. Language for this poet has an aural plasticity which he moulds into units of harmony which are, in light of the poem's subject, especially apt. They give the whole piece a rarefied, enclosed, self-reflecting air. Language, it would seem, is listening to itself, and that wandering "Love" might be, among other things, a love of language for its own sake. Such innocent narcissism (and yet it is also the love of another, "With head to the music bent," a love of something beyond the self through an expression of the self) could conjure up J. F. Byrne's portrait of the young poet at work in 1900 in the National Library: "he would write and rewrite and re-touch, it might almost seem interminably, a bit of verse containing perhaps a dozen or a score of lines. When he had at last polished his gem to a satisfying degree of curvature and smoothness, he would write out the finished poem with slow and stylish penmanship and hand the copy to me."[21]

Plain, simple, conventional—the poem's diction has no surprises: it is a clear distillate of the imagined scene. The syntax is on the same model, being straightforward, unnoticeable, paratactic. Stanzas two and three form virtually (and, in an earlier draft, actually)[22] a single sentence, of which the last six line-units are all adjectival or adverbial qualifications of the main clause contained in the first two lines. What this careful dedication to language creates is a ritual simplicity—something at once refined and unsophisticated, a careful but casual gesture in words. This can be heard in the unassertive nature of the verbs (all except "is," "make," and "wanders" being participles) and the way this is com-plemented by the clean line and firmness of presentation. It is also obvious in the way the colloquial relaxation of "There's music along the river" is given a ritual turn by that Yeatsian "For" and the adagio pace of the line that follows: "For Love wanders there." The vowel play of the whole thing is distinct and im-pressive, the poet sounding vowels and dipthongs (i, e, e, e, u, i, make a rich, pure chord of the first two lines, for example) into elegant harmonic structures.

Here, then, is an example of a poem put together as Stephen Dedalus wanted, "not word by word but letter by letter."[23] And so, for all its conventional evanescence of content, there's a sense of the concrete in the poet's own awareness of and dedication to language. For him, as for the young Yeats, "words alone are certain good." While elements of the actual world have been erased, the language itself has body. (All this must remind of Stephen's composition of his villanelle in *Portrait*.) Such a sacramental commitment to language is consummated in Joyce's prose. But it is proper that its beginnings should be in verse, in poetry. For poetry, to be honest, always begins by being dedicated to, and in some sense being about, language itself, whereas even great prose seems to begin not in this pure air but somehow committed to content, to some expository urge or need. So it is in his beginnings as a poet that Joyce aptly inaugurates the stylistic revolution that would import into the practise of prose poetry's dedication to the word itself, its betrothal to language. The poems of *Chamber Music* are the artist's baptism in craft, his offering up of his artistic life to style.

The next dedication of self revealed by these poems is a dedication to tradition. This is seen in the writer's receptive openness to other voices. In fact, the poems of *Chamber Music* are compounded of "other voices": the poet has no real individual voice. What we hear instead is the voice of tradition (the tradition of love song, love poetry) through which, as appropriate *persona*, this speaker expresses himself. Such a habit of composition reveals something of the natural structure of Joyce's imagination.

Evidence of such imaginative hospitality—which will achieve its perfected form in the catholicity of influence to be heard in the orchestral harmonies of *Finnegans Wake*—appears in the bits and pieces that remain to us of poems preceding *Chamber Music*. Among these is a translation from Horace (a literal taking-on of the voice of another poet), the Yeatsian title of a lost juvenile collection (*Moods*), and fragments from a collection called (after Whitman) *Shine and Dark*, composed in Joyce's last year at Belvedere.[24] Titles such as "Wanhope," "Tenebrae," "Valkyre," and "The Final Peace" suggest a Romantic Gothic influence, and this may be detected in the fragments themselves (e.g., "There are no lips to kiss this foul remains of thee, / O, dead Unchastity!"). This can also be crossed with Keatsian pathos, Yeatsian cadence, Tennysonian gesture: the Lady of Shallott, for example, as well as la belle Dame sans Merci and Wandering Aengus all converge on this harmless, exemplary quatrain: "They covered her with linen white / And set white candles at her head / And loosened out her glorious hair / And laid her on a snow-white bed."[25] Elsewhere, as Richard Ellmann points out, the verse-making can show traces of Byronic posturing or pseudo-Elizabethan simplicity ("For she was passing fair, / And I was passing mad").

Such imitative mood-making was Joyce's apprenticeship for *Chamber Music*, and he showed a proper degree of self-knowledge in preserving none of it except the "Villanelle of the Temptress" from *Portrait*, and an elegant translation of Paul Verlaine (a poet who cast an influential shadow over *Chamber Music*, the poems of which were described by one critic as being "of the same kindred with harps [Yeats?], with woodbirds [the Elizabethans?] and with Paul Verlaine."[26] In the main, however, the nature of this early imitation is a species of parroting, merely miming a manner. As William Archer said after seeing some of the poems, "You feel and imagine poetically, but I do not find that as yet you have very much to say."[27] In *Chamber Music*, not only did he have something to say (about the nature of love and the "journey of the soul"), but he has also a different relationship to his influences. Now they are digested, not just mimed. They do not give Joyce his own voice, necessarily, but a voice that is a genuine compound of traditional accents. His reading, that is, gives him ways and means of translating his own experience into an individual poetic mode. Turn anywhere in these poems and you'll hear echoes of other poets: Nashe, Shakespeare, Herrick, Dowland, Byrd, Shelley, Byron, Blake, the last Romantics of the nineties, Yeats of *The Wind Among the Reeds*, the harder, more "modern" note of Meredith, and even a contemporary Irishman, Paul Gregan, "in whose lyrics he found an affinity" and whose own obvious influences are Yeats and AE.[28] (Gregan's *Sunset Town* appeared around 1900.) A major influence is Ben Jonson, whom Joyce read avidly and "exhaustively" in Paris in 1902, whose distinct simplicity of diction and syntax, as well as his "sinewy qualities and classical exactness" left a clear mark on lucid stanzas like the following: "What counsel has the hooded moon / Put in thy heart, my shyly sweet, / O Love in ancient plenilune, / Glory and stars beneath his feet" (XII).[29] Economy and steadiness of expression here suggest a deliberate chastening and limitation of style, factors which—along with the Elizabethan's irony and elegance—may have drawn Joyce to Jonson.[30]

Since these influences have been documented elsewhere, revealing what Anderson calls Joyce's technique of "multiple theft," I won't rehearse them here.[31] I would like, however, to add to the list a possible influence I have not seen mentioned, namely that of the great Italian lyric poet, Leopardi. Joyce's mention of Leopardi in the essay on Mangan (who is "weaker than Leopardi, for he has not the courage of his own despair")[32] betrays acquaintance and admiration, and although Joyce said, "I dislike Italian verse," his Italian studies must have included some of the *Canti*. With these facts in mind, it is not impossible to hear in the song, "Lean out of the window, / Goldenhair," (V) a faint echo of Leopardi's "To Silvia."[33] In Leopardi's poem the poet also leaves his book and his room to hear a girl's song, just as Joyce's lover-poet does: "I have left my book, / I have left my room, / For I heard you singing / Through the gloom." A second, equally faint Leopardian echo may be heard in the song (XXXIV) that "brings the 1905 sequence [the one Joyce himself arranged: see below] to an inconclusive conclusion."[34] Here the echo of Leopardi's "To Himself" is joined to those of Yeats, *Macbeth*, and the Song of Solomon. Joyce's opening lines— "Sleep now, O sleep now, / O you unquiet heart"—could be a memory of Leopardi's opening, "Or poserai per sempre / Stanco mio cor" ("Now you will rest, my tired heart, forever"), even if that "unquiet heart" of Joyce's derives more directly from Yeats's poem, "The Old Age of Queen Maeve."[35] Joyce's concluding, "Sleep on in peace now," with its conjunction of sleep and death might be an echo of Leopardi's "T'acqueta omai" ("Now rest in peace"), since both of them invoke implicitly the Catholic funerary formulation, "requiescat in pace." Again the Leopardian presence is at best a faint possibility, no more. But with a magpie author like Joyce, such possibilities are in the grain of the work, and none should be too quickly dismissed.

Quotation of this short lyric may help to demonstrate how Joyce digests his influences:

Sleep now, O sleep now,
   O you unquiet heart!
A voice crying "Sleep now"
   Is heard in my heart.

The voice of the winter
   Is heard at the door.
O sleep, for the winter
   Is crying "Sleep no more!"

My kiss will give peace now
   And quiet to your heart—
Sleep on in peace now,
   O you unquiet heart!

Macbeth, the Song of Solomon, Yeats, maybe Leopardi: the echoes are obvious enough. What is worth pointing to, however, is the smoothness with which these various voices have become the one voice of the poem. That this is a poem *about* voices seems particularly apt, its two voices being parts of the poet. In style and substance, that is, the poem enacts the drama of multiple voices becoming one voice, that voice being at once the voice of "Love" and the literary tradition, which throughout this sequence is identifiable with love itself (so that, as poem XXXIII shows, "the end of love is the end of poetry"). In such poems the voice of the lover has no actual identity: it is the voice of that kind of poetry. The poet is betrothed to the tradition, and the lover's persona, as well as the object of his love, is the tradition itself.

    This dedication to the tradition also serves to explain the non-actuality of the woman of *Chamber Music*. "How would I write the most perfect love songs of our time" Joyce rhetorically asked his friend Skeffington, "if I were in love."[36] And in *Stephen Hero*, when Maurice asks Stephen "who the woman [of the poems] was, Stephen looked a little vaguely before answering, and in the end had to answer that he didn't know who she was."[37] In 1909, when the poems had become an important part of the passionate exchange between Joyce and Nora, he tells her that the girl of *Chamber Music* was not her: "She was perhaps (as I saw her in my imagination), a girl fashioned into a curious grave beauty by the culture of generations before her, the woman for whom I wrote poems like "Gentle Lady" or "Thou Leanest to the Shell of Night."[38] Not an actual woman then, but the representative of this kind of poetry, and, by extension, of the literary tradition itself, to which the sequence as a whole is an elaborate act of homage and self-dedication on the part of the young poet. Perhaps this reason, in particular, is why he removed the dedication to Nora, and, in general, why, when he saw the proofs of *Chamber Music* in 1907, he remarked, "It is not a book of love-verses at all, I perceive."[39] In this initial literary action of his career, an act of dedication to tradition itself, Joyce lays the ground of an imagination extraordinarily hospitable to the widest possible range of literary allusions, an imagination to which nothing will seem alien.

At this early stage, however, that "nothing" must be qualified in an important way. For an important footnote to this whole issue concerns not the inclusive but the exclusive nature of the poet's influences. Those influences are, as can be seen at a glance, aggressively non-Irish. Yeats may be a heavy presence. But not the *Celtic* Yeats of *The Wind Among the Reeds*, the book which Joyce regarded with great admiration, saying that "in aim and form" it was "poetry of the highest order,"[40] but rather the Yeats who gathered into himself as a poet of desire and love ("aim") elements of that tradition ("form") which Joyce contrived to let speak through him. And whatever tonal features he may have admired in Paul Gregan's *Sunset Town*, its explicitly Celtic features seem to have left him unmoved.[41] The poet of *Chamber Music* (even its title is unCeltic) stood aloof from the Celtic paraphernalia apparent in the collection of new poets edited by AE in 1904, *New Songs*. With his English, French, and Italian influences on show (Dante's *Vita Nuova*, for instance, prompted Stephen Dedalus to arrange his poems into "a wreath of songs in praise of love")[42] the critics were not going to confuse Joyce with the Celtic School to which Little Chandler in "A Little Cloud" dreams of belonging "by reason of the melancholy tone of his poems."[43] To identify himself further as an Irish poet, Chandler intended to "put in allusions," of the sort, no doubt that crowded the lines of poets like Gregan, Colum, and others among those whom Yeats called "AE's canaries." Joyce's "allusions" are English and classical, both overt and (in the various echoes and borrowings) covert. (Coleridge and Shakespeare seem explicitly alluded to in XXVI). As to Irish allusions, I find only four: "harps" in III, "choirs of faery" in XV, ("choirs," mind you: perhaps a borrowing from Gregan, who refers to "the faery choir")[44]; the not wildly Celtic suburb of Donnycarney in XXXI (perhaps his "Sally Gardens" song), and the satirically barbed "piping poets" of XXVII. Joyce's own eventually measured approval of the poems stresses this Celtic disconnection: "Some of them are pretty enough to be put to music. I hope someone will do so, someone that knows old English music such as I like."[45]

As an initiating gesture in self-portraiture, then, the poems are marked by their refusal to join any club except that of his own choosing (the one, as it turns out, in which most of the competition is dead). It was his encourager and critic, Symons, who noted that Joyce was "not in the Celtic Movement," and "free of schools," observations which had to please this inner emigré, who had gone stylistically into exile before ever he left with Nora from the North Wall in 1904. The poems, in fact, may be the first move in the game of antithesis which Joyce played with Ireland and Irish art for the rest of his life. (But whereas this first move was exclusive and, in a sense, elitist, the later moves were increasingly inclusive and democratic.) The poems manage to suggest at the same time a neutrality (an interest only in style) and a hostility: it is a mixture fertile with possibility, a sort of early summary of how Joyce's imagination actually works. And it shows, too, that the impulse of dedication is also accompanied by an important impulse of divorce, which in itself, however, is an even more deliberate dedication to a literary context larger than that provided by the Irish Literary Revival. As well as being a species of self-excommunication, this dedication to tradition is, as it were, Joyce's First Communion with the totality of a literary past he wanted to emulate and eventually to incorporate.

The third form of self-dedication observable in *Chamber Music* is to narrative. There are two major arrangements of the poems: the published one is by Stanislaus Joyce, whom his brother allowed to organise the sequence, telling him "to do what [he] liked with it." This odd decision, surrendering that last act of will that would arrange the individual pieces into a pattern, suggests the degree of Joyce's own detachment from the poems by 1906, involved as he was in the prose of *Dubliners* and *Stephen Hero*. ("A page of A Little Cloud gives me more pleasure than all my verses," he says).[46] Stanislaus' pattern has a musical logic and bias: he "arranged them . . . in their present order—approximately allegretto, andante cantabile, mosso—to suggest a closed episode of youth and love."[47] Arranged thus, the collection, as Tindall says, "proceeds clearly according to moods."[48] Joyce's own arrangement (preserved in the Yale manuscript) is more essentially and explicitly narrative, proceeding "with greater fidelity to actual experience."[49] It shows an active instinct to organise experience into story shapes, an instinct already alive in 1902 when he decided to divide the suite into two parts, "the first being relatively simple and innocent, the second more complicated and experienced,"[50] on the analogy both of Blake's *Songs* and, even more relevantly, I'd suggest, of the implicit narrative patterns in sonnet sequences such as those of Sidney and Shakespeare. In 1909, when Joyce briefly describes the collection, it is clear that in spite of the published arrangement he still has his own narrative design in mind, into which he has incorporated his brother's changes: "the central song is XIV," he says "after which the movement is all downwards until XXXIV which is vitally the end of the book. XXXV and XXXVI are tailpieces just as I and III are preludes."[51] Since XIV is the seventeenth poem in his own ordering, exactly midpoint in the original sequence, it shows the architectural care for balanced and symmetrical narrative natural to his imagination.

After the dedications to language and tradition, the dedication to narrative may be seen as a bodying forth of his imagination, making it (with its significant performance) present in the world. Narrative, that is, is the more expansive syntax of imagination, shaping the individual elements of the sequence into larger meanings. Since these elements are in themselves essentially musical, Joyce's own arrangement of the sequence brings music and will together, marrying them to one another to produce a unit of richer possibility. *Chamber Music*, therefore, with its musical centre and its narrative circumference, is a miniature model of the imagination that would produce the greater works. It is possible that Joyce's perfunctory permission to Stanislaus to do as he liked with the poems for publication was in part a result of his feeling that this imaginative compound of music and narrative could achieve its full potential for him only in prose, recognising, that is, that the poems, even with his own narrative design in place, were still of necessity dominated by the musical and tonal elements.

Arranged according to his original intentions, however, the poems do tell a coherent story, providing a portrait of the artist as a young lover and, as Robert Boyle says, intending a "projection of the woman he desired to meet in the world outside himself" as well as "a large philosophy dealing with human love."[52] The story is conventionally romantic: the lonely young poet singer with only his own love for a companion, yearns for a girl; he finds her; celebrates her lightly-clad springtime beauty; leaves friends and seeks a haven from the austerities of the world in her "sweet bosom." When "Love is at his noon" he seeks a more fully sexual, fleshly union with her, and seems to find it, in the accents of the Song of Solomon ("My sister . . . my love . . . My breast shall be your bed"). After this climax the shadows increase: desire being satisfied, a sense of death, attended by the "modern" ironic note, sets in: the love affair fluctuates, the woman is seen in a more ambiguous and sinister light, love itself is malicious and tender, is "sweet imprisonment." The end of the affair approaches in autumn, as the lover tries to persuade the beloved that "love that passes is enough." Something in the manner of Yeats's "Ephemera," the love is reduced to memory, and the lover, "for old friendship' sake" welcomes "The ways that we shall go upon." The end of love signifies the end of this kind of poetry; the poet (as we have seen) bids his "unquiet heart" to be at peace. Then, in two "tailpieces" (added by Stanislaus, but which Joyce must have seen would accentuate his own narrative design) the singer goes alone into exile (anticipating the end of *Portrait*), and has an apocalyptic dream that ends with an anguished recognition of his solitude: "My love, my love, my love," he cries to his own heart, to his idea of love, to the lost girl, "why have you left me alone?"

Yearning, discovery, disappointment: the narrative enacted by *Chamber Music* composes a lyrical abstract of Joyce's experience of love in Ireland up to mid-1904 and the meeting with Nora (who, as he told her in 1909, "made me a man").[53] (Most critics assert as a probability that some of the poems concern and are addressed to her, but I remain unconvinced. At very most, it might have been a transformed, rarefied image of her, but no more). Frequenter of brothels and idealiser from a sanitary distance of a few of the girls of his acquaintance, the young Joyce is at the same time desperate for a conjunction of the erotic with the spiritual. In a sense, the narrative charts the failure of that ambition, that hope. Embodying Joyce's early sense of human love and the loss of that sense of it, it is a lyrical narrative about the image of love itself, and as such is the true lineal successor to that love of the Virgin Mary which dominated his boyhood, importing some of that religious fervour into this zone of secular passion. As such it stands between that religious love and his love for Nora. Most important, the sequence shows clearly enough the instinct of Joyce's imagination to fashion those scattered fragments of experience caught and distilled as poems into the larger coherence of narrative. This dedication to narrative represented by *Chamber Music* crowns the other two more primary forms of dedication—to language and to literary tradition—and confirms his imagination (as that to language baptised it and that to tradition enabled it to make its First Communion). After these three sacramental attachments his imagination is ready for future enterprises.

It is in this final form of self-dedication—to narrative—that Joyce also discovers, I believe, the limitations for him of poetry as an art for the expression of reality. Part of the reason why he showed little interest in the poems in 1906 and 1907, as has been suggested or implied, is his awareness that the poems, in spite of their narrative arc, failed to embody and represent adequately the reality that was their subject matter. In the poems, the realities of self, sex, and spirit receive an abstract, distilled expression. He wants a much closer approximation to the actual, and this the poems alone cannot deliver. (He discovers, almost inadvertently, that closer approximation through the letters to Nora in 1909, and the way their coarseness and sexual immediacy could join with the language and sentiments of the poems to form a new, a novel, sense of wholeness. But that, as I said at the start, is another story).

"It is not a book of love-verses at all." By this Joyce means, I imagine, that the poems do not truly or adequately represent the nature of love, and he can only justify them by saying that "at the top of each page I will put an address or a street so that when I open the book I can revisit the places where I wrote the different songs."[54] These mundane addresses or street names (the very stuff of his prose) are for him more evocative of actuality than the poems themselves. For the poems etherealise his subject, distilling and vapourising the experience. And it was (certainly by 1907) the actual experience he was after, and a style that would get as close to that as the nature of language would allow. "Absolute realism is impossible, of course," he conceded not long after the poems were published, but "I would like to put on paper the thousand complexities" in the mind of a young drunken labourer he saw going into a trattoria.[55] True narrative, as far as he is concerned, demands that layered richness of texture, whereas his lyrical habits as displayed in *Chamber Music* are exactly antithetical—distillation, draining away, vapourising.

It is possible to get a closer look at this process, and so to understand a little better his abandonment of verse for prose, by comparing a poem with the experience that gave rise to it. Here is Ellmann's account of the incident that stands behind the poem, "What Counsel Has the Hooded Moon" (CM XII): during an excursion into the Dublin Hills with Mary Sheehy, Francis Skeffington, and other friends, "Joyce, swaggering a little in his yachting cap and canvas shoes and sporting an ashplant, spent most of his time watching Mary. He admired her beauty, and interpreted her silence in company as a contempt like his for the people around her. He did not give himself away now or at any other time, but they exchanged a few words on the way back from the hills. Mary, gazing at the moon, thought it looked tearful, while Joyce, with mild daring, contended that it was "like the chubby hooded face of some jolly fat Capuchin." "I think you are very wicked," said Mary, and he replied, "No, but I do my best." After they separated he tore open a cigarette box (as Stephen Dedalus does for his villanelle) and wrote, "What counsel has the hooded moon."[56] And, now, here is the poem:

> What counsel has the hooded moon
>   Put in thy heart, my shyly sweet,

Of love in ancient plenilune,
    Glory and stars beneath his feet—
A sage that is but kith and kin
With the comedian capuchin?

Believe me rather that am wise
    In disregard of the divine.
A glory kindles in those eyes
    Trembles to starlight. Mine, O Mine!
No more be tears in moon or mist
For thee, sweet sentimentalist.

As you can hear, all the hard sardonic facts have been distilled out of the poem. Even the anti-clerical joke has been given a graceful, enigmatic, stylising twist. Like the fingernails of the God of creation, the facts have been refined out of existence. As Joyce chooses to write poetry, it becomes an agent of, in every sense, sublimation. It is the process described later in *Portrait* when Stephen writes the poem "To E - C-" (for whom Mary Sheehy is the main model): "During this process all these elements which he deemed common and insignificant fell out of the scene. There remained no trace of the tram itself nor of the tram-men nor of the horses: nor did she appear vividly. The verses told only of the night and the balmy breeze and the maiden lustre of the moon."[57] The narrator here exercises an implicit critical judgement on Stephen such as Joyce himself exercised on *Chamber Music*. For he saw that the poems themselves, in spite of their narrative pattern, could not represent the facts of life which he wanted to represent in narrative. His sense of what poetry is, in other words, his own practical aesthetics of verse, will not allow it. And for all Stephen Dedalus' notions of the Incarnation as a metaphor for artistic creation, what his and Joyce's verse does, in effect, is not make the word flesh, but rather make the flesh word. As in the "Villanelle of the Temptress" in *Portrait*, in the poems of *Chamber Music* the facts are rendered down to a few imagistic details, the language is driven by a generalising energy, detaching the "subtle soul of the image from its mesh of defining circumstances."[58] Such an effect is enhanced in the poems by a boneless syntax that simply lets the elements of a poem float together, and by a speaker who is no more than a ghostly presence. Language, music, internal pattern, the playing of old notes—those first two dedications to language and tradition, in fact—are what in the final analysis remove the poems from the area of genuine narrative possibility. This may be exemplified in the first poem of the sequence proper (as Joyce himself would have arranged it):

The twilight turns from amethyst
    To deep and deeper blue,
The lamp fills with a pale green glow
    The trees of the avenue.

The old piano plays an air,

> Sedate and slow and gay;
>   She bends upon the yellow keys,
>   Her head inclines this way.
>
>   Shy thoughts and grave wide eyes and hands
>   That wander as they list—
>   The twilight turns to darker blue
>   With lights of amethyst.

Here all is frozen gesture; language and syntax encase and make conventional the moment, giving it the generality of song. The poem quoted, then, may (as an introduction) be taken as a good representative of the manners governing (and limiting) the whole collection.

In his contemporary work in prose, however, the elements that verse distills out are left in, accentuated. The first place we find this is in what could be seen as a natural transition from poem to prose, those early "epiphanies" which have, more than anything else, qualities we might associate with what is called the "prose poem." It is in the written epiphanies, in fact, that Joyce discovers a management of language that will allow him to pursue his own narrative urge. To take this a step farther, the epiphanies may be seen as the bridge from the poems to the major work in prose. The following example offers a simple comparison with the poem just quoted:

> She stands, her book held lightly at her breast, reading the lesson. Against the dark stuff of her dress her face, mild-featured with downcast eyes, rises softly outlined in light; and from a folded cap, set carelessly forward, a tassel falls along her brown ringletted hair . . . What is the lesson that she reads—of apes, of strange inventions, of the legends of martyrs?[59]

In this slight prose sketch the diction, for all its calculation, does not strain after effects of purity and remoteness, as it does in the verse. This language is more straightforward than the posed simplicity of the poem. The rhythm varies, as the motion of each sentence—turning to a different syntactical impulse—is different. And things are being included, enumerated, given physical body and presence, rather than being forced, under the pressure of poetic sublimation, to "fall out of the scene." The poem is a sort of secret, in code. The prose seems to wish that the reader share exactly what the writer has seen. Here facts are enacted rather than souls evoked. The surfaces are in clear view ("her book held lightly at her breast," the dark stuff of her dress, the folded cap set carelessly forward, a falling tassel, "her brown ringletted hair," rather than "Shy thoughts and grave wide eyes and hands / That wander as they list"). In this dedication to surfaces and the known, as well as in the concluding questions, the sense of the "I" conveyed is of a self mentally alert and sensually attached to the facts. Such qualities, of course, could be part of a poem. But Joyce's own aesthetic presumptions about the nature of verse would not allow them. In prose he could invent his own aesthetics, and not be subject to an inherited set, those that in a sense defined Stephen Dedalus. In a certain sense, *Chamber Music* might be seen as charting some of the limits of Joyce's own identification with Stephen. In prose, the poet of essences becomes the painter of accidents, enabling his imagination—in a way verse as he conceived of it and practised it could not— fully to realise itself. (What verse enabled his imagination to realise, and to begin, was its engagement with language, with tradition, with the idea of narrative—things other than itself.)

In rich and various ways, then, *Chamber Music* is, as he says himself, the beginning of Joyce's "expression of myself" that proceeds through the great works in prose. And valuable and informative (and in its own terms successful) as it is, the accent must always fall on its being a beginning. In it, "the poet Joyce" dedicated himself and discovered his limits, and it brought him nearer to being that quite different creature, the writer Joyce. But it is in the triple dedication represented by *Chamber Music*—to language and craft, to tradition, to narrative—that the fundamental structure of Joyce's imagination is established, and it is by means of this structure that the "writer" becomes truly, in those great works of his maturity, his own early *image* of "the poet," whose life was intense, "taking into its centre the life that surrounds it and flinging it abroad again amid planetary music." From chamber music to planetary music: in such a light, perhaps, it is possible to see the whole career, that life in art, as no more nor less than the ramifying redefinition of "the poet Joyce."

1990

NOTES

[1] James Joyce, *Selected Letters*, ed. Richard Ellmann (New York: Viking, 1975) 26-7, 181.

[2] Richard Ellmann, *James Joyce* (Oxford University Press, new and revised edition, 1982) 127.

[3] Quoted in Ellmann, 479.

[4] I'm thinking especially of "I Hear an Army" in *Chamber Music* and "A Memory of the Players in a Mirror at Midnight," in *Pomes Penyeach*.

[5] *Selected Letters,* 160-61.

[6] *Ibid*, 161.

[7] *Ibid*, 180, 190, 192.

[8] Ellmann, 381.

[9] James Joyce, *Letters*, ed. Richard Ellmann, vol. III (New York: Viking, 1966) 6.

[10] For these and subsequent quotations from reviews, see *Letters*, II, 333.

[11] *Ibid*, 219, 182.

[12] See Oxen of the Sun chapter in *Ulysses* (New York: Random House, 1946) 408.

[13] James Joyce, *Giacomo Joyce* (New York: Viking, 1968) xviii.

[14] William York Tindall, in *Poetry*, 80 (May 1952) 107.

[15] *Chamber Music*, ed. with Introduction and Notes by William York Tindall (New York: Columbia University Press) 1954.

[16] Chester G. Anderson, "Joyce's Verses," in *A Companion to Joyce Studies*, eds. Zack Bowen and James F. Carens (Westport, Connecticut, and London: Greenwood Press, 1984) 129-55. Boyle's essay is in *Women in Joyce*, eds. Suzette Henke and Elaine Unkeless (Chicago: University of Illinois Press, 1982) 3-30.

[17] *Chamber Music*, 88.

[18] *Letters*, II, 217.

[19] *Ibid*, 13.

[20] *Ibid*, 333.

[21] J. F. Byrne, *The Silent Years* (New York: Octagon, 1953) 63-4.

[22] *Chamber Music*, 108.

[23] *Stephen Hero*, (Norfolk, Connecticut: New Directions, 1963) 32.

[24] Ellmann, 50-51, 80ff.

[25] *Ibid*, 81.

[26] *Ibid*, 76, and *Letters*, II, 333. The critic was Tom Kettle.

[27] Stanislaus Joyce, *My Brother's Keeper* (New York: Viking, 1958) 142.

[28] See Ellmann, 83, 121.

[29] For Jonson, see Boyle, 23, and Herbert Gorman, *James Joyce* (New York: Rinehart, 1948) 116.

[30] See Tindall, *Chamber Music*, 31; Boyle, 22-3; Anderson, 138.

[31] See Ellmann, Tindall, Boyle, and Anderson, *passim*.

[32] James Joyce, *Critical Writings*, eds. Richard Ellmann and Ellsworth Mason (London: Faber and Faber, 1959) 80.

[33] Along with echoes from Yeats, the Elizabethans, and "The Lady of Shallott." See *Chamber Music*, 187.

[34] *Ibid*, 221.

[35] Anderson, 147.

[36] *My Brother's Keeper*, 148.

[37] *Stephen Hero*, 36.

[38] *Letters*, II, 237.

[39] *Chamber Music*, 102; Letters, II, 259.

[40] *Chamber Music*, 25.

[41] Many of Gregan's poems are crammed with such features of landscape, mythology, and mood.

[42] *Stephen Hero*, 174.

[43] *Dubliners*, (New York: Viking, 1961) 74.

[44] In one of the poems of *Sunset Town* (40).

[45] *Letters*, II, 219.

[46] *Ibid*, 182. That it is this particular story he mentions (with its subtext of poetic politics) is revealing.

[47] *Chamber Music*, 44.

[48] *Ibid*, 47.

[49] *Ibid*.

[50] *Letters*, II, 27.

[51] Ellmann, 262.

[52] Boyle, 28. His descriptive analysis, on which I have liberally drawn, is most instructive and helpful.

[53] *Selected Letters.*
[54] *Letters*, II, 219.
[55] Ellmann, 266.
[56] *Ibid*, 150.
[57] *A Portrait of the Artist as a Young Man*, (New York: Viking, 1972) 70-1.
[58] *Stephen Hero*, 78.
[59] In *The Workshop of Daedalus*, eds. Robert Scholes and Richard M. Kain (Evanston, Illinois: Northwestern University Press, 1965) 49.

Language and Politics:
A Note on Some Metaphors in Spenser's
A View of the Present State of Ireland

As a sonnet sequence like Sidney's *Astrophel and Stella* or as any of Shakespeare's plays will show, the problem of the relationship between language and reality is very much alive in the late sixteenth and early seventeenth centuries. It is "words, words, words," that Hamlet reads; Troilus tears up the letter from Cressida because it is "words, words, mere words, no matter from the heart"; Cordelia is banished because she "cannot heave her heart into her mouth" as her sisters can; and Lear's pilgrimage carries him from the elaborate language of Titans to the simple acknowledgement of "fair daylight," "I feel this pin prick," and "Be your tears wet?"

An especially revealing version of the problem appears in the relationship between political actuality and the language used to talk about it. In *Julius Caesar*, Shakespeare provides a paradigm for this in Brutus's remarkable meditation upon the reasons for killing Caesar (2.1.10-34).[1] Throughout his soliloquy the philosophic assassin again and again abuses logic, not only in the shifting moods of the verbs, but also in the particular use to which certain metaphors are put. "It is the bright day that brings forth the adder," thinks Brutus, "And that craves wary walking." On one level the observation is a cluster of undeniable facts. As Brutus's next words make clear, it also functions as deliberate trigger to metaphor: "Crown him that, / And then I grant we put a sting in him." Caesar has become a venomous serpent, and his assassination logically follows this metamorphosis:

> And therefore think him as a serpent's egg
> Which, hatch'd, would as his kind grow mischievous,
> And kill him in the shell.

Buttressed by metaphor, political theory can enter the world of political fact with profound, logical simplicity: "Therefore . . . kill him."

By means of a biological-zoological figure, Brutus convinces himself of the necessity of a supposedly analogous political act. The metaphor functions implicitly as argument, drawing one unobtrusively between areas that are not in point of fact related. This moment and the dramatic action of *Julius Caesar* as a whole cast ironic shadows on Brutus's character and its decisions, shadows that throw into telling relief the troubled relationship between political action and a certain kind of rhetoric. As literary critics we may easily assess this fact and speak of it in the comfortable idioms of literary judgement and interpretation. A recent reading of Spenser's *View of the Present State of Ireland*, however, was a salutary reminder to me of the existence of this fact in the world beyond the specifically "literary." Reading Spenser's pragmatic account of the political-military campaign and his plan for a successful conclusion to the whole Elizabethan "Irish Question," I was struck by the way his use of some extremely conventional metaphors (conventional in political discourse, that is) did not so much illustrate the situation as compose a justifying "ground" for the political enterprise as a whole. And while no such calculated ironies as those that alert us to the difficulties of Brutus's position can be supposed to operate in Spenser's text, I was further struck by the fact that *these metaphors themselves* exposed inherent difficulties regarding the use to which Spenser wished to put them, difficulties serious enough to suggest that the view of the world out of which they grow—essentially a world view finding its expression in a certain sort of political theory, a theory that justifies the colonial enterprise—is not in necessary accord with the world of political fact to which they are applied.

I

The metaphors in question are drawn from two related areas—the agricultural and the medical. They deal with the natural world and the human body, and use both in a conventional way as similitudes for certain aspects of the state. Edward Forset in 1606 provides a clear statement of the assumptions on which, for the common understanding of the late sixteenth century, such conventional associations rest:

> Seeing that the uttermost extent of mans understanding, can shape no better forms of ordering the affayres of a State, than by marking and matching of the workes of the finger of God, eyther in the larger volume of the universall, or in the abridgement thereof, the body of man: I account these two to be the two great lights for enquiry and meditation concerning this business [of government].[2]

The appearance of such metaphors in a work like the *View*, therefore, is in no way unexpected. Their very conventionality, however, often blinds to what they are actually *doing*. Such blindness has a particularly serious consequence in a work that is not theoretical but practical, a "view," as the title insists, of the *present state* of Ireland, "by way of conference," as Irenius (Spenser's *persona*) says, "to declare my simple opinion for redress thereof, and establishing a good course for that government."[3] The aim of Spenser's text, therefore, is prescriptive, its metaphors part of a strategy of persuasion, its language an instrument of the colonial enterprise.

Spenser's use of the agricultural metaphor is implicitly justified by his re-current presentation of the Irish as being in a state of wild nature that needs cul-tivation to perfect it. Ireland is always "that savage nation" (91), its people "stubborn and untamed" (4), of "savage life" (156) and "brutish behaviour" (156); they exist in a "beastly manner of life and savage condition" (82-83). Even the Irish moustache (the "glib") bears the marks of a "savage brutishness" (53). It is an easy transition from here to the metaphorical notion of the Irish as uncultivated ground in which a civil state must be planted, a notion appearing incidentally and generally throughout the work. Henry II decided to "plant a peaceable government" among the Irish rather than to "pluck them under" by force (10). There is talk of "planting of laws and plotting of policies" (12), as well as of the fact that "without first cutting off this dangerous custom, it see-meth hard to plant any sound ordinance" (9). The general plan for the estab-lishment of a proper (i.e., English) political system, involves—in the elaborate blueprint for colonization and plantation—a return to literal fact of this particu-lar metaphor.

Apart from its obviously conventional nature, an important if unconscious motive for the use of this metaphor must lie in its essentially benevolent impli-cations. Husbandry is a pacific art, thriving on peace: "Bella execrata colonia— it is most enemy to war and hateth unquietness" (157).[4] In tune with nature, husbandry is also a sufficient sign of the providential moral order as this is re-flected in the order of nature. The state is purified to its ideal condition by the implications of this metaphor, as the emblematic (even if contextually ironic) garden scene in *Richard II* shows. It is by husbandry that the brigands of Book VI of *The Faerie Queene* are to be redeemed, just as the thieves, rebels, villains, and "patchocks" among the Irish will be drawn by the "sweetness and happy contentment" of husbandry away from "their wonted lewd life in thiefery and roguery" (157). Lurking behind the plant metaphor is the unexamined assump-tion that the relationship between the Irish and the English parallels that be-tween the husbandman and his land. A consequence of this figure is the right assumed by one group of people to establish an ordering and, from their point of view, productive mastery over another group. The extension of the metaphor to the animal world brings this notion of the natural right to rule into even sharper focus.

As with the plant metaphor, practical justification for the animal metaphor may be found in Irenius's description of the Irish. Many of the Irish, says Iren-ius, are accustomed "to live themselves the most part of the year in Bollies, pasturing upon the mountains and waste wild places . . . to live in herds as they call them" (49). The very houses of the Irish, he asserts elsewhere, "commonly are rather swinesteads than houses," where the Irishman is to be found "lying and living with his beast in one room and in one bed, that is the clean straw, or rather the foul dunghill" (82-83). Armed with such facts (though they seem dis-putable—which is it, after all, "clean straw" or "foul dunghill"?), the writer can make an easy transition to his figurative treatment of the Irish as animals, the negative connotations of which are clear from the following examples. The presence of the governor among the governed is "a great stay and bridle to them that are ill disposed" (132). The Hibernicised Normans are condemned as "proud hearts" who "do oftentimes like wanton colts kick at their mothers," and who have bitten "off her dug from which they sucked life" (65). A similar critical purpose is clear in the description of the Irish living in the hills, who "think themselves half exempted from law and obedience, and having once tasted freedom do, like a steer that hath been long out of his yoke, grudge and repine ever after to come under rule again" (50).

The assumptions underlying this group of metaphors concern the presumed hierarchical order of natural subordination. Because man—according to this figure—is the apex and epitome of creation, it is his natural, God-given right to subdue to his own ends the creatures of the earth. Since the divinely imbued "principall" of the horse, for example, "is a loving and dutifull inclination to the service of man,"[5] it is man's natural and, given this particular world view, moral right to curtail the freedom of such beasts in order to put them to the use for which God intended them. So, by means of the syllogism implicit in a metaphor which invokes a certain kind of world order, the governing power claims a natural right to act upon the freedom of a subordinate (albeit unwilling) people. The metaphor, therefore, is a purposeful rhetorical gesture extending far beyond its merely illustrative function. In this metaphorical language, the political commitment becomes as persuasive, authoritative, and value-laden as the natural truth sanctioned by belief.

A distinguishing feature of this metaphorical language is its adaptability, moving the reader unhindered between *natural* and *moral* categories. Morally neutral in the context of horse, both "wanton" and "ill-disposed" take on moral overtones in the human world. In the longer of the above quotations, the moral language of "law and obedience" as used in the human world becomes a physical language of "yoke" as used in the animal world (trailing some allegorical edges that enable it also to function in the moral human world), which in turn becomes the more abstract and explicitly political "rule," a word at home in either world. By means of such plasticity of language, the *justice* of a specific kind of rule in the political world has been persuasively presented in the colors of a simple truth drawn from the natural world. The ambiguous, questionable political enterprise is guaranteed by the unarguable natural facts: metaphor has become moral argument.

Spenser's use of the (medical) metaphor of the body politic may be seen in a similar light. In substance the metaphor presents the Irish state and its members as a diseased body, casting the English governors in the role of physicians. In general and incidental usage, the metaphor may be found throughout the *View*. Laws are constantly likened to physic. Their administration is as problematic as the treatment of an illness, which often

> either through ignorance of the disease, or unseasonableness
> of the time, or other accidents coming between, instead of
> good it worketh hurt, and out of one evil, throweth the patient
> into many miseries. (3)

A law can be "too violent a medicine" (32); it can be "very evil surgery," and overzealously "cut off every unsound or sick part of the body, which being by other means due recovered, might afterwards do very good service to the body again, and happily help to save the whole" (81).

But the most virulent disease of the body politic is rebellion. During Lord Grey's time, says Irenius, "there was no part free from the contagion" (19). To settle (cure) a state afflicted by such an illness, the whole task of government is to prescribe and then apply what amounts to a complete medical regimen:

> the which method we may learn of the wise physicians which require that the malady be known thoroughly and discovered, afterwards do teach how to cure and redress it, and lastly do prescribe a diet with strait rules and orders to be daily observed, for fear of relapse into the former disease or falling into some other more dangerous than it. (2-3)

When one governor altered the administrative system of his predecessor, this "manner of government could not be sound and wholesome for the realm" argues Irenius. For it is, he goes on, "even as two physicians should take one sick body in hand at two sundry times, of which the former would minister all things meet to purge and keep under the body, the other to pamper and strengthen it suddenly again" (109).

Employed politically, this metaphor, like its agricultural counterpart, tacitly sanctions the colonial enterprise. Both grow out of the assumption that within the exactitude and economy of God's creation the state is an organic body analogous in its composition to the natural world and to the human body. Just as God cured and colonised chaos so as to bring from it the healthy, orderly body of this universe, and just as the physician brings the patient's diseased body— that little world—to health, so the wise governor leads the body politic from the chaos of rebellion, the sickness of state, to the healthy, rational order of *his* political system. Therefore, it is natural, rational, and moral for the governing power to colonise the sick and savage state. Political colonisation, a phenomenon with ethical implications, is obliquely guaranteed by a rhetorical conjunction that ignores the gap between biological fact and political opinion. As with those drawn from the agricultural world, this metaphor also functions as a rhetorically purposeful purification of the adversary relationship between one political group and another. Metaphor has again become the agent of moral justification, and what is an essentially linguistic reality functions with a clear conscience as the instrument of actual political oppression.

II

The preceding examples illustrate the ordinary and, as it were, theoretical use of these metaphors in the *View*. It is clear, however, that so used they ignore some inherent difficulties. A few of these have already been noted; I now turn to the more serious among them.

Difficulties attending the use of the animal metaphor are of a fairly simple kind. They may be adequately illustrated by the following quotation: "But what boots it," asks Irenius,

> to break a colt and to let him straight run loose at random? So were this people at first well handled and wisely brought to acknowledge allegiance to the kings of England, but being straight left unto themselves and their own inordinate life and manners, they eftsones forgot what before they were taught, and so soon as they were out of sight by themselves shook off their bridles and began to colt anew, more licentiously than before. (6)

The unspoken purpose of this metaphor is to establish a persuasively negative attitude towards "this people." The introductory rhetorical question invites easy agreement with an unarguable truth about the natural world. Then the "so" and the "well handled" translates "this people" into a metaphorical "colt." By doing this, the speaker immediately casts his political opinion into the form of a natural fact, namely, the hierarchical subordination of animal to man. Translated into such a context, the political (and moral) *opinions* embedded in the adjectives and adverbs ("well," "wisely," "inordinate," "licentiously") become as persuasive as the natural beliefs invoked by the metaphor. In such a context, too, positive value attaches to passive forms of the verb ("handled," "brought," "taught"), while the active forms all possess negative overtones ("run loose at random," "forgot," "shook off," "colt"). While these are acceptable in the assumed hierarchical world of human-animal relationships, in the political world to which we are to apply them they serve as a rhetorical argument in favor of the right of one people to deprive another of its freedom.

In spite of its linguistic energy, however (for example, "colt" used as a verb), this metaphor buckles a bit when applied to the world of political actuality. In words like "inordinate" and "licentiously," for example, the more usual moral human meaning outweighs to the point of eliminating the simple physical significance attaching to such words in an equestrian context. In addition, while it is easy to say what "handled" and "bridles" mean in this latter context, it is difficult to establish their *precise* meanings in the world of political action to which they metaphorically refer. And it is this very imprecision which blurs such moral considerations as might attend the exercise of force for political ends.

The problems involved with Spenser's use of the plant metaphors are even more revealing and sinister in their implications. When Eudoxus asks how the necessary task of reformation can be started, Irenius replies:

> Even by the sword, for all those evils must first be cut away
> with a strong hand before any good can be planted, like as the

> corrupt branches and the unwholesome boughs are first to be
> pruned, and the foul moss cleansed or scraped away, before
> the tree can bring forth any good fruit. (95)

Beginning in the hard world of political fact ("sword"), the statement quickly
softens into the metaphorical idiom of political theory. The state is a tree, the
military governor a wise husbandman. The plastic language of the metaphor enables the speaker to deal with political actuality in terms of moral abstraction
("evils," "corrupt," "foul," "good") and agricultural concreteness ("branches,"
"boughs," "moss," "fruit"), both of which draw attention away from whatever
difficult associations might adhere to "sword." The sword is metaphorically
beaten into a pruning knife and its violent implications disappear into the natural
biological benevolence of an act done for the benefit of the tree. The metaphor
translates the actual world into a world of theoretical design. That the metaphor
encounters difficulty in the world of political actuality, however, is obvious not
only at our clarifying distance but also to the other participant in the dialogue.
Eudoxus refers to this solution as a violent "medicine." He then resists the preceding benign translation of sword: "Is not the sword the most violent redress
that may be used for any evil?" he asks. That Spenser, although his own *persona* is Irenius, includes this interrogation at all suggests that he is at least aware
of the critical pressure on this particular use of the metaphor. What follows,
therefore, looks like the most obvious attempt on his part to validate one of the
important rhetorical components of his text. Forced to justify his means, he
turns to the language he has used. "By the sword which I named," he says,

> I do not mean the cutting off of all that nation with the sword,
> which far be it from me that ever I should think so desperately
> or wish so uncharitably, but by the sword I mean the royal
> power of the prince, which ought to stretch itself forth in her
> chief strength, to the redressing and cutting off of those evils
> which I before blamed, and not of the people which are evil;
> for evil people by good ordinance and government may be
> made good, but the evil that is of itself evil will never become
> good. (95)

Like Shakespeare's Brutus debating the assassination of Caesar, Irenius is obviously at great pains to make the language mean what he wants it to mean, to
have it bend the world to a shape and a meaning corresponding to his desire and
need. But Irenius's growing difficulty appears in the increasingly theoretical
nature of his language. Instead of being comfortably embodied in the metaphor
of the state as a tree, the theory he proposes is expressed with much more difficulty (and less conviction) by the abstract distinctions between "evil people"
and "the evil that is of itself evil," or in the equally abstract, almost emblematic
identification between the "sword" and the "royal power of the prince." But the
struggle implicit here between fact and a certain sort of language remains unre-

solved by such a strategy. For on Eudoxus' demand for clarification of "that sword which you mean" (which has already been changed into "the royal power of the prince"), the sword is further transformed into "a strong power [company] of men" (95). The passage as a whole, therefore, reveals a rhetorical progression from fact (sword) to metaphor (pruning knife) to abstraction (royal power) back to fact (strong power of men), meaning many swords. In the same circular way, the factual "evils" first mentioned by Irenius (referring to the actual "troubles" of fomenting "rebellion," see 94) become in turn the metaphorical "corrupt branches" and "unwholesome boughs," then the abstract "evil that is of itself evil," which in a subsequent passage joins the world of fact again and becomes "all that rebellious rout of loose people which either do now stand out in open arms or in wandering companies do keep the woods spoiling and infesting the good subject" (95-96).

Such linguistic juggling shows that the metaphorical language proper to and acceptable in a rhetoric of theory and belief cannot endure in the more problematic context of political fact. By this point, therefore, it's clear that the discussion must center (implicitly and/or explicitly) on the applicability of a certain kind of language to a certain kind of fact. Perhaps the strongest proof that such applicability is in serious doubt is that it is precisely at this stress-point that Irenius abandons the metaphorical rhetoric of *belief* and resorts to the rhetoric of prescriptive *fact*. He turns, that is, to the cooler, more convincing medium of numbers, pragmatic tactics, and considerations of an entirely practical kind (see 96 ff, which are full of numbers of men, amounts of money). In other words, the benevolent ideal embodied by the original metaphor must bend to the practical necessities of a military campaign, for coping expressively with which the rhetoric of fact is perfectly adequate. The unacknowledged irony, however (an irony dramatically uncovered by Shakespeare in Brutus's speech but essentially evaded by the way Spenser conducts his debate), is that the implicit philosophical-ethical guarantor of this political campaign is the *failed* metaphorical rhetoric itself. And it is, as we have seen, the view of the world locked into these metaphors that sanctions and justifies this particular kind of political enterprise. At its deepest level, then, Spenser's struggle here suggests the difficulties and contradictions inherent in any attempt to talk about contemporary political actuality in the idiom of traditional political (and, in a larger sense, cultural) belief.

The medical metaphor itself provides the final illustration of these difficulties. In traditional political theory the governor's need to rule by punishment is often likened to the doctor's need to hurt the body in order to heal it. "To conclude this point of health," says Edward Forset in a section entitled "We may hurt to heale,"

> it is so precious and of so unvaluable a worth, as that when it
> is not so perfect as wee would have it, or when it is somewhat
> impaired, we do not stick willingly to do to our selves farther
> hurt, to the end to heale our infirmities the more soundly. . . .
> So in our bodie of the Commonweale it is not to be disliked,
> that (though there be no great fault found, and all things

> seeme to stand in good order) yet now and then physicall
> courses be used, by opening some veine, by purging of super-
> fluities, and putting to payne some part thereof, for the more
> certeintie of the generall good.[6]

Since the "body politic" is a bloodless fiction, such a similitude (drawn from
verifiably correct facts) in theory is perfectly appropriate. Used in the actual
context assumed by the *View*, however, the moral propriety as well as the accuracy and applicability of the metaphor is open to question. According to the
narrative of the *View*, the body politic that is Ireland has—because of a change
in physician/governors—suffered a "most dangerous relapse" and is "now more
dangerously sick than ever before" (109). Within the confines of theory the kind
of surgical rigour necessary to cure such a condition is easily acceptable. It develops problems, however, in the actual world evoked by Spenser's text. Having
described the country as "one sick body" and its governors as "physicians"
(109), Irenius goes on to say:

> Therefore, by all means it must be foreseen and assured that
> after once entering into this course of reformation, there be
> afterwards no remorse or drawing back, for the sight of any
> such rueful object as must thereupon follow nor for compas-
> sion of their calamities, seeing that by no other means it is
> possible to recure them and that these are not of will, but of
> very urgent necessity. (110)

Because of what turns out to be an essential contradiction between the substance
and meaning of this metaphor, the above passage reveals the breakdown in
functional capacity of this kind of rhetoric used in an actual political context.
First, under the pressure of the actual situation, the speaker alters his earlier
medical terminology to the more explicitly political "course of reformation."
Then, in place of a diction expressive of the natural distaste a doctor feels for
the pain he must inflict, he uses a language bespeaking qualms of a rather different kind: "remorse," "drawing back," and "compassion" carry overtones that
move beyond the physical and into the ethical area. "Rueful object," and
"calamities" remove us even further from the comfortable confines of the exclusively medical metaphor, while the plural "their" and "them" unconsciously
translates the "one sick body" politic mentioned earlier into the multiple bodies
of those members of the state who must be killed. In the context of such obvious
difficulties, the return to the pure state of the metaphor in the explicitly medical
"recure" (especially with "them" as object) is strikingly (and unintentionally)
ironic. For in its mutations the metaphor simply alerts us to the fact that its
metaphorical and actual content are contradictory—one signifying restoration to
health, the other deprivation of life. (A much more recent version of this is, I
guess, the infamous "we had to destroy the village to save it.")

The question remains as to how conscious Spenser was of the kinds of difficulty I'm talking about. Even from the internal evidence of the above passage it seems to me that, while he was not unaware of the problem, he chose (presumably because of the nature of his particular task) to ignore, evade, or (which may amount to the same thing) arbitrarily resolve it. For the passage is riddled with gestures of assertive logicality, from the conclusive "therefore" that initiates it, to the indisputable insistence of "as must thereupon follow" and "seeing that by no other means it is possible." In addition, the speaker also appeals to the transcendent logic of some enforcing fate, allowing "will" (presumably the governor's) to abdicate to "very urgent necessity." It is not the only time in the course of this entire argument that such appeals are made (see, for example, 105, 106, 108). Their frequency, in fact, brings to mind Milton's description of necessity as "the tyrant's plea." As far as the above quotation is concerned, it is also hard not to be reminded again of Shakespeare's Brutus, who begins his examination of the possible reasons for Caesar's murder with the conclusive "It must be by his death," and who proceeds from there to extract justification from some instrumental metaphors.

What happens in the text immediately following the passage I have examined above may be read as confirmation of my argument. For, as with the agricultural metaphors, the hint of the failure or insufficiency of this kind of rhetoric pushes the discussion into pragmatism, into the rhetoric of fact. In this instance the movement is to Eudoxus' straightforward account of the actual problems to be confronted in administering the system. What betrays the strategy as an evasive one is the oddly abrupt way it elbows into the text, without any obvious transition between it ("Thus far then ye have now proceeded to plant your garrisons" [110]) and the passage I have already quoted which it immediately follows. In addition, the actual problems mentioned by Eudoxus are revealing. These mainly consist of the "corruption of captains," a corruption in no way metaphorical but referring to the simple fact of embezzlement. This leads in turn to a practical account of the duties and responsibilities of the colonel in preventing such corruption, and comes to rest, again, in numbers (110-11). Where metaphor falters as the agent of moral justification, the text resorts to the indisputable rhetoric of fact uncomplicated by any moral considerations whatsoever.

III

By analysing one of the rhetorical components of Spenser's text in this way, I have tried to suggest something of the condition and viability at a particular historical moment of certain ways of talking about political experience. This, in turn, is a small but important feature in a larger shift in cultural sensibility concerning the relationship between language and the world, a concern to be found in many explicitly literary texts of the period. Michel Foucault describes this culture shift in part as follows: "The profound kinship of language with the world was thus dissolved. . . . Things and words were to be separated from one another."[7] Dealing as it does with a non-literary text, my discussion may afford some insight into the reasons for Bacon's impatience with certain schematic modes of thought as these are represented in a rhetoric that obfuscated instead of clarifying the world of things, of nature. For "the human understanding," laments Bacon, is

> prone to suppose the existence of more order and regularity in the world than it finds. And though there be many things in nature which are singular and unmatched, yet it devises for them parallels and conjugates and relatives which do not exist.[8]

Spenser's use of certain metaphors in *View* betrays not only this unfortunate human tendency, but the practical injustice that follows from its operation in the realm of politics and, more specifically, in the whole (contaminated) enterprise of colonisation. That the poet of *The Faerie Queene*, in his capacity as a colonial civil servant, shows himself in *A View of the Present State of Ireland* to be a comparatively uncritical employer of such language may provoke us to consider in an even more thoughtful way the rhetorical, aesthetic, historical, and moral assumptions that inform his immeasurably more important poetic text.

1982

NOTES

[1] *The Riverside Shakespeare*, ed. G. Blakemore Evans et al. (Boston: Houghton Mifflin, 1974).

[2] Edward Forset, "To the Reader," *A Comparative Discourse of the Bodies Natural and Politique* (London, 1606; rpt. New York: Da Capo Press, 1973) 2.

[3] Edmund Spenser, *A View of the Present State of Ireland*, ed. W. L. Renwick (Oxford: Clarendon Press, 1970) 169. Subsequent references will be given in the text.

[4] *Colonia* shows how this metaphor stands as justifying agent at the very heart of the colonial enterprise—politics moralized by etymology.

[5] Edward Topsell, *The Historie of Foure-Footed Beastes* (London, 1607; rpt. New York: Da Capo Press, 1973), 281.

[6] Forset, *Comparative Discourse*, 70.

[7] Michel Foucault, *The Order of Things: An Archeology of the Human Sciences* (London: Tavistock, 1966) 43.

[8] Francis Bacon, *Novum Organum*, Book 1, aphorism 45, in *The Works of Francis Bacon*, ed. James Spedding, Robert L. Ellis, and Douglas D. Heath, vol. 4 (London: Longman, 1901) 55.

"Little Room":
Bloom and the Politics of Space

> Out of Ireland have we come,
> Great hatred, little room
> Maimed us at the start.
>
> Yeats

> If I had a house of my own . . .
>
> Joyce to A.F. Bruni

On the 30th of October 1921, Joyce wrote to Valery Larbaud: "I finished *Ithaca* last night so that now the writing of *Ulysses* is ended."[1] Much of this chapter was written in Larbaud's own flat, a place Joyce lived in contentedly from June 3 to October 1. Two days after moving in, he said, "I begin to feel so comfortable that the episode of *Ithaca* is progressing rapidly. A more favourable place for the peaceful ending of such a tumultuous book could not be imagined."[2] This place was, he said to his friend Francini, "unbelievable. Behind the Pantheon, ten minutes from the Luxembourg, a kind of little park, with access through two barred gates, absolute silence, great trees, birds (not, mind you, the sort you're thinking of!), like being a hundred kilometers from Paris. The furnishings are tasteful."[3] His response to this haven of peace, stability and restoration, relieving him from what he lamented as "O this moving job!"[4] (he had moved four times in the previous eleven months), vividly illustrates Joyce's sensitivity to living space, his finely tuned awareness of place, displacement, home, homelessness. As an exile since 1904, when he had left Dublin with Nora Barnacle, his relations with space were—as a litany of his domiciles would show—complicated. "Joyce was a traveler by nature as well as necessity," says Ellmann; "when he had sufficiently complicated his life in one place, he preferred, instead of unraveling it, to move on to another, so that he piled involvement upon involvement." Given such a nature, as well as the various necessities that attended it, it should not come as a surprise that the hero of the novel Joyce is finishing in Larbaud's flat could himself be understood, at least in part, by the way he relates to the spaces he enters, inhabits, and leaves in the course of his odyssey through Dublin on June 16, 1904.

Certainly as *Ithaca* draws to a close, Joyce seems keen to situate Bloom with fastidious exactitude in various spaces. His position in the bed itself is given in geographical terms as "N.W. by W.: on the 53rd parallel of latitude, N. and 6th meridian of longitude, W.: at an angle of 45° to the terrestrial equator."[5]

His physical posture moves from geography to biology, being described as resembling "the manchild in the womb" (737). Thus located, in the large space of the world and the small first dwelling place of the womb ("he rests"), Bloom slides into sleep, and the last we literally see of him is in the large black dot that is offered as an answer to the final question, "Where?" The dot itself is interesting. First, since that question is unanswered, it leaves Bloom's whereabouts in sleep uncertain. Then it is something of a black hole in itself, a space minute and at the same time immense, small but dense, an exit through which Bloom leaves this novel and, presumably (or at least fancifully), enters the sleepworld of *Finnegans Wake*. The last we actually see of Bloom, that is, is as a spatial interrogative and its ambiguous answer. And what such a fact provokes in me as a reader is a curiosity about the other spaces he has been in and out of in the course of his day, and the manner of his being in them and out of them. The rest of my paper is devoted to a few thoughts on some of these spaces and their meaning for our understanding of the novel. For by presenting Bloom as he does at his exit, Joyce is apparently suggesting that in his relations with space he may be understood, at least some of his meaning may be found.

Content as he may appear at the start of the novel, as he potters about the kitchen making Molly's breakfast and pondering the Egyptian mysteries of the cat, it is soon apparent that Bloom's relationship with the various spaces of his own house is not an entirely comfortable one. There is a reiterated wariness in his movements about the kitchen, for example: "he moved about the kitchen softly," "on quietly creaky boots he went up the staircase," and "he said softly in the bare hall" (55-6). It is apparently Molly's presence that obliges Bloom, in part through his own caring nature, to inhabit this space almost as if it were not his own. Noticing he has not got his key he thinks of the "creaky wardrobe" and decides "no use disturbing her" (56). That he has forgotten the key to it, and forgets it again on his second exit, also suggests—in Freudian and other symbolic terms—some sense of dispossession, a sense that doesn't need too much nudging to show its sexual shadow. That we get such a sense *before* anything overt happens to cause Bloom peculiar discomfort in his habitation allows us to imagine that something in his own nature, native to his instinctive self, is in part responsible for the idiosyncratic relationship between him and his various spaces.

Back from his little bit of shopping, however, and at his first entrance into the bedroom, we begin to understand that Bloom's relationship with space also has a source quite outside himself. First there is his behavior, servant-like, in raising the blind, clearing the chair of "her striped petticoat, tossed soiled linen" (62), acquiescing to Molly's peremptory tones of command ("—Hurry up with that tea . . . Scald the teapot . . . What a time you were" [62]), all of which implies that the bedroom is her space, not his. Then there is the unspoken way he observes her "glance at the letter [he's brought] and tuck it under her pillow," the letter at the sight of which, in the hallway, "His quick heart [had] slowed at once . . . Bold hand. Mrs Marion" (61). From Boylan, the letter clearly contaminates this space for Bloom, usurping his rights of possession, setting up a stand-off in sexual politics, since neither he nor Molly acknowledges it, although each knows the other knows the other knows. She doesn't deny that the letter is from Boylan when he asks her, but no more is said. The potential site of peace has been transformed into a field of war, or at least of uncomfortable skirmishing. For this reason, probably, Joyce has Bloom beat something like a comic retreat from the bedroom when he remembers the frying kidney: "He fitted the book roughly into his inner pocket and, stubbing his toe against the broken commode, hurried out towards the smell, stepping hastily down the stairs with a flurried stork's leg" (65). Over the course of the whole day, until he returns to it after midnight, Bloom will remain tethered in intense discomfort to this space, from which he has, at this moment, been cast out.

This central contaminating—"politicising"—force of the forecast adultery also infects the other main room of the house, the kitchen, a room which in many ways is Bloom's native space. Reading the letter from his daughter in the kitchen, he is not only made anxious in a fatherly way for Milly's sexual safety, but also reminded of his own predicament by her mention of Blazes Boylan's song, a reference which immediately crystallises in Bloom's mind as "Seaside girls. Torn envelope" (67). Boylan has entered this space too ("tell him silly Milly sends her best respects," says the letter flirtatiously), and effectively usurped Bloom's place in it. As if to complete the contamination of the house— its pollution by an alien hostile presence that in a sense casts Bloom out, dispossesses him—his otherwise contented episode in the outside jakes ("Life might be so," he thinks about his untroubled bowel movement [69]) is fretted by thoughts of Molly's first meeting with Boylan, a memory that interrupts a leisurely flow of fancy about himself and Molly composing a "sketch" together for *Titbits*. Reminded of Boylan, however, he leaves this space in a hurry: "He tore away the prize story sharply and wiped himself with it . . . He pulled back the jerky door of the jakes and came forth from the gloom into the air" (70). Here, in a small way, is another image of retreat, finishing the *Calypso* chapter on the repeated note of dispossession, of hastily leaving a space taken over by a hostile force. It might not be too fanciful to say that Bloom's native spaces—spaces expressive of the body's need for nourishment, sex, sleep, evacuation—have been colonised by this hostile power in the realm of sexual politics, and that consequently his own present identity runs the risk of extinction. Such a condition is the hazard of colonisation, radically bound up with the issue of space. And Bloom's relationship with these domestic spaces shows how—though free in incidental ways (to feed the cat, to think his thoughts, to walk in the sun, to lust after the serving-girl next door)—he is not in control—as the colonised individual is never in control—of his own living space and living conditions.

Soon after he has left his own (rented) house Bloom visits the house of God. The Irish Roman Catholic God, that is. Going into All Hallows by "the open backdoor" (79), he "entered softly by the rear" (80), his circumspect manner of ingress echoing how he proceeds in his own house. It is Bloom's sense of himself as an outsider to this tribal Catholic space that is immediately stressed, an outsider observing the habits of the natives with naive wonder. First he reduces the instruments of conversion to a slightly comic status: "Crown of thorns and cross. Clever idea Saint Patrick the shamrock." Then he demystifies the

sacral element of Holy Communion: "Shut your eyes and open your mouth...
What? *Corpus*. Body. Corpse. Good idea the Latin. Stupefies them . . . Rum
idea: eating bits of a corpse why the cannibals cotton to it" (80). Later he notices, "Wine. Makes it more aristocratic than for example if he drank what they
are used to Guinness's porter" (81). Bloom's otherness is in focus here: the
mysteries of this religion, what creates this community, exclude him. Detached
by his mild skepticism, he can allow it is all a "Wonderful organisation, certainly. Goes like clockwork" (82-3), an allowance that reveals the essentially
political nature of that organisation: "Squareheaded chaps they must be in
Rome: they run the whole show. And don't they rake in the money too?" (83)
Clearly Bloom does not belong in this space: both priests and people are seen,
are felt as "they" (pronouns always being a barometer to insider/outsider status),
turning the whole institution into a single tribal community, an exclusive family
to which Bloom does not belong: "feel all like one family party . . . They do.
I'm sure of that. Not so lonely. In our confraternity" (81). He understands the
church, then—an institution for which this comfortable, enclosed, exclusive
space stands—in terms of community, confraternity, and family—constituent
elements and metaphors for a political unit from which he feels himself excluded, and feels in that exclusion some unspoken sense of his own solitude.
And as he was aware at his entrance of how the "the cold smell of sacred stone
called him" (80), he has at his exit an equally negative impression, of worship-
pers dipping "furtive hands in the low tide of holy water." And it is hard not to
see his departure from this space again as a kind of relieved escape (or retreat)
"down the aisle and out through the main door into the light" (83).

In the first two spaces we observe him in, then, the terms of Bloom's exclusion are political in the widest sense. Sexual politics excludes Bloom from
his own home; the space of the church is denied him on religious, cultural, even
(by implication, since this is Ireland) national grounds. Throughout the day,
these terms of exclusion will remain constant, as will the fact that his experience
may be understood—as it is here—in terms of the spaces he must enter and
leave.

Let me touch briefly on a few examples. The funeral carriage in *Hades* is
the very image of a tight-knit community, in which Bloom's discomfort stems
from how his three companions cordially salute Blazes Boylan, discuss suicide
from an insensitive Catholic point of view ("They have no mercy on that here or
infanticide," he thinks, remembering his father [96]), roughly smother his attempts to tell a funny story, treat him with incomprehension, or as a stranger to
"their" customs. The Glasnevin Cemetery itself—with its Protestant and Catholic graves, and its national monuments is the space for a tribal rite or a family
event, and while the other men stroll "round by the chief's [Parnell's] grave"
(112), Bloom, in the rear, walks alone, musing. And although it is his own
workspace, the newsrooms of *Aeolus*, too, exclude him from community: he
enters "softly," is ignored by the group, bumped into, hit by a doorknob, told by
the editor to "go to hell," pursued at his exit by newsboys' mimicry and mockery (of his Jewishness and his feminine walk), and is left behind when the
men—brimming with nationalist nostalgia and anecdotage—go off for a drink

together : "All off for a drink. Arm in arm," he thinks (147), aware as always of his own solitude and exclusion.

Burton's restaurant, where Bloom intends to have lunch, is another essentially hostile space. At his careful entrance ("His heart astir he pushed in the door"), he is made aware of repulsive realities: "Stink gripped his trembling breath: pungent meatjuice, slop of greens. See the animals feed. Men. Men. Men" (169). What greets him, in fact, is an extraordinary ordinary spectacle of men eating, grim with concentration, disgusting in their manners, "wolfing gobfuls of sloppy food." Associating male hunger with anger, and linking this with Irishness by a reference to Saint Patrick and "that last pagan king of Ireland Cormac in the schoolpoem [who] choked himself," Bloom's nature is repelled, and he retreats: "Get out of this. Out. I hate dirty eaters" (170). It is the mindless male violence of the spectacle, its frenzied individualism and vulgar egotism that have repelled him. And as he began with the image of a zoo, he ends with that of the jungle: "Eat or be eaten. Kill! Kill!" (170). Vulgar, violently male, the crowded, jostling space has no room for Bloom. Indifferently it expels him like a foreign body.

Without being overtly politicised, the implicit political point about Burton's is that it is a male tribal space, a carnivorous extravaganza that excludes Bloom because of his pacifism and taste. He is far from squeamish and no vegetarian, as we know, but the connection in this instance between meat-eating and more lethal male habits ("Kill! Kill!") is too much for him. In the vulgar conventional sense, he is not man enough. So he beats another retreat: "He backed towards the door. . . . He came out into the clearer air" (170). And even though he finds refuge, a cheese sandwich, and a glass of burgundy in Davy Byrne's "moral pub," when that space is turned into a traditional male community by the chattering, convivial entrance of Bantam Lyons, Tom Rochford, and Paddy Leonard, Bloom leaves: "Mr Bloom on his way out raised three fingers in greeting" (179), the speed of his exit suggested by the conjunction of "going" and "greeting." As Nosey Flynn has observed, Bloom "Slips off when the fun gets too hot," is never one to succumb to the tribal rites. Since, in Ireland, the pub— public house—along with the church (in Irish, *teach pobaill*, public house) was (is) the most important space for the conduct of these rites of community, Bloom's voluntary and involuntary exclusion from such spaces is the effective sign of his separation from that community.

Both the National Library (where he goes in quest of copy for his ad) and the Ormond Hotel (where he goes for a mid-afternoon dinner) are essentially communal, clubbish spaces to which Bloom does not belong. Both spaces signify elements of the dominant culture's inhospitality to him. In the Library, the Literary revival is in full swing ("*We* are becoming important, it seems [says AE] . . . Are *we* going to be read? I feel *we* are" [192, my italics]), and Stephen Dedalus is patenting his own pre-Deriddean brand of derisory deconstruction. In this space of high cultural community, Bloom is a distinctly marginalised figure, a "patient silhouette wait[ing], listening . . . a bowing dark figure following [Lyster's] hasty heels" (200). In addition, he is abused behind his back by Buck Mulligan's anti-semitism ("The sheeny!" [200]) and mocking homophobia, the latter another example of Bloom's sexual exclusion: "O, I fear me, he is Greeker than the Greeks . . . He looked upon you to lust after you . . . O, Kinch, thou art in peril. Get thee a breechpad" (217). Bloom's exit ("his dark back went before them. Step of a pard, down, out by the gateway, under porticullis barbs" [218]) is yet another retreat from a hostile space. And in the Ormond Hotel—with its flirtatious barmaids and its singing regulars—Bloom feels especially uncomfortable at the presence and exit of Blazes Boylan (who is very much at ease, at home here as he will be in Bloom's own bedroom). Again Bloom enters furtively, feeling like an outsider ("Sit tight there, see, not be seen" [265]). He is distressed by thoughts of the approaching encounter of Boylan and Molly, stung by the casual talk of Molly which he overhears, separate from the alcoholic conviviality of the men: "Pity they feel," he says of the response to the patriotic ballad, *The Croppy Boy*, again detaching himself from the national tribe. Like the last sardine on the plate, he is "Bloom alone" (289), and his urge, in another image of enforced flight from an inhospitable space, is to "Get out before the end" and to "walk, walk, walk . . . Freer in air" (286). In sexual and in national terms, then, Bloom is the conscious outsider in this space, *in* but no way *of* the sentimental ethos (both national and sexual) it represents.

All the exclusions so far practised covertly on Bloom by the spaces he enters and inhabits come to a head of explicit expression in *Cyclops*. A sense of insiders and outsiders is established at the very beginning of the anonymous narrative by its casual antisemitism. The public house itself, then, Barney Kiernan's (a sort of nationalist church), is occupied by a group that clearly constitutes a culture community. Bloom is reluctant to enter this space, hanging about outside and eventually "skeezing round the door" (303). He refuses a drink—which would include him in the community—but accepts a cigar, which ensures his remaining outside it. Seen from the angle of the cynical, street-smart narrator, it becomes rapidly apparent that this space is hostile to him in sexual and national/cultural/racial ways. His being cuckolded by Blazes seems common knowledge ("Blazes doing the tootle on the flute . . . That's the bucko that'll organise her" [319]), and his Jewishness allies him with a group the citizen sees as enemies of the nation—"Coming over here to Ireland filling the country with bugs . . . swindling the peasants and the poor of Ireland" (323). When the citizen alludes to Yeats's *Cathleen Ni Houlihan*—"We want no more strangers in our house"—the image of the house embodies as absolutely as possible the exclusiveness of this (monocular) nationalist vision: Ireland is a family space from which the likes of Bloom have to be excluded, for this house has only room for one kind of inhabitant, one kind of 'native', and certainly not for "Virag from Hungary!" (338). What was a political cry for action against the invader ("no more strangers in our house") becomes the verbal justification for repression of those who do not fit the single ethnic, cultural, religious, and political stereotype.

When, at the crux of the exchange, Bloom is asked what a nation is, he responds: "A nation is the same people living in the same place . . . or also living in different places" (331). This significantly spatial (as distinct from political) definition is mocked ("everyone had a laugh at Bloom"), and when the Jew adds that his nation is "Ireland . . . I was born here. Ireland," the citizen spits "a Red bank oyster out of him right in the corner." The spit is Bloom's sentence of exile and excommunication, his expulsion in nationalist terms from the community. It is also, covertly in the narrative, an allusion to Blazes Boylan, whose taste and fondness for Red Bank oysters was noted by Bloom in Davy Byrne's (175), thereby bringing the sexual and national politics of usurpation and exclusion together in one act of dismissive violence, a connection also made when the narrator imagines Bloom unable to function as a man, a soldier, but more likely as a woman ("Gob, he'd adorn a sweepingbrush, so he would, if he only had a nurse's apron on him" (333).

I'll consider Bloom's resistance to all this exclusionary violence later. Right now it is enough to point to the two exits he is obliged to make from this hostile space. The first happens suddenly, almost in mid-sentence, "and off he pops like greased lightning" (333). The second, more apocalyptic, is when Jack Power, Crofton and Martin Cunningham usher him out, and the citizen chases after him, calling "Three cheers for Israel" and "By Jesus, I'll crucify him, so I will"— hounding him with racism and religious oppression, and throwing the biscuit tin for good measure: "And the last we saw," says the narrator, "was the bloody car rounding the corner" in full retreat, the most explosive retreat of the novel so far, but one which simply confirms what's been happening in a more contained and covert but no less real way in Bloom's relationship with the other spaces he's been in and out of.

While the whole of nighttown—the *Circe* space of the redlight district—is a dangerous place for Bloom, and one where the nationalist exclusion is practised (he is called "as bad as Parnell," at one point, and *"Mother Grogan* [alias Mother Ireland] *throws her boot at him"*), the brothel house itself is where his sexual nature, always under threat, comes in for most abuse (making this space parallel to the scene in Kiernan's pub, the sexual equivalent of that national-ist/racial/cultural dispossession). As often happens, Bloom enters the space un-willingly, being drawn over the threshold by the prostitute, Zoe ("He hesitates. She . . . draws him over. He hops" [502]). Immediately, he thinks he sees Boy-lan's waterproof and hat on "the antlered rack of the hall" and so, aptly enough, it is in this scene that Bloom's sexual usurpation by Boylan is consummated. "There's a man of brawn in possession there," says Bello the brothelkeeper (541), underlining the loss of space, while Bloom imagines Boylan inviting him to watch his sexual antics with Molly, become a voyeur in his own house: "Thank you sir, I will sir. May I bring two men chums to witness the deed and take a snapshot?" (566). This is the nadir of Bloom's sexual dispossession, as the scene in Kiernan's was the nadir of his racial/cultural/ religious/national dispossession. After much such abuse, the reiterated insult to his masculinity is completed by his transformation to a woman ("I promise never to disobey" [531 ff]). In this gender transgression he is effectively cast out of this space, since the brothel is built on the lowest common denominator of (hetero)sexual politics. Eventually Bloom flees from the house ("I need mountain air"), and, as climax to all the flights he's had to make from all the hostile spaces he's been expelled from in the course of his day, he is pursued by many of the characters he's run into and afoul of since morning, including the Citizen and Garryowen. The Armageddon of the brothel is a final site of exclusion, brought to its crisis by Stephen's drunken act of smashing the lamp, when "Time's livid final flame leaps and, in the following darkness, ruin of all space, shattered glass and toppling masonry" (583). In this literal breaking up of space, we are invited to see, in symbolic terms, the final and absolute exclusion of Bloom. But from this moment, which he greets with the cry, "Stop!" (583), he is in truth on his way home, reclaiming and redeeming spaces as he goes.

II

In what we have so far seen, Bloom is represented as a victim in the realms of sexuality, nationalism, race, religion, and culture. Were he only a victim, however, the novel and his character would be simply pathetic; it would have a sentimental centre. Clearly that is not the case. On the contrary, Joyce seems to use the relationship between Bloom and these various spaces as the vehicle for larger meanings. I will now turn to what these might be. Basically, the questions to be asked are: How does Bloom in each case of exclusion deal with his circumstances? Does he transform the situation in any way by his response? In the exclusion from certain spaces can he forge another kind of space that somehow counteracts the loss?

In *Calypso*, as we saw, Bloom is usurped from his possession of bedroom, kitchen, and jakes by Molly's affair with Boylan. As well as pain and anxiety, however, he has another reaction. For he has, it seems, removed his daughter Milly from the scene, and for two reasons. The first is that she may be out of harm's way: "better where she is down there: away" (67). The second is to facilitate the affair itself, which is also the reason why he removes himself from the house for the course of the day, deliberately resisting the temptation to return. By his choices and his actions, then, Bloom opens up what I'd call a *moral* space that counteracts the loss of his living space as habitation. The moral space he opens up, of course, cannot be seen in conventional terms. It must simply be characterised as free and human. This humane freeing of the space he has himself been excluded from opens up a broader moral space of individual authenticity—unenclosed, enfranchised. Under these impossible circumstances, Bloom gains the spiritual distinction of acts that can be called altruistic. Such acts amplify the moral space, as the circumstantial and sexual home space is attenuated.

The exclusive church we've seen in *Lotos Eaters* is rendered tolerable in a number of ways. On the one hand Bloom sexualises the space: "Nice discreet place to be next some girl . . . Meet one Sunday after the Rosary" (80-81). On the other hand he aestheticises it by thinking of Church music and Molly's singing: "Some of that old sacred music is splendid" (82). On yet another hand, and most importantly, he responds to his own sense of exclusion and his own scepticism about the space and what it represents with a profound acknowledgement of the basic human condition that underlies it all, even more deeply than the political energies of organisation that turn it into an institution. And that condition is human loneliness. The moral space Bloom opens up on this site of his own exclusion is constructed around the fact that in the midst of an astringent and humorous analysis of the church as a political organisation, he can still sympathise with the even more deeply rooted motivating *human* impulse to belong, to be part of a family, to be "not so lonely" (81). In the space of his tolerant understanding, he is also able to see the other space in a positive light; he will not close himself off from that, he will allow it, just as he allows the church's ceremonial aspects, saying of the way the wine is used, "pious fraud but quite right . . . Perfectly right that is" (82). Cast out of the institutional space, then, Bloom composes a moral space that serves—without his necessarily intending it—as a kind of compensation for his loss.

In regard to each of the spaces earlier mentioned, some such transformation takes place, changing negative victimage into positive moral affirmation (*his* extended and various "Yes"). In the carriage, for example, Bloom's unspoken gratitude to Martin Cunningham's kindness, ("sympathetic human man he is" [96]) opens up the moral space by means of an exchange of human feeling, no less true for being obliged to silence. And in the cemetery itself, amidst the tribal evidences of a cult of death, Bloom enlarges that conventionally enclosing space in two ways: first by the calm and comically unflinching way he looks at death, puncturing such things as the clichés of consolation (105) and opening his own consciousness to the material facts; second by the franker moral gesture of a deliberate commitment to life: "The gates glimmered in front: still open. Back to the world again. Enough of this place . . . Let them sleep in their maggoty beds . . . Warms beds: warm fullblooded life" (114-5).

In the newsrooms of *Aeolus*, the moral space that Bloom opens up is constituted by the peculiarly beavering eagerness and seriousness with which he goes about his particular task of getting an ad. As in the Library episode, there is a peculiar generosity in the attention which Bloom grants to his own mundane enterprise, at odds with the other men's posturing nationalism, intellectualism, futility, and cynicism. The carnivorous Burton episode, with its implications of male violence, is countered by Bloom's openness to the sufferings of slaughtered animals: "Wretched brutes there at the cattlemarket waiting for the poleaxe to split their skulls open" (171). Openness to this sympathy and fellow-feeling, indeed, is what got him fired from the cattle dealer Cuffe's (where he'd worked ten years before), presumably because he had argued for more humane methods for dealing with the animals. As the cynical narrator of *Cyclops* says, "Humane methods. Because the poor animals suffer and experts say and the best known remedy that doesn't cause pain to the animal" (315). Bloom's pacifism, as well as his sense of community and continuity with the animal world, are central here: as a moral position they open up a space directly antithetical to the male violence of that "Kill! Kill!"—which terrible imperatives define the space inhabited by the "dirty eaters" of Burton's.

It is in *Cyclops* that Bloom has most actively to establish a positive counterforce to the energies of exclusion ranged against him, since these energies are so overt. The most notable thing about the chapter is that Bloom rises heroically (and comically) to the occasion. Doing so, he puts into action the moral substance that has been at his centre since the start, letting us see how the private virtues of tolerance and understanding, his plurality of perspectives, can actually operate in the world, can become a valid *political* alternative. Bloom's active resistance to bigotry in this antagonistic space, however, must also mean that by this time in the day he has become more and more sensitive to his own exclusion. (The last we saw of him was at the point where he knew the adultery had taken place, after which he went—unseen by us—to Dignam's house of mourning, where, presumably he also had his own mourning to do.) What he is hearing now becomes a kind of synopsis of all that has happened him, a revelation of the essential injustice underlying it, the hopelessness of it all.

It is at the point where the citizen spits out Bloom's expulsion from the group (332) that Bloom begins his positive assertion of a moral value contrary to those of which he has been and continues to be the victim. And that assertion is of his own *belonging*: "And I belong to a race too, says Bloom, that is hated and persecuted. Also now. This very moment. This very instant" (332). That he makes a specific space for himself incenses the others, since they want him helpless, cast out, excluded. Mentioning the slavery of his race, "sold off in Morocco like slaves or cattle," he insists on the *moral* dimension of this condition—beyond the narrower dimension of the political. So when the citizen asks, "—Are you talking about the new Jerusalem," Bloom can answer with startling simplicity, "—I'm talking about injustice." He goes on to expand this into a despairing formulation of the condition opposite to that which has been victimising him all day. He stumbles awkwardly into the language, but the space it opens up is grand, sufficient: "—But it's no use, says he. Force, hatred, history, all that. That's not life for men and women, insult and hatred. And everybody knows that it's the very opposite of that that is really life."

> —What? says Alf.
> —Love, says Bloom. I mean the opposite of hatred. I must go
> now, says he . . . (333)

Under the greatest exclusionary pressure, forced into the most confined enclosure, Bloom produces the broadest space imaginable, "that that is really life." And by creating a space for "men *and* women" he opposes the implicit sexism that is twin to the rabid nationalism of this hostile, jeering community. His opposition is as absolute as the words *love, hate, injustice*. He meets bigotry with a vision of tolerance, a space of human possibility, a space unavailable in the great hatred, little room of Barney Kiernan's—image of the larger Ireland outside its doors. And as he leaves this narrow space, Bloom is able to expand into a political/racial dimension, creating a world-space out of resounding names— Mendelssohn, Marx, Mercadante, Spinoza, Christ—rattling the exclusionary tactic of the citizen and company and reaching a dazzling climax in "Your God was a jew. Christ was a jew like me" (342). Trapped in the close sectarian space of the pub, Bloom opens up a subversive space of moral possibility that elides the borders between Jew and Christian, this one small gesture making a tolerable space for human beings to live in beyond the lethal enclosures of denial, intolerance, and exclusion. And for his gesture, for the courage of his convictions, for the way Bloom has forced us and the denizens of Kiernan's to at least confront if not cure the little rooms of hate we occupy, the secondary narrative rewards him by whisking him away from this space altogether, assuming him beyond the earth itself: "And they beheld Him, even Him, ben Bloom Elijah, amid clouds of angels ascend to the glory of the brightness at an angle of forty-five degrees over Donohoes in Little Green Street like a shot off a shovel" (345). Beyond the hatreds of Little Green Street and Little Britain Street (site of Kiernan's pub) Bloom is removed, transfigured, translated, into the largest space of that other, blessedly possible (and comic) world.

Finally, in the apocalyptic, Armageddon space of Nighttown, Bloom can oppose the negatively exclusionary hallucinations with positive ones of his own utopian power. He becomes "the world's greatest reformer" (481), his platform a model of political inclusiveness: "I stand for the reform of municipal morals and the plain ten commandments. New worlds for old. Union of all, jew, moslem and gentile. Three acres and a cow for all children of nature" (489). And, at the end of this episode, Bloom exercises his powers of sympathy and fellow-feeling in a practical way, keeping his balance in the charged political space between Stephen and the British soldiers. Standing guard over the fallen Stephen, he composes a picture of heroic attention that is both maternal and "manly," creating a space of inclusive generosity. Into this charged space the vision of his dead son, now eleven, can enter, a gift filling up the space of his fatherhood. As Bloom—wonderstruck and inaudible—calls, "Rudy!" space and time have for a moment been dissolved, and into the world he has opened up with his generosity another world has briefly entered. Containing a trinity of castaways, this small but morally ample space is in a figurative way the restoration of all the spaces politicised in the exclusionary idioms of power. Held in silence like a touching tableau, this last, small, assuaging space contains multitudes.

III

Given how often it is brought to our attention, it should not come as a surprise that Bloom's body is itself a force opposed to the spaces that have excluded him. His body is a site of freedom. In the course of the novel we see it perform a great many natural functions. Three of these, however, are of particular relevance. In the moment at the end of *Lotos Eaters* where he imagines himself in the bath, we have a good example of the way he reclaims his body for himself, redeeming it from the stigma of its own usurpation by the adultery of Molly and Boylan, and redeeming the anxiety of the bed itself. The bath accomplishes the literal and metaphorical restoration of his body:

> He foresaw his pale body reclined in it at full, naked, in a
> womb of warmth, oiled by scented melting soap, softly laved.
> He saw his trunk and limbs rippled over and sustained,

> buoyed lightly upward lemonyellow: his navel, bud of flesh:
> and saw the dark tangled curls of his bush floating, floating
> hair of the stream around the limp father of thousands, a lan-
> guid floating flower. (86)

The body-space of the bath purifies the contaminated bed and womb, and by mixing sexual imagery with the more primary image of birth and cleansing, this space purifies the spaces of the bedroom and the jakes. In its pure individualised hedonism the bath is beyond/before politics, as the body is, and in the freedom of the body Bloom asserts himself ("This is my body," he thinks, in a benignly blasphemous recognition), liberating himself from the sexual politics of which he is the victim.

At the end of *Sirens*, too, Bloom's body is an agent of freedom. Escaped from the uncomfortable space of the Ormond, from its sexual and cultural ex-clusivism, Bloom stops in front of a shop window displaying Emmet's speech from the dock. It reminds him of the seven last words of Christ, a piece of sa-cred music. Simultaneously the men in the bar are singing a nationalist senti-mental ballad. And just about this moment Blazes and Molly are making their own body music. Synchronic with all this hostile action, while reading Emmet's immortal words, Bloom gives a careful, drawn out, satisfying fart. What the fart insists on is how Bloom, exiled to the margins of the sexual and national com-munity, excluded and cuckolded, reclaims the space of his own body, sounding off against national pieties and emotional sentimentalities. Being at home in his own body, Bloom possesses a redemptive space; his body is its own saving grace.

Lastly, in *Nausicaa*, Bloom re-establishes and reclaims through masturba-tion the sexual freedom of his own body. His body, then, accepted without guilt, inhabited with candour, becomes an enfranchised space, physically anchoring those more distinctly moral spaces his reactive gestures have created. ("Did me good, all the same," he thinks; "Off colour after Kiernan's Dignam's"). What he has managed through masturbation is an unpossessive sharing of his body with another (Gerty after all was taking her pleasure too), a kind of pacifist's revenge on Molly. Recovering his own body, too, allows a clear-eyed benevolent rela-tionship with the world: it makes him tolerant of Molly's affair and of her going to Belfast with Boylan, even of the thought of Boylan paying her ("Why not? All a prejudice" [369]). It even redeems the anxiety of Boylan's song that has annoyed him since morning: "Those girls, those girls, those lovely seaside girls," he hums contentedly (371), for isn't Gerty, after all, his own seaside girl? Accepting the full space of his own body (as he told Molly he accepted hers), he smells his own semen, then amplifies into sympathy for women's bodies—his wife's, his daughter's, their periods, their pains (380). And this renewed altru-ism can extend even as far as a gesture of understanding and forgiveness to-wards the citizen: "Perhaps not hurt he meant" (380).

Bloom's body, then, is a primary site of redemptive space, anchoring the spirit. The same, of course, might be said of his mind, which is so staggeringly open to the world, is a space of such obvious democratic plenitude that it needs no illustration. What his mind represents, in fact, as counterpoint to the spaces which effectively silence him, is not a compensating interior monologue, as we usually say, but a space of perpetual dialogue, a dialogue with the world. In the pluralism of his attention he opens a space endlessly hospitable to the voices of the world, so even the most ordinary machine is "doing its level best to speak. That door too sllt creaking, asking to be shut. Everything speaks in its own way" (121). Everything does. And in Bloom's tolerant mind everything also receives precisely what the institutional spaces of his world deny him—a hearing. In his own physical and mental self, then, Bloom is a space that literally embodies values opposite to those politically determined value systems that exclude him.

IV

Following his Odyssean archetype, Joyce intended the last section of the book to be a homecoming. For this reason he set off the last three chapters as a section—a space—to themselves. In this closure that opens into affirmative possibility, we can find a renewed, even redemptive sense of space, one made possible by the tableau of protective generosity that, as I've said, concludes *Circe*.

The cabman's shelter of Eumaeus is "an unpretentious wooden structure" (621). In its austerity the shelter suggests something primary, primitive, a kind of ur-space in which a fresh start can be made. While one can easily imagine the negative circumstance if either were to enter this place alone, together Bloom and Stephen are safe in their own newly established community of companionship and conversation—in the space conversation opens up, of generous exchange. And by seating themselves "in a discreet corner," they create a space of even closer intimacy. Bloom's experience here becomes the main counterweight to what happened him in Barney Kiernan's. For, while the shelter is potentially a hostile environment—with its nationalist proprietor who "obviously had an axe to grind" (640), and its laconic Dubliners with their sexist jokes and nationalist posturings, Bloom may still safely hazard to Stephen his opinions of a reasonable connection between England and Ireland. The mutual space he and Stephen create within potentially hostile territory offers him, in other words, freedom of speech. He is free to speak, and the plain good sense of what he has to say is allowed. His political "philosophy" is guaranteed a hearing:

> —Of course, Mr Bloom proceeded to stipulate, you must look at both sides of the question. It is hard to lay down any hard and fast rules for right and wrong but room for improvement all round there certainly is though every country, they say, our own distressful included, has the government it deserves. But with a little goodwill all round. It's all very fine to boast of mutual superiority but what about mutual equality? I resent violence or intolerance in any shape or form. It never reaches anything or stops anything. A revolution must come on the due installments plan. It's a patent absurdity on the face of it

to hate people because they live round the corner and speak
another vernacular, so to speak." (643)

Bloom, that is, cannot help seeing the political issue in terms of space (room for
improvement, just round the corner), space shared or absurdly struggled over.
Here too, Bloom can reclaim his Irishness, his right to that national space: "—
I'm, he resumed with dramatic force, as good an Irishman as that rude person
[the Citizen] . . . " The recovered space within the cabman's shelter, therefore,
grants Bloom the freedom of speech he had lost in Kiernan's.

Ever the advertiser, Bloom also manages to think of Ireland here in a purely
geographical way, loosening it from the political anxieties that endlessly afflict
that space, by imagining the country in terms of its tourist possibilities:

> There were equally excellent opportunities for vacationists in
> the home island, delightful sylvan spots for rejuvenation, of-
> fering a plethora of attractions as well as a bracing tonic for
> the system in and around Dublin and its picturesque environs,
> even, Poulaphouca . . . but also farther away from the mad-
> ding crowd, in Wicklow, rightly termed the garden of Ireland
> . . . and in the wilds of Donegal . . . Howth, with its historic
> associations . . . rhododendrons several hundred feet above sea
> level was a favourite haunt . . . (628)

What Bloom imagines is a peaceful space, a space open to all, a space that is a
source of pleasure, not competitive, politicised polemics. The political site of
exclusion becomes the post-political condition of inclusion ("the home island"),
with Bloom assuring Stephen that he (the intellectual artist) and the peasant—
the brain and the brawn—"both belong to Ireland," that "each is equally important" (645). Simpleminded as Bloom's terms might appear, what underlies them
is the genuinely charitable division of space, curing the versions of those who
would divide only in order to exclude.

The political-nationalist chat of the other customers, however, bristles with
the usual xenophobia and chauvinism. The Parnell case—that anxious conjunction of Irish politics and sexuality—is treated by them in predictable ways:
"That bitch, the English whore," ruined him (650). For Bloom, however, the
men's laughter and spite evokes not "the faintest suspicion of a smile" (650).
What he objects to is their "blatant jokes" and vulgar laughter, their failure to
understand or have any feeling for the human elements in the political issues.
Because politics, for Bloom, is always close to home. And since his feelings—
both sexual and political—are rooted in a sense of dispossession, it is natural
that such orthodox politics as he once espoused were, we now learn, "involved
with the evicted tenants' question . . . in thorough sympathy with peasant
possession" (657). The step from here to his worry about Stephen as "house and
homeless" is a short one, underscoring the essential integrity of Bloom's sense
of the world. That sense is rooted firmly in an informing relationship with space,
and can receive adequate expression in the liberating space he, with Stephen,

can receive adequate expression in the liberating space he, with Stephen, has managed to create in the cabman's shelter.

Bloom's exit from the cabman's shelter is not a flight, as has so often been the case. Rather he negotiates a tactful, deliberate withdrawal: "The best plan clearly being to clear out, the remainder being plain sailing . . . Bloom, grasping the situation, was the first to rise to his feet so as not to outstay their welcome. . . Seeing that the ruse worked and the coast was clear, they left the shelter or shanty together" (660). The space successfully negotiated—at entry, at inhabitation, and at exit—Bloom and Stephen are, in the open air, physically linked, continuing the intimacy found in the shelter. Arm in arm and talking, they compose an emblem of inhabitable space (curing what Donne calls "defects of loneliness"). Their conversation is in itself a spacious creation. And in this chat, all anxiety gone, Bloom contrives schemes for the future—as if peace were a given. Here is a space of generous exchange and genial intercourse, its idioms being admiration, understanding, the willingness to listen—exactly those conditions prohibited and impossible in the ungenerous, nervous spaces of the rest of the book. The chapter ends with the sight of

> the two figures . . . —one full, one lean—walk towards the railway bridge, *to be married* [in the words of an accompanying song] *by Father Maher.* As they walked they at times stopped and walked again, continuing their tete-a-tete . . . about sirens, enemies of man's reason, mingled with a number of other topics of the same category, usurpers, historical cases of the kind. (665)

The journey home has begun, then, with a benevolent experience of space, a space created by the transforming possibility of companionship and conversation.

The last chapter in which we actually see Bloom is *Ithaca.* In this deliberately flattened cathechetical narrative, what matters, it seems, is the continuous stream of conversation between the two men—so different from one another, yet able in tolerant speech to make a comfortable common space for one another. Between them they create a depoliticised zone, each allowing the other the space for his identity. (The narrative mode itself may also be understood as "depoliticised"—its amazing factual fullness drawing one beyond the realm, always somehow "politicised," of *opinion.*) By bringing this space back into the house, into the kitchen, they purify them. First, Bloom's stratagem for gaining entrance—going over the railings and down into the area and through the area door takes skill, fortitude, strength (he "allowed his body to move freely in space" [668]) and is a deliberate reclaiming of the space he has been excluded from by the adultery. Once in the kitchen, then, and "the enclosures of reticence" removed, they converse easily, since "their place where none could hear them talk being secluded, reassured." In this protected place where peace—enacted and embodied as conversation—can reign, their talk reclaims the spaces of the day, continuing the work inaugurated in the cabman's shelter. The kitchen, that is, becomes a site of redemptive possibility, an ample human space that is a moral source. Home is where the hearth is, a liberated space that grants these migrant inhabitants, these resident aliens, an (as its etymology tells us) abundantly human *focus*.

A couple of fragments in their ranging conversation are of particular interest. One of these concerns the agreement they reach about a philosophy of life. Living, they agree, is "ineluctably constructed on the incertitude of the void." Thus conceived, living itself has to be understood as a relationship to absolute space (the void). Yet, in face of this gloomy view, Bloom is comforted by the knowledge that his own experience may be understood in spatial terms of a more positive order: "That as a competent keyless citizen he had proceeded energetically from the unknown to the known through the incertitude of the void" (697). His journey, that is, has taken him to some more positive understanding: as a voyager he has discovered a space he has made his own, the "known." And the implications of this benevolent colonialism are moral expansion, not contraction.

When Bloom and Stephen proceed from the kitchen into the back garden— "the exodus from the house of bondage into the wilderness of inhabitation" (697)—they emerge from the comfortable human space of their talk, that has redeemed so many hostile human spaces of the day, out into the great space of the world, under "the heaventree of stars" (698). Bloom, whose favorite science is astronomy, maps the constellations for Stephen, making sense of a space that stretches far beyond and above the political. He meditates on their vastness, their light-years of distance, the awe of cosmic space, "in comparison with which the years threescore and ten of allotted human life formed a parenthesis of infinitesimal brevity" (698). For Bloom—as for the Italian poet, Leopardi, in his great poem, *La Ginestra (Broom)*—the spaces of the heavens put human spaces (and endeavours) into perspective. It is this perspective that allows him to understand the political and the sexual for what they are. The space opened up by astronomy gives a sane, ample perspective on the spaces closed off by politics. And so does the space opened up by considerations of size at the opposite end of the scale—the end of the microscope, not the telescope—the infinitude of molecular space "in a single pinhead," or "the universe of human serum constellated with red and white bodies, themselves universes of void space constellated with other bodies" (699). In macrocosm and microcosm, Bloom's reality is—in ways that remove it from the enclosures of politics— spatially apprehended. That the "heavens" are a Utopia, a nowhere, makes them a pessimistic space for Bloom (as they were for Leopardi), but also (as they also were for the Italian poet), a space of freedom, the enfranchising perspective by which he sees all. Finally, as Bloom and Stephen are pissing under the stars, outer space itself is inscribed with Bloom's own name, in the spectacle of a shooting star plunging towards "the zodiacal sign of Leo" (703). And in Bloom's regulated farewell to Stephen at the back gate, the slowly unfolded ritual redeems all those hasty flights from other spaces in the day. For here *he* is the remaining one, the host, at home, hearing—with their buoyant, rhythmic affirmation—"The sound of the peal of the hour of the night by the chime of the bells of the church of Saint George" (704).

Our last glimpses of Bloom alone provide a few final insights into some of the sources of his relationship with space, its place in the recesses of his sensibility. There is, for example, his now recalled, earliest "reminiscence" of his father: "Rudolph Bloom (deceased) narrated to his son Leopold Bloom (aged 6) a retrospective arrangement of migrations and settlements between Dublin, London, Florence, Milan, Vienna, Budapest, Szombathely . . . Leopold Bloom (aged 6) had accompanied these narrations by constant consultation of a geographical map of Europe (political)" (724). In this memory it is not only possible to find a psychological seed of Bloom's nature as wanderer; it also contains an unspoken reminder of the degree to which the named spaces, followed through the politicised geography of Europe, were spaces fundamentally inhospitable to the Jewish migrant, Bloom's father.

Beyond this seminal epiphany, there are three concluding and conclusive images that offer the configured meaning of Bloom's experience in terms of space. One is an image of fear: what he fears most is being reduced by poverty to homelessness, to an enforced residence in Old Man's House (Kilmainham Hospital) or as "the inmate of Simpson's Hospital for reduced but respectable men" (725). Another is an image of desire: his most expansive desire is simply for (to quote his creator) "a house of his own." To be called Bloom Cottage, St Leopolds, or Flowerville (714), (and taking up more space than anything else in *Ithaca* [712-19]), this would be

> a thatched bungalowshaped 2 storey dwelling-house of southerly aspect . . . with porch . . . agreeable prospect from balcony . . . not less than 1 statute mile from the periphery of the metropolis . . . 1 drawingroom . . . 1 sitting room . . . 4 bedrooms, 2 servants' rooms, tiled kitchen . . . lounge hall . . . water closet on mezzanine . . . pantry, buttery, larder, refrigerator, outhouses . . . a tennis and fives court . . . an orchard, kitchen garden and vinery, protected against illegal trespassers by glasstopped mural enclosures, a lumbershed . . . (713-14)

All the indignities of denied space, of dispossession, come literally to rest in this dream of Bloom's own house, a protected ample living space, where he might even become that most peaceful of practitioners, a "gentleman farmer," rising though society to become "at the zenith of his career resident magistrate or justice of the peace with a family crest and coat of arms" (715). Finally, at the other end of the space spectrum from this fantasy of bourgeois respectability, there is the image of a present *voluntary* departure from his home, to become a wanderer on sea and land through attractive localities in Ireland and abroad, under the name Everyman or Noman, the receiver of "honours and gifts of strangers" (counteracting the racial and cultural inhospitality he's been subjected to in the course of his day) and the love of "a nymph, immortal, beauty..." (to compensate for the sexual indignities received). This enfranchised man would forever "wander, selfcompelled, to the extreme limit of his cometary orbit, beyond the fixed stars and variable suns and telescopic planets . . . to the extreme boundary of space, passing from land to land, among peoples, amid events" (728). It is from this image of vast travel, a cosmic wanderer of cosmic space—free, self-compelled, at ease among peoples and events, beautifully in but not of the small political spaces of our little world of history—that he turns to the bed, and turns us back, by a commodious vicus of recirculation, to the beginning of my discussion—where we saw him disappear into his own geographical definition, and thence into the black hole ("Where?") of sleep. Which is where, for the moment, I think, we'll leave him, with, for viaticum, some lines from John Donne's "The Good Morrow" to keep him company, lines that may suggest how he and his creator transformed the "great hatred, little room" of Yeats's Ireland into something—in possibility at least, if not in fact—quite other:

> And now good-morrow to our waking souls
> Which watch not one another out of fear;
> For love all love of other sights controls,
> And makes one little room an everywhere.

I cannot imagine a better blessing to put on Bloom's head, as he goes to that free space, which he has so richly earned, of sleep. It would seem an apt enough valediction, too, perhaps, to lay on the head of his creator, who spent the last month of his life seeking (and successfully gaining) exit permits that would allow him and his family—as the political noose of World War Two tightened around them—to move to the peaceful neutrality of Switzerland. Where, in the house of a friend, he would say, only a few days before he died—still intensely conscious of the rattling implications, human and political, of space, of space denied, free space achieved—"Here you know where you stand, life is settled."

1993

NOTES

[1] James Joyce, *Letters*, ed. Richard Ellmann, vol. I (New York: Viking, 1966) 51.
[2] *Ibid*, 43 (note)
[3] *Ibid*, 45
[4] *Ibid*, 42
[5] James Joyce, *Ulysses* (New York: Random House, 1961) 736. Further references are in my text.

Presence, Absence, Amputations:
Post-Catholic McGahern

"There's nothing more empty than a space you knew once when it was full," says Fonsie Ryan, one of the three brothers who share the centre of one of John McGahern's later short stories, "The Country Funeral." This is a truth Fonsie literally knows in his bones, since he has had both his legs amputated (we're never told why) as a child. In a larger sense, however, it's a truth that McGahern himself has been testing and imaginatively tasting from the start of his career. Much of his major work takes some central absence as its source, and a great many of the stories are marked by moments in which something is glimpsed that might make sense of, or compensate for that which has been lost: moments in which a world that's been deadened by loss is revived and granted value again by the sudden and unexpected apprehension of some affirmative fullness in the way things are. That such moments may be short lived, and that they may be shown to be—from other more sceptical perspectives—illusory, does not negate them. By allowing different views of such visions, McGahern simply insists on the presence of this possibility of spiritual value—of the broken world being somehow made whole—in a context of agnostic circumstance. An important subtext of all such moments is the way they, or their variously inflected consequences, seem to take the place of failed religious belief, take over from Catholic ideology (not to say theology) as the agents of making sense of the world. They are the outward signs—the radical and secular sacraments—of nothing less than a new consciousness; in their composition, McGahern shows himself to be a true revisionist of the Irish spirit.

An early example occurs in *The Barracks*, when the dying Elizabeth Reegan has her own muted experience of what the narrator calls elsewhere "the mystery of life." In a moment free of the "business and distractions" of the day, she is able to experience herself in quietness,

> an interval of pure rest. Such a quietness had come into the house that she felt she could touch it with her hands. There was no stir from the dayroom, where Casey was sunk in the newspapers; the noise of the occasional traffic on the roads, the constant sawing from the woods came and were lost in the quietness she felt about her. The whiteness was burning rapidly off the fields outside, brilliant and glittering on the short grass as it vanished; and the daffodils that yesterday she had arranged in the white vase on the sill were a wonder of yel-

lowness in the sunshine, the heads massed together above the
old green stems disappearing into the mouth of the vase. In
the silence the clock beside the statue of St Therese on the
sideboard beat like a living thing. This'd be the only time of
day she could get some grip and vision on the desperate activity of her life. (London: Panther, 1966; 41)

This recreative, redemptive pause sets Elizabeth aside from public and domestic history (sensed in the newspapers and the clock that beats now in sympathy, "like a living thing"). In this moment of minor-key blessedness, she can
have a "vision" of her life instead of merely living its pain. As an interval of
immanent repose, fully accommodating the actual and in tune with the natural
world, it possesses some undeniably spiritual weight. This seems to be offered
by McGahern as a counterweight to those conventional consolations of the
"always beautiful" rites of religion, whose practical failure overturns Elizabeth's
naive trust "that she'd discover something . . . some miracle of revelation, perhaps." Instead, "she had been given nothing and had discovered nothing . . . She
couldn't pray " (71, 102). The evacuated space of orthodox Catholic belief,
then, is filled up with something for which McGahern gives Elizabeth the
word—"mystery":

There was such deep joy sometimes, joy itself lost in a passion
of wonderment in which she and all things were lost. Nothing
could be decided here. She was just passing through. She had
come to life out of mystery and would return, it surrounded
her life, it safely held it as by hands; she'd return into that
which she could not know; she'd be consumed at last in whatever meaning her life had. Here she had none, none but to be,
which in acceptance must surely be to love. There'd be no
searching for meaning, she must surely grow into meaning as
she grew to love, there was that or nothing and she couldn't
lose . . . All real seeing grew into smiling and if it moved to
speech it must be praise, all else was death, a refusal, a turning
back. . . . All the futility of her life in the barracks came at last
to rest on this sense of mystery. It gave the hours idled away
in idleness or remorse as much validity as a blaze of passion,
all was under its eternal sway. (174)

What's stressed here is the loss of self in a passion of wonder, a sense of
transience, a surrender to the unknown, to mystery. Acceptance of being is
equated with love. The verb most repeated is *grow*, as if to stress the natural
process, to reconcile her to dying by seeing it as a growth (more poignant in that
her illness is a growth, a cancer). Seeing becomes smiling, speech becomes
praise, futility comes to rest in mystery, under its "eternal sway." The language
suggests a translation from the idiom of orthodox Catholicism into a much more
personalised idiom of natural understanding. The space left by the failure of the

Catholic formulae (not aggressively rejected, just calmly felt as inefficacious) is filled by a sense of oneness with the natural world, with a unitary sense of things that sees life with a tranquil, almost Eastern gaze.

Later this tranquillity is tested by the insensitivity of a priest who wants her to pray to the Virgin Mary. In Elizabeth's weary response we see McGahern's confirming the replacement he has made in the above moment: "it was surely the last and hardest thing to accept [versions of her situation] from knaves and active fools and being compelled to live in them as in strait-jackets. To be able to say yes to that intolerant lunacy so as to be able to go your own way without noise or interruption was to accept everything and was hardest of all to do" (180). In fact, Elizabeth does manage to perform such a task of universal acceptance. All that's left of conventional religious practise after this is her love of the rosary, translated into terms of personal appreciation: "what it meant didn't matter, whether it meant anything at all or not it gave the last need of her heart release, the need to praise and celebrate, in which everything rejoiced" (180-81). In this secular ecstasy of final acceptance, release, and the will to praise, the novel gives presence and value to the life of the woman for whom it is an elegy (whose absence, in the way of elegy, it fills). And it does this by dismantling the ideological frame of Catholicism—which would contain that life within "the straitjackets" of its own dogmatic meanings—and supplanting it with some more individually known, tested, accepted truth.

Union with the natural universe opens for Elizabeth Reegan the path to the centre, to the mystery. In other works of McGahern that path is opened not by something that, because it verges on nature mysticism may be seen in a religious light (a quiet competitor to the dominant Catholicism of the context), but by a much more radical opponent to conventional Catholicism—sexual love. The hero of The Leavetaking remembers the first time he made love ("a blessed chance," he describes it as): "I rested within her as if I could not believe I'd entered the rich dark mystery of a woman's body, this feeling of the rich mystery open all night to me far more than the throb of pleasure." Later, the ordinary world itself takes on the quality of miracle: "I sat by the window in the indescribable happiness of wanting nothing whatever in the world over hot coffee and toast and marmalade" (93).

In the larger arc of this novel, then, McGahern plays out the replacement of orthodox versions of Irish history-cum-politics and Irish religion by authentically individual sexual love and the necessarily more complicated view of reality it must generate. On the one hand, the fluent and truthful freedom of the narrator's marriage in an English registry office—for which he is to lose his position as a teacher in Dublin—is contrasted with the rigidity of the official instructions for the teaching of Irish history, in which "it's written down in black and white [that] the cultivation of patriotism is more important than the truth." In this light, history (which according to another character "stays still. It at least is settled" [187]) is a series of unchanging postures ("Britain is always the big black beast, Ireland is the poor daughter struggling while being raped" [186]). To this, the narrative opposes the more complicated fluency and continuity of individual sexual life, underlined by the repeated mantra, "the first constant was water."

In another strategic replacement, the remembered lost rites of the Mass cede to the warm domestic rites of love: thinking of the house and the woman he is going home to at the end of the day, certain images occur to the protagonist. First he remembers his mother's wish for him to be a priest ("In scarlet and white I attend the mysteries of holy Week to the triumphant clamour of the Easter bells" [193]); then he remembers the "second priesthood" of teaching, which is now "strewn about my life as waste." These are immediately followed, however, by the image of the present, the house in Howth where "the table will have bread and meat and cheap wine and flowers . . . We will be true to one another . . . It is the only communion left to us now" (193). Sexual love has created a world of domestic sacramentalism, something of the values of the old ideology rediscovered within these decisively human facts and human actions. Even in the embrace of the new dispensation, however—as can be heard in the tone here and in the implicit allusion to Arnold's "Dover Beach," (a literary "touchstone," I suppose, for the way sexual love succeeds the lost world of religious faith)—the gravity of loss is acknowledged like a phantom limb. And as Elizabeth Reegan salvaged from the wreckage of her religion the emotional comforts of the rosary, the narrator of this novel admits at the end that "even now I feel the desperate need of prayer." In the world of secular sacramentalism that McGahern has managed to bring into being, however, it is the beloved woman who replaces the Virgin Mary as recipient of prayer: "Oh soul full of grace," thinks the man, "pray for me now and at the hour."

In summary, then, this novel charts the replacement of one kind of sacramentalism with another, a fact which gives the "leavetaking" of the title a deeper resonance than it might at first seem to have. Near its start, the narrator has a valedictory experience of Benediction:

> It was soon over, the altar boys in scarlet and white leaving the altar in twos in front of the priest bearing the empty monstrance, light from candles dancing on the gold of his cloak, small human bundle in magnificent clothes. In the sacristy they would be free of the mystery when the boys bowed to the cross and then to one another, as I did too when I was young. (16)

Drained of mystery, this ritual religious blessing is deliberately replaced by the human sacrament of sexual love and its domestic rituals, while the novel closes on a moment that displaces the image of Christian pilgrimage with the perilous journey of human love, recited in the cadences of prayer:

> The odour of our lovemaking rises, redolent of slime and fish, and our very breathing seems an echo of the rise and fall of the sea as we drift to sleep; and I would pray for the boat of our sleep to reach its morning, and see that morning lengthen

to an evening of calm weather that comes through night and sleep again to morning after morning until we meet the first death. (195)

While *The Leavetaking* finds in sexual love and marriage some of the lost values of institutional religion, in *The Pornographer*, sex itself is tested as a site of the mystery, as a replacement for religious loss: within her, says the narrator of the woman he makes pregnant but does not love, "there was this instant of rest, the glory and the awe, that one was as close as ever man could be to the presence of the mystery, and live, the caged bird in its moment of pure rest before it was about to be loosed into blinding light" (Quartet Books and Poolbeg Press, 1980; 39). In this context, however, that possibility is consistently subverted. You can hear this in the actual composition of sentences like the following, in which achievement and loss are syntactically bound together: "We had climbed to the crown of life, and this was all, all the world, and even as we surged towards it, it was already slipping further and further away from one's grasp, and we were stranded again on our own bare lives" (42). Sex itself, in its attempt at a kind of secular wholeness, does not allow one to keep a grasp on the mystery, the world in time loses its precious savor, human life is "bare."

Faced with such barrenness, McGahern reaches the limit of possibility for his secular sacramentalism, a last trace of which is salvaged by the narrator's own stern self-knowledge at the end. "I had not attended properly," he realizes; "I had found the energy to choose too painful. Broken in love, I had turned back, let the light of imagination almost out. Now my hands were ice" (251). In turning, however, to the values of imagination, risk, and human choice (he decides to ask the nurse he's been having an affair with to marry him, and he decides he will return to live in the country, "to try to make a go of it"), he—like the narrator of *The Leavetaking*—finds in himself "a fierce need to pray." And in his awareness of what "prayer" can mean when religious faith has been lost, he is granted a moment of epiphanal insight through which McGahern expresses not only his own kind of mystery, but a form of consciousness that has replaced Catholic ideology with a sceptical humanism that can still acknowledge something other than the simply material in our lives. The narrator is given the chance, that is, to move from pornography to a new style of prayer:

> What I wanted to say was that I had a fierce need to pray, for myself, Maloney, my uncle, the girl, the whole shoot. The prayers could not be answered, but prayers that cannot be answered need to be the more completely said, being their own beginning as well as end. (252)

Here, and in the emphatic resolve to go on that marks the end of the book (the narrator remembers the start of the narrative, that "beginning of the journey—if beginning it ever had—that had brought each to where we were, in the now and the forever"), McGahern shows that even in the world drained of the conventional consolations of religious ideology, human choices can possess a value that reverberates with "spiritual" meaning, as these last words vibrate with a faint echo of the *Glory be to the Father* ("As it was in the beginning, is now, and ever shall be, world without end, Amen").

As far as the subversion of the old dispensation is concerned, then, this particular replacement is the most radical yet, bringing us into a world empty of divine assurance, whose inhabitants can yet live lives given texture and meaning by some of the traditional forms emptied of their traditional content. When one tries to describe the consciousness on view here, the only term that seems adequate is "post-Catholic," suggesting a consciousness imbued by Catholic forms and meanings and assumptions, yet bereft of any primary belief in these, without any of the conventional props to a coherent and reassuring understanding of life that these might, to the believer, offer.

Finally, in two related short stories—"The Wine Breath" and "The Country Funeral"—McGahern returns deliberately to this difficult but at the same time potentially exhilarating terminus. In the first, the protagonist (who is a priest) remembers through a moment of heightened Proustian recall and with "the solid world . . . everywhere around him," a "lost day" from childhood, a day in which he had his most intense experience of "the Mystery." It is the memory of a funeral on Killeelan Hill after the great snowstorm of 1947:

> The coffin moving slowly towards the dark trees on the hill,
> the long line of the mourners, and everywhere the blinding
> white light, among the half-buried thorn bushes and beyond
> Killeelan, on the covered waste of Gloria Bog, on the sides of
> Slieve an Iarainn. (*Collected Stories*, Knopf, 1993; 179)

The day in this radiant memory stands for all purity and perfection, and although in this present he is cut off from it, the priest "felt purged of all tiredness, was, for a moment, eager to begin life again." (The closeness of *Gloria* Bog to Slieve an Iarainn—Iron Hill—suggests the affecting co-existence of high mystery and hard fact in McGahern's vision of things.)

From how McGahern conducts the narrative, it would seem that this funeral marks the passing of a whole way of life. For the dead man, Michael Bruen, "had been a big kindly agreeable man, what was called a lovely man," and, in McGahern's evocation, his farm becomes a version of the peaceable kingdom, a genre painting of plenitude and satisfaction, a secular feast revealing the rich grace of the ordinary and sliding easily into another, religious, world of meaning. Cut off as he is now, however, the priest feels phantom-limbed, lives with the ache of amputation, knows his present time "as a flimsy accumulating tissue over all the time that was lost." His everyday existence is "tortuous," the public world he lives in a scene of violence and outrage and uncertainty: "A man had lost both legs in an explosion. There was violence on the night-shift at Ford's. The pound had steadied at the close but was still down on the day" (185).

In this time-bound present world, from which the faith and the "promise of the eternal" represented by the funeral seem to have withdrawn, it is hard to locate a replacement comparable to those available in the other stories I've been talking about. Yet even at this bleak terminus ("When he looked at the room about him he could hardly believe it was so empty and dead and dry. . . . Wildly and aridly he wanted to curse"), even here McGahern manages to provide some affirmation, some faint but real compensation for loss, and in a medium that is resolutely human. By doing so he once again succeeds in re-imagining Irish consciousness in a revisionist way, absorbing the conditions of something like faith within circumstances that would have to be called agnostic. It is this combination that would seem to lend distinction to what, in McGahern's view, would be our contemporary possibility. For at the end of this story, the priest's bleak epiphany lies in the discovery that the "visitation" he desired "from beyond the walls of sense" is in fact the recognition of his own death. This is the visiting ghost that will drink (as Yeats reminds us in "All Souls' Night") of the breath of the wine: "He might as well get to know him well. It would never leave now and had no mortal shape. Absence does not cast a shadow."

The expanded consciousness the priest shows here is to be understood as a willingness to live with death and to acknowledge absence, as Prospero—to be fully himself—must acknowledge Caliban, "this thing of darkness," as his own. What stems from this revised consciousness, however, is a resurrected gift for seeing the world as it is—in all its variety and as it happens. It is a capacity both to see the facts as they are and to imagine what might be. In this combination there is to be found a generosity of spirit that somehow—within straitened circumstances—touches in kinship the rich remembered Mystery of that "lost time." First the priest has a vivid apprehension of things as they are:

> All that was there was the white light of the lamp on the open book, on the white marble; the brief sun of God on beechwood, and the sudden light of the glistening snow, and the timeless mourners moving towards the yews on Killeelan Hill almost thirty years ago. It was as good a day as any, if there ever was a good day to go. (187)

In the ordinary goodness of the day, in the way that one sentence contains past and present phenomena—different as their meanings might appear to be—within a single white embrace, we may find the resolved humanity of this replenished consciousness. Then, in the last surprising paragraph of the story, McGahern obliges us to see and to feel that the distinguishing mark of this consciousness is its gift for *imagining* other lives—for imagining, indeed, the life not lived—but knowing this not as an unhappy amputation but as a related presence, generously received:

> Somewhere, outside this room that was an end, he knew that a young man, not unlike he had once been, stood on a granite step and listened to the doorbell ring, smiled as he heard a woman's footsteps come down the hallway, ran his fingers through his hair, and turned the bottle of white wine he held in his hands completely around as he prepared to enter a pleasant

and uncomplicated evening, feeling himself immersed in time
without end. (187)

In this wonderfully cumulative period that moves from the small space
"that was an end" to the immense possibility of "time without end," McGahern
lets us share in the capacious "negative capability" of the priest's re-animated
consciousness. In the quiet swirl of tenses—from past through pluperfect to a
virtual present (but I wish he had written 'prepares') and off into a limitless future—we are allowed feel something of the eternal as it informs, as it illuminates, this entirely human moment. The ordinary instant of love, that is, has
been granted something of the spiritual vividness of the remembered funeral, of
"the day set alight in his mind . . . [that] seemed bathed in the eternal, seemed
everything we had been taught and told of the world of God" (180). At this conclusion, then, the day that the priest has already described as "the actual day, the
only day that mattered, the day from which our salvation had to be won or lost,"
the day that was "solidly and impenetrably there, denying the weak life of the
person, with nothing of the eternal other than it would dully endure," this day
has been somehow charged with a force analogous to that emanating from that
unforgettable day of faith and amazing snowlight, has become, strangely, full of
grace, but of insistently *secular* grace.

By locating this peculiar conversion in a priest whose faith has gone dry,
and by insisting on its secularity, refusing to allow the slightest quiver of conventional Catholic belief to get in the way of its surge of world-anchored revelation, McGahern has once again managed to forge a consciousness that truly
lives in a post-religious world of trouble and circumstance (as Keats said)—an
amputated world, if you like, or a world of amputees—but that lives there in a
spirit that, in spite of loss, affirms the value of this material world in its moment
to moment, as a place—to summon Keats again—of "soul making." It is just
such a post-Catholic consciousness that might say with the French poet, Phillipe
Jaccottet, and without any conventionally religious implication, that "this world
is merely the tip / of an unseen conflagration." Or, nearer home, might say with
born-again Kavanagh—whose own post-Catholic awakening on the banks of the
Grand Canal in Dublin surely (although that is another story) left its mark on
McGahern (and on Heaney)—"I turn away to where the Self reposes / The
placeless Heaven that's under all our noses."

Which brings me back to where I started. In "The Country Funeral" McGahern revisits the site of "The Wine Breath." Here is another funeral to Killeelan
graveyard, this one not enshrined in an almost legendary past, but plunged, forty
years later, in the actual complicated present, in an "actual day, the only day that
mattered, the day from which our salvation had to be won or lost." What
McGahern seems to be at here is visiting old ground again with a view to testing
some of his earlier conclusions, subjecting them to a number of different and
opposed perspectives. (McGahern's obsessive habits of *reiteration*—of theme,
character, situation, language—offer a technical example, as it were, of how
deeply the whole enterprise and practise of *revision* is planted in him.) The funeral itself brings together various ways of seeing, chief among them those of

Philly and Fonsie, two of the brothers. Philly, who occupies the centre of the narrative view, is—like a number of other McGahern protagonists—at an existential dead end, searching for something to assuage his parched spirit. (The fact that he is home in Ireland on holidays from his job in the oilfields of Bahrain, as well as the fact that he spends much of his time drinking, give his spiritual dryness a satisfyingly realistic dimension, while these real facts become textured by McGahern's habitual inclination towards the symbolic. That style, indeed, compounding the actual and the symbolic in mutually enriching ways, might be taken as a kind of literary sacramentalism very much in tune with, indeed the apt embodiment of, the thematic presence I am trying to outline here.)

For Philly (whose mind at the beginning of the story, at the first mention of Gloria Bog, had been "flooded . . . with amazing brightness and calm" [377]), the funeral constitutes a moment of speechless revelation:

> I felt something I never felt when we left the coffin on the edge of the grave. A rabbit hopped out of the briars a few yards off. He sat there and looked at us as if he didn't know what was going on before he bolted off. You could see the bog and all the shut houses next to Peter's [the dead man] below us. There wasn't even a wisp of smoke coming from any of the houses. Everybody gathered around, and the priest started to speak of the dead and the Mystery and the Resurrection. (405)

In this view, nature, priest, community, and place all make a single picture, all combining to address some deep new truth to Philly. That the priest speaks of "the Mystery" as well as of the more obvious "dead" and "the Resurrection" forges a link between this and the previous story, suggesting that Philly's view is, although in a more fragmented and colloquially naive mode, roughly analogous to the boy's in the earlier story. The difference is that Philly doesn't belong to the picture in the same way as the boy did, while his "I felt something I never felt" is much more blunt and inchoate than the earlier version ("Never before or since had he experienced the Mystery in such awesomeness"). The point, however, is that Philly does feel *something*, that his contemporary and somewhat brutalised consciousness opens up to some unspoken thing in this ceremony, in this space, although obviously "I felt something I never felt" cannot count as a vision of profound religious implication. But it does, we'd have to say, imply a spiritual response of some sort, a spiritual dimension in Philly's way of receiving the facts.

When Fonsie offers his far more cynical response, however, McGahern draws our attention to the relativity of these reactions, and by implication to the essential absence of any certain, absolute or objective value in the ceremony itself: "the Mystery" of "The Wine Breath" is here seen to depend on the onlooker for its efficacy. For the priest, says Fonsie in his jaundiced, bitter, disappointed way, "is paid to do that," puncturing any possibility of the priesthood as an agent of "Mystery." And furthermore, goes on Fonsie,

> it was no Mystery from the car. Several times I thought you
> were going to drop the coffin. It was more like a crowd of
> apes staggering up a hill with something they had just looted.
> The whole lot of you could have come right out of the Dark
> Ages. (405)

From the car in which the cripple sits, from that removed perspective, this must
have been the mercilessly factual view. In an interesting twist, however, McGahern has complicated the issue by making Fonsie not entirely truthful. For
when, earlier, he actually sees the cortege we are told that,

> In spite of his irritation at the useless ceremony . . . he found
> the coffin and the small band of toiling mourners unbearably
> moving as it made its low stumbling climb up the hill, and this
> deepened further his irritation and the sense of complete use-
> lessness. (405)

What can be seen and what can be felt—the cold fact of the event, that is, and
the feeling it causes—are at odds, and cannot be reconciled. Fonsie's complex
response, then, is even further exacerbated by how the narration itself offers us
the sight of the priest hurrying away from the funeral with the two "most solid
looking and conventional of the mourners. . . . The long black soutane looked
strangely menacing between the two attentive men in suits" (400). By allowing
this vignette into his narrative, McGahern drains the official side of the ceremony of any efficacy, letting priest and conventional parishioners be seen as
mere agents of this mechanical apparatus of power-conscious social obligation
dressed up as religious ritual. (Such a critique of "official" Catholicism reap-
pears at the end of *Amongst Women*, where "Two local politicians who had vied
with one another for prominence all through the funeral now fell back from the
crowd as the prayers began. They walked away to the boundary wall and leaned
together out over the stones in amiable conspiratorial camaraderie, sometimes
turning their heads to look back to the crowd gathered about the grave in undis-
guised contempt" [183].)
    From the narrative "point of view," then, Fonsie's disdain has validity,
properly insisting on the relative nature of the experience, the lack of any objective certainty of value in it. And yet, independent of this sceptical view, and
quite detached from the functionaries (who represent the conventional pietistic
but hollow remains of Catholicism operating as ideology within the community), are Philly's spiritual stirrings, Fonsie's own sense of the whole thing as
"unbearably moving," and even the view of the conventional and repressed
other brother, John, who "said carefully, 'I have to say I found the whole ceremony moving, but once is more than enough to go through that experience'"
(405). So all the brothers are moved in some more or less intense way. But by
exactly *what* it is impossible in any objective sense to say: all that can be said is
that the source in each case is a sort of absence. What McGahern presents as the

brothers' differing knowledge of this absence, however—including the satirical, cynical knowledge spoken by Fonsie—manage to represent a sort of spectrum of post-Catholic consciousness. And such consciousness can, it is suggested, internalise something speechless and of unknown value (but still *there*, like the phantom feeling of an amputated limb). But it can only know this in private, and even then perhaps it leads to nothing, being, as it is in Fonsie's final response, "completely useless."

In the end, however, it is Philly's response, not Fonsie's, that McGahern leaves us with. And that response, no matter how limited or suspect, is an affirmative one. For, like the narrator of *The Pornographer* (who also had a significant, culminating experience at the funeral of his dead aunt), Philly decides to settle in the country, to buy the dead man's house and live there: "'Gloria is far from over . . . I'm going to take up in Peter's place . . . It'll be a place to come home to . . . I'll definitely be buried there some day'" (406-07). It is to Philly, too, to whom the very last word in the story goes: "'Anyhow, we buried poor Peter,' Philly said, as if it was at last a fact" (408).

Coming to rest in *fact*—where this post-Catholic consciousness has mostly to reside—the story nonetheless has granted a last glimpse of something of a different, non-factual kind of value, some small vibration deep in the psyches of each of these men, each one living out painfully an existence of circumstance and complication, but each one also feeling in some unspoken way the truth of Fonsie's off-hand remark that "There's nothing more empty than a space you knew once when it was full." Part of McGahern's achievement is to have raised on that empty space a revisionist simulacrum of contemporary Irish consciousness (more especially Irish male consciousness, though the imbalance has significantly corrected with the publication of *Amongst Women*, a novel that could be read as charting the evolution of what I'm calling "post-Catholic consciousness"). McGahern's achievement, as I say, is to have raised on that empty space a plausible simulacrum of contemporary "post-Catholic" Irish consciousness, phantom limbs and all.[1]

I began this piece by quoting Fonsie's remark about emptiness. What the remark actually refers to is the cutting down of "huge evergreens that used to shelter the church." I find my conclusion in the brief remainder of that passage, where McGahern imagines the following exchange:

> "There's nothing more empty than a space you knew once when it was full," Fonsie said.
> "What do you mean?" [asks the puzzled Philly]
> "Can you not see the trees?" Fonsie gestured irritably.
> "The trees are gone." [says Philly]
> "That's what I mean. They were there and they're no longer there. Can you not see?"

1995

NOTES

[1] The term, "post-Catholic" has become current in recent theoretical and critical studies of Ireland, though I hadn't in fact heard it before using it in this lecture (at the MLA conference in Toronto, 1994).

3

FIGURES IN A LANDSCAPE

Careless Father:
Yeats and His Juniors

> *I'm not interested in poetry: I'm only interested*
> *in what I'm trying to do to myself.*
> WBY to James Stephens

On February 3, 1939, six days after the death of Yeats, his magisterial injunction to Irish poets appeared in *The Irish Independent* and *The Irish Times*:

> Irish poets, learn your trade,
> Sing whatever is well made,
> Scorn the sort now growing up,
> All out of shape from toe to top,
> Their unremembering hearts and heads
> Base-born products of base beds.
> Sing the peasantry, and then
> Hard-riding country gentlemen,
> The holiness of monks, and after
> Porter-drinkers' randy laughter;
> Sing the lords and ladies gay
> That were beaten into the clay
> Through seven heroic centuries;
> Cast your mind on other days
> That we in coming days may be
> Still the indomitable Irishry.[1]

No record remains of the poets' immediate response to this remarkable poetic last will and testament, but it must have been, to say the least, ambivalent. F. R. Higgins, in the last memorial issue of *Arrow*, quotes it with approval, but ten years later Robert Farren can say that the passage infuriated the poets at whom it was presumably aimed.[2] Aside from individual responses, however, the passage is important because it raises the whole question of Yeats's attitude to the Irish poets who would succeed him. It is, as most things with Yeats are, a thorny question. On the one hand is Lennox Robinson's statement that "every young poet looked to him as a model," and that "he was always ready to help in every way the younger artists."[3] On the other, Austin Clarke can say that Yeats's relationship with "the younger generation of poets . . . here in Ireland [was] rather

like [that of] an enormous oak-tree which, of course, kept us in the shade."[4]
Monk Gibbon can even go so far as to say that Yeats "did harm, I think, to the
younger generation of writers in Ireland."[5]

While such statements have their fascination for the student of Yeats and
Irish poetry, it is more to my present purpose to examine such direct evidence as
there is for Yeats's own attitudes towards the poets of the next generation. A
useful way to do this may be to set what he said about his juniors in the context
of his expressed attitudes toward his immediate contemporaries and his Irish
poetic ancestors.

Apart from some possibly mischievous intent, what exactly does Yeats
mean in the lines quoted from "Under Ben Bulben"? What one first notices is
the imperative mood of the piece, giving vivid life to its authority of tone, its
sense of confident leadership. Then the triple repetition of "Sing" underscores
the traditional role Yeats would have the Irish poets adopt.[6] In subject matter,
too, he would have his heirs adhere to tradition, singing established themes. The
purpose—determining role and subject matter—seems a deliberately separatist
one. The initial sprung rhythm insists on dividing Irish from other poets, making
them a race apart. "Scorn" commands a withdrawal that is geographical, historical, and social, a withdrawal from the contaminating company of other poets,
who are contemporary, disfigured, and of lowly antecedents. Being "unremembering," these poets have cut themselves off from tradition, from a past on
which Yeats exhorts his own successors to "cast" (the verb carries two meanings) their minds. As a whole the passage is a denial of the historical present.
The recommended subjects—lords and ladies, peasants and gentlemen, saintly
monks and dissipated drunkards—are a heightened pastiche of imagined history, social classes caught in almost allegorical poses. Together they make a
tapestry of "seven heroic centuries," and reduce Irish history to a few brief lyrical and tragic postures—a poet's emblem of the past. The aim of this reflection
on—or, as the verb "cast" allows, modelling on—"other days" is to ensure a
survival of "the indomitable Irishry" into "the coming days," the future. By
stitching past to future in this deft imagistic way Yeats draws his Irish poets out
of "the filthy modern tide" and gives them and their subject matter a decisive, if
fictive immortality.

By denying the historical present, Yeats seems to want to dominate the Irish
literary future as he had dominated that much of its past for which he himself
had been virtually responsible. The items of Yeats's exhortation all represent
subjects he had himself successfully exploited as a poet. By imposing them
upon the next generation of poets he implicitly tries to make Irish poetry fold in
upon itself, take the same shape as his own poetic career, and its makers be
"Still the indomitable Irishry" of his own imagination. In its willful collapsing
of temporality, its elimination of the fluent vulgarities of the present, the passage attempts to ground an aesthetic in a personally fruitful cultural myth. Ironically, it seems, Yeats attempts to hand on to his poetic successors a notion of
Irish poetry as limiting as the one he had, at the start of his career, set himself
against, and in his successful opposition to which he had laid the ground of
modern Irish poetry, that "rhymed lesson book of Davis" he had helped his gen-

eration to shelve.[7] To the next generation of poets, however, he would offer as compulsory text the (still rhymed) story book of Yeats. Composed with great art, it is a book throbbing with the forms of cultural energy from which he himself had drawn much of his inspiration: the folk tradition, the Anglo-Irish 18th century, the aristocratic Gaels, the vigor of a secular and ecclesiastical past elected in defiant opposition to a present world given over to the despicable vulgarities of Paudeen. That this might also be the appropriate text for his poetic successors to continue, however, is another matter.

It may be argued that the "Irish poets" Yeats addresses in this passage are a collective fiction, an imagined artist to set beside that imagined audience of one which he had, "in scorn" of the actual audience he found in Ireland, invoked in "The Fisherman." And both imagined poet and imagined audience are to be set inside what he himself once called "an imaginary Ireland, in whose service I labour."[8] The "wise and simple" fisherman "is but a dream" made in Yeats's own image to compensate for the failure of "the reality."[9] Similarly, the "Irish poets" addressed in "Under Ben Bulben" represent Yeats's dream of a literary future modelled on his own achievement. This, indeed, had been an early ambition of his. In 1908 he had written, "What I myself did, getting into an original relation with Irish life, creating in myself a new character . . . the literary mind of Ireland must do as a whole."[10] Now, more than thirty years later, he tries to extend this ambition beyond his own death. By neutralising history he would find an immortality for himself and for the culture to which he more than anyone had given a self-conscious identity.

What Yeats had to say in a less formal way of and to his successors in Irish poetry is, to judge by the available evidence, surprisingly little. But even that little bears out the implications I have derived from the passage in "Under Ben Bulben." Before dealing with such statements, however, it is helpful to glance at a few of the very many things Yeats said about his predecessors, since these reveal the shape he wished to put on Irish poetry, a shape on which the "Irish poets" passage is the proper seal.

In "the first published prose piece by Yeats which has survived," Yeats links Mangan, Davis, and Ferguson in the genesis of Irish literature in English.[11] To him these poets represent the stirrings of poetic identity in modern Ireland: "The nation has found in Davis a battle call, as in Mangan its cry of despair; but [Ferguson] only, the one Homeric poet of our time, could give us immortal companions still wet with the dew of their primal world."[12] Ferguson, to whom most of this article is devoted, is the founding father, saviour of the Irish "from that leprosy of the modern—tepid emotion and many aims."[13] This adherence to the past is an indispensable component of the comprehensive aesthetic Yeats, as early as the Eighties, is in the process of making. Such a commitment is entirely national in spirit: "Behind Ireland fierce and militant, is Ireland poetic, passionate, remembering, idyllic, fanciful, and always patriotic."[14] "Remembering" here makes an interesting link with the "unremembering hearts and heads" of "Under Ben Bulben." From the start this commitment to tradition is for Yeats a necessary quality of truly Irish poetry. The worthwhile Irish poetry of the 19th century derives its value from its distinctly Irish features. Ferguson "is the greatest poet Ireland has produced, because the most central and most Celtic."[15]

Moore (whose "national" importance Yeats always ignored) is summarily dismissed from the company of the truly Irish poets, because he "lived in the drawingrooms, and still finds his audience therein. . . . Ireland was a metaphor to Moore."[16] The authentic Irish poets, however, as befits their primary nature, have "a wonderful freshness and sweetness . . . like the smell of newly-ploughed earth."[17] Allingham is included in the pantheon of "our sacred poets ...for he too sang of Irish scenes and Irish faces."[18] All the best writers "base their greatest work, if I except a song or two of Mangan's and Allingham's, upon legends and upon the fortunes of the nation."[19]

There is, however, he goes on to argue, a deficiency of craft in much of this earlier verse: "But side by side with this robustness and rough energy of ours there goes most utter indifference to art, the most dire carelessness, the most dreadful intermixture of the commonplace."[20] The poetry of Young Ireland is often seen as the major offender, a literary past with a debased style which had to be replaced with genuine art. Yeats's task was to tutor his generation in a new mode. He had to make a new poetic tradition, one with as much respect for art as for Ireland: "it seemed then as if our new generation could not do its work unless we overcame the habit of making every Irish book, or poem, shoulder some political idea; it seemed to us we had to escape by some great effort from the obsession of public life."[21] In the "Under Ben Bulben" passage, then, Yeats brings the wheel full circle, leaving as his legacy to Irish poets the subject matter and the sense of style—pride of craft or "trade"—out of which he had since the beginning of his career been trying to mould Irish poetic identity. Withdrawing from the scene in death, Yeats would assert the task's completion, himself embodying and handing on to his successors, whoever they might be, the finished condition of Irish poetry.

So much for his predecessors. In his early remarks upon his contemporaries Yeats's values remain constant. In 1887, for example, he can praise Katherine Tynan because "in . . . finding her nationality she has also found herself, and written many pages of great truthfulness and simplicity."[22] In 1893 he gave superlative praise to Hyde's *Love Songs of Connacht*, which open up a world where "Everything was so old it was steeped in the heart, and every powerful emotion found at once noble types and symbols for its expression. But we—we live in a world of whirling change, where nothing becomes old and sacred, and our powerful emotions, unless we be highly trained artists, express themselves in vulgar types and symbols."[23] Yeats's most notable poetic contemporary is AE. Although his enthusiasm for Russell's work waned after 1900, his early comments are all praise, for "no voice in modern Ireland is to me as beautiful as his is."[24] His poems are "perhaps the most beautiful and delicate that any Irishman of our time has written."[25] Apart from Tynan, AE, and Hyde, Yeats has also early praise for Rolleston, Hopper, Todhunter, and Lionel Johnson. Speaking out of a considered sense of what Irish poets should be at, he praises all these because they are "examples of the long continued and resolute purpose of the Irish writers to bring their literary tradition to perfection, to discover fitting symbols for their emotions, or to accentuate what is at once Celtic and excellent in their nature, that they may be at last tongues of fire uttering the evangel of the Celtic peoples."[26]

Such remarks give an outline of Yeats's sense of the shape he wished Irish poetic identity to take, up to and including his own work and that of his early contemporaries. Paramount among its qualities are the poets' undeviating commitment to their art and "Irishry," and a concomitant rejection—seen in the Hyde passage—of the modern world, its vulgarity and "whirling change." His intention in "Under Ben Bulben" is to draw the *future* of Irish poetry into the same mould, as this mould has been expanded through his own career (by the addition, for example, of those 18th-century "hard riding country gentlemen").[27]

This prescriptive design is also reflected in the two anthologies that Yeats edited. In 1895, *A Book of Irish Verse* appeared. According to one commentator, it represents an "attempt to mold the Anglo-Irish literary past," and, in the words of another, it became "a sourcebook for a number of later Irish anthologies."[28] It is part of Yeats's need to fashion a literary tradition for himself, and to build an audience for Irish literature among "the leisured classes" by separating "what has literary value from what has only a patriotic and political value."[29] Craft is crucial, for "in this century, who does not strive to be a perfect craftsman achieves nothing."[30] His introduction attempted to give tangible form to what Yeats wishes to be seen as modern Irish poetry in English.[31] Once again he exerts his critical power against the poetry of *The Nation*: "the poets who gathered about Thomas Davis, and whose work has come down to us in 'The Spirit of the Nation' were of practical and political, not of literary importance."[32] A slightly revised edition of this book appeared in 1900, and it was reprinted in 1920, the latter event confirming, it would seem, Yeats's wish to see the anthology establishing the orthodox matrix and line of modern Irish verse. It also suggests, at least implicitly, that Yeats avoided any real critical commentary, in public at least, upon his younger contemporaries and juniors. Even in the 1895 Introduction he had been more eager to establish the design of modern Irish poetic history than to comment in an overt way on his own contemporaries.[33] What he does instead is to urge them to "a passion for artistic perfection," lest "the deluge of incoherence, vulgarity, and triviality pass over our heads."[34] Such values, repeated in 1920 and echoed in "Under Ben Bulben," illustrate the firmness with which Yeats held onto his critical design for modern Irish poetry. That the inflexibility of such values will exclude many of Yeats's younger contemporaries and juniors from his design seems obvious.

Such is the firmness with which he held onto these commitments, indeed, that they comprise an essential part of the generalisations informing Yeats's final pronouncements on the tradition of Irish poetry to which he had himself given coherent form. In 1936, Yeats's other anthology appeared, its broader range an indication of his own increased stature since 1900. While *The Oxford Book of Modern Verse* holds many interests for literary historians and students of Yeats, in the present discussion I wish only to address its implications regarding his attitudes towards Irish poets and poetry. In 1936 he also gave a talk for the BBC on modern poetry.[35] Both talk and anthology were the cause of the last in Yeats's long line of literary controversies. Of the broadcast he can say with a touch of pride: "I broadcasted on modern poetry a month ago and have already a crop of enemies because I have left men out or praised their enemies. Even my favourite crony here [Higgins] is cold and if the chill remains he will be a loss."[36]

The broadcast itself suggests very strongly Yeats's wish to dissociate himself from the foreseeable future of Irish poetry. Apart from some measured praise for Louis MacNeice, whom he did not regard in any significant way as an Irish poet, he mentions only one other poet of Irish birth. His reasons for this striking omission are curious, and oddly evasive of the whole issue:

> Many Irish men and women must be listening, and they may wonder why I have said nothing of modern Irish poetry. I have not done so because it moves in a different direction and belongs to a different story. . . . Because Ireland has a still living folk tradition, her poets cannot get it out of their heads that they themselves . . . will be remembered by the common people. Instead of turning to impersonal philosophies, they have hardened and deepened their personalities.[37]

By gathering, but not naming, all those poets who were his contemporaries, his younger contemporaries, and his successors under the umbrella of a single amorphous generalisation, Yeats suggests they are all followers of the official line, all willing elements in the coherent design he has himself composed and continuously insisted upon. The design, he implies, is complete. Essentially he evades consideration of actuality, those unstructurables of historical change and progression which would complicate that design and take it out of his control. Essentially, too, he withdraws Irish poetry from the currents of the world.

In the Introduction to *The Oxford Book*, Yeats's comments on Irish poets, although he does include a few in the selection itself,[38] remain general for the most part, and where particular they are carefully tailored to fit the enduring generalisation. Of two younger contemporaries of the Revival of whom he approves, he has this to say: "In Ireland, where still lives almost undisturbed the last folk tradition of western Europe, the songs of Campbell and Colum draw from that tradition their themes, return to it, and are sung to Irish airs by boys and girls and who have never heard the names of the authors."[39] He says of Synge that he "brought back masculinity to Irish verse," and—referring most obviously to himself—he reminds his readers that "when the folk movement seemed to support vague political mass excitement, certain poets began to create passionate masterful personality."[40] By using "we" in some of his observations, Yeats implies a school of which he himself is the presumed master, going on, however, to refine the "school" almost out of existence: "We are not many; Ireland has few poets of any kind outside Gaelic," he claims, and proceeds to a definite statement, the pragmatic facts of which are difficult, if not impossible to determine: "We are what we are because almost without exception we have had some part in public life in a country where public life is simple and exciting."[41]

Such terms seem as hard to apply to most of the Irish poets then alive and achieving some sort of recognition—Stephens, Clarke, O'Sullivan, Higgins, Kavanagh, MacNeice—as do the epithets "simple and exciting" to an Ireland that, having passed through a war of independence and a civil war, was settling uneasily into the political framework of a modern state in a troubled contemporary Europe. No wonder a reviewer said the book would "shock some of its editor's friends, admirers, and disciples, particularly the youngest of them."[42] Consciously or unconsciously, such critical terms as Yeats uses seem designed to leave Yeats himself—inheritor of a tradition to which he has himself given a coherent design—as master of the field, a king with no successors other than those of his own appointing. As the folk tradition flowed into the work of Colum and Campbell, which work then flowed back into the anonymous folk tradition, so the elected line of Irish poetry out of which Yeats comes runs at the end back into Yeats himself, as he closes the pattern he has initiated.

In fact it is Yeats's seeming choice of his Irish heir-apparent that supports my sense of the idiosyncrasy of his attitude toward Irish poetry after his own. Both in the BBC talk and in his Introduction to the Oxford Book, Yeats praises his friend Oliver St. John Gogarty in terms that set him far above any other contemporary poet. It was not simply that the younger poet paid the older the continued compliment of imitation, saying he was indebted to him for "anything I owe / In the art of making songs,"[43] that made Yeats describe Gogarty as "among the greatest lyric poets of our time."[44] Rather, Gogarty's verse embodies the ideals Yeats wishes Irish poetry to follow, those prescriptive ideals that appear again in "Under Ben Bulben." Gogarty's poetry is "gay, stoical . . . heroic song," qualities inevitably commending it to Yeats's aesthetic sensibility and validating the design for Irish poetry on which he had insisted from the start: "Irish by tradition and many ancestors," he says, I love . . . swashbucklers, horsemen, swift, indifferent men; yet I do not think that this is the sole reason, good reason though it is, why I give him considerable space [17 poems, 12 pages], and think him one of the greatest lyric poets of our age."[45] Even in its extravagant praise of Gogarty, then, Yeats's final, most forceful statement about the Irish poetry that was to succeed him looks back rather than forward. The poems of Gogarty he published do nothing to disturb the design he has laid down, confirming it in either their self-conscious Irishry or their well-learned craft. Immobilising the future this way, the gesture in symbolic terms—while seeming to represent a confirmation of lineal continuity—resembles that slaying of the son by the father which Yeats represented more than once in his treatment of the Cuchulain myth and, with such bitterness, in his last play, *Purgatory*. There, having killed father and son, the old man stands totally isolated in the glare of his own tragic human essence. To speak metaphorically, Yeats seems to have given substance to such an image of himself in his relationship with the younger generation of Irish poets.

Apart from such generalisations, which underline the coherence of Yeats's commands to Irish poets in "Under Ben Bulben" and suggest the consistency and endurance of his aesthetic beliefs regarding Irish poetry, his expressed particular views on the younger generation of poets are very few. This in itself seems significant. John Eglinton, the critic, for example, remembers Yeats as one who "tended to remain aloof from a majority of the younger poets of the period."[46] He was, says Monk Gibbons, "chary of giving an opinion of the worth of younger poets."[47]

The event that stands out most prominently in this regard is Yeats's response to the small anthology of young poets published by AE in 1904. Called *New Songs*, the aim of this volume was "to show some of the new ways the wind of poetry listeth to blow in Ireland today."[48] This event seems to have provoked Yeats into making explicit his dislike of the younger poets. One plausible if unflattering reason for his dislike may be that Yeats was irritated that it was around AE these writers gathered; it was a well-known fact that he called them "AE's canaries."[49] Coming not very long after Yeats's *Book of Irish Verse*, the publication of *New Songs* may have shaken the design he had so carefully composed, pointing to a future this design could not accommodate. In addition, the mainly twilit poetry of *New Songs* may have been too imitative of Yeats's own and AE's verse for Yeats's liking. And although in 1898 he could give AE fulsome praise for his influence on their younger contemporaries,[50] perhaps the suggestion of a "school" under any mastership but his own annoyed him. Whatever the immediate stimulus, the publication of this small volume marks the first important sign of the division between Yeats and the younger poets. As Austin Clarke remembers it, "Yeats regarded the younger generation with disfavour after AE had gathered their early poems in a small anthology."[51] The fact then seems public knowledge, although Yeats himself made no public prose comment on it.

In a letter to AE, however, Yeats reveals some of the possible motives for his dislike. The most important and plausible among such motives, as I've said, is Yeats's opposition, in the persons of these young poets, to a part of his own poetic self which he has left behind. "Some of the poems I will probably underrate," he says, "because the dominant mood in many of them is one I have fought in myself and put down."[52] The new poets were not "manly" enough for Yeats's taste. Like his own earlier verse they exhibit "an exaggeration of sentiment and sentimental beauty which I have come to think unmanly." A criterion like this finds significant echoes in the lines earlier quoted from "Under Ben Bulben," and in Yeats's admiration for Gogarty, clearly posited in large part upon the latter's "manliness." It highlights again the consistency of Yeats's aesthetic thought—and accounts for his notorious exclusion of Wilfred Owen from the *Oxford Book* on the grounds that "passive suffering is not a theme for poetry"[53]—and for those limitations on his thought that effectively separated him from the next generation of Irish poets. In a sense he needed the design too much to forfeit it to the historical process, for it guaranteed his own self-sufficient identity as a poet. In the letter to AE he makes this clear:

> As so often happens with a thing one has been tempted by and
> is still a little tempted by, I am roused by it to a kind of fren-
> zied hatred which is quite out of my control . . . I cannot
> probably be quite just to any poetry that speaks to me with the

sweet insinuating feminine voice of the dwellers in that country of shadows and hollow images. I have dwelt there too long
not to dread all that comes out of it. We possess nothing but
the will and we must never let the children of vague desires
breathe upon it nor the waters of sentiment rust the terrible
mirror of its blade. I fled from some of this new verse you
have gathered as from much verse of our day, knowing that I
fled that water and breath.

In this way, then Yeats externalises an unwanted aspect of his own poetic identity. The terms of his rejection, then, become a principle part of his aesthetic
equipment as a poet. His comments also represent a turning from "much verse
of our day," an elected separation from contemporary currents which finds an
obvious echo in "Under Ben Bulben." In rejecting AE's protegés like this he
separates himself from a collective identity of Irish poetry that cannot be lodged
within the design of the Irish tradition which he has himself organised and to
which, in the passage of instruction to imagined "Irish poets," he will give final
expression.

The quarrel with the younger poets does not stop here. "AE's protegés,"
says Monk Gibbon, "were always anathema to WB . . . to be AE's man was
about the worst recommendation anyone could have with Yeats."[54] Yeats's own
journal for 1909 testifies to the truth of this claim. His objections to these young
artists are social, political, even physical, and match his growing disenchantment with the Irish public as a whole. Russell's followers, he says, are "typical
of the new class which is rising in Ireland: often not ill-bred in manner and
therefore the more manifestly with the ill-breeding of the mind."[55] In Yeats's
view these writers represent the same danger to true art as did the writers of *The
Nation*. Popularity and politics corrupt them as artists: "When they take to any
kind of action it is to some kind of extreme politics. . . . They long for popularity that they may believe in themselves."[56] Here Yeats seems to turn implicitly
from the actualities of Irish life and historical action. Although on an aesthetic
level his quarrel with the younger generation can make sense, it effectively prevents him from knowing or appreciating the Irish poetry that will succeed his
own:

> Went to Russell's Sunday night—everybody either too tall or
> too short, or crooked or lopsided . . . Ireland since the Young
> Irelanders has given itself up to apologetics. Every impression
> of life or impulse of imagination has been examined to see if it
> helped or hurt the glory of Ireland or the political claim of
> Ireland. Gradually sincere impressions of life become imposs-
> ible.[57]

Whatever the justice of the comment, it also suggests that Yeats's literary, and
social, values are decisively fixed in the mould he laid down in shaping an acceptable Irish tradition.

Yeats's final separation from Russell's poets is effected by the bitter little poem he wrote around the same time, in response to AE's request that he write something favorable about the younger writers. Written in 1909, it was originally entitled "To AE, who wants me [to] praise some of his poets imitators of my own":

> You say, as I have often given tongue
> In praise of what another's praise or sung,
> 'Twere politic to do the like by these;
> But was there ever dog that praised his fleas.[58]

After such an insult—the poem appeared in *The Green Helmet* (1920)—there could be little likelihood of a reconciliation between Yeats and the majority of the poets of the next generation. There were exceptions: Gogarty, O'Connor, and Higgins in particular were closely attached to Yeats. Yet, his *general* dislike of (he never in writing actually named the poets he had in mind) and consequent detachment from the poets of the younger generation remained constant.

It is this detachment, I believe, that fuels the magisterial commands to Irish poets in the quotation from "Under Ben Bulben" which began this essay. These poets are a collective fiction of Yeats's imagination, a way of drawing his version of Irish poetry around himself, making it integral with himself and his poetic career, abdicating from historical process, and—perhaps without meaning to—making it necessary for the next generation of poets to carve out their own direction, away from the tree and its shadow. One of the younger poets describes this in a different metaphor: "Yeats hacked a great tributary for himself off the main stream of English literature; many poets of his time were drowned in it. Today our young poets are fighting their way back to that main stream and perhaps later (if they wish), they will carve out their own bywater."[59] After shaping himself to the very end ("Myself must I remake") and—in his epitaph—beyond it, Yeats shapes for himself a literary tradition extending out of a past he has ordered into a future he summons. While the matter of history might elude his mastery (and the greatest of his poems embody his struggle with this fact of life), the matter of self and—so the passage argues—of culture were still in his power. He had once (in 1909) said that "To oppose the new ill-breeding of Ireland . . . I can only set up a secondary or interior personality created by me out of the tradition of myself."[60] It is this "tradition of myself" that Yeats is left with at the end. In it he seems as splendidly alone as one of the oath-bound heroes of his last poem, "The Black Tower," speaking out of heroic fortitude to a collective version of himself, rather than to actual Irish poets who had to establish, after his death, a fresh identity for Irish poetry.

Yeats said himself that "the great thing is to go empty to the grave."[61] His address to the imagined Irish poets ensures that this will be so, since the tradition to which he gave coherent, magnificent design ends with himself. His last symbolic act as a poet is to rid himself of it, to recite it out into the air, into the ears of his own imagined version of a future that cannot come to pass. Writing almost a decade after Yeats's death, one of the poets of the younger generation summarises the relationship which has been the subject of this essay. In doing so he used a familiar image: "Great poets, like great trees, cast massive shadows; poets who grow near them are robbed of their share of the sun; and not till death sets the great bole lying in the grass does the younger leafage succeed to the beaming of fame."[62]

By the time of Yeats's death in 1939, a number of important works by Irish poets who would be the leaders of the next generation (and founding fathers for the poetic generations to follow) had been published. Among the most significant of these were volumes by Austin Clarke—not merely three early Revival-influenced volumes, but also the more original and important *Pilgrimage and Other Poems* (1929) and *Night and Morning* (1938), as well as a *Collected Poems* (1936). In addition, Patrick Kavanagh's first book—*Ploughman and Other Poems* (some of it under the influence of AE, as early Clarke was under Yeats's influence)—had appeared in 1936, Denis Devlin's early volume, *Intercession,* came out in 1937, while by 1939 Louis MacNeice (who, in 1941, would produce a critical study of Yeats) had published *Blind Fireworks* (1929), *Poems* (1935), *Out of the Picture* (1937), *The Earth Compels* (1938) and (in 1939) *Autumn Journal.* But what Irish poetry after Yeats would look like—once the poets of that generation had wholly emerged from the shadow cast by greatness and by a consistent attitude on the part of their great predecessor—still remained to be seen. One thing must have seemed certain, though, even on the evidence of the books I have mentioned. What Yeats in his peremptory last poetic will and testament called "the indomitable Irishry" was hardly how these poets were going to think of themselves or their various versions of Ireland. And it was unlikely that the poetry they needed to compose would "sing the lords and ladies gay" of those "other days" on which Yeats exhorted them to cast their minds. The present world, with all its taxing, complex, and original demands would compel their fresh responses. Neither metrically nor otherwise would they be likely to walk in their father's footsteps.

1979

NOTES

[1] "Under Ben Bulben," in W.B. Yeats, *Collected Poems* (London: Macmillan, 1950) 400. Only Part VI appeared in *The Irish Press.*

[2] *Arrow* was the occasional magazine of the Abbey Theatre. Higgins' essay also appears in *Scattering Branches: Tributes to the Memory of W.B. Yeats,* ed. Stephen Gwynn (New York: Macmillan, 1940) 145-46. Farren's remarks appear in *The Course of Irish Verse* (London: Sheed and Ward, 1948) 75.

[3] In *The Irish Independent,* January 30, 1939.

[4] In 1949. Appears in *W.B. Yeats: Interviews and Recollections,* ed. E.H. Mikhail, vol. I (London: Macmillan, 1975-77) 380.

[5] *The Masterpiece and the Man* (London: Rupert Hart-Davis, 1959) 151.

[6] See Higgins in *Scattering Branches,* 150.

[7] See *Davis, Mangan, Ferguson? Tradition and the Irish Writer* (Dublin: Dolmen Press, 1970) 20.

[8] "Poetry and Patriotism," in *Poetry and Ireland: Essays by W.B. Yeats and Lionel Johnson* (1908; facs. rpt. Shannon: Irish University Press, 1970) 8.

[9] Speaking of this poem later, Yeats describes the Fisherman as "the picture of a man who lived in the country where I had lived, who fished in mountain streams where I had fished." *Uncollected Prose by W.B. Yeats*, ed. John P. Frayne, Colton Johnson, vol. II (New York: Columbia University Press, 1976) 498.

[10] *Samhain*, 1908, in *Explorations* (New York: Collier, 1962) 235.

[11] "Irish Poets and Irish Poetry" (1886), in *Uncollected Prose by W.B. Yeats*, ed. John P. Frayne, vol. I (New York: Cambridge University Press, 1970) 81.

[12] *Ibid*, 90.

[13] *Ibid*, 104.

[14] *Ibid*, 147.

[15] *Ibid*, 103.

[16] *Ibid*, 152.

[17] *Ibid*, 162. A possible echo, here, of Longfellow's sonnet on Chaucer?

[18] *Ibid*, 209.

[19] *Ibid*, 273.

[20] *Ibid*, 249.

[21] In *Tradition and the Irish Writer*, 20.

[22] Frayne, I, 120.

[23] *Ibid*, 295.

[24] *Ibid*, 380.

[25] *Ibid*, II, 123.

[26] *Ibid*, I, 382.

[27] This is not to say that his exhortation to the poets covers the enormous variety and complexity of his career. Rather, it attempts to impose upon the future a fiction, what Yeats would like in some sense to assert as the shape of his career, a shape radically simpler than the actuality had been.

[28] Frayne, I, 360; Richard O'Shea, *Yeats as Editor* (Dublin: Dolmen Press, 1975) 26.

[29] *A Book of Irish Verse*, rev. ed. (London: Methuen, 1900) xv. Yeats's attempt to fashion a fit audience persists throughout his career and is the subject for a separate essay.

[30] *Ibid*, xxvii.

[31] See his important letter of 1895 on this subject in *The Letters of W.B. Yeats*, ed. Allan Wade (London: Rupert Hart-Davis, 1954) 250.

[32] *A Book of Irish Verse*, xxiii.

[33] This is intended as a comparative statement. He has some specific remarks about AE, Lionel Johnson, Katherine Tynan, Nora Hopper, and Charles Weekes (xxviii-xxix); mainly he praises "their deliberate art."

[34] *Irish Verse*, xxvii.

[35] Broadcast October 11, 1936; published in *Essays by W. B. Yeats*, 1931 to 1936 (1937; facs. rept. Shannon: Irish University Press, 1971) 6-28.

[36] Wade, 867.

[37] *Essays 1931 to 1936*, 26.

[38] AE, Colum, Gogarty, Gregory, Higgins, Joyce, MacGreevy, MacNeice, O'Connor, Rolleston, Stephens, Strong, Synge, Wilde. The number, nature, and com-

parative representation of these poets were also triggers of dispute for the many critics of *The Oxford Book.*

[39] *The Oxford Book of Modern Verse 1892-1935* (New York: Oxford University Press) xiii.

[40] *Ibid*, xiv.

[41] *Ibid*, xvi.

[42] See *W. B. Yeats, The Critical Heritage*, ed. A. Norman Jeffares (London: Routledge and Kegan Paul, 1977) 378.

[43] "Elegy on the Archpoet William Butler Yeats Lately Dead," in *The Collected Poems of Oliver St. John Gogarty* (New York: Devin-Adair, 1954) 200. It seems significant that Gogarty's is the only Irish elegy of note on Yeats's death. A reviewer of *The Oxford Book* noted that Gogarty "very closely [resembles] Mr. Yeats himself in his middle period." *Critical Heritage*, 383. Gogarty himself said, "Yeats would offer suggestions that I invariably accepted gratefully." *W.B. Yeats, Interviews and Recollections*, ed. E.H. Mikhail, vol. I (London: Macmillan, 1977) 312.

[44] *Essays 1931-1936*, 27.

[45] *Oxford Book*, xv. For statistics on *Oxford Book* see *Critical Heritage*, 379.

[46] See Edward Boyle-Smith, "A Survey and Index of the Irish Statesman (1923-30)," Unpubl. Diss. Univ. of Washington, 1966 [copy in National Library, Dublin] 54.

[47] Gibbon, 103.

[48] *New Songs* (Dublin, London, 1904), 5. The poets included are Padraic Colum, Eva Gore-Booth, Thomas Koehler, Alice Milligan, Susan Mitchell, Seamus O'Sullivan, George Roberts, and Ella Young.

[49] See Gibbon, 162. He is quoting George Moore's jibe in *Hail and Farewell*.

[50] "I do not believe I could easily exaggerate the direct and individual influence which 'AE' (Mr. George Russell), the most subtle and spiritual poet of his generation, and a visionary who may find room beside Swedenborg and Blake, has had in shaping to a definite conviction the vague spirituality of young Irish men and women of letters." W.B. Yeats, *Memoirs*, ed. Denis Donoghue (New York: Macmillan, 1972) 283.

[51] *A Penny in the Clouds* (London: Routledge and Kegan Paul, 1968) 73.

[52] Wade, 434-35, for this and subsequent quotations from the letter.

[53] *Oxford Book*, xxxiv. The whole issue of "manliness" as a Yeatsian aesthetic—and ethical—criterion is subject for another essay. Enough to say here that the attempt to get beyond its sexist limitations was an important component in the work of later Irish poets. Imagine, for example, what Patrick Kavanagh would make of it.

[54] Gibbon, 190.

[55] *Memoirs*, 140.

[56] *Ibid*, 148.

[57] *Ibid*, 150.

[58] *Ibid*, 221. The published title of the poem is "To a Poet, Who Would Have Me Praise Certain Bad Poets, Imitators of His Mine." *Collected Poems*, 105.

[59] Valentine Iremonger, in *The Bell*, VII, 3 (1943) 256.

[60] *Memoirs*, 142.

[61] Mikhail, I, 204.

[62] Robert Farren, *The Course of Irish Verse*, 147.

Remembering and Forgetting:
Poet and Society in the Work of Austin Clarke

Éire, clamant with pity,
Remembering the old mythology.

What I want to do here is draw a very small sketch of Austin Clarke's evolving notion of the poet, as this can be deduced from the changing nature of the work. I will try to show that despite remarkable changes in the poetry itself—changes which at times occur during long periods of silence—Clarke's sense of the poet's nature and mission remained curiously consistent. And this consistency, I'd argue, entitles Clarke to a status unique among Irish poets who have, since the 19th Century, written in English. Useless as the title itself may be, and reluctant as any poet in his or her right mind would be to bear it, Clarke seems to me to have earned the no doubt ironic right to be known as a "national poet."

I

Clarke's beginnings as a poet are birthmarked by the cultural ideology of the Revival. The epics which constitute his first creative phase are a deliberate response to ideological exhortation. "The discovery of our own mythology and epic stories by the poets of the Irish Literary Revival," he says, "excited my imagination," and it was in an eight-week "state of recurrent imaginative excitement" that he wrote, not long after the Easter Rising, *The Vengeance of Fionn.*[1] While Keats and Tennyson are major influences on the poetic texture of this re-telling of the tale of Diarmuid and Grainne ("youthful bluebelling, lushing and thrushing," was how Clarke later described it),[2] the picture of the poet it offers is mainline Revivalism, descending directly from Standish O'Grady through AE. Of O'Grady's *Bardic History of Ireland*, the book which roused Clarke to an excited pride in the Irish past, AE said, "There was more than a man in it, there was the soul of the people, its noblest and most exalted life symbolised in the story."[3] O'Grady himself praised the tale of Cuculain as "one of the greatest in the whole world," saying its merit "is not mine, but has come to me as a tradition and legacy of our ancestors, the great singers and narrators of old time."[4]

The richly fluent, perfectly anonymous narrator of *The Vengeance of Fionn* is just such a 'medium' for the Irish tale as Revival orthodoxy required. This poet obviously wants to be a voice for that "memory of race"[5] which AE said rose up within him as he read Standish O'Grady. Within the poem itself, the poet Oisín is a mirror for such orthodox notions. A master of enchanting song, he draws his audience to love the old stories; he celebrates the beauties of land-scape; he praises the heroic virtue of the tribe's great men. As a young Irish poet at the start of his career, Clarke is trying to do no less.

Heroic virtue and evocative landscapes are also among the features of Clarke's next 'epic'—the extravagantly Miltonic narrative on the death of Moses, which he called *The Fires of Baal*. Although the tribe this time is not Celtic, and although the poem was "commissioned" by Clarke's Jesuit employ-ers at UCD, when at a unique moment in the anonymous narration the poet re-veals himself, he turns out to be a recognisably Revivalist poet, most likely un-der the influence of AE. Describing Moses' vision, the narrator says, "he saw tremendous forms of doom, / Ranked demi-gods like their great images / Of hammered brass by men and clouded gods. / The mountain gods, that I, who sing, have known / In light and sleep."[6] In *The Candle of Vision* AE stressed the "gift of seership" possessed by "our Gaelic ancestors."[7] He saw poets of the Irish present, like himself, as being "the servants of gods who speak or act through them."[8] Obviously the poet of *The Fires of Baal* is just such a bardic figure (quite distinct from the actual Austin Clarke, lecturer in English at UCD)—singer, visionary, memorialist of the tribe.

This traditional image of tribal bard is strongly in evidence through Book One of *The Sword of the West* ("Concobar," finished in 1918). Even more con-fidently than before, this narrator is the voice of the tribe, namer of great names, medium for "the old hazel tales of the woods and of old loves": "Grave Ferdia the sorrowful and Fergus / brooding his kingly flight, the faithless Celtach / And Fedlimid from grassier kingdoms; many / Whose westward names are lonely cairns; darker / With fate, the proud unhappy clan of Usnach. / They for one woman died and gave all harps / Their sorrow."[9] When the primary narrator hands his narrative over to surrogate singers, these wanderers, dreamers, and tribal memorialists summarise this aspect of the cultural ideology of the Re-vival: "Forever poets in remembering song / Shall be the torches of the dark-ened world." The poet, then, is the medium for the voices of tradition, a pro-cedure Clarke picked up not only from the poetics of AE but from the practice of Herbert Trench's *Deirdre Wed*, where narrative is consigned to the great re-membering voices of the tribe.[10] In Clarke's accumulation of secondary voices, however, the poem's coherence is shaken and it becomes a Revivalist hall of mirrors, imaging a poet who is at one moment a wandering lover-god like Yeats's Aengus, at another a visionary singer, at yet another a heroic dreamer who recounts ecstatically the climactic battle of Moytura.

In the gap between finishing Book One (1918) and writing Book Two (1920-21), Clarke's life suffered shocks which affected his idealised notion of the poet: the death of his father, a sexually provoking but unconsummated af-fair, a mental breakdown and months of hospitalisation, a marriage in a registry office which lasted ten days, the consequent loss of his job at UCD. These are hard facts to swallow for one who would be the voice of remembering song.

Some results may be seen in the poetry and, specifically, in his sense of the nature and function of the poet. The most distinct and dramatic change occurs in section II, where the narrator suddenly reveals himself as a closer version of the poet's actual self than any that's appeared before this.[11] Erotic torment shatters bardic intentions: the "fiery clans" of Section I "Ebb from my song and I am desolate." Like the main voice in *The Wind Among the Reeds* (a major influence), this poet is a solipsistic lover and dreamer who broods upon his lost beloved's "sea-lit face" and "the long tumultuous surge / Of her dark hair," and who knows "I shall never feel her passionate breasts / Beat under mine and silence gathering me / Into her burning deeps."[12] While the narrator eventually draws himself back to his bardic duty,[13] the interlude dramatises the power of Eros to force the poet from his ideal public task, as the same power operating on Clarke's actual life made a dramatic divorce between him and his community.

The rest of the poem deals with Cuculain's sickness and the search of his comrades to find him. The most important of the traditional voices among which Clarke distributes his narrative is the potent unknown bard who appears in Section III and, most tellingly, in Section IV. His function there is to sing the early story of Cuculain and, as it turns out, to serve as elegist for this whole heroic world. Taking dictation from the enduring land itself, he functions as "remembering song," urging the later world to "remember the little clan / That is riding beyond the last reeded shore." Singing an elegy for the hero, he says, "The mournful years / Of these majestic lands burn slowly down. / Their shadows are the harp."[14] Revealed as a god—Aongus Mor—he announces that "I, I am / The voice of song, that will return no more." With such a stress upon endings, Clarke unmakes the image of the poet he has composed out of orthodox Revivalist ideology. The poem becomes an elegy for itself and its poet, who recognises the impossibility of any authentic continuation as a poet in this archaic mode. Among the reasons that might be put forward for his sense of its failure is its remoteness from his actual self and the historical actuality of the world he must live in. Such speculation is at least strengthened by a little poem he wrote later (when exactly is not clear) as a sort of coda to his engagement with the epic material. Echoes to passages in the epics themselves turn these lines into a deliberate epilogue:

> The thousand tales of Ireland sink: I leave
> Unfinished what I had begun nor count
> As gain the youthful frenzy of those years;
> For I remember my own passing breath,
> Man's violence and all the despair of brain
> That wind and river took in Glenasmole.
>   ("The Tales of Ireland," *Collected Poems*, 1930)

II

Clarke's work after these epics may be seen in part as an attempt to revise Revivalist assumptions about the nature of the poet and his relationship with his community. Although the title poem of his next book—*The Cattledrive in Connacht*—is an epic fragment, its style differs sharply from that of the earlier poems, being much more dramatically colloquial in speech, character, and poetic texture. Here the poet seems to repossess the past, rather than being possessed by it. His style historicises the material, re-makes it in modern English:

> He bounced out of bed
> Into the pot. He ran with candlelight
> To waken up the household. All had heard
> With fear that quarrel in the royal blankets
> And filled the hall with yawny light and piled
> Great smoke upon the flags and that proud queen
> Came in before the women and sat down
> Upon a carven chair in her white shift
> And red strapping hair.[15]

No longer an epic Revivalist creator, the poet has become a kind of translator, finding a language in which the old community can think itself anew in English.

The short poems in this collection work in a similar way. They seem to convert Clarke's own experience (travelling around the country in 1921 and 1922) into poetic forms and language that sound like translations from the Irish. They offer a self-conscious picture of the poet as a man of the people, a member of the tribe:

> Black luck upon you Seamus Mac-an-Bhaird
> Who shut the door upon a poet
> Nor put red wine and bread upon the board;
> My song is greater than your hoard,
> Although no running children know it
> Between the sea and the windy stones.
>   ("A Curse," *Collected Poems*, 118)

There's an intense familiarity about this, in its casual allusiveness, its common codes. Establishing a poet's traditional relationship with "the people" (country people),[16] he is making a deliberate attempt to close the gap in the Irish poetic tradition opened by the traumatic transition from the Irish to the English language. Trying to re-experience and re-express the Gaelic tradition in English, his work is a sort of translation—both actual ("The Fair at Windgap") and latent (as in poems like "The Frenzy of Suibhne," "The House in the West," or "The Itinerary of Ua Cleirigh"—"I halted with Yeats / To share the wise salmon . . . I dipped in his plate / Without praise, without wine"). In these and in poems like

"The Lost Heifer" (written "in the mode of the Jacobite songs")[17] Clarke goes beyond translation—unless you think of Pound's "versions"—to bring the Gaelic experience to life in strange yet idiomatically modern English.

Any self-conscious posturing that adheres to this performance in *Cattle-drive* (e.g., "And O, Padraic, you did not know me, / Though we, for a week, / In Baltinglass, / Were drinking with the Wicklow men") is wonderfully exorcised in *Pilgrimage* (1929). This volume contains the first fully mature fruits of the grafting process that took place in *Cattledrive*. Here the traditional persona of the poet is balanced with Clarke's own private preoccupations. Inhabiting the verse in a new way, Clarke makes more profound and complicated the relationship between the poet and his society. At the same time, the task he performs is still that of "remembering song," since he brings into existence here in English a Catholic Gaelic world which the Revival mostly ignored. The poet speaks as a native of that world, rendering its sensibility and texture for us in vivid English. Reaching beyond the achievement of Synge and Stephens (and Hyde and Lady Gregory), the poems represent a reincarnation of the old realities in new forms:

> Grey holdings of rain
> Had grown less with the fields,
> As we came to that blessed place
> Where hail and honey meet.
> O Clonmacnoise was crossed
> With light: those cloistered scholars,
> Whose knowledge of the gospel
> Is cast as metal in pure voice,
> Were all rejoicing daily.
>   ("Pilgrimage")

Here is a marvellous immersion in the old experience, bringing it over into adequate English, while the "we" shows unquestionable community between speaker and surroundings.

Even where there's a critical attitude towards these surroundings, the voice of the poems speaks always as a member of that society. In "Celibacy," for example, Clarke deals both lyrically and dramatically with a problem intrinsic to the Irish (historical) condition, while remaining a part of that environment, a suffering member of that community. It's the sheer verbal energy of this and other poems in the collection—poems, for example, which use the female voices of Queen Gormlai and the Young Woman of Beare to dramatise the perennial Irish dialectic of sexual passion and religious restraint; or poems that catch the pure note of Gaelic political allegory; or the translations proper—which make them so much more than historical pastiche: they are true recreations. In Clarke's "free paraphrase" of *An Mac Leighinn*, for example, you can hear how he domesticates in English the assonantal play of the Gaelic original:

Summer delights the scholar
With knowledge and reason.
Who is happy in hedgerow
Or meadow as he is?

In *Pilgrimage* the poet has no self-conscious role *as poet*. He simply belongs, and speaks out of that clear sense of belonging. He makes out of his craft a world of which he is a native. He composes himself as an Irish poet, reaching out of historical Gaelic into contemporary English. In the verse plays he had the "intense pleasure" of writing between 1929 and 1938, Clarke is practising to an extended degree the art he'd mastered in *Pilgrimage*, making the older world accessible in lively English. His return as a poet, then, in the 1938 volume *Night and Morning* intensifies and deepens and complicates the sense of the poet he has built up so far, and the sense of that poet's relationship with his community.

III

The poems in *Night and Morning* deal with the loss of faith. As the last sections of *The Sword of the West* may be seen as an elegy for the old idealised world of Celtic myth, so *Night and Morning* may be seen as an elegy for the poet's sense of belonging to his community (the community imagined, perhaps, in *Pilgrimage*) in the old way.[18] In part, too, it is a painful critique of destructive elements within that community, elements which divorce the individual from the group. Both as critic and elegist, however, Clarke finds himself speaking not just in his own person, but as spokesman for those in a like condition. Even in these most agonisingly personal poems, the poet is still conscious of his tribal identity. The ubiquity of the first person plural is the most obvious proof of this fact: "This is the hour when we must mourn / With tallows on the black triangle" ("Tenebrae"); "Forgotten as the minds that bled / For us" ("Night and Morning"); "God only knows / What we must suffer to be lost, / What soul is called our own" ("Mortal Pride"). Poem after difficult poem implies by allusion a community with its own codes of reference, its shared values. Even where passionate opposition is the poet's purpose, as in the dramatised voice of "The Straying Student," the manner is that of the outraged individual who criticises his society while acknowledging his own (fallen) citizenship in "this land, where every mother's son / Must carry his own coffin and believe, / In dread, all that the clergy teach the young." The national poet, moving into the present and his own vulnerable self as subject, becomes an inner exile. The resulting complex mixture of criticism and nostalgia marks his sensitive treatment of the faith of one believer in "Martha Blake," and finds a delicate balance in the last stanza of "The Jewels," with which he closes the volume:

The misery of our common faith
Was ours before the age of reason.

Hurrying years cannot mistake
The smile for the decaying teeth,
The last confusion of our senses.
But O to think, when I was younger
And could not tell the difference,
God lay upon this tongue.

Even in the loss of community, then, Clarke still speaks in the voice of the tribe, is still the poet of community. In circumstances such as those in *Night and Morning*, however, or in a national condition which seems a drastic declension from its original ideals and possibility, the likelihood that a poet will continue to find a "common" voice adequate to the occasion isn't great. Abiding nostalgia is dangerous, and one's own critical loss of faith must be moved on from. In a sense *Night and Morning* is a cul-de-sac for a poet like the poet Clarke wanted to be: by dramatising the difficult divorce between poet and community, it removes the very ground of his being as a poet. It isn't really a surprise, then, that after the publication of *Night and Morning* in 1938, he fell into an almost entirely unbroken silence as a poet for the next seventeen years.[19] It's a surprising testament to his quality and stature as a poet, however, that when he finally emerges from this silence the poetry speaks out of as deep an identification with his community as ever. In his triumphant late phase, in fact, he manages to give fresh life and vigor to his unspoken sense of the poet as the voice of "remembering song," though the song is original, the music strange.

IV

Clarke's way out of the cul-de-sac is satire. But satire, if it's only based on a sense of personal victimisation (as, I think, much of Kavanagh's was), can vent its outrage, sting its objects, but cannot pretend to membership of the community it satirises. It will, in fact, disclaim any such membership—as Yeats does magnificently in "The Fisherman" and elsewhere, and Kavanagh does in "The Paddiad" and other poems. Clarke, on the other hand, saves his own soul as a poet by transcending the specifically personal. "As I have few personal interests left," he says in 1957, "I have concentrated on local notions and concerns which are of more importance than we are, keep us employed and last long."[20]

From the start of this new phase in *Ancient Lights* (1955: "Poems and Satires," First Series), the speaker of the poems (basically Clarke himself) belongs irrevocably to the society he lives in, and his authority to castigate it comes directly from his acknowledgement of belonging. The first-person plural is everywhere. The speed and allusive density of the poems testifies to the community the poet assumes between himself and his audience. There is no need to explain anything: he can use a tribal code consisting of his own experience and local events in that common world. He can celebrate the "great men" (in his eyes) of the community—men like Noel Browne and Jim Larkin, whose messages of social justice have been ignored. He can be elegiac about the lost Gaelic world without sentimentalising it ("Somewhere, the last of our love-songs found a refuge"—he says in "Vanishing Irish"). And he can pity the marginalised "poor lovers" who are victims of middle-class bigotry and religious intolerance. He can address his community in a startling variety of tones, in a language grainy and muscular with its engagement in the practical local present. He accepts his own survival into this diminished age, even relishing his membership in this undignified society. And everywhere pity tempers satiric edge—the word occurs nine times in sixteen poems—suggesting the point of deep identification at which Clarke begins this late phase in the relationship between poet and society.

This relationship and these fundamental traits of the verse remain constant through the second and third series of "Poems and Satires"—*Too Great a Vine* (1957) and *The Horse-Eaters* (1960). Expanding his repertory of targets, criticising his society with ever more subtle and various energies, Clarke harps again and again on the corrupt tendency of this age and this society to forget. Generously he allows Yeats his heroic stature, but his description also implies a certain criticism: "Forgetting our age, he waved and raved / Of art and thought her Memory's daughter." By contrast, Clarke—the insider—knows this present age for what it is. And what it is, is a mixture of greed, vulgarity, and collective amnesia, against which he raises the voice of remembering racial conscience. His voice is the outward sign of an inward, savage sense of belonging, to be heard in the bitter irony of "Better put by our History books / And gape" ("Past and Present"). He is resoundingly at home among such local figures, events, icons (which fact itself may account in part for his "difficulty" and for the fact that his stature and achievement have never been much recognised outside Ireland). From miraculous medals to Nelson's Pillar; from the law of usufruct to the Lourdes pilgrimage; from St. Christopher to Wolfe Tone; from contraception to Christmas Eve riots and the spectacle of "Our goodness rotting in their teens"—his language in its blend of poetic muscle and journalistic immediacy gives them all a full, actual life. With savage impersonality Clarke becomes the embattled poet of community, utterly absorbed by his task.

In both these collections, Clarke's racial memory fuels his local tribal satire. The outraged feeling-at-one with his society culminates in three long poems—"The Loss of Strength," "The Flock at Dawn," and "The Hippophagi." What these three speedy, dense poems compose is a collage of autobiography in which self and society are intricately woven about one another, his own history and that of the tribe, the present and the past. In all this startling verse, for which it is difficult to find an appropriate critical language, Clarke—although his accents are cracked, crabbed, satiric and strange—has laid claim to a status as national poet. He does so by choosing, as he says, "With Fionn the music of what happens"—no matter how different the key he makes it in.

V

In the prolific, prodigal decade and more of creative life remaining to him after these three books, Clarke will luxuriate in the craft he has mastered, live richly into the poetic place and personality he has earned for himself, forging a style in which, as Thomas Kinsella says, "nothing is unsayable."[21] In a ripe glow of creative independence he'll revisit epic territory (to revise, recreate, create anew), compose his own Gaelic airs (in "Eighteenth Century Harp Songs"), brilliantly exorcise the ghosts of his mental breakdown and confinement and recovery (in the remarkable *Mnemosyne Lay in Dust*, 1966), and (in a series of sensuous retellings of tales from Irish and Classical myth) indulge himself in a late literary-sexual sabbatical. But always, whatever the subject or the style, the sense of belonging to the community he writes out of (and, so often, against) is in the very grain of the verse. Through all his changes, his progress as a poet has that particular coherence—the coherent sense of what the poet is and what his relationship is with his society, his tribe. It is a sense gathered first from the twilight idealism of the Revival, then altered to meet the needs of his own spirit and imagination in its encounter with the realities of the fallen world he had to inhabit.

Such loyalty and coherence lend Clarke a certain commanding but still not fully acknowledged eminence in the factional world of Irish poetry after Yeats. Kavanagh, of course, has his own loved eminence, but his is different and, in ways, easier to acknowledge. And, in the North, MacNeice has his particular influential place. But it might be possible to argue (if such arguments were ever worth the handsome energies invested in them) that Clarke is the only poet whose completeness and complexity can be seen as somehow comparable to those of Yeats, and that Yeats's dream of being a national poet ("To write for my own race/ And the reality") is—in ways beyond the scope of even Yeats's own speculation—ironically realised by Clarke. At least *some* of these qualities can be detected in the last lines of the aptly entitled *Forget-Me-Not* (1962), a poem which, in Clarke's late eclectic and syncretic mode, mixes a passionate plea for the protection of horses with personal and poetic autobiography, cultural history, and social satire, among other things:

> Our grass still makes a noble show, and the roar
> Of money cheers us at the winning post.
> So pack tradition in the meat-sack, Boys,
> Write off the epitaph of Yeats.
>   I'll turn
> To jogtrot, pony bell, say my first lesson:
>
> *Up the hill,*
> *Hurry me not;*
> *Down the hill,*
> *Worry me not;*

On the level,
Spare me not,
In the stable,
Forget me not.

Forget me not.

1986

NOTES

[1] *A Penny in the Clouds* (London: Routledge and Kegan Paul, 1968) 84, 55.

[2] *Penny*, 90.

[3] Standish O'Grady, *The Coming of Cuculain* (Dublin: The Talbot Press, 1920 [First edition 1894]) x in AE's Introduction.

[4] *In The Gates of the North* (Dublin: The Talbot Press [First edition 1901]) xiii.

[5] *The Coming of Cuculain*, x.

[6] *The Fires of Baal* (Dublin: Maunsel & Roberts, 1921) 28.

[7] *The Candle of Vision* (London: Macmillan, 1919) 151.

[8] *Ibid.*

[9] *The Sword of the West* (Dublin: Maunsel & Roberts, 1921) 6. Much and brilliantly revised for the 1974 *Collected Poems*. In his revision Clarke omits the self-portraiture I deal with, as well as the Revivalist tones and colours. It might be worth recalling that an early Yeats portrait by his father painted the young poet as King Goll, harp and all.

[10] For Trench's influence see *Penny*, 166 ff.

[11] As any comparison between this part of the poem and Clarke's account of "Margaret" in *Penny* will show. See 44, 47-8.

[12] *Sword*, 55. See 53-8. All Clarke saved from this is the strange lyric "O Love, There is No Beauty," which appears in *Collected Poems* (Dublin: Dolmen Press, 1974) 115.

[13] This deserves quotation because of the echoes it raises in the later "The Tales of Ireland": "Her seaward beauty / Is swept into the mighty tide of clans / Returning, and I have remembered the dim gold, / The fiery tumult, and all the majestic sorrow / That wind and river took in Glenasmole" (59).

[14] *Sword*, 93-4. The echo from the early passage of *Sword* quoted on 3 could be noted.

[15] In *Collected Poems*, 137.

[16] See *Penny*, 130 ff.

[17] *Collected Poems*, Notes, 546.

[18] The intensity of his sense of that particular community of Irish Catholicism may be gauged from his account of a Holy Thursday ritual in his childhood in *Twice Round the Black Church* (London: Routledge and Kegan Paul, 1962, 43-52). Here is a fragment: "As we walked up Aungier Street we were aware of the communion of the saints, the communion of the living and the dead: the hosts in heaven; the people passing by the lamp-posts; the furniture stores and ironmonger shops and the hidden millions in Purgatory" (50).

[19] During this time he continued to write verse plays and work in the theatre and on radio and in literary journalism.

[20] *Collected Poems*, Notes, 549.

[21] In Austin Clarke, *Selected Poems*, ed. by Thomas Kinsella (Dublin: Dolmen Press, 1976) x.

A Decade for A.C. (d. 1974)

The likes of you learned the hard way—
In a dark room, one cold stone weighing

Like death on the chest till words shaped
Themselves in scrolls of sound—shipshape,

Secret, salted. You tested your mettle
Against a Free State superflux of miraculous medals

And hungry young ones who put a tongue
(For bitter, for verse) in your mouth, a longing

For (Pity poor lovers, *you said*) justice, justice
Between ourselves, family planning in every sense. Just this

Church and State—cheek-to-cheeking a two-step—
Shrug off, leading uncreated conscience a goose-step

Through the Walls of Limerick into our kingdom
Come and gone. Home truths for the asking: dumb,

We didn't; burned your books instead. Anger is
Good, you said; discipline better. Uncantankerous

At last, you took our measure, deflating the moneychangers
And other stately chancers. But nothing changes—

Look at the cut of us. We need your likes, your clerk-
ly galled compassion, gadfly second best heretic, Austin Clarke.

1984

Affectionate Truth:
Critical Intelligence
in the Poetry of Padraic Fallon

> *. . . the miracle*
> *Taken for granted, being natural.*

Although his critical star in more recent times has never been high, in 1949 it could be said of Padraic Fallon that "many consider him Ireland's best living poet," and just after his death another poet could claim that he was "one of the three or four most considerable poets since Yeats."[1] Certainly he belongs in the company of Clarke, Kavanagh, MacNeice, Devlin and Hewitt as one of the most accomplished voices of that generation which inherited from Yeats the need to give Irish poetry an identity adequate to its contemporary world. It is for his voice I value him, for what Maurice Harmon calls "a flexible and provisional grace of response,"[2] for his rhetorical modesty (and canniness), his judicious imagination, his critical intelligence serving lyrical ends, for the deeply instructive personality that shines through the best poems, even in their often affectionately impersonal style. It is not my intention here to provide an exhaustive critical survey of all the poems in Fallon's *oeuvre*. The present essay, focussing on what I regard as a central impulse in his imagination, is merely intended to open one small door into his considerable achievement.

Behind many of Padraic Fallon's best poems lies an impulse to evaluate, do justice to, estimate and esteem the objects of his attention. More than a rage for order, his work manifests a passion for equity. Marked by a judicious affection, free of sentimentality, speaking their own authentic speech, the poems can bring us a revived consciousness of things we may have taken for granted. While this judgement seems to hold true for a great deal of the work, it may be most clearly observed in a number of poems which claim myth or the mythopoeic as their object. Such poems form a coherent centre to the work, a point from which the rest of it may be appreciated.[3] These poems may be divided into three major areas: his treatment of existing myths; his revelation in ordinary phenomena of a mythic, ritual essence; his reflection on the notion of myth itself and the absence or presence of the mythic dimension in actual experience. While these three areas do not contain all the best or most important of Fallon's poems, they do provide a summary of Fallon's imaginative life, the lyrical embodiment of what I'm calling his critical intelligence.

I

In poems dealing with the myths of Odysseus and of the Virgin Mary, Fallon grants the stories fresh life in the present moment. This he does by means of the intensely domesticated nature of his language, the muscularly matter-of-fact tones of the poems' speakers. In bringing the big stories down to earth he reveals an instinct that is one of his most telling poetic gifts, and part of his imaginative being from boyhood. As he says in the late autobiographical poem, "Lost Man," his youthful need was for "a local God" who was at home in "The weather or the weekday sod . . . amenable to ewes / And quiet moonbodies like fat turnips."[4] By grounding his treatments in ordinary phenomena that challenge the abstractions of conventional piety, Fallon deepens our sympathetic awareness of the tangible human substance of his chosen myths.

In "Consubstantiality," for example, the dramatically plausible voice of Telemachus ventilates traditional enlargements of the myth, giving its figures fresh dimensions and a deliberately 'modern' feeling. ("If heredity / Indeed determine history," he begins, like someone about to have a commonsense altercation with "Leda and the Swan"). This language can also attach a domestic, faintly rural Irish immediacy to the young man's predicament, "Moping / Among the spitting suitors at the fire, / Field and cupboard nearly bare." The true achievement of Fallon's imaginative intention, however, and one that may be taken as representative of much of his best work, is the way the commitment to the quotidian prepares an ascent to a revived and now earned sense of mystery. Strangeness resides in the common phenomena, so the boy can say of his father, "he comes so near my earth our various substances / Seem one, as trembling from the dim cocoon / The butterfly is dazzled leaf and sun." Trafficking between mundane and mysterious realities, Telemachus' voice sounds the note that will become, through various developments, characteristic of much of Fallon's best verse. At once lyrical and reflective, holding rhetorical extravagance in check, it is a speech designed to give expression to what is called in this poem "the blood's philosophy." Responsive to the cadences of ordinary talk, buttressed with a formal yet free rhyme scheme, it is a voice for the rhythmical activity of a mind tuned to the pitch of its own critical sensibility.

The later poem, "Odysseus," shows the direction in which this speech develops. The poet treats the mythical figure with a warm critical candour that at once domesticates him in a landscape more accessible to our common understanding, and at the same time confers on him a new dignity. The poet's aim is that the hero be properly known. The blend of colloquial and formal speech enacts this revision of his character:

> Last year's decencies
> Are the rags and reach-me-downs he'll wear forever,
> Knowing one day he'll sober up inside them
> Safe in wind and wife and limb,
> Respected, of unimpeachable behaviour.

Judgement and affection are the ends of such articulate intelligence, which provides in the phrase "a talent for rehabilitation" a witty proximity to the subject
that is characteristic of Fallon's approach. Characteristic, too is the way the last
line of the poem rises to an apprehension of the real, rugged mystery that persists into the ordinary humanness of the mythological figure, who "will be his
own man soon, without ecstasy." The voice of such utterances is that of the concerned *instructor*, dispelling conventional notions, encouraging a fresh entrance
into the subject.

In "Public Appointment," Fallon again enters the ordinary human recesses
of the Odysseus myth, this time to probe the complex relationship between the
hero and Nausicaa. Here 'explanation' is the lyric impulse in action, as the poet
looks with wry affection on the incident (the hero's respite from responsibility),
revealing his own values and his resigned sense of the value of the world. Lyrical and critical, Fallon's plain poetic speech neatly corresponds to the substance
of the Homeric interlude and its aftermath: after a statute has been demanded "to
that sacred eloquence, / What rose up in the square / Was not oracular, no great
mouthing of stones." The poet's speech itself instinctively draws back from the
'oracular' stressing, as the statue stresses, the human dimensions of the hero,
rooting mystery in the demystified realm of the ordinary love between the two
fated creatures, in the reclaimed zone of their common humanity, so that "The
image that remains . . . Is the haunted man on the main of love, forever / Sailing,
and beside him a virgin at the tiller." By means of such poetic speech, perception becomes instruction, and instruction rises to illumination. Myth is brought
to its everyday senses and we discover its mystery afresh.

Similar imaginative strategies are at work in Fallon's poems about the Virgin Mary. Mary's location at the crossroads of myth and domesticity naturally
appeals to his imagination, and the poems work to clarify her mythic-human
status. In "Virgin," for example, the poet's careful penetration of conventional
piety to reach the tangible reality underlying it leads to a revived sense of mystery ("How the heavens depend on her! / If her weather altered it would mean /
Angels and their wide glories would drip from the air"). Through evaluation and
celebration, Mary is understood afresh as an object of pious devotion, an earth
goddess, and an experience ("as if I had been kissed / And blessed") of sensual
intimacy. Later, in the more nervously charged language of "Assumption," the
poet instructs us in the rich truth residing in a figure centuries of conventional
piety have made bland. Marrying critical scrutiny to heartfelt celebration, Fallon
brings exalted and domestic truths together, his imaginative emphasis insisting
on the vibrant ordinariness at the heart of this mystery. The myth is hallowed in
its humanised reincarnation, as "She takes her pail among the cows / And bolts
her fowls in the fowl-house." Here, and in the acknowledgement that "only her
dreams stir / The peacock presences of air," Fallon creates a space in Irish poetry for the expression of Catholic faith that is neither tortured nor banal. The
critical pose of the poem appears stylistically in the way elegance and urbanity
coexist with plainness, a balance that signals for me one of the most distinguishing features of Fallon's imagination.

The witty, even laconic tone of "Magna Mater" brings this linguistic poise even more fully into the light. Such a tone perfectly conveys Fallon's critical re-evaluation of the myth:

> A dove plus an
> Assenting virgin is
> An odd equation; the bird of Venus, the
> Shotsilk woodhaunter and
> A country shawl
> In congress to produce
> The least erotic of the gods.

Such a mixture of playful agnosticism and authoritative statement takes bland conventionality by surprise. And though the tone may be implicitly critical of the divorce effected by Irish piety between profane and sacred love, Fallon can still end in complex celebration, connecting the Irish countrywoman he describes with Mary herself, humanising the myth and finding mystery inside the mundane. In the Irish countryside "flowers are born with the names of kings" the women "never heard of, pagan fellows." Such colloquialism indicates the common sense that stays in charge of the poem, effectively joining Mary's "country shawl" to the "indestructible / Country mulch" of the mass-going peasant women of the West of Ireland.

II

The second group of poems (those that reveal in ordinary phenomena a mythic, ritual essence) is also shaped in great part by Fallon's urge that things be known in the fullness of their possible reality. In these poems he shows how items in the ordinary world possess their own particular miracle. One edge of this celebratory instinct may be found in the hearty metamorphic extravagance of such early poems as "*Ma Boheme*" (after Rimbaud), and "Mary Hynes" (after Raftery). A dialogue between the fancy-talking Raftery and his down-to-earth lady shows the easy cohabitation, even at an early stage, of the grand and the familiar in Fallon's imagination. His Rimbaud, too, is eloquent and colloquial in expression. In such poems, and in "*Poète Maudit*," Fallon first discovers his need to reveal in ordinary things of the world the "lost and living god" ("*Poète Maudit*") of a mythopoeic, ritual existence. The old sailors of "Maris Stella," for example, at home in their world of the Wexford quays,[5] prompt the poet to a visionary translation that moves easily, like the best of Fallon's work, between eloquence (the light "drowns them in a wintry flash") and plain statement ("the fishermen / Overhaul their gear"). The poet knows in these old men a ritual presence, recognising how they "Add their little rhythms to the sea, / Each man an estuary," just as the old woman of "The Dwelling" is glimpsed as some goddess of domesticity, where "She shines among her satellites."

Such poems, however, only hint at the power that may be felt in "Field Observation," where Fallon's impulse to give things their due takes a natural turn into elegy. The poem moves with wonderful ease between the mundane and the mythic levels of experience, seeing the dead farmer not only as a "whiskered heavy man," but also "Peaceful as Saturn." In its plain solidity of speech the style still possesses a ritual cadence, miming the poet's double vision, richly summoning up the dead man's being:

> Who moved in the gravity
> Of some big sign, and slowly on the plough
> Came out anew in orbit
> With birds and seasons circling him by habit.

As the poet sees him, the mythic range of this man's spirit is anchored firmly in his everyday reality, harmonising the simple facts with the brilliant extensions of visionary revelation.

Such critical-celebratory impulses find another outlet in the later elegy, "A Visit West," where the dead man (Fallon's Uncle Ben) is elevated out of history into an expansive kinship with landscape and climate. The poet recalls him in life, larger than life, "the West / Tumbling over him, his own sky / Strung from his fist." In death he becomes a genius of place, "stabilised among the lesser shades" in "His greenery / . . . his body gone / Into the weather / Without a care." This relaxed idiom of casual metamorphosis seems perfectly natural to Fallon at this point, while the looser lines and various tones of this poem show the poet in full possession of his craft. His gift is for a deliberate but unostentatious fluency, at home between ordinary and mythic worlds. Managing this, as he also does in "Painting of My Father" and "On the Tower Stairs," Fallon strikes at least one of the dominant chords of his imagination, defining his creative identity as one of peculiar modesty and sharp critical intelligence. So, in the poem on his father, he rejects as description the "big translations" of myth, but finds their adequate human equivalents in a simple naming of the man's qualities, who was "daylight's own fellow." In this nominative piety, ordinariness takes on a ritual quality, and the father may be associated with a favourite figure in Fallon's personal pantheon, leaning at noon, "Recomposed on the rail wall / By the City Arms, yarning, true Ulyssean, / Over a shoeshine." Loving, eloquent, and common speech creates a careful warmth of attitude that brings his Ulysses down to earth with a shoeshine.

Celebration finds a different key in "On the Tower Stairs," turning its subject, Lady Gregory, into "A dugout deity, a disconcerting / Earth mother living on." What Fallon honours in her is the power of acute discrimination (what he himself exercises in 'reading' her) which enables her to see "Beyond the obvious anarchy" in Yeats and into "the prophet authentic, / Like midsummer John." From her tangible actuality ("A dumpy vernacular Victoria") he can rise to a note of genuine feeling, at once evaluative, celebratory and warm:

> Her trumpeted house is gone, entirely razed;

But he did raise up another
There on a totem pole in which the lady is
Oracular and quite composed
To outlast everything, live on forever.

Again, what is striking here is Fallon's linguistic tact and rhythmic conviction. His lines have a fine integrity, and his language is exact, hard and unsentimental. Such stylistic qualities guarantee and give enduring life to the poet's will to celebrate the ritual essence in what he most vividly receives from the ordinary world.

III

The poems in the final group I wish to consider contain, as part of their subject, a reflection upon myth itself, its function, the idea of it. In such poems Fallon meditates upon the habits of his own creative instinct and on the source of those habits in the world. From early on Fallon, it would seem, felt the need of some consoling imaginative faith, a longing for a world transfigured by the numinous. The question of the subjective or objective existence of such a world is raised in "If Gods Happen." Emotional and rational sides of his imaginative identity meet in his speech here, putting 'desires' and 'definitions' into necessary conjunction:

If Gods happen
Only when we throw our wild unreasonable
Desires into a kind of definition,
Are they us? And are we then illimitable?

The archetypal figure of the woman is another focus for Fallon's reflective pondering upon myth.[6] Both "The Mothers" and "Women" emerge from some schematic need on the poet's part (felt most apparently during the 1950s) to make large, exemplary sense of things. Such poems, while not great in themselves, fortunately clear the ground for later, better work in which some of the assumptions of the earlier poems are digested or reacted against. What makes for the improvement, for the imaginative enlargement beyond the rather earnest abstractions of these earlier poems, is a change of voice. So the impersonal witty eloquence of "The River Walk" deflates equally the possibility of sentimental excess and of rigid earnestness. The tone is poised, its persona of affable advisor seeming to suit the poet perfectly, granting a pliability to his speech that deftly explores and reveals the subject:

Disturbing it is
To take your stick sedately walking,
Evening in the water and the air,
And discover this; that a woman is a river.
The mythic properties are hard to bear.

Offering instruction that is precise and to the point, he can be both ironic and affectionate towards the myth-making habit itself, countering it with a bluff, humorous realism: "Dangerous, dangerous / This mythology . . . / A woman is a woman, not the earth."

The tart tonal buoyancy of "The River Walk" frees Fallon into a livelier speech for future reflections upon myth, among which reflections are some of his most successful poems.[7] The refined awareness and common sense of these poems, expressed in a practical lyrical speech, make Fallon a singular figure among the Irish poets of his generation. By means of such poems, he enters the Irish consciousness in a unique way, combining a feeling for local landscape with a sophisticated but healthily digested awareness of a larger world of meanings and implications.

"Totem" is among the first of these later reflective lyrics which consider the nature of the mythological and its reverberations in the actual world where the poet lives. An elegy for a dead cow, this poem considers the network of natural connections presupposed by a mythopoeic understanding of the world, what J. G. Frazer, somewhere in *The Golden Bough*, refers to as "the universal framework of things."[8] In locating the mythic inside the quotidian, a function of a certain way of seeing, Fallon is in effect reflecting on the mythologising habit itself. The poem's admirably relaxed speech is rich, deft and delicate enough to divine and celebrate the cow's reality, her largesse of natural implications ("into October she went, the day lying / To its grass anchors / In autumn scent"). Touching the mythopoeic chords very lightly, Fallon grounds his specialised awareness in an intensified language of natural description. This language is further animated by a wit which, in its ambiguity and poise ("A post mortem to go on / Forever in the dogrose / Wherein this old shambling skeleton in rawhide / Is totally translated and taken over") is a correct response to the kind of double experience it wishes to register. A speculative modesty of tone does not allow the poet's high claims to seem excessive. His speech has the confidence of conversation and the quiet authority of belief, "Thus acknowledging the ancient status / Of a quite ordinary creature who yesterday / Was horns not halo."

As Fallon extends his meditation upon myth in the contemporary world he comes to more complex conclusions than those required by the decent (if archaic) beliefs of "Totem." He is brought to the bleaker awareness of absence. "The Small Town of John Coan" wittily compares the vigorous possibilities of a numinous world ("Olympus overhanging the street . . . / Cornuted bulls, and amorous / Birds in the family tree") with the emaciated present, drained of belief, man orphaned by this absence. The mood is one of thoughtful regret for a lost way of seeing and that enlargement of consciousness such a way enabled. More elaborately, but still in the characteristic tones of witty, estimating intelligence, "Monument X" revisits some of the same rich ground. The voice here is one of greater authority and control, expanded by an ironic, self-deprecatory edge. In its firm, undogmatic, muscular plainness, this is the representative voice of Fallon's later style, its taut rhythms giving the proper balance to its intelligent air of critical evaluation:

> Stone has gone, no
> God clamours nowadays to be
> Let out, or even to beat
> Inside barbarously in the menhir's heart.
> Stonehenge is archaeology.

In a tone that deftly mixes irony and affection, scepticism and awe (in a way that might foreshadow aspects of Derek Mahon's poetic voice), he celebrates the old, enigmatic monument in Athenry, finding mythic possibility in the midst of ordinary life. The wry note of the conclusion combines exacting scrutiny with elegiac reverberation, as he silences his comparative mythologising with a brusque efficiency that provokes suggestive epigram and colloquial dismissal: "Enough of that. / Gods live the deaths of one another. / But stone, now, is old hat."

The tone of "Boyne Valley" slides between the elegiac and the sardonic, expanding Fallon's continuing meditation on the absence of mythopoeic consciousness from the contemporary world. (The integrity of his imagination may be gauged by the persistence with which he returns to the same subject, always elaborating upon earlier encounters with it.) In the sacral space denoted by the poem's title, mythic past and present fact sharply collide, their collision given dramatic life by the counterpoints in the poet's language. The mythic hero who was laid in "This hill of metaphor" is gone, "Leaving his head to the stone axe, and the big, broken / Torque of his body to dangle, / Wail, ye women, / God is dead / And picked over by this year's summer students." The poet feels the loss of this mythic consciousness. He is eloquently aware of the absence of the numinous spirit, "Whose secret name was / A flight of months." Between the bereft presence and the world of mythic densities, Fallon clears a space for his own imaginative vision, an outlet for his own speech and his own need to speak. Resigned to what is actual, he says an earnest farewell to the old world and wryly greets, in all its vulgarity, the diminished new. Mythology gives way to history and society, and the distant horn he hears is "Not Herne and his hounds but / Esquires at play." The sheep he sees are not "souls" but "merely ewes," and the earth itself is independent of any mythic presence. His language can display an adequate counterforce to the loss he registers, its laconic tone carrying him to his final ironic look at the contemporary world, the decline of mythic heroism into upper-class house-parties: "Jaguars roll from the meet, trailing / Horseheads and dogfoxes." The apt nerve and sinew of such language tell me that Fallon's concern here lives at the centre of his imaginative con-sciousness, responsible for some of his most thoughtful and successful verse.[9]

Finally, in "For Paddy Mac," the poet turns the relentless light of the critical intelligence retrospectively upon his own mythologising habits.[10] The brisk colloquial speech of the first five stanzas summarises the sort of cultural sentimentality by which the young inheritors of the Literary Revival (Fallon and Patrick MacDonagh among them) were infected, "All messed up with sundogs and / Too many rainbows." Outlining the more sober actuality, his speech com-

mands a down-to-earth directness: "Bunkum, Dear P. The thing was gone, or /
Never was. And we were the leftovers." He produces history in place of the fal-
sifications of 'myth,' insisting in hard deflating tones that the thing be clearly
seen, the myth demystified. The final stanzas of the poem show Fallon's own
sense of himself as a critical, evaluating intelligence, scrupulously dealing out
equitable judgements, amending "the scribbles of the tribe / Lest sheepman and
bullhead / Become a frieze of fathers like stone man." He declares his commitment in the end to human fluency, beyond the consolations of mythology, the
limits of which he keenly senses:

> But this seems certain as I grow:
> Man lives; Gods die:
> It is only the genuflection that survives.

In such a statement Fallon negotiates his graceful exit from the enchanted circle
of myth, his entrance into the purely human, a realm marked for him, as some
later poems show, by mystical apprehension of a decisively personal, idiosyncratic nature. Such later work contains some of his best poetry, as witnessed
by such poems as "Trevaylor," "Brother Twin," and "Lost Man in Me."[11] But
theirs is a different voice, a different way of being in the world, a way that has
digested the critical intelligence and speaks out of a mystical sense of self beyond the supports and reassurances of objective myth. In such a realm, the critical intelligence which gives form and purpose to the poems dealt with in this
essay is absorbed by an urge to speak simply of the difficult truths he has arrived at. He wants, simply, to let them be:

> The virtue of heaven is simply to produce
>
> Anything. It's a music. Birdsongs or bomb,
> It's all equal. In this yin-yang three
> he doesn't ape God but is quite like some
> Kind of eternity
>
> In whose paradox I can sing.
>   ("Lost Man in Me")

   The poems which comprise the subject of this essay, however, offer a secure centre from which to look at Fallon's work, both because of their treatment
of the crucial subject of myth and because of the way this treatment, in its developing phases, exemplifies some characteristic behavior of his imagination.
For at the core of his imaginative life he is a loving judge, eager to see all
things, including his own creative commitment, get their proper due. The poems
I've dealt with here show in a pointed and particular way what is true to one or
another degree about all his best work—the way his imagination, with rare
authority and craft, balances between the largest possibilities of life and its
smallest local details. His most admirable quality as a poet, I believe, resides in

the way he translates such a balance into adequate speech—speech that does justice at once to his feelings and to his critical intelligence. Irish poetry, especially Irish poetry in the generation after Yeats, is enriched by such qualities of enlightened attention, sympathetic intelligence, unostentatious imagination, and authentic speech. Fallon's work, as Seamus Heaney says, "stands in secure and complementary relation to the achievements of Austin Clarke and Patrick Kavanagh."[12] His affectionate truth, therefore, is not only an indispensable part of our recent literary history, but a necessary portion of the inheritance of those poets who have come after him.

1982

NOTES

[1] Devin Garrity, *New Irish Poets* (New York: Devin-Adair, 1948) 204; Anthony Cronin, "An Appreciation," *The Irish Times*, 10 October 1974. See also Eavan Boland, "Padraic Fallon: An Assessment," *Hibernia*, 10 January 1973, 11; Seamus Heaney, review of *Poems, The Irish Times*, 17 August 1974.

[2] "The Poetry of Padraic Fallon," *Studies* (1975) 281.

[3] "Fallon is in search of the myth everywhere and in everything," Micheál Ó hAodha, *Plays and Places* (Dublin: Progress House, 1961) 72. Ó hAodha's treatment of Fallon's radio plays helpfully illuminates a number of issues relevant to the poems. His account is the most extensive treatment so far given this aspect of Fallon's work. See also Ó hAodha, *Theatre in Ireland* (Oxford: Blackwell, 1974) 101-03. [Since my own essay was written, the publication of *Poems and Translations* (Carcanet, 1983) and *Collected Poems* (Gallery and Carcanet, 1990) has made up many of the deficiences in the record, letting us see more clearly the shape and dimensions of the work. A collection of Fallon's critical reviews and essays would also be useful.]

[4] Padraic Fallon, *Poems* (Dublin: Dolmen, 1974). All quotations are from this text.

[5] Place is not mentioned. Fallon keeps his vision "universal." This is often true of poems which are otherwise scrupulous in their observation of naturalistic detail. For this information, as well as for other facts (e.g., those connected with "Totem," "A Visit West" and "For Paddy Mac") I am gratefully indebted to Brian Fallon, the poet's son, whose unfailing generosity with his time and talk about his father's work was both help and encouragement.

[6] Ó hAodha says that a favourite motif of Fallon's work is "that all the poet's songs are about one woman, the goddess, who can never be loved in that physical sense." *Plays and Places*, 71. What this can lead to, of course, is a shortage of actual biographical particularity in the poet's treatment of the subject. There's a sense in which this choice of archetype as subject could be seen as a strategy of evasion, something that keeps some of Fallon's verse from the depths he seems equipped to enter.

[7] The time of this change, the later 1950s, is marked by comparable changes throughout his work. It is during this period that Fallon reaches his maturity as a poet, comes into secure possession of that poetic identity that gives body to and speaks out of the best poems. A full account of this matter will have to await the establishment of a satisfactory chronology of his poems.

[8] The title of this poem presumably derives from Frazer's discussion of totemism.

[9] "The Head," which in terms of language and imagery is certainly one of Fallon's most charged and exciting poetic achievements, belongs to my discussion, in that its fraught, enigmatic narrative seems to imply a movement from a mythic world to one where the mythic consciousness is depleted ("a country narrow low and cold / And very thin like a wire"), but where poetry also raises its voice against this absence ("where the head sang all day"). An adequate discussion of this rich and various poem would require a separate essay, however, and so I omit it.

[10] Patrick MacDonagh (1902-61). Poet. His most notable volumes are: *A Leaf in the Wind* (1929) and the much better *One Landscape Still* (1958).

[11] Maurice Harmon refers to such poems (among others) when he remarks that Fallon's "finest achievement is this attention to the world beyond the visible, within the self" (*Studies*, 1975, 272). I would agree, with reservations, convinced that the poems which form the subject of the present essay are central to any understanding of the nature and achievement of Fallon's imagination.

[12] In his Introduction to *Collected Poems*, 11.

From Simplicity to Simplicity:
Pastoral Design in Kavanagh

Patrick Kavanagh often described his work and his life in the image of a journey: "All we learn from experience is the way from simplicity back to simplicity."[1] It is a traditional image, at root that of an Eden lost and a journey through the infernal places of the world to a recovered innocence, a paradise regained which is like and unlike the original, its innocence more aware, radical, profound, its simplicity "the ultimate sophistication."[2] Although, therefore, he bemoaned the lack of a sustaining myth ("A myth is necessary, for a myth is a sort of self contained world in which one can live," *Pruse*, 268), his own poetic identity is a product, casual as well as deliberate, of one of the most accessible of Western myths, that of the pastoral. The early poems represent an experience of pastoral innocence; the later reflect upon this and repossess it in a new mode. To look at Kavanagh's poetry through the pastoral lens permits the design of that work to emerge in a rich, consistent light.

I

In one of his first engagements with the pastoral convention, Kavanagh is the Adam-poet. Unlike most earlier practitioners in the convention he is not the poet-shepherd, but the poet-ploughman, his version of the convention mediated through Wordsworth, John Clare, and Francis Ledwidge.[3] In his novel, *Tarry Flynn*, speaking of this time, he states: "He did not love nature's works, but he was *in love* with them—and he wished he wasn't, for these things always made him sad, reminding him of something far and forgotten in the land of Childhood before the Fall of Man."[4] Many of the poems in *Ploughman and Other Poems* (1936) give expression to this garden existence in terms at once or by turns natural, mystical, and religious. It is an experience of "quiet ecstasy / Like a prayer," of "Joy that is timeless!"[5] Timelessness and other traditional aspects of the pastoral world are the dominant features of this experience. "Rapt to starriness" he finds himself in "a timeless world. It was an Eden time and Eve not violated. Men were not subject to death. I was happy."[6] The idiom of this experience is that of Christian pastoral at its most intense. The poet is a neighbor "To Seraphim" ("A Star," *CP*, 8) and the light of May might be "Adam's God / As Adam saw before the apple-bite" ("After May," *CP*, 14). In the poems of this period a visionary pastoral world emerges under the poet's awakened, ecstatic scrutiny from the bare facts of the ordinary world. The act of ploughing itself becomes a sacred function, "For you are driving your horses through / The mist where Genesis begins" ("To the Man After the Harrow," *CP*, 27). The poet's condition is that of instant translator, transforming, as the pastoral convention invariably does, the dull metals of the world into the gold of visionary joy.

The Great Hunger (1942) represents an advance in Kavanagh's pastoral journey. The visionary gleam remains, but it is intermittent now, lost in the gray shades of clay that compose the poem's dominant subject. The poem itself might be called "tragic pastoral." The soured life of Patrick Maguire has glimmers of ecstasy that draw upon traditional pastoral for their expression:

> Yet sometimes when the sun comes through a gap
> These men know God the Father in a tree:
> The Holy Spirit is the rising sap,
> And Christ will be the green leaves that will come
> At Easter from the sealed and guarded tomb. (*CP*, 38)

Such lights, however, succumb to the quenching sterility of Maguire's life. They provide us with the poet's awareness of the possibilities inherent in this world, but they cannot redeem the anti-hero from his fate. For the most part *The Great Hunger* portrays the inexorable actuality of earth, an "apocalypse of clay" that slams shut in sterility and dread the gates of a pastoral Eden. It frames an experience of the dark side of Irish Catholicism in terms of the iconology and emotional patterns of traditional pastoral.

Kavanagh's own exile from Eden dated from his settling in Dublin in 1939: "Round about the late nineteen-thirties . . . foolishly enough . . . I chose to leave my native fields" (*SP*, 10). The idiom in which he repeatedly remembers this event highlights its essentially pastoral nature. *Tarry Flynn* ends with "the beauty of what we love . . . the pain of roots dragging up" (188). His early autobiography, *The Green Fool*, insists on the same archetypal pattern, the loss of innocence contingent upon the poet's migration to Dublin: "I have always regretted going to Dublin. I had lost something I could never regain from books" (231). For in the world of Dublin all is changed: "here in this nondescript land / Everything is secondhand" ("Adventures in the Bohemian Jungle," *CP*, 108). Essentially it meant that he had turned from innocence to experience, from the sight of "the Burning Bush / Where God appeared" ("Temptation in Harvest," *CP*, 68) and all the other blessed phenomena of the pastoral world to a world fallen from that primordial grace.

What he found in this world turned Kavanagh into a satirist, and it is as a satirist that he inhabits the second stage of his own pastoral design. In such poems as "The Paddiad," "The Wake of the Books," "The Defeated," "Adventures in the Bohemian Jungle," and "The Christmas Mummers," Kavanagh exorcises his anger at the moral deficiencies and defects of decency and humanity in the world of experience. It is important to realise, however, that the role of satirist also belongs to the traditional pastoral design, being conventionally a posture adopted by the poet (in Spenser's *Shepherds Calendar* and Milton's *Lycidas*, for example) when the visionary possibilities of his original landscape break upon the stony realities of the world.

In contrast to the Edenic garden of innocence which informs the earlier lyrics, the world that comes through in these poems is a kind of hell of the spirit. The journey of the poet is into "the very city of Hate" ("The Road to Hate," *CP*, 89) at the heart of which stands "the devil Mediocrity" ("The Paddiad," *CP*, 90). This world is a "jungle," where "the lions of frustration roar" ("Jungle," *CP*, 96). Its inhabitants are "the defeated," and the poem of this title ends with the poet's anguished response to its perverted values:

> O God, I cried, these treats are not the treats
> That Heaven offers in the Golden Cup.
> And I heard the demon's terrifying yell:
> There is no place as perfect as our hell. (*CP*, 99)

The poet perceives his life in Dublin, at least for the purposes of his poetry, as the demonic antithesis to the ecstatic Edenic experience of his earlier life. Such a demonic netherworld is a necessary part of the full pastoral journey, as this was understood by the Renaissance poets, by Blake, even by Yeats.[7] It is a land of damned sterility, exact counterweight to the almost mystical fertility of the early pastoral landscape. That Kavanagh himself understands his life in such terms may be seen in the allegorical outline of his poem, "The Road to Hate":

> For I know a man who went down the hill into the hollow
> And entered the very city of Hate
> And God visited him every day out of pity
> Till in the end he became a most noble saint. (*CP*, 89)

II

For Kavanagh's career to fit the outlines of the pastoral design exactly there must be a return of some sort to his original condition. Such a return is always more complex than a simple circling, however. In Kavanagh's case it falls into two distinct stages, each of them producing fine poems. Both sets of poems deal with recovery. The first group of poems is written before 1955, the second thereafter. In the first group the poet is possessed by a memorial excitement that rouses his imagination to recapture the likeness of an earlier self and its context:

> And poet lost to potato-fields,
> Remembering the lime and copper smell
> Of the spraying barrels he is not lost
> Or till blossomed stalks cannot weave a spell.
> ("Spraying the Potatoes," *CP*, 78)

This is an endangered possession, however. Like Wordsworth's memorial revelations, like all nostalgia, it is dependent upon things outside the self for its tenuous, threatened existence. With its Wordsworthian connections, this danger is clearest in "Primrose." The poet begins in memory: "Upon a bank I sat, a child made seer / Of one small primrose flowering in my mind" (*CP*, 75). It ends, however, with his admission of the loss of this earlier pristine visionary power: "The years that pass / Like tired soldiers nevermore have given / Moments to see wonders in the grass." The Edenic aspect of it all becomes explicit in "A Christmas Childhood" (*CP*, 71-2). There he recalls "the gay / Garden that was childhood's," and his fall from this blessed condition: "O you, Eve, were the world that tempted me / To eat the knowledge that grew in clay / And death the germ within in!"

In most of these poems it is the loss of his visionary past that preoccupies the poet. In "Innocence," for example, he remembers this loss: "Ashamed of what I loved / I flung her from me and called her a ditch / Although she was smiling at me with violets" (*CP*, 127). The tenuous nature of his imaginative recovery of this time is visible in the concluding stanzas of this poem:

> But now I am back in her briary arms
> The dew of an Indian Summer morning lies
> On bleached potato-stalks—
> What age am I?
>
> I do not know what age I am,
> I am no mortal age;
> I know nothing of women,
> Nothing of cities,
> I cannot die
> Unless I walk outside these whitethorn hedges.

The most striking thing about such lines is the vulnerability of this repossession, with all its Edenic overtones of agelessness and exclusion. The poet closes his eyes to time, revives his childhood ecstasy, and voluntarily accepts its limits. He is an Adam gone back to the garden, opting out of the experience (women, cities) which his exile from it made possible.

The limits of such a condition of loss and memorial re-evocation are every-where visible in this group of poems. Again and again he returns to his denial of his Edenic past, trying to grope lyrically beyond it. In "On Looking into E. V. Rieu's Homer," for example, he remembers

> The intensity that radiated from
> The Far Field Rock—you afterwards denied—
> Was the half-god seeing his half brothers
> Joking on the fabulous mountain-side. (*CP*, 134)

In "On Reading a Book on Common Wildflowers" he again confronts loss and the tenuous repossession of what was lost:

> Let me not moralise or have remorse, for these names

> Purify a corner of my mind;
> I jump over them and rub them with my hands,
> And a free moment appears brand new and spacious
> Where I may live beyond the reach of desire. (*CP*, 137)

Here, as in all these poems, the poet's imagination is under siege. It is only "a corner of my mind" that is purified, and that only for "a free moment." Most of all the condition aspired to is one of necessary surrender of something vital to himself: he must live here "beyond the reach of desire."

It is clear that such poems do not complete Kavanagh's journey. They are going back to "simplicity," as he says himself, but in truth the journey can only be completed by a more radical movement forward, into an acceptance of, a surrender to his own present. In the above poems he expresses loss of vision. But in their Wordsworthian echoes and borrowings, they provide a ready-made frame that drains off the originality from Kavanagh's own profound sense of the experience, his own unique sense of present identity.

The essential confrontation with the present needed to complete properly his pastoral journey occurs in the poems Kavanagh wrote after 1955. It is from this date, in fact, that he himself marks his real "birth" as a poet. The event occurred in Dublin, not long after an operation that in removing one lung cured him of a cancer that might have killed him. "As a poet," he says, "I was born in or about nineteen-fifty-five, the place of my birth being the banks of the Grand Canal" (*SP*, 27-8). The previous group of poems had represented a paradise returned to but not regained. The products of an intensely creative nostalgia, they can hold the past only in imagination, sweet counterpoints to an unpleasant present reality. As he says in "Kerr's Ass,"

> In Ealing Broadway, London Town
> I name their several names
>
> Until a world comes to life—
> Morning, the silent bog,
> And the God of imagination waking
> In a Mucker fog. (*CP*, 135)

Such a return to a world of pre-lapsarian innocence can exist only by virtue of what it excludes. In the poems after 1955, however, Kavanagh is imaginatively impelled towards an ever more ample inclusiveness. In these poems he transforms the image of a journey (back in imagination to a lost Eden) into a condition of simple being. It is a condition not of movement but of stillness he celebrates; not imaginative, imperiled return but the perfect safety of an intensely realised presence. The moment of critical change is a moment of conversion. Fittingly it carries the baptismal blessing of water "Always virginal, / Always original, / It washes out Original sin" ("Is," *CP*, 153): "I sat on the bank of the Grand Canal in the summer of 1955 and let the water lap idly on the shores of my mind. My purpose in life was to have no purpose" ("Author's Note," *CP*, xiv). From this inner conversion, this discovery of what Milton called "the Paradise within," flow those fine and final poems that represent Kavanagh's paradise regained. These poems, with the experience they incorporate, complete the pastoral design of his work. The design is not, as he himself implied it was, a circle ("Curious this, how I had started off with the right simplicity . . . and came back to where I started" [*SP,* 28]), but the more complexly truthful spiral. From this fresh perspective, as he says in a slightly earlier poem, "the main purpose / . . . is to be / Passive, observing with a steady eye" ("Intimate Parnassus," *CP,* 146). Such "wise passivity" is a state in which "God must be allowed to surprise us" ("Having Confessed," *CP,* 149).[8] It is an "anonymous humility," a state of pure being, a radical and practical innocence beyond rather than before experience. It is a state inclusive of all things—neither transcendental as his earliest visionary condition was, nor exclusive and vulnerable as his memorial evocations of his lost Eden were. Here he regains paradise in the present, beyond vulnerability because in a condition of complete surrender. This is his redemption: "Leafy-with-love banks and the green waters of the canal / Pouring redemption for me" ("Canal Bank Walk," *CP,* 150).

Absolute belonging in the present is one of the most important features of the last stage for Kavanagh's poetic identity. It takes him beyond nostalgia, ambition, and envy and allows him to "wallow in the habitual, the banal, / Grow with nature again as before I grew." In "Canal Bank Walk" the poet's visionary intensity finds expression in a language at once tough and lyrical, its diction rising and falling with the pulse of present existence in the real world:

> O unworn world enrapture me, encapture me in a web
> Of fabulous grass and eternal voices by a beech,
> Feed the gaping need of my senses, give me ad lib
> To pray unselfconsciously with overflowing speech. (*CP,* 150)

In this final pastoral state, *being itself* becomes the poet's unselfconscious prayer, a condition that takes him beyond the mystical raptures of the earlier poems (where innocence can be a kind of lit vacancy) and beyond the sensual nostalgia of the middle group, where prayer is memorial posture present in the imagination by virtue of its very absence in actuality.

Kavanagh's final pastoral recovery converts the world to its desire because it surrenders to what is beyond the self, the ego. It is the world itself that now glows with an air of acknowledged mystery: "Fantastic light looks through the eyes of bridges— / And look! a barge comes bringing from Athy / And other far-flung towns mythologies" ("Lines Written on a Seat on the Grand Canal," *CP,* 150). In the pastoral achievement of self-possession the poet finds inclusiveness to be the governing principle, rather than that exclusiveness by which he could possess his lost Eden. Now all things have power to throb with the energies of being: "nothing whatever is by love debarred, / The common and banal her heat can know" ("The Hospital," *CP,* 153).

The terminal truth of this spiraling pastoral journey is love—not a love that leaps through things to their mystical essence, not a nostalgic love for what is lost, but a love that is in and can transform all things, a love it is simply the poet's business to record. He is home at last:

> This is what love does to things: the Rialto Bridge
> The main gate that was bent by a heavy lorry,
> The seat at the back of a shed that was a sun-trap.
> Naming these things is the love-act and its pledge;
> For we must record love's mystery without claptrap,
> Snatch out of time the passionate transitory.
>
> ("The Hospital")

In love like this, the poet is a newly-awakened Adam, the familiar of sickness, mortality, civilisation, and simple pleasure. He is the namer of these things ("I simply chose to name," ["My Powers," *Complete Poems*, 298]), the player in a game with time, the unsentimental, uninnocent recorder of "love's mystery." The poem answers no questions. It records a state of fullness of being that is, in traditional terms, the meaning of the true pastoral return, a return that is no outward journey but a voyage to the paradise within of the truly liberated imagination. Its meaning lies in self-possession and, in Keats's phrase, "soul-making."

This awakened Adam is going nowhere, for "To look on is enough / In the business of love" ("Is," *CP*, 154). It is a state of ordinary mortal things brought to the level of "An enduring story," and including "things above the temporal law." Time and eternity meet here, in a manner quite distinct from the dewy-eyed mysticism of the early poems. An important element in this condition is its generosity, its perpetual blessing, its inclusiveness. The world, especially the world of nature, is charged with this novel energy, an energy at once powerful and lighthearted. The poet is absorbed by the landscape and a voice of knowledge that flows from beyond himself: "beautiful, beautiful, beautiful God / Was breathing His love by a cutaway bog" ("The One," *CP*, 159).

The poem "October" (*CP*, 159) makes the particular inwardness of this state very clear. The season of "leafy yellowness" creates "A world that was and now is poised above time." But in spite of the temptation to nostalgia the season induces—for breeze, temperature, and "patterns of movement" are "the same / As broke my heart for youth passing"—the poet can possess himself in a different kind of peace, a certainty that "Something will be mine wherever I am." In spite of the debts to memory that still stir him, he is essentially independent of time and space, becoming one himself with the season. The fruit of this energetic surrender is true freedom. "It is October over all my life," he says, the line implying not self-pity but liberated acceptance. This condition of oneness, an integral at-oneness with mutability, is the final component of the pastoral design, a design that extends from the early seeing of eternity in ordinary things to this actual being at one with transience itself, not needing "to puzzle out Eternity." As a condition of pastoral fullness it resembles the experience Keats enacts in the "Ode to Autumn."

The final posture of this condition of liberty is that of praise, a purely natural response to the poet's feeling of *atonement*, of being at one with the world:

"So be reposed and praise, praise, praise / The way it happened and the way it is" ("Question to Life," *CP*, 164). Here is the repose of being after the anxieties of desire. It leaves "Nothing more to be done in that particular / Direction, nothing now but prayer—" (Living in the Country: II," *CP*, 169). At this point the pastoral frame closes. Having declared closure, logically silence must follow. His latest work suggests, however, that he was denying, though to no poetic avail, this silence. For in a certain sense his poetic identity has run its course.

III

That the bulk of Kavanagh's work may be understood within the design of his own idiosyncratic version of the pastoral seems confirmed by the presence in it of a detail that often makes its appearance in traditional Christian pastoral. This is the poet's identification or connection of himself with Christ. The poet as priest and Christ figure is a conventional part of Christian pastoral and this Kavanagh has translated into his own terms. Significantly, as with traditional examples of the genre, the identification often occurs in the context of satire.[9]

The connections between poet and Christ appear early in Kavanagh's work. In "Ascetic" he prays "That I may break / With these hands / The bread of wisdom that grows / In the other lands" ("Ascetic," *CP*, 5). He strikes another priestly pose in "A Star," (*CP*, 8). In "Worship" the Christological associations are stretched to almost blasphemous limits:

> Open your tabernacles I too am flame
> Ablaze on the hills of Being. Let the dead
> Chant the low prayer beneath a candled shrine,
> O cut for me life's bread, for me pour wine. (*CP*, 12)

The poet has become a rival to Christ, and whether the poem is one of sexual entreaty or not does not alter the matter. In "Lough Derg" he makes Christ a spirit very like the one he would claim for himself as a poet. For Christ hears, he says, "in the voices of the meanly poor / Homeric utterances, poetry sweeping through" (*Complete Poems*, 121).

In his prose Kavanagh is even more overt about the associations between Christ and the poet. "In every poet," he states in an essay on "The Irish Tradition," "there is something of Christ writing the sins of the people in the dust" (*Pruse*, 234). Elsewhere he is equally explicit: "the great poet equally with Christ offers life more abundantly."[10] In the well known libel action trial Kavanagh exploits again this association: "If I really told the truth," he says, "they would take me up on a high hill and crucify me" (*Pruse*, 214).

It is in the mask of victim that the most extended connection with Christ appears in Kavanagh's work and forms an important part of his poetic identity. In the "Author's Note" to the *Collected Poems*, for example, he says "poetry made me a sort of outcast . . . I do not believe in sacrifice and yet it seems I was sacrificed" (xiii). The hero of *Tarry Flynn* is described as having "to carry a cross. He did not want to carry a cross. He wanted to be ordinary" (68). Real life, with its ceaseless search for patronage, its round of insults, its climactic court case in which the poet was pitted against the forces of mediocrity and what he called evil gave fibre to Kavanagh's Christological associations. "I believe you can only die when you have done whatever you came into the world to do," he once said (*November Haggard*, 47), and on another occasion he compared his indecision about going to Dublin to that of "Christ in Gethsemane" ("Temptation in Harvest," *CP*, 67).

Although he repeatedly insists that "no messianic impulse" (*SP*, 10) drove him to Dublin, his work on confronting the social and cultural realities of that city is full of Messianic overtones. He describes himself in the 1940s as "a mad messiah without a mission or a true impulse."[11] Later ("Author's Note" to *CP*, xiv), he described the time of his anger as one of "messianic compulsion." Certainly many of the poems he wrote before the 1940s and up to 1955 vibrate with some of this messianic fervour. In them he is urgent to flagellate the wickedness he saw around him, a wickedness that, apart from his deep personal hatred for it, also made him, he thought, its special victim.

"A Wreath for Tom Moore's Statue" offers one of the first views of this messianic identification (*CP*, 85). Moore is associated with the vices of mediocrity and complacent middle-class vulgarity. Moore's antithesis, the poet (presumably a version of Kavanagh himself), appears in apocalyptic imagery like a triumphant Christ: "But hope! the poet comes again to build / A new city high above lust and logic." This poem provides an important glimpse of what was to become a full-blown satirical eschatology in the trenchant poems that appeared in the late '40s and early '50s. Kavanagh becomes the scourging, ministering poet, as well as victim and scapegoat of that which he satirises. In "The Paddiad" (*CP*, 90-5), Mediocrity is a devil, the patron of bad art, while Kavanagh himself—a none-too-modest conglomerate with Yeats, Joyce, and O'Casey—is Conscience to this world. At the end of the poem, in spite of much abuse, Conscience is still alive, "Ready again to die of hunger, / Condemnatory and uncivil." Such implicit martyrdom underlines the Christ associations as well as narrows the conglomerate figure to the solitary person of Kavanagh himself.

Further Christological references rise to the surface in these satiric poems. In "The Defeated" the voice of pretentious cultural mediocrity advises the poet to "Leave Christ and Christ-like problems and you'll be / The synthesis of Gaelic poetry" (*CP*, 98). The poet's horror finds expression in an outburst of disappointment reminiscent of Christ in Gethsemane: "O God, I cried, these treats are not the treats / That Heaven offers in the Golden Cup." In "Adventures in the Bohemian Jungle" (*CP*, 101-08) the poet is an innocent conscience at large in the literary-cultural Vanity Fair of Dublin. The implicit identification made here is between the poet truth-teller and the Christ who angrily drove the money-changers from the temple.

The opposition in all these satires is invariably the devil or some version of the devilish. Such almost allegorical oppositions make for many Christological associations in Kavanagh's frequently expressed assumptions about the nature of the poet's mission. For him the status and eternal function of poetry is as "a profound and bold / Faith that cries the inner history / Of the failure of Man's mission" ("Auditors In," *CP*, 123). By the end of a poem called "The Hero," however, he finds that "The sword of a satire in his hand became blunted, / And for the insincere city / He felt a profound pity" (*CP*, 142).

In the later poems, then, it is apparent that Kavanagh moves beyond the need for satire and the instinct to associate himself with Christ. It is significant, too, that such poems are more or less contemporary with his own personal "conversion." He seems, in some sad possession of his own soul, to be able to move beyond "the role . . . of prophet and saviour" and to be able to resist the temptation "to take over the functions of a god in a new fashion" ("After Forty Years of Age," *CP*, 148). In this condition, he comes clear-eyed to the conclusion that "satire is unfruitful prayer" ("Prelude," *CP*, 132). By *incorporating* his association with Christ and therefore leaving it, as explicit persona, behind him, he discovers the totality of his own being. It is a kind of peace, a kind of completeness, and he pointedly couches it in the image of a journey. By this means he turns us back into the framework of his pastoral design, in which this final stage is, as I've said, that of his paradise regained, in truth the possession of his own soul:

> And you must go inland and be
> Lost in compassion's ecstasy,
> Where suffering soars in summer air—
> The millstone has become a star. ("Prelude")

If there is an implicit association between Christ and this accepted self, it is with the Christ who abandoned the world and retreated into the desert (the site of Milton's *Paradise Regained*). Kavanagh leaves behind him "That Promised Land you thought to find," and his final truth is simply "Ignore Power's schismatic sect, / Lovers alone lovers protect" ("Prelude," *CP*, 133). After his conversion, then, Kavanagh, without abandoning the Christian matrix which animates his poetic vision and sensibility, can jettison the explicitly Christ-persona that had carried him to the final stage of his pastoral journey, and so come into the full possession of himself. As he puts it in "Auditors In" (a poem, written in 1951, that anticipates the final stage), he comes "accidentally upon / My self at the end of a tortuous road" (*CP*, 126).

In summary, then, the pastoral convention—with a number of its traditional variants—supplies a coherent frame for the poetic identity Kavanagh's work composes. It does not, of course, account for the poetry, but it does provide a way of organising it critically. It offers a way into the poetry in terms of the poetry itself, rendering it in certain ways independent of its time and place. At the same time it allows us to see that the value of this myth, this conventional design, consists in the particular life Kavanagh gave to it, filling the traditional literary outline with the matter of his own time and place, his own self. In this way he extends the form, substantiating in an unlikely context the enduring validity of this particular mode. He proves that the genre is not merely a literary imposition designed for the convenience of critics, but is a fundamental shaping mode through which the material of a poet's identity can come to coherence, even when on the surface that material seems as inchoate as that often provided by Kavanagh. By the way they reveal a human response solidified into a literary form, then, the impulse and design of traditional pastoral enable us to recognise the degree to which originality and convention are conjoined both in Kavanagh's apprehension of the world and in its creative consequences.

1981

NOTES

[1] *Collected Pruse* (London: MacGibbon and Kee, 1967) 278. Subsequent references to this work appear parenthetically in the text as *Pruse.*

[2] *Self Portrait* (Dublin: Dolmen Press, 1964) 8. Subsequent references to this work appear parenthetically in the text as *SP*. John Jordan, "Mr. Kavanagh's Progress," *Studies*, 49 (1960) 304, notes this pattern, calling it one of "departure, disillusion and bewilderment, enrichment and return." Early as it is, this article remains one of the most perceptive treatments of Kavanagh's work and its shaping choices. In spite of his being recognized as one of the most important poets since Yeats, Kavanagh has attracted scant critical attention in or outside Ireland. See Seamus Heaney, "The Poetry of Patrick Kavanagh: From Monaghan to the Grand Canal," in *Two Decades of Irish Writing*, ed. Douglas Dunn (Manchester: Carcanet Press, 1975) 105-11, rpt. in *Preoccupations* (London: Faber & Faber, 1980); D'Arcy O'Brien, *Patrick Kavanagh* (Cranbury, New Jersey: Bucknell University Press [Irish Writers Series], 1975); Alan Warner, *Clay Is the Word: Patrick Kavanagh, 1904-1967* (Dublin: Dolmen Press, 1974). A recent essay by Terence Brown ("After the Revival: The Problem of Adequacy and Genre," *Genre* 12, No. 4, Winter, 1979, 565-89) offers among other things an excellent summary of the religious and social content of Kavanagh's longer works in verse—*Lough Derg, Why Sorrow?*, and *The Great Hunger*—and glances briefly at the later lyrics. Brown discusses Kavanagh's movement from poetry of social motive and occasion to pure lyrical engagements with the quotidian self and its will to praise, "from society to the intimate histories of self" (588). My own essay is an attempt to identify the pattern that emerges from such content. Where Brown gives a historical "outer" reading of the poetry, my aim is to provide a formal, "inner" reading. The two are, I hope, complementary.

[3] *November Haggard: Uncollected Prose and Verse* (New York: Peter Kavanagh Hand Press, 1971) 34. Hereafter cited parenthetically in the text.

[4] (1949; rpt. New York: Penguin, 1978) 134. Subsequent references to this work appear parenthetically in the text.

[5] "Ploughman," in *Collected Poems* (1964; rpt. London: Martin Brian and O'Keefe, 1972) 3. Most of the other poems referred to in the course of this essay are from this collection, hereafter cited parenthetically in the text as *CP*.

[6] *The Green Fool* (London, 1938; rpt. New York: Penguin, 1975) 194.

[7] It is not my argument that Kavanagh was conscious of these associations. But his work may be read according to the lineaments of this design, a design that may be a deep unconscious part of Western *man's* (it seems a basically male myth) way of perceiving and understanding his experience. The poets give this perception its most vivid form. In

Kavanagh's case, it should be added, the design has written into it the codes of his Catholicism, tilted to fit his own—at once conventional and idiosyncratic—point of view.

[8] This poem and "Intimate Parnassus" pre-date 1955, suggesting that the movement to this stage of Kavanagh's pastoral journey was anticipated by his imagination before the "re-birth." For dating, as well as for poems not in *CP*, see *The Complete Poems of Patrick Kavanagh*, ed. Peter Kavanagh (New York: The Peter Kavanagh Hand Press, 1972), hereafter cited parenthetically in the text as *Complete Poems*.

[9] Spenser's *Shepherds Calendar* and Milton's *Lycidas* come to mind.

[10] "Diary," *Envoy* 4, No. 13 (1950) 89.

[11]In his posthumously published autobiographical novel, *By Night Unstarred* (Dublin: Goldsmith Press, 1977) 18.

"Naming These Things":
A Piecemeal Meditation on Kavanagh's Poetry

I begin by turning away from the form of the conventional essay, which always seems to call for arguments when I want merely observations. Kavanagh himself is my tutor and authority here: "To look on is enough," he says, "In the business of love." I want to believe that's the business I'm in for the moment, his *Complete Poems* open beside me, a rusty railroad spike holding the pages flat. I may as well add the time and place, again instructed by his habit of catching "Things moving or just colour," the shades of the particular moment, that instant one April when "The birds sang in the wet trees," or that kindly June day when he discovered "The word is the messenger of the eye." So, it is Easter Sunday afternoon in Poughkeepsie, New York, and a ragged dark spruce tree leans against the window of my room. None of this egotistical paraphernalia is important, of course, except (as Kavanagh noted of his own life) as an "illustration." It simply shows the poems are alive in the here and now, as indeed they were a few evenings ago, when the poet Galway Kinnell, breaking from his own work, recited by heart two of them to an audience of a few hundred students, most of whom believed Yeats was the start and finish of Irish poetry. Not any more. The next day I found two of them, beginner poets themselves, burrowing among the library stacks in search of "that Kavanagh."

What kept catching my attention this time round was the language of the poems, early and late, its different registers. *Ploughman and Other Poems* (1936), for example, has (at least) two quite distinct idioms. The one that predominates, (a visionary-transcendental mode) is the more obviously lyrical, and provides us with Kavanagh's first official self-portrait, the poet as Seer. You find it in the ploughman's "quiet ecstasy / Like a prayer"; in the poet's decision to "break / With these hands / the bread of wisdom that grows / In the other lands"; or in his delighted recognition that "The maiden of Spring is with child / By the Holy Ghost." In "The Intangible" he pushes out from the explicitly Christian to another, equally religious, field: "Not black or blue, / Grey or red or tan / The skies I travel under. / A strange unquiet wonder. / Indian / Vision and Thunder." In reaching towards the visionary spirit of things, the poet employs a language given him by traditions of conventional religious worship and transcendental mysticism. Its major literary influences are the Catholic faith and AE.

The principle other idiom in *Ploughman* is rooted in, and expressive of the more tangible facts of Kavanagh's personal experience. It is less overtly lyrical, more conversational, saying things like "I saw an old white goat on the slope of Slieve Donard," or, on a tinker woman, "I saw her amid the dunghill debris /

Looking for things / Such as an old pair of shoes or gaiters," utterances that seem wonderfully unemphatic, without rhetorical inflection. A literary influence here may be James Stephens, whose poetic language is so much more concrete, colloquial, and immediate than AE's cloud-shimmering hieroglyphics. The triumph of this idiom, the poem in *Ploughman* which raises it to a new kind of lyricism, is "Inniskeen Road: July Evening." The subtle formal exertions of the sonnet tune and tighten the speech cadences to perfection ("The bicycles go by in twos and threes— / There's a dance in Billy Brennan's barn to-night"). And when this idiom operates at its extended best, as here, it seems able to draw the mystical into its vicinity, making it an ordinary and even more believable part of the poet's experience:

> A road, a mile of kingdom, I am king
> Of banks and stones and every blooming thing.

These two idioms have a richer, more intricate relationship in later work, the first phase of which appears in *Soul for Sale* (1947), which includes *The Great Hunger* (1942). (I name these collections for convenience, for the rough dating they offer, a way of dividing the career. *Complete Poems* [1972], however, is the indispensable text, although the *Collected Poems* of 1964 remains adequate.) In these later poems, the visionary-mystical idiom matures into a language of elegy, mourning the loss of that original transcendent possession, that primary innocence. "Now and then," he says in "A Christmas Childhood," "I can remember something of the gay / Garden that was childhood's." The Christian myth of Eden and Wordsworth's Ode "On the Intimations of Immortality" form the well from which Kavanagh draws his language during this phase. The grammar of this language points us continually into a past that can live only in memory: "The barrels of blue potato-spray / Stood on a headland of July / Beside an orchard wall where roses / Were young girls hanging from the sky" ("Spraying the Potatoes"). Elsewhere the Wordsworthian presence is even more obvious. "Primrose" tells how "Upon a bank I sat, a child made seer / Of one small primrose flowering in my mind," and grieves that the passing years "nevermore have given / Moments to see wonders in the grass." It is in this language that Kavanagh composes the second of his official self-portraits, that of the poet as Exile from Eden. "Temptation in Harvest" is his most searching anatomy of this predicament, a meditation on a visit back to his native place after "five years of pavements raised to art." It is his "Tintern Abbey," but without Wordsworth's emphatic consolations. For him, leaving was merely loss: the language of his pre-lapsarian vision is forced to cohabit with hard facts; the result is at once the end and best achievement of this language-line:

> O Life, forgive me for my sins! I can hear
> In the elm by the potato-pits a thrush.
> Rain is falling on the Burning Bush
> Where God appeared.

A poem like "Memory of My Father" extends the other language-line, that of plainness ungilded by any transcendental possibilities, showing Kavanagh's ability to immerse himself in the objective fact: "Every old man I see / In October-coloured weather / Seems to say to me: / 'I was once your father.'"

Tarry Flynn and *The Great Hunger* are the major works of this phase. (*Lough Derg* has its own special power, and *Why Sorrow?* offers an idiosyncratic example of the opposition between visionary and mundane realities. Neither, however, is complete.) In *Tarry Flynn* and *The Great Hunger*, both the idioms I'm describing dance or wrestle with one another, dramatic embodiments of the kinds of experience which make up Kavanagh's poetic identity. It is an identity grown up enough by this time to see with genuine critical objectivity the forces represented by these different languages. Both these works are reflective summaries of his creative life up to the late 1940s. In *The Great Hunger*, the language of religious vision ("The Holy Spirit is the rising sap") is throttled by that of the awful actuality of Maguire's clay-ridden life: "The graveyard in which he will lie will be just a deep-drilled potato-field." In *Tarry Flynn* the visionary language holds its lyrical own against the comic extremities of ordinary living and the rough vitality of its language. But in the end the book is a valedictory gesture, a farewell to the Garden of the Golden Apples (as it is called in *Why Sorrow?*), another confession of that "Temptation in Harvest" to which the poet succumbs:

> And then I came to the haggard gate,
> And I knew as I entered that I had come
> Through fields that were part of no earthly estate.

I am not at this point interested in the satirical flailing-about Kavanagh did in the '40s and early '50s (another official self-portrait here—the Poet as Scourge of Mediocrity), but in what followed that phase, a period of successful creation which finds its best monuments in *Recent Poems*, published by Peter Kavanagh in 1958 and in *Come Dance with Kitty Stobling* (1960). In this, Kavanagh comes into the fullness of his identity as a poet, shaking off those literary influences I have cited above and releasing himself from their anterior languages. He becomes himself (and in turn becomes a major influence on many Irish poets who come after him).

When, as Kavanagh claimed, he was born (again) as a poet "on the banks of the grand Canal between Baggot Street and Lesson Street bridges in the warm summer of 1955 " (*Self-Portrait*), it was not only his "messianic compulsion" he lost. For he also lost the language that went along with this and other earlier compulsions—a language explicitly Christian and often indebted to Wordsworth. The language of these poems ("I started writing a new kind of poem—with new words," he says in 1957, though in fact he'd probably started a few years before this) is neither the transcendental dialect of the first phase, nor the idiom of nostalgia and visionary bereavement of the second. Languages of absence and loss, these gesture towards what cannot be named or is no longer there. The language of the best poems of the final phase is the language of pure presence, of possession and being possessed. And he owes it to nobody, or almost (I wonder, for example, if George Herbert's "The Flower" hadn't entered his consciousness, most wonderful lyrical account of a recovery from spiritual and poetic dryness to "once more smell the dew and rain, / And relish versing").

My own feeling is that Kavanagh begins to compose this final self-portrait (the word 'official' no longer either applies or matters) with the deliberate manifesto of 1950, "Irish Poets Open Your Eyes" (*Complete Poems*, 236). The echo of Yeats's magisterial injunction is intentional. But Kavanagh's advice is much more demotic, substituting for "Sing whatever is well made" the simple exhortation, "Be ordinary." In place of Yeatsian remoteness he encourages poets to "Enter in and be a part," to see the world that's under their noses, for "Even Cabra can surprise." Most tellingly of all, he counsels them to "Learn repose," a condition which (as noun and verb) he keeps coming back to in the poems of this phase. As he sums it up a decade later in "Question to Life": "So be reposed and praise, praise, praise / The way it happened and the way it is."

While he still resorts in this phase to a vocabulary I'd call religious, now it belongs to and expresses a religion of one: God is not now known or claimed or even aspired to; he must simply "be allowed to surprise us," and the poet does His will by "wallowing" in "the habitual, the banal." Language and self here seem as close to being the same thing as Kavanagh ever managed. His stature depends in part on his persistence in living out the logic of this hard enterprise. This coincidence of language with self accounts for its indicative moods ("I am here in a garage in Monaghan. / It is June and the weather is warm"), the simplicity of its predicates, "I have lived in important places," its unobtrusive ascent to optatives ("O commemorate me where there is water"). In this language without overt influences (though perhaps Mollyjames Joycebloom's "Yes" is somewhere behind it, which Kavanagh called "the most wise word known to the tongue"—he read *Ulysses* around 1950), his sensibility seems somehow at one with the world he inhabits. It is neither the poetry of visionary invocation nor that of valediction. It is, rather, ejaculative, celebrating what is, his here and now: "The Rialto Bridge, / The main gate that was bent by a heavy lorry, / The seat at the back of a shed that was a suntrap." The language of fact has been warmed up till it glows with its own quotidian mystery, and just "naming these things is the love-act and its pledge." It's the language of faith, but in his own fashion. "Gods," after all, as he had said in "Epic," "make their own importance."

•

"Venus with her ecstasy" is not one of Kavanagh's true muses. He never found an adequate language of his own for his explicitly sexual experience: his love poems are usually dismal failures. The best is "On Raglan Road," and this is undeniably a beauty. But its beauty comes in large part from the tune that sounds back of the lines as we read them, from the traditional internal rhymes of song: "The Queen of Hearts still making tarts and I not making hay— / Oh I loved too much and by such by such is happiness thrown away." Aside from this we have the unconvincing exaggerations of an early poem like "Pursuit of an Ideal" (about the "nimble-footed nymph" with "flirt-wild legs" who is elsewhere a "maiden of the dream-vague face" in the shady shades of limpest AE), or the awkward vulnerability of the Hilda poems (in *Complete Poems*, around 1945). The exception is "Bluebells for Love," where the language is charged by his engagement with the natural landscape and a nostalgic recollection of a love-chance missed, given greater poignancy by a use of the future tense:

> There will be bluebells growing under the big trees
> And you will be there and I will be there in May;
> For some other reason we both will have to delay
> The evening in Dunshaughlin.

The love story in *Tarry Flynn* dramatises in comic terms something of the same loss; this poem catches the lyrical, serious side of it. It is the winding together of love and landscape that works here, but it is a unique case. Kavanagh could not discover the poetic idiom to deal with the intricate depths and extensions of the most intimate human relationship.

In the "final phase" I mentioned in the last section, however, *love* is everywhere. But it is a love beyond the specifically sexual, beyond the he and she of it, a love of mere being. Beyond any particular woman, he celebrates the feminine principle itself: "Surely my God is feminine, for Heaven / Is the generous impulse" ("God in Woman," about 1951). This statement sets the tone for the last phase, when he graduates from Eros to Agape, telling himself "You're capable of an intense / Love that is experience." Now when he falls in love it is "with the functional ward / Of a chest hospital," for "nothing whatever is by love debarred." Love is universal affirmation, yes, and the poet's task is merely to look on and "Record love's mystery without claptrap." The best of these fresh, almost Franciscan "love poems" are records of being, no more. For Kavanagh in this phase "love" is conscious being; like Keats in the "Ode to Psyche" he is "let[ting] the warm love in!" In this oriental state the self recedes, becoming tongue, a recording eye and I, only "a single / Item in the picture." In his voluntary accommodation to being he discovers that love is cause and effect, is what makes being in itself a positive and sufficient condition. So being ("Is," written around 1958, is an emblematic title for this period) needs no lyrical transcendence nor the frantic antagonisms of satire: the ordinary, banal world, it turns out, is paradise regained. *This* is what love does to things.

It took him to his limits as a poet. Beyond that, he couldn't "stand and plan / More difficult dominion," which accounts for the painful spectacle of those last years (for all their public recognition and popularity) between *Kitty Stobling* and his death, 1960 to 1967. After Agape, Thanatos. But, like Eros, Thanatos gave him no gift of speech. I back off in dismay.

•

It is time to make some remarks on the (almost) purely technical side. One of the marks of Kavanagh's best work—early and late, lyrical and meditative (I omit the satires, which, however lively or outrageous or purgative, are *technically* not very interesting)—is a surprisingly decisive use of syntax. And his graduation from an earlier to a later kind of excellence in this area is another useful index of his growth as a poet.

Here is a stanza from "Mary," one of the *Ploughman* lyrics; structurally, it is identical to the other three stanzas:I think of poor John Clare's beloved

> And know the blessed pain
> When crusts of death are broken
> And tears are blossomed rain.

First, there is the coincidence between sentence and stanza. This is achieved by a poised, simple syntax. The sentence is without complication: two main clauses are ruled by the verbs "I think . . . And know" placed in dominant positions at the head of their lines and followed by clear direct objects; then come two subordinate clauses, "When crusts . . . are . . . And tears are," with their subjects in the dominant positions. In addition, supplementing the effects of syntax, the balanced lyrical distillation of the thought is confirmed by the straight rhyme, pain/rain, while enjambment offers no surprise, the outcome of the simple conjunctive And/Where/And. Though begun with the "I," the stye is cleansed of "personality," or at lest of that dramatising of personality which is the sound of an individual speech. Here we haven't so much speech as musical utterance (the iambic foot has only two exceptions—"John Clare's" is a spondee, and the third line is catalectic). In spite of its lack of surprise, however, the stanza is successful because of the poet's adequate control of the syntax: he keeps a dancer's muscle rippling through the lines so they refuse to become, for all their regularity, pat or singsong. A sound rhythmic instinct keeps the whole thing pliant.

Even in the early book there's a tendency for this lyrical regularity to push towards the condition of speech while maintaining an unambiguous stanzaic lucidity:

> It is August now, I have hoped
> But I hope no more—
> My beech tree will never hide sparrows
> From hungry hawks.
>   ("Beech Tree")

This is a more complicated stanza than the earlier example. Here the subject shifts imperceptibly from "August" to "I" to "beech tree." Here too the enjambment (which might be seen in any poem as, among other things, a sort of instrument or function of syntax) is an agent of surprise and tension: "But" and "From" as beginnings suggest new breaths, starting again, a fresh thought to complicate the one already there. The cadences, too, are liberated from a given metrical pattern and compose a more shifting, subtle music of dispersed stress.

And, in the way it sets clauses in not quite clear logical relationship to one another, the syntax itself is slightly more dense and surprising than it was before.

The best poem in *Ploughman*, the already mentioned "Inniskeen Road," is even more advanced in this respect. In it the embryonic sense of "personality" implicit in the quotation above is fully and vividly achieved. One reason for this is its supple syntactical organisation, lending density and excitement to a statement that's lyrical and at the same time recognizable as ordinary speech:

> Half-past eight and there is not a spot
> Upon a mile of road, no shadow thrown
> That might turn out a man or woman, not
> A footfall tapping secrecies of stone.

Line and sentence wrestle one another (a more muscular dancing) into a complex poise here. Part of its strength comes from the fact that the innocuous main verb "there is" covers so many clauses. The enjambment, too, works to sustain the tension created by such a strategy: no line except the last contains a complete thought; each line needs the next to fulfill its thought, so there is a continuous pushing forward semantically while rhythm and rhymes keep the line units themselves intact. Syntax, that is, has become a much more powerfully present conductor of the poem than it has been up to this. The result is condensation and a velocity of thought and image and feeling that come across as authoritative poetic power.

In technical terms, the best of the later poetry may be seen as a development of this particular vein of syntactic power (as much as his achievement of what he himself prized as "complete casualness, at being able to play a true note on a dead slack string"—*Self Portrait*). You'll find this in the wonderfully and variously mobile lines of the long poems. Like these from *The Great Hunger*:

> If he stretches out a hand—a wet clod,
> If he opens his nostrils—a dungy smell;
> If he opens his eyes once in a million years—
> Through a crack in the crust of the earth he may see a face nodding in
> Or a woman's legs. Shut them again for that sight is sin.

Or these from *Lough Derg*:

> When he will walk again in Muckno street
> He'll hear from the kitchens of fair-day eating houses
> In the after-bargain carouses
> News from a country beyond the range of birds.

Or these from *Why Sorrow?*:

> It was the gap
> Between the seasons, and the days moved slowly

> With labouring men sleeping on headlands among the nettles
> And long arms that hooked over gates that brightened
> The gravel patches on the June road.

In such expansive, controlled utterances, a limber syntax has become part of the poem's, the voice's, expressive grain.

This is true too of the post-1950 work which, for all its casualness, is still syntactically alert:

> Mention water again
> Always virginal,
> Always original,
> It washes out Original Sin.
>   ("Is")

In the best of these poems it is strong syntax allied to decisive rhythms and rhymes which produces the personal speech characteristic of the later work. Syntactically speaking, his reach expands, becoming more and more capable of drawing many elements into its embrace:

> But satire is unfruitful prayer,
> Only wild shoots of pity there,
> And you must go inland and be
> Lost in compassion's ecstasy,
> Where suffering soars in summer air—
> The millstone has become a star.

What control of syntax amounts to here, its poetic consequence, is Kavanagh's mastery of musical speech. It's easy enough to see and hear in such poems how syntax orchestrates the energetic play of rhythmic unit (line) against sense unit (sentence and its smaller components), lending both buoyancy and sufficient specific gravity to a poem. Yeats is the greatest of Kavanagh's immediate predecessors and possible exemplars in this respect. (The last quotation, indeed, although not a stanza in itself, has an almost Yeatsian look and feel to it, in drive and muscular compactness. It's one of the few points where an inherent connection, amounting possibly to influence, might be detected between the two, Kavanagh otherwise maintaining a definitive, often aggressive or defensive distance between himself and that great blocking shadow.) But the late plays of Shakespeare, which I suppose Kavanagh read, are full of complex rhythmic wholes growing out of the athletic stretch and spirit of syntax, and at moments I am reminded of these too, as I weave or am woven through the poems of *Kitty Stobling* and later. (Or I think, to sound a transatlantic note, of the powerful speech-units, grainy as unplaned wood, of Robert Frost.)

Surprisingly enough, the most accomplished triumphs of Kavanagh's poetic syntax are in his sonnets. Not only is "Inniskeen Road" one, and the later Canal Bank poems and a number of the finest pieces in *Come Dance with Kitty Stob-*

ling (such as the title poem itself, or "Winter" or "October" or "The Hospital" or "Question to Life"), but longer poems like "Temptation in Harvest," "The Defeated," or the second part of "Auditors In" are essentially short sonnet sequences disguised as poems with large stanzas.

Why such a predominant use of this form? In my opinion Kavanagh works so well in the sonnet because it is, in a sense, an external (and traditional) exercise and expression of will to which he must bend his own will, or, better, which acts *as his will* in bending his utterance into formally taut and buoyant shapes. This freedom within well-defined bounds is the perfect space for him, giving firm yet flexible rein to his gift for strong, direct, lyrical-colloquial expression. The movement of the following lines from "Epic" is a fair sample of his power, as he engages with the discipline of the form in an idiosyncratic way, pressing it to fresh shapes inside its traditional contours:

> I heard the Duffys shouting 'Damn your soul'
> And old McCabe stripped to the waist, seen
> Step the plot defying blue cast-steel—
> 'Here is the march along these iron stones'
> That was the year of the Munich bother. Which
> Was more important? I inclined
> To lose my faith in Ballyrush and Gortin
> Till Homer's ghost came whispering to my mind
> He said: I made the Iliad from such
> A local row. Gods make their own importance.

By means of such original syncopations (the equally original punctuation may be simply oversight, and should probably be corrected), such crooked rhymes and such juggling of high and low and middle rhetorics (listen to lines 1 and 4 and 8), Kavanagh forges his own music, his own brand of dancing. As a result, the sonnet is his most consummately achieved choreographic act in the lyric form. And its strength lies in his ability to preserve the form under such pressure, which he does most of all by the limber grace of a syntax that can enable and grant authority to the formal and informal shapes of common speech. As far as the lyric is concerned, this may be his most important legacy, a poetic achievement that joins him to currents of literary form at once traditional and distinctly modern. Such poems show, in fact, how sharp divisions between 'traditional' and 'modern' can be elided, letting each cohabit happily with the other in a single lively contemporary utterance.

•

The question of Kavanagh's influence on later Irish poets arises, naturally. Montague said he "liberated us into ignorance." Kavanagh himself objected to this formulation, and indeed it seems—unless adequately glossed—off target. Heaney's acknowledgement "that reading Kavanagh made him think that he might have something to write about himself" (I'm quoting Darcy O'Brien's book on Kavanagh for the Bucknell series, 67) seems likely to be nearer some enduring truth. Kavanagh's actual public image of the poet-as-embattled-sage (generated by his own behaviour, by his friends and enemies, well-wishers and begrudgers) has been and will continue for a while to be an important factor. But the real heart of his poetic influence must be his use of language in the best work, especially in *The Great Hunger* (ignore his own dismissal of it as "not poetry," as lacking "the nobility and repose of poetry"—his spectrum of critical evaluation was narrow, idiosyncratic, and necessary to the making of his own soul as a poet; but his standards are not sacrosanct, need not be swallowed whole), in some of *Lough Derg* and *Why Sorrow?*, a few of the early lyrics, and many of the poems from his later, post-1950 period. The language-habits of these poems have been a liberating influence on poets as different as Durcan, Montague, Mahon, Heaney, O'Grady, Kennelly, Ní Chuilleanáin, Muldoon—to name a handful. More even than a way of looking or of thinking (though his "we are satisfied with being ourselves, however small" is important—see *Self Portrait*), he taught poets a way of speaking their own various tongues in verse. In this his own example was their encouragement, as his own career might be their caution. He has an abiding place in the modern Irish poetic landscape, the way William Carlos Williams has in the American. What they both offered those who came and come after them was the gift of a rooted speech—a speech, however, that was a true poetic language, not a "local" dialect.

Contemporary Irish poetry is impossible to imagine without Kavanagh. His poetic practice has served as a kind of protective shield against the cramping majesties of Yeats and the minor but infectious rhetorics of the Revival. In form and in language he is a buffer-zone in modern Irish verse, sharing such a state and function with the other important poets of his vexed and hard-pressed generation—with MacNeice, Clarke, Fallon, and Devlin. His practice of what he preached in the following dictum, his finding the language proper to such a practice, leaves many in his debt: "All the poet does is explode the atoms of our ordinary experience." All!

1986

Kavanagonistes

The flash of skunk cabbage in early April
Out of waste ground reminds me of your last
Crop of poems—original, livid, flare of
Feral green: prodigal singing. Those two
Kingfishers ratcheting like mad over Sunset
Lake could be your voice out of the blue
Making an amorous satiric racket in another
World if there is one. And that mourning dove
Alone on a wetback ailanthus branch this morning
Is a warm sienna glow under the rain, passive
And steady-eyed as you were for a little while,
Letting the weather in. You were a real
Eye-opener too, so we see better with our own
Since you went West in fresh garments
Out of Baggot Street, leaving a brave new
World of words to us, pulling the old one
Down about our ears. When the dust settled
In Dublin, London, Inniskeen, you came to rest
Where you belong, in the Prince of Denmark's
*Royal line—*The readiness is all . . . Let be.

1985

In a Topographical Frame:
Ireland in the Poetry of Louis MacNeice

That we were born
Here, not there, is a chance but a chance we took
And would not have it otherwise.

I cannot deny my past to which my self is wed.

That Louis MacNeice is an Irish poet is a fact his critical commentators do not
ignore. Mostly, however, reference to the fact is of an incidental kind and tells
us little about the poetry itself or about the nature and importance of Mac-
Neice's relationship with Ireland.[1] Terence Brown's comment on MacNeice's
exile from his own country may, in fact, be the most revealing of all such comments: "exile from Ireland left him . . . a stranger everywhere."[2] My purpose in
the present essay is to concentrate upon the Irish dimension in the poetry, but in
order to examine the part MacNeice's varied response to Ireland plays in his
work, the effect his relationship with his country has on his verse and on what
might be called his poetic identity, that sense of the self emerging out of the
poems. MacNeice's friend John Hilton once sent a telegram to the poet's parents
which, because of a clerical error, read "Vouch for Louis' nationality."[3] What he
had actually written was "Vouch for Louis' rationality," but as far as MacNeice
as poet is concerned the mistake contains a truth which I hope will be usefully
illuminated by the end of this essay.

I

Apart from his half-humorous claim to be descended from Conor MacNessa,
MacNeice himself often reiterates the importance to his work of Ireland and
things Irish.[4] First among the things that "conditioned my poetry" he placed
"having been brought up in the North of Ireland";[5] his very last radio talk was
about his childhood in Carrickfergus;[6] and he began a late unfinished autobiography with biblical *gravitas*: "In the beginning was the Irish rain."[7] While
MacNeice spent most of his working life outside Ireland, and while the poems
with an explicitly Irish subject matter or setting are comparatively few in number, I would nonetheless argue that these poems and the experience they contain
comprise a most important feature of MacNeice's work. They compose in out-

line a sort of allegorical autobiography of MacNeice's poetic identity, honestly if often obliquely keeping pace with his life.

If MacNeice's world were to be seen in eschatological terms, its heaven and its hell would be located in Ireland.[8] Metaphorically, Ireland represents ecstatic emancipation and dreadful damnation, a spiritual dialectic MacNeice cannot resolve in any simple way. When fused with his childhood, the country becomes a kind of paradise lost elegiacally recalled by the poet bound to the purgatorial experience of time. Such an emblematic design, of course, over-simplifies the complex variety of MacNeice's career as a poet, but may be defended as a means of learning something about the importance of one particular aspect of his poetry.

As far as its social and political realities were concerned, Ireland was from very early on a demonic place in MacNeice's eyes. As a child he saw Belfast as "The city of smoke and dust."[9] It impressed him as being "essentially evil . . . grey, wet, repellent, and its inhabitants dour, rude, and callous."[10] The mill girls frightened him and he feared the men lounging and spitting on street corners, waiting for the pubs to open. Violence is endemic in this society, a social, sectarian, and sexual violence that hardens the realities of living into petrified mockeries of themselves. In an early poem, "Belfast," the poet's horror transmogrifies the city into a wasteland: a chapel is "a cave of gloom," the sea is "salt carrion water," the ship-yard gantries "like crucifixes."[11] Life freezes into the frightening postures of nightmare, people stiffen into inanimate objects (a man is made of basalt and mica, a catholic woman is "shipwrecked . . . before the garish virgin"), and even the ordinary joys of life are "harsh attempts at buyable beauty." This repulsive violence infects life at its cosmic and human sources: "The sun goes down with a banging of Orange drums," and "the male kind murders each its woman." Beyond the "mother-city" the whole North is an equally nightmarish place, a "country of cowled and haunted faces." In another poem he sees Belfast ("devout and profane and hard") in a similar way, a place where the benign juices of life have stopped flowing ("country of callous lava cooled to stone"), a frozen wasteland where even time itself is a solid and solidifying object:

> Time punched with holes like a steel sheet, time
> Hardening the faces, veneering with a grey and speckled rime
> The faces under the shawls and caps.
>
> ("Valediction," 52)

Such imagery turns MacNeice's North into something like Dante's Hell, a place petrified in history, with no outlets channeled by redeeming time. Here the expectation endures "That Casement would land at the pier / With a sword and a horde of rebels," and here too "the voodoo of Orange bands" draws "an iron net through darkest Ulster" (*Autumn Journal*, in *CP*, 31-2). Historical paralysis is mirrored in social immobility, a terrible inability to change:

> And the North where I was a boy,
>   Is still the North, veneered with the grime of Glasgow,
> Thousands of men whom nobody will employ
>   Standing at the corners, coughing. (133)

In this unalterable hell of perfect opposites, eternal antagonisms achieve an exquisite, ridiculous equilibrium:

> Up the Rebels, To Hell with the Pope,
>   And God Save—as you prefer—the King or Ireland. (132)

This infernal immobilising of history is not confined to the North. In MacNeice's eyes the rest of Ireland is also subject to an equivalent corruption of spirit. The important and sufficient cause is that "history never dies, / At any rate in Ireland, arson and murder are legacies" ("Valediction," 52). Historical paralysis, which drives MacNeice away as it drives his *persona* Ryan (in "Eclogue from Iceland") into even more melodramatic exile, is rooted in the fact that Ireland is "a nation / Built upon violence and morose vendettas" (41). Here in Ryan's Dantean vision of political hell is the curse of history at a violent standstill: "My diehard countrymen like drayhorses / Drag their ruin behind them." What repels MacNeice, as it does Ryan, is the saturation of historical time by mindless, bloody repetition. The poet fastens our attention to this by a recurrent imagery of metal and stone, of inanimation. History is an economic treadmill ("They make their Ulster linen from foreign lint / And the money that comes in goes out to make more money," *AJ*, 133) and, socially, a vicious circle:

> A city built upon mud;
> A city built upon profit;
> Free speech nipped in the bud,
> The minority always guilty. (133)

What language and rhythm insist on here is a changeless, unchangeable condition, a non-democratic *status quo*.

The brute, impenetrable primitivism of the peasant and the cultural sentimentality of the Irish middle classes complete MacNeice's picture of Ireland as an infernal wasteland. By birth and upbringing he is cut off from the peasantry, from the "country of cowled and haunted faces." His *persona* Ryan bitterly calls up

> Those eyes which hang in the northern mist, the brute
> Stare of stupidity and hate, the most
> Primitive and false of oracles. (45-6)

From this negative perspective MacNeice understands the peasant as a sensibility suspended in time, a fossilised malevolence infecting historical time with its hate and stupidity. The almost inchoate opening of "Valediction" strikes the same note of speechless terror:

> Died by gunshot under borrowed pennons,
> Sniped from the wet gorse and taken by the limp fins
> And slung like a dead seal in a bog-hole, beaten up
> By peasants with long lips and the whiskey-drinker's cough. (52)

Animal roughness translates the dead man into mere heavy flesh, his murderers into mindless automata, extensions of a landscape that has nothing to do with the more humane possibilities of historical time.

At the opposite extreme to this brutish, mindless malevolence is Irish cultural sentimentality (mainly in the South). It, too, however, is an important element in MacNeice's negative vision of Ireland. For cultural sentimentality also immobilises history, congealing the past into vulgar, outmoded icons of artificial piety, "the trademarks of a hound and a round tower, / . . . Irish glamour . . . sham Celtic crosses . . . souvenirs / Of green marble or black bog-oak" (53). Infecting the historical present with a plastic sentimentalised version of the past, cultural vulgarity draws from MacNeice a stinging denunciation: "Ireland is hooey, Ireland is / A gallery of fake tapestries" (52). He castigates the complacency that will, in spite of the tragedy of emigration, "Take credit for our sanctity, our heroism," those "accepted names" that are only gilded replicas of the qualities they signify. His intense antipathy to ethnic and national complacency fuels his outburst against "Your drums and your dolled-up Virgins and your ignorant dead" (54). What he rejects is frozen time, the constricting to a tiny repertoire of repeated gestures the infinite variety of human and historical possibility. In order to escape this wasteland and restore himself to a more human and humane relationship with historical time, in order not to "have my baby-clothes my shroud" (53), he chooses exile, fluency in time and space, as his only chance of holding onto his own soul.

The poems from which I have been quoting belong mostly to the Thirties. Corresponding to MacNeice's most actively 'political' period, they show one aspect, perhaps a fundamental one, of his need to feel in touch with history. He says of being in Galway when war broke out in 1939, "As soon as I heard . . . of the outbreak of war, Galway became unreal."[12] And elsewhere he tells us that in 1940 he left America to return to a war-time England because "I thought I was missing History."[13] From such a perspective it seems natural enough that certain aspects of Ireland should represent a hell from which he must escape to the fluent historical process of life in England. At the same time MacNeice's view of Ireland was never one of simple rejection. Bitterly negative as some of his feelings were, they were complicated by an intense love for the landscape of the country. Paralleling his rejection is a broad embrace of all that is *free* of history and time—the simple asocial and apolitical fact of space. Seen through this lens Ireland becomes a paradise, the delights of which MacNeice never tires of naming and celebrating.

This visionary tendency predates the poetry. As a child, in order to protect himself against the more unpleasant aspects of his existence, MacNeice was in the habit of constructing "various dream worlds," the first of which was "the West of Ireland."[14] Even the name 'Connemara' "seemed too rich for any ordinary place." What the summoned landscape gives him is a freedom that is at once imaginative and sensual, a place of exuberant generosity and spiritual emancipation:

> It appeared to be a country of windswept open spaces and
> mountains blazing with whins and seas that were never quiet,
> with drowned palaces beneath them, and seals and eagles and
> turf smoke and cottagers who were always laughing and who
> gave you milk when you asked for a glass of water.

Such an epiphanal sense of freedom and perpetuity also rewards his first actual glimpse of the Atlantic, fulfilling the imaginary pattern his dreams had composed. It was, he says, the "biggest thing this side of God," brimming with a sense of "infinite possibility" and "eternity."[15]

Throughout his life and in different parts of Ireland he was to rediscover this ecstatic freedom in the Irish landscape. He describes, for example, a trip to Dublin from England just after the birth of his first child: "I felt I was born again, to be able to go to Dublin on my own. Dodds and I walked up the Wicklow mountains and, as I looked down on Dublin Bay, I felt that the world was open."[16] Here the factual sensation of release verges on the mystical ("born again"), turning the landscape into an occasion of near paradisal release; as he pursues the memory, MacNeice's style rises in lyrical intensity to match the experience: "I was wearing citified suede shoes and finding them afterwards soaked and scratched by heather had a sense of having cut loose; a great wild star of space was smashed in the hot-house window."

The poems themselves everywhere testify to this felt sense of emancipation in the Irish landscape, which they render in approximate but unambiguously paradisal terms. And as the infernal aspects of Ireland are marked by images of mechanical petrifaction, paralysis and immobility, the images that express his paradisal version of the same place are naturally fluent, free, and sensually immediate. In a life constricted by "the monotony of fear" it is in his experience of the Irish landscape that MacNeice finds an occasional, precious freedom:

> For during a tiny portion of our lives we are not in trains,
> The idol living for a moment, not muscle-bound
> But walking freely through the slanting rain,
> Its ankles wet, its grimace relaxed again.
>
> ("Train to Dublin," 27)

This sense of freedom anchors a metaphysical idea in physical phenomena, releasing MacNeice's imagination into gestures of expansive liberality:

> I give you the disproportion between labour spent
> And joy at random; the laughter of the Galway sea
> Juggling with spars and bones irresponsibly. (27)

Granting him in the same poem a freedom at once child-like ("the toy Liffey"), clownish ("irresponsibility"), and visionary ("the vast gulls"), his beloved sea springs him from the dutiful imperatives of history into the timeless, ecstatically contradictory domain of myth. From a world in which history is too much and too unalterably with us, he is released into one where history hardly exists at all. Clonmacnoise, site of the famous monastery, is a fitting emblem for this counterpoint of history and landscape, being "A huddle of tombs and ruins of anonymous men / Above the Shannon dreaming in the quiet rain."[17]

From the vantage point of his delight in landscape MacNeice often translates history into a dynamics of pure sensation:

> I give you the smell of Norman stone, the squelch
> Of bog beneath your boots, the red bog-grass,
> The vivid chequer of the Antrim hills, the trough of dark
> Golden water for the carthorses, the brass
> Belt of serene sun upon the lough. (28)

Experience in this realm is fluent: hard Norman stone becomes subtle smell; the bog, elsewhere a murderous place, is merely the sound and sensation of boots sinking into its softness, the colour of its vegetation. Metal imagery is purged of its inimical associations, so water is richly golden and the lough's "brass belt" is only the benevolent serenity of sunlight. All the senses come to involuntary ecstatic life in this paradise of ordinary pleasures made extraordinary by the poet's vividness of apprehension:

> Fuchsia and ragweed and the distant hills
> Made as it were out of clouds and sea:
> All night the bay is splashing and the moon
>   Makes the break of the waves.
>
> And home-made bread and the smell of turf or flax
> And the air a glove and water lathering easy
>   And convolvulus in the hedge.
>   ("Cushenden," 165)

Fluency of being makes it hard for one thing not to run into another. Verbs, in the present tense and the indicative mood, signify simple presence, a life of dynamic unity. Time seems to be transcended by a total absorption in the sensual moment. A current of entranced life connects all things with a common energy, repeatedly visible in the synesthetic quality and grammatical status of the verbs:

> And the shadows of clouds on the mountains moving
>   Like browsing cattle at ease. . . .

> And splashed against a white
> Roadside cottage a welter of nasturtium
>   Deluging the sight. . . .

> But in Mayo the tumble-down walls went leap-frog
>   Over the moors.
>   ("In Sligo and Mayo," 165)

Objects stand or move in their own sufficient light, the poet's rapt attention granting the visible world the radiance of a paradise of personal vision.

MacNeice's visionary, lyrical sense of Ireland is not confined to the countryside. In such cities as Galway and Dublin political and social realities are not necessarily ignored, but rather placed in the larger context of perpetuity. (Sometimes, and comically, or pathetically, they *are* ignored, as when on the eve of the outbreak of war MacNeice "spent Saturday drinking in a bar with the Dublin literati; they hardly mentioned the war but debated the correct versions of Dublin street songs."[18] Clearly, something in MacNeice was drawn to and enjoyed this sort of sabbatical from reality.) Dublin has its own sensual delights, since even its grey stone seems soft, its bronze is "declamatory," the air is "soft on the cheek," and there is "porter running from the taps / With a head of yellow cream" ("Dublin," 163). As in the country landscape, the inanimate here is animated. In Galway it is the same story of sensual, uncluttered, and precisely observed gifts:

> Salmon in the Corrib
> Gently swaying
> And the water combed out
> Over the weir
> And a hundred swans
> Dreaming on the harbour. (166)

This particular vision of landscape can stretch beyond its actual elements to touch the magical aura of romance:

>   water-shafted air
> Of amethyst and moonstone, the horses feet like bells of hair
> Shambling beneath the Orange cart, the beer-brown spring
> Guzzling between the weather, the green gush of Irish spring.
>   ("Valediction," 52)

The seasonal energy and the other near-magical elements neutralise the historical and political implications of that Orange cart (or see it *only* in a benevolent light). Beyond the exigencies of time ("Her mountains are still blue, her rivers flow / Bubbling over the boulders," *AJ*, XVI, 134), this landscape is constantly passing into the paradisal realm of the perfectly apprehended sensual moment, a realm where the imagination and the ordinary world touch the borders of romance: "O grail of emerald passing light / And hanging smell of sweetest hay / And grain of sea and loom of wind" ("Western Landscape," 255).

What such a landscape offers MacNeice is a pastoral refuge from the unpleasant aspects of the world of history and conscious, elected responsibility. The outbreak of war crystallises his sense of the Irish landscape as an emancipation from the world of ordinary responsibilities and common sense. War paints the contrast in its most vivid colours (it is in dreaming Galway, for example, that "The war came down on us" 166), and although MacNeice is compelled by the war to return to the world of history, he does so wryly, "Eastward again, returning to our so-called posts."[19] One last attempt at escape is, revealingly, headlong into the Irish landscape itself:

> Through the fat fields and the orchards
> And the fan-shafts of the sun,
> Through Dungannon and Augher
> Clogher and Fivemile town
> Making the car roar
> Over the hill's crest,
> Hoping to hide my head
> In the clouds of the West.[20]

In this context, too, one of his most outspoken poems on the subject, "Neutrality" (202), distills much of his imaginative thinking about the double meaning of Ireland to him. It begins

> The neutral island facing the Atlantic,
> The neutral island in the heart of man,
> Are bitterly soft reminders of the beginnings
> That ended before the end began.

Once again Ireland is a counterpoint to the world of history, an attractive antidote to time, a narcotic anachronism from which MacNeice's own sceptical sense of duty and commitment must rouse him:

> Look into your heart and you will find a County Sligo,
> A Knocknarea with for navel a cairn of stones,
> You will find the shadow and sheen of a moleskin mountain
> And a litter of chronicles and bones.

But Ireland's neutrality seemed wrong to MacNeice, an opting out of history in the worst way. The mackerel in the sea around the island "Are fat on the flesh of your kin," he says, and it is this culpable indifference which seals his decision to live away from his island home.

No matter how unwillingly, then, MacNeice did surrender to the claims of history, turning from the fine freedom and sensual pleasures of the Irish land-scape to England's historical actuality. The end of "Valediction" stands as his proper elegiac farewell to something which his *imagination* never abandons:

> goodbye the chequered and the quiet hills
> The gaudily-striped Atlantic, the linen mills
> That swallow the shawled file, the black moor where half
> A turf-stack stands like a ruined cenotaph. (54)

Moving from the accents of Othello to those of Ulysses he recognizes his duty and his quest, his need to resist the pleasures of a country where "the kiss of the past is narcotic . . . the western climate is Lethe / The smoky taste of cooking on turf is lotus." Finally, in an image of buoyant freedom, he acknowledges the antagonism between this paradisal, lyrical world and the world where, driven by other concerns and other duties, he must live his "ordinary" life:

> If I were a dog of sunlight I would bound
> From Phoenix Park to Achill Sound,
> Picking up the scent of a hundred fugitives
> That have broken the mesh of ordinary lives.

But he knows he cannot be the "dog of sunlight" into which the Irish landscape has sometimes transformed him, and so he leaves it with regret, to enter the mesh of history, there to pursue his own more complex and comprehensive truth.

II

MacNeice's poetic relationship with Ireland does not end with the unsustainable infernal and paradisal versions of it just examined. A third version of that rela-tionship remains to be considered, which is perhaps—in terms of his poetry—the most important of all. If there is a dialectic of MacNeice's imagination, then the earlier two versions are thesis and antithesis, this last their proper synthesis.

In the year he died MacNeice gave the Clark Lectures at Cambridge. These were later published as *Varieties of Parable*.[21] In them he put theoretical form on something he had himself already practiced in art, and the final poetic fruit of which is his last and perhaps his best volume of verse, *The Burning Perch* (1963). He himself called it "double-level poetry."[22] As some of the above quo-tations show, his relationship with Ireland lent itself very easily to such a notion. As an icon of exile, a sort of paradise lost, Ireland can be internalized. In the later poetry, especially, it becomes an important element in the symbolic autobiography MacNeice forges in small lyrical fragments. His own life, and with it the Ireland he knew as a child and later, become themselves a variety of parable.

One of the most crucial events in this parable is the loss of an Edenic past. MacNeice expresses his sense of this loss in his prose as well as his verse. An outstanding feature of his childhood was "a second house . . . in a garden enormously large (an acre) with a long prairie of lawn and virgin shrubberies."[23] But even here "there was always a sense of loss because things could never be replaced."[24] There is even a place nearby actually called Eden, but it too is marked by a symbolic shadow: "I always thought of the Garden as I approached it, only to find some dour cement houses and a shop labelled Drugs, which sounded wicked."[25]

The poems pare the actual location of this Edenic dream down to its allegorical outline. In "Autobiography" (187), for example, he says simply

> In my childhood trees were green
> And there was plenty to be seen.

An imaginary Eden quickly supplanted the more prosaic actualities of his life. In dream he translated the West of Ireland into a paradise garden. (So strong were his imaginings that his first actual visit to the West, where both his mother and father came from, "was my homecoming").[26] His childhood imagination, he says in "Day of Renewal" (309), claimed

> a different birthplace, a wild nest
> Further, more truly, west, on a bare height
> Where nothing need be useful and the breakers
> Came and came but never made any progress
> And children were reborn each night.

In "The Strand" (226), an elegy for his father ("A square black figure whom the horizon understood"), poet and father share the symbolic Edenic experience inherent in the Irish landscape (presumably Portstewart), which becomes the agent of their reconciliation.[27] MacNeice's own "steps repeat" as he walks along the beach "Someone's who now has left such strands for good / Carrying his boots and paddling like a child." Time and death expel from the garden, blotting "the bright reflection" in the shore-pools so "no sign / Remains of face or feet when visitors have gone home." Rising out of its fact, the image becomes an adequate symbol of all human transience. In this way, MacNeice transforms the particularity of the Irish landscape into a universal allegory, with no loss of particular feeling. He can do this not only because of the demanding depths of his emotion for his father, but because of the intensity and authenticity of his and his father's feeling for the Irish scene itself.

The allegorical impulse is never far from MacNeice's poetic treatment of Ireland. The western islands, for example (which "endorse the dreams" of "those who despise charts") are "cubs that have lost their mother" ("Last Before

America," 226). Seeing them in this way is to apply the image of personal Edenic loss to the landscape itself. Even when he is glad to be out of Ireland, her very name, like something out of one of his beloved fairy-tales, "keeps ringing like a bell / in an underwater belfry" (*AJ*, XVI, 132). For to be Irish is, as far as he is concerned, to be a citizen "of a world that never was, / Baptised with fairy water" (132). In loss, its image grows in symbolic potency, gathering to itself all his imaginative sense of loss as the special human predicament. Acknowledging this, he insists upon his own involuntary engagement with the land he has voluntarily left:

> In the back of my mind are snips of white, the sails
> Of the Lough's fishing-boats, the bell-ropes lash their tails
> When I would peal my thoughts, the bells pull free—
> Memory in apostasy. ("Valediction," 52)

His own dilemma, then, becomes an allegory of all human exile, which he roots in the plausible facts of what he has himself left behind. We have, he says in "Western Landscape" (257), "lost the right to residence"; we are "visitors," "disfranchised / In the constituencies of quartz and bog-oak / And ousted from the elemental congress." Ireland, then, grounds an imaginative impulse for MacNeice, becomes not merely a fact but an operating element in his poetic imagination.

Accompanying MacNeice's sense of Ireland as the *locus* of his Edenic loss is an even more personal sense of loss—the loss of a self he might have been had he remained. In a number of poems MacNeice virtually composes elegies for this unrealized self. In "A Hand of Snapshots," for example, a series of photographs becomes a gloss on his past:

> Peering into your stout you see a past of lazybeds,
> A liner moving west, leaving the husk of home. . . .
>
> My youth is the tall ship that chose to run on the rocks. (448)

The allegorical possibilities of a self he never became are visible too in his reference to fishing "for something / That he remembers now more by the feel / Of the jigging line than by how it looked when landed" (449). Considering the effect of environment on a two year-old child he once was, he implicitly laments the wrench that will take the man to an end far from his beginnings:

> the blaze of whins, the smell of turf,
> The squelch of mud, the belch of surf,
> The slop of porridge, the squawk of gulls,
> Enter that smallest of small skulls.
>
> Which someday, skull and nothing more,
> Will lie in a box on a foreign shore. (450)

Clearly his decision to leave is a pivotal moment in his life: "Born here, I should have proved a different self" (450). By writing the poem out of this nostalgic consciousness he in some sense internalises the vanished possibility, and by possessing it enriches his chosen self as poet:

> Yet here for a month and for this once in passing,
> I can imagine at least
> The permanence of what passes
> As though the window opened
> And the ancient cross on the hillside meant myself. (450)

In identifying himself with the ancient cross he joins himself not only to a lost personal self, but to some of the cultural ramifications of this loss.

MacNeice's many celebrations of the passing moment, the variety and multiplicity of life, gain special poignance in the light of this actual exile from "the permanence of what passes." His relationship with Ireland puts down in vivid shorthand the precariousness of individual identity, the transitoriness of the world of common and uncommon phenomena. It is a relationship which allows him to hold, but not hold onto "the faces balanced in the toppling wave" ("Train to Dublin," 28), and to "poise the toppling hour" ("Dublin," 164). This deeply felt relationship anchors his parable mode in a living reality.

Working in this mode MacNeice makes crucial use of his Irish childhood.[28] He mines this experience for metaphors of a larger truth, to grasp something permanent in the human condition. It becomes the ground-plan for his symbolic engagement with the concerns of his later life. "Death of an Old Lady" (463) reveals this procedure. In this poem an epiphanal childhood memory (a glimpse of the *Titanic* putting out to sea) is fused with a present occurrence (an actual death) to compose an effective example of the "double-level writing" MacNeice understood as parable:

> At five in the morning there were grey voices
> Calling three times through the dank fields;
> The ground fell away beyond the voices
> Forty long years to the wrinkled lough
> That had given the child one shining glimpse
> Of a boat so big it was named Titanic.

This "shining glimpse" becomes an emblem of childhood itself, its juxtaposition of doomed ship and dying lady summarizing the curve in time which other features of the poem accentuate: "it was grey April, / The daffodils in her garden waited / To make her a wreath."

In other poems of comparable power, the Irish context again serves as a springboard for symbolic meditation. "House on the Cliff" (462), for example, fluently translates a childhood memory into a parable of MacNeice's own, and

man's, mutability and isolation: "Indoors ancestral curse-cum-blessing. Outdoors / the empty bowl of heaven, the empty deep." "Country weekend" (491)
moves from a present act of lighting lamps to a memory shining with the special
lucidity of symbol as the poet "calls back"

> Bustling dead women with steady hands,
> One from Tyrone and one from Cavan
> And one my mother; the soft lights marched
> Nightly out of the pantry and spread
>
> Assurance, not like the fickle candles.

The simple act of reading "in this light" becomes a figure for MacNeice's nostalgia. In its literary allusiveness and symbolic extensions, his early Irish experience comforts the poet in middle age.

MacNeice's return through the purgative conditionals of memory to his
Irish experience is crucial to him as a poet, for it represents a symbolic repossession of a past from which his conscious choice had exiled him. Rooted in
family and place, he locates such repossession in "The Truisms" (507) in a reconciliation with his dead father. Here the myth of departure becomes that of
return, and a death firmly grasped turns into an image of regeneration, convincing because toughly earned, as if in a dream the poet comes upon a strange
house

> And he walked straight in; it was where he had come from
> And something told him the way to behave.
> He raised his hands and blessed his home;
> The truisms flew and perched on his shoulders
> And a tall tree sprouted from his father's grave.

In a way that goes beyond the familial and the personal, this poem suggests very
strongly the importance MacNeice's relationship with Ireland held for his poetic
identity. Recovering his past, finally, becomes a kind of paradise regained, completing the circle of his self within the frame of his Irish experience.

And, indeed, the dominant sense in many of these poems is of coming
home. "Carrick Revisited" (224), a poem written about 1945, shows that this
impulse is not confined to the late poems. Although the theme is here treated in
a naturalistic way, the symbolic ramifications are the same: "the castle as plumb
assured / as thirty years ago . . . / But the green banks are as rich and the lough
as hazily lazy / And the child's astonishment not yet cured." Placing himself
squarely in this "topographical frame," MacNeice acknowledges his identity in
terms of this landscape, "Like a belated rock in the red Antrim clay / That cannot at this era change its pitch or name." In actual and symbolic terms the event
is a homecoming. The very intensity of memory itself is a homecoming, a lock-
ing of past into future to make an acceptable present. This recovery, while it
may not translate elegy into celebration, does provide a certain consolation, the

consolation that something that endures has been repossessed. Such enduring life may be weighed against the evidence of transience and passage. So there is something eternal about the sea at Portstewart: "Round the corner was always the sea. Our childhood / Knew there was more where it came from" (518). Actual and allusive ("Round that corner where Xenephon . . . Knew he was home"), this homecoming turns the paradise lost of childhood and his Irish context into the paradise regained of symbolic consolation.

But, as the sceptic-poet admits in "Donegal Triptych" (445), "To speak of cycles / Rings as false as moving straight." He recognizes that his repossession of the past is a complex thing, only to be accomplished by his own imaginative activity as a poet, reaching beyond the actual to symbolic possibility:

> Here for instance: lanes of fuchsias
> Bleed such hills as, earlier mine,
> Vanished later; later shine
> More than ever, with my collusion.
> Surface takes a glossier polish,
> Depth a richer gloom. And steel
> Skewers the heart. Our fingers feel
> The height of the sky, the ocean bottom. (446)

The wild, lyrical exultation with which MacNeice embraces this homecoming suggests it is his own poetic self he somehow recovers, found in his intense response to his Irish context:

> And salute to our uncle, the Knave of Storms
> Who wolfs the stars and gulps the Atlantic,
> Who cares not a wreck for means and norms
> But winnows nerve and brain to spindrift. (447)

In an imaginative embrace of dissolution the poet recovers himself. Discovering a meaning in passage, he can celebrate the landscape he loves and left, perceiving it now in an allegorical light. Paradise is regained in the full consciousness of its loss and its subjection to time: "let the rain keep sifting / into the earth, while our minds become, like the earth, a sieve / . . . drenched in echoes of our earlier lives" (448). This achievement of identity, the recovery of self inside this particular landscape, has distinct moral overtones, allowing the poet "once more to find communion / With other solitary beings, with the whole race of men" (448). The very impulse that, one may speculate, initially drove MacNeice away from Ireland, is now satisfied by his imaginative return there.

MacNeice's use of the figure of St. Brandan the Navigator forms an almost mystical coda to the paradise regained of his Irish experience. He was always "addicted to the legendary Ancient Irish voyages," he tells us, and the figure of Brandan intrigued him.[29] In what I would understand as the imaginative seal upon his relationship with Ireland, MacNeice seems to project upon the saint imaginative impulses of his own. Brandan is a "spindrift hermit," whose voyage served to "Distil the distance and undo / Time in quintessential West" ("Western Landscape," 256), an achievement MacNeice often seems eager to emulate. Such, however, is the monk's, the mystic's solution, a negation of being, with "all desire fulfilled, unsought." Beyond that there is the real man in a boat among the waves: "one thought of God, one feeling of the ocean, / Fused in the moving body, the unmoved soul, / Made him a part of a not to be parted whole." MacNeice, however, being "neither Brandan / Free of all roots nor yet a rooted peasant," knows he cannot achieve such oneness. And yet the image of the saint haunts him. In "Four Winds" ("West," 494), Brandan's prayer, "coincidence or not," rouses the wind on a still sea. This act of faith confirms him (as it confirms the Ulyssean speaker in "Thalassa," supposedly MacNeice's last poem) in his solitary quest in search of life and—like the poet—in search of himself. It is a quest MacNeice must especially sympathize with, whose prayer on his journey is repeatedly to his own past and its Irish context, the decisive "givens" of his identity:

> Time and place—our bridgeheads into reality
> But also its concealment! Out of the sea
> We land on the Particular and lose
> All other possible bird's-eye views.
>   ("Carrick Revisited," 224)

Because of his unbroken commitment to place, Louis MacNeice managed to compose some of his best work out of his relationship with Ireland. Whether celebratory, nostalgic, or embittered, there was always sufficient feeling in this relationship to prompt poems that are in a special sense independent of the will, poems that gather their own involuntary momentum. MacNeice once said that "the things that happen to one often seem better than the things one chooses."[30] In all its incarnations in his poetry, Ireland provides the imaginative velocity of something "that happens to one," rather than something chosen ("what chance misspelt / May never now be righted by my choice," 225). The poems and parts of poems dealing directly or obliquely with MacNeice's Irish experience, while by no means the largest or even the most significant part of his work, are nonetheless a sort of spine to the rest of his poetry, offering a symbolic diagram for MacNeice's poetic identity. Adrift on the Atlantic, St. Brandan's vessel is impelled by a wind raised by prayer. And, assisted thus by mystery, "The long-lost ship / Flew home and into legend like a bird" (494). By persisting in his relationship with his Irish experience, by repeatedly acknowledging its physical and spiritual importance to him, by imagining it into allegory and parable, MacNeice composed inside the larger body of his work a rich authentic parable of his own poetic identity. And while he may not yet have flown "into legend like a bird," it is true that as a poet he has deeply affected the succeeding generation of Irish poets, especially those from Northern Ireland. Voluntarily and involuntarily he did, in the end, fly home.

1981

NOTES

[1] "The English tended to think of him as Irish; critics referred to his nationality when they reviewed his books." Terence Brown, *Louis MacNeice: Sceptical Vision* (Dublin: Gill and MacMillan, 1975) 13.

[2] *Ibid*, 15.

[3] In an Appendix to MacNeice's autobiography, *The Strings are False* (London: Faber and Faber, 1965) 279.

[4] *Strings*, 152.

[5] *Modern Poetry: A Personal Essay* (Oxford: Clarendon Press, 1938) 88.

[6] See *Time Was Away: The World of Louis MacNeice*, ed. Terence Brown and Alec Reid (Dublin: Dolmen Press, 1976).

[7] "Landscapes of Childhood and Youth," in *Strings*, 216.

[8] England, where the conscious, deliberate struggle towards salvation takes place, would be the Purgatory of such an eschatological framework.

[9] *Zoo* (London: Michael Joseph, 1938) 84.

[10] *Ibid*, 78.

[11] "Belfast," in *The Collected Poems of Louis MacNeice*, ed. E.R. Dodds (London: Faber and Faber, 1966) 17. Unless otherwise stated, all quotations from the poems refer to this volume. Further references are in my text. The volume itself will be referred to as *CP*.

[12] *The Poetry of W.B. Yeats* (1961; Rpt. London: Faber and Faber, 1967) 17.

[13] See William T. McKinnon, *Apollo's Blended Dream* (Oxford University Press, 1971) 32.

[14] This and the quotations which immediately follow are from *Strings*, 216-17.

[15] *Ibid*, 219-20.

[16] *Ibid*, 147.

[17] In Section VIII of "The Coming of War," in *The Last Ditch* (Dublin: The Cuala Press, 1940) 10; excluded from the *Collected Poems*, 1925-1948, and from *CP*.

[18] *Strings*, 212.

[19] See note 17 above.

[20] "Running Away from the War," in *The Last Ditch*, 7.

[21] Cambridge University Press, 1965.

[22] *Ibid*, 8.

[23] *Strings*, 37.

[24] *Ibid*.

[25] *Ibid*, 218.

[26] *Ibid*, 111.

[27] "His father obviously had a deep love for the Irish landscape." Brown, 10.

[28] "In his Irish childhood the coordinates of the poet's imagination were marked out. The contradictions and strains of this world, its extremes of darkness and light were to influence how he eventually saw all of his life." Brown, 28. I hope my own discussion expands upon Brown's seminal insight.

[29] *The Mad Islands* and *The Administrator: Two Radio Plays* (London, Faber and Faber, 1964) 8. References to Saint Brandan occur at a number of points in the first-named play (e.g., 36, 51).

[30] *Strings*, 220.

John Hewitt's "Steady Pulse"

"We pick our path among appearances," says John Hewitt in "The Fool's Cap," "and wisdom safely lies in cautious doubt." For Hewitt, the fruit of forty-five years of poetic growth is a measured wisdom, a modest claim to understanding that's sensibly rooted in a world of palpable surfaces. No extravagant metaphysical adventurer, he is content to know and own up to the limits of his own enduring relationship with the world. Each of the important linguistic elements in the above quotation points to a revealing facet of the poet's nature: "pick our path" suggests care and persistence as well as an engagement with the natural environment; "wisdom" and "doubt" are necessary twins; the adjective confirms the portrait of a poet who will not take too many chances; finally, the verb "lies," an unintended pun, suggests passivity as well the vulnerability to error inherent in the whole enterprise.

In 1968 Hewitt, who was born in 1907, published his *Collected Poems 1932-67*. The two volumes under review (*Out of My Time: Poems*, and *Time Enough: Poems New and Revised*) are his most important productions since that time. Among them, these three books contain his essential poetic output, a small body of work that must nonetheless occupy an important place in any consideration of modern Irish poetry, for itself and for the kinds of influence it has had, along with the work of his fellow Ulsterman, friend, and contemporary, W.R. Rogers, upon some of the younger Northern poets.

The best route to an understanding of Hewitt's poetry is through those poems he has written explicitly on the subject of his own art. He has described his poetry in general as "a quest for identity as an individual, as an Irishman of settler stock, as a Twentieth-Century man." The poems I have alluded to, in a fine mixture of meditation and defence provide insights into the nature of his art and offer a series of stock-taking reports upon the progress of that quest. Appearing in his earliest as well as his most recent work, they are the spine, the backbone of his poetry. In an early poem, "Once Alien Here," he describes the source of his poetic ambitions and the necessary apprenticeship of his resources:

> So I, because of all the buried men
> in Ulster clay, because of rock and glen
> and mist and cloud and quality of air
> as native in my thought as any here,
> who now would seek a native mode to tell
> our stubborn wisdom individual,

> yet lacking skill in either scale of song,
> the graver English, lyric Irish tongue,
> must let this rich earth so enhance the blood
> with steady pulse where now is plunging mood
> till thought and image may, identified,
> find easy voice to utter each aright.

In spite of some faltering—the awkward (slightly Miltonic) inversion of line 6, the weakness of lines 10 and 12—the passage reveals many of Hewitt's characteristic strengths. The steady iambic beat lends itself without strain to the rhythms of a speech at once dignified and colloquial. The rhymes are creative rather than mechanical and give the impression less of calculation than of happy accident. Athletic but not showy, the syntax is flexible enough to sustain a single sentence over twelve lines, allowing its significance to stand poised between enjambed and end-stopped lines. The final impression is of articulate intelligence, an urbanity deftly qualified by the content of the lines, the insistence upon the umbilical bond between poetry, "pulse," and "this rich earth." In expressing the search for an identity that will be the proper amalgamation of public, private, and poetic needs, the lines offer a paradigm to the reader by means of which it is possible to see Hewitt testing himself again and again, with now one, now another of its elements dominant.

Depth is added to the sketchy self-portrait offered above by the long autobiographical poem *Conacre* (1943), in which Hewitt considers his poetic commitment not to the city of Belfast, where he lived and worked at the time, but to a countryside he has never known as a native. Urban phenomena are "not the world my pulses take for true." Like Wordsworth, the apparent master of this phase, Hewitt can delight "only in places far from kerb or street." In spite of the Wordsworthian influence, however, this lover of nature is no extravagant romantic, "but one who needs the comfortable pace / of safe tradition." The continuing need for safety, admirable if only because so candidly acknowledged, steers the poet away from the depths:

> The surfaces of life are safer stuff;
> if weather tear the husk it is enough.
> Should we persist and split the final pod,
> who knows if it reveal the seed of God?

Whatever the motive behind this diffidence, it is a consistent element in his identity, an identity that is in part developed out of reflections upon this fact. He is, as he says in *Conacre*,

> . . . neither saint nor fool,
> rather a happy man who seldom sees
> the emptiness behind the images
> that wake my heart to wonder.

He halts then in the embrace of things, unwilling to explore that provoking "emptiness."

Hewitt's first genuinely successful expression of the poetic identity being forged and reflected upon in these early poems is a poem called "Because I Paced My Thought." Written soon after *Conacre*, it distills the experience of that poem and its consequences into four quatrains that reveal the poet's identity like a signature:

> Because I paced my thought by the natural world,
> the earth organic, renewed with the palpable seasons,
> rather than the city falling ruinous, slowly,
> by weather and use, swiftly by bomb and argument,
>
> I found myself alone who had hoped for attention.
> If one listened a moment he murmured his dissent:
> this is an idle game for a cowardly mind.
> The day is urgent. The sun is not on the agenda.
>
> And some who hated the city and man's unreasoning acts
> remarked: He is no ally. He does not say that
> Power and Hate are the engines of human treason.
> There is no answering love in the yellowing leaf.
>
> I should have made it plain that I stake my future
> on birds flying in and out of the schoolroom-window,
> on the council of sunburnt comrades in the sun,
> and the picture carried with singing into the temple.

"Because I Paced My Thought" perfectly enacts and decisively validates the commitment that is its subject matter. Softspoken, but entirely authoritative, it pushes up out of the depths of its own experience. By *revealing* the self, it lyrically transcends the need to explain it. The poet's honesty finds a matching language, a language at odds with what Stephen Daedalus called "the big words," at one with the things of the natural world, ordinary and as full of grace as "birds flying in and out of the schoolroom-window," and capable of the whispered, unsentimental exaltation of the last line. The poem achieves Hewitt's own independent accent, the tones of honesty and reserve I would most associate with him. Its low-keyed excitement, too, is characteristic, guaranteed by the lucid, meticulous diction, delicate balancing acts of syntax, concentrating and sustaining the pulse of the poem with deliberate parenthesis—"the earth organic"—or ingeniously modulated shifts of metre.

Many of the best and most important poems in the *Collected Poems* rise directly from this central commitment. Bound to its imperatives, however, Hewitt is never "merely" a nature poet. What he writes are meditations, not descriptions. "The Stoat," "The Watchers," "Hedgehog," "The Owl," and "For a September Afternoon of Unexpected Brightness" all have a beauty that comes not only from the poet's eager and attentive eye, but from a meditative note that, while it may owe in substance something to Robert Frost and Edward Thomas, is struck in the balanced, authentic accents of Hewitt himself in, for example, "Hedgehog":

> Patient I waited till the fear was spent,
> and watched the waking from that little death,
> a fellow creature native to my sod,
> nervous and mortal, meant to be alive,
> and eager for the purposes of breath.

The last line here might be an emblem of Hewitt's own ambition as a poet. For him, "the purposes of breath" are, I'd say, some felt obligation to tell an unvarnished truth or two about his own experience and beliefs, setting these—if need be—in a context of certain public realities peculiar to his native environment.

While nature does not alter according to the arbitrary contours of nationality, most poets committed to its celebration locate their "nature" in some specific place—the Lake Country, New England, County Monaghan. Hewitt's location is the Glens of Antrim. When he removed from Belfast to Coventry in 1957—where he was Director of the Herbert Art Gallery and Museum until his retirement in 1972—Hewitt voluntarily cut himself off from a primary source and resource of his imagination. There were, of course, others. But it does seem noteworthy, in the light of the present discussion, that between 1957 and 1967, insofar as this can be gauged from the chronological but undated order of the *Collected Poems*, the dominant elements of Hewitt's poetry are his own family history, a trip to Greece and other parts of Europe, and his own perplexed sense of personal change. While good poems appear in these groups, especially in the family group, the marked change in emphases suggests some conscious or unconscious loss. It is also curious, that between 1957 and 1967 the only direct reflection upon the poet's own art that appears in these poems, most of which have a more deliberately outward tendency than the earlier work, is in the pained "Hand Over Hand": "One measures things by standing near them / and reaching towards them." A more oblique reference concludes "The Modelled Head," in which the poet considers "these alternatives, / to find a new mask for what I wish to be, / or to try to be a man without a mask, / resolved not to grow neutral, growing old."

Whatever the accuracy or value of this crude biographical guesswork, it is a fact that not until after his return to Ireland, in a poem dated 1973, does Hewitt take up again the explicit investigation of his own poetic identity. "On the Canal" is one of the best poems in *Out of My Time*, an uneven collection containing poems written between 1967 and 1974. This particular poem allows us a glimpse of Hewitt's continuity, his links with his own past, and his development as a poet. The old virtues are there, but sparer, more pressured now both in style and substance:

> Slower now, less sure of my footing,
> tired sooner, I must estimate
> new response, reluctant sinew,
> kerb's height, speed of approaching traffic.
> Yet used-response to written words, to
> intended shapes, to coded messages,
> floods in the freeways still; I am equipped
> for report, comment, comparison.

What's notable here is the colloquial, non-iambic yet regular rhythms; the speaking voice of a mannerly, articulate, somewhat flinty human being; the lovely line "new response, reluctant sinew" poised in a way reminiscent of George Herbert on the impeccable adjective; the modest authority of the first-person singular; the effortless edging of strengths, deepened by age and experience into a lucid self-knowledge that can operate at its own borders, its points of contact with the world. The second-last stanza confirms these qualities and carries the poet into an acceptance of his world that is also a lyric celebration of recovery. It is in some sense a homecoming. Rebirth is hinted at: a resurgence of imagination's power in some ritual submission to its primary source and impulse. The canal itself, indeed, unspoken centre of the poem's energy, is an apt metaphor for the best of Hewitt's art—unhurried, steady, binding countryside to city, at once natural and civilised, an enduring presence:

> Loitering here aboard, aware
> of early June's colours, odours, sounds,
> where broad meadows margin the canal,
> senses assemble, mind accepts;
> happy and alert, I can contain
> my world and time, reaching out to touch
> the smooth grooves the tow-ropes scored
> in the long prime of that old stone-bridge.[1]

Bridge and canal, poetry and man: Hewitt has too much tact to nail down these metaphorical equivalences, but a valid reading of the poem will allow for some such illuminating connections.

As I remarked, however, *Out of My Time* is an uneven, fragmented collection. Most of the poems are occasional in the least valuable way: they seem to result merely from the poet's will to write a poem rather than to press upwards from some more urgent recess of passion or commitment. A handful come from deeper regions, manifesting their genesis in a revealing rather than a descriptive use of language. One of them I have quoted. Two other meditations upon the Irish landscape, both written in 1973, also display the rhythmic intelligence of earlier work, as apparent in these lines from "Glendun on a Wet July Day":

> The sounds of running water are its own;
> its nature patient, pliant to all use,

> but not its voices, not its coloured shapes,
> may offer easy symbols, metaphors,
> or simply pleasure, going its own way.

Personal and familial memories are responsible for most of the other successful poems in this collection. Memorial invocations are everywhere. Especially striking is the sonnet to his wife, "Et Tu in Arcadia Vixisti": "leaning, a dark lad against the wall / played to a splay of goats about his knees." This reveals a playfulness with language not normally associated with Hewitt. In his epitaph for W.R. Rogers, too, Hewitt attains to an equilibrium of admiration, tenderness, and estimation that display in little room his gifts of judicious word and balanced line. Memory has become a natural landscape where the poet lives at ease; it is a space where personal and racial truths can nurture one another as they do in "Mary Hagan, Islandmagee, 1919," or a poem to set beside Austin Clarke's "Forget-Me-Not," "The King's Horses" (with its added burden of the Northerner's awareness of political and cultural ambivalence):

> Gypsies they could have been, or tinkers maybe,
> mustering to some hosting of their clans,
> or horse-dealers herding their charges to the docks
> timed to miss the day's traffic and alarms;
> a migration the newspapers had not foretold;
> some battle's ragged finish, dream repeated;
> the last of an age retreating, withdrawing,
> leaving us beggared, bereft
> of the proud nodding muzzles, the nervous bodies;
> gone from us the dark men with their ancient skills
> of saddle and stirrup, of bridle and breeding.

Concern with his family history and his ambiguous cultural position and inheritance are not new themes in Hewitt's work. The first work in *Collected Poems*, for example, is "Ireland," while the fifth, "Ghosts," concerns his grandfather. While the cultural meditations are a continuous obsession, seen to best advantage in *Collected Poems* in "O Country People," "The Colony," and "An Irishman in Coventry," the memorial engagement with his own family does not achieve real prominence until after his removal to England, personal history perhaps compensating in part for the loss of a personalised geography. "Eager Journey," "My Grandmother's Garter," and "A Victorian Steps Out" transform anecdote into meditation, as in the closing lines of the latter poem:

> But in that brash, excited company,
> my grannie marched serene, until she came
> to the church-gate and stopped, her cheeks alight
> with something other than her children's shame,
> all self consumed in that exultant flame.

As the best poems in *Out of My Time* suggest, it is in part his commitment to racial, familial, and personal memories that keeps the pulse of Hewitt's imagination beating during a time when he seems to have been cut off from one of its principle resources. The beauty of his next and most recent book, *Time Enough*, is that in it everything comes together again. The natural world, personal and family history, national and cultural realities interpenetrate one another with, to borrow a phrase of his, "effortless certainty." The title itself predicts a more composed relationship with the world and the self than that of the earlier book.

Technically and emotionally, many of the poems continue and extend the ritual of inner homecoming announced in "On the Canal." Interactions between personal and racial history are here tellingly intensified, especially, in such poems as "Encounter nineteentwenty" or "Nineteen Sixteen, or The Terrible Beauty" in which the poet forces a collision between protected memory and contemporary predicament. In "Nineteen Sixteen" he recalls a teacher telling him as a child about the Dublin Rising and considers the irony of growing up to live through the present horror:

> Yet, sitting there, that long-remembered morning,
> he caught no hint he'd cast an aging eye
> on angled rifles, parcels left in doorways,
> or unattended cars, he'd sidle by.

Factual detail and muted allusiveness tell us that age has not dimmed this poet's specific eye nor dulled his contemplative, sympathetic mind. His earned ability to inhabit the present without regret shows in the way he relentlessly forces even his beloved natural world to confront the unforgiving rigors of history in "Northern Spring":

> . . . and I, older, soiled, thought sadly
> of each spring's innocence,
>
> wishing we could imitate—
> let spring renew us like the year—
> a silly notion, you might say,
> but not without its poignancy
> in this time-tortured place.

Of the many poems in *Time Enough* that owe their life to the poet's personal memories, the least impressive are some longer family-album-style evocations: "The Faded Leaf," "Away Match," "The Lass of Richmond Hill." Their gently anecdotal mode drafts low-voltage rhythms and language into the service of unpressured sentiment. Much more successful are the briefer, defter strains of "My Father's Ghost," "A Great Event," or "The Drift of Petals." To the steady, simple eloquence of these Hewitt can add the distinguished gravity of the following lines from "My Father's Death in Hospital," in which tenderness and outrage find a moving, lyrical solution:

> But this harsh phantom gripping in the dark,
> its every gesture cruelly defined,
> cuffing and jostling him to this cruel end,
> offered no signals to pace out and mark
> the brave submission of a firm-set mind:
> death should be welcome as a waiting friend.

The most impressive group of poems in *Time Enough* belongs to what I have called the spine of Hewitt's verse. Excavations of the poet's self and the poet's art here reach their most complex and intricate level, discovering an identity at once richly true to human and poetic needs. In poems like "A Birthday Rhyme for Roberta" (a poignant epitaph for his wife who died in 1975, Jonsonian in its warm reserve, and containing some verbal echoes of "On the Canal"), "Function," "The Fool's Cap," "A Mobile Mollusc," or "Orientations," it is the self-as-poet who stands at the poem's centre, "The senses sorting out directions well, / not heeding signals he mistrusted." In "Nourish Your Heart" this accomplished self returns us to the commitment of "Because I Paced My Thought." We admire the consistency of the poet's resolution, the firmness of purpose that, even in the more imperative world of this later poem, never descends to the tones of one who is, as Hewitt had once described himself, "dogmatic in assertion and dissent." Standing at the vulnerable border of his relations with the world, it is the senses that compose his genuine identity. The last lines of this poem, in their grave, mannerly, articulate way are to this commitment both elegy and vindication:

> See you miss nothing proffered. Name and store
> and set in order all . . .
> for all you know, or I know, these must last
> the slow attritions of eternity.

The best of this crucial set of poems, and by my reckoning the best poem in *Time Enough* is "Substance and Shadow." In a small but beautifully husbanded space it contains almost all the qualities for which Hewitt is most to be respected: the civilised voice, the alert eye, patient mind, the honest being-in-the-world, rhythmic delicacy and strength, the dignified confessional stance, excitement and reserve, urbane simplicity, verbal fastidiousness without affectation. The poem paints a memorable portrait of the "minor" poet cut off from the bronze or stone achievements of the great, but in its qualities of craft and feeling it drains the epithet of all comparative intent:

> There is a bareness in the images
> I temper time with in my mind's defence;
> they hold their own, their stubborn secrecies;

no use to rage against their reticence:
a gannet's plunge, a heron by a pond,
a last rook homing as the sun goes down,
a spider squatting on a bracken-frond,
and thistles in a corn-sheaf's tufted crown,
a boulder on a hillside, lichen-stained,
the sparks of sun on dripping icicles,
their durable significance contained
in texture, colour, shape, and nothing else.
All these are sharp, spare, simple, native to
this small republic I have charted out
as the sure acre where my sense is true,
while round its boundaries sprawl its screes of doubt.

My lamp lights up the kettle on the stove
and throws its shadow on the white-washed wall,
like some Assyrian profile with, above,
a snake-, or bird-prowed helmet crested tall;
but this remains a shadow; when I shift
the lamp or move the kettle it is gone,
the substance and the shadow break adrift
that needed bronze to lock them, bronze or stone.

Although the poet who wrote these lines is almost seventy, the poem itself, like the "magic spring" in "A Seaside Town" from which "sweet water issued unobtrusively," is alive with the promise of fresh growth. Keeping faith with his own steady pulse as a poet, Hewitt's civil, serious voice makes a just space for itself in the choir of modern and contemporary Irish poetry. Among his "stubborn secrecies" are the ways he might belong to this larger community. While his use of a phrase like "native to / this small republic I have charted out" shows the ironic slant at which he views the political world which surrounds and threatens the "durable significance" of what he does, his persistent self-analysis in the face of doubt is robust enough to parse the difference between that actual kettle and its monumental shadow-translation. He is not, he recognises, a poet of "bronze or stone." But in his ability to face up to that fact and its implications he becomes the honest, authentic poet that he is, offering us a poetry of ordinary human range and concern that in a time of violence is more important than a poetry of stone or bronze—and is likely, at its best, to be more lasting.[2]

1977

NOTES

[1] Kavanagh's canal poems, brimming with their own brand of sacramental rapture, compose a rich counterpoint to Hewitt's deliberately secular celebration. Between them, however, these two poets suggest the spectrum of celebratory response to the natural

world available to the Irish poetic imagination.

[2] [John Hewitt died in 1987. Through the work he published in the last decade of his life, as well as through the critical work of evaluation and appreciation that have attended him since (including the publication of *The Collected Poems of John Hewitt* (1991) and the establishment of the important John Hewitt Summer School, Hewitt has become a deeply significant figure in the cultural and literary landscape of Northern Ireland. While not (in my opinion) their peer in sheer poetic achievement, he takes his place in the company of Kavanagh, MacNeice, Fallon, and Clarke, as another necessary voice of that poetic generation, a voice which—in its mix of elements of Planter stock, Socialist commitment, and regional devotion, as well as in its stubborn (and lonely) individuality—remains both unique as well as representative of something strong and unignorable in the cultural composition of the island.]

"Random Pursuit":
Mining *One* and *A Technical Supplement*

> *It is we, letting things be,*
> *who might come at understanding.*
> *That is the source of our paradise.*

When I was younger I used to try to *understand* Kinsella's poetry, to get exactly what each line, each image, each allusion meant. It was hard going. I remember trying to wrestle to terms with *Nightwalker* when it came out, feeling like Jacob in a weaker moment with his angel. (In a review then I think I voiced the pious hope that, with this weird satiric stuff out of his system, Kinsella would return to delighting us with luminous lyrics. I was, as they say, a bit off.) Then came *Notes from the Land of the Dead*. And then the Peppercanister series, still in process. Strange, strong, expansive verse after the exquisite formal containments of *Downstream* and *Another September* and their "grace, beauty, charm seductive rhythms—all those superficial things" for which he praises Auden.[1] Now, a bit more battered and baffled by the actual, I try not so much to understand as to *experience* the poems. To let them be, on their own terms, and to try to register in myself as fully as possible what those terms are, how the whole poem works. If I'm lucky, such experience will bring about a kind of understanding, maybe even what Kinsella himself hopes his reader will achieve: "If adequately understood and responded to, poetry should add dynamically to the understanding of the reader." I say all this by way of acknowledging that others, including Kinsella himself, will explain much better than I can what exactly things *mean* and do not mean in these two often enigmatic books. What I offer is simpler than explanation: it is a sort of ruminating encounter with the poems, an account of some of my experience as their reader—"eyes bridging the gap, closing a circuit," as Kinsella himself describes reading. "Except," he goes on, "that it is not a closed circuit, / more a mingling of lives, worlds simmering / in the entranced interval." I'm trying to report back a little of what comes to light for me in that "entranced interval."

One. The title first. *One.* A stroke that measures singularity, isolation, suggests a self, a start. One is 1, is I. Not comforting; explains nothing; an open question. I turn the page (of the American, Wake Forest, edition—without the Anne Yeats drawings, so pure 'text') and meet, in italics, *"The storyteller's face / turned toward the fire."* Who speaks with such confident intimacy, yet utters such a curious mixture of things, notes (with pleasing colloquialism) "the World waltzing after" the sun, names what remains to me mysterious—"Bith," and "the voyage of the First Kindred"? Go on, no guides, drawn by curiosity and a faint (in the rhythm? the strange naming? the tone of confident authority?) exhilaration. Next page, next poem, still italics—winding thinly down and overleaf: "Up and awake. Up straight / in absolute hunger / out of this black lair, and eat!" Some one speaking. No context, so I have to experience speaker and what's spoken immediately, without mediation, without explanatory scaffolding. Again the striking confidence of the voice, the energy in that exclamatory "eat!" Some reptilian activity being spoken, perhaps, being enacted, the language creating a world for it. I can admire the words themselves—their kinetic thrust, their texture:

> then with a sudden hiss into
> a grey sheen of light. A pale space
> everywhere alive with bits and pieces.

Meeting these unknowns I have to relax, admire the craft that contrives such vowel music: hiss bits, gray pale space, light alive. Pleasure in that, and in the swift whipping of line into line, the pulse of rhythm (speech, not meter). So while the poem's matter may remain mysterious, I can still experience these tangible pleasures. As the matter clarifies (a snake in action? appetite? Primitive level of self being dramatised?), these pleasures endure and may even—unperplexed—quicken.

And the italics? Puzzling as they are, they at least alert me to the presence of the poet as a maker of meanings, a manipulator of notation, the palpable organising authority. Here, perhaps, they signify a prologue, an emblematic *tableau vivant* to inaugurate the sequence, something aside from the main (human) body of the text. Perhaps its cosmic origination and foreshadowing. Italics appear at the end of the book, too, making an epilogue as enigmatic as the prologue. So the main body of the text is in parenthesis, all that personal and racial history brought to life between an image of pure egotistic appetite and an image of cosmic solitude, of "*obscure substance*," and "*nightmare-bearing tissue*." These seem heavy matters, but to encounter them I'm nourished by language that's tense, light on its feet, immediate speech: "*Down! Like a young thing! / Coil now and wait. / Sleep on these things*." Looking back I see I have explained little or nothing. But I have had an experience that makes me an active reader. However puzzling, the poem is not a puzzle. The poem is an action, an action realised in language, as language. It obliges me, energetically, to participate. As a poet, Kinsella says he feels committed in his poetry to a "dynamic response to whatever happens." His poems can fashion readers with a similar commitment.

Each of Kinsella's books since *Nightwalker* is a calculated chapter in an expanding enterprise of racial, personal, artistic autobiography. From this point of view, the cardinal poems in *One* ("the first stroke of order," as he describes it) are "Finistere" (racial), "38 Phoenix Street" (personal), "Minstrel" (artistic), and "His Father's Hands" (racial, personal, artistic). It seems important to tell myself why I like "Finistere" less, find it less successful than the others. I suppose I care less for its remote, larger-than-life melodramatics (spoken by the poet's artistic ancestor-shadow, the Celtic poet Amergin, as possession is taken of Ireland)[2] than for the more grounded and recognisably local actualities of the other poems. Certainly "Finistere" is a masterful recreation, a kind of translation, bringing over into English that far-off origin of ours, giving it immediate life. In its own way the experience seems lived in. I relish the language, the management of the verse, the palpable vigor and convincing tone:

> We hesitated before that wider sea
> but our heads sang with purpose
> and predatory peace.
> And whose blood was that
> fumbling our movements? What ghostly hunger
> tunneling our thoughts full of passages
> smelling of death and decay and faint metals
> and great stones in darkness?

Grand, mysterious, stirring. Were there a privileged tribal tongue, surely this exalted yet powerfully specific rhetoric of experience and race-memory would be it. It is high articulate invention. In the end, however, it doesn't keep my imaginative interest. It strikes me as curiously *costumed*, remote, the product of the poet's will more than his imagination (although the will is inspired and invigorated by the imagination), made up rather than simply made. As with "The Oldest Place," and those related pieces in *Notes from the Land of the Dead*, there's an enforced quality to "Finistere" that makes me uneasy. I respect the swollen voltages of language and atmosphere. But I can't help hearing the creak of machinery, an odd ironic hint of which Kinsella may be giving in "The Entire Fabric," the poem preceding "Finistere," which sets a stage, brings on an actor-speaker who peers "in mock intensity," and concludes as follows: "Above the temple, in the flies, / a mechanism began to whirr." Finally, what Kinsella may imply in "Finistere" about a line of continuity between himself and the legendary poet (both explorers of the dark), as he may also do with Fintan in "Survivor" (from *Notes*), to me remains essentially unconvincing and of limited interest (because it smacks of willed fiction), as does the allegorical connection between the claiming of fresh tribal territory and the renewal by repossession of the individual psyche. For all of its Jungian associations, it doesn't (yet) convince my imagination: the project in the end seems too calculated, not finally *necessary*. (By necessary here I mean the way I see Kinsella's actual translations as necessary, vital acts, as he says himself, of responsibility to the tradition.)

After such fumbling ambivalence of response, I turn with relief to the poems that examine, with what I would think of as greater necessity and interior vitality, Kinsella's own biographical experience and that of his immediate family. Of the many admirable things to be found in "38 Phoenix Street," "Minstrel," and "His Father's Hands," I will mention just a couple I'm particularly fond of, certain features which keep these poems vividly and vigorously alive in my mind. One of the most arresting of such features, since it fashions the atmosphere and determines the texture and tone of the poems, is Kinsella's successful appropriation of some Joycean techniques to his own use:

> Two little tongues of flame burned
> in the lamp chimney, wavering
> their tips. On the glassy belly
> little drawn-out images quivered.
> Jimmy's mammy was drying the delph in the kitchen.

Here the scrupulous exactitude of *Dubliners* and the first chapter of *Portrait* gets an extra twist of tension through the line units and the flex of enjambment, animating the pace and sound of ordinary speech, faithfully reproducing (without sentimentality) the point of view of the child. It's a style of stark epiphany (a picture of the Sacred Heart "held out the Heart / with his women's fingers / like a toy"), deftly removing narrative scaffolding and leaving the bright essentials exposed.

In "Minstrel," as in Joyce's *Portrait*, personal growth shows in the enrichment of style, appropriately dramatising the increasing complications of consciousness. Facts, while maintaining their status as facts, edge easily into the realm of symbol, emblem: "The fire burned down in the grate. / A light burned on the bare ceiling. / A dry tea-cup stained the oil cloth / where I wrote, bent like a feeding thing / over my own source." This rapt concentration, this state of absolute attention, is Kinsella's signature as artist, who takes over his work (as he says elsewhere) "ever more painstaking care." His language is spare but freighted with its own minute vibrations. "Minstrel," too, marks the genesis of the poet's imaginative conjunction with the overarching world of space: "Outside, the heavens listened, / a starless diaphragm / stopped miles overhead / to hear the remotest whisper / of returning matter, missing / an enormous black beat." The need that links the youthful ruminative poet to cosmic space feels more natural to me than those connections he forges with the world of legendary time. Here the language seems directly responsive to the facts, not laboring to invent them: "A distant point of light / winked at the edge of nothing." This is palpable, immediate, a persuasive union of fact and thought.

In "His Father's Hands" the transformed Joycean manner expands and amplifies again. This time it is one of the lessons of *Ulysses* the poet has learnt, so his style is more closely a miming of consciousness, as it shuttles between flat external description, drama, and simultaneous inwardness. Building a rich pattern, the strands weave over and about one another, and still remain distinct: "I drank firmly / and set the glass down firmly. / You were saying. // My father. / Was saying. // His finger prodded and prodded, / marring his point. Emphas—/ emphasemphasis. // I have watched / his father's hands before him / / cupped, and tightening the black Plug / between knife and thumb, / carving off little curlicues / to rub them in the dark of his palms." Such an easy, effortless, yet steady movement. The exact facts are given their due as themselves, and at the same time subtly taken up into the drama. Style becomes an absorbent energy,

turning facts into narrative, narrative into symbolic revelation. The most dazzling example of such transformation (one that transcends any explicitly Joycean influence and becomes Kinsella's own thing entirely) occurs at the end of
"His Father's Hands." After his account of ancestors proximate and remote, the
poet remembers his grandfather's cobbling block and its amazing end. His image, a repossession, recasts the whole narrative of ancestry and generation into a
single luminous symbol—a vivid burst of bright sexual energy that resides absolutely in the simple fact, waiting to be released by the seeing imagination:

> Extraordinary . . . The big block—I found it
> years afterwards in a corner of the yard
> in sunlight after rain
> and stood it up, wet and black:
> it turned under my hands, an axis
> of light flashing down its length,
> and the wood's soft flesh broke open,
> countless little nails
> squirming and dropping out of it.

This is surely one of Kinsella's most satisfying symbolic moments, where
the facts only need the slightest pressure of adequate language to help them surrender their symbolic burden. At such a moment two of Kinsella's primary convictions and commitments fuse: his "responsibility towards actuality," and his
belief that "Experience by itself, however significant, won't do," that it has to
have "some allegorical drive behind it." The above image of the block has glit-
tered in my mind since I first read it, perhaps because it sums up for me some of
Kinsella's particular gift: the ability to be wonderstruck and factual at the same
time, and to find a language answerable to this twinned condition.

In poems like these Kinsella makes his version of poetry-as-autobiography
unique, authentic, memorable. The life grows mysterious without ever losing or
leaving its common ground. Pliable and unprogrammatic, the epiphanal moments fold naturally into the larger narrative: they are not filleted out and exhibited as privileged lyric illuminations in themselves. They grow out of the life
and the life grows around them. In style and substance these moments of discovery belong to process. "The only thing that one can feel committed to," says
Kinsella, "is the whole process of change and the process of understanding." I'd
say these poems dramatically embody the *process of understanding* the process
of change.

A Technical Supplement appeared in 1976, two years after *One*. It is "a plunge
of a different kind into the nature of things," Kinsella says, "without being
committed to any particular point of view except that of dynamic response to
what happens." What I first stop to admire here is Kinsella's firm resolution to
grow and change as a poet, to alter his angle of entry into experience, to shift
ground, to leave the ground altogether ("plunge"). And the modest scope of his
ambition? Merely, as he reveals in the first poem with almost comic gusto (in-

voking "Blessed William Skullbullet"), to "see how the whole thing / works"—
lovely pause that. His aim here is not so much to record (what Heaney quoting
Oisín quoting Fionn calls) "the music of what happens." Rather, his poetry will
be a "dynamic response" to that music.

A Technical Supplement stands, I'd say, at the very centre of Kinsella's
work because its subject is the heart (and soul?) of his whole poetic enterprise—
the psyche itself in all its various, unprogrammable action ("dynamic response"). Between them, these twenty-six untitled poems embody a speaking
psyche. It is Kinsella's peculiar distinction, that is, to have composed for consciousness itself a right speech, a convincing voice. This achievement, more
than the (also impressive and often startling) contents of the poems themselves,
is what most deeply affects me as a reader, and indeed, as a writer. It's when I
recognise the decisive presence of that strange compelling voice that my pulse-
beat stumbles and I catch myself in a genuine creative shiver. Like Joyce (and
like bits of McGahern), what Kinsella creates here is *psychic tone*, the ability to
affect the reader with the direct palpable presence of a consciousness converted
into language. Although neither one of the best poems in the sequence, nor one
of my own favorites, Poem XX offers a useful model.

> Loneliness. An odour of soap.
> To this end must we come,
> deafened with spent energy.
>
> And so the years propel themselves onward
> toward that tunnel and the stink of fear.
>
> —We can amend that. (Time permits
> a certain latitude. Not much,
> but a harmless re-beginning:)
>
> 'And so the years propel themselves
> onward on thickening scars, toward
> new efforts of propulsion . . . '

The beginning is emotion and sensation, simply noted. In our world we move
endlessly through such conjunctions, separated by category as these two are
separated by the periods. Then the mind opens to receive, to brood, to draw
conclusions. Pause. Then a farther consequence ("And so . . . "), a wider truth,
the thought made physical, married to feeling (the categories running together,
as happens in the fullness of conscious apprehension) by means of that concrete,
kinetic language—propel, tunnel, stink. Pause. A possibility of some revision,
some editing: consciousness curls back on itself, amending, making amends,
seeing some amendment; acknowledging its own existence in time, in process.
Pause, for a "harmless re-beginning." Then revise. A new conclusion from first
premise, less absolute, less dead-end: 'propulsion.' "Propulsion": the word applies to so much in the poem. I'm interested in content here, as who would not

be. But that's only, I might say, an angle of Kinsella's philosophy. What the poem really seems to be 'about' is not the thought itself, but the process of consciousness having this thought, coming to its inconclusive conclusion. This is what I value, what's alive each time I return to it.

Tone in Kinsella is invariably mesmerising. In *A Technical Supplement* it is at its most supple, various, hypnotic. In these poems, each posture, each *state* of consciousness seems to have its own tone. Responding to any of the poems, my first awareness is always of the tone in which the speaker says (usually to himself) what he has to say. Tone is the atmosphere in which the whole piece breathes. Tone is the expressive configuration of consciousness at that moment. It is always wonderfully alive and in motion, determining the faintest shade of meaning. It makes me a listener: I seem to *overhear* these poems. A few examples. In II it is explanatory, scientific, perpetually qualifying its own meanings: "You will note firstly that there is no containing skin as we understand it, but 'contained' muscles / . . . This one, for example, containing—functioning as—" In X it moves from reverie ("To follow the graceful curve of a handrail / and relish the new firmness underfoot") to energetic exhortation: "We have to dig down; / sieve, scour and roughen; / make it all fertile and vigorous /—get the fresh rain down!" In XI it is almost dreamy ("A watered peace. Drop. At the heart"), in XII angry and satisfied ("There isn't a day passes but I thank God, / some others I know . . . didn't 'fulfil their promise'"), in XV hallucinatory, possessed ("I'll pierce her like / a soft fruit, a soft big seed!"). In XXI you can hear the cool tone of literary judgement ("And remember that foolishness / though it may give access to heights of vision / in certain gifted abnormal brains / remains always what it is.") In their distinction and difference these tones (and others— the unexpected gaiety of XVII, for example) dramatise the vital play of consciousness, hold the fleeting moment (of sensation, daydream, opinion, appetite) still for the poet's anatomising inspection. Between them they embody a consciousness oddly compounded of scepticism and authority—a union that results in one of the more important features in my own mental picture of Kinsella's poetic identity.

Authority and scepticism are also the marks of Kinsella's rhythms, here and elsewhere, along with an enviable independence. From Pound, from Williams especially, perhaps from other Americans, he learned how to loosen his line from its stiffer metrical and stanzaic commitments, to let it follow the beat of thought, of feeling, the attenuations or elongations of breath. His rhythms, too, are a sort of "random pursuit" ("I would settle," he says, "for the 'random pursuit' of a poem rather than labour to produce something coherent and recognisable and traditional"). Yet invariably these rhythms possess a sense of purpose and control. Like fishing-line, they lure, hook, and hold my attention, even when the content baffles. In *A Technical Supplement* he is rhythmically at his most suave and muscular, seemingly at ease in many different rhythmic melodies. All seems relaxed, natural, powerfully poised: a sort of predatory readiness. Take, as an example, the utterly colloquial movement of "But for real pleasure there is nothing to equal / sitting down to a *serious* read, / getting settled down comfortably for the night." Or how about the more underscored rhetorical glances of "to note this or that withering in me, / and not to; to anticipate / the Breath, the Bite, with cowering arms, / and not . . . " Almost any sequence of lines will offer examples of an ear tuned to its own music, a music rooted in ordinary speech patterns but often carrying a slight ritual vibration ("It is so peaceful at last: / sinking onward into a free reverie /—if you aren't continually nudged awake / by little scratching sounds"). A brief passage from the extraordinary slaughterhouse poem VI, one of the finest in the collection, should provide a decently representative illustration:

> With the sheep it was even clearer
> they were dangling alive, the blood trickling
> over nostrils and teeth. A flock of them waited their turn
>
> crowded into the farthest corner of the pen,
> some looking back over their shoulders
> at us, in our window.

First of all, the length of the line never settles, so the whole thing is suffused with a slight nervousness. Yet the actual rhythm of each line is quite relaxed, responsive to the colloquial language, unemphatic, the phrasing that of ordinary speech. The rhythmic crown is the enjambment: impeccable, the way it establishes lines of complete integrity which, as they end and we minimally pause, push us towards a surprise every time, deeper and deeper into the subject, into feeling that is without judgement, but brimming with *response* ("At a certain point it is all merely meat, / sections hung or stacked in a certain order"). The enjambed movement of the lines in the longer section heightens the rhythmic tension, as the movement of the two *sentences* works to release it. Between these layered rhythms we are absorbed more and more by the subject, yet the rhythms themselves never distract, never get in our way, never seem to signal their own presence as performance. What Kinsella achieves here (and it is the sort of rhythmic thing he achieves often) reminds me of the way he himself described a performer he admired—the *sean nós* singer, Jerry Flaherty of Dunquin. "Nothing intervened between the song and its expression. The singer managed many difficult things, but the result was to focus attention on the song, not on the performance or on the quality of the voice. It was a special voice, adapted (like a reptile or an insect) to its function. More beauty of tone would have distracted, attracting attention for its own sake. And the singer's act of communication was thoroughly completed by his audience."[3] I suspect that such a description might obliquely apply to Kinsella's own art and performance as well, not only to its control of rhythm, but also to its sternness, its lack of sentimentality, the way it does "many difficult things" without drawing attention to the nature of the performance itself, the way his audience has to "complete" the act of communication. (This last is a curiously modernist touch, which makes a revealing connection between Kinsella's traditionalist and modernist projections.)

The particularity of Kinsella's language—its strict, sometimes punishing exactitude (the sort of activity one should expect, I guess, of a psyche trying to "see how the whole thing / works")—is a tonic pleasure. There's a special excitement in the rapt play of such particularity in *A Technical Supplement*, an excitement which, as it amplifies, convinces me the whole book is in part a weird Kinsellaesque ritual of initiation, a novitiate in *how not to flinch*. In poem II, for example, consciousness prepares itself to encounter the body. It does this by insisting on physical actuality and integrity, in language that itself seems to possess such qualities:

> This one, for example, containing—functioning as—
> a shoulderblade; or this one like a strap
> reaching underneath it, its tail
> melting into a lower rib; or this one
> nuzzling into the crease of the groin;
> or this, on the upper arm, like a big leech;
> even the eyes—dry staring buttons of muscle.

Language here is the sharp instrument of scrutiny, finding the exact word (strap, tail, buttons), the precise image (melting into, nuzzling into) to animate it all, let us see, *experience* it fresh again. The scrupulous exactitude of parts of *One* reaches a kind of culmination in such clinical, yet not cold, particularity. The linguistic style of *A Technical Supplement* is all scalpel and forceps: it cuts into, probes, takes hold of "the nature of things" in their tissue and bone.

And it is the language itself, as it names and images the world, that satisfies. From poem after poem, single details strike out, shine. In IX there is "A crayfish, crusted with black detail, dreamed / on twig tips across the bottom sand," or, in XI, "the sound of water outside / trickling clean into the shore. / And the little washed bird-chirps and trills." The actuality of weather and water-world rides on such description: without judgement, things are minutely and precisely seen, heard, known. Or the particularity of language can draw me into the sensual presence of "A smell of hot home-made loaves / from the kitchen downstairs," and beside this "A sheet of yellowish Victorian thick paper, / a few spearheads depicted in crusty brown ink / . . . added their shiny-stale smell to the baked air / like dried meat" (XVII). The world of *A Technical Supplement* is a world of things seen in the hard uncompromising light of language that won't settle for less than strict precision, a language always yearning to anatomise the actual. And the poet gives his language the same tense turn when not the physical but the metaphysical world calls him to attention, as in that remarkable portrait of another poet (we're not told who) which he offers in XXI:

> Emotion expelled, to free the structure of a thing,
> or indulged, to free the structure of an idea.
> The entirety of one's being
> crowded for everlasting shelter
> into the memory of one crust of bread.

True to actual physical facts and to metaphysical possibilities, able to give the metaphysical a physical presence and pressure ("one's being / crowded . . . "), quick to negotiate between phenomenal and allegorical realities, this is a language of rare particularity, a sufficient, satisfying style. It's true that even where feelings are involved ("That bread smells delicious!") Kinsella's is not exactly the language of feeling but of nomination and analysis, and can consequently leave me thirsty at times for some straight admission of more ordinary emotion, for, as it were, a more surrendered language. Where such language may occur (as in the oddly jolly end of XVIII or the deliberate plainness with which he begins XIX—"It is hard to beat a good meal / and a turn on the terrace, / or a picnic on the beach at evening") it usually seems shaded with traces of a Beckett-like irony, as if the speaker were slightly amused by such reminders of quotidian sensuality and peace. But I guess that such a thirst, the creation of such a thirst, is a discipline in itself. Reading Kinsella, among other of its virtues and values, is a sort of discipline, the discipline of coming to terms with things as, in part, they surely are.

By the time he had finished *One* and *A Technical Supplement*, Kinsella had measured the range and paced the borders of that territory that seems uniquely his. He had opened himself definitively to his own personal and racial past (continuing a process begun in *Notes from the Land of the Dead*); he had opened himself, no less definitively, to his own present, to the psychic and physical facts of his own outer and inner life and the life around him. And he had done all this in his own way, forging his own idiosyncratic language and manner, creating in the process many of the terms in which we have to think of his work, experience it, judge it. Like the strong poet he is, he re-fashions his readers, or forces them to re-fashion themselves. In doing all this he has composed a body of work that calls for celebration, although I suppose—since his own stern "performance" is deliberately unassuaging and, from any more regularly orthodox poetic or philosophic point of view, without conventional beguilements or consolations—I suppose he'd back away from such a notion. No matter. Whenever I think of his later work, two lines (from poem XII in *A Technical Supplement*, one of his many provocative reflections on the craft and art he practices) insist on coming to mind, for they seem to me to sum up his poetic identity and its daunting enterprise:

> There, at the unrewarding outer reaches,
> the integrity of the whole thing is tested.

So far, he seems *farther out* than anyone, and passing—with honours—the test: letting things be; coming at understanding.

1987

NOTES

¹ This and other remarks by Kinsella are taken from the interview with John Haffenden in *Viewpoints* (London: Faber and Faber, 1981) 100-13.

² The best discussion of Kinsella's creative engagement with the Irish *Lebor Gabala* (*Book of Invasions*) is in Dillon Johnston's *Irish Poetry after Joyce* (Notre Dame: University of Notre Dame and Dolmen Press, 1985) 98-101. Johnston's whole exposition of Kinsella is the most illuminating short account I know.

³ From his brief account of Seán Ó Riada in the Commentary attached to *Peppercanister Poems 1972-1978* (Wake Forest: Wake Forest University Press, 1979), 151-52.

Shadow Among the Stars:
Recent Kinsella

Reading the remarkable body of work Thomas Kinsella has fashioned over the past twenty years (since *Wormwood*, say, which appeared in 1966) is a bit like standing outside a closed door, behind which you can catch the hypnotic murmurings of a man talking to himself, maybe in sleep. What impresses is not necessarily an objective "meaning," which may sometimes be grasped at only in snatches, but the hard clarity and conviction of that speaking voice, the articulate authority, however private or eccentric, invested in its rhythms. And this is true whether what you overhear seems directly autobiographical (narrative flashes without a given narrative structure) or frankly metaphysical (the rapt mind sinking to depths or sailing to heights it inhabits alone).

These two new volumes (*Songs of the Psyche, Her Vertical Smile*) are no exceptions. Again the reader is an eavesdropper, listening—in a state of perplexity and exhilaration—to somniloquent soliloquies that probe simple memories or hazard subtle speculations. You overhear in "Phoenix Street," for example, a familial recollection:

> And I have opened the blackstained
> double doors of the triangular
> press up in the corner,
> and his dark nest
> stirred with promises.

The same nervous excitement of rhythm, the same deliberate verbal precision—both signs of Kinsella's obsessive but emotionally responsive urge to get things right—mark the following, initially more remote and intangible lines from *Her Vertical Smile* (a single long sequence, we are told, "on a theme of violence, order and music"):

> and that from even this matter
> (as of man's head rammed against stone
> and woman a mad animal)
> we might yet make a gavotte
> to feed
> that everlasting Ear.

Consider these latest collections as further installments in Kinsella's spiritual autobiography, part of his continuing attempt to make "a strange beauty / in these harsh circumstances." It is a project he has undertaken not only with the stubborn commitment Pound showed to his own mode of difficulty, but with the moral fervour and single-minded artistic integrity of Yeats or Mahler. (Mahler's character and influence—as remorselessly complicated, passionate creator—are partly the subject, partly the guiding spirit, of *Her Vertical Smile*.)

In this enterprise of the imagination his closest kindred, as inventors of individual speech, are Eliot, Joyce, Beckett, and Austin Clarke. His best and most characteristic work starts echoes out of Eliot's metaphysical solitude, Joyce's gritty historical texture lit with epiphanies, Beckett's aggrieved ironic solipsism, Clarke's raw psychic hurt and social rage. But, like each one of them, he is idiosyncratically himself, an explorer pushing insistently on to and beyond the conventional borders of style, making his own way, patiently creating a poetic idiom answerable to his own emergencies.

Shifting tonalities and elastically adaptable rhythms make Kinsella's work, for me, a continuous, if strenuous, pleasure. An astringent pleasure, for his manners—for all their stern decorum—never seek to persuade or allure an audience; his style forever resists being "recklessly fluent and fascinating," rarely resorts to the consoling cadences of a known, familiar music. Although no doubt wishing to be heard, the work seems intrinsically indifferent to that immediate gratification. Its ambition is to perform nothing less than an anatomy of the human system—"getting to the root," seeing "how the whole thing / works." It's an astonishing, uncompromising project, but no conception of incidental difficulty for his audience tempts Kinsella to dilute its seriousness, mitigate its tough, even turbulent reality.

What I particularly admire in these poems, in the work as a series of provisionally cathartic confrontations with the indigestible truths of being human, is Kinsella's ability to commute at speed between the zones of personal history and abstract metaphysics, between the sight of "first light / fidgeting under the leaves" and the insight that "Love is refreshment / in the recognition of pattern." The intense particularity of his own distinctly localized experience ("Miss Carney handed us out blank paper and marla, / old plasticine with the colours / all rolled together into brown") never stops evolving and spreading into realms of allegorical action and apprehension ("The threadbare body gathers / with a new consideration / about the hidden bones").

The astronomical design on the cover of *Her Vertical Smile* suggests that this continuous trafficking between the local and the enlarged figures among Kinsella's poetic beliefs. For in this diagram, "the middle circle is the Earth (*terra*), throwing its shadow among the stars." The poet is forever hazarding the throw of his own terrestrial shadow among the stars, but always in a manner unfailingly sceptical, certain only of the fact he accepts with what grim grace he can (to misquote an early, much-anthologized poem)—the fact that each conclusion is a fresh start, each earned ease the seed of another ache, and always, as he says in "Wormwood," "resuming in candour and doubt the only individual joy—the restored necessity to learn." Absorbed in "self scrutiny" and "self release" and "self renewal" (the title of three poems in *Songs of the Psyche*), the lesson continues.

1986

Riddling Free:
Richard Murphy's *The Price of Stone*

A poet's growth is best measured by the expanding adequacy of his or her language, the way it stretches to receive and register more and more of his or her experience. With this in mind, I welcome *The Price of Stone* as Richard Murphy's best collection so far. From book to book, in fact, Murphy has made his language more supple, more inclusive, drawing deeper and more complex areas of his identity into the light. From the publicly legible surface zones of culture and history which he spoke from in *Sailing to an Island* and *The Battle of Aughrim*, he proceeded in *High Island* to investigate the private self—the self as it exists in community, and the more intimate sequestered self that lives with nature and the vagaries of solitude and love. At every stage of the journey his language has grown to meet the increasingly complicated needs of his exploration, this archeology of self. Now he offers a volume that seems a revising and re-visioning of all he has been and done so far as a poet, a summary coming-clean with his experience. After a life perplexed by homelessness and studded with attempts to compose a right dwelling-place for his displaced identity, Murphy realises as poetic fact a feeling he voiced in 1980. "I feel now," he said, "that my home is in the language." Aptly and ironically enough, this homecoming to language is here achieved through the medium of voiced buildings, speaking stones that compose in their own original terms a kind of biography for the poet.

I

It is the relaxed, rangy action of Murphy's language we can see and hear in *The Price of Stone*—a language various, casual, crafty, civil, and free. And very much at home with its own competence, vitality, well-being. These poems can be jewelled with the unaffected delights of unfamiliar words, letting the tongue savour such exact exotics as *brumal, exuviate, greywacke, cineritious, sloke*. Or the poet can strip his language down to diagrammatic spareness, as he does in "Moonshine" ("Alone I love / To think of us together: / Together I think / I'd love to be alone"), where such plainness suggests the ineluctable geometry of his contradictory emotional state. Or he can dress it up gorgeously to embody the heaped abundance of an old friary:

> Here the rain harps on ruins, plucking lost
> Tunes from my structure, which the wind pours through
> In jackdaw desecration, carping at the dust

And leprous sores my towers like beggars show.

Witty, inventive, fit—the language of *The Price of Stone* is full of such remarkable animations. It is the means the poet uses to revive his world, enabling it—
literally, in the sonnets which compose the second section of the volume—to
speak in tongues. So even while it maintains the shapely forms of verse, the
language of these poems succeeds more consistently than ever before in being
speech—speech that can be natural and playful and dramatic at the same time;
speech that suggests a relationship between Murphy and his audience more intimate, informal, and unencumbered by self-consciousness than it has been in
the past.

For me, the language at work here creates the feeling of being truly in touch
with the poet inside the lines. Before this, the poetry, even when I admired it
most, made me feel like a looker-on, cut off from the embodied experience in
the way the wonderfully watchful poet is marooned outside the erotic action of
the seals in "Seals at High Island." But everywhere in *The Price of Stone* I feel
palpable communication: the warm, beating immediacy of the language is always drawing me in. Here, from many possible examples, is one from a poem
that celebrates Murphy's dead friend, Tony White (whose beloved free spirit
seems an almost tutelary presence in the book, in its lavish offering of whole
home truths): the poem is called "Bookcase for the Oxford English Dictionary":

> All the words I need
> Stored like seed in a pyramid
> To bring back from the dead your living shade
> Lie coffined in this thing of wood you made
> Of solid pine mortised and glued
> Not long before you died.

Whether I point to the solid diction that properly registers the made thing; to the
rippling syntax that can enclose so much within a single unclouded, unpunctu-
ated and melodic sentence; or to the capacious image broad and deep enough to
be a pyramid, a coffin, a womb, and an actual bookcase; whether I concentrate
on the word-music composed by each line-ending, or on the freight of unspoken
yet tangible feeling between that "I" and "you," the way "I need" opens a path
of surprising yet satisfying turns that closes in the gentle but absolute finality of
"you died," a path along the trajectory of those near or full rhymes—whatever I
choose to single out for admiration here, I am struck and struck again by how
directly and simply Murphy's skillful but natural management of the language
communicates its truth, how intimate a view of his experience the language allows me.

The sonnets that compose section two—all but one "spoken" by a building
that's had some epiphanal connection with Murphy's life—have in their language the same warm immediacy of address. You can hear it in this random
sample from "Beehive Cell":

There's no comfort inside me, only a small
Hart's-tongue sprouting square with pyramidal headroom
For one man alone kneeling down: a smell
Of peregrine mutes and eremitical boredom.

Once, in my thirteen hundred years on this barren
Island, have I felt a woman giving birth,
On her own in my spinal cerebellic souterrain,
To a living child, as she knelt on earth.

This voice is at once wise and entirely colloquial. Its language is fully lived in,
all rhetorical gestures subdued to its main purpose of communicating its story, a
wonder of life and death. At ease with itself, it inhabits the truth of its experience, stretching effortlessly from the unemphatic casual opening—"There's no
comfort inside me"—to the startlingly technical yet still organic fullness of
"spinal cerebellic souterrain." Beyond such large effects lie other playful shim-
merings, like the hint of a pun in "peregrine" above, or witty verbal gestures
such as that in his description of the annual penetration of sunlight into the tomb
at Newgrange: "Once a year it may strike me, a pure gift / Making light work, a
mound of greywacke lift." Throughout *The Price of Stone* Murphy's language,
without falsification, makes light work of its burden of experience.

II

Aside from this remarkable ripening of language, *The Price of Stone* is notable
for the way it brings into focus what is perhaps the central thematic design in
Murphy's work. In a poem in *High Island* called "Gallows Riddle," the Tinker
says to the Hangman, "Now my tongue must riddle me free." It is a line which
could stand as the poet's address to his own complicated fate. For the life presented in the poetry seems to be lived on the human equivalent of a geological
"fault," neither completely solid nor broken, but irreparably divided and perpetually at risk of dissolution. For this reason, it seems to me, Murphy's poetic
enterprise from the start has been to riddle himself free of the puzzle of doubleness and division in his own nature and identity. And this, no doubt, is what
generates his obsession with building, with making things "integral" (a word
that recurs), and with the craft of well-made verse itself.

In his first collections Murphy engages with cultural and historical double-
ness/division. As probably the last poet to whom the vexed hyphenation,
"Anglo-Irish," can be properly applied, it's appropriate that in this early work
he should reflect (implicitly and explicitly) on the meaning of the term as it determined his own more publicly legible experience. In *Sailing to an Island* he
tries, by what looks like sheer force of poetic will, to migrate from one side of
the identity equation to the other. He writes elegies from the "Anglo-Irish" side
of his nature ("The Lady of the House," for example), and writes poems of symbolic passage which will, he hopes, harbour him in the "truly Irish" (his own

term) community of which he longs to be an integral part. In the title poem itself, the poet is a kind of cultural explorer, an outsider who may be "jealous of
these courteous fishermen . . . for knowing the sea / Intimately." After the inconclusive conclusion of that poem ("The tide has ebbed . . . Here is a bed"),
"The Last Galway Hooker" is the poet's earnest induction into the network of
the tribe, a process concluding on a jauntier, more optimistic note: "So I chose
to renew her, to rebuild, to prolong / For a while the spliced yards of yesterday /
. . . Old men my instructors, and with all new gear / May I handle her well down
tomorrow's sea-road." The suggestion implicit here is that the renewal of the
boat is a renewal of Murphy's own identity, fitting it up for the future. "The
Cleggan Disaster," then—in its vivid particularity as well as in its celebratory
and elegiac drive—is his inaugural performance as bard of his sea-board adop-
tive community.

Yet the poignantly unspoken but indelible meaning of all three of these
poems resides for me in their speaker's failure to become what he calls "truly
Irish," audible in the prevalence of the Anglo-Saxon line with its metrically emphatic caesura (unconscious image of division on Murphy's pulse, in his ear),
and heard in the oddly inauthentic interior speech of Concannon, hero of "The
Cleggan Disaster" ("Spears in hundreds / Are hurtling against my head. Was it
south of us it shone. / Lucky the keepers are safe. What a lonely life."), both of
which give a curiously "foreign" or "estranged" flavour to the events recounted,
the uneasy feeling that, for all the skill of narrative, the matter and the medium
are somehow at odds with each other. This can be detected, I'd say, at places in
"The Last Galway Hooker" ("Fastest in the race to the gull-marked banks, /
What harbour she hived in, there she was queen,") or in lines like the following
from "The Cleggan Disaster," where the simile seems a touch pastiche: "The
wind began to play, like country fiddlers / In a crowded room, with nailed boots
stamping / On the stone cottage floor, raising white ashes." In their own terms,
these are successful poems. They demonstrate, however, more than the poet
intends them to, revealing in stark outline the very split in his consciousness and
personality which they are designed to heal.

Murphy's next volume, *The Battle of Aughrim*, was an attempt, as he says
himself, "to see my own conflict in historical terms." However, in spite of the
fact that the poem shows the evolution of Murphy's poetic language (being
tougher and more dramatic, more resilient and in closer touch with the grainy
nature of things), it does not illuminate in any deep way the historical dilemma
(with the exception of a vivid *lyrical* insight into the contrasting relationship
with the land experienced by the Planter landlord and the native Irish). More importantly, it does little, as far as I can tell, to alter or cure Murphy's own dilemma of division and doubleness, a dilemma he feels as his identity, his cultural
and historical fate. The historical probe, sensitive as it is and elegantly as it is
carried out, does not reach into the vexed recesses of the poet's own condition.

In *High Island*, however, Murphy leaves the world of public meanings and
enters that of his own private drama. Where the two earlier books were strenuous engagements with community, full of people, the poems of *High Island* inhabit solitude (even where community is implied). In the more deeply recessed

areas of the self, however, the poet discovers division and doubleness at least as acute as what he'd experienced in the public domains of the earlier poems. He finds it in the richly detailed poems about his childhood in Ceylon, with their fearful throbbing sense of foreignness and difference and guilt. And he finds it at the core of his own sexual nature (there's a curiously pervasive sexual atmosphere throughout the book)—a discovery he lodges in vibrant poems about corncrake and stormpetrel and mating seals. So the corncrake is a "little bridegroom," with a "defenceless home" and a mate "silently sitting on her nest / And producing your offspring." One stormpetrel throbs "till daylight on your cryptic nest" and its song "ends in a gasp," while another sings "A solo tune" and "Is dying with passion / For someone out there to come quickly." And the seals that mate in the sea off High Island become, under the poet's astonished gaze, an emblem of sexual mutuality: "She opens her fierce mouth like a scarlet flower / Full of white seeds," and "When the great bull withdraws his rod, it glows / Like a carnelian candle." The oblique hints in such poems flower into the candid account of a doubled or divided human sexual nature in "Sun-up," where, in order to assuage his pain of loss, the speaker says to his departed lover, who has returned to the woman with whom he lives,

> Is she delighting you in bed
> In her caravan on a cutaway road?
> Does the sun give you the same kiss
> To wake you, with her at your side?
>
> I kiss you both, like the sun,
> I kiss your hands and your feet,
> Your ears and your eyes,
> Both your bodies, I bless them both.

This then, in brief, is the thematic design I'd see articulated by these three books: in the very depths of identity—cultural, psychological, sexual selves all marked by it—there appears a sense of doubleness / division which remains visible but essentially unresolved. And this brings me back to *The Price of Stone*, a collection of poems which, like symphonic music, seems to carry this thematic recurrence to a fine and defining close. It does this not by resolving the dilemma, but by composing an honest poetic world in which all the elements of division / doubleness are simply acknowledged as necessary components of the poet's identity and integrated into it. In this way, Murphy composes a self-portrait more complete and coherent than any he's drawn before. Poem after poem in both sections—in one the poet a speaking "I," in the other a listening "you"—displays the same relentless essay at the truth about himself, a truth which simply contains the fact of doubleness/division as just another element in this single human life. This cumulative truth is presented directly or (in the sonnets) in the more indirect utterances (in a variety of attitudes and tones) by the various buildings. (These sonnets remind me of traditional riddle poems. In this case, however, the answer is given in the title. It could be instructive and amusing, in fact, to imagine away the title and then read the poem, guessing at the identity of the "speaker.")

In the poems that comprise the first part of the book, the theme seems one of deliberate unmaking, or at least reveals the will to wreck the carefully composed self—externalised as buildings—which has become the poet's life. In "Arsonist," for example, the protagonist is trapped by the house he has built ("Each random stone made integral / Has bonded him with debt") while in "Care" he sees how even good intentions can have fatal results. Throughout these poems, Murphy keeps expressing conditions of irreparable contradiction, attempting to embody in language a sense of his own doubled and contradictory being. Even the portrait of "Mary Ure" depicts her as a creature of contradictions, reading "Lady Lazarus" "in a blue silk gown / So thin the cloudy wind is biting to the bone / But she talks as lightly as if the sun shone."

Murphy's instinctive deftness of language and form here, however, show how he is able to take in and transform or redeem contradiction by the lightness of his touch, and by its candour. So peaceful sheep "like to graze on headlands / High up looking down on a raging sea." So the crying child in "Shelter" helps the speaker "make the dark inside / Glitter with sheaves bound firm to keep out storm. / Hear how they rustle as we lay them down: / Their broken heads are trashed clean of grain." The making of the urns in "Niches" is described in a similarly contradictory way: "A woman threw them lovingly, glazed them in tears." Beautiful, they are "bone-ash jars." Similarly, in "Stone Mania," the poet confronts the contradiction that his passion for building prevented him from living in the present: "How much it hurts to see the destruction that all good building, even the best, must cause." Even love itself is contradictory, being a kind of homelessness that has to be confronted, negotiated: "Although we have no home in the time that's come, / Coming together we live in our own time. / Make your nest of moss like a wren in my skull."

Murphy's friend, Tony White, was the antithesis of the dominant paradox. As a countering paradox, "His presence made the darkest day feel clear," he brings love and death together in some redemptive way: "Because his kind of love taught me to live / His dying I forgive." Tony White embodies opposites, but without anxiety or stress; his life is a fullness out of contradictions; the opposites do not short-circuit each other ("It was his style / To play as well / Carrying a creel on his back or Coriolanus"). And the bookcase he has made contains "All the words I need / Stored like seed in a pyramid / To bring back from the dead your living shade." In such poems, Murphy gets a hold of his bedevilling opposites and sees them as the way life is, and sees that his job is to give utterance to them, to get beyond the hyphen of division to some satisfactory singular nature.

The paradox of the doubled self is most revealingly caught in "Displaced Person." All the contradictions come to roost in this *dual* person: "To show I'd nothing false to hide/ And make you feel the truth of love I lied." Neat as an epigram, the style mirrors the subject, being clipped, irrefutable, perfectly poised between opposites. Contradiction becomes a dizzying thing, but captured in the simplicty of lovemaking itself. This paradox (holding two in one) becomes

Murphy's clue to the nature of the world. For now, everywhere he looks he sees contradiction, a doubled reality. "These are the just / Who kill unjustly men they call unjust. / These are the pure in heart / Who see God smeared in excrement on walls. / . . . These are the martyrs / Who die for a future buried in the past" ("Amazement"). In the private world, in the world of poetry itself, the same sense of contradiction rules. And so the dying poet in the last poem of Section One "seem[s] so far away, though near me now," while the same poem ends on the following paradoxical note: "And this is you, / Who put flesh into words that can't renew / The life you lavished making them ring true."

The poems in this section, then, offer a diagram of the various worlds the poet knows and inhabits—that diagram having as its constant the notion of intractable contradiction. And along with this acknowledgement comes the revelation that fullness of being consists in this exquisitely balanced state. The language of the second half of the volume (in the section entitled "The Price of Stone,") tells the poet's story through the mouths of buildings connected with his life. It is a language radiated, as it were, by this fact of contradiction. Underlying all these sonnets is one diagrammatically simple fact, that the speaking building, by addressing the poet as "you," allows the writer to be both objective and subjective at once, able to be entirely objective about himself as subject. In this way doubleness and contradiction are given a single voice and body, which in turn gives us a doubled perspective on everything: "The tomb I've made becomes a vivid road."

Most of all, it is Murphy's obsessive yet always civil desire to get at the truth about the self—to get at the truth, to admit to the truth, to find a language answerable to the truth—that makes *The Price of Stone* so distinct and distinguished a volume. Themes and concerns of the earlier books recur, but all is now autobiography, whether in the scattered recollections of childhood and growing up in Ireland and England, or in the apology for isolation, or in the poems about Tony White, or in the connection with an Anglo-Irish relative, or in the doubled sexual nature embodied in emotionally ambivalent terms by the first building, a "Folly":

> My form is epicene: male when the gold
> Seed of the sun comes melting through my skin
> Of old grey stucco: female when the mould
> Of moonlight makes my witch-pap cone obscene.

Or it can appear in the way the same complex state of things, the same ambiguity of being, is delicately treated of in the poet's own experience as a "Displaced Person"—a treatment that seems to draw some of its tact and exacting precision as well as its sweetness from the triangular situation in Shakespeare's sonnets which it seems to echo—"Those years ago when I made love to you, / With fears I was afraid you knew, / To grow strong I'd pretend to be / A boy I'd loved, loving yourself as me."

Another feature of related and compelling interest in this collection was the way Murphy's habits of language became themselves emblematic of a double life. Again and again, the speaking building utters itself with a sort of witty doubled tongue, recycling clichés at every turn. An abandoned lead mine chimney says, "Now I lack / The guts to pour out sulphur and hot air." A portico, in a series of *double entendres*, describes the sexual happenings it witnesses: the cruising men "Perform on flutes groping, mute melodies / With a seedy touch of ithyphallic art." The destroyed Nelson's Pillar describes the explosion that ruined it: "the blast wore / Red, white and blue in a flash of puerile skill." The Wellington Monument is "Needling my native sky over Phoenix Park," while the male "Gym" speaks in sexually loaded terms, its "fabric, full of cock and bull." And since many of the poems are memorials to the Anglo-Irish way of life, and to its passing ("Paraplegics live here now, and love my faults" says the "Family Seat;" "Planter Stock" is falling down and wears "fuchsia tweed, an ancient ivy coat;" "The Rectory" is decaying, even in memory), I wonder if Murphy's cunning use of language here—its wit and irony and doubleness— isn't a sort of contrapuntal energy to exercise against all the images and evidence of decomposition in the subject. By such verbal action, that is, Murphy can both be inside the actuality and rise above it, authentically the voice that *sees off* the Anglo-Irish. Certainly the fact that a tinker's tent is "Wattled with hazel cut from the remotest / Copse of a departed ascendancy demesne" seems emblematic, both of these buildings, and what they represent, being outcasts on the landscape. (And, in an altered key, both of them being, perhaps, Murphy's muted echo of and ironic awakening from Yeats's dream of the noble and the beggarman.)

In these poems, too, there is an unabashed reclaiming of his own life by the poet. This can take the form of affection for his youngster self ("A peeled rush, dipped in tallow, carried light / From the dark ages, kissing you goodnight"), while the youth discovering himself in his objections to war, is reminded "How selfishly you serve your own heart's bent." These buildings are the stages, the building blocks, of the developing artist (and of the sexual being, so a public toilet [in "Convenience"] is "The public servant of men's private parts . . . Your profane oracle." Through these poems, too, the poet can be emotional and confessional in a new way, while a poem like "Friary" enlarges the cultural / historical exploration, the essential archeological nature of the book—since the Christian friary is built where a druid wood once stood. Continuity and difference seems the point he's getting at, so "the rain harps on ruins," and a beehive cell has its penitential austerity marvelously sexualised by the fact that a woman (once in 1300 years) gave birth there.

It would be easy to go on citing poems with approval, both for their thematic point and their incidental elegance of expression, for there are abundant riches and satisfactions in this latest volume. Perhaps it is enough to say that the book offers the rare pleasure of witnessing the lively operation of a language adequate to its task of unfolding a life. In the last poem in the book, its final sonnet, Murphy brings up the rear of his architectural procession by speaking in his own person. Properly it is a poem of birth, for the whole book is, as I take it, about a sort of rebirth, and it is right to be brought to its conclusion in a voice that has been reborn out of all this experience. What this last poem celebrates is the birth of a "Natural Son." In it, Murphy justly turns all that stone he's paid the price of back into living flesh:

> No house we build could hope to satisfy
> Every small need, now that you've made this move
> To share our loneliness, much as we try
> Our vocal skill to wall you round with love.
>
> This day you crave so little, we so much
> For you to live, who need our merest touch.

Recognising, in the purely human moment of this birth, the way buildings are limited and "vocal skill" can only do so much, and recognising in the birth of this "natural son" a core of being that's independent of all conventional determinants and their propulsion towards doubleness, Murphy releases *himself* from the enclosing walls—built of family, race, sexual norms and social expectations—of his own past. What he affirms with that "merest touch" at the end of this poem, at the end of this collection, is his own wholeness.

1985

"Of So, and So, and So":
Re-Reading Some Details in Montague

What I propose to do here is look closely at a few passages in Montague's poetry which I have always found compelling. I want to see, and try to explain if I can, why these particular passages appeal to me in the ways they do.

The first piece is from what is probably the best, and best-known, poem in the 1961 volume, *Poisoned Lands*, which begins as follows:

Like dolmens round my childhood, the old people.

Jamie MacCrystal sang to himself,
A broken song without tune, without words;
He tipped me a penny every pension day,
Fed kindly crusts to winter birds.
When he died, his cottage was robbed,
Mattress and money box torn and searched.
Only the corpse they didn't disturb.

First, I love the truncated, verbless grammar of the opening line, the way it turns the title—which it simply repeats—into a gesture of strong but not strident affirmation (the *sound* ensures that, all those soft consonants and open vowels seem nurturing, protective). Lovely, too, the way the poet tucks his own childhood between the two impressive (quasi-parental) entities—ancient monuments and "the old people" (the definite article in this phrase adds a dimension of grandeur to adjective and noun)—rhythmically isolating it, but putting it protectively within a traditional line of descent.

One of the triumphs of the stanza that follows is the way it shifts tonal gear and register out of the expansive rhetoric of the poem's opening line into the restrained indicative simplicity of description. Nothing could be more straightforward than Montague's manner here, showing how well he had learned the lessons of Kavanagh and of William Carlos Williams. Sentences lay themselves out without syntactical difficulty, each line at once a unit of rhythm and of sense, as natural as speech. The opening line of the poem—oddly structured, grammatically impacted, a passionate push for summary and fullness—reminds me of someone suddenly breaking into speech after long silence. The stanza, however, is the painstakingly simple speech of someone who wants to get things just right, precise, true to the facts. The language here is physical and factual: it resides among the surfaces of things and actions, entering no speculative depths, offering no overt commentary. The eye and the ear of the poet are alive to the facts of the matter: by presenting these facts unadorned he bears best witness to his subject. Almost without adjectives, the diction is plain, colloquial, to the point. The only two adjectives—"broken" and "kindly" (which is in truth an elastic adverb)—are chosen with exquisite justice and tact, since between them they seem to epitomise Jamie's nature and condition. Because of such tact, the picture Montague gives seems, for all its economy, complete.

Part of its completeness comes from the way the stanza is divided in two. The first part describes the qualities of the man himself—his harmless kind habits, his solitude, his enduring heart. The second part—"When he died"—portrays the social environment which preys upon Jamie MacCrystal in death. Montague is equally alert to both of these realities, describing the cruelty in a dispassionate yet understanding and feeling way (the feeling is in the pathos of these details of mattress and money box). The passive impersonality of the verbs, the dispersed anonymity of "they," reveal his reluctance to set himself up in any way as judge. His role, rather, is that of witness, and he performs it flawlessly. So the private, personal, and social being of the dead man has been exhibited, as well as the environment in which he lived and died. The poet has found an adequate language, a language to acknowledge properly the real presence of this local character. The stanza composes an "historical" vignette, with the poet's own remembered self as an unobtrusive yet authenticating part of it.

Another source of my pleasure in this passage is observing the deftness and delicacy with which Montague coaxes the actual details towards emblematic status. For it seems to me that everything mentioned in connection with Jamie MacCrystal, all those personal details, may also be given a representative reading and interpretation. Seen in this way, Jamie is the last relic of a civilisation and way of life. Singing to himself "A broken song without tune, without words," he becomes an image of solitary craft, a whole tradition of music, song, even poetry dying away in his tuneless, wordless music. He reminds me of Wordsworth's "Solitary Reaper," although his predicament and what it represents are more pathetic. (Wordsworth may not understand the song he hears his reaper singing, but he knows the song itself has coherence—"For old, unhappy, far-off things / And battles long ago"—and suggests a live tradition). For Jamie's song is its own subject, is limited to his own hearing, is in every sense an end in itself. By putting the issue of song at the start of his poem, Montague stresses the emblematic nature of the truth he wants to reveal: making his own music out of that cultural loss, he underscores his elegiac point and, perhaps, the deeper point of renewal. By taking upon himself the task of elegiac celebration, the poet both acknowledges the loss and establishes out of it a fresh beginning.

It's possible to detect some similar double sense "passing on" in the next detail, which also exists at factual and emblematic levels: "He tipped me a penny every pension day." In this quotidian image I can find at least a trace of ritual, a sort of laying on of hands, the old singer giving his gift to the boy who would become the poet. (A more self-conscious version of this appears in "The Country Fiddler," from *A Chosen Light*). Obviously one doesn't want to overstress these possibilities, since the success of the poem lies, for me, in its beautifully balanced distance from any whiff of ideology, in the way these larger points remain latent. But Montague's sureness of touch here, the confidence with which he can summon up the real (the social, even sociological factuality of "pension day") and give it some extra air of the absolute, allows, without straining the text, for such extensions of meaning as I've mentioned. In this emblematic sense, then, the poem is not only an elegy for a culture but also a rite of poetic initiation. What's implicit and needs to be teased out at the start, however, becomes, as we'll see later, quite explicit in the last stanza.

The next line, "Fed kindly crusts to winter birds" has two possible metaphorical enlargements. First, those "winter birds" are an appropriate enhancement of the images of terminal song in the first two lines. As icons of hunger and need, they properly belong to this emotional landscape. As recipients of another kindness, another gesture of almost parental solicitude, they become kin to the boy. Second, they embody an active connection between the old man and the natural world, a relationship of an essentially benevolent kind. This sets up a category of description and understanding that continues through the portrait-stanzas following this one. All of "the old people," in fact, are bound closely to the natural world: Maggie Owens "was surrounded by animals"; on "the mountain lane" where the blind Nialls lived, "heather bells bloomed, clumps of foxglove"; Mary Moore's gatehouse is "crumbling" back to the state of nature, while "she tramped the fields"; and even Wild Billy Eagleson had "his flailing blackthorn." On the emblematic level these references suggest a vital continuity between the natural world and the civilisation these people represent. What Montague is instinctively insisting on here is the essential wholeness of that culture, a culture that inscribes an organic connection between man and nature, as well as, indeed, between dolmens and the old people. These old people are as native to their landscape as plants and animals (and dolmens), as integral to the natural world as Wordsworth's leech gatherer in "Resolution and Independence," who resembles "a huge stone" or "a sea-beast crawled forth," is "motionless as a cloud," an elemental particle of "the weary moors," and who is, like Montague's people, relic and reminder of another time, living into an age that has "dwindled long by slow decay."

The emblematic possibility of the next two lines (the account of the robbery) may be related to this idea of a fallen, a decayed age. The cruel treatment of the dead man suggests how an age of genuinely civilised benevolence can sink into one of savagery. And yet the mildness of Montague's language—the declarative sentence itself (with its initiating temporal adverb, "When") an image of inevitability—suggests the poet's own resignation before such unarguable proof of *process*. Given the deliberate (grammatical) absence of human agents, it might almost seem as if time itself, an inexorable and impersonal force, were responsible. What this manner manages to delineate is the sudden violent extinction of certain values—values of community—their blatant absence from this post-mortem world.

[It is worth making a small digression here, to point out that such a preoccupation with loss will mark many of Montague's later poems, notably "Hymn to the New Omagh Road" in *The Rough Field*—where human agency is more in evidence and the poem is making, satirically, an ideological point—and in two poems of a more truly philosophical bias in *The Dead Kingdom*—"Process" and "Gone," both of them songs to "the goddess Mutability, / dark Lady of Process, / our devouring Queen." This engagement to loss is a strong consistent thread throughout the work (a dominant and plangent note in the poems about the breakdown of his first marriage that appear in *The Great Cloak*), making elegy one of Montague's most effective and affecting modes. In "Like Dolmens Round My Childhood, the Old People," this "engagement to loss" receives early expression significantly in a context that is both cultural and personal. What happens to Jamie MacCrystal, then, may be seen as an image of process writ large, the poet's own deep, unspoken sense of loss given violent embodiment. The pathetic felony is emblematic of a larger truth, a truth extending in different directions out of Montague's imagination. It suggests not only a world of cultural loss and decay, but also implies a world in which benign beginnings have unhappy outcomes. This latter sense of things, one could speculate (assisted by Montague's own later poems, poems in which he describes being abandoned as a child by his mother, and the absence of his father: In "A Flowering Absence" and "A Locket," from *The Dead Kingdom*, for example, "All roads wind backwards to it. / An unwanted child, a primal hurt"), is generated by an imagination trying to deal with the psyche's own appalled sense of being orphaned, in the grip of loss, at an irremediable loss. Some such interior motivation, deeper, more elusive and more mysterious than analytic expression can render, may account for this poem's existence in the first place, and for its occupying—as readers invariably feel it occupies—such an obviously cardinal spot in Montague's own genesis and evolution as a poet. He may simply be peopling his (cultural) past with parents. (End of digression.)]

The final line of the stanza is also amenable to emblematic expansion. First of all, the simple fact reveals something of the true nature of the thieves, possessed by some residual moral feeling, is it? or by a delicate, if unlikely, scruple of taste, or merely by superstitious awe. In its own spare way, the line provides a quick sketch of a disintegrating community, the collapse of which is made seem all the more grievous and lamentable in this single quasi-religious observance, this hungover, morally hollow form. Linguistically, too, the line goes beyond its matter of fact. The word "disturb," after all, may betray an irony on the poet's part, an irony subtly leveled at the communal depravity. For does it have a simple physical meaning? Or does it have the more emotionally animate sense of 'distract,' 'call away the attention of'? (which, being obviously impossible in the case of a corpse makes the scrupulosity or residual civility seem ridiculously formulaic), or is it meant in the emotional sense of 'upset,' an equally ridiculous proposition? Indeed the corpse—and this meaning may also be built into the line—is the only one not disturbed by the whole event, an event which in truth, at its most representative and emblematic levels, disturbs a whole fabric of existence, a total way of life. Such possible authorial irony is another indication of Montague's sense of the representative nature of this small event. And, because of the ambivalent possibilities of meaning here, his own status as witness rather than judge remains essentially undisturbed. As with the picture of Jamie MacCrystal itself—the details of which can so easily grow into emblematic meanings—palpable delicacy of presentation is everything, in the last line's potential for larger implications.

A final note on this line concerns its curious construction. "Only the corpse they didn't disturb": rhythmically satisfying, it is syntactically peculiar. Both the satisfaction and the peculiarity, however, reveal the poet's own implicit feeling of being a part of this broken community, a sense of belonging that he dramatises by adopting such a distinctly colloquial locution. In his use of language— the recording instrument, the agent of memory, even the means of healing personal psychic wounds that, as it turned out, also impeded speech ("my tongue became a rusted hinge / until the sweet oils of poetry / eased it and light flooded in," he will say in "A Flowering Absence")—in his use of language the poet puts himself at one with his subject, endorsing its actuality, its emotional authenticity, and its emblematic significance.

The next passage I want to consider (but not at such length) is also from "Like Dolmens Round My Childhood, the Old People," from the end of the poem.

> Ancient Ireland, indeed! I was reared by her bedside,
> The rune and the chant, evil eye and averted head,
> Formorian fierceness of family and local feud.
> Gaunt figures of fear and of friendliness,
> For years they trespassed on my dreams,
> Until once, in a standing circle of stones,
> I felt their shadows pass
> Into that dark permanence of ancient forms.

I suppose the first thing to say about these lines is that they reveal the source from which the rest of the poem actually flows. Because of the event described here (we do not know when it happened, only that it happened "once"—as in "once upon a time"), the earlier stanzas have taken the form they do, have come into being at all. What first compels my attention here, however, is the vivid shift in tone brought about by that exclamatory opening. The last word in the preceding stanza is "death" and its final image is one of striking immobility, enlarging the pathetic figures of the old people who have died into emblematic "Silent keepers of a smokeless hearth / Suddenly cast in the mould of death." (The majestic calm and cultural implication of this image—tribal remnants struck dumb in front of the quenched fire of a whole way of life, a civilisation— is proof of how Montague can shuttle between the actual and something beyond that, can perceive in the actual its ritual shadow, can find for the actual a language that can, without betraying its actuality, elevate its status to that of ritual, into what he calls in another early poem, "redeeming patterns of experience," intending that first word as noun and verb).

The unexpected scorn of "Ancient Ireland indeed!" shatters such a mood, thrusting the poem into a fresh direction, another idiom. It shows remarkable agility on the part of the poet, a confident streamlined fluency capable of emotional reversals and rapid shifts of attention. This lively, aggressive utterance punctures a conventional notion usually approached in attitudes of piety and homage. (In the later poem, "The Siege of Mullingar"—from *A Chosen Light*— he sees a whole generation, in the Sixties, perform a similarly debunking act, this time on "Romantic Ireland"). By dismissing the conventional version, however, Montague clears the ground for a more personal version, as we'll see, of the same entity, providing another "take" on "Ancient Ireland." In addition, the idiosyncratic individuality of his voice here acts as a bridge between the more or less objective narrative—descriptive mode of the earlier stanzas and the intensely subjective manner of this one.

Subjectivity is the norm here, and the manner memorial. Everything is translated into the emotional vibration it had for the boy who became the remembering, recollecting poet. First he claims his own intimate relationship with "Ancient Ireland," having been "reared by her bedside." Maternal, grandmaternal, filial—however the relationship is named, the metaphor insists on its intensely familial nature, enabling the poet to provide for himself a (representative) cultural parent. In this context, the gender of "Ancient Ireland" seems especially revealing since Montague might just as easily have written "*its* bedside" (as in Yeat's refrain about "Romantic Ireland": "It's with O'Leary in the grave,") but chose to write—deliberately or involuntarily—"her" instead.

In the next two lines, completing the first sentence, the potentially peaceful connotations of "bedside" are—in a condensed version of the pattern that shapes most of the poem—destroyed by a number of violent appositional phrases. This brief litany of "ancient" conditions suggests an in-grown, grimly enclosed, superstitious society, cruel by nature, violent in its habits. (It is, incidentally, a much more negative picture than that created by the particular portraits themselves, as if this generalisation, in a sense, *preceded* the more genially detailed memories of the individual people.) The litany also implies a quick connection between private and public worlds, a rooted attachment to the past, cultural continuity, and a continuum of a palpable kind persisting between the worlds of matter and of spirit.

Meeting an accumulation of facts as powerfully, and for the most part negatively, evocative as these are, allied to the images of rearing, bedside, and motherhood which precede them, a reader might justifiably imagine a traumatic relationship between the child and his environment, both the general human environment—society, culture—and, by extension, the more immediate environment of the actual parents. Such a traumatic possibility is in fact endorsed by Montague in other poems, from the poem which precedes "Like Dolmens" in *Poisoned Lands*. "The Sean Bhean Bhocht" (1957)—"As a child I was frightened by her"—to the two poems from *The Dead Kingdom* (1984) that I have already mentioned—"The Locket" and "A Flowering Absence." What's so important to me about "Like Dolmens Round My Childhood, the Old People" is the fact that in it Montague dramatises, and therefore distances into understanding, the early wounds, both the wound of fear caused by the strange primeval otherness of "the old people," and the deeper wound of personal abandonment, being made a prey to such strangeness, being virtually orphaned. Indeed, it is probably fair to say that the primary wound is compensated for and "displaced" by the obsessive and frightened attachment to the old people, such a form of emotional substitution being an apt strategy for a psyche that must itself have felt—moving from Brooklyn to Northern Ireland, then from his mother to his father's relatives (see "A Flowering Absence")—the acutest ache of a double displacement.

In the mysterious epiphany that ends the poem, the poet finds the true cure for these wounds, or at least the beginnings of such a cure. He also finds in it one of his own critical beginnings as a poet, since the moment of its occurrence—in "real" time—was, I suspect, one of the single most enabling moments in the life of Montague's imagination. It occupies the concluding five lines of the poem. What these lines dramatise is an exorcism and a birth. What's exorcised is incapacitating fear; what's born is poetic consciousness. The old people were "Gaunt figures of fear and friendliness," trespassing for years on the child's dreams. Larger than life, with an ambivalent emotional effect, they are a source of psychic uncertainty, embodying the child's fear of the unknown. In this case the unknown has, so to speak, a cultural body. The fear it causes is not unlike the ambivalent fears Stephen Dedalus (at various moments in *Portrait*) feels towards the peasantry and what they represent. Here is the very young Stephen's response to the peasants in Clane: "It would be lovely to sleep for one night in that cottage before the fire of smoking turf, in the dark lit by the fire, in the warm dark, breathing the smell of peasants, air and rain and turf and corduroy. But, O, the road there between the trees was dark! You would be lost in the dark. It made him afraid to think of how it was." Warm by the fire; lost in the dark: here are Montague's "figures of fear and of friendliness." In Stephen's later, more anguished brooding, it might be possible to find something of the dilemma of Montague's evolving imagination. After the satiric barb thrown at "Mulrennan" (a version of Synge) and the "old man" with "red eyes" who spoke Irish and was from the West of Ireland ("Ancient Ireland indeed!"), Stephen says in his diary, "I fear him. I fear his redrimmed horny eyes. It is with him I must struggle all through this night till day come, till he or I lie dead . . . No. I mean him no harm." Stephen leaves Ireland without really resolving this important issue for himself. Montague's resolution, on the other hand, is this poem, for which he is prepared by the experience described in the closing three lines.[1]

After the figures have "trespassed" on the most intimately private space of his dreams (becoming, I suppose, emanations of dread and of a desire for the human comfort of belonging), the poet is granted the gift of an exorcism that is authentic understanding, freeing him into a knowledge of *meanings*. In this silent and singular moment ("once") located at a ritual center, a standing circle that has to be womb and omphalos, he "felt their shadows pass" into that dark permanence of ancient forms. Verb and enjambment here both stress the motion that must accompany exorcism, a sense confirmed by the last line, with the shadows entering—a sort of image of possession—into the stones, and through them into the even more remote, but still vitally connected, "permanence of ancient forms." In this given instant of awareness, the old people become "the old people," at one with the icons of tradition and continuity (the dolmens), shadowy facts become permanent forms. And it is through this recognition that he comes to understand them also as emblems of a common loss, the sort of thing he gives expression to in the rest of the poem, these individuals glimpsed as exemplars of a traditional world that in their poor attenuated selves is at its last gasp. Seen in this way, the people may at least be dealt with as he actually deals with them in the poem, the manner, emotional texture, and assured vision of which derive from the moment dramatised at its conclusion. So the poem is a full circle, returning at the end to the first awareness of the condition stated in the opening line. By means of this epiphanal gift, Montague has managed to ritualise his sense of loss and exorcise many of the fears that surrounded it: the old people, transient and vulnerable, become a dark permanence, "ancient *forms*" that are themselves a consolation. Through this whole process his imagination, or at least a significant part of his poetic consciousness, is born. And this imagination, this poetic consciousness, is responsible for a great many of the poems that will come later. The moment is as important to Montague as the moment Wordsworth describes in Book One of *The Prelude*, the incident of the stolen boat. Montague's gaunt, trespassing figures could be related to the "huge peak, black and huge" which became for Wordsworth "huge and mighty forms" that were "a trouble to my dreams." Montague's last line, too, has something of a Wordsworthian amplitude, not unlike that "dim and undetermined sense / Of unknown modes of being" in the stolen boat passage.

The two passages I've just explored give something of the feel of Montague's imagination—its attachments, preoccupations, modes of procedure. They show, I'd say, the degree to which his sense of cultural vulnerability and loss—the sort of thing to be found in poems at every stage of his work—may grow out of some even deeper personal region of the spirit, a region where the issue of loss is a private matter co-extensive with the whole sentient personality itself. This is what gives these poems their rare emotional power, a power that does not necessarily inform poems where the issue of loss takes on—as it does in parts of *The Rough Field*, for example—a more explicitly ideological tinge, producing poems whose source seems to lie in the will rather than within that complex range of perceptions and receptions we call imagination. The passages also show one of Montague's most admirable traits—his ability to turn the keenly, lovingly observed actual detail into something larger, more representative, emblematic. Such an ability testifies, perhaps, to his awareness of inhabiting a border country between history and myth, a subject that would require an essay on its own. In the present case I'd only point to the malleable vitality of his language, the way it enables him to occupy a number of contiguous zones of thought and feeling without any sense of strain. The passages might also reveal a poet who was, at least in his early phase, a responsive reader of Wordsworth. Finally, these lines and stanzas demonstrate the degree to which poetry is for Montague a necessary, deeply instinctive response to loss. Here, by imaginatively entering into the otherness of culture, he is essentially dealing with loss, offering (first to himself) some provisional restoration.

I want to expand this meditation (if art is "a warm brooding," as the poet—in a fine maternal metaphor—says it is, then maybe that's what criticism should be, too) by considering closely a few lines which may help me probe a little more the nature of what I most admire about the work of Montague's imagination. The lines are the last seven from *11 rue Daguerre*, which is Part I of the title poem from the 1967 collection, *A Chosen Light*:

> There is white light on the cobblestones
> And in the apartment house opposite—
> All four floors—silence.
>
> In that stillness—soft but luminously exact,
> A chosen light—I notice that
> The tips of the lately grafted cherry-tree
>
> Are a firm and lacquered black.

In the passages I quoted from "Like Dolmens Round My Childhood" it's possible to see the workings of imagination *in the world*. The way the poet focuses on the people he names and describes, the way their accidental natures become representative of meanings larger than themselves, mark the imagination's entrance into the world of history—of culture and society, of time. The role of the imagination is to seek out significance, finding a meaning for these transient inhabitants and the world for which they stand. I believe the lines just quoted above, however, put one in touch with the true lyrical centre of Montague's art, the imagination focussed on things for their own sake, the meaning utterly intrinsic to the object. It is a condition or point of consciousness where "the object of attention is the particularity of nature, and the imagination is disposed to reveal it in its plenitude, with the result that the objects contemplated take to themselves a certain radiance which marks the feeling they inspire."[2] In the passages from "Like Dolmens" we see the source of imaginative action, the imagination's dedication to the world; in the lines from "A Chosen Light" it is the pure presence of imaginative being that confronts us, and the poet's acknowledgement of this "certain radiance."

Tactful, unobtrusive, as silently watchful as the mood of the poem itself, these lines suggest a refined collaboration between eye and speech, the eye acknowledging what Terence Brown calls "the existential tingle of material objects,"[3] while the speech refuses to do much more than name the phenomena—cobblestones, house, cherry tree, silence, light. A more or less neutral form of the verb "to be" is pervasive; the strongest verbal assertion resides in the speaker's own relaxed but ready attention, "I notice" (an intransitive usage even less aggressive than the alternative "I see," since it takes no direct object). The wonder-word in the passage is "chosen." Is it simply an adjective formed out of the past participle of the verb, as in "the chosen people?" Or does it have a greater degree of verbal assertion, meaning that Montague has himself 'chosen' it, an implicit gesture of mastery? It is not the answers to such questions that

What really matters is the poise of the word between such meanings, that brief enchantment of language the poet thought enough of to use as the title of his book. The language is all eyes and ears, making 'stillness' (absence of movement and sound) synaesthetically synonymous with 'light', "soft but luminously exact." By means of such language, the poet at once inhabits and is absent from this moment.

What I love about this language is its calm reciprocity with the world of facts, of objects. The objective world seems splendidly *available* to a speech that is at once simple, deliberate, and polished. What Montague finds here is a language for and of pure awareness, a language emerging from the core of primary knowledge that must be one of the generative places of imagination. It's the space he inhabits in "The Trout" (also from *A Chosen Light*), describing the fish "where he lay, light as a leaf / In his fluid sensual dream," and the remembered self as "so preternaturally close/ I could count every stipple." Here is the lyrical center of his art—an art of absolute attention to the living thing in the moment—which he describes in "A Bright Day" (from *A Chosen Light*) as "a slow exactness / Which recreates experience / By ritualising its details." This language starts from things themselves and the mind's rapt attention to them, so "even the clock on the mantel / Moves its hands in a fierce delight / Of so, and so, and so." It is the perfect silence ("In that stillness . . . I notice") that houses the heart of Montague's imaginative being, close to what Yeats must have been thinking of when he described the (creative) mind as "a long-legged fly" that "moves upon silence." And in the poem "Division" (in *A Chosen Light*), Montague knows it as "my own best life"— not that "bitter, predatory thing," the head, but "the hypnotised field-mouse / Housed beneath its claws."

Thinking into such details as those in the lines I've quoted from *11 rue Daguerre*, and trying to figure out what they tell me about the nature of Montague's imagination, two further things are of particular interest to me. The first of these is simply literary: I wonder what kind of literary kinships this small passage might suggest. The second is more personal: I wonder what it tells me, whether intending to or not, about the poet's deepest and least mediated apprehension of existence. I'll end this meditation on Montague by briefly considering each of these issues.

The first ghost conjured by the lines is Kavanagh's. Intense attention lodging in plain speech is one of the principal legacies Kavanagh left to Irish poets:

> A boortree tried hard to
> Let me see it grow,
> Mere notice was enough,
> She would take care of love.
>   ("Ante-Natal Dream")

Montague has often acknowledged this aspect of the older poet. Indeed, it is to that he was most likely referring when he said (controversially) that Kavanagh had "liberated us into ignorance," since by "ignorance" I suspect he means a capacity for pure, uncontaminated awareness of the actual, the quotidian. Such an awareness is a decisive element in Kavanagh's own aesthetic, clearly seen in "The Hospital"—where, after a litany of ordinary objects, he declares that "Naming these things is the love-act and its pledge; / For we must record love's mystery without claptrap."[4] In the poem, "Waiting" (from *A Chosen Light*), Montague echoes these sentiments when he says of his own literary habits, "This low-pitched style seeks exactness, / Daring only to name the event." The lines I've quoted from *11 rue Daguerre* perform an intense excavation of a single moment of awareness, everything coming to a point in the tips of that cherry tree. In this exacting entrance into the moment—to acknowledge its presence, testify to its simple being—Montague seems to be obeying instinctively another of Kavanagh's poetic injunctions, the one that instructed poets to "Snatch out of time the passionate transitory" ("The Hospital"). Given such implicit connections, I suspect that Kavanagh's willingness to be still in the face of the objective world ("The only true teaching / Subsists in watching / Things moving or just colour"—"Is") was tutor to Montague's central lyrical energy.

What might distinguish the younger poet from his master (one of his masters) is the way his sensibility, even where it is chiming with Kavanagh's, has a greater tendency to aestheticise (or, to use his own word, "ritualise") the moment and what inhabits it. Kavanagh's notice is just notice: "A year ago I fell in love with the functional ward / Of a chest hospital: square cubicles in a row / Plain concrete, wash basins—an art lover's woe" ("The Hospital"). (The rhyme, of course, is a force of "arrangement," but what it arranges is the poem—a sonnet—not the objects in the poem). Montague's descriptions, on the other hand, are more likely to be an "art lover's" delight. Cobblestones and white light, house and silence, black lacquer tips of the tree and a luminous exactitude—these elements seem to settle naturally into a framed, orderly picture. There's an inescapable and not unconscious refinement to the sensibility that thus arranges (very delicately) the world, rather than simply acknowledging it. Because of the nature of Montague's imaginative receptivity, the things of the world, as they enter his attention, somehow fall into place. This, I think, distinguishes his imagination from the more expansive tolerances of Kavanagh's, from Kavanagh's account of an actuality bristling with interior energies. While the causes and consequences of such differences would be revealing, the similarities I've noted simply underline the influential presence of Kavanagh at the lyrical center of Montague's verse.

A couple of minor influences might also be touched on. The unhurried factual accumulation ("There is white light on the cobblestones . . ."), the utterly unjudged description, the definitive absence of commentary or evaluation—all these qualities evoke, along with their touches of Imagism, the tradition of Japanese haiku, poems which create a pellucid atmosphere of purified attention around an otherwise unremarkable and mundane moment. The "lacquered black" tips of the cherry tree (perennial haiku subject) also suggest a certain Japanese effect, as if here Montague were trying to find something of the ritual precision of the haiku. Effects such as these, however, might also be under an influence closer to home—that of the Early Irish poets, whose poems of uncluttered radiance (moments of pure being uttered in a manner at once intense and simple) have always been deeply admired by Montague. He has called them "vernacular poems as delicate as haiku," and would surely approve of Flann O'Brien's praise of their "steel-peen exactness"[5] (a quality particularly telling for him, given the "luminously exact" nature of his own "chosen light"). In addition, he has translated into English a number of their elegant and innocent celebrations of the natural world:

> The whistle
> of the bright
> yellow billed
>   little bird:
>
> Over the loch
> upon a golden
> whin, a blackbird
>   stirred.
>   ("Belfast Lough")

Another possible influence on the lyrical habits responsible for such lines as those quoted from *11 rue Daguerre* is that of Synge. For what Montague is at here—which is fairly representative of his most intense and, for me, most satisfying lyrical mode—seems not unlike what Synge is at in the shining prose of *The Aran Islands*. A passage of Synge's like the following, for example, seems to blend facts, ritual, existential awareness of objects, and the poise between feeling and seeing, in more or less the same proportions as they are mixed in Montague:

> the walls [of a kitchen] have been toned by the turf smoke to a soft brown that blends with the grey earth-colour of the floor. Many sorts of fishing-tackle, and the nets and oilskins of the men, are hung upon the walls or among the open rafters; and right overhead, under the thatch, there is a whole cow-skin from which they make pampooties. Every article on these islands has an almost personal character, which gives this simple life, where all art is unknown, something of the artistic beauty of medieval life.[6]

Particularity such as this, edging into ritual, is certainly a determining element in the passage quoted from the rue Daguerre poem. It may be found in an even more obviously influential way in "The Answer" (*A Chosen Light*), where the poet stands in a country cottage, "tasting the neat silence / of the swept flags, the scoured delph / on the tall dresser where even something / tinny like a two-legged, horned alarm-clock / was isolated into meaning." Also in "The Answer," the hint of a connection with Synge might be extended. For the politeness of the old woman's Irish, as she gives "the answer," her "ritual greetings" and her general demeanor—all exemplifying "the only way, / the way of courtesy"—could call to mind a remark of Synge's on "the courtesy of the old woman of the house," and how he "could see with how much grace she motioned each visitor to a chair, or stool, according to his age, and said a few words to him."[7]

The pure affecting glitter of phenomenal presence; the recognition in an actual environment of ritual grace: these are the qualities Montague might have taken, consciously or unconsciously, from Synge. Furthermore, in his "Song for Synge," what he values in Synge is the way "Creation bright / each object shines and stirs," a precise condensation of some of the very qualities he may have learned, at least in part, from Synge. Synge, that is, could have encouraged in him an intensified state of awareness, that state in which things "shine," as well as a heightened sensitivity to the ritual possibility within objects, the "stir" in them that generates ritualising patterns. (It may also have been Synge who helped bring this pure lyric sensibility to the borders of cultural, even ideo-logical, awareness and expression—as happens in "The Answer"— since those are the borders on which Synge's own lyrical imagination is at home).

What I would finally say about this whole more or less speculative issue of influences is that, in the conjunction of Kavanagh and Synge as lyric influences (an ironic conjunction, in that Kavanagh took many a critical swipe at Synge, accusing him of being "mock-Irish"), Montague manages to marry a natural "insider's" response to the world with the more sophisticated aesthetic habits of the enchanted "outsider." Under two such influences, Montague's lyric sense receives excellent training, tuned early to the real world and to his own re-sponses to it.

The lines quoted above from *11 rue Daguerre* are a sign, as I said, of Monta-gue's passionate attachment to the particularity of the moment and the momen-tary particular. I want to end by briefly considering this attachment. The mo-ment in question occurs at the close of the same poem. What precedes it is an experience of process, the sight (in the garden) of "tendrils of green" that are "desperately frail / In their passage against / The dark, unredeemed parcels of earth." By juxtaposing the opening image of stillness against this image of "frail" but definitely kinetic energy, the poet draws the moment out of time, out of process, into a small island of being abstracted from the flow. Such an act seems native to Montague's imagination, a necessary reflex that becomes crea-tive habit, a distinct presence and strategy in many of his best poems. In the very early "Irish Street Scene, with Lovers" (from *Poisoned Lands*), for example, "the world shrinks" to the compass of an umbrella, "its assembly of spokes like points of stars, / A globule of water slowly forming on each." Such minutely observed data contrasts with the normal street scene, stands up against passage the way "the glittering cry / of a robin . . . balances a moment." Or in that flaw-less poem, "The Trout," the whole mesmerised, sensual action takes place inside a few moments epiphanally teased out of time, the poet "savouring my own ab-sence." In "The Wild Dog Rose," a similar strategy and habit may be found sprouting from a narrative of violence and horror, becoming an emblem of in-explicable consolation:

> Briefly
> the air is strong with the smell
> of that weak flower, offering
> its crumbling yellow cup
> and pale bleeding lips
> fading to white . . .

Such a strategy and habit compose epiphanal moments like those visible in the small spots of time preserved in memory's amber in "Salutation" (from *The Rough Field*)—"The damp coats of the scholars/ Stood breathing in the hall." Or else the poet can create the rapt, self-forgetting attentiveness that etches the image of the snail in "Small Secrets" (from A Slow Dance), "rippling along / its liquid self- / creating path," or the even more richly evocative moment in "Almost a Song" (from *A Slow Dance*): "At mealtimes / huge hobnails sparkled / a circle in the stiff grass / as we drank brown tea, bit / buttered planks of soda bread."

In spite of differences in content and context, what these examples have in common is a commitment—as total as it is exclusive—to the living moment. Implicitly they insist on the moment's own efficacy, asserting against the devouring, clouding energies of time and process the moment's luminous, intrinsic value. In each case—and they could be multiplied—the compound condition that's been revealed has on one side an awareness of inevitable loss, and on the other a countering or consoling assertion of the value of the moment, with the poet's own habit of attention *enabling* that moment. It is possible, I believe, to see in all this a shaping base to Montague's imagination: a psyche conditioned by the sense of loss, seeking to temper that sense—and the sense of futility that may attend it—by its rapt attachment to the almost extra-temporal moment. Where culture may provide the poet with surrogate parents, this more primary and pre-cultural condition may provide him with no less than a feeling of meaningful existence. Such moments, that is, may convert "being" into "meaning."

Nowhere is this habit of imagination more active than in Montague's love poems, as if sexual love itself were a point of concentration for all these forces. (Given the central position of women—Woman?—in the history of his psyche—as this has been revealed through his own poems—it is hardly surprising that this should be the case.) Most of Montague's best love poems, indeed, are either elegies, or celebrations of the moment—both of which impulses most likely grow from the one imaginative or psychic root, from the one complex way of receiving the world. This may be seen in his earliest love poem of original power—"All Legendary Obstacles" (from *A Chosen Light*)—where the terrible energies of process (time and space and weather) are finally overcome in one minutely observed moment of emotional relief, observed not by the poet himself but by "an old lady" who (like an eluded Fate) remains on the train that has brought his lover, and

who marked
A neat circle on the glass
With her glove, to watch us
Move into the wet darkness
Kissing, still unable to speak.

The same breathless (and speechless) dissolution in the moment may be found in the more erotically charged "Tracks" (from *Tides*): "As I turn to kiss / your tight black / curls, full breasts, / heat flares from / your unmarked skin / and your eyes widen." Always, these moments are threatened ("I shall miss you / creaks the mirror / into which the scene / will shortly disappear"), since sexual love—"a greeting / in the night . . . a form of truth . . . an answer to death" ("Love, A Greeting," in *Tides*)—is itself the prey of time and flux and circumstance. So affairs wear out, marriages collapse and shatter, proving the pattern of loss, provoking the poet to elegy. The best of his love elegies is the poem in *The Great Cloak* called "Herbert Street Revisited," where celebration of the moment and elegiac acknowledgement of process, of loss, are—for one singular, emotionally flawless instant—the same thing. Beginning the poem outside the house in which he has spent part of his married life ("someone is leading our old lives!"), he goes on to evoke some of the most vivid elements that constituted, and now reconstitute, that time and the texture of that stage of the marriage. (That the poem is "*for Madeleine*" provides, by accident, an initiating Proustian dedication to memory itself, a journey of the mind and heart "in search of lost time.") "Herbert Street Revisited" ends with a tender summoning of things past ("So put the leaves back on the tree, / put the tree back in the ground"), an unsentimental conjuring trick to outwit time and loss, a lovely moment of pure memorial magic, a triumph (*the* triumph) of pure lyricism:

And let the pony and donkey come—
look, someone has left the gate open—
like hobbyhorses linked in
the slow motion of a dream

parading side by side, down
the length of Herbert Street,
rising and falling, lifting
their hooves in the moonlight.

I seem to have wandered far from my starting point in *11 rue Daguerre*. But in truth not too far, for here again the poet—standing outside his "home" at night—finds himself in the contemplation of things, a lyrical contemplation enriched, this time, by its directly elegiac context. This time he is more explicit in affirmation, but what he's affirming is the same thing: the value of the object itself in its living moment—the only talisman we can know against the inexorable and inevitable reality of loss. In poems such as these—explicit and implicit acknowledgments of loss and affirmations of being—Montague reveals an im-

portant truth about the nature of his imagination and its creative sources and
resources, a truth I have been circling about in these few pages. At his lyrical
best,[8] he can embody a profound sense of loss *and* of affirmation *and* of celebration in a single poem, even in a few lines within a single poem. And in such
lines, in such poems, he can summarise his sense of the world and show us "The
only way of saying something / Luminously as possible." When this happens,
and it happens often, he illuminates us all.

1989

NOTES

[1] Oddly enough, Montague says he was going to use this latter Joycean passage as
epigraph to his collection of short stories, *Death of a Chieftain*. See his "Work Your
Progress," *Irish University Review*, 12 (Spring 1982) 49.

[2] Denis Donoghue, "The Sovereign Ghost, part 1," *Sewanee Review*, 84, 1 (1976)
103.

[3] Terence Brown, *Northern Voices* (Totowa, New Jersey: Rowman and Littlefield,
1975) 152.

[4] Patrick Kavanagh, *Collected Poems* (London: MacGibbon and Kee, 1964) 152.
The following quotation is also from this volume ("Is," 154).

[5] "In the Irish Grain," Introduction to *The Faber Book of Irish Verse* (London: Faber
and Faber, 1974) 23. The O'Brien quotation may be found in Seamus Heaney's essay,
"The God in the Trees," *Preoccupations* (London: Faber and Faber, 1980) 181.

[6] John M. Synge, *Collected Works*, ed. Alan Price, vol. 2 (Gerrards Cross: Colin
Smythe, 1982) 58-9.

[7] *Ibid.*

[8] To my mind, Montague is at his best as a lyricist, though he himself might sometimes balk at whatever suggestion of confinement this might imply. In his poetry, the
narrative instinct or need that composes *sequences* like *The Rough Field*, *The Great
Cloak*, and *The Dead Kingdom* seems to me at times a bit too willed a thing, seeking to
establish order and pattern and understanding in a more imposing way than that in which
he often *inadvertently finds them* in and through individual poems, poems that are lyrical
reflexes to deep needs and habits of feeling and expression in the more involuntary and
unrehearsed zones of his psyche. The sequences as sequences, that is, can sometimes
seem less than the sum of their parts. Maybe his own *natural* tendency is revealed in a
1985 interview, where he says that his imaginative habit is "to let the lyric come as it
will, let the spirit blow where it listeth, and now and then you can see some larger pattern" ("Elegiac Cheer," *The Literary Review*, 31, Fall 1987, 29). Some of the "larger
patterns," however, seem less simply "seen" than deliberately "composed." I should add,
however, that the poet's appetite for design is obviously, for himself, a necessary and
imaginatively enabling element, which probably makes the critic's quarrel with it irrelevant (as well as, to judge from my own experience with various issues of taste and
judgement, subject to qualification at a later date).

"To the Point of Speech":
The Poetry of Derek Mahon

The publication of *Poems 1962-1978* confirmed Derek Mahon's reputation as one of the most important voices in contemporary Irish poetry.[1] Unlike Seamus Heaney, Thomas Kinsella, and John Montague, however, Mahon is scarcely known on this side of the Atlantic. Reviews of his work have occasionally appeared, but these have, for all their commendations, done little to make him a felt presence.[2] Yet Mahon's compelling independence of voice and vision; the elegant mastery of craft that marks everything he writes; a range of imaginative commitments that link him not only to major Irish poets of the preceding generation like Louis MacNeice and Patrick Kavanagh but also with Auden, with Robert Lowell, with the Matthew Arnold of "Dover Beach," and the Wallace Stevens of "The Idea of Order at Key West"—all these and other excellences have made him indispensable to any comprehensive understanding of Irish poetry at the present time. And although there is probably a need for a general introduction to his work, I have chosen instead in this essay to meditate upon one important element of his poetry. By doing this, I hope to illuminate the value of the work as a whole, and to suggest some ways in which we may as readers bring to it a measure of the attention it deserves.

The strongest impression made on me when I read any poem by Derek Mahon is the sense that I have been spoken to: that the poem has established its presence in the world as a kind of speech. In addition, I am aware that its status as speech is an important value in itself, carrying and confirming those other, more explicit values which the poem endorses as part of its overt 'meaning.' What I hear in these poems is a firm commitment to speech itself, to the act of civil communication enlivened, in this case, by poetic craft. Listen, for example, to a few lines of the elegy for MacNeice, "In Carrowdore Churchyard":

> Maguire, I believe, suggested a blackbird
> And over your grave a phrase from Euripides.
> Which suits you down to the ground, like this churchyard
> With its play of shadow, its humane perspective.

The mannerly plainness of this direct address makes the speech itself a tribute to MacNeice as well as a revelation of Mahon's chosen way as a poet of being in the world. Here is wit in the delicate, inventive animation of the cliché, modesty in those self-effacing hesitations. Intimate and polite, such speech is a gesture of admiration and reconciliation, its perfect pitch and balance denying the excesses of feeling and form which would jeopardise the whole enterprise:

> All we may ask of you we have. The rest
> Is not for publication, will not be heard.

I hear in this speech (some of the qualities of which are probably derived from the influential practice of MacNeice himself) a tenacious commitment to what is private in experience. Intimacy is the desired end of such poetry—with the dead poet (an intimacy of shared idiom, gratitude for the gift of speech) and with the reader—but such an intimacy as permits the experience to have a "public" expression without losing its essentially private nature. This kind of skater's balance, this decency of deportment, locates Mahon's deepest instinct for form, an instinct which makes its presence felt in the actual body and pressure of his poetic speech.

Mahon's belief in speech as value and as an epitome of identity is clear in those poems in which he invents another speaker. In "Van Gogh in the Borinage," "Bruce Ismay's Soliloquy," and "The Forger," he gives each of these outsiders a voice of his own: in speech, he seems to be saying, human identity finds itself. These poems act out (and act out of) the pressing need to be articulate in difficult straits. By converting distress into a distinct clarity of utterance, each speaker raises his speech to a value in itself, a civil declaration of independence against the forces of disastrous circumstance. The general model might be Van Gogh, tempering the ugliness of "pits, slag heaps, beetroot fields" with a vividness of perception that illuminates the ordinary and communicates it in a speech possessing its own tough grace:

> A meteor of golden light
> On chairs, faces and old boots,
> Setting fierce fire to the eyes
> Of sunflowers and fishing boats,
> Each one a miner in disguise.

For Mahon, then, poetry is speech, an act—perhaps the fundamental act—of true communication between one human being and another (or others: Van Gogh speaks to his brother; Bruce Ismay and the forger, Jan Van Meghrem, deliver their distraught yet dignified confessions to the world). Even in love poems (like "Preface to a Love Poem" or "Bird Sanctuary") love itself is a search for a way of speaking to the other, who is "the soul of silence," a way

> To say 'I love you' out of indolence,
>   As one might speak at sea without forethought,
> Drifting inconsequently among islands.

Love poem, elegy ("The Death of Marilyn Monroe," "The Poets of the Nineties," "Homage to Malcolm Lowry"), translation (Villon, Jaccottet), autobiographical vignette ("My Wicked Uncle"), and extended verse letter ("Beyond Howth Head," "The Sea in Winter")—all such poems seem informed by the same belief in poetry as speech. This belief also determines the nature of those poems which emerge from what I see as the central dilemma in Mahon's poetic consciousness. To simplify, it is a dilemma that manifests itself as a struggle with the difficult exigencies of historical circumstance, a struggle which ends in the rejection of history itself and those values it urges upon us.

As one moves through *Poems 1962-1978*, one can see how Mahon's growing disenchantment with historical circumstance is grounded in his vexed and complex relationship with the North of Ireland. In poems like "Glengormley," "The Spring Vacation," and "Ecclesiastes," the complicated nature of the relationship is effectively accommodated by the speech of the poem. He is compelled to acknowledge the fact that he belongs to this place. "By / Necessity, if not choice," he admits in "Glengormley," "I live here too," and in "The Spring Vacation" (dedicated to Michael Longley; original title: "In Belfast") he advances from astute criticism to uneasy acceptance:

> One part of my mind must learn to know its place.
> The things that happen in the kitchen houses
> And echoing back-streets of this desperate city
> Should engage more than my casual interest,
> Exact more interest than my casual pity.

Speech here seems like Mahon's own way of making himself honest. Its peculiar forthrightness of presence makes it the proper medium for communicating difficult truth. It is speech that negotiates the strain in the poet's complicated response, just as it is the vigorously ironic cadences of his speech in "Ecclesiastes" that actively disengages him from his native place. Significantly enough, this separation itself is perceived in terms of speech—a refusal to surrender to historical circumstances which would require a certain constriction of expression:

> Your people await you, their heavy washing
>   flaps for you in the housing estates—
> a credulous people. God you could do it, God
>   help you, stand on a corner stiff
> with rhetoric, promising nothing under the sun.

Instead of such promises, it is freedom of speech (the opposite to "rhetoric") that Mahon craves. In later poems, such freedom of speech becomes part of that value for which he undertakes inner and outer exile: the speech of the poems themselves becomes a space emancipated from the destructive environment of history.[3]

This release from history is at the heart of the most important poems in the collection. In contrast to history's clamorous demands, Mahon offers the subdued affirmations of a civil speech. Whether these poems have an invented *persona* or speak in the voice of the poet himself, their speech is consistently a value opposed to the values of historical circumstance. In careful, polite tones, the speaker in "The Last of the Fire Kings" informs us he is "through with history." He would pass to a new world, "Not knowing a word of the language." In its deliberate patience, its poise and lucidity of syntax, his speech opposes that noisy world of "Sirens, bin-lids / And bricked-up windows" from which he turns. His speech has the cadences of reasonable conversation, a kind of communion impossible inside the din created by "the fire-loving people":

> Five years I have reigned
> During which time
> I have lain awake each night
>
> And prowled by day
> In the sacred grove
> For fear of the usurper,
>
> Perfecting my cold dream
> Of a place out of time
> A palace of porcelain
>
> Where the frugivorous
> Inheritors recline
> In their rich fabrics
> Far from the sea.

Such a poem obviously contains an indirect reflection on Mahon's own relationship as a poet with the North. In a comment he once made on another poem ("The Studio"), he mentioned "the oblique, and possibly escapist, relationship of the Artist to his historical circumstances, particularly where these circumstances include a violent and complex political upheaval."[4] The lines quoted above give in their speech a fullness of life to this complicated relationship. Escape from history is, in part, a journey into the secure composure of such a style of speech, with its direct tone, its frankness, its fluency of movement between plainness and unusual eloquence.

What might be called the ritual of such expression achieves an even more vivid existence in "The Snow Party" (dedicated to the poet, Louis Asekoff) the details of which establish in summary form the two opposing forces in Mahon's extended meditation on history. Speaking this poem, the poet stands on a border between barbarous violence and civil peace, his unhurried, precise speech an attempt to endorse the value of the latter:

> Bashō, coming
> To the city of Nagoya,

Is asked to a snow party.

There is a tinkling of china
And tea into china;
There are introductions.

Then everyone
Crowds to the window
To watch the falling snow.

Here, it is as if the urge for quiet, plain utterance itself enacts the poem's theme. Politeness of tone and indicative simplicity of grammar reflect the sanity and ceremony of the occasion. Verbs are almost invisible: the strongest one is "crowding," and this, in the present context, conveys a sense of courteous community rather than jostling disorder. Ritual discovers the shining at the heart of ordinary events, redeeming the infections of the violent world that surrounds this oasis of peace with its uproar, though even this uproar is communicated in the same modest, polite tones of infinite courtesy:

Elsewhere they are burning
Witches and heretics
In the boiling squares,

Thousands have died since dawn
In the service
Of barbarous kings.

The quietness of this communication graduates naturally to an emblematic silence, the falling snow bringing man and nature into civil accord: "there is silence / In the houses of Nagoya / And the hills of Ise." The speaker need do no more than tell us: further assertion would do violence to the delicate fabric of the poem. In such speech you can hear the poet turning away from the unspeakable chaos of history toward the besieged but peaceful retreats of his own imagination. Inside these quiet stanzas beats a desire for peace which, in the honest intensity of its expression, achieves the status of a moral value. In its reasonable politeness and unsentimental exactitude such speech is at once a withdrawal from history and a calm, unflinching meditation upon it.

Like other refugees and exiles from history, the mushrooms in "A Disused Shed in Co. Wexford" have learnt "patience and silence." Rich, casual, beautifully specific, the speech of this splendid poem first accommodates their silence, then provides them with a voice of their own with which to make a special claim upon our attention. The poem inscribes a journey from silence to speech, that entry of imagination into an object which in Mahon's poetry almost always culminates in the object itself achieving a kind of speech. Through gestures of controlled eloquence ("What should they do there but desire? / So many

days beyond the rhododendrons / With the world waltzing in its bowl of cloud")
the poem moves discreetly to the realisation that the poet is in fact being addressed, is being asked to speak for these victims of historical amnesia, these
forgotten creatures:

> They are begging us, you see, in their wordless way,
> To do something, to speak on their behalf
> Or at least not to close the door again.
> Lost people of Treblinka and Pompeii!

Here, as elsewhere, Mahon's authoritative use of the first person plural enhances
my sense of the poem as immediate address, an immediacy confirmed by that
mannerly "you see." Such civil soft-spokenness not only gives vivid dramatic
life to the exclamatory surprise of the last line; it also allows one to endorse its
riskily expansive gesture. The precise allusion has been earned (in part by the
fact that the horrors named have different sources—one the result of human
peril, the other a product of human disaster). The poem ends, then, by transforming the speaker into a listener. The speech which the poet allows to the
mushrooms and all their corollary creatures confirms our sense of his imaginative engagement with the world as a species of conversation. It is, I might say, a
condition of sustained desire that balances, in a way at once nervous and reassuring, the act of speech with that of listening. These castaways of history are
connected to us by the plangent urgency of their address. Its unaffected simplicity reveals the depth of their distress and the intensity with which they are present to the poet. We enter a circle of sympathy as we listen:

> 'Save us, save us,' they seem to say,
> 'Let the god not abandon us
> Who have come so far in darkness and in pain.
> We too had our lives to live.
> You with your light meter and relaxed itinerary,
> Let not our naive labours have been in vain!'

Such a speech holds our attention by its spare intensity, its refusal to sentimentalise its subject. In this poem, Mahon converts the whole relationship between
history and the individual into a part of speech, which it is the poet's business to
parse and make present in the world.

Silence is a necessary element in this retreat from history. The fact that
history may be understood as contaminated speech must be one source of Mahon's recurrent preoccupation with silence. So, in "Beyond Howth Head" he
refers to political jargon (especially, according to himself, that of the Vietnam
War)[5] in the following terms:

> And everywhere the ground is thick
> With the dead sparrows rhetoric
> Demands as fictive sacrifice

To prove its substance in our eyes.

Silence, then, becomes a salient gesture against a world diseased in its very capacity for honest communication. So the extravagant "destruction of all things" in "Matthew V 29-30" ends "in that silence without bound" where no offence will remain, and—in "The Antigone Riddle"—man is opposed by the silence of the natural world, where

>   the windfall waits
> In silence for his departure
> Before it drops in
> Silence to the long grass.

Likewise, the bleak speakers of "Going Home" have given up "Inventing names for things / To propitiate silence. / It is silence we hug now." And in the curiously tranquil apocalypse of "The Golden Bough," silence marks a new beginning: "There will be silence, then / A sigh of waking / as from a long dream."

The speech of these poems reaches in this regenerative silence toward some act of tactile worship, an engagement with objects for their own sake. It cannot escape notice, indeed, that, for Mahon, the withdrawal from historical circumstance stimulates an intense attachment to the world of simple objects. So "The Banished Gods" "sit out the centuries / In stone, water / And the hearts of trees." Here, close to elemental things, they dream

> Of zero-growth economics and seasonal change
>   In a world without cars, computers
>   Or chemical skies,
>   Where thought is a fondling of stones
> And wisdom a five-minute silence at moonrise.

Thought becomes simple tactility, the affectionate acknowledgement of the object-world; wisdom is silence. Here is a speech that eschews verbs almost entirely, as if for Mahon the verb itself were an act or instrument of aggression. He will not interfere with the object's simple presence; his speech embodies his desire for a fresh, untroubled beginning in a relationship with such a presence.

Silence and a new speech of continuous accommodation (antithesis of the hectoring rhetorics of historical circumstance) belong to the ideal world of Mahon's imagination. So the hermit who speaks in "The Mayo Tao," having turned from history to the natural world, "lives in a snow-lit silence," spends his days "in conversation / with stags and blackbirds," and is an expert on "the silence of crickets." He makes a fresh beginning out of this silence and its accompanying engagement with primary objects, with "frost crystals" and "stars in the mud." The reason he gives for such an attachment may also be understood as Mahon's own explanation for his commitment to the "mute phenomena" of the world: "There is," his hermit speaker claims,

> an immanence in these things
> which drives me, despite
>   my scepticism, almost
> to the point of speech.

The communal voice in "The Apotheosis of Tins" must be heard as a projection of this same commitment. These creatures too have been exiled from history:

> Deprived of use, we are safe now
>   from the historical nightmare
>   and may give our attention at last
>   to the things of the spirit.

Voice here is simply the occasion of the objects' presence: it is how this presence registers in the world, under the peaceful light of the verb "to be": "This is the terminal democracy / of hatbox and crab / of hock and Windowlene." This speech is itself an act of surrender to the comically various world of humble phenomena, animating them with that witty linguistic dexterity characteristic of all Mahon's work.

As I have said, then, the retreat from "history" pushes the poet toward a deep commitment to "object." And the speech of the poems is at once the expression of this commitment and its confirmation. Such speech celebrates presence, turning away from those "meanings" which history asks the poet to espouse. His affection for the phenomenological world makes itself felt in an almost neutral lyricism of naming. Making no harsh demands of us, his speech claims our attention by the simple luminosity of that which it names. Such a love for the object grows more intense as the surrounding circumstantial life grows bleaker. In "Consolations of Philosophy" and in "An Image from Beckett," it is the extremity of death itself which gives the loved particular sheen to objects. In the perspective provided by the grave, ordinary objects shine with a startling vividness. The subdued voice that utters them allows them an unmeditated presence in our sight:

> Oh, then a few will remember with delight
> The dust gyrating in a shaft of light;
> The integrity of pebbles; a sheep's skull
> Grinning its patience on a wintry sill.

Love in such a context is unsentimentally direct, enlivened by the unobtrusive arrangements of rhyme, unhesitating in its simple indicative speech. Here, as in the following lines from "An Image from Beckett," warmth and exactitude purify to toughness this lyrical nostalgia: identity is a tone of voice:

> In that instant
> There was a sea, far off,
> As bright as lettuce,

> A northern landscape
> And a huddle
> Of houses along the shore.
>
> Also, I think, a white
> Flicker of gulls
> And washing hung to dry.

This voice expends itself in the act of naming ("Naming these things is the love-act and its pledge," as Kavanagh says);[6] the speaker is there only in the delicate pressure exerted by that qualifying "I think." Emotion is a quality of cadence, a tone, the way the objects press into the world as words, impress themselves upon the air. On this illuminated border between life and death, speech is a careful negotiation between hopelessness and belief, a belief—even when the worst is admitted—in some residual abiding value:

> It was good while it lasted,
> And if it only lasted
> The biblical span
>
> Required to drop six feet
> Through a glitter of wintry light,
> There is no one to blame.

Calm, plainspoken, unobtrusively eloquent: it is truly in the poet's speech we find the affectionate stoicism the poem, with infinite tact, urges upon our attention.

That vivid existence of objects which Mahon opposes to the conventional values of history is in itself the dramatised subject of "Lives." As elsewhere, the object is granted a voice to recount its various incarnations. The "I" of the poem is the metamorphic essence of "object," its speech the persistent current of being that animates its lives:

> First time out
> I was a torc of gold
> And wept tears of the sun.
>
> That was fun
> But they buried me
> In the earth two thousand years
>
> Till a labourer
> Turned me up with a pick
> In eighteen fifty-four

And sold me
For tea and sugar
In Newmarket-on-Fergus.

Buoyantly independent of history (even while immersed in it), the life of this object comes to us as pliable speech—colloquial, well-mannered, with its own excitement and its own melancholy. The concrete simplicity of speech itself becomes an analogue for the presence of the object, and this conjunction achieves an authentic release from the anxiety of historical circumstance, even from geographical fixity: "I was a stone in Tibet, / A tongue of bark / At the heart of Africa." Speech here is not so much about the object as it is the object's actual mode of being. This may be seen in an even more radical way in "Deaths," where the very breath of the poem is composed of the objects desperately named:

Who died nails, key-rings,
Sword hilts and lunulae,
Rose hash, bog-paper
And deciduous forests,
Died again these things,

Rose kites, wolves,
Piranha fish . . .

Commitment to the object, it seems, is a commitment to a certain sort of speech, a speech that in its intense accommodation of the world of objects enacts a gesture against historical circumstance that would simply use, abuse, or cast out the object. Imaginative existence-as-speech, that is, enables Mahon to move beyond his struggle with history toward a condition where the object is its own justification. His poetic speech is simply, then, an acknowledgement of this discovery, his way of endorsing that which he takes to be *authenticity of being* in the world.

By getting rid of even the last vestiges of a human voice, some of the poems in the final section of *Poems 1962-1978* try to achieve an even closer association between word and object. Speech in a poem like "Light Music," for example, is almost transparent, surrendering its identity to the simple acknowledged presence of the object:

A stone at the roadside
watches snow fall
on the silent gate-lodge.

At their best, the brief poems of "Light Music" have a sort of luminous neutrality, verless inhabitants of space rather than time, objects of the eye rather than voice: "Gulls in a rain-dark cornfield / crows on a sunlit sea." Mahon has described this language as a deliberate choice, a sort of "tabula rasa on which careful plain words might be placed."[7] Such plainness informs "Autobiographies," "The Return" ("And often thought if I lived / Long enough in this house / I would turn into a tree"), and "The Attic":

> At work in your attic
>   Up here under the roof—
> Listen, can you hear me
>   Turning over a new leaf?

Speech here starts again from the very centre of the self, as an appeal for a listener. Such speech seems to be the agent of a newly created self, as if the poems represented a fresh phase of Mahon's experience of the world: beyond the struggle with history and his discovery of the object lies the struggle with and discovery or rediscovery of the self. The speech of these poems is *self*-centred in a painfully unmeditated way. Here Mahon stands outside the complexities and civil strategies of the earlier work, simply exposing the self in a speech that neither affects nor allows itself any protection:

> I lie here in a riot of sunlight
> watching the day break and the clouds flying.
> Everything is going to be all right.
>   ("Everything is Going to Be All Right")

In this later work, poems dealing with his married life in Surrey are, again, suggestive of someone starting over, leaving behind some of that debonair wit and verbal elasticity which marked the earlier work. Although this retreat into Surrey (from London) realises in fact some of the ideals posed fictionally in earlier poems, the poet's condition, curiously enough, is that of one looking for speech, trying to establish conversation (as in "Dry Hill"). In "The Return" there is a courageous plainness, agent of a confessional instinct that realises the dangers inherent in its own impulses:

> I have watched girls walking
> And children playing under
> Lilac and rhododendron,
> And me flicking my ash
> Into the rose bushes
> As if I owned the place.

Inside this speech I hear the poet's own discovery of *himself* beyond the violent circle of history. The tone suggests a fresh start, a beginning which permits his re-engagement with the world and, through a renewed speech, an affirmation of older values. So, even in a context of impossible violence (beyond Surrey and back in Northern Ireland), speech can be a commitment to the immanent loveliness of the world. "The Chinese Restaurant in Portrush," for example, offers an image of peace in spite of the vulgar and violent actualities of the North. Its straightforward speech embodies the reconciled consciousness of one who has learned to locate what can be loved *inside* the actual, the way immanent beauty resides inside ordinary objects. His speech here is one of celebration, of alertness to the actual, of honest elegy, and of the acceptance of all these as elements in a single consciousness of the world:

> While I sit with my paper and prawn chow-mein
> Under a framed photograph of Hong Kong
> The proprietor of the Chinese restaurant
> Stands at the door as if the world were young
> Watching the first yacht hoist a sail—
> An ideogram on sea-cloud—and the light
> Of heaven upon the mountains of Donegal;
> And whistles a little tune, dreaming of home.

In these last poems of the collection, Mahon shows us an identity revising itself toward a fresh alignment with the world, and registering this transformation in a speech of experimental plainness. Speech itself, that is, as it has been throughout the volume, is both identity and philosophical disposition; a total mode of being in the world. It is at once the means of carrying the struggle with history to a reasonable conclusion, and it is itself the redemption from that engagement.

What I have called a single consciousness of the world is what informs many of the poems in Mahon's most recent collection, *Courtyards in Delft* (1981). The struggle with history can still be a present concern, but as an object of meditation now, in a speech calmed by this condition, and not as a dramatic urgency prodding the poet's own psyche into action. So, in "Rathlin Island" the poet repeats a phrase of "The Last of the Fire Kings," but as an observer, as someone for whom this struggle is over: "Bombs doze in the housing estates / But here they are through with history." The island is a silence "slowly broken / By the shearwater, by the sporadic / Conversation of crickets." As in other poems, this natural silence and natural speech (that "conversation"), this no-man's-land beyond the violent borders of history and its "unspeakable violence," is imagined as "the infancy of the race." What such a meditative posture and answerable style convey, however, is a sense of the poet's present acceptance of things as they are, a natural outcome of his almost programmatic commitment to the phenomenological presence of ordinary objects in the ordinary world. In its fluent, unruffled mingling of plain and lyrical elements, one shining inside the other, as it were, the speech embodying such acceptance perfectly realises the vision that recognises, in spite of all circumstantial opposition, the immanent, desirable beauty of the world. A renewed, unabashed commitment to rhyme and stanza pattern gives further buoyancy to such speech. Awareness is all, and it can light up even the grimly circumstantial shades of a "Derry Morning":

Here it began, and here at least
It fades into the finite past
Or seems to; clattering shadows whop
Mechanically over pub and shop.
A strangely pastoral silence rules
The shining roofs and murmuring schools;
For this is how the centuries work—
Two steps forward, one step back.

In its supple range, speech here seems released into self-possession, beyond the claims of any external commitment except to the minutiae of the speaker's own enlightened awareness of the world. In such speech I detect the actuality of that new beginning which so many of the earlier poems had made a speculative possibility. Here—tutored by the plainness of those poems in the last part of *Poems*—is a tougher, more experienced version of that civil elegance informing the earlier work. Here is a strengthening of the capacity for speech as the enabling means of poetic communication between the speaker and those who choose to listen. The accepting energy of such speech appears in the epigraph to "North Wind," from Nadine Gordimer's *The Late Bourgeois World*: "'If I had gone to live elsewhere in the world, I should never have known that this particular morning . . . continues, will always continue, to exist.'" The poem itself finds in plain speech the beauty of things, even inside a context of disaster:

Yet there are mornings when,
Even in midwinter, sunlight
Flares, and a rare stillness
Lies upon roof and garden,
Each object eldritch-bright,
The sea scarred but at peace.

With its quiet reasonableness, its fastidious care to pick the right word, its assertive modesty, such speech seems the perfect agent of the kind of complex reconciliation to be found here.

The title poem of this volume, a poem in praise of a painting by Pieter de Hooch, might stand as a summary and model of this condition. The qualities Mahon chooses to admire in the painter tell us of what he values in his own work: "Oblique light on the trite, on brick and tile—Immaculate masonry . . . scrubbed yards, modest but adequate . . . the trim composure of those trees." Speech here is the agent of meditation, both on the things of the world and on the art that best construes them. It is a speech that resists the verb and embraces the adjective and noun—the locations of being, presence. Here, in Mahon's precise utterance itself, is "the chaste / Precision of the thing and the thing made," where "Nothing is random, nothing goes to waste." By admitting that such a vision is exclusive of the shadier complexities of experience, the speaker manages to make his own meditation an inclusive act. For he knows that "This is life too, and the cracked / Outhouse door a verifiable fact." Spare, exact, lyrical, engaging, this speech becomes a capacious version of the world. As such, it is capable of including the self—along with a consideration of the relationship between self and history that provides a source for the struggle with historical circumstance marking the earlier poems. In addition, it is a celebratory assertion of the immanent loveliness in the everyday objects of the world. Possessed of that "elegiac clarity" that Huizinga attributed to Dutch painting, the speech perfectly echoes the poet's way of being inside his whole existence:

> I lived there as a boy and know the coal
> Glittering in its shed, late-afternoon
> Lambency informing the deal table,
> The ceiling cradled in a radiant spoon.
> I must be lying low in a room there,
> A strange child with a taste for verse,
> While my hard-nosed companions dream of war
> On a parched veldt and fields of rain-swept gorse.

Verse and speech here become affirmative instincts counterpointing the dream of war impelling those hard-nosed companion/ancestors who will—directly or indirectly—colonise South Africa and Northern Ireland. What's notable, however, is the way the stanza allows the lyrical and historical impulses this moment of cohabitation: the speech of the whole thing becomes a species of understanding.

Finally, in "Table Talk," Mahon allows his commitment to the "mute phenomena" of the world be itself the object of scrutiny and comment. His own work-table speaks to him, turning him into a listener (as in "Disused Shed"), a condition implicit in a commitment such as his. Direct speech is the mode he chooses for this deliberate reflection upon his work and his progress in it. The object posits its identity in a voice of its own, a speech of its own. The poet is someone who is spoken to. Such a condition seems infinitely satisfying to an imagination which has constantly discovered and renewed itself and its own covenant with the world as a style of speech, speech as being and speech as value. The following quotation is, I believe, a fitting illustration and confirmation of what I've been saying about Mahon's work in the course of this essay. "And yet I love you," says the table, "even in your ignorance,"

> Perhaps because at last you are making sense—
> Talking to me, not through me, recognizing
> That it is I alone who let you sing
> Wood music. Hitherto shadowy and dumb,
> I speak to you now as your indispensable medium.

To grasp Mahon's work as speech is a necessary first step toward its proper understanding and appreciation. For while so much of its content deals with a withdrawal from history—especially from that complex variety of it tragically indigenous to the North of Ireland—the form of the poetry, in its acute urge to make and sustain civil communication, is a radically political statement. Both in form and content, moreover, his commitment keeps us in touch with what truly matters: the importance of the object in its own unique life, and the desire to speak to one another in tones that are those of simple exchange, not confrontation. I hear such speech as one of the most profound responses it is possible to make to the embattled conditions of border living, where, whatever idiom you choose, you have defined yourself as someone's enemy. (A context in which it's almost imperative to accept the exhortation Seamus Heaney uses as an ironic title: "Whatever you say, say nothing.") I receive Mahon's poetry, his poetic speech, as a persistent (even if unconscious) attempt to negotiate his own way through these impossible and unspeakable conditions, and by so doing to show us how we might move beyond them. His poetry is a constant reminder that civility is still possible, that the world awaits our attention and speaks to us in its own way, that "vodka and talking / Are ceremonies," that facts, and a speech that adequately makes them a part of our world, have their own redemptive possibility. These poems, and those acts of speech that they comprise, are grounds for a condition that is one of Mahon's most definitive characteristics—a sort of battered optimism that finds one of its more moving expressions in "The Sea in Winter" (dedicated to Desmond O'Grady), in imagining

> One day, the day each one conceives—
> The day the Dying Gaul revives,
> The day the girl among the trees
> Strides through our wrecked technologies,
> The stones speak out, the rainbow ends,
> The wine goes round among the friends,
> The lost are found, the parted lovers
> Lie at peace beneath the covers.

Mahon's dispatches from the embattled regions where he's been, however, are no facile reassurances that all is well with the world. It is, he says in "Girls on the Bridge," "an insane / and monstrous age, . . . / And we have come / Despite ourselves, to no / True notion of our proper work." This is a world where, as his two verse-letters especially show (their very existence formally emblematic of his will for immediate communication, communion), a world where the individual is perpetually at risk. And yet, in spite of all this, a true buoyancy of spirit remains possible, its telling sign the undefeated urge to speak and the truly civil presence this speech realises in the world. In his wish to speak to us, and sometimes for us (the authority of his use of the first person plural is notable), he manages in his work to embody a kind of optimism validated by the authentic desperation of its circumstances and the unflinching honesty with which he confronts them. Without sentimentality, his poems make that offering of the self that is true speech, that enter into genuine relationship with an object (which lives in his way of speaking about it, out of it) and with an audience of fellow-creatures who become, in their listening, a community. He brings us in every sense "to the point of speech," and we should have no choice but to hear him out.

1982

NOTES

[1] Published by Oxford in 1979, it contains Mahon's three earlier Oxford volumes—*Night Crossing* (1968), *Lives* (1972), and *The Snow Party* (1975)—as well as more recent work. My references and quotations will all be to and from the collected volume. Such revisions as appear there, and they are numerous and various enough, are not my concern in the present essay. See Blake Morrison's review of *Poems 1962-1978* in *TLS*, February 15, 1980, 168, for a brisk treatment of the range and nature of these revisions. [Since the publication of *Poems 1962-1978*, of course, Mahon has published a number of collections, chief among them being the *Selected Poems* (1991) and *The Hudson Letter* (1995) and *The Yellow Book* (1997). Particularly in his last, in which he has allowed the more Juvenalian side of himself free rein, he has made some innovative swerves away from the lyrical road on which most of his work has traveled. He has not lost, however, either the plangency or the panoptic ability informing that lyrical mode.]

[2] See the review of *The Snow Party* by Michael Berryhill, in *Éire-Ireland* 12, 1 (1976), 144-52, and Brian Donnelly's "From Nineveh to the Harbour Bar," *Ploughshares*, 6, 1 (1981) 131-37.

[3] Exile: he is from Belfast and has lived in Dublin, Paris, Toronto, Cambridge (Massachusetts), London, Surrey, Coleraine, and at present, in London again. [Since the time of writing he has lived for a period in New York, in Rome, and is now domiciled once more in Dublin.]

[4] In *Choice*, Desmond Egan and Michael Hartnett, eds. (Dublin: Goldsmith Press, 1979) 80. If one were to do a study of Mahon's influences, the names of Joyce and Beckett, as well as that of Andrew Marvell, would have to be mentioned, all of whom have had a share, I would say, in tutoring his own encounter with history.

[5] In one of our conversations.

[6] "The Hospital," in *Collected Poems* (London: Martin Brian & O'Keefe, 1964).

[7] In a letter to me.

Opening the Field:
Michael Longley's *Gorse Fires*

In the noisy competitive jostle of contemporary Irish poetry, Michael Longley's place seems quietly assured, unquestionable. *Poems 1963-1983* secured a reputation that had grown from book to book—from the precocious craft of *No Continuing City* (1969) through the increasingly mature work of *An Exploded View* (1973) and *Man Lying on a Wall* (1976) to the more dense, demanding, troubled poems of what I'd regard as his single most substantial volume, *The Echo Gate* (1979). Open any of these books at random and you'll hear the unmistakable sound of a Longley poem, those impeccable verbal manners that make him one of our truly distinct and distinguished contemporary voices:

> Birds, such heavenly bric-a-brac
> Without their guts, without their fears,
> Despite the vital powers they lack
> Have here maintained their proper cloth,
> Have held their equilibrium
> So perfectly, so many years,
> Shed nothing but momentum,
> Their only weather dust and moth.
> ("The Ornithological Section")

> Also a bus-conductor's uniform—
> He collapsed beside his carpet-slippers
> Without a murmur, shot through the head
> By a shivering boy who wandered in
> Before they could turn the television down
> Or tidy away the supper dishes.
> To the children, to a bewildered wife,
> I think "Sorry Missus" was what he said.
> ("Rounds")

> It was right to hesitate before
> I punctured the skin, made incisions
> And broached with my reluctant fingers
> The chill of its intestines, because
>
> Surviving there, lodged in its tract,

Nudging the bruise of its orifice
Was the last egg. I delivered it
Like clean bone, a seamless cranium.
                                    ("The Goose")

I picture his hand when I stroke the dog,
His legs if I knock the kettle from the hearth.
It's his peculiar way of putting this
That fills in the spaces of Tullabaun.
The dregs stewed in the teapot remind me.
And wind creaming rainwater off the butt.
                        (*Brothers*, "Mayo Monologues")

My deep pleasure in these quotations—as well as in dozens like them—derives
especially from the way the language embodies an insistent and instinctive civility of address, a reflective decency of expression, a habit of articulate concern
that unites emotion and intelligence in an idiom of awareness directed with
equal intensity out at the world and in at the self. In their quiet good manners,
all of these lines testify to a belief in the efficacy of a certain modest eloquence,
in the power of language to register accurately (and thereby make more understandable, maybe even more tolerable) different aspects—natural, political,
erotic, social—of the world. Longley's way with language, that is, is at its best
the agent of authentic moral quest and insight, constitutes in itself a moral way
of being in the world.

In getting to such a position of authority, Longley had to outgrow some of
his own early gifted facility, to leave behind the blandishments of certain elements that tempted him into showy metaphorical performances of exquisite but
often insubstantial finesse. A stanza from "No Continuing City" might serve as
an example; the subject is ex-girlfriends, "Girls who linger still in photostat":

From today new hoardings crowd my eyes,
Pasted over my ancient histories
Which (I must be cruel to be kind)
Only gale or cloudburst now discover,
Rippling the billboard of my mind—
Oh, there my lovers,
There my dead no longer advertise.

In studied verbal gestures such as these, genuine emotion is embalmed: the performance in itself is what invites our attention and approval. Witty as they can
be, these methods and habits of lyrical expression offer a language that is in
excess of its occasions. It is part of Longley's growth as a poet that he manages
to bring his language and its occasions into a beautifully modulated equilibrium,
the kind of delicate but firm balance apparent in these luminous lines from
"Swans Mating":

This was a marriage and a baptism,
A holding of breath, nearly a drowning,
Wings spread wide for balance where he trod,
Her feathers full of water and her neck
Under the water like a bar of light.

Here an eloquent control of syntax, rhythmic variety inside syllabic uniformity, simplicity of diction and image, a tone of impeccable discretion and a water-colourist's clarity of attention to detail, all weave themselves into a style at once sophisticated and in touch with wonder, as the language itself reconciles wild and civilised dimensions. Right through *Poems 1963-1983* the best work maintains such brave yet buoyant poise, adding up to an achieved poetry of reconciliation—letting us see in manner as well as in matter that the difficult issues of the private and public world (from sexual love to political murder) may be written of (and out of) in language that accommodates passion and intelligence, in accents that shun extremities and inhabit with richly conservative grace the middle way.

Given his achievement, fluency and stature, Longley's virtual silence as a poet between 1979, when *The Echo Gate* appeared, and earlier this year [1991] when *Gorse Fires* was published, invites some attention and comment. (The "New Poems" section in *Poems 1963-1983* is a break in the silence but does not constitute a new volume.) Lodged as it has to be in a web of psyche and circumstance, a phenomenon like this will resist any certain interpretation or understanding (think of the long silence of Austin Clarke). The work itself, however, may offer some clues. While *No Continuing City* begins with "Epithalamion" and ends with "Birthmarks," the next three books reveal a striking preponderance of images of death. "The dying fall, the death spasm, / last words and catechism" are the first words of *An Exploded View*, which ends with "Ankle-bone, knuckle / In the ship of death." *Man Lying on a Wall* opens with "Check-up" and ends in "Last Rites," while *The Echo Gate* starts with "Obsequies" and concludes in a remarkable image of inverted birth, the speaker of "Codicils," who is "the sole survivor /—Without location or protocol—/ Of a tribe which let the fire go out" and who tries (unsuccessfully) to explain "Why I am huddled up in mourning / And, like a baby, sucking my thumb."

Within these books, too, in spite of their buoyant performative skills and civilised virtues, a great many poems seem preoccupied with death and immobility, infections which taint the whole available world. The speaker of "Alibis," for example, imagines himself as someone who had "folded my life like a cheque-book," and in "Options" the speaker says, "I might have cut off my head / In so many words," the suicidal image implicating his style itself. In later poems, both erotic love and love of nature are located perilously close to a world governed by death. Thus the poet can speak of a mountain as "raven's territory, skulls, bones," or of "the slow descent of the scrotum towards death," of the fact that "to reach her I must circle / This burial mound." Such a vision can make "a hospital of the landscape" or see love-making as how "We grind the ears of corn to death between our bones," or as an image of frightening inversion and terminus: "We kiss forever and I feel like the ghost of a child / Visiting the mother who long ago aborted him" ("Dead Men's Fingers").

Although these desperate straits are negotiated with characteristic dignity and stylistic verve, without resort to hectic emotionalism or self-pity, one impression a reader could be left with at the close of *Poems 1963-1983* is of a poet acutely conscious of being in a cul-de-sac, turning and turning at dead ends where even nests (in "Light behind the Rain") become graves and the body itself is a "wake-house." As the speaker of "The Echo Gate" says,

> I stand between the pillars of the gate,
> A skull between two ears that reconstructs
> Broken voices, broken stones, history . . .

Silence seems an understandable enough response to such a sense of the world and of the self, such an awareness of a style that could no longer be an agent of liberation or enlightenment. Now, with the publication of *Gorse Fires*, the silence has been decisively broken.

The title of the volume is itself a symbolic action. Brilliant and encumbering, the gorse is burnt off in spring to open a field and render the land more usable. Everything about the brilliant, brief title poem suggests renewal, a starting over: "Cattle out of their byres are dungy still, lambs / Have stepped from last year as from an enclosure / . . . I am travelling from one April to another." The image of destruction, of salutary purgation, is balanced by one of regrowth and new beginnings: "Gorse fires are smoking, but primroses burn / And celandine and white may and gorse flowers." A dead end has become a rite of passage, a process of initiation.

Whatever its cause, this sense of renewal is to be found first in style, in the most radical stylistic shift Longley has so far made. Through the earlier work there always ran a tense lyrical nerve that heightened every expression. Such heightening is a Longley signature:

> But even in our attic under the skylight
> We make love on a bleach green, the whole meadow
> Draped with material turning white in the sun
> As though snow reluctant to melt were our attire.
>   ("The Linen Industry")

I admire the gorgeous composure of these lines, their composed elegance, the way the image is discreetly unfolded, yet how meaning is carried decisively into the light. This same lyrical nerve—an intensifying presence that insists on the essentially written nature of the lines—also inhabits graver matter:

> There can be no songs for dead children
> Near the crazy circle of explosion,
> The splintering tangent of the ricochet,

> No songs for the children who have become
> My unrestricted tenants, fingerprints
> Everywhere, teethmarks on this and that.
>   ("Kindertotenlieder")

In this precisely articulated sentence, it is once again the discretion of its written manners that impress and move me—the way it accumulates meaning, its ritual *gravitas* of repetition and movement. The sentence has Longley's characteristically controlled demeanor, gently circling and clicking into place. The extension of a metaphor (circle, tangent; unrestricted tenants) mixes intelligence and feeling to create an effect at once loving and calculated, striking an equilibrium that seemed in those earlier collections to be the natural expression of their author's sensibility, a sensibility that depended on such carefully managed written dispositions of the world in order to make acceptable sense of it. Style, in such terms, became its own consolation. If there was a risk in such strategic manners it was, as I've said earlier, that they could degenerate into mannerism, into rhetorical fluency and wit at the expense of some more substantive possibilities.

In contrast to this heightened and heightening lyrical nerve, the poems of *Gorse Fires* for the most part seem to me to be marked by a musical plainness that derives not from the careful manners of a consciously written style but from the looser (and, it might be said, in the best sense, "prosier") behaviour of a spoken mode. The best poems in this volume are a style of speech: they *sound* very different from the earlier work. Listen, for example, to the opening lines of "Between Hovers":

> And not even when we ran over the badger
> Did he tell me he had cancer, Joe O'Toole
> Who was psychic about carburetor and clutch
> And knew a folk cure for the starter-engine.

The very intimacy of the communication, its relaxed manner, pushes against the lyrical grain, though without losing its definite rhythmic momentum, or its wit, or its affection.

While this intensely plainspoken music has an enabling ancestor in the "Mayo Monologues" from *The Echo Gate*, there are important differences. In the "Monologues" the spoken style was a species of mimicry, another kind of (character-creating) performance, a script. In *Gorse Fires*, however, it is the poet himself who possesses this style: it embodies his own fresh way of receiving the world. In many respects, indeed, I think it reflects some fresh judgements he's made about the nature of the poetic performance. The spoken, colloquial manners of these poems cut against the grain of the sort of lyrical performance that marked the earlier work. The performative element is subdued here, as if the facts of the matter plainly presented were performance enough. In technical terms, this new music of the relaxed speaking voice is marked by simpler diction and a rhythmically looser, longer line. Open *Poems 1963-1983* anywhere and you're likely to find a poem with ten syllables or less per line. (Interesting exceptions are the early "Alibis," or the lovely version of Tibullus's "Peace"—the response to the classical verse-line has to be important—or a few later pieces like "Martinmas" or "Dead Men's Fingers," which begin to break up the earlier, more conventional lyrical music.) In *Gorse Fires*, on the other hand, most of the poems have a palpably longer line of twelve or more syllables. The contrast in effect is immediately audible if you compare the following two passages:

> I pull up over us old clothes, remnants,
> Stitching together shirts and nightshirts
>
> Into such a dazzle as will burn away
> Newspapers, letters, previous templates,
>
> The hearth too, a red patch at the centre
> That scorches the walls and our low ceiling.
>
>   ("Patchwork")
>
> The ghosts of the aunt and uncles I never knew
> Put in an appearance when I meet my cousin.
> Charlie, big in the Union, straightens his plus-fours.
> Hugh is curing home-grown tobacco in the garage
> While my grandparents lie upstairs, out of sorts.
>
>   ("In a Missisauga Garden")

The length of line in the second piece, and its relaxation (as if breathing in time to the ordinary unfolding of an action and the account of that action) achieve effects entirely different from the denser, more deliberately controlled breath of the earlier quotation. As far as verse is concerned, that is, it might be said that in *Gorse Fires* Longley breathes more easily.

Another aspect of the book that suggests a fresh departure is the sense it gives of something closer to surrender to a kind of randomness of response than has marked Longley's work in the past, something less overtly calculated (as speech is usually less calculated than writing) in the individual poems, which often have the feel of small fragments of experience being brought into sharp focus for a moment, then released. Almost as counterpoint, the architectural organisation of the book as a whole is intensely considered and controlled: principles of opposition and amplification are everywhere at work, expanding personal themes (for example) by setting them next to larger literary versions of, roughly, the same thing. What this amounts to in terms of structure is carefully wrought collage—poems playing off one another not so much as in a "richly varied sequence" or "an extended poetic sequence" (to quote the blurb and a recent reviewer) but as in a collage: the meanings do not necessarily build on one another, amounting to some cumulatively assembled multiple meaning by the end (as happens, say, in a sequence like *Station Island*). In *Gorse Fires*, as in a collage, the parts gain their effect to some degree by their placement, the fragments fitting angularly together to form a single picture, a self-portrait of the artist starting over. Still a poetry of reconciliation, the poet has chosen new modes of reconciling the elements in his life of feeling, reading, being in a landscape: the reconciliations (often part of the actual matter of the poems themselves) are less engineered, more simply allowed as elements in a larger, essentially unspoken, narrative.

Partly responsible for this sense of the book as collage is the fact that almost half its poems are extremely short (ten lines or less): Among these are poems like "Washing":

> All the washing on the line adds up to me alone.
> When the cows go home and the golden plover calls
> I bring it in, but leave pegged out at intervals
> Dooaghtry Lake and David's Lake and Corragaun,
> Gaps in the dunes, a sky-space for the lapwings
> And the invisible whiteness of your underthings.

"The Hip-Bath," is marked by its brevity:

> My body has felt like a coalminer's black body
> Folded into the hip-bath, a blink of white eyes
> And then darkness, warm water coloured by darkness
> And the hands that trickle down my dusty spine.

Delicately crafted pieces such as these are all condensed *aperçus*, responding either to the world outside or inside the poet. Elegant, exact, technically deft (the subtle rhymes of the first hovering at the edge of audibility, the assonantal patterns of the second as sure as the harmonies an accomplished pianist makes, fingering chords). Each one of these short poems holds up to the light something that seems stumbled on almost by accident. In the earlier work, short pieces (or poems made up of separate short segments) such as "Thaw" or "Botany" or "The Corner of the Eye" or "Carrigskeewaun" might be seen as predecessors. But where the earlier work tends toward the condition of epigram anchored in external observation (e.g., "Snow curls into the coalhouse, flecks the coal. / We burn the snow as well in bad weather / As though to spring-clean that darkening hole. / The thaw's a blackbird with one white feather"), the short poems in *Gorse Fires* seem centered in the self, often radiating out into the world and then returning to the self. They seem, I would say, to compose more of a mental journey. (Even where the self is absent—as in pieces like "Eva Braun" and "Geisha"—the sense of mental journey is still strong.) Where the earlier pieces are epigrams and sketches, that is, the poet's notebook has here been used to record *penseés*. The self has been accommodated as part of the world, not as its definer. The willingness creatively to inhabit fragments implies the notebook quality of what is going on here, and suggests someone keeping pace with his life rather than simply using it as look-out, as a blind.

This new relationship with the fragmentary seems to me to be one of the surest diagnostic marks of the collection. For even the most notable among the longer poems—those remarkable renderings of certain episodes in the *Odyssey*—are also in essence fragments, each discrete event implicitly resonating with an element in Longley's own life. The brief sequence, "Ghetto," is also composed of fragments (a miniature collage within the larger collage of the whole book), while other larger pieces such as "In a Mississauga Garden," "An Amish Rug," or "The Ice-Cream-Man" touch in a glancing but effective way the familial, erotic, and political realms of his experience. By placing poems in significant relationship to one another (a poem about the poet's mother, for example, alongside one about Odysseus's mother, and the same with poems about the fathers), he composes an oblique collage self-portrait that is stronger, more vivid, than any of those implicitly composed by the earlier volumes, a self-portrait in which the essential *pietas* of Longley's response to the various areas of his world is most clearly and satisfyingly seen for the intense emotional, intellectual, and moral position that it is.

It is not only as an act of vivid self-portraiture, but also as an enterprise in poetic self-renewal and rebirth, that *Gorse Fires*, lays powerful claims on our attention. While it may not be as strong or compelling a volume as *The Echo Gate* (which seems to me more various, substantial and—because of its creative unease, its unresolved tensions of feeling—more rawly interesting), it does contain individual triumphs of imagination and expression unmatched elsewhere in Longley's work. Among these for me are the astonishing images that fill out "The Butchers" (e.g., the women "like long-winged thrushes / Or doves trapped in a mist-net across a thicket where they roost, / Their heads bobbing in a row, their feet twitching but not for long"); or the grave but buoyant, long-lined syntactic majesty of that poem and others drawn from the *Odyssey*; or the poignant litanies of "Trade Winds" and "The Ice-Cream-Man" (their ritual utterance of names expressing helplessness in the face of violence and death). And although it may not be as stylistically charged to deal with the horror of its subject as is the nervous, aptly jagged and dislocated style of Celan, I've come to appreciate "Ghetto" [set in Terezin] as a miniature marvel of tenderness and expressive care, its dry-voiced plain speech containing its own ache of helpless grief:

> There will be performances in the waiting room, and time
> To jump over a skipping rope, and time to adjust
> As though for a dancing class the ribbons in your hair.
> This string quartet is the most natural thing in the world.

Among other things indelibly printed on my memory I would also mention the understated brilliance of "Couchette," at once beautifully detailed and witty and grave ("With my wife, son, daughter in layers up the walls/ This room on wheels has become the family vault"), and the marvelously moving last lines of "Laertes," where all of Longley's elegies for his father come together in an image of male tenderness and grief that makes this poem one of the best he has ever written:

> Until Laertes recognised his son and, weak at the knees,
> Dizzy, flung his arms around the neck of great Odysseus
> Who drew the old man fainting to his breast and held him there
> And cradled like driftwood the bones of his dwindling father.

In the face of such rhythmic inevitability, such a spare and exact image ("driftwood"), before that amazing verb and adjective ("cradled" and "dwindling"), criticism is rendered redundant. And the volume contains enough such pleasures and illuminations to make it in itself (aside from the fact that it is a sign of a strong poet's fresh and refreshed start) something to rejoice over.

While I'm in no doubt over my admiration for this new departure of Longley's and the fine poems it has produced, I am also aware of some limitations to the collection. A number of the short emotional evocations (e.g., "The Man of Two Sorrows," "Icon," "Il Volto Santo," "Glass Flowers," "Cathedral") seem light in implication or a bit strained; the pleasant occasional poem, "Font," ends weakly; and the addition of the explicitly biographical part II to "Eurycleia" diminishes, for me at least, that poem. In themselves, the *Odyssey* pieces are splendid things, and suggest that a Longley version of the whole poem could be a revelation. They are masterful in their sympathetic, modestly magniloquent entrance into the larger literary experience and the ways the poet mines out of this some implicit connections with his own life. However, the "connection with the ambiguities of life in Northern Ireland" mentioned in the blurb (as if to extend the import of the poems, to make them more than they are) seems arbitrary and unnecessary. Even "The Butchers" seems to me to be related as much to the cleansing that Longley's own imagination has to perform in order to write *Gorse Fires*, than to the butchery in the North. While the sheer appalling presence and consequence of violence are strikingly rendered, and while this, by understandable association, could connect with the horrors in the North, the moral dimensions of each case seem too remote from one another for easy or persuasive analogy. In these *Odyssey* poems Longley's imagination has been strong enough to encounter one of the greatest works of literature and— enabled by that source and his own rich resources of language and feeling—to draw poems of his own out of the encounter, poems that connect with his own experience in revealing ways and then live their own life in their own language. That is achievement enough, and nothing else should be required of them (which is not to say that analogies may not be drawn between Homeric incidents and aspects of life in the Northerrn context: my point is simply that in these pieces that analogy sometimes seems more strained than efficacious).

Reservations such as those I've mentioned could only be made in the context of approval and admiration for a strong poet working at his best—which is what I think Longley is, and is doing, in *Gorse Fires*. The volume is a turning-point and milestone in a distinguished career, and one of the most exciting things about it is that it's impossible to say what direction it forecasts for the future. Having cleared his field by fire, the poet has granted himself a fresh, exhilarating freedom. In the opening poem of the book he declares his condition with a lucidity of expression characteristic of the volume as a whole:

> I am making do with what has been left me,
> The saltier leaves of samphire for my salad.
> At midnight the moon goes, then the Pleiades,
> A sparkle of sand grains on my wellingtons.
>
> ("Sea Shanty")

What's been left him is a world that reaches from his wellingtons to the Pleiades; from Laertes' "duncher" (a flat cap, in Belfast dialect) to the "bog-meadow full of bog-asphodels" where Hermes leads the souls of the dead; from family life to the large designs of a literary masterpiece; from the murder of a neighbor to the wildflowers of the burren. It is a world, as it were, without end, an open world in which this renewed, reconciling, vital imagination can—happily for us—continue to live and flourish.

1991

Real Things:
The Work of Eiléan Ní Chuilleanáin

. . . grace, the instant overloaded . . .

I've been an admirer of Eiléan Ní Chuilleanáin's poetry ever since a poem of hers won an *Irish Times* prize in 1966. It's the quiet confidence of her voice, its modesty, its convinced seriousness and toughness, its thoughtful discretion and its refusal of easy options that I especially like, as well as the kind of hard but at the same time (and in every sense) careful light in which she bathes her scenes. Her work has a fine intellectual clarity, but also a lucidity of image and narrative (or narrative fragment) which lends a lyrical finesse to whatever she says. In volume after slim volume (she is the most exacting pruner of her own work) she has accumulated a body of exquisite and substantial work that places her among the most accomplished poets now writing in, or out of, Ireland.[1]

Her work is also difficult. It is often hard to say what a poem "means." The world she creates in a poem has an enigmatic centre: one sees the facts clearly enough, but the purpose and point of these clearly realised facts aren't easy to pin down. She herself is aware of this difficulty, although her explanation of it seems not quite accurate. "Poetry," she says justly, "is something that demands a lot of concentration." Fair enough. She goes on then to say, "I feel that I'm writing both in an idiom and, to some extent, using references that are available to an Irish audience. And it seems to me not likely that those beyond that audience would understand it very well."[2] It seems to me, however, that many in her designated audience might also find a lot of difficulty in reading these poems. This, indeed, she is probably acknowledging when she goes on to remark, "I suppose I have been uncompromising in the sense that quite often I write difficult poetry . . . difficult in the sense of complicating to the reader." So the premise is a kind of difficulty, although for those who cherish the poems this is also what lends them their own particular flavor, makes them as compelling as they are.

Going through all of Ní Chuilleanáin's work before reading her latest volume, however, I found myself trying to account for the nature of that difficulty. I was trying, that is, to account for my state as a reader, able at the same time to be possessed by admiration and unsettled by puzzlement, to love what I was getting and yet be disturbed by the sense that I was not "getting it." One result of this attempt was a page scribbled with impressionistic reflexes to the poems, a roughly articulated series of qualities and a few random but, to me, revealing phrases culled from the poems themselves. Here, in no particular order, are the qualities, or words pointing to qualities: architecture / light; miracle / loss; objectivist / dreamer; tense form / free form; past / persist; shock / quietude; reflection / narration; history / withdrawal; voyage / cell; evocation / exposition; lucid / difficult; ground / abstraction; male / female; seeing / "seeing"; quarry / axe; patient / urgent; self-assured / unfinished; allegory / parable; analytic / holistic; acts / monuments; frame / open air; road / maze; splinter / web / honeycomb / cupboard; wilderness / well; exposition / concealment. And here are some of the quotations I jotted down beside these "qualities." They are not supposed to illuminate them in any special way; they simply struck me at the time as having some general relevance to the way the poems were working for me. "Help is at hand / Though out of reach." "The house persists." "A maze / of angels and families." "The moral of the ship is death." "The road stretches like the soul's posthumous journey." "The girl gave birth in a ruin." "Hope / And no warnings." "Grace, the instant overloaded." "The exile . . . is an unpeopled poet staring at a broken wall." "Pierced and visible." "Geometry of guilt." "Amphibious twilight." "Lost according to plan." "I watch the bones and they begin to shine." "A voice glittering in the wilderness." "A voice / Breaking loose." "Her voice, a wail of strings."

What the above paragraph offers, I guess, are subjects and titles for possible essays on the poetry of Eiléan Ní Chuilleanáin. Before leaving them to the common domain, however, I'd like to add a gloss to some of them.

Architecture / light: In so many Ní Chuilleanáin poems one of the first things to strike a reader is the presence in it of some architecturally rendered space. Since it is the opening poem in what amounts to an early selected volume (*The Second Voyage*), "The Lady's Tower" might be taken as a kind of signature piece, beginning with a strongly articulated sense of composed space:

> Hollow my high tower leans
> Back to the cliff; my thatch
> Converses with spread sky,
> Heronries. The grey wall
> Slices downward and meets
> A sliding flooded stream
> Pebble-banked, small diving
> Birds. Downstairs, my cellars plumb.

Buildings are all over the poems: houses, convents, monasteries, churches, cells, even whole cities (in *Cork*). While in formal terms these buildings suggest a commitment to clarity of organisation and expression—something that is apparent in Ní Chuilleanáin's strong, straightforward syntax—in substantive terms they can suggest the solitary life or the life of the group—the hermit or the family, whether the family is secular or ecclesiastical, condensed or expanded. The buildings can even be in ruins, but the spirit of their foundation and the presence of their architecture remains. The buildings, too, are usually meeting-places, established intersections where worlds—often the world of the spirit and the world of the body—come together. The palpable force and solid presence of architecture itself, so reassuringly there, can stand as some form of endorsement for this intersection (and therefore continuum) between these separated worlds. So architecture is sacramental, a solid outward sign of some inward truth: a monument, often literally, to an act of faith. In Ireland, too, architectural ruins and remains—both civic and sacred, political and spiritual—are a kind of stony shorthand for history itself, speaking emblems of what has happened. And so it is the presence of architecture in the poems that extends, as art, Ní Chuilleanáin's specific engagement with Ireland and her general remark that "in terms of Irish history I'm very interested in the sacred in history." Buildings of one form or another, that is, are her means of imaging in complex ways these primary preoccupations.

I have linked light with architecture. Like buildings, light is ubiquitous throughout Ní Chuilleanáin's poetry. Look at *The Second Voyage*, for example, or *The Rose-Geranium*, and you will find on almost every page some reference to an aspect of light. In formal terms I'd say this ubiquity of light has something to do with the lovely fluency of the poems, their exact and exacting clarity of line, the sense we get from Ní Chuilleanáin's language of a serious interest in communication. No matter how mysterious the poem may be, it never gives the impression of wanting to mystify us: the language, the sound patterns, the lines, the management of image, all seem powerfully directed, intently purposeful. As far as substance is concerned, the omnipresence of light—like that of architecture—suggests to me the imagination's strategy for living in two worlds at once. For while light is that which allows us to be in confident contact with the daily world, the here and now, it is also the element (as the Greeks called it, the fifth element) which keeps bringing us intimations of whatever it is that amplifies the quotidian, stretches us into other possibilities, into the possibility of "the other." Finally, light and architecture together are a coupling and a counterpoint that generate the world as we perceive it, and it is "the world as we perceive it" that might, with a little license, be described as Ní Chuilleanáin's subject.

The notion of "the world as we perceive it" leads easily to seeing / "seeing." By this double use of "seeing" I don't simply mean to imply that Ní Chuilleanáin is a "seer," although that is part of it, for her poems are constantly sliding from the physical to the spiritual realm, seeing through matter into mystery (while the manner remains very matter-of-fact). What interests me, however, and seems to stand at the source of her creative habits, is a gift she has for shifting perspective, for seeing the real, the actual, at an odd but revealing angle. Beyond her great gift for seeing the physical world in and for itself, that is, she has this gift for transformation, but a transformation that never seems to do violence to its subject. It is one quality of imagination among those most responsible, I'd say, for her becoming the kind of poet she is. Although implicit in all she does, she may from time to time allude directly to this habit. In one poem, for example, she strokes "clean wood," and "looking into the grain / Wavered and kinked like hairlines, what I see / Is the long currents of a pale ocean / Softly turning itself inside out." In another she says, "Here where I sit so still / I can see the milk in my glass is tidal," and in yet another that "Somewhere an eye sees him as a whirlpool of glass." Such moments of rapt metamorphosis are everywhere, suggestive of a marvelous instability in the world of the seen, a habit of looking that is inseparable from a sense of the flux at the very heart of things:

> I look out on darkness and walls that move away,
> I am seen, I reflect the starlight, but blinded
> I seek for depths as planets fly from the sun,
> What holds me in life is flowing from me and I flow
> Falling, out of true. ("Waters Below")

Feeling and seeing are intimately connected in this transforming nexus of apprehension, this shifty zone where things become other than themselves. In "More Islands," for example, she mentions how a child "feels the sea in the waves of her hair / And icebergs in a storm of lemonade," while "Sea-Squirrels" contains the following imperative: "Look in its red eyes: you will see / Peacocks mincing along a bridge / Fountains like snow descending." Perhaps the loveliest of all references to transformative sight and feeling appears in *The Brazen Serpent*, where, in "Fireman's Lift," we hear a delicately pitched echo of Kavanagh's "This is what love does to things" (from "The Hospital"). The poem concerns a painting of the Assumption of the Virgin and, at an oblique angle to this, the death of the poet's mother:

> This is what love sees, that angle:
> The crick in the branch loaded with fruit,
> A jaw defining itself, a shoulder yoked,
>
> The back making itself a roof
> The legs a bridge, the hands
> A crane and cradle.

What is so satisfying about all this is the way the physical world keeps getting its due: it is the lovingly recorded particularity that presses first upon our attention; only then, in a deft continuum, does transformation begin. The seeing and the "seeing," the visual and the visionary, are easy and at home together in this imagination and in the language it finds to give it body in the world.

The other connected features in which I was especially interested were narration / reflection and allegory / parable. These, too, touched on some of the more complicated ways in which Ní Chuilleanáin's poems work. A great many of the poems have a narrative spine, are a narrative or, more likely, a narrative fragment. They say, "This happened." Here are some examples: "'When all this is over,'" said the swineherd, / 'I mean to retire . . . '" "Alone I walk in a wood above Holyoke . . . " "When you pass the doorway / You are going underground . . . " "Underneath the photograph / Of the old woman at her kitchen table . . . " "I was standing beside you looking up / Through the big tree of the cupola . . . " In some sense the narrative voice, narration itself, is not unlike architecture, in that it can be a means of establishing the secure ground of the experience which is the poem's subject. It can also create difficulty, however, since it may not be given a visible or comprehensible context: it may simply be there—a story or a picture existing (for us, though presumably not for the speaker) in its own terms only. How, for example, are we to understand what exactly is going on in poems like "Ransom" (from *The Second Voyage*) or in "Chrissie" or "The Pig-boy" (from *The Magdalene Sermon*) or in "A Glass House" from *The Brazen Serpent*, or in "The Real Thing," which begins,

> The Book of Exits, miraculously copied
> Here in this convent by an angel's hand,
> Stands open on a lectern, grooved
> Like the breast of a martyred deacon.

In this quotation, for example, it is impossible to know who the speaker of the narrative might be, while "this convent"—like many narrative allusions confidently presented to us—is veiled in referential obscurity. Confronted by such conditions of ignorance, a reader simply has to hang on to what's given, and enter (with a small act of faith) the moment of mystery and exhilaration.

Having established such a strong, if puzzling, narrative as the premise of her poem, what Ní Chuilleanáin is then often inclined to do is extend the narrative into a species of reflection, which can compound what is already difficult. For it is not a question of the narrative and the reflection existing in quite separated containers. The borders between them are laid over one another, so no division is seen. Narrative and reflective voices become a compound single thing, something which absorbs us, and which we must often find enigmatic. The poem "Consolation" for example, begins with "His wife collects the rifled / Remains," but ends with the following lines, that hold a different kind of strangeness:

> She hears the words, the repeated story:
> There was no assassination, the fire in his brain
> Came only from the red of the dyed cloth.
> There was a pillared space when he was dying,
> A voice and a response. It was not a hunt and a blow.

And the beautifully moving "Fireman's Lift" moves from a fairly ordinary narrative opening, which describes two people standing in a church, to the following reflective dismantling of the narrative scaffold:

> We saw the work entire, and how the light
> Melted and faded bodies so that
> Loose feet and elbows and staring eyes
> Floated in the wide stone petticoat
> Clear and free as weeds.

> This is what love sees, that angle.

So, just as the abrupt narrative opening itself can sometimes throw a reader off balance, the relationship between narrative and reflective elements in the poems can also lead to a sense of mystery brimming with emotional suggestion (the fact that "Fireman's Lift" is also a kind of elegy for the poet's mother adds to the emotional conviction and vibration). Narratively located, physically grounded, we nonetheless find ourselves afloat in an atmosphere of enigma. And it is this sense of being at once anchored and afloat—a sense deriving both from the odd handling of narrative itself and from the peculiar way narration and reflection relate to each other—that I most appreciate in my experience of these poems. As readers, it would seem, we have to give ourselves up to the poem's voice as we would put ourselves into the hands of a guide we trusted to lead us through a strange place. (Given the gist of what I've been saying so far, it's interesting to see that one of the opening poems in the new collection is not only called "The Architectural Metaphor," but that it begins, "The guide in the flashing cap explains / The lie of the land." This last phrase, incidentally, might be conjured with in ways that could call the whole work of criticism into question, although—as is often the case with these poems, which rarely flag their ironies or subversive strategies—it is impossible to say whether this is intended or not.)

My final set of paired qualities is allegory / parable, which is not unrelated to narrative/ reflection. For, as I've just suggested, while the events, stories, or anecdotes in Ní Chuilleanáin's poems invariably possess factual clarity in themselves, they do not always possess a correspondingly easy clarity of significance. (It would, however, be wrong to see this is a fault. It is merely a resistance proper to some poetry, a feature of the poem that reveals its independence, its organic integrity, its final—like a self—inscrutability. In Ní Chuilleanáin's case, the particular nature of this resistance is also what makes her unique. For in the Irish context, at least, no one is like her. The qualities, for example, of McGuckian, Muldoon, and Carson—all three enigmatic and baffling in their own ways—are quite distinct from hers. In this respect, the contemporary poet I'd place her closest to might be Geoffrey Hill, although her supple—containing but unconstraining—forms are very different from Hill's more compact, tight-lipped formality.)

The resistance to easy understanding which we can often feel working in a Ní Chuilleanáin poem can tempt critics to read her in a fairly formulaic, allegorical way. So one recent commentator says that Ní Chuilleanáin's "poetic voice tells the audience—the Irish people—that they cannot elude their country's social conditions and political forces," and that "the shift in the thematic pattern . . . suggests that native culture maturates into an act of native acculturation." The problem with allegorical readings like this is that they tend to swerve away from the body of the actual poem into a construct of the critic's own, to the lineaments of which the particulars of the poem are bent, or—if they won't bend to the desired shape—they are conveniently ignored. As a medieval and Renaissance scholar and teacher, the poet herself is familiar with and no doubt hospitable to the strategies of allegory (particularly, I'd say, to the ranginess of the kind found in Dante and in much of Spenser, where meanings are maintained, floating, within the vivid narrative solution itself and not necessarily crystallised out as "solutions" to a narrative puzzle). But the operation of many of her poems may more usefully be seen in terms of parable than those of allegory. For while parable may be a species of the broader term "allegory," its operation is quite distinct from the usually narrow modern understanding of allegory (as a kind of underfed poor relation to symbolism). For in parable there doesn't have to be an exact equation between all the narrative elements and some given external meaning. The "historical" or "narrative" surfaces of parable contain the point within themselves, it is not easily extractable. And whereas quick visibility of meaning and explanation is what the dealer in allegory often wants, there is usually something enigmatic about parable ("any kind of enigmatical or dark saying," is how the OED defines it), something puzzling about its moral point, something that defies easy explanation. (Think of Christ's parable of the prodigal son, or that of the land-owner who paid his laborers the same wages for different work.)

The parable habit seems to be with Ní Chuilleanáin from the start, implicit in her way of looking at and expressing her world. Poems from *The Second Voyage* like "Survivors" or "The Ropesellers" or "The House Remembered," for example, have a distinct "parable" manner, as does "Celibates":

> When the farmers burned the furze away
> Where they had heedlessly lived till then
> The hermits all made for the sea-shore
> Chose each a far safe hole beneath rocks,
> Now more alone than even before.

While you might reduce this to an "allegory" for the disappearance of faith, the factual particularity seems weighted against such a one-dimensional reading, although it may contain such a meaning. Such a parable mode seems to operate, too, even when the subject is more personal, closer to some presumed biographical self of the speaker, a rendering of an experience actually remembered, as in "Quarant' Ore" from *The Magdalene Sermon*:

> At the dark early hour
> When the open door of the church
> Is pumping out light
> The sacristan is at work unfolding
> The stacked chairs, he carries them
> Out of the porch, into the glow.

This parable mode (which can sometimes remind of the later poems of Louis MacNeice, who called his Clarke Lectures "Varieties of Parable," who preferred reading Spenser to almost any other poet, and who spoke of the parable mode itself as "double-level writing") is everywhere apparent in the splendid poems of *The Brazen Serpent*, whether in the ecclesiastical evocation of "The Real Thing," the enigmatic family memory of "The Secret," the extraordinary handling of male and female in "Man Watching a Woman," or the intense condensation of personal grief in the elegiac "A Hand, A Wood":

> I am wearing your shape
> Like a shirt of flame;
> My hair is full of shadows.

And since the point about parable is that it won't allow easy translation into a summary meaning—as readers we are obliged to the body and soul of the verse, not able to choose one at the expense of the other—it seems a native and proper mode for Ní Chuilleanáin's imagination. It is the mode, I'd say, that best belongs to the kind of thing she wants to do as a poet, the kind of thing that allows her to deal most adequately with the historical, the political, the biographical, the spiritual, and the moral dimensions of experience, without slighting any of them.

As for this most recent volume, *The Brazen Serpent*—in strength of achievement it seems to me to continue the fresh trajectory she established in the poems of her last collection, *The Magdalene Sermon*. Possibly composing a deliberate diptych, both volumes show the same tightness of expression, sharpness of vision, and the same fiercely controlled moral seriousness. Both titles, too, are Biblical in reference, the most recent one alluding to the moment in The Book of Numbers when the capricious God of that text, having plagued the discontented Israelites, grants them a cure for the sickness he has visited upon them. Such doubleness and enigmatic power, I might add, is precisely the kind of matter that lends itself to parable: we have the "facts" but the exact meaning of the facts, the moral message we're to take from their recitation, is never entirely clear, unless it is simply the absolute power of the Deity to dispose of people as He wishes. If this is the case, indeed, one might see a continuity of narrative style—and purpose—between the terrible histories of the Old Testament and the milder, but no less morally demanding, stories told by Christ and recorded in the Gospels of the New Testament. The fact that the Book of Numbers concerns the wanderings of the Israelites in the wilderness may also be quite relevant to the general tone of the poems in this volume, as may the fact that just before the incident of the brazen serpent itself Moses has brought forth water out of the rock. Issues of thirst and its austere satisfactions seem never to be too far away from these poems, nor from the general workings of Ní Chuilleanáin's imagination.

The poems in *The Brazen Serpent* demonstrate a great many of Ní Chuilleanáin's virtues. The language is clean, pointed, chaste, taut, spare, but sensuously physical and instinct with feeling. While she seems to move in a deliberate narrative way, there is real speed in the management of narrative—a quiet leaping from stone to stepping-stone across a story (an image which reminds me of the zig-zagging underwater path of sticks that would bring a crannóg-dweller home). There's a muscle of strangeness underneath the apparently normal surfaces:

> The bus is late getting into my home town.
> I walk up the hill by the barracks,
> Cutting through alleyways that jump at me.
> They come bursting out of the walls
> Just a minute before I began to feel them
> Getting ready to arch and push. Here is the house.

As can be seen in these lines—with their spare account of the action, their unlikely but powerful animations, their shifting sentence length and momentum, their odd switch of tense, their abruptly simple finality—there's something tense, condensed, distilled about Ní Chuilleanáin's imagination, something at once speedy and controlled, something richly physical but which refuses to allow any waste in a poem. Many of the pieces in *The Brazen Serpent* stand among her best work, including "Fireman's Lift," "The Architectural Metaphor," "The Real Thing," "The Bee and the Rapeseed," "Following," "Woman Shoeing a Horse," "Man Watching a Woman," "The Pastoral Life," "A Hand, A Wood," and "Studying the Language." Poems like these have confidence, deeply achieved language manners, a fully imagined world. They give an extraordinary sense of the way a thoroughly physical world has edges which touch the unknown, thresholds connected with spiritual possibility. More than any other Irish poet, indeed, Ní Chuilleanáin coaxes us to feel the palpable presence of the spiritual. This happens in Heaney, too, of course, most powerfully in *Seeing Things*. But there's always in Heaney a sense of the struggle between pragmatism and mystery, and it is out of that drama that some of his best work emerges, having earned its authentic immersion in the spiritual. Ní Chuilleanáin is not engaged in the same drama: "difficult" as they are, her poems seem to live in and bear their own complicated witness to a world in which the realm of the spirit is—as it is in religious parables, although her versions stop at the borders of the transcendental—a given. This is not to offer a judgement or even an opinion about the status of "faith" or "belief" in her life. It is simply an attempt to describe something about the poems and the sense of the world they communicate.

Many of the poems in *The Brazen Serpent* are written *out of* not *about* that uncanny zone where physical facts rub shoulders with mystery. This is apparent in the remarkable "Following," in which a memory is revived and the strange reality it contains may be felt in the pressure of the language itself:

> So she follows the trail of her father's coat through the fair
> Shouldering past beasts packed solid as books,
> And the dealing men nearly as slow to give way—
> A block of a belly, a back like a mountain,
> A shifting elbow like a plumber's bend—
> When she catches a glimpse of a shirt-cuff, a handkerchief,
> Then the hard brim of his hat, skimming along,
>
> Until she is tracing light footsteps
> Across the shivering bog by starlight,
> The dead corpse risen from the wakehouse
> Gliding before her in a white habit.

For all the staggering physicality of its description, the poem delivers its almost Gothic vision in an utterly quiet, unemphatic way, making it all the more dramatic and credible, the porous boundary between worlds as unassuming as the white space between stanzas. In "Woman Shoeing a Horse," too, there is an extraordinary bringing together of the sense world and the world that reaches beyond that: "I could see by her shoulders how her breath shifted / In the burst of heat, and the wide gesture of her free arm / As she lifted the weight and clung // Around the hoof . . . / . . . But the noise I could not hear was the shock of air / Crashing into her lungs, the depth / Of the gasp as she turned with a ready hand." Plain, yet densely packed with verbal surprises, the lines push the physical and the spiritual into an odd, convincing alignment. And, characteristically, while they resist any of the conventional blandishments of the lyric, they are intensely lyrical.

In light not only of "Woman Shoeing a Horse" but of many other poems in this and earlier collections, it is important to acknowledge the degree to which Ní Chuilleanáin insists upon the feminine dimension of the world. Without dogmatism, with no particular agenda to be enforced, it is simply there—a female way of seeing and being, and a way that seems to be dissolved in the larger category of the human. Poems like *"Vierge Ouvrante,"* "Woman Shoeing a Horse," "That Summer," "Home Town," "No Loads / No Clothing / Allowed / In the Library," "Saint Margaret of Cortona," "Passing Over in Silence," "The Water Journey," "The Real Thing," and "La Corona" are all profound engagements with and entrances into female experience, while "Man Watching A Woman" is a remarkable account of relations between men and women, as striking for its understated tone as for its vivid content. She has said the dichotomy between masculine and feminine is not for her a very real dichotomy, "except that I think imaginative literature is constantly transforming and transgressing boundaries and always being interested in ways one can get a perspective which isn't entirely masculine and isn't entirely feminine." True as this may be, it's also true to say that the luminous attention of so many of these poems seems mostly focused on the experience of women, letting the *interior* truth of that experience be felt—as physically and persuasively as a young girl's experience while watching the older woman bake is captured in the following lines, lines that seem both ordinary and yet tinged with parable possibility:

> The hand squashes flour and eggs to hide the yeast
> And again it folds and wraps away
> The breathing, slackening, raw loaf
> That tried to grow and was twisted and turned back.

What comes through so much of her work is an immense, sympathetic understanding of women, especially of women in their work. Marked as much by its objectivity as by its passion, this understanding resists sentimentality in its quest for a wholeness of response, and calls to mind a remark by the feminist theorist and critic, Donna Haraway. "Feminist objectivity," says Haraway, "is about limited location and situated knowledge, not about transcendence and splitting of subject and object." Limited location and situated knowledge: it is from such a perspective that Ní Chuilleanáin's feminism might best be understood.

The Brazen Serpent contains the work of a poet in the mature fullness of her power. It is a book of unaggressively presented mysteries, a stirring mixture of the practical and the numinous, in touch with this world and its sensuous paradoxes ("the dry fragrance of tea-chests / The tins shining in ranks, the ten-pound jars / Rich with shrivelled fruit") and at the same time connected to some charge of mystery: for "Where better to lie down / And sleep, along the labelled shelves, / With the key still in your pocket?" Ní Chuilleanáin's poetic voice is an inner tongue that still lives in the same world as we do. We may not always understand circumstantially what it is saying, but we trust in the presence of that key in the sleeping pocket. In a poem called "The Real Thing" (about a supposed relic of the brazen serpent itself) occur the following lines:

> True stories wind and hang like this
> Shuddering loop wreathed on a lapis lazuli
> Frame. She says, this is the real thing.
> She veils it again and locks up.

Even from such a small example it's easy to see how, in the strict but sensuous economy of her language, Ní Chuilleanáin charges plainness with strangeness, while her fine ear for the buoyancy and weight of the line, her skill at an abrupt but joltless turn, and the businesslike way she continues a narrative lend density and speed to whatever she does. It is lines like these, both in their balanced expression and in what they say (the miraculous and the practical in daily touch with one another), that let us know beyond question that Eiléan Ní Chuilleanáin is the real thing. For almost thirty years her work has been an indispensable feature on the map of Irish poetry. Private as it is, her poetry opens up something of the nature of Irish consciousness itself. At the close of *The Brazen Serpent* (she has, incidentally, a great sense of the architecture *of a book*, how the parts—the side-chapels?—fit into the larger design of the whole), in a poem called "Studying the Language," appear these valedictory lines: "I call this my work, these decades and stations—/ Because, without these, I would be a stranger here." Without the peculiar qualities of her verse, without its profound mixture of the secular and the sacred, the contemporary and the traditional, the worldly and the ecclesiastical, the Catholic and the existential, we would all, I think it is fair to say, be more likely to be strangers here. She keeps alive, by living through in gleaming splinters of her own kind of narrative, a whole zone of our collective experience, of which her poetry is, and will be, a reliable record.

1995

NOTES

[1] This essay was intended as a review of Eiléan Ní Chuilleanáin's latest volume, *The Brazen Serpent*.

[2] *Irish Literary Supplement* (Spring 1993), Interview with Deborah MacWilliams Consalvo.

Wrestling with Hartnett

Is seo í Éire, is mise mise.
This is Ireland, I'm myself.

From the very early Sixties, when his first poems were published in the UCD magazine *St. Stephen's* (edited in 1960 by the enigmatic Kerryman, Jeremiah Nolan, and for a couple of years after that by the far from enigmatic me), Michael Hartnett has been a considerable, indispensable figure in the landscape of Irish poetry. And although very little has been written about his work in the intervening thirty years or so, it has always been in Ireland a powerfully felt, compelling presence, both for his fellow-poets and—in spite of its inherent difficulties and its complex habits of negotiation between two languages—for the ordinary reader. Now Gallery Press in Ireland and Wake Forest Press in America have brought out a *Selected & New Poems*, which should go a long way towards sharpening that amorphous, if important sense of "presence" into a spare but satisfactorily revealing portrait of the poet in his work. (John Shinnors' impressive half-mask of Hartnett's face, which stares with chilling intensity from the cover of the present volume, seems an apt emblem for what the collection represents and achieves.)

The chessboard main hall in Earlsfort Terrace. Clouds of talk and cigarette smoke any week-day morning during term time. 1961, '62, '63, '64. The poets (all male; only Eavan Boland—and she was in Trinity—seemed at the time to break that mould, although we knew of Caitlín Maude): Jerry Nolan, John Moriarty, Richard Riordan, Tommy McCann, Macdara Woods, Paul Durcan, Michael Smith, Michael Hartnett. The students of history, of literature, of economics; the talking heads; the intellectuals. A litany of names, a procession of faces. Mick Nunan, Paddy Walsh, Nora Graham, Pat Clery, Liam Hourican, Dymphna Nee, Paddy Cosgrave, Ronan Fanning, Donal Dorcey, Paul Carney, Sunniva O'Neill, Tom Garvin, Jane Hogan, Dermot Fenlon, Tony Clare, Ruth Dudley Edwards, Michael Gill, Seán Murray, Jane Hogan, Dara McCormack, Brendan Walshe, Muireann McHugh, Máire McHugh, Fionnuala Flanagan, Creda Cremin, Donal Mooney, Hugh Keegan, Martin Rogerson, David Jordan, Fennel Betson. Others: faces without names, names without faces. Student politicians like Gerry Collins and his cohorts stalking heron-eyed and three abreast down the long corridors. Smell of ink, sweat, and books in the whispering Library. Murky productions of Beckett in the Little Theatre. Readings of *Under Milk Wood* in Gai's Restaurant. Jesuit-loathing Jerry Nolan giving offense with a poem that called Christ "our Easter egg." Paddy Walsh giving even more widespread offense with an article referring to the rosary as "the pop song of Catholicism." Short stories being too sexy or too blasphemous for the printers to print them without an imprimatur (granted) from the harried, garrulous, good-humored college chaplain, Fr. Tuohy. John Moriarty startling the audience at the English Lit. by folding Dionysus in with "the Crucified." A poetry reading by Thomas Kinsella which put some lines from "Mirror in February" among our mantras: "They are not young who reach the age of Christ," he told us, and "I fold my towel with what grace I can, / Not young and not renewable, but man." Paying Patrick Kavanagh three guineas for a "Writer at Work" piece in *St. Stephens* ("I have a fair share of experience of talented writers and I have never caught any of them working"). The Physics Theatre before a class: crowded, rowdy, falling silent. Denis Donoghue lecturing *ab alto* on *King Lear*. J.J. Hogan blankly intoning line after line of Milton's blank verse. Lorna Reynolds enthusing in her richly modulated Anglo-Irish accents over the intricate delights of Crashaw or Herrick. An acerbic, probably hung-over John Jordan mixing hate and love in equal measure for Spenser's *Faerie Queene*, or turning to chastise a nun in the second row ("Please don't point that crucifix at me, Sister. I'm not the Devil, you know"). Roger McHugh blandly, benignly, inaudibly calling attention to what Joyce referred to as the "cloistral, silver-veined" qualities of Newman's prose.

Thirty and more years later, these scraps of college memory are still with me. I wonder what Hartnett remembers? What I remember of him is a small, compact figure in dark tweed jacket or overcoat, one hand in pocket, the other holding a cigarette. Large ears. A face of lovely planes, angles. The dark hair combed forward to a little twist on his brow. Woodkern or novice monk, deep in English or Irish conversation. Serious, watchful, intense, something dark and a bit secret there, no matter the smiles and talk over pints in Dwyer's or Hartigan's or McDaid's. Already a known poet. Was he there because, as we'd heard, John Jordan had discovered him, helped pay his fees? We never found out. It didn't matter. The poems started to appear, and they mattered. He had a voice of his own, its own kind of assurance, a light but exact and suggestive lyrical touch, through which he could convey a real, if partial self. What others were at seemed more melodramatic, more garish. He surprised us, being so sparely yet so distinctly there: "I asked this city / for a little thing. / My voice moved / among the alien people." Young gestures, yes, but somehow trustworthy, evocative, formally pleasing. A gesture like "Four hounds went south / one had your liver in his mouth. / Poor Acteon," or like the following (from a 1962 poem, called "I will Rise with the Hawk," dedicated to John Moriarty): "if we are destined to be birds / then I must be one of prey / and you must be, say, / a defenseless one / symbolic of love." When I come across lines like these again it is—no matter what Hartnett's subject might be—Dublin and UCD in those days of the early Sixties that I remember, and the presence there of a gifted poet who could, we felt, put his heart in his mouth:

> I have exhausted the delighted range
> of small birds, and now, a new end to pain
> makes a mirage of what I wished my life . . . .
>
> Small birds, small poems, are not immortal,
> nor, however passed, is one intense night:
> there is no time now for my dream of hawks.

As well as the daunting fact that he is a poet who writes in both English and Irish, one of the reasons why there's been so little critical work on Hartnett probably has to do with the vagaries of publication. In the case of poets such as Montague, Kinsella, Heaney, Mahon, Ní Chuilleanáin, Boland or Muldoon—to name a few of the most obvious—individual volumes appear at regular intervals, gradually accumulate, and may then be neatly decanted into volumes of selected work. This allows the lines that might compose the trajectory of a "career" to be seen with some clarity, and this clarity in turn encourages, as well as enables, critical response, not to mention critical reputation. The history of Hartnett's publications, on the other hand, is a bit of a jumble. (To a lesser degree this was also true of Paul Durcan, which is why the *Selected Durcan* published some years ago by Blackstaff was not only a relief but the beginning of a more coherent critical account of the poet and his work. It was also the case, to a drastic degree, of Padraic Fallon.) Given this jumble, it may be useful to offer a quick bibliographical outline of the predecessors to the latest Gallery/Wake Forest volume. (A useful Editor's Note at the end of the Gallery edition refers to, and then unravels the "notoriously complicated publishing history" of Hartnett's work.)

In 1968 Dolmen Press published a collection of love lyrics called *Anatomy of a Cliché*. The translation of *The Hag of Beare* came out from New Writers' Press in 1969. This was followed in 1970 by the New Writers' Press *Selected Poems*, containing sections of work from 1958, 1964 ("Madrid"), 1966, 1967 ("West Kensington"), "Wake Poems," "Four Sonnets," and the 1969 "Notes on My Contemporaries." In 1972, New Writers' Press published his version of the *Tao* (which had appeared in the literary magazine, *Arena*, in 1963). *Gipsy Ballads* (a version of Lorca's *Romancer Gitano*) was put out by Goldsmith Press in 1973, and in 1975—a watershed publishing year for Hartnett—Goldsmith released the bilingual *Cúlú Íde / The Retreat of Ita Cagney*, while Gallery Press put out *A Farewell to English*, which contained the poet's declared intent to write thenceforth in Irish. In 1977, then, Dolmen published a selection entitled *Poems in English*, comprised of selections from *Selected Poems* (1970), *Gipsy Ballads*, *A Farewell to English*, and *The Retreat of Ita Cagney*, as well as the *Tao* and *The Hag of Beare*. Also in 1977, Gallery, in conjunction with Deerfield Press (Massachusetts), published a pamphlet, *Prisoners*. Hartnett's first volume in Irish, *Adharca Broic*, came out from Gallery in 1978, and in 1979 Gallery published *Daoine*. Volume One of *Collected Poems* appeared in 1984 in Ireland from Raven Arts Press, and in 1985 in England from Carcanet. Its sections were "1957-1960," "1962-1965," "Anatomy of a Cliché," "Thirteen Poems Written in

Madrid 1964," "1966-1970," "Wake Poems," "Notes on My Contemporaries 1969," "Sonnets from the Dark Side of the Mind," "The Retreat of Ita Cagney," and "A Farewell to English." In 1985, Hartnett returned to composing in English with *Inchicore Haiku* (Raven Arts), which was followed later that year by *Ó Bruadair*, his translations of selected poems of Dáibhí Ó Bruadair (d. 1698), from Gallery. Volume Two of *Collected Poems* appeared from Raven Arts in 1986, and from Carcanet in 1987; this contained his translations and versions from the Irish, the Chinese, and the Spanish. Also in 1987, Gallery Press released *A Necklace of Wrens*, a bilingual volume which included the poet's own translations of the poems in *Adharca Broic*, of *Cúlú Íde*, and of a series of new poems (some of which had already appeared in *Collected Poems*, Volume Two), written first in Irish and then translated ("re-made" might be better) into English. Chief among this latter group were the startling *An Phurgóid* ("The Purge," first published in Irish by *Coiscéim* in 1983) and *An Lia Nocht* ("The Naked Surgeon"). The English volume, *Poems for Younger Women*, came out from Gallery in 1988, and Gallery published *The Killing of Dreams* in 1992, and *Haicéad* (translations of the work of Pádraigín Haicéad, d. 1654) in 1993. It's easy to see from this brief sketch the problems attending any attempt to get a clear picture of Hartnett's work. As editor of *Selected & New Poems*, Peter Fallon has managed to provide from this mass of material in two languages a coherent account—a pared down self-portrait—of the poet, while clearly suggesting the scope and variety of the work as a whole.

Hartnett's view of the critic is harsh and accusatory. "What's a critic, in living Bridget's name?" he asks towards the end of "The Purge." "Will 'objective correlatives' explain? / What is left when his piping ceases? / Dregs and spit, echoes and treacle." But a critic, it seems to me, can also be someone whose aim is to come to terms with the work in question, which may be done by trying to come to those terms that will best reveal and illuminate the nature, texture, and quality of that work. In what follows I'll be trying to come to terms, in both senses, with the work of a poet I admire, a poet whose best poems can be a source either of pleasure or of puzzlement, and sometimes of both of these together. It is not—as I have found and as my title admits—an easy task. For the trajectory made by Hartnett's work so far is not a neat uninterrupted arc. It is more like a journey that starts, stops, starts again, doubles back on itself, pursues false paths, tries different approaches, feels its way into the clear, then presses deliberately and forcefully ahead. The poet, that is, doesn't proceed easily along the open road; certainly there is progress (the growth from his beginnings to his latest work is pronounced and real), but the way it is achieved suggests more a man moving about in a maze.

Hartnett begins as a romantic lyricist with an imagist edge. His eye is sharp, he can surprise with an odd image, his voice is straightforward, syntactically simple:

I know you cannot rise.

You are unable to move.
But I can see your fear,
for two wet mice dart
cornered in the hollows
of your head.

              ("Sickroom")

The defining touches for me in this picture are the words "wet" and "cornered."
The first is shorthand for the palpable physicality of Hartnett's imagination; the
second suggests the degree to which he can find for emotions a physical language. The effect of the whole stanza is also characteristic, revealing as it does a
rapt attention focussed on material bodily facts, as well as a baffled energy
moving rapidly and eagerly about in a confined, confining space. Whatever
changes and amplifications the poetry will go through in the next thirty years,
such qualities remain to mark it as peculiarly his.

In some of these early poems—which can move from a self-consciously
romantic image of the poet to satiric pieces directed against the sexual puritanism of the Catholic church or the awfulness of the city ("Dublin Inferno")—it's
possible to hear elements of the early Pound of *Personae*, as well as the harsher
accents of Patrick Kavanagh. Whatever the influences, however, the poems
themselves could sometimes be weakly derivative in language and pose. This
weaker side of the work between (roughly) 1960 and 1970 seems to come from
an inflated sense of self-as-poet, a too-easy adoption of a "tribal" voice (the
phrase "my people" recurs), and a hectic imagism that produces lines like "My
soul felt like an exposed nipple." In fact, the poems chosen for Hartnett's first
volume, *Anatomy of a Cliché* (1968), show many of these early weaknesses:
curdled excesses of language, self-infatuated sexism ("although / we have built
philosophies / I will honour you with sex . . . "), and a kind of clumsy self-
regard in search of appropriate "eloquence." It is a language of male display, in
touch with verbal gestures, but out of touch with itself, with real feeling, and
with any plausibly realised other. Most effective is the piece originally entitled
"IX" ("Bread" in *SNP*). In its simplicity, particularity, and subdued tone, this
poem shows up by contrast the strident, affected, and overblown qualities of
what doesn't work in much of the rest of *Anatomy*, as well as in other less than
successful early pieces:

Her iron beats
the smell of bread
from damp linen,
silver, crystal,
and warm white things.
Whatever bird
I used to be,
hawk or lapwing,
tern, or something
wild, fierce or shy,

these birds are dead,
and I come here
on tiring wings.
Odours of bread . . .

The disparity between successful and unsuccessful early work suggests to
me that a couple of versions of "the poet," are jostling for position in Hartnett's
creative life, in his imagination. One is the spare, still quite tentative lyricist,
tuned by a keenly sensuous hold on things, and with a romantic, slightly extravagant but formally contained, sense of self. This may be seen and heard in
pieces like "Bread" and "Sickroom" and "For My Grandmother Bridget Halpin." The other is more of a gaudy decorator, a derivative, claustrophobic,
mildly oracular declaimer, a sort of blocked self seeking to hide behind larger-
than-life verbal posing, the sort of thing to be found in *Anatomy of a Cliché*, in
the poems written in Madrid in 1964, and elsewhere. What comes through in
this latter version is a kind of advanced world-weariness, couched in a language
of sexual frustration and moral self-righteousness: "For we have heard a myth /
in Western Europe, / that there are some men / who take wives." "We," "myth,"
"Western Europe," "some men" "take wives"—the whole thing is a hollow
pose, a verbal gesture without much substance or responsibility.

The "Sonnets from the Dark Side of the Mind" (two of the best of
which have been retained in *Selected & New Poems*) are also infected with this
delphic urge, a kind of cryptic hollow booming ("I am not free. I am bound by
bread / to concrete chariots. My time is sold / for smallest coin, my acreage for
beads"). Such poems suffer from a sort of "Ozymandias" complex, a "Second
Coming" complex. The self-image of the poet as truth-teller, shaman, law-giver
is too heavy a burden for the poetry to bear. Archaic and musclebound, the language clots, curdles, grows claustrophobic. "Secular Prayers" (only one of
which is retained in the *Selected*, as epigraph) are similarly contaminated, opting
for the empty, orotund accents of a made-up piety. This, like much of what
doesn't work for Hartnett in this first phase, is a poetry preying on itself, forcing
things to carry significance. It is speech-making rather than communication, and
usually derivative, as in this fruity Yeatsian gesture: "I have loved you: / there is
none more beautiful."

The most successfully achieved version of the early voice appears in some
poems written between 1966 and 1970, in pieces like "'Don't go,' they said," "I
was volcanic . . . " "Base to Smaller," "A Small Farm," "There will be Talking,"
"I Heard Him Whistle," and "Green Room." In poems like these (most of which
are in *Selected & New Poems*), emotional directness is concordant with a lyrical
language of image and restrained action. The following lines are from "Green
Room" (a title happily tamed from its original, "No, That Cell is for Maniacs"):

There is no voice for him
but the fern arms gentling to the window.
It is so foamed with green lace here

> that we call his room
> 'the green tapestried room.'

The balance of this voice, the way its emotional impulses are matched by carefully delineated facts, may also be heard in "A Small Farm," the poem which inaugurates *Selected & New Poems* on a properly autobiographical note:

> I was abandoned to their tragedies
> and began to count the birds,
> to deduce secrets in the kitchen cold,
> and to avoid among my nameless weeds
> the civil war of that household.

There's a keen plainness to such language, as if the poet had chastened the self-regarding melodrama of his rhetoric, but kept its kernel of intensity. The language here, as in the more publicly oriented utterance of certain of the "Notes on My Contemporaries," is not without its ritual gestures, but these have body, substance, integrity. Other successful poems in the early phase possess something like a miniature narrative impulse ("Maiden Street Wake," for example), or a voice of direct address, as in "For My Grandmother, Bridget Halpin":

> You never saw the animals
> of God, and the flower under
> your feet; and the trees change leaf;
> and the red fur of a fox on
> a quiet evening; and the long
> birches falling down the hillside.

This early phase of Hartnett's work, then, contains two quite distinct modes or voices, only one of which seems, poetically, to work. By embodying a competition between two versions of "the poet," however, the early poems also reveal—in the fact of the contest itself—the sound of a writer trying hard to write himself into a voice that will be responsible for the expression of his life. The unspoken ache at the heart of many of these overtly melancholy poems is the ache to find an adequate voice, a voice able to negotiate between a hidden, vulnerable self (which speaks a language of over-simplified directness: "I hate this country. / I hate the joy, the loquacity") and a self that's hardened into a remote, ritualised mask, into a rhetorical carapace. This not only means that the poet is willing to take expressive risks that may fail, but that—looking for himself in language—he will be satisfied with nothing less than an idiom unmediated by anything except its own sense of style and ritual, a language capable of stating exactly and fully the human condition of the speaker. He seeks a style adequate to the full expression of the individual's emotional and intellectual and spiritual condition, adequate to his relationships with himself, with others, and with the world. This quest itself, I'd say, is the common thread that runs like a bright, raw nerve through all of Hartnett's work: it is this that makes his career (I mean his life as a poet) exemplary, and his work important to us.

The transitional phase of Hartnett's work is represented by *A Farewell to English* and *The Retreat of Ita Cagney*—both of which belong, as publications, to 1975. What distinguishes many of the poems in *A Farewell to English* from earlier work is their distinct sense of purpose. While the earlier work seemed in part marked by a searching, this collection is marked by a sense of discovery. There is, for example, "Struts" which seems to be an allegorical exploration of poetry, the poet's task, and the relationship of the poet to tradition. (A fresh inclination to use allegory and parable is a distinct mark of this new phase, and one which Hartnett will keep, and develop, in later work.)

> We are climbing upwards into time
> and climbing backwards into tradition,
> the sudden message on a rope
> evoking the cosiness of soft-lit rooms,
> the comfort and the smell
> of sharing ancient overcoats.
> Sometimes a rope gives,
> implodes unweighted in the hand,
> and then tradition, time and fire
> mix in a spinning blur:
> the hill unskins the knuckles.

The extended image is a parable for poetic engagement. In its intense physicality as well as its implications the rock-climbing metaphor suggests coolness, attention, scrupulosity. There seems to be a trace of Beckett in this way of expressing the world, which may also be found in "The Buffeting":

> That night
> I crouched in a small alcove of heat
> under a rough cloth rubbed hard
> by years of limbs shivering,
> recycling the same breath,
> the same comforting smells.
> I had escaped the bastinado.
> But only for a while.

Other poems (such as "Early One Morning" or "Signal from the World") have a Beckett touch, too, as if Hartnett had gone on a penitential Beckett diet. There's the curious detachment of the Beckett hero—the passionless subjective voice, the world beyond understanding ("Sitting here: for hours: / venturing sometimes to the concrete inclines / . . Just lying beside jute sacks among the grooves, / lying beside the giant flakes of paint.") And there is, in the actual manner of such poems, Beckett's own love for the parable, for the sharply particular but allegorically representative action.

Perhaps connected with this (possible) Beckett influence is a new *narrative* energy and purpose that marks a number of the poems in *A Farewell to English*. The poet enters the elements of his own past in a more objective way, with language tightly reined in to the actual narrative facts, rather than evaporating among the emotions. In "Horse Breaking Loose" this leads to a compact intensity ("All this violence and men running passed me by / with lashing whips of wire / and long outlandish coats / with voice and weapons most barbarous and uncouth"), while in "Pig Killing" the narrative element becomes buoyant, showing a lyrical lightness of touch, as Hartnett makes his own of a corner of Kavanagh. After the pig has been slaughtered,

> I kick his golden bladder
> in the air.
> It lands like a moon
> among the damsons.
> Like a knife cutting a knife
> his last plea for life
> echoes joyfully in Camas.

Here the free verse form achieves a brilliant objectivity through economy, straight description, and the speed with which it tells the story. And, beyond such lyrical naturalism, "The Oat Woman" reveals the ritual order to which the ordinary actions of Hartnett's remembered world can be brought: "Their coats lay down in sculpture, / each with a tired dog: / thin blades quaked at blunt whetstones: / purple barked at blue." (Some of these fresh effects may be the result of Hartnett's immersion, as translator, in the poetry of Lorca. The Spanish poet may have taught him how to yoke imagistic strangeness to a clear narrative drive, the shape of the story holding the strangeness in, the mundane and the extreme finding common ground, as they do in "Ballad of the Moon": "The moon comes into the forge / in her dress of hoop and flower. / The child stares, stares at her.")

One of the impressive things about *A Farewell to English* is the way personal, formal, and (for want of a better word) political aspects of Hartnett's imagination come together. In "A Visit to Castletown House" the political point is formalised and feels the influential pressure of a Yeatsian stanza, while in "A Visit to Croom 1745" it is vividly dramatised:

> Five Gaelic faces stopped their talk,
> turned from the red of fire
> into a cloud of rush-light fumes,
> scraped their pewter mugs
> across the board and talked about the king.

The relaxed sound of unaffected talk is what strikes me here—a fresh formal dimension, beyond both the bad and the good early lyricism. And this talk gathers both personal and political notes into itself, turning them into a single, convincingly anchored, "native" voice.

This is the voice that will carry Hartnett forward, and one can hear it again in parts of the unevenly successful title poem itself, especially in the lovely incidental music of the second section—which begins, imaginatively, in Kavanagh country, not too far, I'd say, from the Inniskeen Road:

> Half afraid to break a promise
> made to Dinny Halpin Friday night
> I sat down from my walk to Camas
> Sunday evening, Doody's Cross,
> and took off my burning boots
> on a gentle bench of grass.
> The cows had crushed the evening
> green with mint.

Here a relaxed expository narrative is quickened by its lyrical touches, its concrete names, its sensuous engagement with landscape and place. But it's the way Hartnett moves beyond Kavanagh's lyricism into some deeper, more demanding, indigenous territory of his own that seems especially important here, as he sinks not his hands but his whole self into tradition. Confronted by "These old men [who] walked on the summer road / sugán belts and long black coats," he experiences a kind of *aisling*, a dream vision, although it's the men's terrible actuality that's overwhelming. Effortlessly, then, the road to Camas turns into Hartnett's road to Damascus: the old men are the lightning bolt, with "black moons of misery / sickling their eye-sockets, / a thousand years of history / in their pockets."

The rhyme between "misery" and "history" here is sufficient index to Hartnett's political point. His politics are the politics of personal recognition, something making its inexorable claim on him, calling for a response. And response, as we'll soon see, becomes responsibility. The place-names themselves ("Croom, Meentogues and Cahirmoyle"—their recitation a kind of elegiac refrain) participate in this cultural reawakening, being all intimately connected to Gaelic poetry. In a scene that mixes the most mundane occurrence with something close to a hard visionary substance, the poet shows how fluently he can move between the personal and the public, the self and the sense of tribal meaning. This release from solipsism, to which there have been plenty of suggestive prologues, is here accomplished in a marvelously simple, unassuming, but convincing and persuasive way, a way that marks this whole volume as pivotal in his imaginative life, not merely for the turning away from English which it declares, but for the manners in which the poet accomplishes its best pieces.

As a whole, however, "A Farewell to English" itself is an uneven poem, with some sub-Kavanagh satire, a few clumsy swipes at Yeats, and myopic, exclusive, pseudo-mystical claims for the Irish language, "For Gaelic is our final sign that / we are human, therefore not a herd." This latter claim is spurious, it seems to me, since "our" humanity depends not on the language we use, but on how we use the language we have, whatever it is (a point integral to the creative relationship Hartnett will later set up between Irish and English). As for the swipes he makes at "our bug-bear, Mr. Yeats," these too easily ignore the connection between his own poem and Yeats's great poem of rejection, "The Fisherman" (not to mention other examples of Yeatsian influence, for good—as in "Castletown House"—and bad—as in *Anatomy of a Cliché*). The satire, too, as I say, is in Kavanagh's shadow, which makes Hartnett much less effective than, for example, Clarke was in his later work or than Kinsella was in "Nightwalker" and many of the poems that followed it. Not until "The Purge" does Hartnett grow into a strong satirical voice of his own.

Whatever about its damaging flaws as a poem, however, "A Farewell to English" in its entirety is an invaluable document, letting us into the inner workings of a crucial moment in Hartnett's imaginative development, a moment of Yeatsian "re-making," as the poet commences his journey from one language to another, walking to Camas instead of sailing to Byzantium. In "The Fisherman" Yeats says he had hoped "to write for my own race, / and the reality," but finds he must, in the end, invent an audience of one. In the affecting last section of "A Farewell to English," Hartnett moves in the opposite direction:

> I have made my choice
> and leave with little weeping:
> I have come with meagre voice
> to court the language of my people.

Where Yeats turned to "the tradition of myself," Hartnett—binding determination to humility—will submit himself to the communal tradition inherent in the Irish language itself. It is a new beginning and it has remarkable consequences. "Style" says Synge, "comes from the shock of new experience." The style that comes from Hartnett's new experience amplifies his poetic achievement and helps him to a fresh, more expansive engagement with his world. It is a style that negotiates in remarkable ways between Irish and English; a style that, at its best, makes a unique sound and unique sense in the world of contemporary Irish poetry.

Ideally, in order to comment in any adequate way on Hartnett's poetry since *A Farewell to English*, a critic should have much more and better Irish than my few school remnants. But an essay like this can't ignore what is his major work, and so I'll hazard some observations about what seem to me to be its distinguishing features. First—and perhaps most importantly to his success and survival as a poet—I believe that the deliberate turn from English to Irish allowed Hartnett to find formal comfort in immediate speech, to find a way in which speech itself could be formally managed without loss of immediacy. In Irish, that is, he discovered (was given) a mode of address that answered his dual need for muscular formality and nervous immediacy of expression. For these are the qualities I myself think I am hearing in such Gaelic poetry as I, however dimly, know. Invariably, this poetry seems to carry the sound of confident speech, of a speaker's confidence of being heard, even when, as in so much of Ó Rathaille or Ó Bruadair or Haicéad or Raftery, the subject itself is loss—loss of culture, of place, of language itself. (One of the reasons behind this may be that in the Gaelic tradition, as Thomas Kinsella has said, "poetry played a much more direct part in the spending of people's lives than we are accustomed to in the English or any other Western tradition. Poetry was a significant part of living, of how Gaelic culture responded to its experiences, great and small, national, parochial, and domestic."[1]

What I mean by "the sound of confident speech" can, I think, be heard in Hartnett's early works in Irish, in the lyrics of *Adharca Broic* and the long poem *Cúlú Íde*. In the lyrics he seems to begin again in simplicity:

> I mo bhuachaill óg, fadó fadó,
>   d'aimsíos nead.
> Bhí no gearrcaigh clúmtha, fásta,
>   is iad ag scread. (*An Muince Dreoilíní*)

[literal: "When I was a young boy, long ago, / I found a nest. / The little birds were fledged, grown, / and they were screeching."]

Simple and direct as well as neatly formal, the poem seems bent on immediate communication. It may even be that the poet has a strong sense of audience here, a sense that he is not talking to himself but to an essentially coherent community. This can be heard, I believe, even when he is speaking critically of aspects of this community, as he does in a poem called *An Séipéal faoin Tuath* ("The Country Chapel"):

> Is capall uaigneach an pobal seo
> ag dul amú san fhichiú haois
> comh tuathalach le fear ag rince
> le bean rialta ag bainis.

[literal: this people is a lonely horse / going about in the twentieth century / as clumsily as a man dancing / with a nun at a wedding."]

Here the Gaelic itself—concrete, plain, direct, musical, straightforward, simple, familiar, recognisable, shared—is a sign of the speaker's ease of communication, while the formal aspects of the lines (their assonantal patterns, their tangible—mostly iambic—rhythm) give this communication something of the orderly design of ritual. The same sense of confident and immediate address, formally shaped, may be heard in the Irish of *Cúlú Íde*—in its narrative directness, its concrete imagery, and in the sense one has as a reader of being *told* something in as simple yet vivid a way as possible:

> Ní raibh de bhainis ann
> ach anraith is arán.
>   Luíodar gan codlata
>   gan Bhíobla, gan ola:
>   lámh an fhir go dlúth
>   mar ghearrcach in nead a gruaige.

[lit: "It wasn't anything of a wedding / just bread and *anraith*. / They lay down without sleeping / without Bible, without oil [blessing]: / the man's hand as close [still] / as a fledgling in the nest of her hair."]

Qualities like these suggest that the recovery of and creative immersion in Irish granted Hartnett access to a zone of confidence where he could feel a satisfying coincidence between what he wanted to say and the means of saying it. A zone of imaginative expression in which the formal and the natural seemed to meet and be at one. In many senses, I'd say, he had found his tongue. Given my limited understanding of what's actually going on formally and substantively in the Irish, however, all I've just said can be no more than speculation, relying on the reflexes of instinct and intuition. I hope I'm on more solid critical ground in what I'm about to say regarding what Hartnett himself makes of the qualities I've mentioned, when he turns his own poems in Irish into poems in English.

In his translations from Ó Bruadair and Haicéad and Ó Rathaille Hartnett's concern is to give a sense in English of the older poet's Irish voice. "I did not want to afflict the poet with *my* voice," he says: "to do that, too much of what survived in my version would be distorted."[2] Something else entirely seems to be going on, however, when he translates or re-makes his own Irish into English. What this is may best be seen in his three splendid long poems—"The Retreat of Ita Cagney," "The Purge," and "The Naked Surgeon." Since each of these poems, as well as the whole issue of Hartnett's relations with the two languages, would demand a separate essay, my aim here has to be quite modest. It is to suggest something about the nature of his language in these re-makings: what it's like, how it relates to its subject, how it relates to and affects a reader. Here is the opening of "The Retreat of Ita Cagney":

> Their barbarism did not assuage the grief:
> their polished boots, their Sunday clothes,
> the drone of hoarse melodeons.
> The smoke was like the edge of blue scythes.
> The downpour smell of overcoats
> made the kitchen cry for air:
> snuff lashed the nose like nettles
> and the toothless praising of the dead
> spun on like unoiled bellows,
> She could not understand her grief:
> the women who had washed his corpse
> were now more intimate with him
> than she had ever been.

> She put a square of silk upon her head
> and hidden in the collars of her coat
> she felt her way along the white-washed walls.
> The road became a dim knife.
> She had no plan
> but instinct neighed around her
> like a pulling horse.

Since the Irish from which this is re-made is in three regular stanzas, the first thing to note is the unrhymed irregularity of the English lines. Beyond this difference, however, the following particular qualities of the English strike me as taken over from the Irish: the intense physicality of the language, a powerful sense of bodily presence in the words themselves, the extraordinary animation of the environment through vivid images, and a peculiar sensation—thick and almost cinematic—of "close-upness," of tangible proximity to what is spoken. In addition, the lines convey a powerful sense (which increases as the poem goes on) of living inside the protagonist's consciousness as she experiences her grief in sharply physical terms. They also give us, I'd say, the overall impression of being, as readers, immediately addressed, of being told something in an abrupt, unmediated, and unaffected way.

Hartnett's English voice here expresses itself in a manner that is both intimate and strange. Foregoing the external formality of the Irish "original," it nonetheless manages to capture something of its ritual nature, while holding on to those qualities of concreteness of image and diction, as well as to the velocity and urgency of immediate address that belong to Irish poetic expression. And while the English is faithful in meaning to the Irish, what comes over to my ear is less what I'd call a translation than a creative re-making in which the English has been "informed," even transformed, by the Irish and is, therefore—or at least gives the impression of being—a kind of hybrid thing. As such, it could be seen as an accurate embodiment of the poet's own consciousness, caught in what Kinsella has called (in the essay I've already cited) "the two-tongued Irish tradition in its late twentieth-century manifestation."

The narrative content of "The Retreat of Ita Cagney" concerns the clash between individual choice and institutional morality—represented by the collusion between the forces of the Catholic church and those of conventional social piety—especially in the realm of sexual love. It is a subject that Hartnett had often touched before, but never with such depth of insight or feeling, never with such a richly realised sense of its sheer physical reality. Presumably part of this enrichment was due to the way in which the Irish language itself allowed him to enter the subject with an intensity of emotional understanding he might not otherwise have had. (I wonder if the fact that Ita Cagney, a widow, lives in a new union unblessed by the church and feared and loathed by society might be seen as some sort of reflection of the relationship in Hartnett's work between the English and the Irish elements.) However it's looked at, the poem in English is a remarkable feat of imaginative sympathy and ethical discernment.

In his next major poem made over from the Irish, "The Purge," Hartnett turns away from the explicitly ethical realm and towards the realm of the aesthetic, focussing the energies of his new style on the subject of poetry itself, on the poet's own task and condition, his obligation to start over again, to re-make himself as a poet. (At times while reading this poem I was reminded of Synge's energetic, forceful language as he too cleaned his slate, forcing poetry to be "brutal before it could be human," saying farewell to the "gods and skinny *shee*" of the Revival. While his relation to the Irish language and to Gaelic culture was very different from Hartnett's, it may be true to say that not since Synge—with the exception of Austin Clarke—has there been such a programmatic, and instinctive, attempt to bring the two languages into a vital creative union.) Early on in "The Purge," the speaker announces his project:

> I'll have to clean and flay my talk—
> without a purge great penances will fall,
> my poems become mere wind and noise
> and I will lose my human voice.
>
> Joyfully young poets dance among their books
> but daft the dance of old poets deaf and dumb—
> those mimics in their tinkers' shawls,
> those bauble-stealing crass jackdaws,
> those carpenters of crippled chairs,
> those scap-lipped brassers, streetwise, on the game.
> Pity him who first compared
> a poet to a bird:
> he insulted plumage to the skies—
> swallows' droppings blind his eyes.

What strikes me first about this is its immediacy of address, the confidence of the speaking voice, the unembarrassed reference to the self as the direct subject of the poem. This quality of vocal self-possession comes over from the Irish, as do the rapid couplets that suggest urgent speech. From the spoken immediacy of the Irish, too, comes the fresh, conversational, colloquial vigour, the sound of a person actually talking, no matter how formal the actual construction of the poem may be. Poetry itself, indeed, is referred to as "talk" (*caint*), a talk that can move from the contained outrage of "Tradition squats on me at night, / an ancient thing and lizard-like, / shouting 'free verse! alliteration! assonance!'" to the brisk colloquial patter of "Isn't it grand to meet with Plato / or drink with Emmet, the darlin' of Erin? / or have a chat with Christ the Saviour." This converted style also enables a rapid movement between public and private issues, between the speaker's own poetry and the habits of poets in general.

Taken over, too, is the hard factual physicality of the original, which in English becomes even more extravagant than it is in the Irish (*béal gearbach striapach na sráide* [lit. "scabby streetwalker mouth"] becomes "those scap-lipped brassers, streetwise, on the game"). Once again there's a kind of mixture of intimacy and strangeness about this English, something slightly askew about its emotional speed and colloquial verve, something that suggests the hybridising of forces in a single consciousness. A small emblem of this hybrid action may be seen in the relation between the English phrase "clever wind and noise" and the Irish original, which is *gaoth is glicbhéarla*. For *glicbhéarla* literally means "clever [or, in American, "smartass"] English," which suggests that while the speaker is talking in Irish about being a poet, becoming responsible to a new language, the language he's also thinking of being a poet *in* is English. So the two tongues are entirely implicated in one another, both of them having the task of expressing/registering the speaker's single consciousness in his "human voice." This conviction of a "human voice" is the most compelling aspect of these new poems. It conveys the sense of an urgent and authentic presence in the language, a sense that the language is the full expression of a consciousness. The formal energy, too, prevents it being simply confessional, except in the way, perhaps, that Berryman's *Dream Songs* are confessional. The speaker is a *persona*, "the poet," not simply the biographical Michael Hartnett, and this double identity results in the refreshed freedom of the voice.

From ethics to aesthetics to faith: this seems to be the curve of Hartnett's imaginative arc as he moves from "Ita Cagney" through "The Purge" to "The Naked Surgeon," as if the poet wished to explore in and with his new language the most serious and pressing aspects of his world. "The Naked Surgeon" is a richly thoughtful, deeply felt, interrogation of God ("listen God, are you there?" he says in English, which in Irish was "Listen, God, I'm talking to you"). It is a sustained pursuit of meaning in a world in which faith grows cold. Another "translation," its expressive virtues in English are not unlike those in the other two long poems, although it is formally more lyrical, more consistently structured (stanzas throughout), and tonally more restrained (more, in a way, "classical") than the other two. Such formal concentration, however, does not interfere with its immediacy of speech nor with its startling imagery, as the poet explores in a condensed way his own life, turning its phases to allegorical shapes. Section 5, for example, is an allegorical re-enactment of his struggle with alcohol. This, at least, is how I'd read it, translating its imagery into references to St. Patrick's Hospital, founded by Swift. (At times the poem reminds me of Clarke's *Mnemosyne Lay in Dust*, which is about another visit to St. Pat's. Hartnett's directly allegorical manner is quite unlike Clarke's, but they both have at times a similarly direct emotional tone of voice.)

> My first trip to the house of thatch—
>
> home of the Slaughter Lad
> who condemned his own kind—
> a hammer vision showed him how
> to escape the bird-lime.
> I was called, no scalpel packed.
> I threw a saddle on the dark

and galloped to the threshold of his mind.

What's important in this case is the way the allegorical element, the sense of parable, comes over naturally from the Irish into a speedily idiomatic English that seems at once familiar and a little tilted, and into an oddly impulsive, original imagery. The Irish, that is, always reads (to me) as more ordinary, more normative than the English, which always seems at an angle to the norm (an interesting angle that keeps me attentive, slightly off-kilter, a bit unsettled). I find this angular quality to be one of Hartnett's most compelling features, creating that fusion of the foreign and the familiar, that union of the intimate and the strange, that's a characteristic mark of his mature verse.

My general point here—tentatively made because of my own insecurity in talking about the Irish "originals"—is that this new English that Hartnett speaks as a poet is one result of a radically innovative relationship he sets up between the English and the Irish languages, a relationship that in its richly fertilising, blended quality might stand for the personal and representative consciousness of the poet himself. (I find in this aspect of Hartnett's work some parallels to John McGahern, whose relationship to the Irish language is nothing like the poet's, but whose odd qualities of voice in the novels and short stories also signals a speaking consciousness that is at once personally idiosyncratic and hauntingly representative.) Whether my observations are right or wrong in their particulars, the fact of the matter remains that in these three poems in their English incarnations Hartnett re-made himself as a poet in the English language. And, in the best work written over the decade and more since their publication (in some of the work in *The Killing of Dreams*, that is, and in parts of the new long poems that conclude the present *Selected*), he has continued to practice with distinction this revised art of his, becoming the nervous master of its vivid, idiosyncratic, trustworthy style.

As to the *Selected & New Poems* itself: It is a gift to all of Hartnett's admirers, as well as to those readers who are approaching his work for the first time. The poet and his editor have done a scrupulous job of selection, pruning the excesses and leaving, as I've said, a spare self-portrait of the developing artist. Since a *Selected* is a sort of anthology, a reader familiar with the whole work will probably have some quibbles. Personally I thought the selection could have been less austere: I'd maybe have added such pieces as the early "All that is Left . . . " as well as the lively sonnet, "Here be the burnings . . . " and "Pig Killing," and the Beckett-like "Struts." A few more of the *Inchicore Haiku* (which show the poet effecting a monastically attenuated re-entry into English) would have done no harm, and, for its documentary value, the whole of "A Farewell to English" might have been included. And it seems a pity to deny readers of this volume at least some of the livelier, astringent pleasures of "The Purge." If space were needed to allow some of these additions, I think I might fillet and keep only the more bravura passages from the last poem ("He'll to the Moors"), which seems in its entirety less coherent and less impressive than the other new pieces. (A note on the identity of its subject would also have helped.) But these are only quibbles, and the editor's final note (in the Gallery edition) makes them redundant, in that it is an assurance of a Hartnett *Collected Poems* sometime in the future. As it stands, the present volume gives a convincing account of the range and quality of the poetry, and should serve on both sides of the Atlantic to establish Hartnett as one of the best, most interesting, and most authentic poetic voices of his generation. There is no one like him. And when I read a recent poem like "A Falling Out" or "Sibelius in Silence," both of them containing at their best some serious and startling meditations on the art of poetry itself, I am struck again, as I am by all of his best work, at just how tenaciously he has—ever since those early days in UCD—kept faith with his art. His most successful work is always a testament to that simple fact. In spite of the radical changes he has made in himself as a poet, this is what connects in a coherent way the capacious voice that conducts later poems like "The Purge" or "Mountains Fall On Us" to the emotionally scrupulous, small lyrical voice of a very early piece like "I heard him whistle . . ."

Early on in this essay, I described Hartnett's poetic manner in the image of "a baffled energy moving rapidly and eagerly about in a confined, confining space." But now when I think of his work I also often think of a man on a journey. It is a journey like that of the monks who set out in sail-boats, possessing little more than their faith and their craft, but determined to keep going wherever the wind and the waves (and what was behind the wind and the waves) would take them. In the image of these voyagers I find something of Hartnett's mixture of risk-taking and trust, of confidence and desperation. Which is why, I suppose, I love the note of arrival on which he concludes his vexed examination of conscience in "The Old Catechism":

> However. There is a house I've heard of—
> where the herbs are always fresh
> and where, at last, pain and panic are dismissed,
> and you can walk in, take off your aches,
> sit down, discard your fear,
> and say: 'Hello God. I'm here.'

In these lines—with their unshowy but eloquent echo (I suspect) of the old Irish poem *M'air iuclán hi Túaim Inbir* (variously titled "God's House" or "The Ivy Bower" or "The Oratory")—you can hear Hartnett's own distinctive voice, that lyrical, muscular, slightly off-centre but idiomatic style of address which sounds like no one else. As a poet he has not stood still, but taken those risks of change that have given an odd and sometimes difficult shape to his career so far. But in his stubborn unpredictability he has never stopped—and presumably will go on—surprising us. And whatever about God, we know, and we're glad to know, he's here.

1995

NOTES

[1] "Another Country," in *The Pleasures of Gaelic Poetry,* ed. by Seán Mac Réamoinn (London: Allen Lane, 1982).

[2] "Wrestling with Ó Bruadair," in *The Pleasures of Gaelic Poetry.*

Prime Durcan: A Collage

In the light of things as they are.

Seeing Things

Leaving an art gallery or museum of art after looking at paintings for a couple of hours, I often find I'm seeing the world differently, at least for a little while. I notice the shapes and volumes of things—all those cones and pyramids, oblongs and triangles that the things of the world can render down to. I see with a revived eye the extraordinary fact of colour in the world—those glints of gold and silver in a sea of green grass, the way a window can be an explosion of turquoise when the sun hits it, the black, maroon and magenta geometry of a woman's scarf as it curls across the curve of her shoulder, the intense vitality of yellow in a twist of lemon peel, the cat's malachite eyes. It isn't just a case of life imitating art. It's more a question of the inspired and calculated facts of art waking us up to the vast particularity of things, to what MacNeice called "the drunkenness of things being various," to the infinite dazzle of their surfaces as well as to the sensuous, indefinable order that seems to inhere in them. Most of all, I suppose, it is a question of briefly seeing the world through the painters' eyes: the world will take its cue from the painters I've been especially impressed with, will look back at me in the way I imagine it must have looked to their interrogative and creative gaze.

Something analogous to this happens to me after I've been reading a lot of Paul Durcan's poetry. I start to see the world at the Durcan angle. Things I would not normally pay much attention to begin to strike me as slightly bizarre. The world, like Aliceland, grows curiouser and curiouser. Recently, for example, while reading Durcan's work for this essay, I attended a concert by an American-Irish music group called Celtic Thunder. Their fiddle player is an Asian-American, and their pianist mixes jazz improvisation with Irish melodies. This young man is also a champion stepdancer and his high leaps in the middle of a reel or a hornpipe brought thoughts of Nijinsky and Birdman Sweeney to mind. I say I attended the concert; in fact I gave a reading before the music, so the flyer for the evening read "Eamon Grennan Followed by Celtic Thunder," a stage direction to challenge "Exit pursued by Bear." The next day I went to a concert given by the South African *a capella* singing group, Ladysmith Black Mombasa, whose striking mixture of individuality and community in their singing, as well as the astonishing spectacle of their "tiptoe guys" dancing (a form of Saturday night silent hopping and kicking developed by the miners to elude the detection of guards in their camps) fused energy and constraint in spellbinding ways. Their bright shirts, dashikis—brilliant lozenge patterns on an amber ground—reminded me of vestments on figures in illuminated Irish manuscripts. And the other night, while taking a taxi home from the train station, I told my driver—a Jamaican—I was from Ireland. "My grandfather's Irish," he said. "His parents came over from Ireland with him. My name's MacMorris." So there I was driving down Main Street in Poughkeepsie with this gentle young black man of Irish descent, and thinking of his splenetic namesake in Shakespeare's *Henry V*—the Irish Captain MacMorris—who (asked, as Leopold Bloom was asked, "What is your nation?") has this to say of his native land: "My nation! What ish my nation? Ish a villain, and a bastard, and a knave, and a rascal—what ish my nation? Who talks of my nation?"

The confluence of these events—which under other circumstances I might not have paid much attention to—made me think I was living in a Durcan poem. Which in turn made me consider, a little enviously, what Durcan would do with such material. For, as a poet, he seems to live in constant touch with such slightly skewed spins on normal reality. When he holds more or less ordinary events up to the light, they glow in odd ways, revealing facets of meaning most of us could never imagine. It is his genius to discover the truly peculiar soul in things, and to celebrate or castigate this as its moral nature demands. (Although he has been called a great comedian, he is in fact a relentless—and relentlessly buoyant—moralist: weird as its projections are, the map he makes of the world is a moral map, his tendencies as a poet instinctively utopian.)

Incidents such as those I've just mentioned remind me that I know of no other poet who can do Durcan's sort of poetic justice to the connections offered us by everyday life, the kind of ordinary weirdnesses thrown up by our own unremarkable experience. These events were not particularly exceptional in themselves: they were marked by a certain amount of coincidence, I suppose, and a measure of the unexpected. In essence they embodied an idea of conjunction: conjunction within the phenomena themselves (the Asian-American playing the Irish fiddle, the Jamaican with the unlikely Irish grandfather), and a related kind of conjunction created by the observing mind (associating the South African singers with illuminated pages in the Book of Kells). Durcan's poems exist in a region ruled by this dual idea of conjunction, speaking out of it in a poetic dialect that is unmistakably his own. Because I'd been reading him, I noticed things as I did. His poems transformed the way I saw, thought about, understood the world. Only the strongest poetry has such powers of transformation. Some poetry, pretending to such power, tries to enforce transformation, bullying us to see the world as its maker sees it. Poetry like Durcan's, however, has transformation as an involuntary by-product. It works on us in the same way as a visit to an art gallery does. When we enter the actual world again after looking at the work of a painter we love, the world (so known, so new) takes our eye by surprise. Likewise, when we've been reading Durcan for a while our world loses its steadiness and familiarity, to become a place unchanged in its

essence but shaken now by comic fits and unexpected perplexities, simply riddled with astonishment.

Things Past

I'm trying to remember something of those early days in UCD, when Durcan
arrived in 1961 or '62 and met up with the poets there—with Macdara Woods,
John Moriarty, Michael Hartnett, Michael Smith. I remember something of the
aura that hung around him—something at once gloomy and bright and unpredictable. And I remember how, once, he emerged through blue clouds of cigarette smoke and a Babel-stew of talk in Dwyers' pub at the corner of Leeson
Street and Stephen's Green, beamed up close at me in a way that Guinness had
something to do with—his curly hair tousled, his face bony, aquiline, hugely
smiling—and shouted, *a propos* a line in a poem of mine that had just appeared
in a college magazine, "Eamon, you're a saint! you're a *saint!*" and then vanished back into the scrum of drinkers and roarers, leaving me to wonder why I'd
been canonised. The line in question, I remember (and remember only because
of this incident), described a dead woman in her coffin being "rolled like a stone
to the tomb," and I think the simile caught his fancy, as well as the sound,
maybe, and the rhythm. But it's his impulsive generosity and enthusiasm that
keep the moment (and the line) alive in my memory—that hearty willingness to
praise, as well as the odd, wildly extravagant terms of the praise itself.

As for the poems of his that I saw at that time—pieces he published in *St.
Stephen's* or the *University Review*—I recall nothing but their generalised atmosphere of melancholy, the slightly exotic air of their gestures. I haven't got a
copy of *Endsville* (which was published by Michael Smith's New Writer's Press
in 1967), but I suppose the one poem from it that appears in the latest "New and
Selected Poems" (*A Snail in My Prime*, 1993) is a representative sample of the
best of that early work:

> Of my love's body I think
> That it is a white window.
> Her clothes are curtains:
> By day drawn over
> To conceal the light;
> By night drawn back
> To reveal the dark.

What I'd notice about this now is the deliberate clarity of the saying. There's a
kind of purposeful plainness about the statements, in spite of the oddly impacted
syntax of the first two lines, the surprising main image itself, and the enigmatic
meaning of "the dark." The manner suggests a politely meticulous speaker
who's keen to convey his meaning—to *communicate*—in as precise, immediate,
and unambiguous a way as possible. And no matter how richly complicated,

how difficult, or how intellectually and emotionally various Durcan's subsequent poems and their meanings become, I'd be inclined to say that this well-
mannered wish for plain communication underlies all his work. Like a traveler
returned from strange parts, he is always concerned to share the nature of the
journey and the true state of where he's been.

Old Hat

What follows are excerpts from pieces I've written about Durcan's work over
the years.[1]

1. Observe, too, Paul Durcan becoming one of the most original Irish poetic
voices, doodling in the margins of *Teresa's Bar*—Celtic crossed with Marvel
Comics.

2. . . . For all the outrage, desperation and darkness of its content, anatomising
public and private ills in a language of startling directness—comic, pathetic and
angry by turns or all at once—*The Berlin Wall Café* is a tonic, an exhilaration, a
surge of imaginative energy as irrepressible as whatever manages, when we're
stormbeaten, to keep us going." Putting on voice after voice as if they were hats
(a wife, a lover, a priest, a Catholic father, a melancholy Russian, the perturbed
son of a man with five penises, a witness to loving anarchy, a loutish business-
man, a gas-meter man who thinks "it would be / Uplifting to meet the Dalai
Lama," various newscasters, a loving, distressed, penitent husband, among others), Durcan reminds me of the Fool in *King Lear*—trying to make sense of the
storm, mocking the world of respectable corruptions, keeping the rest of us
sometimes in stitches, but always bringing us to our right senses. The poems are
clown-scripts in deadly earnest, by means of which the poet enters the disastrous
world of men and women at the mercy of one another or bullied by the various
life-denying hypocrisies-in-residence of Church and State. Maybe Durcan is, as
he's been called, a visionary poet. Certainly there are moments of exalted vision
to be found here (the naked happy anarchy of the "Man Smoking a Cigarette in
the Barcelona Metro," for example, or the moving applause for fathers in "10:30
a.m. Mass, June 16, 1985"), but it seems better to call Durcan a great listener.
His best achievement, it seems to me, is to put our lives into recognisable
speech, speech that rollercoasts between the weird and the familiar, now bra-
zenly colloquial, now ringing with echoes of literary tradition . . .

. . . Mainly spoken in a voice that is as close to Durcan's "own" as we're likely
to get, the poems in the marriage section of *The Berlin Wall Café* add up to an
extended penitential elegy for what was once whole and is now broken. In these
poems Durcan gives a fresh twist to the term "confessional poetry." According
to Kavanagh, verse was the only place where a man could confess with dignity.

Durcan carries this a stage farther by dismantling and casting out that dangerous category—dignity. And perhaps the most remarkable fact about these surprising and disturbing confrontations with the accidents and essence of marriage is that they make successful use of some of the comic forms of drama and dramatic narrative which the poet uses for those poems dealing with the public domain, encircling them with an intensity of personal feeling and private revelation sharper and deeper than any he has touched before. . . . These poetic (albeit one-sided) anatomies of love, marriage and family are the most extraordinary utterances on the subject yet to have appeared in Irish poetry, nor do I know anything in modern British or American poetry to put beside them. In them, Durcan has found a strange, satisfying way to perform the full range of his feelings—to go public with them, to dramatise them, and at the same time to convince of their absolute privacy, their intimate actuality. Allegorical of the woe and wonder that is in marriage, the poems are also a stunning explication of the one unique, unrepeatable relationship between this man and this woman . . .

. . . No one in contemporary Irish poetry has been "gifted with so fine an ear" for the sound of Irish speech. I imagine him as sired, in this respect, by Kavanagh, by Myles na gCopaleen, and by Joyce: Kavanagh for the plain speech, the tune on a slack string; Myles for the wicked exactitudes, the deadpan scenarios that get weirder and weirder; and Joyce for the energy and variety of it all, and for the way that speech reveals consciousness . . .

. . . Some of the poem-scripts don't seem animated by a core of necessary drama and so, like jokes told before, don't outlast their telling ("The Man with Five Penises," for example, or "Archbishop of Dublin to Film Romeo and Juliet," or the soberer "Bob Dylan Concert at Slane, 1984"). And sometimes Durcan doesn't seem quite to know how to end a poem: otherwise strong and surprising pieces like "Girls Playing with Boys" or "The Pietá's Over" or "On Falling in Love with a Salesman in a Shoeshop" sort of trail off at the end in an indecisive way. But these are small faults in a collection that's a triumph of coherence, of feeling, of language, and of style.

3. When I read or hear the poems of Paul Durcan, it is like listening to a man standing at a boundary and, in the accents of a refugee or a displaced person, crying out over our arbitrary world of borders—whether those borders are sexual, political, tribal, social, or geographical. I read his poems as scripts which—with something of the buoyant anarchy and anarchic buoyancy of Chagall, that painter's wild and sudden and loving weightlessness—undermine and rearrange our fixed, that is bounded, sense of the way things are. In his ventriloquent voices I hear the Cumaean Sibyl or the Hag of Beare speaking in the commonplace and contemporary Irish accents of the chapel, the pub, the office, or the shopping mall. And, good satirist that he is, he is always writing love poems—scolding and loving, trying to chant the borders down. He is a denouncer of boundaries, demotic prophet of a world without them.

4. . . . To get a little closer to Durcan's specific poetic effects, I'll concentrate on a couple of features that first affect me when I read individual poems: metaphor, and the poem's movement. . . . Probably the first things that strike me about Durcan's metaphors are their extremity, their extravagance, their naive and "primary" air. Here are some random examples:

> Swags of red apples are his cheeks;
> Swags of yellow pears are his eyes;
> Foliages of dark green oaks are his torsos;
> And in the cambium of his bark juice lies.
>
> ("Polycarp")

> And I'd sit in her lap with my hands
> Around her waist gulping her down
> And eating her green apples
> That hung in bunches from her thighs
> And the clusters of hot grapes between her breasts.
>
> ("Fat Molly")

> Under her gas meter I get down on my knees
> And say a prayer to the side-altars of her thighs,
> And the three-light window of her breasts.
>
> ("The Day Kerry Became Dublin")

> I turn about and see
> Over the windowpane's frosted hemisphere
> A small black hat sail slowly past my eyes
> Into the unknown ocean of the sea at noon.
>
> ("Hat Factory")

What all these passages have in common is their benign violence of metaphorical language. In each case Durcan deliberately transfigures the world normally seen, so that it embodies a truth higher or deeper than the one on usual view. In each case the means are simple: the subject becomes something else—an orchard, an oakwood, a fruitful feast, a chapel, a flying ship, an unknown ocean. Stated as fact, none of these "vehicles" is odd or esoteric in itself. In fact, there's an almost childlike naiveté about them. Addressed initially more to the eye than the mind, these images speak to something or somewhere quite primitive in us, full of primary colours and sensations (red, yellow green; bunches, clusters; hot; slowly). When you consider what is being described in such terms, however (a male or female body, a hat, daylight), then the extravagant nature of this "simplicity" (underlined by the undemanding grammatical and syntactical forms, which put no impediments between utterance and understanding) strike home. In an act of joyous subversion, these figures of speech unmake and then remake the known world. . . . Insisting on something deeper than the factual layer of reality we call history, they proclaim the truth of sensual and emotional

possibility. They make a world that surprises us, that shocks us into an awareness of such possibility. The fusion of extravagance and naiveté is designed not
only to awaken us to a refreshed version of the world we conventionally inhabit,
but to coax us to embrace the possibility of this new world in ourselves: how
can it not be within our grasp when it appears, is offered, in such a simple, almost childlike way? This is how the world could be, were we rightly awake. So
something of an evangelical tilt determines metaphors like this, a fact that, if
recognised, might open up the otherwise encumbering notion of Durcan's being
a "visionary." Metaphors such as those quoted above give concrete point to
Derek Mahon's observation that Durcan is "a seeker and, in Rimbaud's sense, a
seer." What Durcan sees is a world transformed, released from the old limiting
laws of singular, inflexible actuality. . .

. . . I would say there is something of Chagall (also a seer) in Durcan's habits of
metaphor, in the way the ordinary world (its ordinariness known in the plain,
colloquially direct, uncomplicated language) is altered to become a zone of
metamorphic energies. In this colorful and kinetic transfiguration of the world
by the word, Durcan activates a Blakean (or, nearer home, a Bloomian) hope for
an existence that is all positive energy, all flow, all active peace. As invocations
of a latent and fertile goodness in the natural possibility of the world (though
human nature, not Nature, is Durcan's subject), these metaphors and their like
are an attempt to insert that possibility into the damaged realm of the actual (and
a way of fusing, maybe, the spirits of Kavanagh and Austin Clarke). Such metaphors achieve some of the same or similar effects as do Chagall's disturbances
of gravity and expectation, his running together of lyrical, narrative, and autobiographical elements, his political gestures that are at once intimate and expansive. (See, for example, Chagall's *The Painter and His Wife* [1969], *The Martyr*
[1939], or *Around Her* [1945].)

As with Chagall, too, the effect of many such metaphors in Durcan is celebratory. Both artists (of course at their different levels of sheer achievement)
embody the extravagance of secular prayer in the comic mode. In work like this
the world is renewed, liberated, made over in imagination; the distance between
indicative and optative moods is eliminated. In deference to the larger laws of
feeling, the old binding laws of nature are suspended. Both Chagall's amazing
collocations and Durcan's metaphors testify to this truth of imagination, and the
innocent force of their desire is underlined by a kind of naive awkwardness that
marks the style in each case, granting, I suppose, further proof of its sincerity.
The way Chagall invites us to look at a painting may help in the reading of a
typical piece of Durcan metaphor-making like the following:

> Our children swam about our home
> As if it was our private sea,
> Their own unique, symbiotic fluid
> Of which their parents also partook.
> Such is home—a sea of your own—
> In which you hang upside down from the ceiling

With equanimity, while postcards from Thailand on the mantlepiece
Are raising their eyebrow markings benignly:
Your hands dangling their prayers to the floorboards of your home,
Sifting the sands underneath the surfaces of conversation,
The marine insect life of the family psyche.

                         ("Windfall, 8 Parnell Hill, Cork")

The extended life of this metaphor is characteristic of Durcan's procedures in a
number of ways. The fairly simple transforming turn of the first two lines
("swam . . . as if . . . sea") is more and more twisted as the passage continues,
implicating more and more elements; the image gains a life of its own, and we
are, as we are in a painting by Chagall, in a realm that hesitates between allegory and dream. The passage from "Our children swam about our home" to
"The marine insect life of the family psyche" is a gradual thickening of metaphor, the poet's own surrender to its generative logic. And, as in the earlier examples, the metaphor is an expression of difference, the poet's way of putting
an emotional truth that defies or simply eludes more rootedly normative habits
of expression. The nature and activity of Durcan's metaphor, that is, imply and
give solid body to a belief in the (otherwise inexpressible) spiritual and emotional dimensions of ordinary experience. Indeed, as the ordinary is luminously
opened up (deepened, set flowing), spiritual and emotional dimensions are made
one, identified. Metaphors like this are Durcan's way of getting beyond the limits of representation and touching those of revelation. Among other things, his
metaphors are his poetic acts of faith, hope, and charity.

    A poetic world of such extremities and such simplicities as those consti-
tuted by Durcan's metaphors seems designed to make us see our experience
with newborn eyes—newborn, that is, in spirit and in feeling. Whether his subject is autobiographical or political, private or public, the nature of his metaphors will always attack those outworn, conventional, and spiritlessly habitual
ways of receiving experience that are the death alike of public and private life—
of our life as citizens and as beloved and loving creatures. In this way, Durcan's
metaphors are at the single root of his double being as a poet, equally fundamental to his satires and his celebrations. They are proclamations of a different
world, a world in which good and evil, joy and sorrow, are tangible absolutes,
actors in a perpetual psychomachia where—as he says of "the dark school of
childhood"—"tiny is tiny, and massive is massive" (*En Famille*, 1979,") . . .

. . . What I am calling the "movement" of Durcan's poems is another of the
elements that first compels my attention as a reader. I am intrigued by the way a
poem opens, proceeds, concludes; how it gets from point to point; how it charts
its course. Reading it, listening to it, I am struck by how, in spite of its quick
and often surprising shifts of direction, I never lose my way. I am interested in
the way the poem can contain a narrative, but how the narrative is usually absorbed by, dissolved in, the narrator's feelings (exalted, lyrical, dejected, angry,
satirical) about the story being told. This conjunction of story and feelings about
it (a condition that also seems to underlie formal and substantive qualitites in the

painting of Chagall) gives an oddly *radial* quality to many of the poems. Images and metaphors generate digressions, and this trajectory of movement (an operation on and in space) in turn produces a peculiar tempo (operation on and in time). So one is never lulled or assuaged or allured by a poem of Durcan's. Rather one is always conscious, sometimes uneasily, of being moved (in many ways) from one point or area (or emotion or conviction) to another.

Since this feature of a poem cannot be discussed in excerpts, I will use "On Seeing Two Bus Conductors Kissing Each Other in the Middle of the Street" by way of illustration:

> Electricity zig-zags through me into the blue leatherette
> And I look around quick and yes—
> All faces are in a state of shock:
> By Christ,—this busride
> Will be the busride to beat all busrides.
>
> Sure enough the conductor comes waltzing up the stairs—
> The winding stairs—
> And he comes up the aisle a-hopping and a-whooping
> So I take my chance
> Being part of the dance:
> I say: "A penny please."
> "Certainly, Sir" he replies
> And rummages in his satchel
> Until he fishes out a tiny penny,
> An eenshy-weenshy penny,
> Which he hands me crooning—
> "That's especially for you Sir—thank you, Sir."
>
> So there it is, or was:
> Will the day or night ever come when I will see
> Two policemen at a street corner caressing each other?
> Let the prisoners escape, conceal them in a sunbeam?
> O my dear Guard William, O my darling Guard John.

With the title as a springboard, the poem gets off to a flying start. The first stanza plunges us into the speaker's responses to this curious event. The movement is from stimulus to response to observation to further response (electricity, look, faces, exclamation). Speed is intensified by spoken immediacy, accentuated by the present tense, the "yes," the impulsive "By Christ" (apt, as it turns out, in a tract on brotherly love), and the enthusiastically colloquial "busride to beat all busrides." The movement is itself a quick zig-zag and obliges us to wonder "what next?" We realise we are in the grip of a hectic teller of tales.

The first six lines of the next stanza form the next phase. Again the movement of the sentence—broken into metrically uneven lines that respond to the segment-logic of the phrase, the telling breath—is a speedy zig-zag, marked by

loud rapid rhythmic action (waltzing, a-hopping, a-whooping) and assisted sub-
liminally by the parenthetical reminder of the winding stairs. Quick, slightly
crazy and maybe-not-there-at-all references (to Yeats in "winding stairs" and
"part of the dance," to the marriage ceremony in "up the aisle") further make the
movement helter-skelter, yet always forward, coming to rest in the distinct, simple, actual request, "A penny please" (what the passenger normally says—or
used to say when "a penny" could still buy a bus-ticket, an archaic economic
fact that Durcan may be making part of his comedy).

The normality of this exchange ("'Certainly, Sir,' he replies") then swerves
swiftly into the anarchic event, described, however, in a perfectly straightforward anecdotal manner: the conductor, instead of taking, gives the narrator-
passenger a penny. By this time the world is topsy-turvy, but then there is yet
another curve, into the parenthetical baby-talk ("eenshy-weenshy") that retards
the narrative but heightens the comic suspense. Finally, the comedy crests over
the crooning gesture and the extravagantly solicitous manner. As a reader I'm
being presented here, at high speed, with a series of most unlikely occurrences—all unlikely because (*because!*) they are so expressively charitable. The
speed and dodgy trace of the narrative hide its satire in strangeness: awakened
by comedy I find—through this rapid mental run-around—that the point is satirical.

The final stanza steps back from the comic event to make the satiric point
more decisive, and the reader has to leave the field of narrative and enter a more
speculative zone. In the longer, steadier lines, movement slows to a more meditative pace, then veers into the subversive possibility of two policemen (more
sinister embodiments of authority than bus conductors) "caressing each other."
This in turn—by means of a grammatical and syntactical skidding that, unusual
in Durcan, reminds me of Muldoon—moves into a sort of prayer, thence to a
dramatised exchange (but who speaks?) of erotic endearments between the two
solidly named Guards. And then, suddenly and surprisingly, it is over.

Even in this brisk description it's easy to see that the movement of the
whole poem is rapid and dashing—hare-like in shifting direction yet always
advancing to its proper end. In such a movement, I suspect Durcan is appropri-
ating something of the performative skill of the oral poet, who can preserve a
spine of anecdotal purpose while swerving through strange, abrupt, not immediately explicable transitions. The presence of the speaking performer is what
gives unity (and its own acceptable logic) to this variety and speed. And it is this
(imagined) speaking presence that makes such movement real and convincing,
tuning me (as I listen to the "script") to the subversive satire of the poem even
before I begin to deal with it in a more analytical way. The poem's movement,
that is, exercises a primary (and—given the suggestion of orality—primitive)
power, bringing me to a sort of pre-cognitive understanding. By responding to it
in this way I am participating in its comic anarchy in—from the conventional
point of view—a dangerous way . . .

. . . Both in metaphor and movement, then, Durcan's work manifests a drive
toward a different world of expanded moral, spiritual, and emotional conscious-

ness. Even at its most private (as in the marriage poems) it can be a public exhortation toward renewal. This condition is identified and aspired to by means of radical satire and celebration, by comic subversion and high but basically simple rhetorical gesture. Both metaphor and movement, at the centre of his work as I see it, show the work to be a creative attempt to bully, lovingly, the Republic into becoming a different world. In the animated metaphors and the restless movement of these poems it is possible to detect—through the oddly commanding voice of a comic scapegoat—an enterprising, surprising, courageous drive toward grace. In Durcan's way of "being present" he performs an important job for and in Irish poetry and, more largely, Irish life. As vividly as any, his poetry shows the possibility for a rich and complicated connection between the two.

Nourishment: Kavanagh, Keats (*Keats?*)

The influence of Kavanagh is two-fold: formal and substantive. It affects the way the poems take shape, and it affects the way Durcan sees, takes in, and speaks back to the world. From Kavanagh comes a trust for the actual and the ordinary, as well as the courage to see that love can inhere in the actual and the ordinary. An originating text could be "The Hospital":

> A year ago I fell in love with the functional ward
> Of a chest hospital: square cubicles in a row,
> Plain concrete, wash basins—an art lover's woe,
> Not counting how the fellow in the next bed snored.
> But nothing whatever is by love debarred,
> The common and banal her heat can know.
> The corridor led to a stairway and below
> Was the inexhaustible adventure of a gravelled yard.
>
> This is what love does to things: the Rialto Bridge,
> The main gate that was bent by a heavy lorry,
> The seat at the back of the shed that was a suntrap.
> Naming these things is the love-act and its pledge.
> For we must record love's mystery without claptrap,
> Snatch out of time the passionate transitory.

A great many of the qualities of this sonnet find their way into Durcan's verse, among them the vision it contains (whereby the most mundane facts of material life—ungilded by sentimentality or "art"—take on an edge of radiance, an aura of spiritual importance), and the casual colloquialism of the language itself, which is the perfectly apt expression ("beyond claptrap") of that vision. In addition there's the humor ("how the fellow in the next bed snored"), the eye for unremarkable detail (the gate "bent by a heavy lorry"), the willingness to make a large, even abstract, emotional gesture, but in simple terms ("This is what love does to things"), and the candour of the poet's own commitment ("For we must record love's mystery").

There are differences, of course. Kavanagh, for example, often relied formally, as he does here, on the compact enclosure of the sonnet to give coherent and satisfying shape to his experience. Durcan (with the exception of his idiosyncratic engagement with the ballad tradition), is much more thoroughly committed to the open form, letting the material—and perhaps the requirements of the speaking voice—give shape to the poem.[2] (The open form itself, however, may owe something to Kavanagh's own practice in *The Great Hunger*, while both poets took instruction in the use of supple open forms from modern American poetry.) Another difference is that Kavanagh is much more conservative in his use of image and implication. One can only imagine, for example, what Durcan would do with the suggestions built into the language of the first line and a half of "The Hospital," how he might follow to much wilder and weirder extremes the hint of that unusual passion and the bland normality of its phrasing ("I fell in love with the functional ward of a chest hospital . . . "). Yet, even with such differences, it is easy to see why Durcan should say that Kavanagh was one of two artists who "changed everything for me," teaching him "that life was fundamentally good . . . that there was nothing that was not fit matter for a poem . . . and that poetry was most nearly poetry when it was most nearly prose."[3]

Durcan's sense of the goodness of life comes through everywhere: even his satire and his elegies are celebratory acts. But while the initial stimulus for this is admittedly triggered by Kavanagh, the shape it achieves is very different from that given to it by the older poet. For Kavanagh located this celebratory force in himself, in his recovered or remembered response to aspects of the natural world like the Canal, in his own capacity to find a kind of Zen passivity and a capacity for praise ("So be reposed and praise, praise, praise / The way it happened and the way it is"). The locus of Kavanagh's freedom (and the source of his conviction about the goodness of life) is this admitted self—which is, however, only "a single item in the picture," is a self freed from selfishness. This ability to be and celebrate an unabashed self (even if it leads to that dead end which Kavanagh himself hit as a poet, as the last pieces in *Collected Poems* suggest) is what liberated Irish poetry after Kavanagh in inestimably valuable ways. While Durcan absorbed that influence, however, he avoided its more dangerous consequences by refusing to remain in the glasshouse of the self. His conviction of life's goodness has an extraordinarily broad application. His celebrations always reach deliberately beyond the self to the other, validating lives outside his own.

Kavanagh's pioneering post-romanticism—his acceptance not only of the local and the ordinary but also of the contradictory self—might be described in Keats's term, "Negative capability . . . that is, when a man is capable of being in uncertainties, mysteries, doubts, without any irritable reaching after fact and reason." (*Letters*, Dec. 22, 1817) "The day I walked out on Reason," says Kavanagh, "was the best day of my life." And "To Hell with commonsense" he says, and "to hell / With all reasonable / Poems in particular," for the soul needs to be honored with "arguments that cannot be proven." In the Irish tradition, this willingness to exist in doubt and uncertainty is the necessary counterpoint to Yeatsian certainties, to the magnificent prejudices that hammered Yeats's extraordinary body of work into a unity Kavanagh could never achieve. By establishing this decisive break with Father Yeats, however, Kavanagh himself fathers a great deal of contemporary Irish poetry, his line most easily traced, I'd say, into the very different work of Heaney and of Durcan.

In Durcan, Kavanagh's version of "negative capability" leads to a much more robustly dramatised self than anything in the older poet. In fact, it might be said that what Durcan adds to the concept of negative capability is, consciously or unconsciously, Keats's own notion of "the poetical Character":

> It is not itself—it has no self—It is everything and nothing—It has no character—it enjoys light and shade; it lives in gusto, be it foul or fair, high or low, rich or poor, mean or elevated ... A poet is the most unpoetical of anything in existence, because he has no identity—he is continually in for and filling some other body ... the poet has ... no identity—he is certainly the most unpoetical of all God's creatures ... When I am in a room with people ... the identity of every one in the room begins to press upon me, so that I am in a very little time annihilated—not only among men; it would be the same in a nursery of children ... If a Sparrow come before my Window, I take part in its existence and peck about the gravel.
> (*Letters,* Oct 27, 1818, Nov 22, 1817)

This ability to leave the self and totally inhere in another existence is surely what enables those poems in which Durcan inhabits character dramatically, becoming a multitude of perfectly realised voices, among them the voice of Ireland "Before the Celtic Yoke," or that of the archbishop "dreaming of the harlot of Rathkeale," or the inimitable ballad whisper of "The Kilfenora Teaboy":

> Oh indeed my wife is handsome.
> She has a fire lighting in each eye,
> You can pluck laughter from her elbows
> And from her knees pour money's tears;
> I make all my tea for her,
> I'm her teaboy on the hill,
> And I also thatch her roof;
> And I do a small bit of sheepfarming on the side.

An essential list of these voices would also include Micheál Mac Liammóir, Sister Agnes writing home about the reverend mother's pregnancy, the middle-class male horrors who speak such poems as "The Propellor I Left in Bilbao" and "Charlie's Mother," or the amazing recitative between the parish priest of Tullynoe and his housekeeper. As if to further underline the poet's surrender to otherness, a great many of these voices are women, among them "The Woman Who Keeps her Breasts in the Back Garden," the upper-middle-class affectation of the woman who asks, "What Shall I Wear, Darling, to *The Great Hunger*?" and—most astonishingly rich and strange—the Haulier's wife who meets Jesus "On the Road to Moone," and that magnificent monologist from the dead, the nun who tells the story in "Six Nuns Die in Convent Inferno":

> How lucky I was to lose—I say, lose—lose my life.
> It was a Sunday night, and after vespers
> I skipped bathroom so I could hop straight into bed
> And get in a bit of a read before lights out.

Revealing "the poetical character," this inhabiting of other beings is itself also a kind of negative capability, a deliberate dramatising of negative capability. Since Kavanagh could only lyricise his negative capability, and reflect on it, Durcan's invention of a world of other voices shows how he absorbs and amplifies towards his own unique ends those inclusive lessons of attention and generosity which he learned from his master.

Coming from the Pictures

Durcan's dramatising capacity (which makes many of the poems feel less like conventional "dramatic monologues" than like miniature scripts) is also what makes possible all those poems he has written on / after paintings—most notably in the two collections *Crazy About Women* (1991) and *Give Me Your Hand* (1994). With growing (and outrageous) authority, these poems are another sign in Durcan of Keats's "poetical character." For in them the poet usually inhabits one of the figures in a painting, frequently a minor figure or detail, and from this locus of identity speaks some peculiar revelation, most often at a blindingly oblique angle to what would normally be seen in (and as) the painting itself. Rubens' great *Samson and Delilah*, for example, opens in the following startling way: "I am a master barber / Trained in Cleveland Ohio, / Working in Antwerp, Belgium . . . " Sometimes the speaker even exists outside but in some decisive relationship with the painting, as in "A Cornfield with Cypresses," which begins, "Let me make no bones about A Cornfield with Cypresses— / Make clear straightaway who I am. / I am the painter's mother." Seen in the light of Keats's concept of "poetical character," the paintings become Durcan's way away from the self, although this not-self can utter in oblique or direct ways many of Durcan's own recurrent preoccupations, as these have been gleaned from poems in "his own" voice. (That voice, too, of course, is itself a kind of dramatised fiction, another example of "poetical character": there is always a sense of some gap between the speaker of any poem and the actual Paul Durcan, a gap of a sort that Kavanagh—except to some degrees in his satires—doesn't manage. This is true even in the poems that record, in his own and others' voices, the breakdown of Durcan's marriage: the experience has been *rendered* in some way, making him and his wife figures in a landscape of parable.)

One of the things that interests me in the way Durcan treats paintings he makes poems from is how the treatment is at once subjective and objective. On the one hand, the picture is inhabited as Keats inhabits the sparrow pecking about the gravel. But there's a sense in which the painting is also obliterated by what Durcan speaks out from the interior, speaks out of what he finds there for himself. So, in one of his best poems of this kind, "The Riding School" (the painting is by Karel Dujardin), he speaks in the voice of the groom in the painting, but his subject has become art and the Northern violence ("My song is nearing the end of its tether; / Lament in art whose end is war"), neither of which could be seen as "belonging" to Dujardin'a work. And so, in "Lady Mary Wortley Montague," it is the voice of the lady's clavicytherium that says ("My role each evening / [is] To stand nude in the bay window"), while Joshua Reynolds' portrait of General Sir Banastre Tarleton gives rise to a meditation in the voice of the subject's father on his son's prowess as a rugby player and his death from AIDS. People and things are given voices in these poems, voices that grant life and expression to an assortment of curious existences. By his simultaneous commitment both to subjective and objective truths, it might be said that what Durcan is doing here is letting the artist, the poet, function as an agent of liberation. For the existences in question, which belong to the paintings which trigger the poems, are in a sense set free—by the poem's independent voice—of the enclosure into which the original work of art has confined them, to which it has abandoned them.

Ideas such as these may allow us to see the "painting-poems"—so idiosyncratic, so astonishing in their inventiveness, their humor, their often powerful seriousness—as a sign of Durcan's conception of art, a conception of art which is a development of Kavanagh's aesthetic. For that aesthetic refused the sense of enclosure, wanted desperately to break down the sense of artifact as an exclusive space, a confinement, a Grecian Urn or a golden bird, wanted to make art in some way coterminous with life. "A man, (I am thinking of myself)," says Kavanagh—in what Durcan has described as "one of the holy texts," the "Author's Note" to his *Collected Poems*—"innocently dabbles in words and rhymes and finds that it is his life." So Durcan, by breaking into the sacrosanct enclosure of the paintings, is freeing something he has found there, something latent in the artwork itself, something that illustrates his conviction about the continuum between art and life. By extending Keats's notions of "poetical character" and "negative capability," mediated as they were through something indispensable in Kavanagh, Durcan in these painting-poems (as well as in other areas of his work) manages to establish an aesthetic of his own, which might be loosely described as an amplified poetics of the common touch. In the modern Irish tradition, Kavanagh inaugurates this tendency by his deliberate movement away from the language manners of Yeats and the Revival. Durcan carries this movement even further—by populating his poems with an extraordinary assortment of demotic voices, and by establishing a convincing continuum between the world we ordinarily inhabit and the other world of the work of art.

Rejoyce

Everything I said above about Keats might also, of course, have come to Durcan (and Kavanagh) from another source, closer to home. For Joyce's *Ulysses* is a book Durcan, like Kavanagh before him, reveres, and it is in *Ulysses* that one could find sources for many of the elements I've been describing. The notion that life is fundamentally good, for example, as well as the notions of negative capability and poetical character are embodied in Leopold Bloom, while the stylistic inhabitation of others—people, things, thoughts, whatever—is what makes the Circe/Nighttown chapter the extraordinary carnival of metamorphoses it is. Aside from these, Joyce's astounding capacity for voice-invention must have left its mark, even if we go no farther than the collision between flagrant and fragrant colloquialism to be heard in the movement from the crass narrator of the Cyclops chapter to the genteel tones of Gerty MacDowell in Nausicaa.

In the notion of "openness," the influence of Bloom may be most keenly felt. For Bloom's openness to the other, human and otherwise, is apparent throughout the novel. Whether he is sympathising with "Poor Mrs Purefoy's" pregnancy ("Sss. Dth, dth, dth! Three days imagine groaning on a bed with a vinegared handkerchief around her forehead, her belly swollen out! Phew! Dreadful simply!"), wondering about the blind youth's sense of smell, listening to the typesetting machine "doing its level best to speak," or hearing the creak of a door "asking to be shut," Bloom is perpetually engaged by the world outside himself.[4] And the simple formulation Joyce gives him in order to reveal this definitive and endearing feature could also apply to Durcan's strategy of multiple voices, rooting it in a particular, and particularly receptive, response to the world: for "everything," says Bloom, "speaks in its own way."[5] Nor is Bloom's perpetual going out from himself, his openness to the polyglottal nature of the world, escapist in the ordinary sense: he does not use it in order to censor his pain about Molly's infidelity, or his aches over his own life, although it can sometimes serve as therapeutic distraction. It should be seen, rather, as the action of "the poetical character," while Bloom's almost infinite tolerance—the moral extension of his sympathetic nature—is "negative capability" in action, standing up against the purveyors of egotistic and nationalistic "facts and reasons," his whole existence a testament to unirritable persistence in the hard life of uncertainty.

As far as *stylistic* instruction is concerned, *Ulysses* contains numerous specific elements that likely marked Durcan's work. Chapters such as Cyclops and Nausicaa, as I've said, are treasure troves of speech possibility in their two radically different registers of the colloquial. A random dip into the first produces the following gem of unaffected Dublinese: "And begob there he was passing the door with his books under his oxter and the wife beside him and Corny Kelleher with his wall eye looking in as they went past, talking to him like a father, trying to sell him a secondhand coffin."[6] An equally random encounter with Nausicaa finds this very different sound: "Gerty MacDowell who was seated near her companions, lost in thought, gazing far away into the distance was in very truth as fair a specimen of winsome Irish girlhood as one could wish to see."[7] Such influxes into his work of Dublin speech in its different registers (most of his voices, I'd say, have a definite Dublin colour and texture) should remind us that Durcan's own insistence on his Mayo roots need not distract from the fact that he is—along with Clarke, Kinsella and, more recently, Paula Meehan—a quintessentially Dublin poet.

Beyond this stimulus to distinctive speech, *Ulysses* must also have prompted Durcan's natural inclination towards the metamorphic. In the Circe/ Nighttown chapter, metamorphosis is everywhere: whether a bar of soap sings or a bicycle bell shrieks, everything not only "speaks in its own way" but is able at the slightest provocation to turn into something else. A ceaseless, dreamlike fluency of matter and character dissolves all borders, rattles all categories out of themselves, so the certain concrete world becomes infinitely plastic, fluid, uncertain, and the borders dissolve even between such stubbornly separate entities as this life and the next world, or male and female genders. The sheer exuberance and abundance of these transformations have, I imagine, made a deep and deeply creative impression on Durcan, accounting in part not only for the variety of his inventions and the ease with which he adopts male and female voices, but for the amazing fluency of matter within the poems themselves. So Mayo may be seen in the light of Asia Minor, Christ is abroad on the road to Moone, a woman keeps her breasts in the back garden, a father and son get married "in the church of Crinkle near Birr," a man of forty "has spent all his life reclining in his wife's lap, / Being given birth to by her again and again," and a daughter can daub slime on the face of her snail father lying "under the great snail cairn of Newgrange."

Mimic and metamorphic, therefore, it is easy to see how Joyce's style would be crucial to Durcan's evolution of his own poetic strategies, while the moral nature of Joyce's hero, Bloom, would be equally crucial to the moral configuration Durcan puts on his world. For, in Bloom, Joyce offers an exhilarating mixture of unflinching materialism and utopian idealism, a tolerant nationalism (when asked, "What is your nation?" Bloom insists, but in tones very different from the apoplectic MacMorris, that it is "Ireland . . . I was born here, Ireland") married to universal humanism and humane-ism, a condition of rarely achieved balance between understanding and judgement. It is an equilibrium Durcan—in his very different, often hidden way—is after.

Vox Pop & the Meaning of It All

In stringing together these bits and pieces from Keats and Kavanagh and Joyce, my purpose is not to suggest that Durcan is doing the same thing over again, or doing it in their shadow, but that he has in one way or another been nourished by what is implicit and explicit in their work or in their notions of poetry, of the poet. I believe that ideas such as these have been his creative sustenance, that they make possible and sustain his own idiosyncratic art.[8] And when I ask myself what central and more or less general feature of his art is most explicitly owed to these ideas, I keep returning to the concept of *extension*. For what the Keats ideas, the Kavanagh practice, the Joyce style, the Bloom way of the world have in common is a notion of extension. And extension is a defining mark of Durcan's work: whether in the notice he pays to an overlooked detail or in the way he brings normally hidden voices to articulate life, he is always extending our sympathy for the ordinary, the local, the trivial, the mundane.

The possibility of extending consciousness (this poet's version, I suppose, of Stephen Dedalus's ambition to forge in the smithy of his soul the uncreated conscience of his race) may also be what directs Durcan's striking public recitals of his own poems. For in the intense plucking apart of the phonetic components of language that these entail, his voice draws inexorably to our attention the slightest detail of linguistic presence. The smallest trace of *coloratura* in a vowel or a diphthong is heard for itself, as is the decisively aspirated or sibilant finality of a consonant, or the slightest modulation of tone or accent—allowing whole characters, whole forms of life, to come alive in slow motion, embodied by his language and its aural resources (for, as he well knows, *everything speaks in its own way*). Such art is surely an art of extension, enlarging our sense both of the world and of the word. It is an art at once meticulous, reassuring, and estranging. Meticulous in the quality of its attention, reassuring in the way it restores what has been overlooked to its properly acknowledged place in the world, and estranging because the quality of the performance makes the language feel odd and unfamiliar to us. While on the page Durcan's language may seem, for all its strangeness, to be anchored in everyday colloquial usage, in the poet's own inimitable performance it becomes a *ritual* of the colloquial.

Beyond its own specific local meanings, then, each poem as performed by the poet has an additional significance, a significance that might be attached to his work as a whole. For in these performances (which carry their own measure of instruction to us as readers, strong hints on how to hear the poems when we read them to ourselves) the ordinary is granted—in an extraordinarily vivid and immediate way—the quality and status of ritual. And finally, in a neat reversal and paradox (forms peculiarly appropriate to the instinctively Christian interior of much of Durcan's work, its weightless migrations through time and space), this act of estrangement is really an instrument of renewed recognition, creating a fresh association and connection with the subject. On the page and in performance Durcan's poems re-connect us with the world, so that in the end connectedness itself is his subject—whether he writes out of his even-handed resistance to public atrocities in Northern Ireland , or out of the divided private region of his broken marriage, fractured family life, the aching gap between father and son. With connectedness as its implicit theme, his work extends our sense of the world, just as his own connection to Joyce and Kavanagh allows him to extend *his* creative world, and by doing so to establish a body of poetry that has become central to contemporary Irish art and, in turn, contemporary Irish consciousness. In his work, that is, he extends what we might call our tradition, and by doing so extends, in his own remarkable way, us all.

Soul Music

Thinking about her own belief in God and in certain acts of religious piety, Molly Bloom presumes that her husband would "scoff if he heard because he never goes to church mass or meeting he says your soul you have no soul inside only grey matter because he doesn't know what it is to have one."[9] Unlike Leopold Bloom (whatever about Joyce), Durcan seems to have what we might call belief in "the soul." Belief, in fact, whether its status be theological or otherwise, is a mark of his stance towards experience and the world from early on. As he says in "The Butterfly is the Hardest Stroke,"

> I have not "met" God, I have not "read"
> David Gascoyne, James Joyce, or Patrick Kavanagh:
> I believe in them.

It is this quality of belief that lends its peculiar touch of authenticity to Durcan's best work. Whether located in a region of conventional belief (such as the church in "10.30 a.m. Mass, 16 June 1985"—Bloomsday!—or "The Crucifixion Circus, Good Friday, Paris, 1981") or in a sexually animated but guiltless environment conventionally at odds with (Irish) religion ("Teresa's Bar," for example, or the bedrooms in "Phyllis Goldberg," and "Lifesaving," or the erotic night-kitchen in "Around the Corner from Francis Bacon"), a great number of the best poems testify to an affirmative faith in that "fundamental goodness" of life which he learned from Kavanagh, a faith to which he, like Kavanagh, often gives a "feminine" character. In terms of style, too—in the way the poems embrace the language and what might be called its sacramental possibility (using its ordinary resources to reveal an extraordinary world)—Durcan at his best communicates belief in what he is saying, and the intensity of faith gives buoyancy as well as conviction to his lines, no matter how weird or unlikely their contents. Whereas the work of Derek Mahon might be described as a poetry of profound scepticism shot through with thin and intermittent flickers of belief, and the work of Seamus Heaney might be seen as a poetry of belief tempered by a stubbornly sceptical naturalism, the work of Durcan seems to live in an unqualified region of faith.

But not of transcendence. This faith is comic, self-aware, human, irrational, a blithe transgressive mix of the here and there, the then and now. It is a faith, too, that trusts itself sufficiently to make mistakes, to take risks, to sound silly. Finally, it is a faith that finds characteristic serio-comic expression in one of his most recent and, it seems to me, best pieces, "A Spin in the Rain with Seamus Heaney." "I have always thought," he remarks, as he and Heaney play a desultory game of ping-pong, "that ping-pong balls— / Static spheres fleet as thoughts— / Have flight textures similar to souls." Surprising as this association is, it is no surprise that it leads to a connection between soul and poetry. For isn't that what it's all been leading to? Certainly it is what this poem comes to rest in, ending as it does with Durcan's withdrawal into the place where soul poetry intersect, the musical space where poetry becomes not only an expression of the spirit, but a moral agent:

> As darkness drops, the rain clears.
> I take leave of you to prepare my soul
> For tonight's public recital. Wishing each other well.
>
> Poetry! To be able to look a bullet in the eye,
> With a whiff of the bat to return it spinning to drop
> Down scarcely over the lapped net; to stand still; to stop.

To stop. Yes. And but of course to—as Beckett says—go on.

1996

NOTES

[1] The pieces from which these have been taken are: "A View from the Bridge: Irish Writing 1977-78," *Éire-Ireland*, XIII (1978) 141-47; "The Community and the Individual," *The Honest Ulsterman*, 81 (1986) 65-73; Introduction to a 1992 reading by Durcan at the 92nd Street "Y" in New York City; and "Two Part Invention: Reading into Durcan and Muldoon," in *New Irish Writing*, edited by James Brophy and Eamon Grennan (Twayne, 1989) 203-29.

[2] An interesting piece could be written on Durcan's ballads. He has made over the form in his own image in a string of poems, such as "Polycarp," "The Kilfenora Teaboy," "Teresa's Bar," "Lord Mayo," "Backside to the Wind," "Fallen Blackbird," "Making Love outside Arus an Uachtaráin," "Drimoleague Blues," "Fermoy Calling Moscow," "Going Home with Sylvia," "Forty-eight Hours in Bed with Joanna," "Brother Can you Spare a Valium," or "Anna Swanton," to name some of them. A distinctive side of his work, that is, consists of these idiosyncratic, slightly off-centred examples of the ballad form. This choice of his may reflect something of Durcan's populist tendencies.

[3] Interview with Mary Dalton, *Irish Literary Supplement* (Fall 1991) 20.

[4] *Ulysses*, Random House edition (1946) 159, 120.

[5] *Ibid*, 120.

[6] *Ibid*, 316.

[7] *Ibid*, 342.

[8] Durcan has acknowledged the painter, R.B. Kitaj as another major source of nourishment and change in his work, and another essay might be devoted to the connection. Kitaj's vivid ways of combining the confessional with the bizarre must have impressed Durcan, as must his mixture of the sexual and the spiritual. I imagine a remark Kitaj has made somewhere about the confessional mode in art may have struck a responsive chord in the poet: "My idea of art is that it conceals and reveals one's life and that what it confesses is, as Kafka called it, 'a rumour of true things.'"

[9] *Ulysses*, 726.

A World of Difference:
Reading Muldoon

On the edge but implicated

Often hard to get a firm purchase on, reluctant to surrender its meanings, the poetry of Paul Muldoon is nonetheless enormously attractive. There's a remarkable openness about it, an agnostic accommodation of many worlds, of multiple points of view. It is at once genial and cool, intimate and oddly remote, both revealing and discreet. At one moment it can be a hall of allegorical, distorting mirrors that reflect in their own unlikely way political or psychological or metaphysical truths. At another it can be a simple gesture of direct emotional power. Many of its best moments manage to be both of these, and more, at once. It has distinct narrative ambition, not just in the longer poems like "Immram" and "The More a Man Has, the More a Man Wants" but also in the way many of the shorter poems are implicit narratives, miniature stories, or the way poems in a single book can echo one another and accrete into larger units. It is also, however, intensely committed to lyrical minutiae and lyrical fragments: an impressive sense of design never throttles an acute, compelling sense of detail. Muldoon's is also a poetry that believes in the efficacy of fiction, well and truly grounded in factual data. His imaginary gardens are hopping mad with real toads. After five books (and he is still an enviable distance from his fortieth birthday)—each energetically different from its predecessors and with its own distinct unity—his original, idiosyncratic, entertaining and disturbing voice has to be one of the most notable features on the landscape of contemporary Irish poetry.[1]

Having chosen to write about Muldoon's work, I was immediately presented with a large number of possible topics. Should I concentrate on his inventive way with traditional Irish material, for example—his witty revision of the vision poem, the *Aisling*; his splicing of Gaelic narrative to American detective story; his fusion of contemporary events in Northern Ireland and native American trickster tales? Should I concentrate on the metamorphic nature of his verse, whether in the narrative or lyric mode? His interweaving of political and sexual areas of experience, often with violence as common denominator, also caught, and held, my attention. The proximity of violence and ordinariness in the Northern situation—the way Muldoon lets us feel the true texture of that situation in such conjunctions—was also a possible subject, as was the presence in the poems of apparently hallucinogenic experience. The theme of the father also presented itself, a figure recurring in many of the poems and in many different masks. Or, on the more strictly formal level, should I deal with Muldoon's metrical individualism, his wonderfully sure ear for the right music of a line or his extraordinary use of the sonnet form, the myriad changes he rings on it with the ecstatic abandon of an intoxicated Quasimodo? Any of these offers itself as a perfectly reasonable and proper topic.

As I considered my own reactions to the poems, however, I decided to explore in more depth a topic that seemed to me simpler and in a way more fundamental than any of those I have mentioned. This was the point in most of the poems where I located my own primary pleasure and fascination, a point preceding and underlying other, more cognitively explicit elements in the poems and responses in myself. On reflection, of course, this observation of mine should have come as no surprise (although almost everything in a Muldoon poem comes as a surprise). For what I kept noticing in the early stages of my encounter with any of these poems was what any strong poet will make me notice—namely his or her handling of the language. In the present case that general consideration had to be even more deliberately refined: the particular elements of language that insisted on my earliest, startled attention here were grammar, syntax, and tone of voice. It was Muldoon's peculiar handling of, or behaviour in these three areas that first began to shape my response to the experience offered by the poem. In these three zones of language, I believe, it is possible to discover—almost before it becomes conscious of itself—Muldoon's instinctive apprehension of the world.

Grammar, syntax, tone of voice: I have chosen, pretty much at random, one poem in which to observe how these three elements operate. I would imagine it is more or less representative. From *Why Brownlee Left* (1980), it is called "Making the Move."

> When Ulysses braved the wine-dark sea
> He left his bow with Penelope,
>
> Who would bend for no one but himself.
> I edge along the bookshelf.
>
> Past bad Lord Byron, Raymond Chandler,
> *Howard Hughes: The Hidden Years*,
>
> Past Blaise Pascal, who, bound in hide,
> Divined the void in his left side:
>
> Such books as one may think one owns
> Unloose themselves like stones
>
> And clatter down into this wider gulf
> Between myself and my good wife;

A primus stove, a sleeping bag,
The bow I bought through a catalogue

When I was thirteen or fourteen
That would bend, and break, for anyone,

Its boyish length of maple upon maple
Unseasoned and unsupple.

Were I embarking on that wine-dark sea
I would bring my bow along with me.

Before I get anywhere near the meaning of this poem I am struck, slowed down, by its curious grammatical action. The sentences have an odd, unorthodox, slightly refracted quality. For one thing, the subject—usually the most anchoring aspect of a statement or sequence of statements—keeps shifting. Beginning as Ulysses, it quickly becomes Penelope (or does the *who* refer, however oddly, to the bow? In either case what I have to experience is the sudden transformation of an object, a grammatical object, whether direct or indirect, into a subject). Then, *I* is the subject, giving way, in a subordinate clause, to *Blaise Pascal*. This in turn cedes to *such books* (following that slightly enigmatic use of the colon), which gives way as subject to the impersonal *one*, then to *primus stove*, *sleeping bag*, and *bow*. On closer inspection, however, these last three turn out most likely to be indirect objects of *I edge . . . Past*. Then *I* becomes subject again, followed by, in the subordinate clause, the understood *bow*. Finally, bringing the poem full circle, the *I* is the subject of the last sentence, in a context that has this last subject (stressed by metrical need in the penultimate line) usurping the action of the first subject, Ulysses.

While I am still trying to get a grip on the subject, I notice—with a slight heightening of unease (or a certain sort of wary exhilaration?)—that its shifty mobility (apt enough in a poem called "Making the Move" and invoking the archetypal voyager) is repeated in the way the verb behaves. For both tense and mood are marked by extreme inconstancy. The first four lines, for example, have three verbs in the indicative mood, two of them in a simple past tense and one in a simple present. The mood and tense of the other verb—*would bend*—are indeterminate. Is it a conditional mood or a past continuous? At some level it has to be a sort of future, since at Ulysses's departure Penelope's not bending is in the future. A past future, perhaps? The present of *I edge* shifts to a past participle (*bound*), then to a simple past (*divined*). After this there's another shift, this time to a present subjunctive (*may think*) and a series of simple presents (*owns, unloose, clatter*). From here we are taken to a past (*bought*), a past imperfect, and a past continuous (*would bend*—or is it a conditional?). The final sentence brings the whole poem to ambiguous rest in a subjunctive and an unambiguous conditional.

However brief and rough this account, it is possible to see from it that Muldoon has taken the two grammatical elements to which we look first for our bearings in most sentences—subject and predicate—and has seriously shaken up whatever conventional expectations we might have of them. He will not allow me, as a reader, to settle down with my normal assumptions of how language should behave. A result of this bewildering, almost indecently kinetic nature of subject and verb is a speedy unsettling of any firm sense of identity, and an equally rapid undermining of any sure sense of time or of the status of action. In the world the speaker brings to life, uncertainty seems a natural law: both the logic of time and the condition of being slip their moorings, and subjective identity itself keeps sliding in and out of the speaker's grasp. But this grammatical unsteadiness never seems to overcome the world of the poem, never reduces it to merely chaotic randomness; rather the world is constituted by such unfixed elements. However much it may disorient the reader, this grammatical indeterminism implies on the part of the speaker a way of knowing experience that is both clear-sighted (each detail lucidly observed) and tolerant of confusion (the void, after all, is *divined*). And because grammar always adumbrates an epistemology, this particular grammatical variety reveals—perhaps involuntarily—a radically sceptical epistemological posture. The world, that is to say, is known in a number of different ways at once, no one of these excluding or taking precedence over another. And since grammar—as what we take to be a definitive given of language—is one of language's most decisively social attributes (i.e., unquestioningly shared; incorrect—as we say—usage normally has social or sociological implications), its unorthodox (not "incorrect") activity here suggests a certain estrangement on the part of the speaker, a sense of being removed from a community of assumptions, isolated, exiled from the centre to the edge, at sea. Before ever touching the *apparent* (surface or narrative) meaning of the poem, then, I can know a considerable amount about the experience it contains and embodies.

The poem's syntax has an equal part to play in shaping my primary (pre-"meaning") response. Technically, of course, it is "the second part of grammar" (OED), dealing with "the established uses of grammatical construction" (OED). For my present purposes, however, I want to separate it from "grammar" and deal with it on its own. Syntax is a spatial and temporal energy governing the shape of a sentence, disposing the (grammatical) elements in a certain way. Put simply, it is the where (and therefore the when) of how the words are in relation to one another. I suspect it is less socially determined than what I have been calling grammar, more malleably responsive to idiosyncratic manipulation by the individual writer/speaker. It suggests more emphatically the operation, or at least the collaboration, of the individual will in the production of meaning, in the effort to make particular sense in language of a given world, a given "being."

The syntax of the first three lines, the first sentence, of "Making the Move" is unexceptional. This is so in spite of the way the third line skids away from the upright organisation of the first two, just enough to give the reader a small pause, a brief hesitation, minor perplexity. The following fifteen lines, however, which make up a single sentence (showing Muldoon's muscular control of line/sentence relationships), put a number of syntactical dubieties in my way. The comma at the end of the first line, for example, sets the inaugural statement off from what follows. After this slight, almost subliminal, oddity, the syntax proceeds in a normal way for four lines, phrase added predictably enough to phrase, the parenthetical extension of "Blaise Pascal" ("who, bound in hide") neatly tucked in. After the colon, however, things begin to go curiously awry. The colon itself is a crucial syntactical instrument: it sets up certain expectations of the way what follows it relates to what precedes it. The first four lines after the punctuation here are unsurprising in themselves and form a syntactically straightforward sentence (subject, predicates, objects—each element deftly and rhythmically fitted to a single line). But what precisely is the relationship between this and the earlier element of the same sentence? I *suppose* it is a species of enlarged apposition, but the peremptory speed with which one of these elements is laid down alongside the other lends a tense, nervous quality to their conjunction. The syntax yokes the elements together without any facilitating gestures of explanation or connection. It immediately implicates me as a reader in some primal awareness of *something unsaid*. (This is confirmed, I suspect, when I later notice the way philosophical or theological *void* evolves into [inter]personal *gulf*: the syntax tunes me to hear more accurately, more feelingly, what the diction and its imagery hint at.)

The next six lines form the last major unit of the poem's long central sentence. Immediately I read them, their syntax ignites uncertainties in my mind. The largest of these concerns the precise nature of the relation between this unit and what has gone before. These connected statements follow a semicolon, but how do they belong to the sentence as a whole? It takes me more than one reading to see that, like the books and metonymic authors mentioned earlier, they are all objects of "I edge . . . past." Syntax works, therefore, to distance object from subject and main verb in an unusual way. It orchestrates a sort of gapped discourse. It forces me to experience a gulf between subject/verb and object (objects, indeed, that seem at first to be subjects themselves).

Individual syntactical particles of these six lines compound the unsteady and uncertain state I am left in by the problems of the larger unit. For one thing, the frustrated expectations of a fulfilling verb upsets my reading at the end of the first line and throughout the extended description of the bow. The apparent construction seems to prepare for a statement that never occurs: the objects seem organised for something that never happens, a destination never arrived at. The syntax involved in the description of the bow, then, also bears some peculiar marks. The paratactic disposition of clauses, for example, keeps me reaching for the "point" of the description, which seems to be perpetually postponed. This sense of postponement is intensified by the way the last two lines sound like an explanatory afterthought, with a further syntactical oddity to be found in the fact that the *cause* of bending and breaking for anyone (the unseasoned and unsupple wood) is placed after its effect. It is also possible to argue that the line, "That would bend, and break, for anyone," bends or breaks the natural syntactic push of the sentence with a kind of parenthetical aside (an aside, however, of central thematic and emotional importance). The management of the statement in these last two lines also heightens the syntactical tension of the whole unit. For by postponing the adjectives, placing them after what they modify, the speaker would seem to be inverting the normal order, although in truth what is happening is that the two lines are actually the object of *bend* and *break* (or are they an adjectival clause qualifying *bow*?). The postponement also adds a possible ambiguity as to precisely which noun ("maple" or "length") the adjectives modify, with a slightly different nuance in each case. So, on top of everything else, syntax naturally disturbs grammatical understanding.

From all this it is easy to see that the six lines are, to say the least, syntactically uneasy, a fact accentuated by the rather curious punctuation (an instrument of syntax): no comma where I might expect one, after "fourteen," and the decisive presence of two commas where they might not have been expected (before and after "and break"). But, then, in the last two lines of the poem, syntax is restored to something straightforward and firmly controlled, a single compound sentence—meticulous in its observance of syntactical norms—bringing the poem to a strong full stop. Couched in conditionals as it is, there is about the syntax itself a kind of unflinching steadiness, a firmness of resolution.

What, in syntactical terms, have I learned from this poem? First I learn something about the poet's sense of the relationship between things. No element in itself is difficult to understand. But the precise nature of their coexistence, the way they add up to a larger unity of complex sense, is problematic. Syntax also suggests the nature of the poet's own particular power over the world he has invented. In Muldoon's case that power lies in maintaining cool control over shifting elements, elements related to one another in unlikely, unpredictable ways. And although relations between objects in the world he offers are dynamic, changing, complex, often strange, the world itself does have design. By means of his syntax the poet comes at sense in this world, both by ordering things in orthodox ways and by upsetting conventional expectations. Muldoon's syntax suggests a double sense of being-in-the-world: on one level things are in their usual places, it is a normal world; on the other, things are unusually located, joined in unexpected ways. And although relations between objects in the world he offers are dynamic, changing, complex, often strange, the world itself does have design. The dynamics of the verse derive in part from shuttling between these two levels, more or less at home in both of them.

Syntax, too, is responsible for the rhythm of the poem (emphatically in evidence in the penultimate couplet), for the way the lines beat, the phrases engage one another. It is the means by which the poet's apprehension of the world (this apprehension being fundamentally an interior rhythmic reality) becomes most articulate. So what Muldoon's musical (i.e., deliberately rhythmic) syntax amounts to is a twofold fact: his awareness of a world in which the relations between things is not what is expected, and his assertion of his own right to arrange the elements as he wishes to suit his purposes. Syntax is power, the poet's authority. In this case it reveals a problematic world and the poet's sense of his own autonomous power to respond to that world in his own way. So world and self—poetic self—are both embodied by this syntax, both given their due. In the way it registers a mode of being, then, Muldoon's syntax adumbrates an ontology.

Moulded by grammar and syntax, a reader's initial experiences of a Muldoon poem can be, as I say, unsettling. Syntax and grammar make the familiar (as all the elements are in themselves) strange. As instruments of estrangement they imply that such an estranging sense of things persists in the very grain and fiber of Muldoon's apprehension of experience. (An analogy for this process of estrangement, this rattling of the known and the familiar, may be found in his inventive handling of the sonnet form. In poem after poem—especially in *Mules, Why Brownlee Left*, and *Quoof*—he dissects the convention, ranging over a multitude of its formal possibilities. In strictly formal terms, that is, the poet again locates himself "on the edge" in deft, fairly radical experimentation, but "implicated" in the conventional source itself. Another analogy—this time a purely linguistic one—may be seen in his use of cliché. Perpetually retreading their balding familiarity, he gives new and curious life to such bland formulations of as "best of both worlds," "as the crow flies," "I would give my right arm." Doing this, he at once stands at the very centre of linguistic habit and on its cutting and renewing edge.)

The third quality or element in my initial response to a Muldoon poem tempers the unsettling experience of grammar and syntax. For, in the midst of its odd, unconventional activity, the poem's tone of voice is ordinary and beguiling, building up my confidence in the normality of the presented world. The tone of voice reassures me that a certain steadiness is to be found in this world; that whatever the problems attaching to things, it is all right for them to be that way. No matter how grammar bewilderingly shifts or how syntax unsettles my sense of expected relationships, the tone of voice remains even, just telling me, in a way that is both reserved and intimate—unemphatic and detailed, no odd tonal gestures, no sudden shifts of register—a few apparently personal facts.

This voice embodies a kind of unflappable sanity among slightly skewed circumstances. It creates a tone at once intimate and formal, moving between the mannerly impersonality of "Such books as one may think one owns" and the more relaxed, personal "myself and my good wife." It can distance into impersonal narrative, as the first lines do; take us closer to the spectacle of personal action ("I edge along the bookshelf"); startle us into an awareness of an emotionally charged situation ("this wider gulf / Between myself and my good wife"); and end on an almost plangent note of personal feeling ("I would bring my bow along with me"). But, different as they are, these three registers slide easily and unobtrusively into one another, each one striking the reader as something familiar, something with the resonance of direct address that is intended to convey information and feeling but in an unsurprising, even genial way. Muldoon himself has referred to "a range of tones," and he singles out "that sweet, inveigling voice" in which "the speaker quite often says, 'Come on in. Please come in, and sit down and make yourself at home.' Usually what happens then is that the next thing you know you get a punch in the nose. In fact, you know

there's been some shift, some change, some dislocation."[2] But for all its minutely graduated shifts, changes, and dislocations, and in spite of that punch in
the nose, it is this carefully controlled and impeccably, almost pedantically,
modulated tone of voice that continues to reassure us as readers that we are in a
knowable, even local world, no matter how its elements behave or relate to one
another, no matter how metamorphically strange or alien it may become. As
distinct from the more palpably designing tones of argument, exposition, demonstration, interrogation, celebration, or lamentation, the tone of "Making the
Move"—as almost always in a Muldoon poem—is basically the inviting and
assuaging one of *narrative*, of telling a story, sharing an anecdote, proffering a
confidence. The absence in this particular case of contextual information or explanation has a double effect: it makes of Muldoon's a *new kind* of narrative,
and it makes me, as a reader, even more grateful for and dependent on that reassuring tone of voice.

The tone of voice is what contains my other two primary elements, grammar and syntax. I mean "contains" in two ways: the tone is an envelope and the
other two elements exist inside it; and tone neutralises the risk of their reducing
the presented world to a chaotic question, a swirl of unresolved relations. Such a
tone of voice allows for a continued civil existence in the face of a world that
shifts about in unsteady, unsettled, and unsettling ways. The air of the poem,
generated by its tone of voice, is benign. In it, the other oddly disposed elements
can abide, without reducing the whole fabric of this world to meaninglessness.
Tone of voice is the suffused nature of the speaker, an *achieved* nature that rises
out of a full, unflinching awareness of the complexities represented (and dramatised) by grammar and syntax. Tone, that is, represents and dramatises the
speaker's hospitality and openness to the world, even when *what* he says is enigmatic. So this tone of voice enables me to welcome and take pleasure in what
may remain impenetrably private. It lets me be intimate with enigma, to share,
with something like communal satisfaction, a family secret.

Tone, finally, is the signature of feeling. It is the audible body of feeling
that in this case is variable and unspoken, yet presses indirectly into the pragmatic naming of things with intimate personal associations. The tone of the
poem indicates the delicate nature of the feeling—its reluctance to name itself,
yet its discreet eagerness to be known. And in the last three couplets the tone,
although still unruffled and discreet, touches, just, an almost confessional level
of personal intensity. It could be said, then, that tone of voice registers as *feeling*
(vulnerable but tolerant) that compound experience of perplexity and deliberate
will which is lodged in the poem's grammar and syntax. In this way the three
elements I have been dealing with are bound together to become one single *primary* (for me) experience of reading the poem. It seems important that this primary response should culminate in *feeling*, both a feeling *inside* the world of the
poem and a feeling *about* the experience in that world. It is as if the poet's various (conscious and unconscious) strategies on what for me is a primary level of
the poem's existence—strategies, that is, of grammar, syntax, and tone of
voice—are all a means of at once concealing and revealing emotion: concealing

its precise nature; revealing its complex range, depth, and variety. So in the very linguistic innards of the poem, the poet is a free agent, odysseying fluently among the inner and outer reaches of his own experience. It is not surprising that this should seem connected to Muldoon's own opinion of "a writer's job," which is, he claims, "So far as any of us can . . . to be a free agent, within the state of oneself, or roaming through the different states of oneself."[3]

"Making the Move" seems to be about parting, fortitude, maybe betrayal, some complicated sense of hurt. It includes a snapshot of the speaker's present interests, and an evocative memory. It glances off the hard facts of personal relationship. It dramatises the activity of a curious, hospitable, restless consciousness, feeling its way (as that primus stove and sleeping bag suggest) into solitude, a solitary existence. Half to itself, half to an impersonal audience, it speaks its strange experience in a deceptively mild-mannered way. Full of sharply delineated facts, it remains elusive about the actual emotional condition of the speaker. It leaves a reader sympathetically connected with quite a number of things, but unable to establish, as it were, a hierarchy of commitment among them. Commitment, finally, is to the unjudged experience as a whole: that is what the poem gently compels. All this, I believe—what has to be a large part of the poem's "meaning"—is implicit in the fusion within the poem of grammar, syntax, and tone of voice.

Such a fusion makes reading a Muldoon poem an exhilaratingly active experience. Such a fusion also allows me to see how the phrase "on the edge but implicated"[4] lies at the very root of the form of life constituted by the poem. The speaker of "Making the Move," for example, is on the edge of his experience, at its periphery, curiously impersonal about it. He is also "on the edge," at some extremity of experience—an end, a beginning. At the same time he is "on edge," as seen in the unexpected and unconventional way he presents that experience. (That he *edges* along the bookshelf lends a literal endorsement to this notion.) "On edge," then, is a bridge from "on the edge" to "implicated." It points to the implicitly perceived difficulty of the world and the emotional pressure of the voice responding to it, both of which reveal how the speaker is necessarily bound to this world, is a feeling part of it, implicated in it. "The move" he is or may be "making" is away from the achingly familiar. It seems fair to say, then, that grammar, syntax, and tone of voice let me know in an immediate and unavoidable way the true depth of meaning in the phrase "on the edge but implicated." They show it to be a basic description of Muldoon's reception of the world, in the grain and fiber of his being.

"Making the Move" is a fairly "unloaded" poem. It does not enter overtly into the more significantly loaded zones of sex, politics, or metaphysics the way many of Muldoon's poems do. Its subject matter is not laden with references to obviously important public or private areas of our world. Yet what I have been saying about three of its stylistic features contains a useful general truth about Muldoon's work. The elementary nature of grammar, syntax, and tone of voice throws light on the activity of his imagination in those more substantively sophisticated areas of psychology, metaphysics, aesthetics, cultural commentary, love, sex, elegy, and politics. Ubiquitous witty scepticism; strong and often refracted feeling; esoteric knowledge; politely anarchic refusal of any tribal or narrowly political alignment: these are among the qualities that make him the compelling and considerable poet he is. These, and an endlessly inventive delight in crowding his world with credible fictions, give to his poems their particular and peculiar configurations. But it is his special qualities of grammar, syntax, and tone of voice that underlie and embody the complex nature of his sexual, cultural, metaphysical and political understanding. Estranged and intimate, anarchic and believing in order, tolerant of individual idiosyncrasy, strange and reassuringly familiar, violent and quotidian, utterly factual and depending "on more than we could see" ("Early Warning," in *Why Brownlee Left*)—Muldoon's poems are a strong, imaginatively confident response to an ambiguous, unsteady, endlessly uncertain sense of experience. In political terms this can refer to the state of Northern Ireland; in metaphysical terms it can refer to the contemporary state of our world and our being-in-the-world.

No matter what the precise referential nature of Muldoon's subject matter, however, grammar, syntax, and tone of voice will suggest a constancy in his response to it and his apprehension of it. Coming awake as a poet in the wake of (especially) Heaney and Mahon, Muldoon has had to find and claim his own poetic space. Looser, more stylistically various, more extravagantly agnostic than they are, he has immersed himself more deliberately in the destructive element. And his work rises out of it speaking—in what are essentially *un*speakable (political, emotional, and metaphysical) states—his own finely tuned contemporary truth. What I have tried to suggest here is the way this truth—whatever its nature or substance—is rooted in his poetic manner, in those rudimentary elements of it that first impress me when I read almost any of his poems. Grammar, syntax, and tone of voice create a sense of being—in many senses—"on the edge but implicated." And growing as they do out of the ground of these enabling elements, his poems make—in every sense—a world of difference.

1989

NOTES

[1] The five volumes, all published by Faber and Faber (London), are *New Weather* (1973), *Mules* (1977), *Why Brownlee Left* (1980), *Quoof* (1983), and *Meeting the British* (1987). This last was also published, as was *Quoof*, by Wake-Forest Press, Winston-Salem, South Carolina. Faber has published a *Collected Poems*, an expanded version of which has also been published in America, by Ecco Press (1987). [More recent volumes have been published in the United States by Farrar, Straus, & Giroux.]

[2] *Irish Literary Supplement* (Fall 1987): 37; P.M. interviewed by Kevin Barry.

[3] *Ibid*, 36.

[4] From *Viewpoints: Poets in Conversation with John Haffenden* (London: Faber & Faber, 1981) 134.

Works and Days:
Wordsmith Muldoon

No contemporary poet lives more thoroughly in the language than Paul Muldoon.[1] By this I mean a number of things, among them the exuberant relish with which he savors the taste and texture, the sound, the weight, and the lovely, self-spawning semantic fertility of words themselves. I mean the way his use of the language has become so inimitably his own, has become so recognisable a *voice*, a voice that—in its colloquial relaxation as well as in its wilder, weirdly inventive energies—gives convincing expression to consciousness itself, to a consciousness I as a reader trust and believe in, a consciousness that is not confessional, but is—for all its ventriloquism and quicksilver mastery of densely plotted narrative—remarkably unmasked, present, honest, immediate to itself and others. (In this, leaving narrative aside, he reminds me of John Ashbery, a poet whom he does not otherwise resemble.) And finally I mean that, as his most recent work shows (in its seemingly more overt autobiographical impulses), his life and the language are vividly implicated in one another at every turn. Or at least this is so in the dazzling and compendious collage of parts of it (especially its childhood, adolescence, and young manhood) that he composes in the long poem, "Yarrow," which occupies most of his latest volume, *The Annals of Chile*. All these meanings of "living in the language" have rightfully won for Muldoon the eminence and reputation he currently enjoys both among general readers and his fellow practitioners.

None of this is to suggest that Muldoon's work (whatever about some of the commentaries upon it) is intellectually rarefied or dryly "academic." Although it does speak from and to a distinctly postmodern sense of things (in its decentering of narrative, its rupture of certainties, its fragmentation of consciousness itself), and although it brims and glitters with an astonishing amount of idiosyncratic and esoteric knowledge, he takes the harm out of such extravaganzas by means of his believable, politely genial voice, making a heady, often comic mix of pedantry and scepticism, private allusion and easily shared assumption, colloquial expression and fastidiously intricate formal manoeuvers. Like that of a man telling jokes and surprising stories while performing handstands on the high wire, Muldoon's performance (and it's always that, although he makes the intensely *formal* coincide with *normal*, the art itself seem nature) results in exhilaration and a certain elation in the reader. (If the reader is one of those fellow-practitioners I've mentioned, it can also make for a certain amount of that ordinary occupational hazard of the scribbling classes, professional envy.

His rhyming alone—sly, unexpected, and spot on—has been a cause of much hair-loss and gnashing of teeth.)

The Prince of the Quotidian (which I always see first as *The* Price *of the Quotidian*, a title which would not have run the same risk of looking like self-regard) contains a month's worth of small poems—one a day—that register something of the substance and quality of the poet's daily life with his wife and child, his friends, his professional acquaintances and duties (he directs the creative writing program at Princeton). Whatever their ultimate value as poems, and they are of varying quality, these pieces—like a painter's sketches—are fascinating for what they reveal about the artist's ordinary concerns, the more or less unmediated matter of his life, and, of course, about his art.

As far as the "matter" of the life is concerned, we learn something about Muldoon's love for the unusual, "even the smell of cloves // and chloroform / that sweetens Elizabeth" [New Jersey], as well as his intensely developed senses (that smell couldn't be more specific, but who'd ever stumble on so exact and evocative a description of it?). We learn some of his familial and household pleasures (watching a video with his wife, feeding the finches bacon rind and millet), some of the more gregarious activities of the sophisticated suburbanite (parties, visiting antique shops, going to the opera). We get a sense of a life led contentedly enough with American friends, but in touch, too, with the jostlings of Irish literary politics and with the intrusive perturbations of violence in the North. We even get an uncharacteristic touch of self-righteous indignation in portraiture (corresponding, I suppose, to the slightly sour-minded caricatures that can turn up in an artist's sketchbook). Among these freeze-frame spots of time there is a quick shot of the expectant father's nervous anticipation, as well as a larger take—ending the sequence on a subversive, deflationary, pre-Lenten note—on the poet's anxiety about his own enterprise ("there's not an image here that's worth a fuck," chides a ghostly visitor, reminiscent of some of Heaney's abrasive chastisers in *Station Island*: "Who gives a shit about the dreck / of your life").

What lends all this more or less ordinary matter vividness and life is Muldoon's shaping energy, his verbal buoyancy, his power over colloquial expression, his formal elasticity, his extraordinary rhyming skills. In a word, his style. In a way both calculated and unguarded, *The Prince of the Quotidian* lets us into a corner of the poet's workshop, giving us a glimpse of the way this intriguing, kinetic, compulsively metamorphic consciousness lives and works. Here, "living in the language" means translating the facts of daily life into patterns of meaning that are as much linguistic and literary as they are biographical—patterns, indeed, that elide the borders between these categories. (A great deal of Muldoon's work consists in just such an elision of borders, which may be the essential *political* subtext of all he writes. His rhymes, as well as his startling metaphors and similes, participate in this. Much of the thrust of the work consists in demonstrating *likeness* between what are assumed to be *unlike* phenomena, a valuable lesson if it could be learned in Belfast, Jerusalem, or Sarajevo.) In the following small sample you can see how Ireland and America, Irish and

English, nature and technology are coaxed into friendly, productive cohabitation (as, in Muldoon's independent yet obedient—and brilliant—translations of the poems of Nuala Ní Dhomhnaill, the dual reality of "Contemporary Irish Poetry" finds a single, common ground):

> As I coasted into the tunnel
> of the Pennington car wash
> I glanced at my copy of *Feis*
> by Nuala Ní Dhomhnaill:
>
> a wave broke over a rock
> somewhere west of Dingle;
> my windshield was a tangle
> of eel-grass and bladderwrack.

The Prince of the Quotidian is full of such surprising transformations and at-onements, which (along with the other revealing features I've mentioned) are what make this volume—understandably lightweight by comparison with his other collections—entirely worthwhile.

Nothing lightweight or sketchy, however, about *The Annals of Chile*. Because Muldoon does something new in every volume (while still *evolving* in a comprehensible way), it is hard to compare on a value scale the books among themselves. For me, however, the latest volume is perhaps the most richly satisfying. Formally the book is a *tour-de-force*. In fact it's many *tours-de-force*. In an early interview, he remarked that "the only use I can see for formal structures is to help the writer himself decide the shape and size of the canvas. What has to be said determines its own form, or should do . . . I don't scan, however, but use a purely intuitive process within each line. My only concern is that the lines are speakable." Intuition, formal shapes, speakability: these are still the co-ordinates of Muldoon's design. And, as far as form is concerned, in the present collection he dazzles more than ever with his sheer technical skill, speeding from orthodox and unorthodox uses of the rhyming couplet to his own variations on the villa-nelle (in "Milkweed and Monarch") and the sonnet ("Footling," for example), to the rattled *ottava rima* of the splendid elegy, "Incantata" (in which he follows, on his own terms, the formal stanzaic lead of another Irish elegy—Yeats's "In Memory of Major Robert Gregory"), to the vastly compounded, hypnotically cross-rhyming variations on the sestina, sustained through the 150 pages of "Yarrow" (which ends in some glancing blows of *terza rima*, a scheme he also employs in the ebullient and touching "Cows").

As a joyous compendium of forms, the collection shows just how deeply Muldoon has heard Yeats's injunction to Irish poets to learn their trade, and reveals how much a master of his craft he has become. Here, by way of partial illustration, is a stanza from "Incantata," in which plain phrasing and speech-syntax is fused to effective rhymes and half-rhymes, and rhetorically amplified by the way the sentence grows into the capacious breadth (and breath) of the stanza (another Yeatsian lesson well digested):

> I thought of you again tonight, thin as a rake, as you bent
> over the copper plate of 'Emblements,'
> its tidal wave of army-worms into which you all but disappeared:
> I wanted to catch something of its spirit
> and yours, to body out your disembodied *vox*
> *clamantis in deserto*, to let this all too-cumbersome device
> of a potato-mouth in a potato-face
> speak out, unencumbered, from its long, low, mould-filled box.

All this technical wizardry and witchery would come over as somewhat brittle and just showy, of course, if the poems didn't assure us of their intellectual and, especially, their emotional *bona fides*. In the past, Muldoon has been accused of a lack of feeling; it's been said that the formal super-competence comes at the cost of emotional conviction. But, while I admit to finding *Madoc: A Mystery* somewhat hard going, I've never subscribed to this point of view. What I've always valued about Muldoon's work, in fact, is the way it manages, through formal means, to gain access to reliable feeling. I find this in early lyrics like "Wind and Tree," "Ma," "Making the Move," or "Why Brownlee Left" or, later, in poems such as "Quoof," "Wishbone," or "Cherish the Ladies"; I find it in that exquisite little elegy, "Coney," in the longer elegy, "The Soap-Pig" (a rehearsal, if that's the word, for the much more ambitious and fulfilling "Incantata"), and in many other poems, lyrical and narrative alike.

In a number of the poems in *The Annals of Chile* this electric union of form and feeling seems to me to be at its most complete and satisfying so far. This is especially true, I'd say, of "Cows" (one of my favourites), the incomparable "Incantata" (which, as well as being a moving, unsentimental celebration of the life and art of Mary Farl Powers, passionately explores, as "Lycidas" does, the problem of the relationship between art and feeling and death), and much of "Yarrow," especially those moments where the poet's elegiac sense is roused and finds an answerable language, moments where the vanished but remembered past (his own, his mother's, that of the enigmatic S—) is conjured into the present in all its plaintive, but concrete and unself-pitying detail:

> The bridge, the barn: the tongue of a boot once lus-
> trous with mink-
> oil;
>
> a rocking horse's hoof; the family tree from Ada;
> all swept away in the bob and
> wheel
>
> of the sonata for flute and harp,

the wild harp hanged on a willow by Wolfgang Amadeo;
again and again Lear enters with a rare

and radiant maiden in his arms
who might at any moment fret and fream,
'I am the arrow that flieth by day. I am the arrow.'

The whole poem is punctuated by such moments, sometimes anchored to the phrase "That was the year . . ." (lifted from Kavanagh's "Epic," and recurring like a mantra for the remembrance of things past). Meanwhile it advances a jumpy but coherent narrative, its spots of time rendered in a sort of *pointilliste* mode, the collage of the whole gradually, but inexorably and recognisably, accumulating into a strobe-lit portrait of the artist as a young man. As a poem in which the emotional centre keeps touching his mother, the work is also an elegy. It is the poet's response, that is—in that manner of abrupt coherence that is Muldoon's—to the injunction which (via the speaking horse of Armagh, on loan from the earlier "Gathering Mushrooms") he had laid upon himself at the end of *The Prince of the Quotidian*:

'Above all else, you must atone
for everything you've said and done

against your mother: meet excess of love
with excess of love; begin on the Feast of Saint Brigid.'

I don't know whether "Yarrow" was begun on February 1, but it has surely obeyed that Yeats-inflected injunction. The volume as a whole is dedicated to the memory of Brigid Regan, the poet's mother, memorialised by her maiden name. The long poem is richer and more various than I've suggested in this brief comment. Fashioning an illuminated map (like those you'll find in London or Paris of the underground rail system) of what Wordsworth called "the growth of the poet's mind," the poem zigzags between its diverse elements: books by Robert Louis Stevenson; the landscape of rural Armagh; the family's sweet or fraught domestic interiors; the big world of rock music and unsettling public events (such as the Profumo case and the suicide of Sylvia Plath); the drug-speckled student and bohemian subculture; *King Lear*. Negotiating this shifty, turbulent world with the panache of a champion canoeist going through white water, the poem charts in a comprehensive and convincing way the coming to imaginative consciousness of the poet who has given us seven books (not counting translations, a libretto, an anthology) and twenty-one years of remarkable output in verse.

Coming as it does after twenty-one such productive years, *The Annals of Chile* marks Muldoon's coming of age as a poet, his entrance into a capacious (and still vastly "promising") maturity. For all its tricks and sleights of tongue, there is something wonderfully and bracingly honest about his poetic voice; for all its speedy and bedazzling fictions, it tells the truth. And "truth"—no matter how many quote marks we qualify it with—is what poetry is about and after. That in Muldoon this "truth" has found a serious, stubborn, independent, and paradoxically reliable voice is something we can all celebrate, as we celebrate his artist's good conviction that "art may be made . . . / of nothing more than a turn in the road where a swallow dips into the mire," and yet this same quotidian art is what

> builds from pain, from misery, from a deep-seated hurt,
> a monument to the human heart
> that shines like a golden dome among roofs rain-glazed and leaden.

In this union of realism and idealism (more borders down), Muldoon's confident and courageous voice—supple and immediate, that is, with the courage of its own convictions—makes a world-in-art that is, by any measure, worth celebrating.

1996

NOTES

[1] This piece is a review of *The Prince of the Quotidian* (Wake Forest Press), and *The Annals of Chile* (Farrar, Straus, & Giroux).

Mazing McGuckian

I love how the poems of Medbh McGuckian provoke a mixture of exhilaration and perplexity, how any one of them can give the sense of a journey at high speed through a strange but compelling, often dazzling landscape. I relish their sensuous surfaces—all those textures and colours, the dream-space of synesthesia that has to be surrendered to because, as she conjures it, it becomes the most natural thing in the world. Most of all, of course, I admire how as a poet she lives in the language, how the language leads its own passionate, affective, mesmerising life in her poems. And, although I always find it hard to get a fully coherent hold on whole books of hers, I take *Captain Lavender* to be her most substantial and impressive collection so far, the one in which more poems than ever before unite a specific gravity of feeling to a specific density of language in immediately satisfying and powerfully generative ways.[1]

How does she do it? When I read McGuckian, that's the question that keeps needling and stimulating me, keeping me alert and curious, attached to the words on the page. Or, maybe better, "how does it work?" How does a poem— at once puzzling and gratifying—hang together? How does it create its peculiar effects? How does it give pleasure, and what is the nature of the pleasure it gives? What is it telling us about the world, and what is the connection between the matter—what it tells us about the world—and its manner? I want to begin by addressing briefly this more or less general (but at the same time most particular) issue since it seems to me that any useful evaluation will first take into account the way McGuckian operates as a composer of poems, and since so many of her critics and reviewers either balk at this necessary first task or complain about the unreasonable, even impenetrable difficulty of her working surfaces. What is striking to me as a reader is that even if I find the "meaning" of a poem impenetrable, inaccessible, unavailable to conventionally rational analysis, I do not find myself therefore denied pleasure. It's just that the pleasure belongs to categories for which I haven't yet found the right description.

A McGuckian poem usually begins abruptly, and by doing so lays forceful claim on your attention. Here are some examples: "The flowers I picked were a bloodstream / I was standing in." "I love to live in afternoon / because of its mysterious stairs." "All the angles of the twigs / seemed such twilight gossip / in their impure purple." "A white melancholy sits in the lesser chair / at the front edge of time." "Bereft of my flowers early in the season, / I found you condemned to spend whole seasons, alone." Such openings plunge a reader immediately into an unknown element. The circumstance of the speaker is plainly given, but what precisely that circumstance is or means in customary terms is

hard to say. So we begin by losing our bearings, and in doing so we find ourselves dependent on the speaker. In each of the above moments, for example,
although each one may begin in some recognisable state (picking flowers, loving the afternoon, the look of twigs, melancholy, a loss of flowers) there is immediately—in the way the apparently expository statement unfurls—something
odd, something at odds with our everyday sense of things. How are flowers a
bloodstream, and how do you stand in it? What are the "stairs of afternoon"?
How do the angles of twigs become "twilight gossip"? What is the "lesser
chair" less than, and what is the front (or back or side) edge of time? In the last
example, who is speaking, and to whom, and what might "bereft of my flowers"
really "mean"?

The abruptness of these beginnings is not due to some sudden declamatory
or otherwise rhetorical form of address. It is simply a result of there being a
world already in existence which is calmly, but in surprising terms, spoken out
of. With McGuckian we are always *in medias res*: things are going on; the continuum of the speaker's existence is interrupted by this voiced and worded
fragment of it. Every beginning seems to propel us into some brightly lit corner
of a narrative to which no other access has been provided, a narrative that never
seems to strain after completeness or closure, that has something of the quality
of a stained glass window in smithereens: we know there is a "story" there but
we're excluded from the whole readable shape of it.

Abruptness has something to do, too, with tone. Each of the above poems
begins in a curiously confident tone of voice. There is no suggestion that the
speaker is trying to mystify or astonish. The unruffled normality of the tone, in
fact, is directly at odds with the peculiarity of what's being said. What is being
said, it seems, makes entirely understandable sense to the speaker, just as a sentence like "In Sandycove, by nine o'clock on Tuesday morning, the tide had
covered the rocks" would make sense to most of us. With McGuckian, however,
it's as if the speaker, in this normal tone of voice, is speaking a curious dialect
of her own, the syntax of which is that of the common tongue but the vocabulary and turns of phrase of which are opaque and strange to us. The abruptness
of the opening, that is, comes from a curiously muted collision (gentle, not violent: it has nothing to do with the purposefully rattling juxtapositions of the sur-
real) between categories, a collision that draws us into a world in which fixed
boundaries are elided and everything is in flux.

There may be something implicitly sexual, too, about the poem's abrupt
mode of address: it takes you off-guard and, at the same time, rouses your interest; stopping you in your tracks, it coaxes you to go on. It provokes a sense of
relationship, half enigma and half conspiracy, that could be seen as analogous to
what goes on in a certain kind of sexual exchange. In addition, the rhythms established by any of McGuckian's openings are themselves quite unsettling, being usually composed of a strong, subtle, but nervous marriage between a
phantom iambic beat and ordinary, unmodulated speech. As with the other elements I have mentioned, such a conjunction produces a kind of perplexity in me

as a reader, a curious state in which I seem to be in possession of something perpetually flitting from my grasp.

Beyond beginnings, among the other things that create "difficulty" in a McGuckian poem are the curious fluidity of pronouns without known referents, and the dazzling rapidity with which the poem can commute between subjective and objective conditions. As far as pronouns are concerned, it is very hard sometimes to say exactly who the 'you' or the 'he' or the 'it' or the 'they' actually refers to, and without this knowledge a reader is forced to swim in a present of implicit faith, trusting to the poem itself to 'explain' itself. Some poems, beginning with an 'I' and a 'you,' will later introduce a 'he' or a 'she' unexpectedly and often inexplicably, as if the narrative of personality were a floating story not entirely within the speaker's control. In others, the pronouns 'you' or 'he' or 'she' don't attach themselves to a personal identity that's decodable in a "narrative" way from the poem itself. (A lover, a spouse, a friend, a known or unknown other—what is the status of the person located by the pronoun?) Some lines from "The Most Emily of All" may illustrate what I mean:

> If you call out 'house' to me
> and I answer 'library,' you answer me
> by the very terms of your asking,
> as a sentence clings tighter
> because it makes no sense.

In addition, it is often difficult to separate subjective from objective: what is going on in a poem can seem to hover between these usually contrasting states. As usual, an image of McGuckian's own may be the best illustration: in one poem, she says," Even if you were outside, where summer was, / you would still be inside every leaf," and in another, "Though she swore / That she did not carry / Another man's child under her heart, / My seed is a loose stormcoat / Of gold silk, with wide sleeves, in her uterus." Subjective and objective here dissolve their boundaries and, in John Donne's word, "interinanimate" each other. It may indeed be the rapidity with which this interchange takes place in the perceiving nervous system of the poet that creates such a kinetic, concentrated, and (to borrow Elizabeth Bishop's word) "unlikely" world in every poem.

Finally, high on my own list of qualities that give to any McGuckian poem its distinct feel and flavour is the idiosyncratic way the sentence is handled. For when I read a few poems in succession, I am aware not only of the rhythm of word and line—the usual lyric syncopations—but also of the over-beat of sentences as one follows another in a purposeful unfolding towards the poem's conclusion. Whether short or long, calm or more impetuously pitched, each sentence first builds its own little room of action, an almost self-enclosed space where some sense (clear or opaque, but in its own way decisive) is being made. Then, because the overarching impulse of the whole structure—the thought/ feeling which the poem both knows and is discovering as it goes—has not been exhausted, needs another "beat" (which may in turn need another), a fresh sentence begins and is carried through to its conclusion. Often, but by no means always, sentence coincides with stanza, thereby constructing another unit of rhythm and verse-architecture. Here are a few examples, to give a small sense of what I mean. (But since every poem, I believe, sets up its own peculiar relationship between sentence, line, and stanza, I wouldn't claim any necessary representative status for them.) The first is a passage from "The Snow Speaker":

> So little of the earth, you
> open the earth for me.
>
> Having no more need of me
> than I of you,
> I am as alone with you
> as without you.
>
> I try to love the sky
> as the sea's accomplice,
> but nothing human
> can help us know the stars.

Here is a stanza from "The Blue She Brings with Her":

> Your eyes change colour as you move
> and will not go into words. Their swanless
> sky-curve holds like a conscious star
> a promise from the wind about the blue
> she brings with her. If beauty lives
> by escaping and leaves a mark, your wrist
> will have the mark of my finger in the morning.

And here is the title poem from *Captain Lavender*:

> Night-hours. The edge of a fuller moon
> waits among the interlocking patterns
> of a flier's sky.
>
> Sperm names, ovum names, push inside
> each other. We are half-taught
> our real names, from other lives.
>
> Emphasise your eyes. Be my flare-
> path, my uncold begetter,
> my air-minded bird-sense.

In all of these examples, I believe, the propulsive energy of the poem is generated by the poet's instinctive drive towards sentence-making. Syntactically supple and determined, fluid and tense, each sentence is a kind of sudden embrace, complete in itself, both cut off from and yet in some tonal and emotional way connected to its fellows. The effect of their accumulation is a curious one, a harmony derived from the counterpoint of solitude and the hope of intimate exchange. Just as the individual elements in a sentence are in a sometimes puzzling relationship to one another, and yet—by the confident syntactical manner—make a persuasive unit of sense, so the sentences themselves add up to the emotionally persuasive and satisfying unit of the stanza, first, and finally the poem.

So, from its usually enigmatic title on (the relationship between title and what follows is often very obscure: the way the title "belongs" to the body of the poem can be a puzzle; in fact the category of "relationship" itself may be at the root of many of the palpable difficulties in these poems), each McGuckian poem is a maze without the kind of outlet a prose paraphrase or a recognisable meaning and referent would offer. We have to be reconciled as readers to living in this perplexing space. To cope with such difficulties, it is necessary to read her slowly, to work against the velocity of the poem itself, teasing it out piece by piece, seeing what each highly *charged*—a word which, like "fraught," has its origins in "load" and "burden"—what each highly charged element means (actually, symbolically, allegorically: these categories of interpretation flow easily into one another in her work) within the little cosmos of the poem. Trying to state as clearly as possible the nature of the difficulties may be a help, however. For if we know these are the kinds of things that happen in a McGuckian poem, then the difficulties may be diminished: we will not be looking in her poem for something she is not doing, that her kind of poem doesn't want to do.

From what's been said, I think it will be clear that any poem by McGuckian makes and inhabits a world of elided borders, a world of language seeking some approximation to the fluctuating ripple-and-glitter-world of feeling itself, a world that refuses those certainties by which the rest of us try to steady our sense of reality in the either/or of categorical choice. And as far as the connection between this manner and the matter and meaning of her work is concerned, it does not take too much ingenuity to see how such a stance towards language, fact, and feeling—such a radically lyrical destabilising of conventional assumptions—would be not only a mimetic rendering of the fluid and fluctuating nature of consciousness itself, but would also be both a response to and an expression of a sense of responsibility in the idiosyncratic environment of Northern Ireland. In that sense, I'd say, McGuckian's poems are as expressive of their fractured environment in as full and as complex a way, as fully "political" a way, as are the poems of Carson and Muldoon or Heaney and Mahon.

As for *Captain Lavender* itself, it contains, as I've said, some of her strongest work to date. Especially in the first part of the collection, which directs itself mostly in her own elegiac terms to her parents, there are poems of great accomplishment and beauty. Listen, for example, to the astonishing conclusion of the beautiful "Porcelain Bells" (dedicated to the poet's mother):

> When you find your way out
> of the jewel-groove of your limbs
> and the used-up breeze goes past
> your icy eye-lid,
> already no longer anyone's,
> I will dive you back to earth
> and pull it up with you.

One of the things that makes for the success of this and other poems in *Captain Lavender* is that its fraught lyricism is scaffolded securely by a distinct narrative purpose, not lost in the mirror-world of its own effects. Strange as the above elements may be—from the oddity of the images to that very moving, unorthodox use of the normally intransitive verb, 'dive'—the narrative relationship between them and their source in the speaker's feeling is clear. What the poet seems to have grown into, in other words, is an ability to increase narrative visibility, without stilling that pulse of strangeness which keeps the poem alive and beating. The same could be said of what goes on in many of the poems that have her father as their subject: in the brilliant and compact "The Wake Sofa," for example, or in "The Aisling Hat" ("Over your face a cognac eagleskin / was tightly stretched, my cart-horse, / dray-horse, drew your heavy chariot"), or in the intensely moving "Elegy for an Irish Speaker," where the poet addresses "Miss Death" directly, and where—thickening the poem's meaning and effect—McGuckian's own sense of language and her art comes through in the dominant idiom of grief:

> Roaming root of multiple meanings,
> he shouts himself out
> in your narrow amphora,
> your tasteless, because immortal, wine.
> The instant of recognition
> is unsweet to him, scarecrow word
> sealed up, second half
> of a poetic simile lost somewhere.

The death of the father also informs many of the poems in the second part of *Captain Lavender*, although here the scope seems to have been amplified to take in the larger political issues of the province. At times I do not feel that these publicly *directed* poems work as well as the more privately aligned: "Flirting with Saviours," for example seems clotted, while parts of "The Colour Shop," as well as "The Radio Traitor" and "For the Wind Millionaire" seem too programmatic. Perhaps the reason for this is that the kind of intense subjectivity of McGuckian's work (which at its best can give solipsism a good name) is less finely tuned to the *actual* frequencies of the public world, her lyrical manners less well adapted to handling the stonier facts of political life in any direct (insofar as her imagination could ever be "direct") way. Which is not to say that her poems, whatever their subject, have not their political edge. But they possess this in their own unique way and therefore—in the same unique way—belong naturally to any comprehensive and, in the broadest sense, political understanding of the North. It is just that those with a more overtly private source work better—for me, at least, and, I should add, for the moment.

I feel obliged to add that last caveat ("for the moment") because when I linger over poems that don't work for me now, I know I may later find in them fresh revelations, successful work. For McGuckian's poems call for close, loving, reiterated and lingering attention, which may account for the fact that many reviewers have a hard time not being simply baffled by the poems, and not saying much else. The poems ask for time and a quality of attention that are not always easy to find. (A blurb that talks about poems in "the guise of conversations" doesn't help: the one thing McGuckian's poems are not is "conversations," although they are always spoken. Conversation, however, is not at all what's going on: the poet is the only speaker.) But any reader who grants the necessary time and attention will discover how *Captain Lavender* extends Medbh McGuckian's range, increases her stature, and confirms her reputation as one of the best poets now writing in what goes on being an extraordinary flourishing of poetry on this island.

1995

NOTES

[1] Although it outgrew its origin, this essay began as a review of *Captain Lavender* (Gallery, 1995; Wake Forest, 1996).

4

BIGGER PICTURES

Gathering Poets:
The Ins and Outs of It

1. WHIMFUL BOOK

In its second edition I hope *The Faber Book of Contemporary Irish Poetry* will be given its proper title: *Ten Irish Poets*, selected by Paul Muldoon.[1] That should bring a lot of blood pressures back to normal, which have been roused to boiling by the book's present misleading announcement of itself as a representative picture of *Contemporary Irish Poetry*, edited by Paul Muldoon. For the volume in no sense offers a clear or fair picture of contemporary Irish poetry, nor has Paul Muldoon performed the real job of an editor, merely that of a selector with plenty of good taste and some curious blind spots. Anyone in Ireland with a titter of sense on the subject will see this immediately, and can therefore take the book as a gathering of many fine poems. But in England and America, prime marketing targets for the collection, titters of sense on this subject are rare enough, so, given the book's title, Muldoon's top ten will constitute, unchallenged, a definitive map of the post-Yeatsian Irish poetic landscape, and that's too bad. The landscape, even if you take only its most prominent features into account, is more complex, various and exciting than the present gathering of poets and poems suggests.

I should say right away that I have no objections to those poets Muldoon has chosen to include, however I might quarrel over the allotments of space or quibble about particular choices among the poems. But I'm surprised by the omission of a *few* poets whom I'd say a more or less impartial editor would have to see as necessary elements in any adequate account of the subject. I'm not arguing for a gather-'em-up, for a whole battalion of Kavanagh's standing army of ten thousand to have a poem or two apiece. That sort of standardless catholicity would be just as bad as what has happened here. Muldoon's decision to give a rich sampling of each poet's work was a good one. But an editor, even a mere selector doing his or her work under a banner like this one, has two unshirkable responsibilities: to be true to honest personal prejudices, and to be equally true to the subject itself. Nothing will persuade me that Muldoon has accepted this second responsibility in any objective spirit. What he offers here is as whimful (a word he once used of his own imagination) and as myopic as Yeats's extraordinary performance in editing *The Oxford Book of Modern Verse*, with his notorious exclusion of Wilfred Owen and others because "passive suffering is not a theme for poetry," his daft claims for Oliver St. John

Gogarty as "one of the great lyric poets of our age," and his total ignoring of Austin Clarke.

In addition to Muldoon's chosen ten, any adequate account of "Contemporary Irish Poetry" is impossible without the following names: Austin Clarke, Denis Devlin, John Hewitt, Padraic Fallon, Richard Murphy, Eiléan Ní Chuilleanáin, James Simmons, Michael Hartnett, Eavan Boland, Paul Muldoon. Each of them, aside from being an individual poet of achieved excellence, has contributed something *necessary* to the picture. Without them, the picture is incomplete and unconvincing. Obviously my list isn't infallible, and would be altered by another player of this game of 'who's in, who's out, who's up, who's down.' But let the criterion be *necessity*, and I suspect most people familiar with the subject would add a short list something like mine to Muldoon's too-truncated offering.

With telegraphic brevity, let me try to suggest why any "Book of Contemporary Irish Poetry" should include those I have named. Muldoon's own exclusion, of course, is a special case, the result of misplaced editorial modesty. But he should have overcome it. He is, and must know it, one of the most startling, original, inventive and important voices on the current scene, and the picture he offers of that scene is the poorer without his odd, exhilarating presence. Austin Clarke's absence is the gravest flaw in the book. It's inexplicable to me that Muldoon is lacking in appreciation for all that verbal power, satiric bite, Clarke's inspired, extravagant resurgences. More than any other Irish poet, Clarke has ensured that Irish poetry after Yeats has confronted and occupied its contemporary historical, political, cultural environment; he has enabled (in ways that complement the achievements of Kavanagh and MacNeice) an alignment between poetic speech and intellectual imagination. Having been a poet of Yeats's world, he made himself a poet of ours. More than any other, his absence invalidates the book's title.

Padraic Fallon is, for his intelligent, quietly confident speech in such poems as "Totem," "The Head," "Monument X," "Boyne Valley," or "To Paddy Mac," a crucial voice in the generation between Yeats and the present, an articulate critic of aspects of Revivalism confronted by the contemporary world, and at the same time an instructive link between two worlds. Like MacNeice, Kavanagh and Clarke, Fallon stands at the head of contemporary Irish poetry, mediating between us and what went before them, domesticating Yeatsian sublimities, Yeatsian grandiloquence. Denis Devlin, in spite of the fragmentary and uneven nature of his (brief) career, also serves as a conduit for Irish poetry into the contemporary world. His intellectual suppleness, his originality of manner, his metaphysical sophistication, and his instinctive wrestle with the implications for Catholic culture and sensibility, of what it means to be modern—all such considerations make him a necessary feature of our recent literary landscape.

John Hewitt, happily still writing, is another unique and necessary voice. His attempt to give speech to the colonist consciousness, to utter himself as an articulately personal lover of the Northern province—its landscape, its traditions, its embattled present—makes the best of his poems satisfying things in themselves and important documents in the past fifty years of Irish poetry. Richard Murphy has, in four or five volumes of work, forged an appropriate poetry for a specifically "Anglo-Irish" consciousness, probably the last poet who will ever do so. The poems in which he wrestles with the ambivalent reality of his cultural (and of his personal and sexual) identity belong by necessity to our mixed tradition. The picture is lacking without them. James Simmons' voice—of the North, in the Protestant (and agnostic) tradition, formally playful, at once literary and domestic—is at its best a valuable presence, an active resistance to forms of caste and forgetfulness that can plague both parts of the island.

As the first of the women in our short tradition to establish their equality with the best poets of their generation, Eiléan Ní Chuilleanáin and Eavan Boland belong by right in any anthology of contemporary Irish poetry deserving the name.[2] Poets first, they also (voluntarily and involuntarily) stand for a radically evolved female reality in the wider world, and they have given this reality an adequate poetic voice. Michael Hartnett's work—shuttling between the Irish and English languages—has made impressive entries into the Irish psyche for the past twenty years. His language is curious, lyrically angular, raw, learned, with a distinct accent of its own. In 1974 James Simmons said that Hartnett was, in the North, "the most widely admired Southern poet." Times, it seems, have changed.

That six of my eight names are from the Republic is a merely necessary corrective to the fact that Muldoon's critical compass seems fixed at poetic North. Seven of his ten are from Northern Ireland (and five of them appear, along with Muldoon himself, in the recent *Penguin Book of Contemporary British Poetry*). Ultimately, it's true, these labels don't matter: a good poem's a poem for a' that. But, in the world that may be less informed of the actual truth of things, labels have a bad habit of sticking (one of the facts that may have fuelled Seamus Heaney's polite refusal of pride of place in the Penguin book). The full range of contemporary Irish poetry is badly contracted by this Faber book. That this diminished version of the subject should gain the currency assured it by the hard facts of publication and publicity, should gain internationally some sort of canonical authority, are sad, damaging, but unavoidable truths. It is a pity that neither Muldoon's critical sympathy nor (perhaps) Faber and Faber's budget could have allowed for a larger book.

Another regrettable omission is a genuine preface by the editor. Because I admire Muldoon's poetry very much, I imagine he must have extremely interesting reasons for disregarding Clarke and excluding Murphy, for ranking Tom Paulin higher than either of them. (Indeed, given the only critical criterion here available—the relative allotment of space—for why he rates Paulin higher than any of the included poets except Kavanagh and MacNeice. Yeats told us why he esteemed Gogarty as he did. It would have been only fair for Muldoon to say exactly why Paulin's work has the particular superiority he implies it has. The poems, in this case, do not speak for themselves.) But this editor offers nothing except the wet squib of an exchange between MacNeice and F.R. Higgins, taken from a BBC broadcast of 1939. In this, MacNeice's "common sense view of poetry" clearly wins out over Higgins's twilight-silly mysticism, his buckleppin' babble of magic and "blood-music" and "the awful sense of respect for words." Not only are the terms of the whole fatuous exchange heavyhandedly irrelevant to Irish poetry today, they also have little or no bearing upon the poems that follow this excuse for a preface.

This anthologist, like Joyce's artist-God of creation, sits invisible behind his handiwork, paring his fingernails. Such detachment works wonderfully in the elusive world of Muldoon's own poetry. But it is frustrating—not so much elusive as evasive—when it is the posture adopted in the editing and prefacing of anthologies. Of his own poetry he has said, "I have no allegiances except to tell it like it is." A pity not to apply the same principle to the work of anthologising. Whatever else *The Faber Book of Contemporary Irish Poetry* does, it does not "tell it like it is."

After the quarrel, what? In the context of a general approval of the actual selections, I have just a few quibbles (the bread and butter of reviewing any anthology). The Kavanagh selection would have been enriched by the Canal poems, pivotal in his own career and fine representative expressions of his later phase. In place of that particular passage from "Autumn Sequel" or the "Eclogue for the Motherless" which seems forced in spots, I'd like to have seen some more of MacNeice's lyrics—"The Casualty," or "Death of an Old Lady" or "After the Crash," "Birthright," "The British Museum Reading Room" or that lovely elegy for his father, "The Strand."

While it's good to see "His Father's Hands" and "Tao and Unfitness at Inistiogue on the River Nore," some of the more difficult poems from *A Technical Supplement* (say the slaughterhouse segment) or later work would have enriched the Kinsella selection. I was sorry, too, not to see "Beyond Howth Head" or "The Sea in Winter" among the Mahon poems included, since the epistolary form in both of these so clearly embodies Mahon's commitment to civilised speech, his will to communicate deep private and public truths in as intimate a way as possible. To omit the Mayo sequence from the Longley selection is a pity, since in these poems Longley pushes into riskier, less linguistically urbane zones than in any other part of his work.

While I'm glad Muldoon chose to include Paul Durcan, I wish the selection he made were a better one, more representative of the wilder, bolder reaches of Durcan's imagination. This rather stingy offering would have been immeasurably improved by the substitution of a number of poems from the last two collections for the Mac Liammoir elegy, a poem which is not among Durcan's best. And while it's fair enough for Muldoon to include Tom Paulin in this elite group, the size of the selection seems out of proportion, generous to a fault (44 pages; Durcan gets 12, Mahon 31, Montague 34, Heaney 42). I'm glad the dialect stuff is not there, but even some of the poems that are here (e.g., "Thinking of Iceland," "Cadaver Politics," "From," "The Hyperboreans") seem willed out of energies more polemical than anything else. The McGuckian selection is a fair sampling of that quirky, erotic imagination, which manages to be at once both robust and shimmering. The Heaney and Montague selections are basically very good, very satisfying, though the sketch of each poet might have been interestingly complicated by the inclusion of those poems from *The Great Cloak* in which Montague allows the wife to speak in her own voice, and by some of the more strangely accelerating and mysterious pieces from the third section of Heaney's *Station Island.*

Because of absences like these, and the absences of such original voices as those of Clarke, Hartnett, Muldoon himself, Ní Chuilleanáin, this collection, in spite of all the fine work it contains, makes contemporary Irish poetry seem a safer, less original and risky and inventive thing than it really is. This is especially odd and regrettable, it seems to me, given the editor's own radical energies as a poet, his oblique, compelling ways into the world.

Yet in fairness it must be said that the selections suggest the health and soundness of the subject they collectively embody. They grow out of a distinctly serious view of the large world and the small, and display a healthy variety of serious commitments to their common craft. Any anthology (the vexed question of titles aside) that contains poems of the caliber of "The Great Hunger," "Woods," "His Father's Hands," "Herbert St. Revisited," "Mossbawn," "Courtyards in Delft," "Making Love Outside Áras an Uachtaráin'," "Inniskeel Parish Church," "Swans Mating," and "The Seed Picture" needs no apology. It is the expression of a rich, various, complicated, verbally buoyant world.

What, then, given even the limited nature of this selection, does it tell about Irish poetry? Before suggesting anything, let me lighten the probably overearnest language of this review by a batch of quotations, each one of which should show something of the quality of the individual poets, who should be easy to identify. Linger over them.

Water honeyed

in the slung bucket
and the sun stood
like a griddle cooling
against the wall

of each long afternoon.

*

The fields were bleached white,
The wooden tubs full of water
Were white in the winds
That blew through Brannagan's Gap on their way from Siberia;
The cows on the grassless heights
Followed the hay that had wings.

*

Flat on the bank I parted

Rushes to ease my hands
In the water without a ripple
And tilt them slowly downstream
To where he lay,
Tendril light,
In his fluid sensual dream.

*

I was born in Belfast between the mountain and the gantries
To the hooting of lost sirens and the clang of trams:
Thence to smoky Carrick in County Antrim
    Where the bottleneck harbour collects the mud which jams
The little boats beneath the Norman castle,
    The piper shining with lumps of crystal salt;
The Scotch Quarter was a line of residential houses
    But the Irish Quarter was a slum for the blind and halt.

*

'I've become so lonely I could die'—he writes,
The native who is an exile in his native land:
'Do you hear me whispering to you across the Golden Vale?
Do you hear me bawling to you across the hearthrug?'

*

the big block . . .
. . . turned under my hands, an axis
of light flashing down its length,
and the wood's soft flesh broke open,
countless little nails
squirming and dropping out of it.

*

now dream
of that sweet
equal republic
where the juniper
talks to the oak,
the thistle,
the bandaged elm,
and the jolly jolly chestnut.

*

The mayflies' opera is their only moon, only
Those that fall on water reproduce, content
With scattering fog or storm, such ivory
As elephants hold lofty, like champagne.

*

This was a marriage and a baptism,
A holding of breath, nearly a drowning,
Wings spread wide for balance where he trod,
Her feathers full of water and her neck
Under water like a bar of light.

*

I lived there as a boy and know the coal
Glittering in its shed, late-afternoon
Lambency informing the deal table,
The ceiling cradled in a radiant spoon.

Different voices. Differing registers of poetic speech. What can be said of such a collage of fragments? In all I detect a decisive commitment to communication: no matter how private the matter, there's little wilful obscurity. I note an adherence to the things of the natural, phenomenal world, outdoors and in, a love of place that could easily slide into political anguish. Above all, I'm struck by a tender keenness of observation that carries an awareness of some potency inside things: a light; some valorising energy. Speaking this sense, they use a language that is muscularly in touch with metaphor. Entirely secular as they are, these poets seem to keep obliquely in their lines a last glimmering residue of what we still have, probably, to call faith. It's interesting to imagine that they might, between them (and beyond the raw, clumsy opposition between F.R. Higgins's "magic" and MacNeice's "common sense") compose something like a poetics of contemporary faith. Given the service this much abused word is forced into in both parts of this island, it is salutary to see it emerge in this form among the poets.

To conclude: *The Faber* (or any other) *Book of Contemporary Irish Poetry* remains to be compiled. But once shorn of its misleading banner, the book presently bearing that title is a good collection, one that gives hope for and allows for satisfaction in the present and future state of Irish poetry. What's needed now, however, is a penitential second (revised) edition, expanded to include the missing but necessary poets, with some shifts of emphasis and space in the present selections, and enlivened by the addition of a real Introduction by the present editor. Then it would be a volume worthy of its declared subject, properly equipped to "tell it like it is."

1986

2. SAMPLER

In editing this special Irish supplement for *Verse*, I have brought together a number of poets who are in their forties or younger, have published at least two books, and are among the better known of their contemporaries, nationally and, in some cases, internationally. First a roll-call: Eavan Boland, Harry Clifton, John F. Deane, Seamus Deane, Peter Fallon, Seamus Heaney, Tom McCarthy, Medbh McGuckian, Derek Mahon, Eiléan Ní Chuilleanáin, Frank Ormsby. It's clear that these poets in no sense constitute a group, a school, any recognisable literary family or faction. They are, it is true, "Irish poets," but aside from Northern and/or Southern citizenship the term refers to little more than a sense of physical and cultural geography, an alignment of consciousness capable of infinite variation—as the differences between, say Medbh McGuckian and Peter Fallon would suggest. In fact the Irish literary spectrum at the moment is not characterised by distinct or coherent groupings—nothing like the Martians in England or the New York "school" in America. One of the few that comes to mind is that made up of some of the poets published by Raven Arts in Dublin, whose work displays a decisive (sometimes rhetorically heavy-handed) social passion. It's also possible that a growing number of poets who are women feel united by their gender in ways that shape their verse, which could therefore be seen as specifically feminist. Beyond that, it seems a question of individuals getting on with the task of making the best poems they can.

That there's a surprising number of these individuals (published by an equally surprising number of healthy presses, such as Blackstaff, Arlen House, Gallery, Dolmen, Raven Arts, Brandon, Dedalus, Goldsmith, and in magazines like *Cyphers, Poetry Ireland Review, Honest Ulsterman, Belfast Review, Tracks, The Salmon*) is worth mentioning. And behind the poetic "generation" represented here (regrettable absences being among others, Paul Muldoon, Michael Longley, Gerald Dawe, Paul Durcan, Tom Paulin, Michael Hartnett) there's another one springing up, marked by energy, purpose, and a confident sense of its own indigenous identity. The trail of modern Irish poetry (in English) blazed by Yeats's major successors—Clarke, MacNeice, Kavanagh, Fallon, Devlin— and broadened by the generation of Kinsella, Murphy, and Montague, has become a busy four-lane highway. No doubt time will sift and sort all out, revealing achievement and diminishing numbers, but for the moment it's possible simply to welcome such a lot of lively action.

On the particular evidence of the poems that follow, what can be said to any critical purpose of the present gathering? In terms of style I'd note a certain confidence in lyrical language itself, a trust in the traditional resources of poetic form. Except for the most overtly difficult and indubitably private, these poems seem to share an implicit assumption of being heard and understood by an audience occupying some common ground. Even in the case of the most private and difficult of the poets (McGuckian, Ní Chuilleanáin, Seamus Deane), the lyrical language seems trusted to bear the weight of enigma and fraught intimacy, as it is not, say, in the work of Thomas Kinsella, who moves beyond the lyrical into a sparer, bonier idiom of his own.

The single point I'd hazard on content may be related to the above observations on style. Many of these poems, that is, seem to speak out of some implication in community. The speaker in Eavan Boland's poems, for example, is often a witness to community (most often a community of women), to the condition of an individual within that community. Seamus Heaney's voice opens porously to its communal surroundings—cultural, political, or intimately personal. Whatever he does, Heaney seems a Proteus of communal fealty, without ever losing his own rich, absorbent individuality. Thomas McCarthy builds his sense of (often political) community from a private core of love and family, extending it in an amused, bemused way to the notion of explicit literary community. Peter Fallon's voice lives inside concentric circles of community—a familial memory, the local group, a communal action, a vision of mythical, legendary and topographical establishment and continuity. The most prominent word in his vocabulary is "we." In Frank Ormsby's work the note is of community threatened by violence, the embattled continuance of ordinary life in the midst of extraordinary occurrences. John F. Deane speaks as an oblique witness to the way the world can shatter communal possibility.

Even those poets who seem to live in the intricate web of their own secret imagery and language—I think of Medbh McGuckian's excited indifference to all but the most intimate stirrings of her own rapt imagination; of Seamus Deane's voice brooding on the margins, enfiguring a sort of pure isolation of the head in its obsessive pondering on a few remnant phenomena; of Harry Clifton's grieving over a Western world in physical and emotional tatters, beyond the possibility of any redemptive community; of the vulnerable sense of isolation to be found in the work of Eiléan Ní Chuilleanáin—even these seem somehow in voluntary or involuntary exile from a sense of community: that absence seems a live beat between their lines. And in Philippe Jaccottet, Derek Mahon has found and translated with ebullient elegance a poet who may share Mahon's own sense of ubiquitous imperilment, who speaks as a sort of allegorical man surviving on the saving graces of wit and irony in a world where authentic community is no longer possible.

In such a small space as this introduction I'd be unwilling to risk opinions on the meaning of all this. Perhaps it's enough to say that this issue of community or its variously provoking absence is an integral thread in the imaginative fiber of all these poets connected by what I have called, roughly, cultural geography and citizenship(s). It is as if they were all responding to some common impulses that lie much deeper than anything we might call ideology. Such a thought raises the question of the relationship between art and its cultural, political, even national grounds, a powerfully relevant question in Ireland at this distinctly revisionist moment.

1986

3. CONTEMPORARY SCENE

For this special issue of *The Colby Quarterly* ("Contemporary Irish Poetry"), I ransack my bookshelves, rummage in the heap of volumes stacked on the desk or spilled over the floor. Books of recent Irish poetry, published by Salmon, Dedalus, Gallery, Blackstaff, Raven, Wake Forest, Ecco, Farrar, Straus & Giroux, Faber, Anvil, Penguin, Secker & Warburg, others. Volumes published by poets from Ireland and Northern Ireland, poets from the whole island. (How vexed the language is, our habits of naming thrown constantly into contortions of embarrassment. Speak, and someone is excluded, offended, enraged, hurt.) Volumes in the English language and volumes in the Irish language. Volumes by men and—more and more—volumes by women. The stream that began in the late 1960s (when the beginnings of New Writers' Press and the—still thriving—Gallery Press augmented the regular trickle of volumes from Dolmen Press) and swelled through the '70s and '80s, has by now become something of a flood, the breadth and depth of which may in part be judged by the growth of "Irish Studies" (especially in American colleges and universities), by the proliferation of cultural/literary festivals and summer schools all over Ireland itself, and by the numerous anthologies of Irish poetry that have appeared on both sides of the Irish Sea and on both sides of the Atlantic Ocean. (This geographical allusion might neatly suggest the *centrality* of Ireland and its literary productions—as antidote, perhaps to the more usual sense, "post-colonial" and all that that implies, of its *marginality*. But perhaps "centrality" is not the word: it's likely we are neither central nor marginal but simply *in-between*.)

Picking at random among the heap that now lies higgledypiggledy on my desk and on the floor, I open the latest volume (Salmon, 1992) by a poet from Galway, Rita Ann Higgins, whose intense, subversive, angry, laconic voice is a considerable contemporary presence. These lines are from the title poem ("Philomena's Revenge"):

> 'Mad at the world'
> the old women nod
> round each other's faces
>
> But it was more
> than that
> and for less
> she was punished.
>
> That weekend
> she didn't leave a cup alone
> every chair hit the wall,
> Philomena's revenge.
>
> Soon after

she was shifted
and given the shocks.

Abrupt and brutal, the short lines open a crack on women's experience of suppression and rage, and the ignorance that attends it. It is this world that Higgins keeps probing—fierce and humorous, a demotic *Goddess and Witch* (the title of an earlier collection) from the urban sprawl beside Galway Bay. This is not the voice of what many American readers have come to expect of "Irish Poetry" (a phrase, like the phrase "Irish Poet," which should perhaps be followed, as "Mayo" once was, by the ejaculative "God help us!"). But it is truly there, it utters something actual in the psyche of contemporary Ireland, registering (in the words of Edna Longley) "its economic and spiritual deprivation."

Dipping again among my books, I open *Fleurs-du-Lit* (Dedalus, 1990), a collection of zippy lyrics by Tom MacIntyre, their lean stanzas buzzing on some linguistic Speed of their own, their anchorage in Gaelic tradition, their sails snapping in gusts of contemporary fragmentation:

Tickle an ear
he hops up and down
like an egg in a ponger,

I'm the Monsoon-Horse,
hums the clear of his eye,
I'm the Martinmas Gander,
I sleep like a thrush,
I don't look at calendars,
I'm your permanent bash
and The Patron of Hauliers.
("Baby in the Fire")

While MacIntyre's landscape is dreamlike, flashy, fitfully erotic, full of playful echoes of phrases that reside just at the edge of our consciousness, something quite different is going on in *The Wrong Side of the Alps* by Anthony Glavin (Gallery, 1989), the second half of which is the remarkable sequence—*Living in Hiroshima*—which manages to inhabit the bleak impossible landscape of horror in a language not inadequate to its almost unthinkable occasions. One of its minute, two-couplet sections is entitled, "In Plato's Cave":

'Our present historical velocity . . . ' Godspeed!
Can there be sunlight now without contamination?

My analyst sighs—no comment, he can wait . . .
The ceiling flickers like a video screen.

Such poetry attempts to inhabit and articulate the unspeakable, and demonstrates the refusal of contemporary Irish poets to be contained by the boundaries of the island, the confines of explicitly "Irish" subject matter. (The quicksilver post-modern quixotica of Muldoon are probably the best known and most finished example of this.)

Still rooting, I come upon the latest volume of Michael Hartnett (*The Killing of Dreams*, Gallery, 1992)—whose poems have been disturbing and delighting me since the first time I saw them thirty years ago in UCD, and whose voice, which once cast off English altogether (in *A Farewell to English*, 1975), inhabits English forms in his own mordantly ironic, idiosyncratic way:

> White as squid among the roseate prawns
> his fingers placed with prim finesse
> the seaweed in a green coiffure
> about the diamond ice
> and gesticulating back he eyed his work
> and pursed, 'It's finished; very nice.'
>
>   ("Mountains, Fall on Us")

Hartnett's tone, the pulse and timbre of his voice, seem peculiarly tuned to local understanding, to a sense—in spite of a sharply individual mind and sensibility—of being related to (even in isolation) a "home" community. That even "at home" can seem to our new crop of poets a foreign place, however, foreign to conventional literary expectations, is shown in some lines from the next volume I leaf through—Michael O'Loughlin's *Stalingrad: The Street Directory*:

> If I lived in this place for a thousand years
> I would never construe you Cuchulainn.
> Your name is a fossil, a petrified tree
> Your name means less than nothing.
> Less than Librium or Burton's Biscuits
> Or Phoenix Audio-Visual Systems—
> I have never heard it whispered
> By the wind in the telegraph wires
>
> Or seen it scrawled on the wall
> At the back of the children's playground.
>
>   ("Cuchulainn")

O'Loughlin's grainy urban meditations have opened up (in his three collections from Raven Arts Press) a particular—astringent but compassionate—zone of consciousness as well as social geography.

Randomly stumbled on, the examples I've used above could easily be replaced with others (by poets like Sara Berkeley, John Hughes, Macdara Woods, Moya Cannon, John F. Deane, Sean Dunne, Gerald Dawe, Joan McBreen, Peter Fallon, Ciaran Carson, Pat Boran, Theo Dorgan, Paula Meehan *et al.*), all of them demonstrating a comparable liveliness of language, depth of engagement with the subject, confidence of speech. In their work, as in that of O'Loughlin and the others I've quoted from, the world that contemporary Irish poets encounter and make known to us (sometimes by making strange for us) must oblige us to revise at least some of our safer, more established notions about— God help us!—Irish Poetry. It is qualities and energies such as these—revisionist, I suppose, in the best sense—that I value in the poetry being at present written all over the island, a poetry that at its most accomplished (in the work of Kinsella, Montague, Murphy, Heaney, Ní Chuilleanáin, Mahon, Boland, Muldoon and others among the established figures of the past twenty years) is honestly preoccupied with the world of individual consciousness and the world of external fact, honestly seeks a language that will do some sort of unsentimental justice to these two zones of being, however the weight of attention and engagement is actually distributed between them.

Whether the site of attention is the local "domestic" world—of family, lovers, the back garden, a street, a house—or the larger world of more public ("political") confrontations, or the interior world of consciousness itself, what impresses me is the fine articulate energy of so many of these poets, an energy that is various, intense, confident of itself in the very act of utterance. And such a largesse of poetic production, poetic speech, makes me think that at last the English language itself—fully, unabashedly, unselfconsciously—has become a "native" Irish possession. (That at the same time a freshly thriving poetry in the Irish language forms one of the most prominent features of the literary landscape of the island is hardly mere coincidence, and gives proper piquancy to the cross-pollination that occurs in the current spate of translation of Irish poets from Irish into English—most notably, but not uniquely, in the case of Nuala Ní Dhomhnaill—and even, occasionally, from English into Irish.)

Once upon a time, Stephen Dedalus listened to the speech of the English Dean of Studies at UCD and thought to himself, "My soul frets in the shadow of his language." For better, for worse, that fretting lasted a long time. It may be argued, as Michael O'Loughlin has done, that "Kavanagh was the first fully-fledged Irish poet in the English language—that is, an Irish poet whose relationship to Irish nationality and to the English language was not problematic" (*After Kavanagh: Patrick Kavanagh and the Discourse of Contemporary Irish Poetry,* Raven Arts, 1985). That independence in Kavanagh, however, was won at a certain cost: it is what makes him the indispensable forerunner, and at the same time what limits his own discourse, his own world, the odyssey of his own questing, irascible, troubled consciousness. For the poets aside from (and after) Kavanagh, however, the fretting continued: it is in Kinsella, Montague, Murphy, in Heaney and of course in Hartnett; there are traces of it in Ní Chuilleanáin and Boland; and there is even a curious touch of it in Mahon and Longley (although it would be interesting to consider the precise nature of the felt relationship with the English language of poets from a Protestant background—North or South— and poets from a Catholic background, as this may be found registered in their poems).

But the energy and sheer plenitude of Irish poetry in English at the present moment (let posterity do the work of criticism; for now I'm just letting myself relish the fact of the matter), its confidence of voice, its fluency of speech, seem to have taken us beyond the Joycean fret, beyond that long moment of creative/linguistic anxiety (which Joyce himself, of course, got beyond in his own scrupulously anarchic, awakened way). The language, all these poets seem collectively to be saying (whether they are writing and publishing in Ireland or England or America or anywhere else—where, for example, is Harry Clifton this minute?), the language is *ours*. And not ours in a spirit of post-colonial revenge, but simply, naturally ours, our natural way of taking possession of the worlds we inhabit and that inform us. Without, I hope, being over-fanciful, I can hear in the collective speech of these poets, in the immediacy of their utterance-as-speech, a restoration of what I think I am hearing when I read, even with my inadequate Irish, a poem by Ó Rathaille or Ó Brudair or Ó Suilleabháin, by Raftery or Mac Giolla Ghunna or Eibhlín Dubh Ní Chonaill: the sound of the language of the tribe, a sound that closes the gap between the language of the *polis* and that of the poem, a single speech spectrum that can include (without rendering into some spurious unity, into a single "countrified" or "mid-Atlantic" Irish accent) the surgical astringencies of a Kinsella, the humane boundary-elisions of a Heaney, the passionate urbanity or outrage of a Mahon, the baroque vertiginosities of a McGuckian, the heady, jocoserious play of a Muldoon, the subversive intimacies of a Durcan, or the colloquial indignation of a Rita Ann Higgins.

Between all these poems and poets, the collective consciousness (in all its multiplicity, beyond what Gerald Dawe calls "the illusion . . . of being forever of the one place and of the one people" [*How's the Poetry Going?* Lagan Press, 1991]) is finding its map in language, a language more varied, even, than the landscape of the island itself. And while this may not have an immediate and direct effect on what we call the body politic (the question of whether poetry "makes nothing happen" remains an open one), something of its real achievement may at some time filter into—by opposition, if not by endorsement—what will come to be "Ireland" (quote marks, to let our *virtuality* be known), whenever and however and whatever that will be. There is a poem by Michael Davitt, published in a recent issue of *Poetry Ireland Review* (whose editor, the poet Máire Mhac an tSaoi, expanded the presence of Irish language poets in the magazine, as her successor, Peter Denman, has continued to do) that touches from another angle on a thought that may not be too far from this one. For a lovely moment, during an electrical blackout, Davitt—as I understand the poem (entitled "Debheascana"/"Diglossia")—has a glimmer of *unity*, of a common dual tongue, and that tongue is *talk*:

> Ag féachaint amach an fhuinneog dom ar ball
> Bhí Raghnallach ina Dhún Chaoin oíche Nollag.
> Coinneallphobal.
>
> Is cuimhníos ar Corr na Móna fiche bliain o shin . . .

Is d'ól mo dhá chluais an mhioruilt debheascna:
Sruthchaint threadach na Seoigheach,
Gaeilge.

[Outside the window later on / Ranelagh was Dun Chaoin on Christmas Eve, / A candle community // And I thought of Corr na Mona twenty years ago . . . And my two ears drank the miracle of diglossia: / The tribal speech—flow of the Joyces, / Irish.] (translation, Gabriel Fitzmaurice)

Talk is "Irish" and is community, and wherever any of us is writing we are all *trying to talk*—trying in our various ways, our personal dialects, to talk ourselves and our world into existence, into coexistence. The simple fact of dual language—of the island containing poets writing in two languages—becomes itself an image of possibility, the possibility of accommodation and the richness that is its consequence. The variety of personal dialects insists on this possibility as a fact, at least in that world of language that the poets must inhabit.

The variety of these personal, map-making dialects is especially vivid if one compares any representative gathering of contemporary poems (a cross section, say, of a number of anthologies) with the 1925 *Golden Treasury of Irish Verse* edited by Lennox Robinson. In this monument to Revivalist taste and achievement, almost all the poems speak what seems—at this distance, anyway—to be a single more or less common dialect, whether the subject is Ireland, love, religion, political passion, or a love of the land, and that dialect is not a personal one but a possession of the community, of the *literary* community. Maybe it's simply a question of taste and fashion and the way these tune one's ears, but the poems in Robinson's collection seem more monotonic, everything sounding a bit Padraic Columish ("Mavourneen, we'll go far away / From the net of the crooked town, / Where they grudge us the light of day"—"The Beggar's Child") or Nora Hopperish ("Mavrone, Mavrone! the wind among the reeds, / It calls and cries and will not let me be; / And all its cry is of forgotten deeds / When men were loved of all the Daoine-sidhe"—"The Wind Among the Reeds").

One reason this is so, I'd say, is because most of the poems in Robinson's collection look away from the consciousness of the speaker towards some external subject, which is then painted in the proper lyrical colours (usually various shades of green). It is what set the young Samuel Beckett's teeth on edge: "The device common to the poets of the Revival and after," says Beckett, "in the use of which even beyond the jewels of language they are at one, is that of flight from self-awareness" ("Recent Irish Poetry," *Disjecta*, Grove Press, 1984). It is in fact a shock in the midst of such lyrical facility to come across the tough, interrogative, unflinchingly personal tones of "Easter 1916" and "The Wild Swans at Coole," tones which accommodate the perplexed, struggling, self-questioning consciousness of the speaking poet. For the most part in Robinson's *Golden Treasury*, though, the struggle to speak is over by the time the poem is written, and so the sound of these poems is smoother than speech, a pasteurised lyrical convention that will not accommodate individual consciousness in individual speech.

Our own contemporary poets, on the other hand—whatever their final value, and however many of them would pass the rigorous exam set by Beckett—speak in many different voices, invent dialects that seem quite distinct from one another, would be very hard to confine to a single critical description. In their variety and number, in fact, they render the category to which many of them aspire ("Irish Poet") virtually useless as an instrument of description, never mind evaluation (although it will no doubt continue to perform such functions for a good while yet). What they provide between them, however, is a many-voiced choir of often vivid, often casual, sometimes important, occasionally crucial *talk* about the world and the self in it.

That something of value may come from this talk is, I think, known by the poetry itself at some instinctive level, and so we keep at it, keep chipping away at the rockface of what Pound with winning simplicity called "the art of getting meaning into words." The *effort* at real human speech—no matter what dialect of it we speak—is a value in itself. If, as Derek Mahon has said (in an oft—repeated formulation), a good poem is a paradigm of good politics, it is so, I suppose, because of its patience and tolerance, its wish to accommodate as much of the world as possible, its interest in getting things exact, its attempt to make precise discriminations that do not amount to a scale of exclusive and excluding values. Because, that is, of the balances it holds, because it grants everything in it a right to exist, allows everything in it to make a difference. And if I extend Mahon's point, I might add that a *poetry* that is multiple, plural, accommodating of variety, tolerant of difference, eager to have all the voices heard, could also be the paradigm for a more humane political possibility.

As the fuss over various recent anthologies shows, however, that possibility in poetry itself has not yet necessarily affected for the good those who make the agendas, those who define the communities, those who determine who's in, who's out. But the possibility is there for a larger-hearted view of things. I suppose the fact is that we are still witnessing the falling into place and shape of an *identity*, and just as, in the political world, that struggle to define an "official" identity can foment civil war, or the continuing debate of democratic government, so in the literary world it can create quarrels, claims and counterclaims, an appetite for a seat at the conference table, a hunger to be in. Internecine squabbles (hard to forget Yeats's "great hatred, little room") constitute the negative side of all the vitality and variety, all that productive energy.

This is an inevitable if regrettable part of the picture as, on the most mundane level, poetry gets mixed up with publicity, and a thirst for recognition grows universal and unquenchable. Literary editors of the major newspapers publish reviews of only a fraction of the books of poetry published. And even with the best will in the world they *can* publish little more than a fraction. A result of this is that "Poetry reviews in many Irish newspapers," according to the poet Sean Dunne, who is also a journalist, "are literature's answer to the Big Mac" (*Poetry Ireland Review*, 32, 1991). And of course, in this scuffle for headlines—for the good word in the most public place, for the positive opinion of the right critic—real worth and real value can easily get lost. There is inevitably a business and a hype side to it all (the prizes, the short lists, radio and TV appearances), neatly summarised in the title of Gerald Dawe's *How's the Poetry Going?* and in his comment that, in contemporary Ireland, "the burden of market values is being put formidably upon literature to do the work of politics." But from the long enough perspective, I suppose (and aside from the fact that the various skirmishes and controversies do suggest that poetry *matters* in Ireland in a way that is probably not true in America), such competitive jostling is just so much fluff, is—to use a phrase Kinsella used in a more notorious connection—a "journalistic entity." (See his Introduction to the *New Oxford Book of Irish Verse*.) Posterity, that unfoolable if not infallible set of taste buds, may judge all this noisy jockeying for power (a symptom of the malaise being Desmond Fennell's widely read pamphlet on the meaning of the popularity of Seamus Heaney) as part of the history of cultural maturation. But it will make its own judgements about the poems and the poets that last.

In its own collective critical way, the present gathering of essays and articles for *The Colby Quarterly* suggests some of the ramifications of Irish poetry at present, touches some of the issues I have just glanced at. What might be seen as a subtext of a number of these offerings (Antoinette Quinn's on the lesbian poet, Mary Dorcey, for example, or Dillon Johnston's on the presence of America in Muldoon and Montague, or Peggy O'Brien's on some literary precedents—significantly American—for the unsettling erotic element and linguistic adventure in McGuckian) is the way boundaries are breached (whether boundaries of gender or place or subject or sexuality or language) and the way, in breaching those boundaries, the poetry of contemporary Irish poets is insistently pushing out the defining and confining limits of its own field. (This could also be true of a particular collection like Seamus Heaney's most recent volume, *Seeing Things*, in which the accommodating fluency of the poet's language manages—with its tactful mix of heft and buoyancy—to navigate, to negotiate, between the realm of the *here and now* and that of the *over there*.) Such an essentially outward looking impulse may be seen, too, in Peter Sirr's brief account of some contacts between contemporary European and Irish poetry, suggesting activity in the realm of translation that stretches poets beyond the geographical limits of Ireland and absorbs influences from the continent (influences often mediated by the volumes of translations—often done by Irish poets—published by Dedalus Press).

Our little gathering might also be seen to contain, in the interviews with Joan Mc Breen and Paula Meehan and in the brief autobiographical piece by Pat Boran, an illustration of the way the younger, "emerging" poets have—by going beyond conventional boundaries—established a fresh set of relationships with what came before them. Listening to these voices of a fresh generation of poets, and listening to what the critics have to say about the various issues raised, one is made aware at the very least of the vitality and variety of Irish poetry (in both languages, as Peter Denman's essay on Biddy Jenkinson and Nuala Ni Dhómhnaill makes clear) at the present moment, while Adrian Frazier's analysis of a few prominent recent anthologies offers a glimpse of serious power struggles taking place underneath the vitality and variety of the verse itself. Of course, given the wide choice of possible subjects (whether in terms of theme, technique, author, or issue), a collection of essays like this one can offer little more than a tiny sliver or two cut at arbitrary angles off the larger body. But even in these small samples, I hope, something of the life of the whole thing may be known. And for the moment, at least, it is the life of it that matters.

In "Hopes and Fears for Irish Literature," Yeats said, "Here in Ireland we are living in a young age, full of hope and promise—a young age which has only just begun to make its literature." That was in 1892, exactly a hundred years ago. We can no longer talk of a "young age," and the public "hope and promise" of the island has been blighted by social distress and political violence both in the North and the South. Nothing in literature can at all "compensate" for such facts. It is possible, however, that in the undeniable energy and genuine talent of the new poetry—talent and energy that in my opinion give the lie to Declan Kiberd's rather grudging editorial assessment of "Contemporary Irish Poetry" in the wonderfully abundant *Field Day Anthology of Irish Literature*— something at least of that "hope and promise" may again be found, if only the hope, and the promise, of making sense of ourselves. We'll see.

1992

NOTES

[1] Review of *The Faber Book of Contemporary Irish Poetry,* edited by Paul Muldoon, in *The Honest Ulsterman*, Winter 1986.

[2] I am only thinking of poets writing in English. In Irish, Máire Mhac an tSaoí and Caitlín Maude would have a similar distinction.

The American Connection:
An Influence on
Modern and Contemporary Irish Poetry

There were a number of ways of approaching this subject—the relationship between Irish and American poetry. Specific themes and issues, for example: time and space; the way history is present to both poetries; how Irish and American poets deal (differently) with their respective geographies. Or the connection in both countries between poetry and politics (how poems by Kinsella or Montague or Heaney or Boland or Muldoon—in which some explicit or implicit political pressure may be felt stirring, shaping, sensitising the material—might compare with poems by Kinnell or Levertov or Simic or Hass). The related issue of community edged into a question: is there a distinct sense of *community* within the work of many Irish poets (in spite of what Kinsella has said about "a scattering of incoherent lives"),[1] while it is a palpable absence in recent American poetry? The notion of faith (in what?) in a broad sense was another beguiling possibility, throwing open the Pandora's can of worms of "secular" imagination and some other kind: the figuring of immanence and transcendence in the poetic firmaments of the two countries. The status of Irish and American poetry—both "post-colonial," but *how*, precisely—*vis-à-vis* the English tradition (in general or from the more limited point of view of Romanticism) was also a topic worth investigating. Aside from all these, there were the more strictly *formal* possibilities: poetic use of the English language in 20th Century Irish and American verse, for example; or a comparison between the way an Irish poem and an American poem actually conduct themselves on the page (as seen, perhaps, in a passage of Whitman and one of Yeats, something by Kavanagh and by Williams, a piece by Kinsella set beside one by Ashbery or some Jorie Graham, a Heaney poem beside a poem by Pinsky, one by Ní Chuilleanáin alongside one by Plath, something by James Merill next to a few stanzas of Derek Mahon).

Having considered such possible subjects, however, I found myself thinking more about a simpler and more straightforwardly historical issue: the way, if at all, American poetry of the past century has nourished the body of Irish poetry in English during that time. Such an exploration, more fundamental than the others I've mentioned, could serve as a base or preliminary study for them. This, accordingly, became the topic of the following essay.

I was first awakened to a tangible connection between Irish and American poetry during a reading given by Thomas Kinsella at Vassar College, in 1974 or
'75. Kinsella spoke of his own emancipation as a poet being due to the enabling
influence of William Carlos Williams. "Doctor Williams," as Kinsella insisted
on calling him, freed him from the restrictions of the iambic line and offered
him by example the possibilities of a new music. When I asked Kinsella to read
"A Country Walk" for my class in Irish Literature, he baffled them by bemoan-
ing its limp iambics, and would only read it under protest. He also spoke of
Pound, of the *Cantos* as exemplary poetic action, praising their inclusiveness
and their enigmas. It was no harm, he explained, for a reader to have to *work* at
a poem; no harm to be compelled to discover some new facts, the actual meaning of some esoteric allusion or scrap of mandarin Chinese. Such a fit reader, it
has struck me since, is precisely the reader Kinsella himself hopes for, a ready
traveller in those often bewildering realms of personal and cultural history
which his poetry since *Nightwalker* has opened up.

   Since that time I've been aware of the American influence as a real presence in the work of contemporary Irish poets. It is not hard to support such a
feeling. John Montague, for example, has often voiced his debt to poets like
Ransom and Creeley and Robert Duncan. Seamus Heaney's year in Berkeley
(1970-71) not only introduced him to the poetry of Duncan and Snyder and Bly,
and the meshing of cultural, political and mythological frames of reference it
managed, but led also to "a release I got just by reading American poetry, in
particular coming to grips with Carlos Williams," and to "a more relaxed
movement to the verse."[2] All this on top of the touches of Frost, Roethke, and
Lowell that can be found in and between his lines. In Eavan Boland's recent
poetry it is hard not to hear cadences, detect images, recognise language, feel
the pressure of attitudes which must owe something to Sylvia Plath and Adrienne Rich, while Paul Muldoon's dazzling displays of eccentric ventriloquism
reveal an imaginative hospitality to a whole spectrum of American poets, from
Frost to Berryman, Pound and Stevens, to Ashbery and Charles Simic. Michael
Longley, too, would hardly deny a drop of Emily Dickinson or John Crowe
Ransom among his civil stanzas, and Derek Mahon could probably stand to be
told that traces of Stevens, Lowell, and Pound were detectable among his. And
in the idiosyncratic, vatic and comic voices of Paul Durcan it may be possible to
hear echoes of Ginsberg and Ferlinghetti. Approximate as they may be, I suspect most readers would find themselves roughly in agreement with these
claims, all of which add up to the simple fact that modern and contemporary
American poetry has had a strong, substantial influence on the poetry at present
being written in Ireland.

   What, however, of the past? The subject of this paper forced me to consider
the sources of such influence, to wonder how far back it went, what its history
might be, or its meaning. What follows is a preliminary sketch of the territory
opened up by such questions. As usual, it's necessary to start with Yeats. At first
it may seem odd, but then right, that the young man who in March 1887 sat in a
house in Harold's Cross and dreamt of starting "a school of Irish poetry" could
reveal to an anonymous correspondent his belief that "Whitman is the greatest

teacher of these decades."³ A teacher, as it later appears, of cultural nationalism, and so a natural model for the young Yeats. And since Whitman is "very American," even though "America was once an English colony," it follows of necessity that "it should be easy for us, who have in us that wild Celtic blood, the most unEnglish of all things under heaven, to make such a literature."⁴ To this explicitly nationalist and ideological stimulus, Yeats added his heightened sense of Whitman as the poet-as-outcast, at odds with his society, "neglected and persecuted," hounded by moralists in spite of being "the most National of her poets," and the victim (as Yeats would in time come to see himself) of an "uneducated and idle" public.⁵ In such a role (a sort of literary Parnell), as well as in his role as teacher, Whitman is to Yeats something like what Ibsen is to the young Joyce. He alerts the Irish poet not only to the possibilities of creating a new literature, but to the concomitant need (central to the Revival) to create an audience for that literature.

Beyond ideology and image, Yeats must also have felt the stylistic pressure of Whitman. The poet who would in time refer to his poems as "my true self" must surely have been struck by the emphatic revelation of personality in the work of the American. In fact, Whitman's "he who touches this book touches a man" is in 1892 a term of praise in Yeats's critical writing.⁶ And by citing with approval the "wild irregular verses of Todhunter's 'Banshee'" as a cross "between Walt Whitman and the Scotch Ossian," Yeats almost manages to turn the American into an honorary Celt.⁷ Finally, that *Leaves of Grass* is so vigorously a *speaking* book, a book of impassioned speech ("my own voice," says Whitman, "orotund sweeping and final")⁸, must have been a conscious or unconscious encouragement to a poet eager "to make the language of poetry coincide with that of passionate, normal speech."⁹ By a fine irony of literary history, then, what Yeats will come to see as the particular, civilised distinction of his case— "Gradual Time's last gift, a written speech / Wrought of high laughter, loveliness and ease"—owed something in its beginnings to a barbaric Transatlantic yawp.¹⁰

Whitman is not the end of Yeats's connection with the American muse. Ezra Pound came first (to Europe) to learn from Yeats. Being Pound, he ended up teaching the older poet a thing or two.¹¹ In a sense—Pound, who called Whitman "a pig-headed father," but also acknowledged "We have one sap and one root" (how Yeats, in his despairing search for a literary father, must have envied such assured kinship)—begins American literature for the second time. It seems natural enough, then, that Pound should help Yeats re-make himself, begin again. Not only did he give Yeats a less eccentric view of literary history (convincing him that between the Greeks and Elizabethans there was more than "a great blank"), he also urged his verse towards something sparer, harder, more aggressively present to that world, "harsher and more outspoken."¹² In addition to the fact that the two poets met around 1909, such qualities (seen in *The Green Helmet* and *Responsibilities*) suggest that Pound's influence took over where that of Synge was broken off by Synge's death (March, 1909). Pound's own comments on these two volumes echo, I would imagine, Yeats's feeling about the new elements in his verse. They contain, says Pound in a review, "a manifestly new note;" they have "prose directness;" they show "his work becoming gaunter, seeking greater hardness of outline."[13] Yeats's own view of Pound, uttered shortly after their first meeting, suggests the sort of benefits he would reap from his contact with "this queer creature."[14] Pound is close "to the right sort of music for poetry," he says to Lady Gregory, "music with strongly marked time and yet it is effective speech."[15]

Where Whitman, then, was one of Yeats's important teachers in the establishment of his first poetic self, Pound taught him to re-make himself and move towards the style of his maturity, during a time when he "thought that anything good in poetry would come out of America."[16] It seems fitting, therefore (as well as another ironic twist in the thread of literary history), that it has often been Pound and later American heirs of Whitman who have assisted more recent Irish poets to free themselves from the power- (or prison-) house of Yeats—the rich, seductive, varied magniloquence of the mature and later verse.

Although Louis MacNeice wrote a book about modern poetry, and although like everyone else in the Thirties he undoubtedly felt the influence of Eliot, and although he actually lived and taught in America before the war, he shows little interest in or knowledge of American poetry. And what he does know he seems negative about. Among other things, he distrusts the spirit of Whitman, whose optimism offends him and whose tendency to formal excesses ("a wrong-headed attempt at spontaneity")[17] threatens MacNeice's own (more or less rationalist) bias towards common sense. He punctures Pound's Imagist manifesto at every point, and objects to the method of the *Cantos* because their "passion for the particular detail conduces to a total blur."[18] When he comes to write a long poem of his own (*Autumn Sequel*) in what one might think could have been an American, loose-limbed manner, he is at pains to insist his model is Spenser, not the *Cantos*. Nor does he have anything good to say about Ransom ("a dainty contemplative whimsicality, centered on domestic objects," that "brought a metaphysical attitude into the nursery"), or cummings (nothing but "tough-guy sentimentality").[19]

Such a wholesale lack of sympathy is probably due to MacNeice's own search for some sort of contemporary common-sense classicism. From such a point of view (sharpened by a certain Northern canniness and restraint), American poetry has to seem a stew of excesses: excesses of emotion ("sentimentality"), of openness ("wrong-headed spontaneity"), of particularity ("blur"), and of craft ("whimsicality"). What the undeniably vital principle of Whitman (with whom he yoked D.H. Lawrence) needed, argued MacNeice, was to be properly *girdered* "with a structure supplied partly by reason, partly by emotion intelligently canalised to an end, partly by the mere love of form."[20] Terms such as these—added to the fact that MacNeice probably didn't *need* American poetry because he felt comfortable with the classics, the English tradition, and a comparatively limited ("traditional") sense of the meaning of "form"—ensure that the poets of America don't ever truly enter the bloodstream of MacNeice's verse. Why this should remain a somewhat surprising fact is because what he says of Whitman and Lawrence ("poetry keeping pace with their lives and with their beliefs as affecting their lives")[21] could be applied, though in a different *formal* spirit, to some of his own intentions as a poet.

As with just about everything else in Austin Clarke's career, his connection with American poetry is oblique, occluded, enigmatic. Given his explicit commitment to the "Irish Mode" and his early relationship to the Revival and Revivalism, it is a surprise to find Americans at the very source and opening of Clarke's imaginative life as a poet. While these early influences may seem, in the larger picture, slight enough, they are nonetheless worth mentioning.

After what he calls his "experiences of nature," it was Longfellow's *Hiawatha* which first awakened the poet in Clarke, giving him his "first experience of the evocative power of verbal rhythm."[22] In stylistic terms this may not have been a particularly "American" experience, but there was also, to judge by a comparatively late poem, an early encounter with Whitman. It is in "Old Fashioned Pilgrimage" (written after the pivotal *Mnemosyne Lay in Dust*, which had emancipated his memory and given him the freedom of his whole past) that Clarke recalls his startled early discovery of Whitman:

> I heard his free verse come
> In a rhythmic run of syllables that spread around me, loud
> And soft . . . I was a
> Boy, turning that once forbidden book, *The Leaves*
> *Of Grass*, word-showered, until my body was naked and self-proud
> As I looked it boldly up and down, vein-ready, well-stocked;
> Joy rising.[23]

Whitman is here vividly connected with Clarke's discovery of his own sexuality. And since Clarke's sexuality is so bound to his imagination, to his life as a poet—either in celebratory, satiric, or desperate ways—Whitman's forbidden book can be reasonably associated with Clarke's growth into and as a poet, even his discovery of a sort of verbal Eden, innocent and extravagantly sensual. Beyond the auto-erotic intensity of this response to *Leaves of Grass*, the connection with Whitman is further endorsed by Clarke's awareness of the American poet's passionate commitment to a common social being, his image of universal fraternity, of "Europe, America, Asia, Africa together."[24] In Clarke's own case, on the other hand, it is the blunting of precisely these sexual and social possibilities (more specifically understood on his terms) that hurt him into poetry. So Whitman's exemplary nature is, for Clarke, suggestive of some Paradise Lost of human freedom.

Later than the encounter with Whitman, Clarke's experience of Poe is also, however, crucial to his development as a poet. So, at least, it would seem from "Old Fashioned Pilgrimage," in which he also visits the shrine of Poe's "small white cottage." A dream reveals the way Poe's poetry was implicated in the most sexually traumatic circumstance of Clarke's young manhood. Poe's romantic fever of desire is a disease Clarke feels he himself suffered from, most notably in the unconsummated affair with "Margaret," known from the autobiography, *Mnemosyne*, and from some curious intrusions into the early epics.[25] It was this condition ("Cornelia, in the candlelight, uneasy / With love, thin pallor and gloom, under her nightgown, half seen") that drove him into a breakdown

and St. Patrick's hospital. Recalling it in the Poe-induced dream, he can comment on it in critical terms, blaming the whole unnatural catastrophe on the rigorous strictures of the Catholic Church: "O could the Church have allowed us
pessary, thin cover, / I would not so abuse what others coveted" ("Pilgrimage,"
CP, 358). So Poe's women are a displacing code for "Margaret." And by locating him in sexual sites, giving a focus to his imagination for what could not be
achieved in "life," Poe's work propelled Clarke inadvertently towards becoming
the poet he grew into after the "Margaret" affair, a poet acutely aware of the gap
between desire and mundane facts, aware of the originating power of blocked
erotic energy. In the hidden but essential parts of himself, that is, both Poe and
Whitman offered Clarke a reality he had, no matter in how curbed or distorted a
way, to get into his own work. Often this reality pushes against the more voluntary and deliberately accommodated influences of the Revival, and has to wait
until the later poetry for more direct expression.

Poe, Longfellow, and Whitman, then, seem to have left distinct marks on
what lies under and before Clarke's growth as a poet; on his nervous sense of
rhythm, his sexual identity and distress, the anger that leads to satiric vitality
and personal reticence. In addition, and much later in his career as a poet, there
is Pound. Beginning in repugnance, Clarke's recorded attitude to Pound describes an arc of increasing approval, rising from his 1940's description of the
Cantos as "a gigantic poetic notebook in which [Pound] has jotted down, with a
minimum of rearrangement and simple parallelism, everything that strikes his
fancy in the midst of his extensive reading."[26] What Clarke objects to here is a
lack of formal order, the apparent disorder of Pound's method naturally disturbing a poet who is himself (see *Night and Morning*, 1938) obsessive about
tight closed forms posited upon principles of metaphysical and aesthetic selection and willed limitation.

By 1950, however, a more benevolent note creeps in. Now Pound's "rag-
bag of the centuries" is "a gigantic patchwork quilt to keep young poets
warm."[27] Finally, by 1960, after Clarke's own re-emergence as a poet with a
renewed relationship to the whole notion of form, he can seem almost envious
of Pound's openness, of "his poetical forms . . . so ample in their freedom that
they seem devoid of technical controls."[28] At the same time he was ready, predictably enough, to praise Pound's "energy and zeal," his "quarrel with his own
country."[29] And Pound's surrender to plenitude may arguably have had some
impact on the latest work of Clarke, in some of which ("Old Fashioned Pilgrimage" itself, for example) the expansive manners of Pound and Whitman may
have been drawn into the circle of Clarke's own laden expression.

On the speculative side, too, though one would not want to push this too
far, it's possible to detect connections between those acts of creative *translation*
performed by Clarke as well as Pound. This could be true of Clarke's late adap-
tation of Ovid ("The Dilemma of Iphis"), which is reminiscent in voice of some
of Pound's great translations. It might also be true of some of those much earlier
translations by Clarke, his adaptations and re-animations of the Irish (in *Cattledrive in Connaught,* and in *Pilgrimage*), where the Irish poet seems to perform something of the same service for Celtic and Medieval Ireland as Pound

(in *Personae*, 1908-1910) did for Provençal and Medieval Italian literature. Like Pound, Clarke both brings the old works into a recognisably modern idiom, and at the same time "translates" some of his own experiences into the poetic idiom of the earlier culture. Without direct evidence, of course, this has to remain a possibly interesting parallel of literary achievements, a farther, if speculative link between the Irish and the American poet. All in all, however, these acquaintances suggest that in the grain of Clarke's poetic achievement there is a definite American presence, both in the deeper layers of the imagination and in the more distinctly tangible areas of form.

Nothing suggests an early American influence on Padraic Fallon. Some critical views, however, as well as a number of poems of his maturity show that Fallon used Ezra Pound to help him cast off the obviously heavy (and disturbing) burden of Yeats. What he takes from Pound seems at once formal and substantive. His praise for Pound's "loosening verse line" and open form, for example, is posited on the ability of such formal instruments to accommodate all aspects of the individual in a way that is not available to the "careful stanzas" of Yeats.[30] Pound offers Fallon encouragement for his own emerging, aesthetic bent towards a "free-for-all [of] personal language."[31] Stimulated by American practice, he argues against the English Auden's rationale for closed forms, and he sounds like a Black Mountaineer with an Irish accent when he declares that the poem should make "its own rules of rhythm and pattern . . . personal to the poet."[32] There's a remarkably prescient and refreshing quality to Fallon's further critical remark that "each poem is different from any other and demands its own kind of language and approach."[33]

This aesthetic pragmatism (which makes Fallon sound more like the contemporary of Montague and Kinsella than their elder by a generation) was enriched even more in 1957 by the Irish poet's discovery of William Carlos Williams. In this case, the American influence prompted arguments for a poetry of "normal human range," free from the larger gestures of Yeatsian magniloquence, since "The big tower," as he says in one poem, "would have us / Make our verse like his, sing / Jubilant Muses."[34] The effects of such critical and theoretical views are most in evidence in the agile relaxed fluencies of such poems as "The Head," "For Paddy Mac," or "Painting of My Father" ("So you wanted little of me towards the end, / Barbering, a light / For the old pipe, / And an ear, my ear, any ear, when you spilled over / The intolerable burden / Of being a very old man"). The particular influence of Pound may be detected especially in "Stop on the Road to Ballylee." In this poem, recording a journey to honour Yeats's centenary, Fallon can be seen, ironically, embracing the poetic legacy of Pound in the poem's patchwork as it moves between the voice of the mind, a Latin text, and the external spectacle of patients in the grounds of an asylum. The subject matter itself has to be an oblique declaration of the reason why such a formal stretching is necessary—otherwise how encompass a world of such daunting variety, a world that will not lend itself to neater formulations, no matter how masterful their rhetoric.[35] Poems like these underline the serious ways in which Padraic Fallon (a poet whose true value and importance have still not been properly recognised) serves as a conduit for the American presence in contemporary Irish poetry.

Denis Devlin is the most deliberately cosmopolitan of the poets in the generation immediately after Yeats. Although it is the European influence that's usually cited in this regard (Valéry in particular),[36] the American influence, which helped him become "one of the pioneers of the international poetic English which now prevails on both sides of the Atlantic" (as his American commentators said of him),[37] is impossible to overlook. His collegial friendship with American poets such as Tate, Warren, and Ransom had to foster such an influence, which seems also to have been a way (as was his use of the Europeans) to avoid the difficult shadow of Yeats. The American pressure on the work may be felt in a comparison between the first and second volumes of Devlin's verse. The following stanza is from *Intercessions* (1937):

> Me seeing the seen, the prestige of death drives faint,
> Coupled asynchronous like time and knowledge.
> Lunar scaffolding, a decrepit star falls,
> Rotting eyelashes fall through fetid wind.
> > ("In the Last Resort")

It is a task to unravel the stiff, hermetic obscurities of these lines. Linguistically muscle-bound, their rhythmic push is nervously staccato, far from speech. The poems in the next book, however, (*Lough Derg*, 1946) are "more accessible in their increasing ease both in line and language," qualities which may be attributed to a specifically American influence—to Tate, Warren, maybe Stevens, Hart Crane.[38] Here is how "Ank'hor Vat," a poem in that volume, begins:

> The antlered forests
> Move down to the sea.
> Here the dung-filled jungle pauses.
> Buddha has covered the walls of the great temple
> With the vegetative speed of his imagery.

It is easy to see how the clotted syntax, turgid abstractions and claustrophobic lines of the earlier mode have given way to a colloquial yet dignified ease, an expression quick and unencumbered, moving in varied lines along the edge of direct 'prose' statement. This "Americanisation" of Devlin's work (a shift which heightened, I believe, the native drift and ability of his imagination) is even more apparent in "Annapolis," where direct speech and relaxed narrative manner remind of Frank O'Hara. This is how it begins:

> 'No we can't get a license for liquor, being too near the church,'
> Said the waiter. The church looked friends enough
> On its humble grassy hillock. So I said: 'Excuse me
> I must have a drink.' And I rambled on down West Street

> To eat and drink at Socrates the Greek's.

Finally, the American presence in Devlin's work can be confirmed by the "Projective" openness of the later "Memoirs of a Turcoman Diplomat," with its echoes of Pound's Mauberly, or of some of Stevens's dandyish effects, a touch of Ransom's sly, spry pedantry:

> Tuck in your trews, Johannes my boy, be led by me,
> These girls are kind. And we're all the rage now,
>> whiskey-flushed men of our age,
> The callow and the sallow and the fallow wiped off the page.

It is influences like these that nourish Devlin's own various, sophisticated voice and chameleon manner—his eclectic, thoughtful, idiosyncratic habits of imagination which left their mark on poets like Montague and Kinsella. By such distinct means he helps to blaze a path away from Yeats—who in terms of a certain sort of influence could be a dead end for an Irish poet—a path marked out at least in part by the Americans.

Oddly enough, perhaps, it is Patrick Kavanagh, poet of the parochial, who is most vocal in that generation about his debts to American poetry. For this reason one has to take with the usual spoon of salt (necessary accompaniment to a great many of Kavanagh's *ex cathedra* critical pronouncements) the poet's response to the question, "What do you think of modern American literature?" The answer was a single shot from the hip: "Trash."[39] The truth of the matter is that Kavanagh drank deep at this Transatlantic well, and was the first Irish poet to bring American influence into its post "modernist" phase, post Pound and Eliot, that is. As for the other poets mentioned, for him too this influence seems to be one way out of the Yeatsian cul-de-sac.

Kavanagh's submission to American influence falls into two phases. The first brings him into contact with the Imagists and Gertrude Stein. The lucid, hard-edged quality of the Imagists "excited my clay heavy mind," he says, while Stein's "work was like whiskey to me, her strange rhythms broke up the cliché formulation of my thought."[40] Both in the Imagists and in Stein he found the encouragement to be "hard and clear," undecorative, to *present* image and "to make full use of free verse."[41] He admired the work of J.G. Fletcher, most likely valuing its ability to be emotional in a direct, unsentimental way.[42] The fact that Imagism "praises by showing" edges the influence out of the formal and into the area of feeling, of a particular attitude to the subject.[43]

Basically, then, Kavanagh first went to technical and emotional school to the Americans, learning what he could from the poets in Conrad Aiken's anthology, *Twentieth Century American Poetry*. By 1947 he is knowledgeable enough to say that for him the best American poets are "Dickinson among the women, after Millay, a sentimentalist [not necessarily, as Kavanagh uses the term, pejorative], and among the men some very good such as Frost, Wallace Stevens, E.A. Robinson, Jeffers, John Peale Bishop, Hart Crane, Richard Eberhart, and young Harry Brown, a new poet influenced by Yeats. All these men are perhaps in the Main Stream."[44] Thanks to this tutorial in American poetry, Kavanagh could move from the brief stanzaic structures of his first book to the larger visionary reach and suppler technical accomplishment of *The Great Hunger*. Here's a stanza from an early lyric, "A Star":

> Beauty was that
> Far vanished flame,
> Call it a star
> Wanting better name.

It's easy to hear the gap between that sort of thing and lines like the following from *The Great Hunger*—with their more casual formalities, their sense of spoken language, their quick shifts of perspective:

> Maguire knelt beside a pillar where he could spit
> Without being seen. He turned an old prayer round:
> 'Jesus, Mary and Joseph pray for us
> Now and at the hour.' Heaven dazzled death.
> 'Wonder should I cross-plough that turnip-ground?'

Kavanagh's second phase under the influence of American poetry departs from the Main Stream, connecting up with the overflowing tributary generated by the Beat poets. This coincides more or less with his own poetical "re-birth" in the mid-50s. He sees their work as an antidote to what he objects to in the "artificial verbalism" of Richard Wilbur and others, and his attitude to them in 1958 is part mockery, part envy: "That rascal Allen Ginsberg has made news with the beat generation . . . You only have to roar and use bad language. I am genuinely thinking of having a go."[45] Later he says he still likes "the fun and games of a lot of contemporary verse . . . even people like Ginsberg to some extent, funny stuff."[46] It is the vitality he admires: Ferlinghetti, he says, is 'alive' (as opposed to 'very dead' Robert Lowell).[47]

What Kavanagh gets from the Beats is the encouragement to exercise his own talent in a *relaxed* way—beyond lyrical posture and beyond even the great colloquial performance of *The Great Hunger*—for "they have all written direct, personal statements, nothing involved, no, just statements of their position. That's all."[48] It was this sort of encouragement which led him to the "direct, personal statements" of such later poems as the Canal sonnets, "Is," "The Hospital," and "Auditors In": here even rhyme is relaxed statement:

>   I am so glad
> To come accidentally upon
> Myself at the end of a tortuous road
> And have learned with surprise that God
> Unworshipped withers to the Futile One.

The Americans, then, marshaled Kavanagh the way that he was going, along a path that was deliberately (and for later Irish poets most helpfully) charted away from the more rhetorically imposing figure of Yeats. Nourished by the Americans, Kavanagh found a poetic voice that did not falsify his powerful sense of the actual or betray his conviction that "what is called art is merely life." That his American schooling was of central importance to him as a poet is sadly confirmed by the fact that, when he runs dry at the end, even "an American anthology" can grant him no inspiring jolt:

> I have perused an American anthology for stimulation
> But the result is not as encouraging as it used
> To be when Walter Lowenfels' falling down words
> Like ladders excited me to chance my arm
> With nouns and verbs.
>
> ("In Blinking Blankness")

The strongest and most lasting effect of the random, often haphazard, usually occasional uses of American influence by these four important poets in the generation after Yeats (that the Northerners MacNeice and Hewitt seem untouched by this influence is a fact that may at some point be worth following up, as another indicator of differences between poetry written out of distinct historical and cultural traditions [and conditions] in the island), is to aid in the establishment of a fresh base for Irish poetry in the modern world for which Yeats felt such contempt. American poetry, that is, helps steer Irish poetry in a direction quite distinct from that pointed to by Yeats's last wilful testament and exhortation in "Under Ben Bulben." Whether the Americans are "base-born products of base beds" or not, it's clear that these Irish poets do not "scorn" them (and we remember that Yeats himself began with one radically modern American as teacher, and proceeded to the school of another). Rather do the Irish poets make their own uses of certain Americans on a journey that moves away from Yeats and towards their own identities as poets of contemporary Ireland and the contemporary world. In one way or another, Clarke, Kavanagh, Devlin, and Fallon lay the ground between them for two major poets of the next poetic generation—John Montague and Thomas Kinsella (Richard Murphy's apparent freedom from that influence might, of necessity, be part of the discussion that would include MacNeice and Hewitt)—to flower fully within the sphere of American influence. Taking for granted the working of this particular influence in their immediate predecessors, impelled, both by their reading of these predecessors and by their own experience, towards the Americans, they have richly re-discovered this influence for themselves and incorporated it organically into their work.

Both Kinsella and Montague deepen and extend the American influence in a conscious effort to become truly modern Irish poets. The American influence also helps them break from their first influences—French poetry in Montague's case, Yeats and Auden for Kinsella. More than their predecessors, these two have made American poetry a distinct, articulate part of their own development as poets. Even in personal terms the two seem emblematic of new conditions in this literary relationship: Montague was born in American, and later literally "went to school" (at Yale, Iowa, Berkeley) to American poets. Kinsella—between 1965 and the late '80s—lived part of every year in America.[49]

"Ireland," Montague has said, somewhat mischievously, "is an island off the coast of Europe, facing across three thousand miles of water towards America."[50] Aside from having spent his first six or so years there, he spent some poetically formative years, 1953-56, attending Yale, Iowa, and living on the West Coast. Given his respect for Pound, Eliot, Stevens, Williams, and Crane ("probably the best generation of poets since the Great Romantics"),[51] it was natural for him to turn to America. Ransom, at Yale, he says, was "instrumental in changing my destiny,"[52] Williams once "hugged me like a son;" Snodgrass, Bly and others were at Iowa with him; Lowell and Wilbur were known on the East Coast, and Ginsberg and Snyder on the West: meeting them, "I seemed to have completed the spectrum of my own generation of American poetry."[53] Williams helped him towards a "low-pitched style [that] seeks exactness," ("Waiting," in *A Chosen Light*), while in the work of Robert Duncan he was encouraged in a natural tendency of his own—a habit of touching the ordinary with ritual grace, a glimmer of myth. It was also most likely Duncan who tuned him to the depths of possibility in the term "political poetry."[54]

From early on, Montague saw the American influence as a necessary complement to the Irish: "I am not saying that Ezra Pound is necessarily more important than Egan O'Rahilly for an Irish poet (one has to study both) but the complexity and pain of the *Pisan Cantos* are certainly more relevant than another version of 'Preab San Ól.'"[55] Both content and form in American poetry helped Montague realise his own poetic identity, learning from that "complexity and pain" of Pound and from the "new music" which Pound and Williams brought into English verse, prompting the realisation that the iambic line was no longer able to register "the curve of modern speech."[56] In form and language, as well as content, American poetry has helped Montague become what he calls "a global regionalist," a poetic citizen of the world.[57] And at a deeper level, it helps him do greater justice to his own doubled, or tripled, identity—Ulster-Irish-American. It may be, indeed, that the American influence / presence / nourishment helped Montague deal with the ambiguities inherent in such a layered identity, helping him distance himself creatively (i.e. with no loss of feeling) from the intimate intensities of his personal, communal, or political subject matter. In addition, by crossing Lowell with Snyder, Creeley, Ginsberg, and Duncan, he imports into Irish poetry a rich array of poetic resources for dealing with the autobiographical. In writing about the self he has learned to be lyrical and detached, a combination not as truly available to him in the expansive sonorities of Yeats nor in the much more relaxed but often rawly personal exposures of Kavanagh (who as a lyric poet remains much more *vulnerable* than Montague ever seems to be).

The result of Montague's reception of the Americans may be seen in the following stanzas. First, these lines from an early poem:

A rainy quiet evening, with leaves that hang
Like squares of silk from dripping branches.
An avenue of laurel, and the guttering cry
Of a robin that balances a moment,
Starts and is gone
Upon some furtive errand of its own.
                    ("Irish Street Scene With Lovers" 1952)

In this descriptive "scene," external texture is what matters, as it does in the rest
of the poem. The self is nowhere, all is external, adjectival. Even the title ac-
centuates the analogy with painting. On the other hand, the opening stanza of
Montague's quintessential Sixties (in Ireland) poem—the poem that, maybe
more than any other, registered a waking up, "The Siege of Mullingar"—suggests something of the way his style relaxed under American influences:

At the Fleadh Cheóil in Mullingar
There were two sounds, the breaking
Of glass, and the background pulse
Of music. Young girls roamed
The streets with eager faces,
Pushing for men. Bottles in
Hand, they rowed out a song:
Puritan Ireland's dead and gone
A myth of O'Connor and Ó Faoláin.

There's a distinct new sound here, something that goes beyond description
and enters the realm of action. Rhythmically it is very relaxed, yet there's a tension in the phrasing itself, as in those young girls "pushing for men." The plain
diction has a ritual edge to it (pulse, roamed, the breaking), culminating in the
elegiac, slightly comic refrain that deconstructs Yeats and "September 1913." In
this pliancy of expression, lyrical narrative has taken over from description,
enhancing the deliberately un-iambic movement towards an easy, elegant, but
decisively unYeatsian balancing of stanza and sentence. The openness the poet
seems to be celebrating is inherent in his own formal management as well as in
the life freshly surging around him. So Montague's encounter with Irish matter
in idioms that live under the influence of American poetry helps him to his own
voice, his own poetic identity, free not only of the Revival, but of Kavanagh too,
as in the following lines from a later poem:

A slight fragrance revives:
cycling through the evening
to a dance in Gowna—Lake
of the Calf, source of Erne—
with one of the Caffrey's.
Our carbide lamps wobbled
along the summer hedges, a

warm scent of hay and clover
as, after the dance, I kissed
my girl against a crumbling
churchyard wall.

("A Slight Fragrance," *The Dead Kingdom*)

Here the brief lines bolster the mythic allusion with ordinariness, as Montague shows Williams' or Synder's feel for effective brevity. A narrative bone keeps lyrical description honest, while the run of the lines, gathering towards a sentence, prohibits any iambic dependence. This is the Kavanagh of "Inniskeen Road" salted with a rack of American suggestions. This is Montague's own possession of the "new music" he has mentioned.

Which brings me back to that most idiosyncratic of contemporary poetic musicians, Thomas Kinsella. From the start, says Kinsella, "the things behind form were what bothered me, having to do with content, exploratory form—the sequence rather than the finished single object . . . longer, sequential forms, open-ended—so that the effort can continue inside a more stable continuum."[58] Like Yeats with Pound, Kinsella managed to remake himself under the influence of, again, Pound, then Williams and, most likely, Lowell. In adhering to the "wonderfully enabling free forms" of the Americans, Kinsella felt he was turning to the center of modern poetry in English.[59] For, as he says in 1966, "at some point [during the last twenty-five years], the growth point of contemporary poetry shifted from England to American."[60] The Americans helped him proceed beyond the influence of Yeats and the influential "grace" of Auden, to "find much more satisfaction in the form of Ezra Pound's *Cantos*. Finally I don't think graceful postures are adequate; you have to deal with the raw material."[61] Dealing with the "raw material," the Americans liberated him into a "dynamic response to whatever happens."[62] Like Yeats, who was a profound example in this respect, these American poets encouraged Kinsella to think of the *totality* of a poetic career, as they helped Montague towards his commitment to the poetic *sequence*.

Probably the most important lesson Kinsella learned from Williams was to bring form and content together in especially fertile, fructifying ways. This was "a kind of creative relaxation in the face of complex reality; to remain open, prehensile; not rigidly committed."[63] In a poetry where "commitment" is difficult to avoid (Yeats's stratagem was to be absolute, serially, for different things; very little about his magniloquent stanzaic adventures suggests "creative relaxation"), Williams's kinetic scepticism offered a way out to Kinsella, a Keatsian lesson translated into American. Creative agility, imaginative openness: in the substantive and formal consequences of such terms, Kinsella is the Irish poet who has most internalised them. These American lessons sanction to Kinsella's own mind the continuous, open-ended nature of this enterprise. And, seen in this light, his work (as well as that of Montague) owes much (aside from the *Cantos*) to such American examples as *Paterson, Notebooks, History,* the *Maximus* poems, *Howl, Kaddish, Dream Songs,* and of course to the granddaddy of them all, *Leaves of Grass.* Such American sequences taught both these Irish poets how to forge a language and a form adequate to the particular span and nature of their personal and public experience. And taught them, too, how to be implicitly more "political," in the broadest meaning of that word.

In its development and change, Kinsella's work is most exemplary of the way the American presence can affect Irish poetry. (Even more than Montague, he discovered and made use of it after his own early style was firmly established.) The following brief passages—the first from "Mirror in February" (1962), the second from "Worker in Mirror, At His Bench" (1973)—may serve to illustrate this.

> Below my window the awakening trees,
> Hacked clean for better bearing, stand defaced,
> Suffering their brute necessities,
> And how should the flesh not quail that span for span
> Is mutilated more? In slow distaste
> I fold my towel with what grace I can,
> Not young and not renewable, but man.

What may be heard first in this passage is the iambic insistence of the line, the deliberate sense of closure, the firm architectural snap as it shuts on that conclusive foot. Abstractions are obvious, too, "brute necessities" being both spare and eloquent (if a bit self-consciously *gestured*), as is the slightly posed syntax of the rhetorical question. The emblematic account of the landscape is also worth noting: the poet reads the surroundings in a way that goes back to "That time of year thou May'st in me behold" and beyond. It is a given trope, brilliantly handled. The nature of the experience, therefore, is being clearly seen from the outside, and in all this Kinsella is the masterful manager of given conventions, of what he himself calls "received forms and rhyme."[64]

In what sounds like his own version of some of the tenets of Projective Verse, Kinsella describes his later poems as "[having] a form which ought to be felt as a whole, rather than in, e.g., stanzaic expectations. Each poem has a unique shape, contents and development."[65] The impulse, he says, is "merely to understand, not to impose order."[66] Where "Mirror in February" seeks "to impose order," I'd say "Worker in Mirror, at His Bench" reflects the impulse "merely to understand," trying to show something like Williams's "creative relaxation in the face of complex reality."

> It is tedious, yes.
> The process is elaborate, and wasteful
> —a dangerous litter of lacerating pieces
> collects. Let my rubbish stand witness . . .
> Smile, stirring it idly with a shoe.
> Take, for example, this work in hand:
> out of its waste matter
> it should emerge light and solid.
> One idea, grown with the thing itself,

should drive it searching inward
with a sort of life, due to the mirror effect.
Often, the more I simplify,
the more a few simplicities go
burrowing into their own depths,
until the guardian structure is aroused . . .

Most satisfying, yes.
Another kind of vigour, I agree
—unhappy until its actions are more convulsed:
the 'passionate'—might find it maddening.

In this passage Kinsella is committed to no climactic truth, but to a "dynamic response to whatever happens" (rather than "the music of what happens"). Here everything is interiorised, the mind's voice seems much closer to its source than in the earlier poem. Matching this, the iambic line has been broken into a line that's more responsive to phrase/sense units, and to units of breath. Rhyme is gone, lyrical diction is gone, and syntax is fractured and hesitant, articulating the way the mind itself proceeds. Consciousness here turns into speech, with almost no intermediaries, and reflects upon itself, not upon some world external to it. We're less aware of the thing made than of the making itself, as tones shift and unspoken nuances slide between one utterance and the next. Metaphor seems not at all imposed, but found in the language itself as a direct response to perception (as in "guardian," "waste matter," "aroused"). There is no sense of a finished architecture, an architecture of finish, of conclusions. All is process, and this is confirmed by the ending of the poem, which is simply an unfinished period ("from zenith to pit / through dead"). Consciousness is speaking here, not being spoken about. I might even hazard that it is the American revolution in his own verse that enables Kinsella to get beyond the poetic influences of Yeats and Auden to the prose virtues of articulated consciousness that Joyce offers in *Ulysses*. If for Stephen Dedalus the shortest way to Tara is via Holyhead, the shortest way to a native Irish consciousness in modern poetry may be via Paterson, New Jersey, and Hailey, Idaho.

After the deliberate attachment of Kinsella and Montague to poetry written by Americans, it's been easier for Irish poets to take American influence as a natural feature of their own verse. So the enlargement of Seamus Heaney's style by the benevolent presences of Frost, Lowell, or Elizabeth Bishop—his accommodation within the borders of his own disciplined habits of what he calls "the drift of contemporary American verse"[67]—doesn't come as a surprise. In moral as well as technical terms, too, Lowell's has been as instructive a career to Heaney as the starker model of Mandelstam, while in books like *Station Island, The Haw Lantern,* and *Seeing Things,* the American habit of sequence-making has left its mark. Derek Mahon's best work, too, with its sceptical ironies and plangent lyrical intelligence may carry some signs of Lowell, Hart Crane, Richard Wilbur and Elizabeth Bishop. And in the remarkable poems of Paul Durcan, I think most of us would hear a voice that betrays something of the emancipated

energy of the Beat poets—part bardic, part comic-strip, part spiritual efferves-
cence.[68] In a more incidental way, Ciaran Carson has acknowledged that the
spell-binding narrative strategies of his recent poems are indebted to the long
fluent line of the American poet C.K. Williams. And even the rapt enigmatic
manners of Medbh McGuckian may, or so the critics say, owe something to
Hart Crane (and, I would add, to Emily Dickinson and Marianne Moore).

While showing an increasingly American presence in Irish poetry, these
more recent individual connections do not signal any radical innovations or significant new departures. In the work of Eavan Boland and Paul Muldoon, however, the American influence has—as it has at other pivotal moments over the
past hundred years—brought important new elements into Irish verse.

Feeling herself orphaned in her own predominantly male native tradition,
Eavan Boland found in the American tradition a powerful and persistent female
presence. In that remaking of herself that entailed turning away from her earliest
lyric manner, Boland seems to have drawn in particular on two poets—Sylvia
Plath and Adrienne Rich. First—to fashion a more recognisably female voice
speaking specifically female truths—it is to Plath she turns, to the Plath of reck-
less self-exposure, of nervous extremities vehemently controlled by compressed
lines and closed-circuit stanzas. The Plath you can hear in this snatch of "Me-
dusa":

> Green as eunuchs, your wishes
> Hiss at my sins.
> Off, off, eely tentacles!
>
> There is nothing between us.

In *In Her Own Image* Boland adapts this voice to her own uses, to chart some
general truths about the female condition and to speak about the female body
and a woman's relationship to it in a novel, often bitter, but unflinching way.
Her "Tirade to the Mimic Muse" sets the purgative tone:

> I've caught you out. You slut. you fat trout.
> So here you are fumed in candle-stink.
> Its yellow balm exhumes you for the glass.
> How you arch and pout in it!
> How you poach your face in it!

Writing such "rhythms of struggle, need, will, and female energy," Boland
amplifies her range in *Night Feed*, drawing this time on some of the quieter,
more domestic tones and cadences of Plath. In the later poems of *The Journey*
and *Outside History*, however, she moves out of earshot of Plath and into range
of Adrienne Rich. Rich's politicising of women's territory has also fed Boland's
critical stances, while the Irish woman's choice of a public role as poet has in
part been enabled by the American's exemplary career. Rich's poetic language
is much less hectic than Plath's, and this has led, I'd imagine, to the more qui-

etly accented speech of Boland's recent poems. Certainly this later work seems like a tuned response to Rich's own self-instruction in that splendid feminist allegory of hers, "Diving into the Wreck": "I have to learn alone / to turn my body without force / in the deep element."

Boland's work—tutored by her chosen American connections—has helped younger Irish poets who happen to be women find their voices and their courage. In this it has altered the map of Irish poetry. That map isn't so much altered as re-invented by the startling work of Paul Muldoon. And it almost goes without saying, that in this first thoroughly postmodern imagination in Irish poetry the American presence is palpable from the start. Muldoon's ludic mode co-opts a whole rack of American presences to his own purposes. The eclectic early narrative, "Immram," for example, splices and old Irish voyage tale to tough-guy detective stories in the manner of Raymond Chandler:

> She was wearing what looked like a dead fox
> Over a low-cut sequined gown,
> And went by the name of Susan, or Suzanne.
> A girl who would never pass out of fashion
> So long as there's an 'if' in California.

Likewise, "The More a Man Has, the More a Man Wants" grafts onto a dark tale of violence in the mean streets of the North of Ireland some elements from native North American trickster stories. And Muldoon's latest opus *Madoc, A Mystery*, narrates in his own mysterious and mischievous way an hallucinatory encounter between Europe (more specifically the British Isles) and the New World. This is only a sample, but it's enough to show how deeply America is implicated in Muldoon's work, so deeply as to make specific debts to specific poets a moot point. He himself has said that "it's important to most societies to have the notion of something out there to which we belong, that our home is somewhere else." His own discovery of America as one such "out there," has turned that "somewhere else" into a home, into a brave new world of possibilities that enable him to deal—in ways as compelling as they are oblique—with some of the most pressing political issues of his own native Northern Ireland.

Because the eclectic collage excitements of America have illuminated Muldoon's work from the start and in such a seemingly natural and undogmatic way, he represents a logical conclusion to this story. His work, indeed, may be taken as emblematic of the speed with which one can now move between Ireland and America. Times Square, after all, is not too many flying hours from Harold's Cross. But in the hundred years or so since Yeats sat in that house in Harold's Cross, thinking of Walt Whitman and a school of Irish poetry, the poetry of Times Square (or Harvard Square or San Francisco Bay) has been a consistently nourishing source to which Irish poets have turned and by which they have been replenished. Although it hasn't been the only influence, what we now know as modern Irish poetry in English would be very different without it.

But why has this been the case? In the modern and contemporary poetry of Great Britain, after all—leaving aside Auden, Thom Gunn, and some recent poetry by women—no such deep and extended connection with America seems to exist. It's probably not possible to answer with any completeness that question. But in the story as I've told it, two common threads seem to have run through the examples. Yeats, remember, was influenced by Whitman in what we might call ideological ways and by Pound in more explicitly aesthetic/stylistic ways. Likewise, in all the other cases I've mentioned, stylistic and "ideological" elements seem closely bound. For, in all of them, American influence seems synonymous with freedom—whether freedom from a colonial condition, freedom from socio-cultural or racial clichés, freedom from a powerful predecessor, freedom from a confining state and state of mind into a mode of freshly expressive consciousness, freedom from that confinement caused by the politics of gender, or freedom from any and all the easy labelings of cultural, political, and poetical rhetorics. Since to treat properly the implications of this fact would need another essay, I'll simply end with a fairly rudimentary formulation of "stylistic" and "ideological" factors that have played their part in this game of influences. The formulation combines two descriptive statements. The first is John Montague's revisionist description of Ireland's geographical location: "Ireland," said Montague, "is an island off the coast of Europe facing across three thousand miles of water towards America." The second statement belongs to Thomas Kinsella, who in 1966 observed that "at some point in the last 25 years, the growth point of contemporary poetry shifted from England to America." What I deduce from these two statements—taking them lightly enough and yet seeing some subversive nerve twitching under each of them—is that the variously inflected American connection I've been describing is merely a logical part of the continuing (perhaps now completed) effort at achieving the comprehensive autonomy of Irish poetry in the English language.

1990

NOTES

[1] Thomas Kinsella, *Davis, Mangan, and Ferguson? Tradition and the Irish Writer*, (Dublin: Dolmen Press, 1970) 57.

[2] James Randall, Interview with Seamus Heaney, *Ploughshares*. 5. 3. (1979) 20.

[3] W.B. Yeats, *Collected Letters*, eds. John Kelly and E. Domville, vol. I (London: Oxford University Press, 1986) 9.

[4] *Letters*, 339.

[5] *Ibid*, 408, 409.

[6] In "A New Poet" (review of poems by Edwin Ellis). See *Uncollected Prose of W.B. Yeats*, ed. John Frayne, vol. I (New York: Columbia University Press, 1970-1976) 234.

[7] "Dr. Todhunter's Irish Poems" (review, 1892, of *The Banshee and Other Poems*), in Frayne, 216.

[8] "Song of Myself," *Leaves of Grass* (New York: Penguin Books, 1982) 42, 73.

[9] W.B. Yeats, *Essays and Introductions* (New York: Macmillan, 1961) 521.

[10] "Upon a House Shaken By the Land Agitation," *Poems* (1951) 93.

[11] "Of an evening in Woburn Buildings, it is reported that [Douglas] Goldring thought that Pound had succeeded in reducing *Yeats* from master to disciple." Frank Tuohy, *Yeats* (London: Macmillan, 1976) 47.

[12] A.N. Jeffares, *W.B. Yeats, Man and Poet* (London: Routledge & Kegan Paul; New Haven: Yale University Press, 1949) 176-77.

[13] Ezra Pound, "The Later Yeats," in *Literary Essays of Ezra Pound* (New York: New Directions, 1968) 379.

[14] Letter to Lady Gregory, December 10, 1909, in Allen Wade (ed). *The Letters of W.B. Yeats* (London: Rupert Hart-Davis, 1954) 543.

[15] *Ibid.*

[16] Tuohy, 147.

[17] *Modern Poetry* (London: Oxford University Press, 1938) 71. MacNiece says that Whitman "Is all for affirming everything, he forgets to negate" (72), and he claims that Whitman's poetry demonstrates "'democracy' in the worst sense" (72).

[18] *Ibid*, 164.

[19] *Ibid*, 186.

[20] *Ibid*, 18.

[21] *Ibid*, 203.

[22] *Twice Round the Black Church* (London: Routledge and Kegan Paul, 1962) 162.

[23] *Collected Poems* (Dublin: Dolmen Press, 1974) 358-59.

[24] *Ibid.*

[25] See, for example, *Mnemosyne Lay in Dust* in *Collected Poems*, 336, and *A Penny in the Clouds* (London: Routledge and Kegan Paul, 1968) 44. Also see Part II of "The Death of Cuchullin" in the first edition of *The Sword of the West* (Dublin: Maunsel and Roberts, 1921) 53-59. Clarke excluded this from the revised version in *Collected Poems*.

[26] G. Craig Tapping, *Austin Clarke: A Study of His Writings* (Dublin: Academy Press, 1981) 229.

[27] *Ibid*, 230. The quotations here are from reviews for *The Irish Times*. See Tapping's Appendix for full list.

[28] *Ibid.*

[29] *Ibid.*

[30] *The Bell*, 17. 8 (1951) 59.

[31] *Ibid*, 17. 11 (1952) 53.

[32] *Ibid.*

[33] *Ibid*, 54.

[34] "Stop on the Road to Ballylee." *Poems* (Dublin: Dolmen Press, 1974) 61.

[35] Given the voice and general manner of this poem, it may even be possible to see its locale as a covert allusion to Pound in St. Elizabeth's. But no external evidence I know of supports such a speculation.

[36] See Denis Devlin, *Selected Poems*, edited by Allen Tate and Robert Penn Warren (New York: Holt, Rinehart and Wilson, 1963), Introduction, 13.

[37] *Ibid*, 14. The work of Devlin's friend and contemporary, Brian Coffey (1905-1995), should also be mentioned, whose "Missouri Sequence" (1962) and *The Death of Hektor* (1979) show the influence of Pound and Eliot.

[38] John Montague, "The Impact of International Modern Poetry on Irish Writing," in *Irish Poets in English: The Thomas Davis Lectures on Anglo-Irish Poetry*, ed. Sean Lucy (Cork and Dublin: Mercier Press, 1973) 149-50. Both Montague and Kinsella have always insisted on the importance of Devlin's example to their own broadening of poetic horizons.

[39] *November Haggard: Uncollected Prose and Verse of Patrick Kavanagh*, ed. Peter Kavanagh (New York: Peter Kavanagh Hand Press, 1971) 96.

[40] *The Green Fool* (London: Penguin Books, 1975) 244. He adds, "it was in the American poets I was chiefly interested."

[41] Pound's Imagist Manifesto, cited in John Nemo, *Patrick Kavanagh* (Boston: Twayne, 1979) 40-41. See also 38-41.

[42] See *Lapped Furrows: Correspondence 1933-1967 Between Patrick and Peter Kavanagh*, ed. Peter Kavanagh (New York: The Peter Kavanagh Hand Press, 1969) 111. Kavanagh raises this and subsequent points in advice to his brother about a series of lectures on modern poetry, in August 1947.

[43] *Ibid.*

[44] *Ibid*, 113. The oddest omission from his list is William Carlos Williams, since Kavanagh, in a sense, ended up doing for Irish poetry what Williams did for American— bringing poetry home to ordinary life in an authentically ordinary language with a capacity for genuine lyrical lift-off.

[45] *Ibid*, 219.

[46] *November Haggard*, 91, (from an interview in May, 1964).

[47] *Tri-Quarterly*, 4 (1966) 109. In a symposium "Poetry Since Yeats: An Exchange of Views," at Northwestern University, which broke up in disorder with Kavanagh arguing against Kinsella (and everybody else) over the particular merits of contemporary poetry. This might be an emblematic moment in the history of American influence on modern Irish poetry.

[48] *Ibid*, 110-111.

[49] Before this, only Devlin had had any practical exposure, being Irish Consul in New York from 1939 to 1947.

[50] "The Impact of International Modern Poetry on Irish Writing," in Lucy, 144.

[51] *The Literary Review*, 22 (1979) 173.

[52] "John Montague: An Interview," *Verse* (Oxford) 6 (1986) 35.

[53] *TLR*, 22 (1979) 157.

[54] This is an assumption I am making, knowing Montague's admiration for Duncan (See *TLR* above, 157-58 and in Lucy, 157), and Duncan's profound ability to fuse political and personal issues.

[55] In Lucy, 153.

[56] *Ibid*, 156.

[57] Title of interview in *TLR*.

[58] *Viewpoints*, 104.

[59] *Ibid*, 106.

[60] *Tri-Quarterly*, 4 (1996) 105.

[61] *Viewpoints*, 104.

[62] *Ibid*, 108.

[63] *Ibid*, 106.

[64] *Ibid*, 108.

[65] *Ibid*, 109.

[66] *Ibid.*

[67] *Ploughshares* 5.3. (1979) 19. He has also had his political / poetical consciousness tuned by these West Coast encounters.

[68] The poems of James Liddy, who has lived for many years in America, reveal similar influences, while their gay sexuality also connects them with distinct strains of

recent American verse, as can be seen in "The Voice of America 1961," in which he addresses "Daddy Whitman."

Public Positions, Private Parts:
Sex and the Erotic in Irish Poetry,
from Cúchullain to Nuala Ní Dhómhnaill

When Crazy Jane talks with the Bishop, she opposes the churchman's anti-sexual piety by saying "Yes!" to the body. Urged to "Live in a heavenly mansion, / And not in some foul sty," she reminds his Lordship that "Love has pitched his mansion in / The place of excrement; / For nothing can be sole or whole / That has not been rent." That was around 1930. Less than a decade later Austin Clarke addressed the ecclesiastical powers and their secular agents on the Censorship Board in a little poem punningly entitled "Penal Law": "Burn Ovid with the rest," the poet wrote, "Lovers will find / A hedge-school for themselves and learn by heart / All that the clergy banish from the mind, / When hands are joined and head bows in the dark." Thirty years or so after this, Paul Durcan was wondering "what deValera would have thought / Inside in his ivory tower / If he knew we were in his green, green grass / Making love outside Áras an Uachtaráin." The poet knows the answer: "I see him now in the heat-haze of the day / Blindly stalking us down; / And, levelling an ancient rifle, he says, 'Stop / Making love outside Áras an Uachtaráin.'" More recently still, Nuala Ní Dhómhnaill—connecting herself to the Russian poet Marina Tsvetaeva and speaking in the accents of a feistily reincarnated Gaelic Eve—opposes a number of the entrenched orthodoxies of Ireland: "We are damned, my sisters," she announces, "we who accepted the priests' challenge / our kindred's challenge, / who ate from destiny's dish / who have knowledge of good and evil / who are no longer concerned. / . . . We preferred to be shoeless on the tide / dancing singly on the wet sand / . . . than to be / indoors making strong tea for the men."

Common to all these examples is how sexual and erotic energy resists the powers of church and state and, indeed—in the last example—private and family life. Common to them, too, is the sense that poetry, by giving voice to such sentiments, might provide its citizen readers with an alternative understanding of the world, a way of being in the world that answers more satisfactorily to human need than the dogmatic restrictions of official power.

I

In Ireland things were not always thus. Consider, for example, how the first of the "tales before the *Táin*" begins: "Nes the daughter of Eochaidh Salbuid of the yellow heel was sitting outside Emain with her royal women about her. The druid Cathbad . . . passed by, and the girl said to him:

> 'What is the present hour lucky for?'
> 'For begetting a king on a queen,' he said.
> The queen asked him if that were really true, and the druid swore by god that it was: a son conceived at that hour would be heard of in Ireland forever. The girl saw no other male near, and she took him inside with her.
> She grew heavy with child. It was in her womb for three years and three months. And at the feast of Othar she was delivered.

In this story of the conception and birth of King Conchobar, religious and political forces (in the person of the druid) are easily aligned with the forces of sex (helped by the druid's wit and the woman's opportunistic impulse). The sexual is acknowledged as a normal element of the world, in tune with the community's larger value systems. As far as the saga literature is concerned, such accommodation is borne out in Cúchullain's prodigious sexuality—both in general and in the particulars of his marriage to Emer and his affairs with Fand and Aoife—and in the frank and outspoken sexuality of Queen Medbh. In this pre-Christian world, the great issues can be grounded in erotic feelings and outcomes. Although there might be gender struggles, the depiction of such struggles suggest the important role sexuality itself played in this world. And for all its chauvinist extravagance, Cúchullain's sexual drive—or overdrive—is an unavoidable aspect of his heroic stature, his career "full of triumph and women's love." Even where there is conflict between the erotic and a public value such as loyalty to the Prince—as there is in the stories of Deirdre and Naoise, or Diarmuid and Grainne—sexuality itself has its unquestionable, undeniable place in this world.

The literary sign of this acceptance is the direct, powerful, unabashedly physical manner in which the erotic and the sexual find poetic expression. Cúchullain's wooing of Emer, for example, commences in a remarkable duet of sexual metaphors, while Deirdre's desire for Naoise is wonderfully direct, as is her lament for him dead: "I loved the modest, mighty warrior, / loved his fitting, firm desire, / loved him at daybreak as he dressed / by the margin of the forest. // Those blue eyes that melted women . . . " In substance and style, the ancient literature endorses the sexual and erotic assumptions of the community to which it belongs.

Naturally, the spiritual colonisation of the island by Christianity made a difference in how erotic and sexual aspects of life were seen. The primary difference lay in the separation of a celibate from a sexually active world, a separation responsible for those exquisite monastic poems of the early Middle Ages, as well as for that remarkable lyric testament to the potential conflict between devotion to Christ and devotion to Eros, the poem Liadan makes on the loss of her lover Cuirithir. In spite of such a separation, however, the literature of the

Gaelic secular tradition right up to the 18th Century still gives a strong sense that the erotic has its accepted place within the social and cultural framework. One could make a choice of a worldly or an "otherworldly" life, but there was no necessary antagonism between the erotic in itself and the culture at large. So the *Dánta Grá* of the later Middle Ages—European love poetry with an Irish accent—were not only written by men confident of their social place, but by those who registered no contradiction between social reality and the erotic forces expressed in the poems. Such assumptions seem part of the Irish tradition right up to that poem composed by a woman in 1773, the *Caoine Airt Uí Laoire*, parts of which sound as if they are in a direct line from Deirdre's lament for Naoise. Eileen Dubh's impassioned utterance and physical immediacy shows not only how implicit in the Gaelic tradition such erotic lyricism could be, but also (in this tradition) how natural a continuity could exist between the erotic and the domestic: "How well your hat suited you . . . Oh my soul's darling . . . My steadfast love / when you rode into town / sturdy and strong / the shopkeepers' wives / bowed and scraped / knowing only too well / how good you were in bed / what a fine cavalier / and sire for children." (Trans. Eilis Dillon).

While Eileen Dubh's poem represents continuity with the old tradition, the last major work *in* that tradition, *The Midnight Court* (1780), is about the end of the easy presence of the erotic and sexual both in the culture and in the literature. Implicitly as well as explicitly, Merryman's poem laments the squeezing of the erotic out of Irish life. Although its narrator shows a histrionic fear of sex, the poem's ironic purpose is to praise the power of sexuality (especially female sexuality) and to assert the sexual as a redemptive energy, a redemption that can take place only by the submission of the celibate clergy to the laws of Eros. The poem presents the sexual as a means of healing the country's ills, a private means underlying any public political solution to these same ills. Plagued externally by political domination, and internally by clerical celibacy and the cultural habit of late marriages—both of these connected with condemnation of the erotic impulses themselves—late 18th Century Ireland, or so the poem proposes—could be liberated by a healthy dose of sexual activity. The erotic, implies Merriman, could be a means of emancipation. Through his poem, it's as if the Gaelic tradition itself is speaking its piece of final wisdom.

In the 19th Century, as Irish literature makes the vexed, uneasy transition from the Irish to the English language, the erotic figures in curious ways. Sanitised in the *Irish Melodies* of Thomas Moore and allegorised in the political verse of Mangan and the poets of the Young Ireland movement, it becomes, strangely enough, a force for the establishment of national consciousness. For Moore's songs to traditional airs are full of a discreetly sexual "Irish" emotionalism, while his very emblem of romance—Robert Emmet and Sarah Curran—inspires a kind of nationalist pathos which allows the erotic (fitted out for the drawing rooms of respectability) to function as a badge of national feeling. Likewise, a poem like Mangan's "Dark Rosaleen" (in a mode derived directly from the Aisling poets of the Gaelic tradition) converts the erotic to nationalist allegorical meanings, religiously tinted and more explicitly linked to the possibility of violent revolution than they ever would be in Moore.

At the beginning of modern Irish literature in English, then, the erotic—transformed in certain ways, but still (because of the phenomenon of translation) in fairly close touch with the Gaelic tradition—becomes a means of establishing a community of both private and public national feeling. Poetic treatment of the sexual and erotic, that is, could be seen as an endorsement of Irish nationalism and therefore as subversive of the colonial status quo. Thus displaced, the erotic is allowed a place and function in Irish consciousness that doesn't challenge orthodox morality. (A corollary to this fact must be the way in which such treatments screen the reader from any *actual female* presence. So the nationalist uses of the erotic and the sexual generates, to say the least, problems—problems which have only begun to be truly addressed by recent, mainly feminist criticism and truly resolved by the contemporary artistic practices of women. This particular aspect of the problem, however, does not concern me *per se* at this point.)

There was a bit of a spin put on all this in the late 19th-century, however, when another significant bridge between Irish literature in Irish and Irish literature in English was built out of *The Love Songs of Connacht* as translated by Douglas Hyde. For while the *Songs* (composed between the 17th and 19th century by both men and women) show the persistent life of the erotic in the native tradition, and while as translations they are a deliberate act of cultural nationalism, they also on occasion reveal how the erotic, as private experience, could put an individual at odds with his or her community, as it does, for example, in Tomás Costello's "Una Bhán":

> And sure I would rather be sitting beside thee than the glory of heaven . . .
> O fair Una it is you have set astray my senses;
> O Una it is you who went close in, between me and God.
> Was it not better for me to be without eyes than ever to have seen you.
>
> I would rather than two sheep if I had one Una Bhán . . .
> I had rather be beside her on a couch, ever kissing her,
> Than be sitting in Heaven in the chair of the Trinity.

By the late 19th Century, then, the erotic in its literary expression can be either a force of national and/or individual consciousness. The possibility of conflict between these two versions of the erotic creates, as I have said and as you might imagine, a problem. For as "national" and "Catholic" became increasingly identified, the potential conflict between national and individual consciousness found an emblematic focus in the sphere of the sexual and erotic. And it is in the dynamics of this problem (I incidentally believe, though I won't pursue) that some of the drama of the Irish Literary Revival works itself out, (with Synge, of course, as a major protagonist). Which, naturally, brings me to Yeats.

II

Yeats begins and ends as a love poet, a poet-servant of the erotic powers. As early as *The Wanderings of Oisín* the presence of the erotic in his work has some sub-textual implication. For while Oisín's Celtic identity encourages a positive nationalist response, the erotic nature of the narrative encourages quite another, the hero's romantic love for Niamh set against that sterner love represented by St. Patrick. Since Niamh versus Patrick is a version of Eros versus Christ, Oisín himself represents an unsettling amalgam of sexual and nationalist meanings. A similar amalgam, at a more personal level, may be found in the poems of *The Wind Among the Reeds* (1899), where the erotic has a new role, becoming a primary building block in the composition of individual identity, of the poet's own speaking consciousness. Among the last desire-filled gasps of the Petrarchan tradition, this collection is also the first sustained breath of an Irish poet asserting independent coherent consciousness in a language, imagery, and landscape recognisably Irish. That early published versions of the poems were "attributed" to Irish poets of the Gaelic tradition (with elaborate explanatory notes) implies that this speaker's single consciousness incorporates the older tradition, establishing, as it were, erotic continuity between the two languages, with Aengus, the Celtic god of love serving as a kind of patron spirit to the whole collection. Rooting his monodrama of desire in Irishness and the erotic, Yeats forges an identity in which these two elements are in harmony. Much of the rest of his poetry of love and sexuality, however, is generated by a sense of the conflict between the sexual and a certain version of Irishness.

Such a conflict appears in the great body of love poetry Yeats wrote directly and obliquely to and about Maud Gonne after *Reeds* and up to the end of his life. While in *Cathleen Ni Houlihan* he rendered Maud as that emblematic Ireland herself for whose lethal love men sacrifice themselves, thereby joining erotic and political tropes in a single figure (and putting himself in the line of 19th century *aisling* poets), in much of the rest of the love poetry Yeats is effectively trying to recapture his beloved from the nationalist embrace, to have Eros, or Aengus, subvert the power of Cathleen. In many of these poems, private erotic obsession becomes an implicit critique of nationalist obsession, not to eliminate it but to make it more complex, more responsive to ordinary human needs and demands, not to become "a stone in the midst of all."

For, partly thanks to Synge, Yeats knew that genuine freedom had to be anchored in private (rather than public and overtly political) consciousness and that this—as Synge kept illustrating in his plays—was done by means that were fundamentally sexual and erotic. Such is the basic burden of Yeats's 1911 poem "On Those that Hated the Playboy of the Western World, 1907":

> Once, when midnight smote the air,
> Eunuchs ran through Hell and met
> On every crowded street to stare
> Upon great Juan riding by:

Even like these to rail and sweat
Staring upon his sinewy thigh.

While the sexual is an intrinsic part of almost all Yeats wrote, and while
such explicit concentration has to be somewhat scandalous in a country as
Catholic as Ireland, no matter how it is being otherwise governed, the great subversive outbursts—of poems that are deliberately using a contemplation on the
sexual and the erotic to challenge some orthodox public assumptions—occur
after the establishment of the Free State, when the Protestant/pagan poet observed the way the new state curtailed liberty and constricted consciousness in
its official attitudes to sex and matters erotic. Triggered by his hostility to such
attitudes, the Crazy Jane poems (in *Words for Music Perhaps* in 1929) become a
profound, broad-spoken meditation on sexuality itself, in opposition to the national powers that be. Implicitly setting up the sexual as a counter-truth to some
of the inhibitions on individual conscience and consciousness practiced by the
broader culture, he also, in 1934, composed his ironically entitled *Supernatural
Songs*, rewriting in them the battle of Oisín and Patrick. In these poems, Ribh
(an Irish monk with Indian influences) insists on the sexuality of Godhead and
all creation against the "abstract Greek absurdity" of Patrick's Christianity.
Through Ribh, Yeats fills the universe, nature, and humanity with sex, sex, and
more sex, in flagrant opposition to those orthodox attitudes which would erase
it. Freedom of consciousness is confirmed, insists Yeats, by affirming the centrality of the erotic in being. Ribh and Crazy Jane are different versions of a
voice that blesses wholeness of body and soul in a visionary eroticism of the
imagination.

From Oisín to Ribh, then, in ever widening gyres, Yeats progressively establishes the church of Eros to oppose the various orthodoxies of what becomes
the (ironically named) Irish Free State. His scandalous creed is that everything
that exists "Stands in God's unchanging eye / In all the vigour of its blood; / In
that faith I live or die." And scandalous, too, is the sexual realism of these late
sequences: not-so-crazy Jane and Ribh bring scatology and mysticism into a
single visionary embrace, to compose a world that is erotic to the core. A world
that—in the poem Yeats would have placed at the end of his *Last Poems*—is to
be seen through the lens of the sexual. For at the close of the poem called
"Politics"—after he has considered the political nature of the world—he is taken
by the sight of a young girl (bringing to simple sight all the visionary energies
of the other poems) and cries out, "But O that I was young again / And held her
in my arms."

III

From Yeats to the present, the sexual and the erotic have been active, distinct,
and important elements in Irish poetry. What I want to suggest is that they have
also been among poetry's most consistent means of "political" action, opposing
cultural and political forces that limited individual freedom or in some other

way diminished the fully human. In what remains of this essay I'll offer a summary account of this, in which my purpose is to be suggestive rather than exhaustive or comprehensive. In what I have to say I'm going to take for granted that in issues such as the Constitution (with its assumptions about women and the place of the Catholic Church) and Censorship the state laid its public hands on the private parts of its citizenry, and that one result of this was to make the whole issue of sexuality a sort of national neurosis that retarded the evolution of a mature "national" consciousness. While volumes of social, cultural, and political history deal with this, my concern is with how poetry responds to this historical circumstance, this being, in turn, part of a larger literary response, the prose version of which was inaugurated by Joyce and carried on by, among others, Kate O'Brien, Edna O'Brien, and John McGahern.

Although Austin Clarke's early poems are in the shadow of Yeats's *Reeds*, it is the hard facts of Catholic morality and sexual guilt that fuel his explorations in the erotic zone. Early sexual trauma—which led to a nervous breakdown culminating in a period in St. Patrick's Hospital—triggered Clarke's "reading" of medieval Ireland in an effort to find out how the repressive sexual *mores* of modern Ireland might have evolved. What he discovers is that the contest between Christ and Eros is an early feature of Irish Christianity. Sex obsesses the imagined priests of *Pilgrimage* (1929):

> On pale knees in the dawn,
> Parting the straw that wrapped me,
> She sank until I saw
> The bright roots of her scalp.
> She pulled me down to sleep,
> But I fled as the Baptist
> To thistle and to reed.

Giving a voice to figures such as Queen Gormlai or "The Young Woman of Beare," Clarke links himself with the Gaelic tradition. By doing so, he demonstrates the vibrant and enduring humanity of sexual love, gives psychological and physical substance to the erotic (significantly in the voice of the woman), thereby broadening and deepening individual consciousness in opposition to the moralistic rigidity of the Irish state/church. His Young Woman of Beare seems to be the erotic principle itself, antagonist of "the clergy," and she speaks as a victor in the battle between Eros and Christ: "I am the bright temptation / In talk, in wine, in sleep. / Although the clergy pray, / I triumph in a dream." The sheer erotic energy of these women's voices is itself subversive of the sexual censorship entailed by social and religious orthodoxy in the Ireland of the time. In the 1938 volume, *Night and Morning*, Clarke shows how strangling the erotic leads to a throttling of consciousness, although "the stern law of the clergy" cannot totally subdue such energies, since even if Ovid is burned, lovers will go on, willynilly, practising—in defiance of state condemnation—their art, learning "by heart / All that the clergy banish from the mind."

In 1955, when Clarke emerged from a seventeen-year poetic silence, it was as poetic antagonist to the dogmatic moralism of a controlling State. Much of his imaginative anger in this phase is directed at the state's laws on sexuality, and their unhappy consequences. This is most poignantly expressed in a poem called "The Envy of Poor Lovers":

> Pity poor lovers who may not do as they please
> With their kisses under a hedge, before a raindrop
> Unhouses it; and astir from wretched centuries,
> Bramble and briar remind them of the saints . . .
>
> Lying in the grass as if it were a sin
> To move, they hold each other's breath, tremble,
> Ready to share the ancient dread—kisses begin
> Again—of Ireland keeping company with them.
>
> Think children, of institutions mured above
> Your ignorance, where every look is veiled,
> State-paid to snatch away the folly of poor lovers
> For whom, it seems, the sacraments have failed.

As far as the poet is concerned, cruel laws—essentially directed against erotic energy itself—pollute the marriage-bed as well, and are a flaw in institutional religion:

> But shall the sweet promise of the sacrament
> Gladden the heart, if mortals calculate
> Their pleasures by the calendar? Night-school
> Of love where all, who learn to cheat, grow pale
> With guilty hope at every change of moon!
>   ("Marriage")

In Clarke's poems, the erotic and sexual become a politics of resistance, audible in the taut cadences themselves, the uncompromising off-rhymes, the disciplined voice. What he criticises is the absence of sexual education and its replacement by condemnation, so everyone suffers except the pietistic powers of church and state. His later poetry—after the purgative work of satire is over—revels in richly descriptive celebrations of the androgynously bodied erotic itself, presenting the experience of sexual love as a paradise of physical mutuality. In poems like "Iphis," "The Wooing of Becfola," "The Healing of Mis," or "Tiresias," sexuality itself is a joyous and gorgeous (if idealised) healing power. Presenting it thus, Clarke makes his final subversive gesture against those state- and church-sponsored prohibitions which would repress it.

As in Clarke's work, there is a sexual wound with national implications at the heart of Patrick Kavanagh's poetry. Although each poet responds to the wound in his own way, their work has in common an overt or sub-textual opposition to the sexual conditions they found in the Ireland of their time. Kavanagh's documentary poem, *The Great Hunger* (which can be read as a tragic postscript to *The Midnight Court*), records the death of Eros in rural Ireland. Between the pincers of peasant life and priestly condemnation, erotic possibility is squeezed from Maguire's life: his sex becomes "an impotent worm on his thigh," religion is "a rope . . . strangling true love," and Ireland, at least rural Ireland, is a land of sexual famine. *The Great Hunger* is a poem of protest and indictment, its purpose the exposure of a communal malady for which the poet can find no cure: deprived of Eros, clay is the word, clay is the flesh, and "the apocalypse of clay / is screamed in every corner of the land."

Leaving the famished land of Maguire behind him, Kavanagh solves the peasant's dilemma for himself both by becoming a poet and by displacing the actual erotic into a metaphorical relationship with the natural world, a relationship that sets him "beyond the reach of desire" and in "the daily and nightly earth." Situated thus, he can develop a relationship that is both sexual in its implications and metaphors, yet in actual fact "safe." "Where can I look," he asks, "and not become a lover / Terrified at each recurring spasm." Sexualised as the language is, and as the relationship with the natural world may be felt to be, it remains a sign of the failure of the sexual and erotic in the interpersonal human world. In later poems (such as "Is" or "The Hospital") he farther displaces this dangerous entry into a quasi-mystical relationship with ordinary being itself, with everything in the phenomenal world: "A year ago I fell in love with the functional ward / Of a chest hospital. . . . For we must record love's mystery without claptrap, / Snatch out of time the passionate transitory."

By finding a spiritually satisfying way to set free his erotic impulses in the ordinary world, Kavanagh avoids the moral risks and scruples built into sexuality in the Irish context. Avoiding moral conflict, he becomes a kind of mystical voyeur: "To look on is enough" he says, "In the business of love." Finding blessedness in the ordinary, marrying the erotic to the holy ("without claptrap") Kavanagh manages to turn a casualty of the wars of Eros into a triumph of poetic personality. His loss of the erotic in practical human terms becomes the source of his speaking consciousness, thus giving his achievement exemplary status, power, and implication. His drama of racial conscience is the drama of erotic loss, and out of this the recovery of the self. Having dramatised the crucifixion of the erotic instinct in Maguire, he dramatises in himself a paradise regained of redirected erotic energy in the redeemed, self-created personality. His final poetic posture is post-erotic repose: "So be reposed and praise, praise, praise / The way it happened and the way it is." As counter-truth to the hard Puritan truths of the state, his redemptive, non-personal version of the erotic is an instrument of liberation.

In the work of two other poets of this first poetic generation after Yeats, the erotic takes on a more immediately personal coloration. As expressions of liberated consciousness, however, the very different poems of sexual love written by Louis MacNeice and Denis Devlin extend poetry's resistance to conventional attitudes. An existentialist of the erotic—articulate, sceptical, secular—Mac-

Neice's insistence on the benevolent ordinariness of the sexual subverts moralistic attempts to stigmatise it, as well as romantic attempts to sentimentalise it. In his love poems he will—directly and in a matter-of-fact way—address a particular woman, often cutting across the grain of the conventionally romantic. At other times, the beloved becomes an image of what's possible in the world, an image of mobility, suppleness, accommodation.

For MacNeice, love is at war with time, provides a stay against its confusions, maybe a momentary stillness in flux. In a way different from the rest of his Irish contemporaries, too, MacNeice manages to write directly of a sexual affair, and to write of love that can mix the domestic with the erotic. He can be at once ordinary and impassioned, saying, "I shall remember you in bed with bright / Eyes or in a cafe stirring coffee / Abstractedly and on your plate the white / Smoking stub your lips had touched with crimson." At once homage and evaluative critique, his love poem is always emblematic, being—like the rest of his work—a deliberate attempt to incorporate the whole man into the poem, to make the poet an ordinary man speaking directly to another person: "Because you intoxicate like all the drinks / we have drunk together from Achill Island to Athens . . . " In its plainspoken refusal to allow the sexual to become moralised or sentimentalised out of existence, MacNeice's work (in the *Irish* domain of Eros at least) is, whether deliberately or not, a mode of resistance.

While very different in texture and feeling, the intellectually sensuous, symbolist love poems of Denis Devlin are also subversive in their effects, being the lucid affirmation of an independent, uninhibited consciousness. Devlin shows a sense of civilised sexuality, not tortured by moral difficulty. His "Venus on the Half-Shell," for example, is both erotic and impersonal—a commentary on the force itself of love, while his "Edinburgh Tale" is a covert narrative, a love poem, a direct address remarkable for its unadorned intimacy; "your heart saying the same word over and over again to itself like a happy child." His is the love poetry of a metaphysician, its accent that of intelligence itself—guiding the articulation of love, of being in love, of the attitude to the self and the beloved: "And her I would meet / as though I were unconscious / In vacant bright-columned streets / And beings in love's tunic scattered to the four winds / For no reason at all / For no reason that I can tell." His "The Colours of Love" addressed to his wife is a kind of *summa*—an exploration of the relation between love and death in the light of marriage:

> I raise my arms to that mistress planet,
> Venus, whose hunting priests explain
> My heart and the rush of legend on it,
> Making me man again!

Devlin's and MacNeice's love poetry—taking for granted the erotic as a normal, unquestionable part of human behaviour and experience, and accepting that the love poem is the purest voice of the private self—demonstrate that for them Eros is the liberator from that inner colonisation of the spirit which can keep people in a kind of moral captivity. In this zone, then, their work counterpoints that of Clarke and Kavanagh, while at the same time implicitly proving a similar point: that in the Irish realm of sex and the erotic, poetry is an agent of resistance to conventional assumptions, assumptions which—as seen in the cases of Clarke and Kavanagh—can be morally limiting and personally debilitating.

IV

Because of what the poets I've mentioned so far achieved, freedom of *personal* expression in the erotic and sexual sphere can be taken for granted by the next generation of poets. For Thomas Kinsella, Richard Murphy, and especially for John Montague, however, the intimately personalised erotic and sexual continue to serve as an implicitly subversive means of expanding consciousness.

In Kinsella, the erotic and the sexual are quickly taken up into a larger meditation on consciousness and history. Personalised in the relationship with his wife, the sexual stands as an emblematic origin for the struggle towards articulate consciousness, a total knowing of the world. The sexual from the start is implicated with suffering and death: until "The other props are gone. / Sighing in one another's / Iron arms, propped above nothing, / We praise Love the limiter." In "Phoenix Park," sexual love becomes a source of the ghostly "structure" he seeks, testing him in an intense and intimate way about the connections between mind and body. Erotic love—taken for granted and moved beyond—sets him on the road of contemplation, is limiter and tutor of his spirit:

> Midsummer, and I had tasted your knowledge,
> My flesh blazing in yours; Autumn, I had learned
> Giving without tearing is not possible.

His mind shoots beyond the erotic into the metaphysics of flesh and blood, the morality of endurance. "Propped above nothing" as it is, love is Kinsella's educator on the journey to pitiless self-knowledge, being, like his own poetry, a "delicate, scrupulous art," which in the fullness of consciousness establishes a truth that resists the constricting, authoritarian, anti-individual "truths" of the state and the surrounding culture, truths that settle for so much less than the dangerous total knowledge of love.

Richard Murphy's use of the erotic is personal and public. Intimations of the special nature of his own sexuality appear in his vivid account of mating seals: "She opens her fierce mouth like a scarlet flower / Full of white seeds; she holds it open long / At the sunburst in the music of their loving." This keen attachment to the particularity of the female (the sexual, almost genital palpability of "her fierce mouth") is matched by the dazzling phallic account of the male: "When the great bull withdraws his rod, it glows / Like a carnelian candle set in jade." Such alertness to the two makes an emblem of doubled sexuality that could well act as prologue to later poems in which Murphy's own sexuality— either directly or indirectly—is the subject. In his plainspoken clarity about the sexual, Murphy strikes his own subversive note, his freedom of scandalous expression implicitly subverting the taboos implicit in authority's view of sexual matters. The private, he implies, makes its own laws. In "A Nest in a Wall" he celebrates the simple act of being in bed with another. In this he is deliberately sensuous, as untroubled as Auden by anything except the transitoriness of the flesh itself and the love it begets:

> I float a moment on a gust sighing forever
> Gently over your face where two swans swim.
> Let me kiss your eyes in the slateblue calm
> Before their Connemara clouds return . . .
>
> Your country and mine, love, can it still exist?
> The unsignposted hawthorn lane of your body
> Leads to my lichenous walls and gutted house.
> Your kind of beauty earth has almost lost.
> Although we have no home in the time that's come,
> Coming together we live in our own time.
> Make your nest of moss like a wren in my skull.

Murphy's erotic world, containing the taboo (in the Irish context) elements of homosexuality and perversity, portrays in brief flickers the underbelly of erotic life. What Murphy may be doing here, and throughout *The Price of Stone*, is putting dangerous aspects of the erotic into a social perspective. In these indirect utterances (e.g., "Convenience")—spreading the accents of Eros among these buildings, giving the mute stones a voice, voices—Murphy discovers his own kind of candour, the candour to admit "how selfishly you serve your own heart's bent," where the word "bent" is itself a sexual pun, indicative of Murphy's deft and epigrammatic way of confessing and concealing at once.

In their tolerant accents of civilised understanding, Murphy's poems implicitly celebrate the free play of sexual difference. In *The Price of Stone,* as I say, he broadens this spectrum of tolerance, showing up the scandalous underbelly of the sexual—and insisting on the multiple nature of sexuality itself. His speaking buildings become instruments of social awakening, and the erotic and sexual—often in scandalous forms—become a tutorial in difference, asking for nothing except that civilised tolerance which his own civility of address encourages. His poetry offers a world in which the enclosures and exclusions patented by moral orthodoxy need no longer apply.

The most developed exponent of the erotic and sexual in poetry since Yeats is John Montague, who moves continuously between public and private truths, and for whom the expression of the private truths of his sexual experience can often be seen as a deliberately educational attempt to expand the limits of Irish consciousness and to pierce what he calls the "miasma" and "fog" hanging over Irish life in the '50s, by "transgressing the Irish inhibition on the matter of sex." Psychologist, mythographer, and sociologist of the sexual, Montague examines the possibility of a full life in sexual terms. When, in the epigraph to *The Great*

Cloak, he says that he writes love poems "as my province burns" he asserts the right of Eros to its own place in the world.

From the start, it is love in an Irish context that compels him. In the early "Irish Street Scene, With Lovers," "Virgo Hibernica," and "Country Matters" he looks at the various faces (romantic, mythical, squalidly realistic) love can wear in an Irish context. Then, in "the Siege of Mullingar, 1963" he marks a pivotal moment, seeing in the young people at the traditional music festival some basic shift in consciousness, Eros returning to Ireland in the "eager faces" of the young girls who "roamed the street . . . shoving for men," as well as in the young lovers who "Lay on both sides of the canal / Listening on Sony transistors / To the agony of Pope John." Written to the music of death and resurrection, the poem is one of erotic beginnings, since "Puritan Ireland's dead and gone, / A myth of O'Connor and Ó Faoláin." The poem's title, too, gives it a resonantly historical flavour (with sexuality rather than military force the agent of liberation), while the occasion itself, the Fleadh Ceóil, connects it with the Gaelic world—whose attitude to sex, Montague says, he is "just bringing back."

In many later poems the poet celebrates the pleasures of sex itself and the pleasures of a woman's body, while in a poem like "Life Class" his slow unveiling of the female body is a lecture in erotic appreciation. Opening up the realm of the sexual he becomes its secular celebrant, celebrating not just its mysteries, but its ordinariness, educating his audience in the normal goodness of sexual life and activity. His tone is one of demonstration—Look, he says, this is not a source of shame, still less of sin: it is a site of pleasure, mystery, and ordinary goodness in the world. For him, the sexual is the path to a more tolerant and truly human experience of the real. Ultimately his lesson is that sexual love is an "answer to death." Sex therefore emulates religion as a way of giving value and meaning to the world. It is "a form of truth," an expansion of consciousness, and Montague's poetry in praise of it signals an emancipated imagination, a psyche dealing with the delights and difficulties of sexual life on its own terms, unpropped and unpuzzled by institutional commandments or assumptions.

By enacting his own sexual life in the public light of poetry, Montague participates in the opening of Irish consciousness to a world larger and more complex than that determined by institutional religion or the church/state culture born from it. Arguing always for what he calls the "body's intelligence," he works to exorcise that hatred of the eroticised human body that brought on the great hunger of Kavanagh's Patrick Maguire. In the next poetic generation the poets (or at least the male poets) can more or less take the sexual and erotic for granted for themselves, while in different ways all the poets (both male and female) can investigate the various meanings the erotic might have in their particular "political" contexts—whether the politics in question are those of gender, or of the Republic, or of the North of Ireland.

V

For Seamus Heaney, the sexual becomes an *exemplum* of relationship, of trust in difference, of what human consciousness can be. In the early "Lovers on Aran," for example, he turns the landscape into a sexual metaphor, seeing the waves "sifting from the Americas // To possess Aran" and seeing Aran "rush / To throw wide arms of rock around a tide / That yielded with an ebb, a soft crash." This give-and-take means that each element "drew new meaning from the waves' collision. / Sea broke on land to full identity." As part of "relationship," love is seen as a chosen limit: the erotic flourishes within the limits of relationship, and within the everyday: "So Venus comes," he says in another poem, "matter-of-fact." The erotic is a normal part of the quotidian, as well as deep in the heart of the mystery of everyday things: a ditch being opened, a frozen yard-pump thawed by fire, the landscape itself—all can be intensely sexualised. Marriage is naturally continuous with such erotic serenades, part of the feminised music of what happens. There is much matter feminine in the second part of *Wintering Out*, the poet investigating his own love, his own erotic self, inside the larger context of women's world. Poems like "A Winter's Tale," "Maigh-dean Mara," "Bye-Child," and others sound the female music of love-making, birth, death, wombs. In dealing with such matter, Heaney seems to seek wholeness, an authentic human and humane complexity, the foundation of genuine relationship.

While the erotic educates Heaney about wholeness and complexity in the realm of personal relationships, and a sort of lyric fullness in the natural world, it also tutors him about complexity, failure and *possible* wholeness in the realm of politics. The ritual dead in *North*, for example, represent among other things the dark side of the erotic state, while the poet's ambivalence of what is presented as a (problematic) sexual response in a poem like "Punishment" embodies the intense difficulty of the political situation, the difficulty of mixed feelings, of trying to get the relationship straight. The exhumed woman suffers the wind which "blows her nipples / to amber beads," and he can say, "I almost love you," while confessing his complicitous silence before the girl of his own time, punished for "tribal" disloyalty. In such poems, the sexual and the political are fused in curious, often unsettling ways, while the poet gives voice to his condition of being caught between desire and inaction, between feeling and voyeuristic detachment. In these poems, I believe, Heaney has discovered one of his measures—that of seeing into the sexual shape of something previously seen in its polite and political surfaces. And since political failure is the failure of relationship, so its cure could be located in some analogue for the erotic relationship that achieves harmony in the complex recognition of difference and the mutual rights deriving from difference.[1]

Running parallel to Heaney's preoccupation with the political (and perhaps contrapuntal to it) are poems which celebrate the erotic side of his relationship with his wife. Love comes through a powerful evocation of bodies in "Otter," and, in "The Skunk," his celebrations of the body and of married sensuality achieve a comic note at the end: "stirred / By the sootfall of your things at bed-time, / Your head-down, tail-up hunt in a bottom drawer / For the black plunge-line nightdress." This love accommodates jealousy and indifference, finds the ordinary worthy of rhapsodic response, the poet's frank delight in the ordinary life of love creating a light that's affectionate, comic and erotic all at once. What these poems establish is a true sense of relationship, the sense of something like *talk* between equals, which even if not actually recorded in the poem stands as its enabling source. So the woman can be seen with a decisive realism as "bitter and dependable," and the poet can "see the vaccination mark / stretched on your upper arm." This achieves a kind of summation in "Glanmore Revisited" where he records "Year after year our game of Scrabble: love / Taken for granted like any other word."

One of Heaney's recurrent concerns is how difficulty can be charted through to survival. The sign of his unsentimental optimism lies in the fact that the erotic itself, in a context of companionable love, is what survives:

> Last autumn we were smouldering and parched
> As those spikes that keep vigil overhead
> Like Grendel's steely talon nailed
> To the mead-hall roof. And then we broke through
> Or we came through. It was its own reward.
>
> We are voluptuaries of the morning after.
> As gulls cry out above the deep channels
> And you stand on and on, twiddling your hair
> Think of me as your MacWhirr of the boudoir,
> Head on, one track, ignorant of manoeuvre.
>
> ("Coming Through")

Heaney's love poem, then, serves to anchor the self in the real world, in the ac-tions of conversation, in relationship, in equality. He is not a recorder of the high disastrous passions, but of the quieter reaches of understanding and bal-ance. His is a tempered Eros, but Eros still. And while it's true that sexual love takes its place inside a constellation of other imaginative commitments, it may have been the experience of such love that first—through difficulty and discov-ery—brought him also to his crucial insight about the marriage between the marvelous and the ordinary, on which, in recent volumes, he has put his own inimitable spin, love itself being something "taken for granted like any other word / That was chanced on."

The erotic for Heaney is an emblem of rootedness in the actual, as well as representing a passage or transit to deeper, mysterious reaches of the self. And while it educates him to what is possible in the political zone, it also illustrates the desperate and enduring complexity of the political quarrel. An awareness of sexual and erotic reality is what teaches him about fullness as well as limit, in self-realisation, and in realisation of the nature of the world in its political actuality and spiritual possibility. And by connecting the political with the sexual in an idiom of relationship as he does, he makes subversive use of the sexual to underscore the intimate human truth inside a political reality in the grip of intransigent tribal abstractions. In his imaginative response to and his poetic use of the sexual and the erotic, that is, Heaney fulfils his high sense of poetry's loaded, complicated responsibility to the world.

In his earlier work, Michael Longley is an exclusively private celebrant of the sexual, a civilised mannerist attempting to articulate the place of the erotic in private life. A sort of priest of love, he is a materialist with a spiritual tinge, surrounding the matter of love with hieroglyphs of the natural world, its animals and landscape. In a poem like the lovely "Swans Mating" he can establish a close-up of copulation itself, a little like the way Murphy does in "Seals at High Island," with a touch of Montague:

> This was a marriage and a baptism,
> A holding of breath, nearly a drowning,
> Wings spread wide for balance where he trod,
> Her feathers full of water and her neck
> Under the water like a bar of light.

In the context of Northern Ireland, this unabashed privacy will eventually become a radical gesture, a gesture on behalf of life, so even his delicate dismantling of the female body—becoming, as he often does, a rapt fetishist of its parts—can take on oppositional power, the erotic antithesis of endemic physical violence. A sort of grammarian of the female body, he examines and gently names its parts: "Your nipples under my fingertips / Like white flowers on a white ground," for example, or "Poems in the palm of the hand, life-lines, / Fingers tapping the ridge of the shinbone, / The bridge of the nose, fingerprints, breath." Persistently pitting Eros against Thanatos, he eroticises private life to the core, knowing it is all to hold on to in the midst of violence. And even when love poems proper are few, Longley can still register love as his lamp and centre, his poems continuing to stress the presence of sexuality in the world and in culture, in a language charged with implicit sexuality of its own, transforming the world ("the orchids have borrowed her cunty petals").

The quietly intense privacy of Longley's work is erected against public violence, the insistent, often enigmatic particularity of his poems a gesture against the lethal generalities of the North. Such poems are on the side of peace, and so it is no surprise that in "Ceasefire"—his version of a moment in the *Iliad*—he describes enemies at the point of reconciliation as lovers: "When they had eaten together it pleased them both / To stare at each other's beauty as lovers might, / Achilles built like a God, Priam good-looking still." He has said (during a reading at New York's American Irish Historical Society) "As I get older it's a challenge to go on writing love poetry." This can be taken as a private and a public point. But he has gone on doing it, and his work bears out his own description: "But love poetry may be at the heart of what I do, the core of the enterprise. It is the hub of the wheel: everything else branches out from it." As poetry quietly insistent on love's right to a world of time and space, to enduring human attention, his work bears its own kind of undeniable witness, resisting the culture of violence by which he is surrounded.

In the work of James Simmons, the erotic also has private point and public implication. The private point is a kind of assertion of the self in the world. Singing of "natural forces: / Marriages, divorces," he tells his own (usually one-sided) story. In the public arena he wants to have a revolutionary effect—using the erotic to undo some of the constricting assumptions of Northern puritanism, "insisting," as Edna Longley says, "that making love is better than making war or your peace with God." In addition, his hymns to sexual life are an implicit attack on death-mongering, while his adaptations to a contemporary Northern context of *The Hag of Beare* and the *Lament for Art O'Leary* show his understanding of continuity in the Irish tradition, and of the erotic and sexual as indispensable to how poetry can bring private and public worlds together.

Simmons' sexual explicitness, his clear narrative element—given clean point by the formal scrupulosity and musical muscularity of his verse—is a powerful challenge to the puritanically minded. His *persona* is a sort of sexual Everyman, recording his state of heart, mind, and genitals as frankly as he can. In a sequence like "Marital Sonnets," he probes the wound of the unhappy marriage in manners that are formally tight and idiomatically assured, while his celebrations of sexual joy are direct and vivid, as a poem like "The Honeymoon" quickly shows:

> Our best man swore you would be black and blue,
> and, true enough, love's frightening. You do
> violent-seeming things; but no one's hurt,
> playing by the rules. We rise from dirt,
> stink, struggle, shining, have suffered nothing.
> No wonder they say that God would have us loving.

Celebratory and demotic, Simmons places the erotic firmly in the ordinary world and at the centre of the human tragicomedy—of which he is protagonist and chorus. The subversive end is clear, and was, as he himself has said, to "create the free hygienic mind, / rid of the guilt and infantile self-hate / that we were subject to." Eros is the liberator, and he is the not-so-secret agent of Eros. The erotic is a means to authentic individual freedom of body, consciousness, spirit, a freedom in which sexual delight can become a sufficient world.

Paul Durcan's engagement with the erotic also works in two ways. On the one hand he celebrates in an almost sacramental manner its redemptive power. But for Durcan, as for Simmons, the private erotic quickly takes on public implications. Beginning in a style that always reminds me of Chagall, he first celebrates the erotic content of his relationship with his wife, then moves quickly to making the erotic subversive through a deliberate attack on Irish prudishness, taking over in a comic mode the more tragic satiric vein of Clarke. Emblematic fictions and comic scenarios, his poems aim at the redemptive expansion of Irish consciousness by a deliberate, comic *re-eroticising* of the country. In "Fat Molly" for example, Molly is an Irish servant of Eros, inducting the poet into sexual life:

> I'd say Molly was about thirty when I went to her
> And she taught me the art of passionate kissing:
> From minuscule kisses to majuscule
> On lips, breasts, necks, shoulders, lips,
> And the enwrapping of tongue around tongue.
>
> ("Fat Molly," 38)

The fact that this is supposed to occur in the year 744, and "On the other side of the forest from the monk-fort at Kells" anchors the poem in the older tradition, making the kind of link with the Gaelic world which has previously, as we've seen, been one of poetry's ways to draw the erotic and sexual into modern Irish life. (His heroine's name makes a further, more modern connection, with Joyce.)

At the bottom of Durcan's ambition is a wish to eroticise Irish Catholicism out of its old and into a new existence. He does this by sexualising many of the icons of the culture, turning the High Cross of Moone into a maypole and Jesus himself into "a lovely man, / All that a woman could ever possibly dream of; / Gentle, wild, soft-spoken, courteous, sad; / Angular, awkward, candid, methodical; / Humorous, passionate, angry, kind; / Entirely sensitive to a woman's world." Also, in a poem like "My Beloved Compares Herself to a Pint of Stout," he undermines the dominant masculine ethos of the culture by translating the male icon of the pint of stout into a woman speaking her own erotic nature ("I look around to see her foaming out of the bedclothes . . . 'So sip me slowly, let me linger on your lips, / Ooze through your teeth, dawdle down your throat'"). And, as if he is baptising Ireland's original roots in the waters of Eros, the title poem to his last collection has him transmigrating into the body of a very erotic snail in Newgrange. The public implication of a redemptive erotic attitude could be no clearer": "At my life's end, I writhe / For the sun to fatten in the east / And make love to me; / To enter me / At 8.58 a.m. / And to stay inside me / For seventeen minutes, / My eyes out on stalks. / You feel like a spiral / Inside me; you feel / Like three spirals inside me."

Aside from this deliberate sensuousness—Durcan's celebratory eroticism—his Eros, like Clarke's, is an agent of subversion, deflating some of the tyrannical pieties of the Catholic state. "Making love outside Árus an Uachtaráin" is emblematic in this respect, a poem to place beside Clarke's "The Envy of Poor Lovers." It is a subversion of deValera's Ireland, a kind of companion piece to Montague's "Siege of Mullingar," with the anarchic, but positive energy of the lovers in direct antithesis to the puritan Ireland of deValera with his "ancient rifle" leveled at the lovers:

> But even had our names been Diarmaid and Gráinne
> We doubted deValera's approval
> For a poet's son and a judge's daughter

Making love outside Áras an Uachtaráin.

The fact that Durcan's poems also often examine in critical/comical ways the sociology of women's position in Ireland is connected with the ways he deals with the erotic, for it is often in the realm of sexuality itself that his fables of women and their lot are situated. In such fables Durcan attacks the dominant male chauvinist ethos of the culture: "the do-it-yourself men boors / Who despise men with feminine souls." By subverting religious and secular male chauvinism, Durcan intends, in part at least, to feminise the Irish world and Irish consciousness, and to celebrate the variety of sexual possibility.

VI

In the actual world, of course, this feminisation—thanks to the Women's Movement—has been in process over the past twenty-five years or so, altering Irish culture, transforming Irish public and private life. In fact, the Women's Movement effectively began the *unmaking* of that predominantly male Ireland that generated many of the difficulties to which the poems I've been talking about were responses.

At this juncture, however, it is also necessary to say that no matter how sexually enlightened the poems of some male poets are, their implications may still be limited by the poet's own complicated relations with actual women—especially with wives, with lovers. And that the poems themselves, in their treatment of women, can be at times one-sided and shortsighted. Poets like Durcan, Heaney, and Montague, indeed, make such limitations part of their subject matter, often in the form of confession and contrition. Nonetheless, the limitations remain, since no matter how imaginatively sympathetic these poets may be to the feminine, they stand outside it, can only see and feel it as the other.

No matter how much liberation of consciousness these poems by men might achieve, then, something like full freedom could only come when poems by women established the actual presence of the female in her own voice, making her own sexual and erotic realities known from the inside. Only then, when those who have so often been the direct victims of a sexual tyranny built into the culture (with its religious, political, and familial subordination of women), only when these women themselves claim a voice for their own reality, assert that reality with confidence (a confidence male poets have by virtue of their gender), only then can it be said that true freedom of consciousness exists in Irish life. As far as poetry is concerned, such freedom has moved closer, in part, because over the last twenty-five years—paralleling the growth and energy of active feminism—there has been an ever-increasing number of women who are poets writing their own truths, and changing the tradition as they do.

I want to conclude by looking at how the most prominent of these poets advance and swerve from what the male poets have been doing, and bring the story I'm telling to a close. For as women insert the evidence of their own bodies into the equation, reclaiming themselves as they do so, they create a fully politicised Eros and a fully eroticised "political" world, widening the Irish world for and by the real presence of the female. And in this way, the sexual in poetry continues to be an agent of subversion and change as regards the larger world. The four poets I want to talk about fall into two poetic generations. Eiléan Ní Chuilleanáin and Eavan Boland came to maturity through the '60s and they inhabit a different imaginative world from that of the younger Medbh McGuckian and Nuala Ní Dhómhnaill. The aim of the older two poets, I'd say, is reclamation; the aim of the younger two is affirmation.

An unspoken purpose of Eiléan Ní Chuilleanáin's poetry is to reclaim women's bodies, to make them visible in history again. To reclaim the body prior to its erotic possibility, making a female space and making (from the inside out) a feminised world. In composing a homeground for women, she invents her own erotics of austerity. Where women's reality has been rendered almost invisible by male accounts, simply being "the square of white linen / that held three drops / Of her heart's blood," her aim is to make visible "The real thing, the one free foot kicking / Under the white sheet of history." The consequence of such an aim is the intense feminisation of the world.

Viewed from such a perspective, Ní Chuilleanáin's "Lady's Tower" feminises Yeats's tower, deconstructing its phallic monumentality into a female building of curves and movement—all roots, all sliding changing bobbing dreamy delighted action. The way she makes space for (and from) the female body is a fundamentally political act, subverting a world in which women's place is mostly unacknowledged. Her poems are a sort of starting over—from the realisation that "Our history is a mountain of salt, / A leaking stain" to a revived, strangely oblique but pressingly authentic, sense of the body. Under the sign of Mary Magdalene, Ní Chuilleanáin creates "a voice glittering in the wilderness" to speak the gospel of women—often mixing religion and the sexual in new ways. It is in the voice of Magdalene that she delivers an epigraph to her own procedures, granting austerity itself an erotic tinge: "I watch the bones,'" she says, "and they begin to shine." Her poems free the female body into a freshness of being—found, for example, in her description of a woman shoeing a horse:

> I could see by her shoulders how her breath shifted
> In the burst of heat, and the wide gesture of her free arm
> As she lifted the weight and clung
>
> Around the hoof.

In such purposeful acts of reclamation we find the pulsing secret life of women in their own bodies; we find the wholly human that is female, and the female that is wholly human.

In Ní Chuilleanáin's work, the female body is often reclaimed for its own sake, independent of any erotic implications, as if the business of reclamation had to get behind the erotic in order to take effect. The female, in a sense, precedes the erotic. In the work of Eavan Boland, the act of reclamation is a deliberate de-eroticising of the female body, since its erotic version, so her argument would go, is an instrument of the woman's subjection to the male world, a male fiction which keeps the woman in captivity. A poem like "Suburban Woman" marks the point where Boland first sees how the woman's life can make her a "courtesan to the lethal / rapine of routine," where "The kitchen lights like a brothel," and the unmade bed is only a memory of "an underworld of limbs."

Boland's ambition is to write this woman into another story. A poem like "Tirade for a Mimic Muse" is a litany of unmakings:

> Eye-shadow, swivel brushes, blushers,
> Hot pinks, rouge pots, sticks,
> Ice for the pores, a mud mask—
> All the latest tricks.
> Not one of them disguise
> That there's a dead millenium in your eyes.

For the speaker of these poems, the erotic is undone by "the hubbub and shriek of daily grief" and the "trashy whim" of "love and again love and again love," while in "Anorexic," flesh itself "is heretic. / My body is a witch. / I am burning it." With the fervour of Hamlet rebuking both his mother for her sexuality and Ophelia for wearing make-up, Boland's verse performs a primitive exorcism, unmaking the male version of the female body in order to start again. Gone are the sweet, sometimes over-calculated fluencies of her earlier work. In their place are the more crabbed cadences of responsive speech which, if it's not colloquial, is not deliberately lyrical, but more dynamically performative. One way this comes about may be in the poet's splitting of the self in two—a she and an I, a woman who suffers, and a woman watching, taking notes, making judgements, commentary: "Defeated, we survive, we two, housed // together in my compromise, my craft / who are of one another the first draft." The self is saved by the poetry, and the two—poet and woman—set up house together. In this house, however, one won't find domestic joy, nor erotic bliss, "no magic here." The loss (whatever it is, for its precise nature remains occluded) is only compensated for by finding a voice. Thus, speaking in this generalised voice of almost impersonal female rage, the poems from *In Her Own Image* seek to burn away the sentimentalities that inhabit male erotic versions of the female body. These poems are acts of amputation, an *auto-de-fé* that consumes the female body in a bonfire of male-determined vanities.

After this necessary rite of purgation, Boland manages in *Night Feed* to speak a woman's life on some of its own terms, a life of connection between mother and child, of domestic harmony, familial love, and "the sort of light / jugs and kettles / grow important by." That it is a life from which the erotic—though not love—seems mostly experienced as absence may be significant (an absence that may in part be explained by experiences touched on in certain poems dealing with childhood memories, in which the sexual is a sinister, threatening force, as it is, for example, in "The Black Lace Fan My Mother gave

Me"). Some of Boland's later poems and polemical prose—rebuking male Irish poets *en masse* for composing something she calls "the Irish poem" exclusive of women and women's concerns seem to me to belong more to the politics of literary place than to a true engagement with the politics of gender. Within the politics of gender, however, her best work has been an important and exemplary presence, helping Irish poets who are women inscribe themselves into the "national" poetic tradition on their own terms. Her poetry, that is, performs in its more aggressive and confrontational way an act of "political" reclamation complementary to that performed by Eiléan Ní Chuilleanáin.

By means of Boland's unmaking of the male erotic, by means of her purgative negations, and the reclamations carried out by her work and by Ní Chuilleanáin's, a genuine *reaffirmation* of the sexual and the erotic in women's experience can take place. And this reaffirmation is what the tradition needs, I would argue, to heal itself, to fulfil whatever possibility was inherent in what those male poets have done who, since Yeats, have opposed public orthodoxy and dogmatic moralisms of one kind and another, and engaged their imaginations with the sexual and the erotic element in order to bring about a truly liberated human Irish consciousness.

The work of Nuala Ní Dhómhnaill and Medbh McGuckian brings, I believe, this story to a kind of close (as well, of course, as representing a new beginning). For in their work we find a fully eroticised poetry written by women. McGuckian puts into practice what Boland often preaches, remaking the poetic language "in her own image." In their shifty syntax and "floating metaphors" her poems embody a distinctly female mode of expressing female consciousness. In a language that is itself "eroticised" she emancipates female sexuality into its own fluent version of itself:

> In my all-weather loneliness I am like a sparrow
> Picking leftovers of rice in a mortar,
> A dark cicada clinging to a branch,
> The empty space created by your kiss . . .
>
> You overflow, sleeping on your back:
> My lap is bent upon itself, my bulbs
> Are fleeced, my wishbone wings are tied.

Idiosyncratic, liberationist, her language re-eroticises female experience so even a house can be transformed into an erotic experience, so "Under the hip-roofed thatch, / the bed-wing is warmed by the chimney-breast . . . " from which it follows that it is

> . . . possible once more to call
> houses by their names, Annsgift or Mavisbank,
> Mount Juliet or Bettysgrove . . .
> . . . I drink to you as Hymenstown,
> (my touch of fantasy) or First Fruits,

impatient for my power as a bride.
("The Soil Map")

With her own brand of self-confidence, McGuckian claims the world for the female principle: her poems are reflexes of the surprised body finding an answerable language for its own startlements and its own repose. Assuming their own power rather than erecting themselves against some other power, her poems fulfill the possibility of sexual freedom intuited and wished for by earlier poets. Her fully embodied female voice—with its traces of the speech of Shakespeare's late heroines (Marina, Perdita, Miranda) and of the cadences of Virginia Woolf—affirms the primacy of the sexual in human experience. As a visionary of the erotic, she charges everything with desire, sexual substance, femaleness—stretching the notion of the erotic in important ways. On her soil-seed- and soul-maps all territories are erogenous zones:

> I think the detectable difference
> between winter and summer is a damsel
> who requires saving, a heroine half-
> asleep and measurably able to hear
> but hard to see, like the spaces
> between the birds when I turn
> back to the sky for another empty feeling.
> ("Hotel")

That McGuckian's poetry suggests the freedom of women's consciousness (including a powerful consciousness of the woman's body and the body of the other) is enough to reveal its political implications. This is the body language of the erotic imagination: "I had / Smoothed the cream of youth, or manhood, / Into my arms, my body, the kiss / Of a spent-salmon where / The earth is never wet." Her metamorphic energy achieves freedom as fluency both of body and language, a true liberationist erotics, subverting any lingering assumption that the erotic is not a natural zone of habitation for women (and, by extension, for men). Her gravity-defying style is a result of her female consciousness, since, as she says herself (in a *Southern Review* interview, Summer 1995), "A woman is so naturally fluid and her mind is so dominated by her body that for a woman to write real poetry as men have traditionally been able to do—is difficult." Floating within its own instinctively erotic solution, however, her work provides another, female model of poetic possibility. Her dazzling mobility can cross all borders, so even death can be eroticised:

> How like death and unlike death
> the reeds and silks of your kiss rendered
> unrecognisable by death
> . . . the wafer of your mouth, the body of
> your mouth, your body's mouth, your mouth's

body . . . nothing will now disturb our night.

At an allegorical level, the multiplicity represented by her mobile style and its erotic action becomes an image of fresh possibility in an Ireland crippled north and south by the violence of dogmatic singularity and exclusion, and by the congealed politics that is its consequence.

When Nuala Ní Dhómhnaill says, "I write sexy poems in Irish," she implicitly subverts three orthodoxies—that of the English language, that of official gaelgeóir attitudes to the "purity" of the Irish language, and that of conventional assumptions about sexuality in general and female sexuality in particular. What Boland burned back to skin and bone, Ní Dhómhnaill restores to flesh and blood, to a healthy sense of its own self-possessed, sexual, eroticised self. In a more direct, less enigmatic way than McGuckian, she not only re-eroticises the female body and the male body, but the body of relationship between them.

As a poet, Ní Dhómhnaill begins with declarations of sexual independence, setting up an exemplary self against the puritan norms of womanhood imposed by the male church and its subservient national culture. From the start she celebrates the female body in an uninhibited way, smacking at times of the song of Songs ("my hair is henna-brown / and pearls from my neck hang down / and my navel here conceals / vials of the honey of wild bees"). Like McGuckian, part of her freedom is that she can also celebrate the man's body, implicitly asserting her equality with male poets by taking over their lyrical habit of turning the beloved body into a landscape (so a lover's "nude body is an island / asprawl on the ocean bed"). In doing this, too, she puts herself in touch with the female voices of the Gaelic tradition (from Deirdre to Eileen Dubh), whose actual, Irish language she is using. Like Longley or Montague, she delights in naming the parts of the beloved body: "Your back, your slender waist, / and, of course, / the root that is the very seat / of pleasure, the pleasure source." What she adds to such celebratory delight is a sense of irony, often sliding off at the end into a playfulness that reminds of the relationship itself, reminds that this is not (as it often is in male poets) mere solitary gazing. A good example is *"Fear"* (in Eiléan Ní Chuilleanáin's translation, "Looking at a Man") in which, after a litany of praise, she concludes,

> You're the one they should praise
> In public places,
> The one should be handed
> Trophies and cheques.
> You're the model
> For the artist's hand,
> Standing before me
> In your skin and wristwatch.

Treating the erotic in comic and tragic, celebratory and silly ways, Ní Dhómhnaill can be sensuous, realistic, or unashamedly dependent, running a broad gamut of sexual possibility, giving the sense of a consciousness that's whole, intact, liberated and in possession of a speech adequate to its liberated need. Speaking thus from the woman's angle, she subverts the orthodoxy that would stigmatise any public expression of sexuality, while at the same time she deflates the sentimental male habit of erotic idealisation. In such an affirmative voice she writes women into the erotic world in a new way.

In addition, and not unlike Durcan, Ní Dhómhnaill can either eroticise or dismantle some elements in the treasured iconology of the Irish tradition. So sex with her lover, for example, can be an evocation both of Newgrange and of an early church like the Gallarus oratory:

> A ray of sunshine comes
> slender and spare
> down the dark passageway
> and though the gap
>
> in the lintel
> to trace a light-scroll
> on the mudfloor
> in the nethermost
> sealed chamber.
> Then it swells
> and swells until a golden glow
> fills the whole oratory.
>   ("Feis/Carnival," trans. Muldoon)

Or else her poem on the Annunciation can remind the Virgin "that never was it known / that a man came to you / in the darkness alone, / his feet bare, his teeth white / and roguery swelling in his eyes." Or she can be a monk's bright temptation, or even subvert Cúchullain himself, putting down his prodigious sexuality as no more than a chauvinist story in mythic form. In reclaiming the spaces of myth for women, she can even deconstruct the Sean Bhean Bhocht, undoing that most lethal of male infatuations with Cathleen Ní Houlihan:

> And those first smitten by the light of day
> While she danced in the fire
> Were doomed to be burned out, dazzled and frazzled
> With all-consuming love for her
> So that it came to pass that they were mowed down
> In their hundreds, left and right, not with love
> That you or I know, no, not with ordinary love
> But with a gnawing, migraine-bright black lust
> And galloping consumption.
>   (trans. Ciaran Carson)

By eroticising or dismantling the cultural landscape through the medium of Irish, Ní Dhómhnaill also frees the modern Irish language from the puritan grip of its official sponsors, reminding of its true nature. For Irish, she says, "isn't prudish. The language is very open and non-judgemental about the body and its orifices." It is for this reason that—embodied by a fully eroticised female imagination working in Irish—the work of Ní Dhómhnaill brings to a logical conclusion the evolving act of subversion that began in the work of the male poets who attempted to broaden and deepen the possibilities of Irish consciousness, to forge the conscience of the race into a shape and a texture more in tune with a holistic humanity than the versions promulgated by a state in which political and ecclesiastical powers colluded to keep people in a condition of human immaturity. The line of erotic poetry I have been following here, I'd argue, establishes a sort of Resistance, a counterforce, a radical opposition to many of the orthodox assumptions and pieties of the various culture communities that have made up both states in the island.

This version of the story ends with Ní Dhómhnaill and McGuckian because by this point Irish poets, whether male or female, straight or gay can be as erotic as they like without feeling their poems have to somehow take on some larger orthodox power. (That a recent issue of *Poetry Ireland Review* was devoted to "*Sexuality*" illustrates this fact.) For the truth is that by now (I mean "at last") a certain amount of public social life has matured towards a more liberal understanding of individual human freedom (at least the freedom to debate the issues without fear) especially within the realm of sex. And so, when the history of modern and contemporary Irish poetry (in English and in Irish) comes to be written, it will have to contain a chapter describing how that poetry—by its complex and sustained devotion to and presentation of the sexual and erotic in human life—made its own articulate and heartening contribution to the possibility (at least) of a saner, more tolerant, and freer, even more joyous, community for the men and women of the island.

I thought of ending with verses (in Irish) by Cathal Ó Searcaigh, who says in one love poem, "I'd deny the Gospels for your sake" and whose erotic celebration of his lover's body is carried out in terms of Catholic ritual, showing how the expression of sexuality (gay sexuality in this case) can continue to be an agent of "political" subversion. In fact I've chosen to end, however, with the translation of a poem (*Lúghnasa*) by Michael Davitt, which seems to celebrate a sexual freedom that dissolves boundaries and rejoices in an erotic condition that is "amphibian":

> August
> A broad-beamed stately mannish woman
> and a silkie man
> took a spin of an August evening
> along the empty strands
>
> stippled light and shade

turning inside out
between silhouette and sand

a shot of Vladivar a cigarette

her rollicking down to the tide
in her moonstruck hide
his soft shoe shuffle at her hooves
till he bested her on the crest of a wave
and they set themselves up as pillars of salt
and swam through a swell of pubic hair
pleasure-gland to pleasure-gland

until at least one wound
among so many wounds was salved

a pair of amphibians in the oomph of quicksilver.

In its dissolution of sexual borders, in its electric connection with the old Gaelic world through the poem's title (attaching this contemporary couple to the Feast of Lúghnasa with all its sexual and erotic implications), Davitt's poem—in itself and in Paul Muldoon's witty and meticulous translation[2]—might represent the mark towards which the line of poetry I have been talking about has all the time been tending, a mark where sexual love itself (herself, himself), might be standing, without fear, and smiling.

1997

NOTES

[1] In the recent "Mycenae Lookout," from *The Spirit Level*, the conjunction of sexuality, political violence, and what "loyalty" might mean, is an originating given for the poem's haunting narrative fragments, briskly brought to a head in an image from "His Dawn Vision," in which "a man / Jumped a fresh earth-wall and another ran / Amorously, it seemed, to strike him down."

[2] I have not dealt with his own work in this discussion, but I should add that Muldoon himself is a poet whose novel and liberating riffs on the subversive and transgressive operations of sexuality could occupy another essay. (The sexual vibrations of Lúghnasa, of course, are at the heart of Brian Friel's recent play.)

Passwords:
Prizing Heaney

I was getting my first sense of crafting words
and for one reason or another, words as bearers
of history and mystery began to invite me.

"Feelings into Words"

I remember as a first-year graduate student writing an essay on "The Figure of the Poet in Spenser's *Shepherdes Calendar*." I began it with two phrases—*the brightness of brave and glorious words* (from Spenser), and *words alone are certain good* (from Yeats). I forget the essay that followed, but these two phrases came to mind when I was asked to say something very brief here about Seamus Heaney's work.[1] For—although the poet himself has seen the problems that lie inside these formulations and their like, and although so much of the poetry is an alert, athletic wrestling with such problems—it is nonetheless to his words themselves, as words, and to his own obvious relish for them that I return again and again for nourishment, invariably finding in them the kind of elasticity and surprise that provides enduring satisfaction.

For Heaney himself, I believe, such a satisfaction derives from the poet's own intense personal faith that his life and language are somehow bound up inextricably in one another. Evidence for this can be found in that miniature myth of origin which he shaped for himself in "Mossbawn," the opening essay of *Preoccupations*: "I would begin with the Greek word, *omphalos*, meaning the navel, and hence the stone that marked the centre of the world, and repeat it, *omphalos, omphalos, omphalos,* until its blunt and falling music becomes the music of somebody pumping water at the pump outside our back door. It is Co. Derry in the early 1940s." From *omphalos* to *pump*: the word and the world (centre of the earth, or a backyard in Co. Derry) gush into one another in enlivening, enabling ways.

For a reader, such a satisfaction is to be found in the poems and the criticism alike. Opening any book of the verse at random, I am sure to find words that either register the physical world almost on its own physical, auditory terms (think of the "gross-bellied frogs" all the way back there in "Death of a Naturalist," with "their blunt heads farting"), or that register a refined, palpably felt moral discrimination (consider that extraordinary, simple and strange account the poet gives in "Clearances" of his mother's dying: "The space we stood around had been emptied / Into us to keep, it penetrated / Clearances that suddenly stood open. / High cries were felled and a pure change happened"). Some of this must have a subliminal or umbilical connection with a (Joycean/Catholic) sense of incarnation, the word made flesh, the world "worded." In the criticism, too, the same sense of verbal presence, heft and accuracy is always striking, and striking home, as when he remarks how the verses of mad Sweeney sound a "double note of relish and penitence," or how Keats's vowels (in a line from "To Autumn") "seem like nubs, buds off a single *uh* or *oo*, yeasty growths that are ready at any moment to relapse back into the original mother sound." Given such habits, then, it makes sense that he should say in "Crediting Poetry" (his Nobel speech) that "the effort [of the poet] is to repose in the stability conferred by a musically satisfying order of sounds."

It's no wonder that the passage in *Portrait of the Artist* where Stephen Dedalus encounters the Dean of Studies and his tundish is among Heaney's necessary touchstones (and not just because the relevant entry in Stephen's diary is for April 13, Heaney's own—and Beckett's—birthday, a coincidence that would have tickled the superstitious, birthday-alert Joyce). For his whole career has been a movement, it seems to me, away from fretting in the shadow of the English language (his first pen-name *Incertus*) to a robust, interrogative, always affirmative rejoicing (yes) in its possibilities of music, manner, and meaning. As part of such a movement, it is right to recall a poem of landscape reclamation like "Anahorish," its Irish meaning become the poet's own nominative possession ("my 'place of clear water'"), its (anglicised) transformation into "soft gradient / of consonant, vowel meadow" an act of exact reconciliation between the languages and—by extension into an unspoken optative mood—between other more pressing (political rather than toponymical, although these two are never separate) oppositions.[2]

And right now, reading Heaney's more recent work, I wonder what unfolding he will perform on the word "soul," with its various amplifying metaphors and spirit-synonyms, and I imagine him in pursuit of a language that would (with Yeats's phrase in mind) do some sort of *justice* and offer some sort of *reality* to that tricky monosyllable, as he does in thinking of a great philosopher's death, how "at the centre of the city and the day / Socrates has proved the soul immortal" ("'Poet's Chair'"). This simple assertion cannot satisfy the poet, however, who must acknowledge the gap between that daunting possibility and the difficult here and now of living, a here and now in which what we *must* know (rather than what we *would* know) has to be faced up to and fully articulated: "But for the moment everything's an ache / Deferred, foreknown, imagined and most real." At the root of all this is the observation I have used as epigraph, where the poet remarks on how language was what, for him, connected "history" to "mystery." Firmly grounded, but reaching for the rarer element, words—from this point of view—are all winged centaurs.

For me, as I am sure for many other older as well as younger poets, this sheer bodily and spiritual living into the language has been, in every sense, one of Heaney's greatest gifts. Some years ago, writing a poem I would dedicate to him (in part because of its subject matter, its tentative connection—or so I

imagined—with some of what he was at in his own work), I sought about to end
it on a "Heaney note," which meant foraging for certain words and a certain sort
of cadence. What I came up with in the end (to conclude the description I had
given of men working on a roof) was "and they ply, they intercede." The many
meanings of "ply" seemed to me then (and still do) to touch on important aspects of Heaney's work and craft. The OED offers, among others, *to mould, to
shape, to bend, to yield, to bend in reverence, to bow, to apply, work busily at,
to wield vigorously, to exert a faculty, to keep on with questions,* and adds to
these the nautical meanings of *to beat up against the wind, to tack, to steer, to
move onward.* And there is, of course, its presence in *implicate* and *explicate,*
not to mention *plight.* A reader or a writer might meditate an hour or so on each
of these definitions and its reverberations in Heaney's own work, noting how
their accumulated meanings could make a design in which issues now of craft
and now of moral texture and alignment were being—turn and turn about—
coaxed into the light. As for "intercede": the various meanings, secular and
religious, it reaches into and out of include all kinds of *going between*—in the
sense of trying to cross borders, pass between realms, carry a just account,
amplify a commitment to truth with sympathy and understanding—which again
seem peculiarly apposite to the content of Heaney's verse, and in increasingly
rich, and complex ways.

Although I function here as a "critic" (meaning by that word no more nor less
than a careful, responsible reader willing to report as concretely and accurately
as he can on what he finds in a text) there is something in me that doesn't really
want to know Heaney's work too analytically or too well. This is because, as a
poet, I just want to take it in, roam around in it, get close to hear its small
breathings, stand back to take in some of its bigger pictures. I want to let it be,
not know too much (in intellectual or analytic terms) about it, about what's in it,
what it's doing, how it's doing it and so on. In addition, I find myself daunted
by the sheer verbal textures of the work itself, textures beside which some critical vocabularies can seem dry, a bit out of touch, or mannered, or cast in the
dogmatic postures of an agenda quite separable from the work itself. A further
shying of my critical consciousness comes from knowing that when Heaney
himself works as a critic he is always acutely conscious of such textures in the
work of those poets he attends upon, making the act of critical reading itself the
art of being answerable to his subjects in rhetorically adequate ways. As a result,
his critical essays are acts of linguistic discovery, finding and finding again the
language most aptly and exactly responsive to his particular subject.

In both prose and verse, then, Heaney's work—even if simply taken at the
level of the word itself—is everywhere marked for me by generosity, capacious-
ness, and that sort of expansive human response to experience and to language
for which I can only find the word *porousness.* In his own deliberate fashion,
that is, he seems always to be trying honestly to open up to the world as it comes
to him, and to open up to himself in the act of responding, and to open up his
language in a sufficiently conscientious way so as to do justice to both these
zones, of object and of subject. It is this quality of *porousness,* I believe, that

enables him to maintain that state of moral vigilance which, in turn, obliges him to interrogate his own past and present choices as a poet. And it is that quality, too, that allows him to absorb new knowledge about those choices, knowledge that can prompt change (of direction, attitude, understanding) rather than—as it did in the case of Kavanagh—irritable rejection. *Porousness*, at least for me, implies a substance that is sturdy, solid, but not still. That it tilts me, not irrelevantly, towards the verb 'to pore over' is a further satisfaction.

When the Nobel announcement was made, however, the word that came to my mind was *enlarge*. In being thus recognised, Heaney had, I felt—and in every sense of the word—enlarged all of us in Ireland and in Northern Ireland. *Enlarge*. It was, I later thought, a word—especially in the hopeful context of ceasefire and peace process—that might describe how Heaney's own work, his imagination's enterprise, might carry us beyond Yeats's description of the island as a place of "great hatred, little room" towards a more tolerant understanding of shared space, maybe even a somewhere that is, as he says in a recent poem, "neither here nor there, / A hurry through which known and strange things pass / As big soft buffetings come at the car sideways / And catch the heart off guard and blow it open." As far as life on the island is concerned, such an enlargement of the heart might do much in the realm of ordinary human action. And beyond that realm, in the zones of poetry itself, the same word, *enlarge*, might even—as far as his fellow-poets are concerned—suggest a freeing of some sort, an enlargement into a world in which the line from one poet to another was a liberating rather than, as it has sometimes been in the past, a restraining and inhibiting force.

Of course the truly admirable thing about Heaney's richly inflected regard for the capacious possibilities of language itself is his concurrent knowledge of its limits, his conviction (I think) that in Yeats's phrase, "words alone are certain good," an ironic (and maybe Irish) emphasis might fall on *certain*. This seems clear from a couplet in the recent affectionate elegy composed for his friend, Joseph Brodsky. For, in contemplating the death of one whose life was a continuously renewed dedication to language, he has to speak in an idiom of acknowledgement, has to speak the unpalatable but unavoidable truth: "Even your peremptory trust / in words alone here bites the dust." It is a measure of Heaney's essential composure, of his ability to bring aesthetics and ethics into a felt but unfussy equilibrium, that—even while biting into such bitterness—his language can still yoke that marvellously Latinate *peremptory*, to the colloquial keenness of *bite the dust*, can still skim delight from the surfaces (but they are never just surfaces) of the language, still relish what he is doing. "*Certain* good," fair enough. But good. Or, to use his own morally scrupulous, characteristically colloquial, wry but double-edged formulation at the end of the recent poem, "Tollund," (in *The Spirit Level*): "not bad." Indeed.

1996

NOTES

[1] In the Spring 1996 issue of *The Harvard Review*, to celebrate Heaney's 1995 Nobel Prize.

[2] Addendum: How deeply language and politics are twinned in his thinking can be seen even in his recent comment on the agreement reached between the parties in the North, when he said that "language itself seems to have gained a new friskiness through the signing of the inter-party agreement." (From his response, published in *The Irish Times*, 11 April 1998.)

AFTERWORD

In the Kitchen with Yeats

Since the poet is never the man
who sits down to breakfast,
never that bundle of fragments,
but the composed whole bloke
buzzing iambics behind a closed door,
I suppose he wasn't one to linger
if ever he visited the kitchen—
his sense of smell confined
to incense, honey, wine
and other emblematic fragrances.
So what would he make of me
in this cottage kitchen on his birthday
stirring a sauce for pasta, one hand
holding a wooden spoon, the other
his Collected Poems, *a fresh edition?*

With one ear I listen
to the homely little splutter
of tomatoes, spices, garlic, a diced onion
as they bubble
towards their unity of being,
while with the other I can hear
the clear, austere music
of "The Wild Swans at Coole,"
the ache of its defeats beating
through that one lost rhyme each stanza,
and through those clean lifelines of his
that keep cheating us out of ease
but lead to grace. Wooden spoon

tapping the skillet, I close my eyes
to get the poem by heart, making
its cold companionable manners
my own as long as that music lasts,
while all the while the cottage

fills to steamy brimming
with smells that distill into the air
some vegetarian notion of the soul,
and fills with the ceremony of sound
he stirred into the stock
of his own marrowbone soup—
to keep us, even in lean times,
warm. When I close the book

and leave the sauce to simmer,
the whole place breathes
a single compound smell
of garlic tomatoes onions oregano
pepper cinnamon wild thyme, all
in a base of olive oil and crowned
with a leaf or two of bay. Later—
wondering how he might have relished
the scent of his own ascending dinner
winding up the winding stairs—
I'll spoon the wine-dark mixture
over fettucini, sprinkle parmesan
(aged nine months), prop up
his book against the bowl, and eat.